Frontiers of Globalization Research

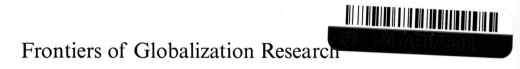

Ino Rossi

Editor

Frontiers of Globalization Research:

Theoretical and Methodological Approaches

With updated postscript

 Springer

Ino Rossi
Department of Sociology and Anthropology
Saint John's University
Queens, NY 11439
USA

Library of Congress Control Number: 2006923907

ISBN-10: 0-387-33595-1   e-ISBN-10: 0-387-33596-X
ISBN-13: 978-0-387-33595-7   e-ISBN-13: 978-0-387-33596-4

Printed on acid-free paper.

9 8 7 6 5 4 3 2 1

springer.com

Preface

Every generation has its own social, economic, or political challenges, and globalization is a powerful combination of all three. This is one topic that inevitably pops up in public media as well as in daily conversations, and one that we find difficult to discuss with clarity and equanimity. This volume amply demonstrates that even academic discourse is far from having reached a consensual understanding on foundational issues regarding the study of globalization. This is to be expected given the complexity of the issues in question and the richness of our disciplinary traditions. The hope is that the diversity of perspectives discussed here will enable the reader to appreciate the strength and complementarity of alternative points of view and research strategies.

We must be grateful to the contributors to this volume for having found time in the midst of their "globalizing" schedules to offer us a primer of first-hand research and/or a re-examination of the theoretical and methodological principles that have guided their globalization journey. The list of contributors has been augmented by leaps and bounds, as a result of consultations and debates. Repeated exchanges and revisions have produced a set of papers that are purposefully focused on theoretical and methodological issues that scholars face in globalization research. My gratitude goes to the "early" contributors for having patiently waited for the "late" deliverers and newcomers: I have continued to seek insightful and provocative essays until the very end as the unfolding of the process has generated new theoretical and methodological issues.

There are many other people whom I must thank. I was unsuccessful in my repeated attempts to obtain an essay or a commentary from a representative of the World Polity perspective. However, John Boli has been helpful with comments, especially in the early stages of this project. Unfortunately, his administrative and publishing commitments have prevented him from writing a full-fledged essay. The patient and supporting series editor, Teresa Krauss, of Springer, and her competent editorial staff have provided competent support for the completion of this project. My "enduring" graduate assistants, Veronica Ticas and Christian Francis Tran, have helped me greatly in editorial matters, and some of my colleagues have occasionally "volunteered" to listen to my probing on globalization matters. Neither they nor my son, Paul, who kept wondering whether this book would ever make it to the press, have been told about my numerous hours spent in front of the PC to think through a lot of difficult issues. My wife Irene has assisted me over the years through my bouts with French structuralism, dialectic sociology, and disaster studies, and currently, globalization. Not only my perseverance, but also my style and editorial chores have benefited a great deal from her supportive understanding and skills.

With the realization that the globalization debate is still in its early stage, I hope that this contributed volume will facilitate a multiperspective and a cross-disciplinary discourse on a complex process with all its ramifications and potential trajectories. One hopes also that the imbalances and tensions of the globalization process that have been documented in this volume will foster a genuine dialogue among all its protagonists, winners and losers alike.

Addendum for the softcover edition

This softcover edition incorporates corrections and updatings that have been submitted by Jonathan Friedman, Douglas Kellner, Leslie Sklair, and the editor of the book [see in particular the insert in pages 434–436 on empirical tests of Beck's notions of second modernity and individualization].

The reader who may find theoretical disquisitions in this volume a bit overwhelming should not blame the unconscious bias of the editor, but his conscious editorial policy. At the formative stages of globalization research we must know what we mean by "globalization" and how to study it. Without such a "foundational" discourse, any systematic and cumulative body of knowledge on the globalization process and anti-globalization movements is not really possible.

Suggestions on how to improve this collective effort might contribute to make our globalizing world a bit less disorienting.

St. John's University,   Ino Rossi
January 2008   *rossii@stjohns.edu*

Contents

Contributors

JANET ABU-LUGHOD
New York, NY, USA

MARTIN ALBROW
Center for the Study of Global Governance, London School of Economics,
London WC2A, UK

JEFFREY C. ALEXANDER
Department of Sociology, Yale University, New Haven, CT 06511, USA

MARGARET S. ARCHER
Department of Sociology, University of Warwick, Coventry CV4 7AL, UK

GIOVANNI ARRIGHI
Department of Sociology, The Johns Hopkins University, Baltimore, MD
21218-2685, USA

CHRISTOPHER CHASE-DUNN
Institute for Research on World-Systems, University of California-Riverside,
Riverside, CA 92521, USA

RANDALL COLLINS
Department of Sociology, University of Pennsylvania, Philadelphia, PA
19104-6299, USA

JONATHAN FRIEDMAN
Department of Social Anthropology, University of Lund, Lund. 4, Sweden

RAYMOND GREW
Department of History (Emeritus), University of Michigan, Ann Arbor,
MI 48105, USA

ANDREW JORGENSON
Department of Sociology, Washington State University, Pullman, WA 99164

DOUGLAS KELLNER
Department of Social Sciences and Comparative Education, University of
California-Los Angeles, Los Angeles, CA 90095-1521, USA

KARIN KNORR CETINA
Department of Sociology and Anthropology, University of Constance,
Constance, Germany and The University of Chicago, Chicago IL 60637,
USA

GEORGE RITZER
Department of Sociology, University of Maryland, College Park, MD 20742-1315, USA

JAMES N. ROSENAU
Elliott School of International Affairs, The George Washington University, Washington, D.C. 20052, USA

INO ROSSI
Department of Sociology and Anthropology, Saint John's University, Queens, NY 11439, USA

SASKIA SASSEN
Department of Sociology, University of Chicago, Chicago, Illinois 60637, USA

ROBERT K. SCHAEFFER
Department of Sociology and Anthropology, Kansas State University, Manhattan, KS, 66502, USA

LESLIE SKLAIR
Professor Emeritus of Sociology, London School of Economics and Political Science, London WC2A 2AE, UK

RUDOLF STICHWEH
Soziologisches Seminar, Universität Luzern, CH-6000 Luzern 7, Switzerland

JOHN URRY
Department of Sociology, Lancaster University, Lancaster, LA1 4YD, UK

Introduction
Rationale of the Volume and Thematics of the Contributions

INO ROSSI

Genesis and Rationale of This Volume

Globalization has attracted the attention of the social sciences since the early 1980s. Given the recency of the topic, it is no wonder that there are plenty of controversies on what "globalization" means, on the theoretical and methodological approaches for studying it, and on the diagnoses and solutions of problems attributed to globalization. This book focuses on the formulation and discussion of alternative definitions, modes of theorizing, and research methodologies in the field of globalization.

The intellectual itinerary that led to this book began with the organization of a series of sessions on theoretical approaches to globalization: first, on the occasion of the 2002 International Conference on Globalization that was promoted by the late Richard Harvey Brown of the University of Maryland, then on the occasion of the 2003 and 2004 meetings of the Eastern Sociological Society. The interest in those sessions and the debates that they generated prompted me to pursue the idea of a book that would systematically examine the theoretical bases of the globalization discourse and make explicit as much as possible the strategies for its study: these were the two explicit indications I gave to the prospective contributors to the book. I did, however, contact a larger group than the attendees to the three mentioned conferences in an effort to secure a representation of as many approaches to globalization as possible. Three years of correspondence, discussions, exchanges, and revisions of papers should assure the reader that this book is not a haphazard collection of conference papers loosely related to each other.

On the contrary, these papers ought to be approached as systematic formulations, often interactively produced, of alternative approaches to the study of globalization. Most of the contributors are sociologists, but the contributions of Jonathan Friedman (an anthropologist), Raymond Grew (an historian), and James Rosenau (international relations) bring a touch of interdisciplinarity. Obviously, an extensive representation of all social sciences could not be compacted in a single volume.

The essays are organized in three parts: in the first part there are theoretical papers on globalization, in general, and on cultural globalization, in particular; the chapters of Part 2 deal with theoretical and methodological issues in the areas of economic and political globalization; the chapters of Part 3 discuss research strategies and methodological issues encountered in the empirical study of globalization. The chapters were placed in different sections of the book on the basis of their major emphasis, although most of them contain elements relevant to more than one section of the book. When I introduce the chapters of one section, I utilize elements of chapters located in other sections when they are relevant to the theme of the section. Hopefully, this crossreferencing will help the reader to use this volume, not in a piecemeal fashion, but as an integrated totality. A detailed index will further enhance the usefulness of this book as a systematic introduction to central issues in the field of globalization.

The introduction to Part 1 is a bit more extensive not only because the chapters deal with foundational issues, but also because theoretical elements from chapters located in other sections of the book had to be brought into the systematic discussion.

Part 1:   Theoretical Perspectives

Part 1 deals with conceptualizations, definitions, and frameworks for the analysis of globalization.

In the first essay, "Globalization as an Historical and Dialectical Process," I present a framework that analyzes globalization as a multifaceted and conflictual process. The historical, conflictual, macro- and microperspectives on globalization are integrated into one comprehensive framework for the study of technological, cultural, political, and economic processes and their interrelationship. The essay begins with the Weberian conception of societal order as consisting of cultural, political, and economic principles of social organization. The prevailing principle of social organization (cultural or political or economic) determines the type of society with which we are dealing with, (respectively, a prevalently cultural, prevalently political, or prevalently economic society). These societal types are analytic models and not evolutionary stages through which every society must evolve. I claim that the dominant principle of social organization tells us also whether transsocietal ties (globalization) are respectively mostly cultural or political or economic in nature. The most recent type of globalization is economic globalization in the form of capitalist globalization that has produced commercial, industrial, and financial variations of capitalism, all of them based on finance capital.

In analyzing primarily Western types of societies I focus on a threefold level of societal concerns (see Table 1.3): (a) the local level of ethnic/religious/community concerns; (b) the level of national concerns (national heritage, national sovereignty, national identity, nationalism); (c) the level of international concerns regarding mostly issues of international economy. The conflictuality of globalization derives from two main structural factors: (a) conflicts or adaptive interactions among the cultural, political, and economic principles of social organization within each one of the three levels of societal concerns (local, national, international) (b) conflicts among the local, national, and international societal concerns. These conflicts occur in each society, but they are greatly augmented at the level of cross-national transactions by the fact that different societies are at different levels of socioeconomic development. For some nations cultural/religious issues are a priority, for other societies a nationalistic image and autonomous political regime, and for other societies global economic competitiveness.

The analytic models I developed are helpful for the analysis not only of macro issues, but also for understanding the formation of psychocultural identity in a globalizing world. Finally, the interaction between agency and structure (cultural, political, economic structures) within nations and cross-nations is singled out as a resource mechanism to negotiate conflicts and forge an intercivilizational path for a viable global future. The multidimensional and dialectic models presented in this essay can serve as a platform to interlink the perspectives and various levels of analysis contained in the contributors' papers.

The other chapters of Part 1 deal with the micro (Knorr Cetina), systemic (Friedman, Sklair), and supersystemic (*eigenstructures* of Stichweh) perspectives on globalization as well as with the conceptualization of globalization as a set of self-organizing complex systems (Urry).

A Major Bone of Contention Throughout These Papers Is the Definition of What Is "Global"

I begin from conceptualizations that use traditional categories of analysis. Saskia Sassen (see her essay in Part 3) argues that global spatialities and temporalities are partially overlapping and inserted and interacting with national relations. Privatized intermediary institutional arrangements for handling cross-border operations evolve into an institutional world that parallels the state and denationalizes its functions.

James N. Rosenau also uses traditional tools of analysis, but he starts from a totally different premise: "All the dimensions of globalization are sustained by individuals at the microlevel as well as by diverse organizations at the macrolevel." Rosenau defines the central task of globalization theory as one of developing propositions that link microinteraction (among individual actors) and macrointeractions (among states and organizations). The overall assumption is that globalization does not entail any new specific process beyond the actions and interactions of individuals, states, and organizations. In contrast to Sassen's position, he seems to shy away from the notion of overlapping, partially intersecting, imbricating relationships between the micro- and macroorders of interaction.

In "Microglobalization" Karin Knorr Cetina argues that globalization is based upon structures of connectivity and integration that are global in scope, but microsociological in character. With the notion of microglobalization Knorr Cetina suggests that the texture of a global world becomes articulated through microstructural patterns that develop in the shadow of (and perhaps liberated from) national and local institutional patterns. Insofar as they are "liberated from national and local patterns," the "fields of practice that stretch across all time zones" seem to be "emergent" realities. Knorr Cetina hastens to clarify that the "emergent" reality is *sui generis*, because following are the characteristics of global microstructures: they are "light," institutionally speaking; they appear to facilitate a certain non-Weberian effectiveness; they cannot simply be reduced to networks; and they tend to be temporal structures because the systems of microglobal structures exhibit "flow characteristics." All these characteristics make them unpredictable, playful, temporal, self-organizing, and, even, intertwined with chaos (here Knorr Cetina refers to Urry's position). The new terrorism is a major exemplifying case of a global microstructure, and so are some global financial markets, for example, the foreign exchange market. The analysis of microglobalization helps one to collect and assess empirical evidence for the architecture of a world society. Knorr Cetina suggests also that time mechanisms and temporal or sequential complexity substitute for the loss of spatially differentiated stability and articulation in global systems.

One may raise the question of how temporal, flowing, and underinstitutionalized microglobal structures can be the building blocks of the global architecture of the world. I discuss the implications of this question for global theorizing in my last essay.

Interestingly enough, Sassen speaks of a semi-privatized institutional world that is parallel to the local and national. For Sassen the global is only partial, because it is partially embedded in the national, and the latter is becoming more and more denationalized. For Knorr Cetina the global is parallel to the national as an emerging pattern of interaction, however fluid and temporal it may be. A logical question to be raised is how to resolve the controversy over the "emerging and parallel" versus "the partial and embedded" notion of the global when compared with Roseau's assumption that all dimensions of globalization are sustained by interactions among individuals (microinteraction) and interaction among organizations and states.

Rudolf Stichweh provides a solution to this dilemma. In his chapter "Structure Formation in World Society: The *Eigenstructures* of World Society and the Regional Cultures of the World," Stichweh starts his analysis from the notion of society as based on communication and from the conditions of access and exclusion from communication. Co-existence of societies and civilizations is an old phenomenon, but since the 15th century the European–Atlantic system has incorporated the rest of the world in one system. The unity of the world has not been accomplished by reducing cultural differences (McDonaldization thesis) or by incorporating—and preserving—cultural differences within the world system (Einsenstadt's theory of multiple modernities). Both of these positions entail continuity with previous societies.

Stichweh utilizes Parsonian and Luhmanian ideas when he suggests that intercivilizational encounters occur not via clashes (Huntington), but via functional differentiation. Stichweh discusses many "functional systems" of modern society: world economy, world science, world law, world literature, education, mass media, sport, tourism, and so on. These structures differentiate a certain functional aspect of communication and produce a global semantics. Modern *eigenstructures* and *eigencultures* consist of generalized symbols that are based on the binary code of communication; the latter is disembedded from the material content of social relations. Moreover, these differentiated functional subsystems of communication are based on principles of functioning that are multiple, flexible, and transcend family, geographical, and cultural connections and imply transfers of personnel and knowledge. For all these reasons these symbolic systems overcome regional and cultural boundaries and penetrate world's regions with global semantics. Other examples of *eigenstructures* are formal organizations, networks, epistemic communities, world events, and world city markets.

These structural forms are producers of diversity because they impose new structures over local and national structures, whereas the local is not necessarily a guarantor of diversity. The new social and cultural patterns do not replace preexistent cultural diversity, but they overlay old structures that are incorporated through a higher form of integration. It is not a question of a substitutive, but of a cumulative and multilevel model of structure, where the new structures (*eigenstructures*) reduce the informational relevance and frequency of activation of the old structures without extinguishing them. Some of the structures of world society go back to antiquity and Medieval Europe; these old structures interact with and make possible world society to the extent to which the old structures are themselves articulated and compatible with the world system.

Stichweh's heavy reliance on the disembeddedness of the symbolic systems of communication is consistent with the discussion on the "disembedded" nature of digital communication in the concluding essay. Moreover, Stichweh's position on the cumulative nature of *eigencultures* seems to be consistent with the findings of cross-national world value surveys that document the persistence in developing societies of traditional values and national values together with the gradual embrace of modern and postmodern values (see Inglehart's survey findings quoted in Rossi's essay on the dialectics of globalization).

Our theoretical itinerary has so far revealed differences that can be (partially) related to different starting points of analysis. Whereas Knorr Cetina and Stichweh focus on culture and digital communication, Sassen argues that the processes of economic globalization shape the cultural, political, and "subjective" dimensions of globalization. These different starting points of analysis lead to different definitions of global processes; if the distinctive characteristic of globalization lies in economic processes, we can understand why Sassen states

that the (unexplained) spatialities and temporalities of the global, that are produced by economic globalization, are not "emergent", but partially "imbricated"
(overlapping and interacting) with the national; in other words, they are a matter of political economy, and the global is only a partial, although strategically
important, set of relations. After all, IGOs such as the World Bank and IMF
are intergovernmental organizations that are imbricated with the functions of
national governments.

Similarly, if the starting point of analysis is interaction in the behaviorist
sense, it follows that global transactions are sustained by and inseparable from
the actions of individual, state, and corporate actors (Rosenau). On the other
hand, if we focus on transnational interactions that are based on and sustained
by the digital media of communication, the specificity of globalization consists
of emerging structures of communication and interaction (different from local
and national processes, Knorr Cetina and Stichweh). However, for Knorr Cetina
global structures of interactivity are parallel (and flexible and horizontal) to
national and local groups, whereas for Stichweh they are superimposed on local
and traditional structures; the latter ones are subsumed by a higher informational order without being eliminated. Neither Knorr Cetina nor Stichweh is
preoccupied with coordinating the national with the global level of analysis
inasmuch as the latter is an emerging order, whereas this is a central task for
Saskia Sassen.

One wonders how Knorr Cetina and Stichweh would deal with the issue of
denationalization of sociocultural and political domains that is central in
Sassen's analysis. Yet, Leslie Sklair will likely find Sassen's approach state-
centric, and hence not effective for the analysis of globalization as Sklair
conceptualizes it.

The next question to be examined is: what are the relationships among microglobal interactional structures? Some authors invoke the notion of system to interre-
late the cultural, economic, and political dimensions of the global (Sklair);
Friedman also uses the notion of system, but in a metaempirical and relational
sense; others use the notion of flows (Knorr Cetina) and of self-regulating and
co-evolving systems (Urry).

Leslie Sklair in "A Transnational Framework for Theory and Research in the
Study of Globalization" offers a systematizing framework of the field of globalization and opens up the discussion of the cultural, economic, and political impact of
globalization. He argues that much of the confusion in the literature is due to the
failure to distinguish between generic globalization and its historical forms, actual
or potential. He defines "generic globalization" in terms of the electronic revolution, the subsequent creation of transnational social spaces, and the emergence of
transnational cosmopolitanism.

The paper distinguishes analytically among three competing approaches
that have dominated theory and research in the study of globalization, namely
internationalist (state-centrist), transnationalist (globalization as a contested
world-historical project with capitalist and alternative forms), and globalist

(capitalist globalization as a more or less completed and irreversible neoliberal capitalist project).

The internationalist (state-centrist) approach is rejected on the grounds of theoretical redundancy and empirical inadequacy. The globalist approach is also rejected for its failure to theorize correctly the role of the state and the interstate system in sustaining the hegemony of capitalist globalization. The transnational approach is perceived to be the most fruitful, and it is based on the concept of transnational practices in the spheres of economics, politics, and culture-ideology. The transnational research strategy focuses on the characteristic institutional forms of transnational practices in these three spheres (major TNCs, the transnational capitalist class, and the culture-ideology of consumerism, respectively). Sklair argues that the transnationalist approach opens up conceptual and substantive paths for theorizing and researching alternative globalizations. Capitalist globalization cannot succeed in the longterm because it cannot resolve two central crises, those of class polarization and ecological unsustainability on a global scale. This makes the TNCs, the transnational capitalist class and the culture-ideology of consumerism wideopen to the attacks of an ever-widening antiglobalization movement that increasingly takes on anticapitalist forms.

Sklair explores one path out of capitalism through the connections among capitalist globalization (where we are), what can be termed co-operative democracy (a transitional form of society), socialist globalization (where we should be heading), and what can be termed the culture-ideology of universal human rights. Such a transformation could be achieved by the gradual elimination of the culture-ideology of consumerism and its replacement with a culture-ideology of human rights. This means, briefly, that instead of our possessions being the main focus of our cultures and the basis of our values, our lives should be lived with regard to a universally agreed system of human rights and the responsibilities to others that these rights entail. This does not imply that we should stop consuming. What it implies is that we should evaluate our consumption in terms of our rights and responsibilities. For this project to have any chance of success in the long run it will be necessary to experiment theoretically and practically with the electronic revolution, transnational social spaces, and transnational cosmopolitanism. The chapter concludes with an example of a research framework that links theory and substantive issues in the field of architecture and the built environment. His unit of analysis (transnational practices) is applied to the study of the capitalist global system in economic (TNCs), political (TCC or transnational capitalist class), and cultural institutions (consumerism). Sklair generates working hypotheses related to seven major debates surrounding capitalist globalization and his essay ends with an outline of a systematic research framework.

Douglas Kellner in his chapter placed in Part 2: "Globalization, Terrorism, and Democracy: 9/11 and Its Aftermath" wants to overcome dichotomizing pro versus con discourses and proposes a critical theory of globalization that distinguishes between progressive and emancipatory features, and oppressive and negative attributes of globalization. Kellner argues that the September 11 terrorist attacks and the subsequent wars in Afghanistan and Iraq illustrate contradictions and ambiguities embedded in globalization that demand critical and dialectical perspectives. Showing the ways that globalization and a networked society were involved in the 9/11 events and subsequent wars in Afghanistan and Iraq, he argues that the terrorist attacks and the ensuing Terror War show contradictions in the nature of globalization; both positive and negative features of globalization are evident, and the free and open society, the Internet, and global flow of people, ideas, and commodities are full of ambiguities: they allow terror and destruction, commerce, and democratization.

Kellner states that

> Worldwide terrorism is threatening in part because globalization relentlessly divides the world into have and have-nots, promotes conflicts and competition, and fuels long simmering hatreds and grievances, as well as bringing people together, creating new relations and interactions, and new hybridities. This is the objective ambiguity of globalization that both brings people together and brings them into conflict, that creates social interaction and inclusion, as well as hostilities and exclusions, and that potentially tears regions and the world apart while attempting to pull things together. ...

Kellner's emphasis on the contradictions and ambiguities of globalization is consistent with the premises of my dialectical approach that is based on the many conflicts of globalization.

Other authors appear not to find too convincing, or relevant or, perhaps, too old-fashioned, the notion of dialectics and they readily discard the notion of "system" to opt for a more open-ended view of globalization as a set of flows and self-organizing and co-evolving systems.

Urry's chapter, "Globalization and Complexity" breaks away drastically from traditional social science categories by taking inspiration from chaos theory. He starts from the notion that new technologies produce global times and dematerialize distances between places and people. He systematizes the discourses so far emerged on globalization on the basis of five concepts (structure, flow, ideology, performance, and complexity) to opt for the last one. Taking inspiration from complexity sciences, he conceptualizes globalization as a "series of co-evolving self-organizing systems." The dynamics of these self-organizing systems is best understood not via structure and agency, micro–macro, system-world or life-world or recurrence or cause–effect relationships, and this is a pretty clear wholesale dismissal of the positions we have discussed so far. Co-evolving and self-organizing systems are transformed through iterations (large-scale, nonlinear and branching-off transformations) without necessarily implying an agency. The self-organizing systems are connected by complex relationality, continuous changes, and sudden new structures; they are in a state of orderly disorder, irreversibly evolve via positive and negative feedback with the environment, and co-evolve with agents and the environment. Such global systems are characterized by unpredictability and irreversibility; they lack finalized equilibrium or order. Iterative patterns of social ordering can heighten overall global disorder. Complexity theory is drawn upon to show how global systems operate on the "edge of chaos." *Empire* by Hardt and Negri (2000) describes well the imperial sovereignty of the flexible and systemic structure of the single logic governing the world without governance. *Empire*, however, does not explain the internal dynamic, and especially, its operation in conditions of disequilibrium. For Urry, *Empire* is an "attractor" in the sense that societies are attracted to and compete with each other on the world stage. Urry states that "societies as empires develop new practices as systems develop . . ." and take . . . "new shapes moving in and through time space."

At this point, the global has become not only an emergent, but a chaotic and unpredictable self-evolving system: there appears to be some convergence between Urry's notion of globalization and Archer's statement on the "rapid, unregulated, and potentially explosive transformation" brought on by globalization; yet, the two authors start from different theoretical premises.

Against Reifications: Globalization Understood from the Concrete

Adopting a structural-Marxist perspective, Jonathan Friedman advocates a global systemic approach that denies a reified status to the global. In his chapter, "Global Systems, Globalization, and Anthropological Theory," he begins with an historical excursus on anthropological theory where he criticizes the 1970s' focus on institutions and cultural meaning in society, the latter being approached as a closed and self-contained entity. Structural-functionalism, neoevolutionism, and Maoist Marxism equally rejected the notion that the constitution of a society can be explained by something larger than the society in question. The same closed perspective was present in the structural Marxism of that time which focused on the social reproduction of a given society in terms of its internal contradictions (he mentions himself and Maurice Godelier as examples of this approach; for essays by Godelier see *Structural Sociology* (Rossi, 1982) and *The Logic of Culture* (Rossi, 1982a)).

The importance of the global perspective began with Eric Wolf in the 1970s and in the ethnographic practice of some anthropologists, including Friedman himself. The globalization discourse is clear in the works of R. Robertson, A. Appadurai, and U. Hannerz, but it has considerable shortcomings: the global is conceptualized as a culturally autonomous field, as a new phenomenon in history, sometimes considered in evolutionary terms, and studied from an empiricist and behavioral perspective. Friedman sees a sharp difference between this global approach and his own global systemic approach; in the latter, "the global refers to the total social arena within which social life is reproduced, and the global systemic refers to the properties of the complex cycles of global social reproduction, the way in which they constitute local institutional forms, identities, and economic and political cycles of expansion and contraction." In this framework the local is always part of the global, and this does not mean that the local is produced by the global. On the contrary, the global is nothing else than the local on a higher plane. The global refers to the properties of the systemic processes that connect the world's localities, and this includes their formation as more or less bounded places. There is no global space floating above the local. The global is a purely structural concept in the sense that local institutions, identities, economies, and cycles of economic and political expansion and contraction are to be understood as an articulation of historically specific sets of practices together with the larger field of forces and conditions of reproduction. The local is understood as one aspect of larger relationships.

The relations constitute the parts, inasmuch as relationships to the whole are immanent in the parts; the latter are generated by the systemic properties of the larger global space; the priority of the whole over the parts is present in Hegel, Marx, and Levi-Strauss's works; for the latter see Rossi (1974, 1983, 1993). Friedman avoids the shortcomings of empiricism, evolutionism, and diffusionism and considers globalization as old as human social organization; in fact, social organization is really explained only when the relations among its constituent components (or its underlying structures) are understood or, in other words, when empirical social structures are apprehended in their logical organization (Rossi, 1983, 1993). This "logical organization" refers to the nonvisible systemic properties among visible (behavioral) relationships such as "expansion and contraction, the formation and demise of center-periphery relations, the cyclical and dialectic relations between cultural identity and global hegemony" (these relationships are analogous to the properties of business cycles). Hence, the notion of "glocal" is a misplaced concreteness, because the "global" is not a place different from the "local"; the global exists only in its local effects; the global is a perspective, an insight into the organization of the local.

I think that Friedman's perspective is analytically sound and effective in explaining global relations, global consciousness, and the emergence of cosmopolitanism. But aren't the cultural and organizational products of the global, for instance, the IGOs, something different from and constraining the local and national? Aren't the microglobal structures of Knorr Cetina referring to an important emergent global dynamics?

For Friedman, internal and external (global) relations have been always there as constitutive forces of social reproduction of a given society, so that globalization is not a new phenomenon. According to Friedman, Sassen understands the importance of the globalization of capital flaws but only for explaining global transformations and not the emergence of the global. Friedman focuses on the historical specificity and the cyclical nature of the new global system characterized, among other things, by the geographical decentralization of economic accumulation, and cultural and political fragmentation; this is a cyclical and recapitulatory system. This systemic perspective renders superfluous a state-centered perspective to analyze globalization; on this point Friedman concurs with Sklair's position. His perspective allows him to offer also engaging critiques of some common conceptualizations of hybridity, "creolization," nation-state, transnationalism, and various other anthropological notions.

Jonathan Friedman discusses the ethnographic implications of his position: culture cannot be approached as an abstraction or a "superorganic". "If the global is not a place, but merely a set of properties that informs and reproduces the local, field work must deal with the existential and the concrete as much as with cultural objects." In fact, "The local is always an articulation between a specific historical and cultural and localized set of practices and its larger field of forces and conditions of reproduction."

Jonathan Friedman also elaborates on some methodological prescriptions for studying historical cycles of self-reproduction, including a phenomenological insight into processes of structuration and underlying ordering processes.

The discrepancies among the theoretical positions we have discussed may be partially understood by relating them to the empirical (Sassen, Rosenau), phenomenological (Knorr Cetina), systemic (Stichweh), and structural-Marxist perspectives (Friedman). Perhaps the notions of emerging spatiotemporalities that are separate and overlapping (Sassen), or in the shadow of (Knorr Cetina), or superimposed (Stichweh) on the local and national can be accepted as preliminary conceptualizations of the global as the objective relationships that condition the social production of the local (Friedman); but real understanding is achieved only through "structural analysis." For me empirical and structural analyses are two moments of the theorizing of the global.

The caution against the reification of the global is more than an artificial byproduct of a structuralist ploy à la Levi-Strauss. We saw this principle clearly stated by Rosenau and it is a central canon of the globalization perspective even for Martin Albrow.

Martin Albrow's chapter, "Situating Global Social Relations," reports on his London fieldwork in working-class housing and in international phonecalls, where he saw social practices being shaped by specific territories, by the nation-state, and by even larger entities. The social identity of social actors derives from a much wider social order than the village, town, region, or country. Affirmations of identity are made in reference to a frame outside the national territory. The homeless, women, blacks, whites "are located in global social relations." They recognize they have various issues in common and that these issues are the bases for common understandings and collective action. Even their national identity emerges in a global framework. "Nationality is quite essentially a tertiary relation. Tertiary or global relationships (such as identity relations with strangers) are constitutive elements of social practices that do not occur in a national context, but in an open field or flux of cultural, economic, and political relations."

> Albrow reconsiders of older community-based ways of thinking about society where social relations were dichotomized as primary and secondary. We can add a tertiary category to take account of identity relations and their potential global scope, and recast the conceptual scheme into three nonprioritized categories of intimacy, instrumentality, and identity.

Albrow refers to the postmodern emphasis on actor's narratives as a locus of lived experience and identity. This marks a shift in the conceptualization of social relations. The old Chicago school of primary and secondary relations implied spatial and temporal criteria (for instance, physical proximity, face-to-face relationships); for Marx social relations are based on class. With the postmodern emphasis on identity we have a shift from class, essentialism, and space/time-based social relations to social relations based on intimacy, instrumentality (relations in terms of calculated advantage), and identity (socially ascribed identity independent of spatial and temporal categories). Albrow's redefinition of social relations is an intriguing one, and, certainly, entails a notion of global that is somewhat consistent with Rosenau and Friedman's notions that the local is constituted in global relations.

Conclusion to Part 1

These chapters represent a progression from microstructures to macrostructures, from structures to systems, and from historically cyclical systems to open, unpredictable, and self-organizing systems with a final "return" back to the concrete and to the local. Underlying these analytic differences are the empirical, evolutionist, phenomenological, structuralist (à la Levi-Strauss), and the ethnographic perspectives à la Geertz (Albrow). In this sense the essays of this book provide applications, extensions, and refinements of the large spectrum of socioanthropological theories.

Yet, it is interesting that we have some sort of theoretical triangulation on the notion that the global is concrete and nonreified from three different theoretical perspectives: Rosenau's interactionism, Friedman's structural Marxism, and Geertzian ethnography as applied by Martin Albrow.

We have too often referred to conflicts underlying global trends. Global conflicts are not just cultural and civilizational in nature but they are also economic and political, as we discuss in Part 2 of the book.

Part 2:   Economic and Political Processes

Economic Integration, Disintegration, and Uneven Development

The field of economic globalization abounds in controversies. The first two chapters of part two deal with the crucial issue of whether globalization brings a new level of integration to the world or whether it increases economic disparities. We can say that we have greater integration in the sense of increased interaction among the world's nations (Chase-Dunn and Andrew Jorgenson); but on the vital question of whether all nations share equally in the economic benefits produced by increased economic transactions the answer is negative.

Christopher Chase-Dunn and Andrew Jorgenson focus on long-term processes of trade integration in their chapter, "Trajectories of Trade and Investment Globalization," where they discuss the definition and operationalization of various dimensions of global integration: economic, political, and cultural. They distinguish political globalization (or the political discourse about global integration and competition aimed at justifying policies) from structural globalization that they define as an increase in spatial scale (expansion) and in the intensity of political, economic, and cultural interactions. The greater integration and interdependence of the world is presented as an attribute of the whole world-system. Previous research has shown that trade globalization is a cyclical phenomenon with the highest peak being reached in recent times. Chase-Dunn and Jorgenson in this chapter want to determine whether international capital flows and investments increase with the size of the world economy. The increase of structural integration is measured by the ratio of increase of transnational interactions over intranational interactions. Focusing on trade, they measure the average "open trade" globalization in terms of country ratio of GDP to imports. Chase-Dunn and Jorgenson also discuss measures of political globalization and investment globalization (another measure of economic globalization); the latter is conceptualized as the sum of all international financial transactions (involving claims of ownership and control of debt) over the size of the world economy (the sum total of national GDP). Having discussed the problem of lack of data, they offer further refine-ment of measurements, including various types of investment income. Finally, they analyze the data for the period for which adequate data are available, 1938–1999, and they find that after World War II there has been an upward trend of investment globalization; this has sharply increased since 1970 when regulations over international investments were established together with a deregulation of international monetary arrangements.

In a previous longer version of their papers, Chase-Dunn and Jorgenson had explained the cyclical nature of trade globalization:

> Our research shows that economic globalization is a cycle as well as an upward trend, and so periods of high economic integration in the past have been followed by periods of de-globalization. This shows that the reduction of transportation and communication costs is not the only cause of globalization; the latter is affected also by the institutional structures of global governance associated with the rise and fall of hegemonic core states.

The authors' reference to institutions of global governance recognizes the inseparability of economic and political processes and the avoidance of monocausal economic determinism.

Christopher Chase-Dunn and Andrew Jorgenson provide a well-documented illustration of what Arrighi calls temporal unevenness. Whereas Chase-Dunn focuses on structural integration as measured by increased interaction of trade and investment activities, Giovanni Arrighi focuses on ideological globalization. In his chapter, "Uneven Development and Globalization," he argues that much of what goes under the name of globalization is a reflection of the temporal and spatial unevenness of the processes of capital accumulation on a world scale. "Uneveness" brings to mind the opposite of integration; in fact, for Arrighi temporal unevenness concerns what some observers call long phases of predominant prosperity and predominant depression, and others call global turbulence. Spatial unevenness concerns the distribution and redistribution of prosperity and depression among the world's regions and political jurisdictions. Both kinds of unevenness originate in major clusters of innovations that recurrently restructure the world politically, economically, and socially.

The first part of the chapter deals with temporal unevenness, focusing specifically on financialization and ideological globalization as instruments of competition and class struggle in the global North. Post-World War Two expansion benefited the Third World countries up to the 1970s, because they received high prices for their commodities and could rely on an abundance of cheap investments. Since 1980 the ideological globalization of Margaret Thatcher and Ronald Reagan drastically curtailed cheap capital and corporate taxes and increased interest rates and corporate freedom. The consequence was a worldwide recession with a contraction of demand for commodities and a decrease of cheap investment capital. At the same time, the so-called "development project" of post-World War II had encouraged import substitution within developing countries, but it was substituted in the 1980s and 1990s by the procapitalist or market-friendly strategies of privatization, free trade, and free movement of capital; the latter were promoted by the "Washington consensus." The result was a worldwide recession and a stagnation of low- and middle-income countries: the rate of growth of per capital income of these countries fell from 2.5% from 1960–1979 to 0% from 1980–1998. So much for an increase in structural integration: the key issue is which country is in control of structural integration and which countries benefit or suffer from it.

The second part of the chapter deals with spatial unevenness that focuses on the differential impact of financialization and ideological globalization on the global South and global North. The period of "development project" favored manufacturing over agriculture and the service sector, for productivity reasons; the hope was that industrial convergence would narrow income differences between First and Third World countries. Industrial convergence occurred: whereas in 1960 the proportion of GDP produced by manufacturing in the Third World countries was 74.6% of that of the First World, in 2000 it was 17.1% higher. However, during these 40 years the income gap between the southern and northern hemispheres has remained unchanged: the per capita GNP of Third World countries was 4.5% of that of First World countries in 1960 and 4.6% in 2000. (These measures are weighted by population growth, which is much higher in the newly industrializing countries.) Arrighi argues that these two apparently contradicting trends are consistent with Schumpeter's theory of competition under capitalism and Raymond Vernon's closely related theory of the "product cycle".

In conclusion, it was political globalization that produced the income divide between the northern and southern hemispheres, and political globalization was dictated by the need to reverse the sliding power and prestige of the United States after the two sharp increases in oil prices. The increased interest rate rerouted massive capital toward the U.S. currency, increased the U.S. debt, and denied capital to the developing world. There was an exception: Southeast Asia took advantage of U.S. demand for cheap commodities. The chapter concludes with a discussion of the success of China and India who participate in structural globalization on their own terms. China succeeds on the global scene by substituting inexpensive educated labor for expensive machines and expensive managers as well; inexpensive educated labor is important also for China's research and development. Because of their size and educational capital, China and India can control the conditions of globalization, but not sub-Sahara or Latin America. In the final analysis, the prospect for economic development in the Third World countries is rather gloomy, with the exception of the two major countries of China and India.

Robert Schaeffer's chapter, "Globalization and Disintegration: Substitutionist Technologies and the Disintegration of Global Economic Ties," also focuses on a negative consequence of economic globalization, as the title itself suggests. Schaeffer's approach is grounded in world-system theory and in theories of "agro-industrial development" advanced by environmental scholars (Goodman, Sorj, and Wilkinson) who have contributed to the "sociology of agriculture" school. He grafts together elements of both schools for two reasons: he thinks that the world-system perspective needs a better appreciation of the role of technology as a force for change, which the sociology of agriculture provides; and, because environmental scholars need a wider understanding of the import of technological change, which the world-system perspective provides. His approach advances the work of agriculture school sociology by applying their theoretical insights about "dematerialization," not only to agricultural resources, but also to mineral resources (oil and metals).

Schaeffer starts from the premise that the emergence of the capitalist world-economy in the 16th century set the stage for an ongoing globalization of economic and political institutions based in Europe. The world economy that emerged experienced fairly long periods of expansion and contraction. Some expansionary periods have been characterized by a tendency to integrate production, trade, investment, and technology around the world. The periods from 1880–1914 and 1970–2000/present have been identified as two such periods, which have been theorized in a diverse literature (not exclusive to world-system theory) as "globalization". But although there has been considerable economic and political integration or globalization in the most recent period, two important technological developments—what I have called "substitutionist" and "dematerialist," after Goodman, Sorj, and Wilkinson—have contributed not to integration, but to a disintegration of long-standing economic ties between core and periphery. *Substitutionist* technologies are those that are used to replace one raw material input with another. *Dematerialist* technologies are those that reduce raw material inputs through conservation, waste reduction, and recycling. Using a theoretical framework derived from world-system theory (particularly the relation between core and periphery) and operational concepts from the sociology of agriculture (particularly dematerialization), this chapter examines the impact that new core technologies have had on peripheral producers of sugar, tropical oils, coffee, copper, gold, and oil. Chief among these technologies are high fructose corn sweeteners, wireless and fiber-optic telecommunications technologies, financial instruments, and energy-saving technologies. Schaeffer argues that new technologies in the core have contributed to a series of problems in the periphery: falling commodity prices, widespread unemployment, declining state revenues, trade deficits, currency devaluations, and growing indebtedness. These developments have resulted in a weakening of economic and political ties between core and periphery.

Schaeffer's approach to globalization differs from that of many scholars because he does not think that global change has a singular, universal social meaning. Instead he argues that global change—like that associated with dematerialist and substitutionist technologies—has diverse social meanings in different settings; the new agroindustrial technologies wreak different kinds of havoc around the world.

The chapter, then, examines the implications of these developments for theories of globalization and future empirical research. First, it argues that the development of new core technologies will likely accelerate in the coming years, contributing to the process of disintegration. Second, it maintains that although some new economic ties will be forged between core and periphery—chiefly by the development of export-manufacturing and tourist industries in the periphery—they will not replace or compensate for lost ties based on primary goods production. Third, the ongoing disintegration of economic ties will contribute to a growing reluctance by the core to invest economically or intervene politically in the periphery. The dissolution of important economic and political ties is a development that Schaeffer characterizes as "indifferent imperialism." Finally, the disintegration of important economic and political relations between core and periphery will bring an end to the core efforts aimed at "modernizing" or to "developing" the periphery, and will close the book on the theories of development that informed them.

In conclusion, although the globalization of investment, production, trade, and technology does provide some benefits to the periphery, the chief beneficiaries of globalization have been countries in the core of the world system. From this perspective, globalization has resulted in a greater integration of businesses and states in the core, but has simultaneously resulted in disintegration and a distancing of the core from the periphery.

Arrighi and Schaeffer's critical assessment of the inability of the South to catch up with the North documents some of the imbalances and conflicts on which Rossi's dialectic view is anchored. These chapters foreshadow Kellner's chapter on the political ambiguities of globalization.

World Governance, Terrorism, and Democracy

The area of political globalization is no less complex and controversial than the area of economic globalization. The chapters of this section deal with two central issues: is global governance possible and are global capitalism and democracy compatible.

In her chapter, "Social Integration, System Integration, and Global Governance," Margaret Archer argues that the penetrative power of economic, political, and cultural changes that go under the label of "globalization" have made all of us "denizens of one world," but not "citizens" of it. Archer makes a distinction between "social integration," that is, social relationships between people—individuals, collectivities, and groups on the global scene—and "system integration," that is, structural relationships of contradiction or complementarity between the parts (institutions) of global society. Archer argues that both are simultaneously dropping to low levels of integration, which represents a formula promotive of rapid, unregulated, and potentially explosive transformation. According to Archer, the state once supplied legitimate channels and a relatively stable context for institutional operations (system integration), and a relatively secure environment for individual life-projects (social integration); these two types of integration regulated each other within the territorial boundaries of the state that provided, among other things, one national labor market, a national educational system, and citizenship. Ideological conflicts also produced mutual regulation, and so did the interface between state and civil society.

The delinking of economy and culture from the state brought disintegration without introducing a new integrative mechanism.

> . . . The problem raised by globalization concerns guidance and participation. The absence of guiding agencies has been highlighted by sociologists in terms of a 'runaway world' (Giddens) or 'risk society' (Beck). The lack of participatory mechanisms has been captured by the concept of 'exclusion'. If participation means having a say through open channels, then the human family is worse off in these respects and it is becoming more so, although the costs are unequally distributed around the globe. To be affected by globalization, without any ability to exert a counter-effect, is the lot of the vast majority of the world's population. It means that global penetration is negatively related to participation. Not only is it unaccompanied by new forms of government and governance, it systematically disempowers those previous and hard-won agencies for guidance and participation—representative democracy, the institutions of civil society, trade unionism, and citizenship—which, until now, were associated with development; that is, the truly novel consequence of early globalization. To some sociological commentators, all that had seemed solid had melted, into the ether. What globalization left was a gaping void between free-floating global networks and the atomized individual, the two connected only by Internet. . . .

With the delegitimation of the state (and the state becoming less and less important to people) trends toward privatization and the exclusion of large social segments have emerged. Archer also faults neoliberalism that justifies the quest for cheap labor, deal-making with weak states accompanied by corruption, the flight of the technical elite toward industrial countries, the disintegration of indigenous populations, cybercrime, fundamentalist movements, and ethnic tribalism (p. 13).

What are the prospects of a Global Order? We lack a single agency for global governance, but we have the recognition of a finitude of resources and of the dangers of nuclear conflagration. Hence, we all recognize that we have common interests, rights, and obligations (p. 14). The new social movements under the aegis of "global civil society" (my use of the term) offer some hope of countering nationalism, fundamentalism, and disintegrating economic processes. Margaret Archer is, however, rather pessimistic about the possibility of a "cosmopolitan democratic community," because social movements are denied a role in decision making, and the IGOs are at the mercy of national interests.

One may want to raise the following questions: at whose expense was national integration achieved under the state? Was regulation imposed by strong social strata over weaker ones? Archer raises the issue of what the conditions of new integration might be (namely, the bringing together again of social and systemic integration): it may well be that a common framework of co-existence may emerge from the recognized world's dangers. One wonders whether Archer pays sufficient attention to the declaration of universal human rights, the doctrines of international regimes, the emerging globalism and cosmopolitanism (see the works of J. Meyer and the "World Polity" group), the spreading of democracy, and global civil society as factors that may foster a greater integration of the world. Besides, many authors may question Archer's assumption about the delegitimation and the fading power of the state. (On this issue see the last essay in this volume)

The following chapter is relevant to this question: can a universally acceptable notion of democracy provide a global normative framework?

Douglas Kellner offers a sharp critique on the notion of democracy in capitalistic America and entertains a dialectic and critical discourse that points at certain convergences with the dialectic argument of Rossi's first chapter in this volume. In his chapter, "Globalization, Terrorism, and Democracy," Kellner argues that the terrorist attack of 9/11 and the ensuing war on terrorism show contradictions in the nature of globalization that requires a rigorous critique.

> I want to argue that in order to properly theorize globalization one needs to conceptualize several sets of contradictions generated by globalization's combination of technological revolution and restructuring of capital, which in turn generate tensions between capitalism and democracy, and haves and have nots. Within the world economy, globalization involves the proliferation of the logic of capital, but also the spread of democracy in information, finance, investing, and the diffusion of technology. Globalization is thus a contradictory amalgam of capitalism and democracy, in which the logic of capital and the market system enter more and more arenas of global life, even as democracy spreads and more political regions and spaces of everyday life are being contested by democratic demands and forces. But the overall process is contradictory. Sometimes globalizing forces promote democracy and sometimes inhibit it, thus either equating capitalism and democracy, or simply opposing them, are problematical. . . .
>
> Hence, I would advocate the development of a critical theory of globalization that would dialectically appraise its positive and negative features. A critical theory is sharply critical of globalization's oppressive effects, skeptical of legitimating ideological discourse, but also recognizes the centrality of the phenomenon in the present age. It affirms and promotes globalization's progressive features, while criticizing negative ones and noting contradictions and ambiguities. . . . (p. 8)

Kellner stresses the importance of "reflecting on the implications of September 11 and the subsequent Terror War for critical social theory and democratic politics, envisaging a new global movement against terrorism and militarism and for democracy, peace, environmentalism, and social justice."

In conclusion, the chapters of Part 2 point to positive and negative aspects of globalization and in this sense reinforce the premises of a conflictual and dialectic view of globalization. It is also interesting to see in Kellner's work a reference to global civil society; this is a factor that plays an important role in my dialectic framework for the analysis of globalization.

Part 3:   Methodological Approaches to the Study of Globalization

This section contains chapters related to the study of globalization as an historical and as a contemporary process.

The perspective on globalization as an historical process was briefly introduced by Rossi's essay at the beginning of the book. Raymond Grew offers a provocative analysis of key issues entailed by an historical analysis of globalization; the issues he raises present serious challenges to the discipline of history as well as to social sciences. Grew argues that the historical study of globalization can make use of established methods and specializations, but it requires asking new questions of the past and integrating empirical research with theory, especially through the use of comparison.

The overwhelming attention paid to theoretical issues by the contributors to this volume is consistent with the key importance given to them by John Boli (in private correspondence), Grew, and myself. Grew clearly states that the central problematics for globalization research is not related to methodology, but to proper theorizing. Globalization forces historians to ask new questions, and to make use of theory and comparison as well. This is a challenging call for the discipline of history that is well known for shying away from theorizing.

Grew suggests that the new questions can lead to the discovery of previously overlooked historical evidence of global relationships; such evidence should be used to produce testable hypotheses about globalization as an historical process. The results can be expected to challenge many current assumptions about globalization and, more important, to raise fundamental questions about established historical interpretations and also about contemporary globalization.

As mentioned, the social science chapters in this volume pay overwhelming attention to theoretical issues, especially to the proper definition of global relations; but theoretical issues inevitably surface even in chapters that deal more directly with questions of methodology. The methodologies referred to or used in this volume reflect the diversity of approaches prevailing in social sciences: statistical methodologies (Chase-Dunn and Sassen), historical analysis (Friedman, Sklair, Arrighi, Archer), ethnographic analysis (Friedman, Albrow), "grounded theory" (Rosenau), phenomenological analysis (Knorr Cetina), dialectic and critical analysis (Rossi and Kellner), as well as structural Marxism (Friedman).

This theoretical and methodological diversification that is typical in the social sciences is reflected in different research strategies in the field of globalization. Some authors, such as Sassen, prefer to start globalization research from the global, whereas Rosenau and Albrow start from the local, and others deny any real distinction between the two (Friedman).

Saskia Sassen's chapter, "Theoretical and Empirical Elements in the Study of Globalization," entails a heavy usage of statistical data, and new analytical concepts.

She begins with an analysis of the interaction and overlapping between the national and the global. Her point of entry is the global and she focuses on three elements to develop instruments for theorization and empirical specifications of globalization. The empirical instantiations of each of these elements lend themselves to detailed studies and a variety of research techniques, including some developed by anthropologists.

In the first section Sassen develops the question of place as central to many of the circuits constitutive of economic globalization; she conceptualizes the global economic system as partly embedded in specific types of places and partly constituted through highly specialized cross-border circuits. The second section develops some of these issues by focusing on microenvironments with a global span and what this entails for understanding the local. These microenvironments may actually be oriented to other such microenvironments located far away, thereby destabilizing the notion of context that is often imbricated in that of the local and the notion that physical proximity is one of the attributes or markers of the local. The third section concerns the national as instantiated in national states and the consequences of the partial embeddedness of the global in the national described in the first two sections. Her interpretation of the outcome is a partial denationalization of what has been constructed over the last century or more as "national" (in the sense of the national state, not national people) territories and institutional domains.

The headings and subheadings of her chapter provide a good idea of her key analytical concepts: "Place in a Global and Digital Economy," "The Material Practices of Globalization," "Global Cities are Centers for the Servicing and Financing of International Trade, Investment, and Headquarter Operations," "New Geographies of Centrality and of Marginality," "A New Transnational Politics of Place?," "Sited Materialities and Global Span," "A Networked Subeconomy," "The Intersection Between Actual and Digital Space," and "Denationalized State Agendas and Privatized Norm-Making."

Saskia Sassen has been using economic data, but more recently she has expressed the need to incorporate cultural data to carry out adequate globalization research.

James N. Rosenau in a short chapter called "Toward a Viable Theory of Globalization" offers "a grounded-theory" strategy to theorize about globalization starting from the smallest instances of interaction. He starts from the premise that "all the dimensions of globalization are sustained by individuals at the microlevel as well as by diverse organizations at the macrolevel." It follows that the central task of globalization research for him is to ascertain how leaders and officials (macroperspective) and the numerous individuals composing the public (microperspective) influence the other's orientations and behavior. If we assume "that all globalizing actions originate with individuals who may then form aggregate entities that engage in salient behavior, then it clearly follows that an adequate theory of globalization must perforce allow for micro–macro interactions." This position counters the usual attention that is given to the macroperspective.

To carry out his micro–macro perspective Rosenau suggests starting with the question, "Of what is this an instance?" where "this" "refers to anything we observe, whether it is in personal, professional, political, or global life and irrespective of whether it occurs in our immediate environment, is read in print, or is seen on television. If the instance is seen as indicating that cultural flows can move from west to east as well as east to west, globalization theorists can avoid the trap of assuming that globalization consists of the spread of American values and are thus in a better position to integrate the cultural dimension into their theoretical framework. He concedes that this "journalistic method" does not provide any guidance on how to integrate insights about cultural flows with generalizations and, hence, how to generate micro–macro theoretical propositions. "For this purpose a more encompassing micro–macro perspective is needed, one that combines the fruits of the what-is-this-an-instance question with a scheme that identifies the sources of globalization and generates hypotheses as to how they might operate in a micro–macro context."

Starting from the definition that globalization consists of "all those processes whereby flows expand across national borders, flows of goods, ideas, people, pollution, drugs, crime, disease, technology, and a host of other phenomena that are part and parcel of daily and national life," he identifies eight sources of flows; these sources contain micro- and macrocomponents that aggregate at four levels: micro, macro, micro–macro, macro–macro (see his complex table). The eight sources of flows are: Microelectronic Technologies, Skill Revolution, Organizational Explosion, Bifurcation of Global Structures, Mobility Upheaval, Weakening of Territoriality, States, and Sovereignty, Authority Crises, and Globalization of National Economies. These flows are analyzed through a 32-cell matrix (eight sources, each with four levels of aggregation).

I find that this approach can produce a practical tool for the empirical documentation of interaction flows. However, the linearity of flow sequences is a gratuitous assumption that needs to be demonstrated, because there are actions and counter-actions all along the flows. I also do not see a clear analytical distinction made among the cultural, political, and economic sources of flows and their dialectical interface. On the basis of my framework (discussed in the first essay of this volume), I find it more intellectually cogent to document the dialectical interaction within and among cultural, political, and economic flows at the local/national/international levels of societal interaction. Responding in a personal communication to my essay on the dialectics of globalization, Rosenau finds that our two approaches are complementary. Certainly, some operational complementarity can be worked out, but I would prefer operational guidelines that are derived from a clear analytical distinction among cultural, political, and economic flows.

Rosenau has added a methodological third step in his essay prepared for this book. Applying his micro–macro interaction theory to power relations, he rightly asserts that power is not a possessional attribute, but depends on the relation between those who exercise authority and those toward whom the authority is exercised. At the core of a viable theory, therefore, are relational phenomena.

Power analysis can be avoided by abandoning the concept of power and replacing it with two concepts, capabilities for the possessional factors and control for the relational factors. Such a conceptual adjustment ensures that the outcome of situations will be addressed and analyzed. It will enable observers to probe what possessions the parties to a situation bring to it and how the conduct of each party is founded not only on their relative possessions but also on the perceptions of the motives underlying each others' efforts to control the outcome of the situation.

This consideration is certainly true of any social interaction, in general, and of global relations, in particular. This relational perspective is also central to a dialectical view of globalization. The relational perspective, however, can be understood as an analysis of sequences of behavioral (observable) interactions and overtly ascertainable exchanges of meaning. One can, however, push the relational perspective to the level of deep structures or constitutive relations that underlie empirically observable structures (à la Levi-Strauss) and à la Friedman. Friedman states the following.

> Because the global is embedded in real lives, although its properties may not necessarily be experienced directly in those lives, it is not another place or level of reality, but an aspect of social reality, and thus, ethnographically accessible. . . . If the global is not a new place, it is certainly a perspective on social reality . . . If it is not something that has suddenly occurred, it is an insight into the organization of the world, an insight in the deep logic of things.

In a summary of his chapter, "Situating Global Social Relations" Martin Albrow argues as follows.

> Ethnography, if conducted on the basis of traditional assumptions about the community as a basic unit of society and the local as the natural site for research, will have difficulties in taking globalization as a field of research. In recent years both globalization and the politics of identity have fore grounded social relations as the most effective conceptual lens for viewing contemporary changes in society. In ethnography this has led to a new emphasis on the porosity of place and the world wide interconnectedness of people in a locality.

Albrow's methodological stance is Geertz's "thick description" of the concrete and the requirement that any theoretical concept must be translatable or documentable in terms of "the description of the meanings that acts have for actors." We must be aware that the boundaries of class, status, and power are continuously renegotiated in a global framework that is beyond the boundaries of the village, "community," town, regions, and nation-state. Our social relations are "mediated by the rest of the world" (and reinterpreted accordingly); social relations are free-floating "in the flux of global social relations." Global social relations are objective, namely they have an impact on peoples' lives; global social movements and protests, among other things, document this very well.

Albrow draws several ethnographic strategies from his notion of global relations: (1) avoidance of the dichotomy of close–distant relations, because, for instance, social trust and social capital that are so important in social relations are cast in a wide framework of expectations. (2) we need to introduce "socioscape" and "sociosphere" to grasp the quality of relations in a noncommunity-based locality. "Local space" ought to be replaced with socioscape, because visibly local social relations make sense "as an ecological ordering of physical distances, as an administrative ordering, usually of occupations and of potential relations born of proximity;" these relations have an environmental and aesthetic reality and an identity of place; (3) "sociospheres" are extensions of social relations over time and space that only occasionally result in face-to-face interaction; they are the networks, communities, or collectivities in which social actors participate, but beyond our vision. Only socioscapes are visible because that is where visible actors meet; socioscape is the materialization or momentary instantiation of inter-secting sociospheres; (4) social relations are deterritorialized in the sense that their material conditions and environmental bases are not fixed or inherently bounded by localities. Milieux are social and environmental, but exchangeable and extendable in the sense that they transcend physical localities (e.g., an academic environment, a business environment); (5) finally, social relations are constraining and real in their consequences. It is, then, clear that the ethnographic study of social relations is now an effective method for developing a theoretical framework for understanding society under globalized conditions.

These are important concepts that ought to guide a globally conscious ethnographic research. In my view they appear to be useful as guidelines to move from the empirical ethnography of the territorialized microinteraction to the progressively more and more deterriorializing micro–macro and macro–macro levels of interaction, and, finally, to the level of the relationships of similarities/differences/oppositions underlying the micro–macro and macro–micro arch of analysis. At the same time, these globally generated guidelines seem flexible enough to study semi-institutionalized and thin microglobal structures (see Knorr Cetina's paper), the layers of overlapping structures (Stichweh), and the evanescence and unpredictable complexity of co-evolving and self-organizing systems (Urry).

This brief overview of the book's contributions has shown that globalization research has produced new conceptual tools to link traditional and novel theoretical perspectives. Globalization research has produced an elaboration of traditional perspectives, the emergence of new ones, and has generated new research strategies. The reader must judge for herself or himself the validity of these claims by experiencing first hand globalization research through these original essays.

References Cited and Bibliography

Hardt, Michael and Antonio Negri. 2000. *Empire*. Cambridge MA: Harvard University Press.

Rossi, Ino, ed . 1974. *The Unconscious in Culture: The Structuralism of Claude Levi-Strauss in Perspective*. New York: Dutton.

——, ed. 1982. *Structural Sociology*. New York: Columbia University Press, 1982.

——, ed. 1982a. *The Logic of Culture: Advances in Structural Theory and Method*. South Hadley, MA: J. F. Bergin.

——, 1983. *From the Sociology of Symbols to the Sociology of Signs: Toward a Dialectic Sociology* (translated in Japanese). New York: Columbia University Press.

——. 1993. *Community Reconstruction after an Earthquake: Dialectical Sociology in Action*. Westport, CT: Praeger.

Part 1
Theoretical Perspectives

1
Globalization as an Historical and a Dialectical Process[1]

Ino Rossi

The purpose of this chapter is to provide a comprehensive understanding of the various facets of globalization. Globalization is explained as a multicivilizational and technologically sustained process that is driven by conflicts among different cultural traditions and by competing interests among nations and among social strata within nations. Globalization is approached from a macro, micro, and historical perspective. Because all these perspectives are represented in the contributions to this volume, this essay may help the reader to see the relation-ship among the contributions and, therefore, attain an integrated understanding of the volume.

The ambition of this chapter goes a bit further. A comprehensive view of globali-zation is achieved by focusing on the conflictual interaction between the vertical and horizontal parameters, so to speak, of intrasocietal and intersocietal processes: the vertical parameter refers to the interaction among the local, national, and international levels of societal functioning; the horizontal parameter refers to the interaction among the cultural, political, and economic principles of social organization within each level of societal functioning.

In the first part of the chapter I construct a typology of societies to identify three major kinds of globalization. In the second part I use the typology to discuss the dialectical interaction among intrasocietal, intersocietal, and intercivilizational

---

[1] I acknowledge the suggestions and criticisms of Janet Abu-Lughod, Giovanni Arrighi, John Boli, Raymod Grew, and Frank Coppa to an early draft of this essay. I am the only one responsible for my selective hearing.

processes. I conclude with a discussion on the "agency-structure" relationship to generate insights on how to mobilize societal resources for the resolution of global conflicts.

Globalization in Historical Perspective

Globalization has been referred to as the "widening, deepening and speeding up of world-wide interconnectedness in all aspects of contemporary social life, from the cultural to the criminal, the financial to the spiritual" (Held & McGrew, 2000: 2). Throughout human history contacts among different societies and civilizations have produced positive outcomes (through the borrowing of cultural elements, technologies, and other strategies for living) as well as negative outcomes (as a long history of conquests, oppressions, uneven developments, and conflicts amply demonstrate). A typology of human societies that is based on the dominant principle of social organization helps to identify the engines of intersocietal contacts in different types of societies.

Types of Human Societies

To avoid misunderstandings from my historian friends and historically minded social scientists, I clarify that I speak of "types" of societies in the sense of Weberian "ideal types" that I define as follows: analytical constructs based on the accentuation of one or more cultural, economic, or political events or traits as representing and synthesizing an historical period and/or the dominant characteristics of a given society. Because historical periods differ from each other on too many particularities of people, issues, circumstances, and events, the only way to compare one period to another is to focus on salient characteristics or events. For me the salient characteristic of a given type of society is the principle of social organization (cultural, political, and economic). Which principle is deemed to be "salient" is interactively determined by the perspective of the social scientist and the observable or documentable characteristics of the historical periods or societies that are compared. Those models, or ideal types, that explain most events with the least complex models will survive for use in further interpretations. This kind of validation or refutation is in human sciences somewhat analogous to the neopositivist notion of falsification; the latter, however, strictly speaking applies only to models based on statistical averages and not to "ideal types" (Rossi, 1974: 97).

The salient characteristics used to construct an ideal type or model can overlap or cross over more than one historical period. For instance, certain capitalist elements were present in Roman Palestine (an order to a banker to pay money held in account to a third party was the equivalent of our check), and in the classic Islamic empire (for instance, the bill of exchange) (McKay et al., 2004: 261). These practices, however, in combination with double-entry bookkeeping and business partnerships, among others, culminated in the new historical trend that we call the commercial capitalism of the Italian city-states (see below). There are, of course, many variations and mixed types of societies that do not fit squarely in just one model or type.

Ideal types are not evolutionary stages that all societies must experience in their development (as with the threefold typology of Comte and other evolutionists). Nor do I claim that any type of society is a necessary prerequisite for any other type of society, although historically one type of society may have transformed into another type in a given region of the world.

Following is a threefold typology of human societies based on the predominance of the cultural or political or economic principles of organization (see Table 1.1).

The three principles of social organization are consistent with the three principles of social order as formulated by Max Weber: the cultural order (status), the political order (power), and the economic order (class). This line of thinking has been continued and elaborated by Bourdieu, Collins, and Giddens, among others, with the notion of cultural, economic, and political capital (See Rossi, 1993: 19 ff). I use "capitalism" as the principle of organization of "economic societies," because I claim that with the advent of the capitalism of the medieval Italian city-states new economic forces emerged that slowly evolved as distinct, and often times, opposed to political forces. In other words, with capitalism new economic principles of organization began to give a distinctive dynamics to the society as a whole and eventually transformed it.

Table 1.2 shows that the three principles of social organization are present in all societies, but that their order of importance differs in the three different types of societies.

The solid horizontal arrow in Table 1.2 indicates that in cultural societies the primary organizational thrust derives from cultural institutions, the secondary one from issues of governance and social order, and the third one from economic concerns. Analogous considerations apply to the other two types of societies. The dotted lines indicate the feedback and adaptive pressures of the other principles of social organization.

Types of Globalization in Different Types of Societies

My attention here is on the relationship between the dominant principle of social organization and the engine of intersocietal connectedness. Different historical phases of globalization have been proposed by different authors such as Roland Robertson (1992), Held et al. (1999), Scholte (2000), Hopkins (2002), Robbie Robertson (2003), and Osterhammel and Peterson (2005) (see also Grew's chapter in this book).

TABLE 1.1. Typology of human societies.

Types of Societies	Principle of Social Organization
Cultural	Kinship, religion
Political	Centralized authority
Economic	Capitalism

TABLE 1.2. Differential importance of principles of social organization in different types of societies.

Type of Society	Principle of Social Organization		
	Kinship, Religion	Centralized Authority	Capitalism
Cultural	1	2	3
Political	2	1	3
Economic	3	2	1

1 = The most important principle of social organization.
3 = The least important principle of social organization.

I hypothesize that the dominant principle of societal organization determines the type of globalization or cross-societal ties. This hypothesis is based on the simple reason that societies put their efforts into acquiring and trading items that are most important to their functioning and/or are more meaningful to their members. On the basis of this principle we can distinguish three major "types" of globalization (with, of course, a variety of possible subtypes and mixed types): in cultural societies the most important items circulating across societal boundaries are cultural in nature, in political societies the main cross-societal linkages are political in nature, and in economic societies the trade of goods is the dominant cross-societal link. In transitional or mixed types of societies we expect to find a mixture of these cross-societal links. Because space limitations prevent a full historical analysis, I limit myself to a few illustrative examples.[2]

Cultural Societies and Forms of Cultural Globalization

Historical examples of *cultural societies* are aboriginal societies where political and economic activities were governed by kinship principles (the council of the elders) and were preceded and followed by religious rituals. Properly speaking, the distinction among the cultural, political, and economic principles of social organization does not apply to aboriginal cultures. Anthropologists state that in

---

[2] In rereading the contributions I realized that Jonathan Friedman's chapter in this book conceives globalization in Braudelian terms as a world-systemic phenomenon related to cycles of expansion and contractions. He gives as examples the political rise and fall of the Roman Empire, the capital export of Macedonian expansion, the commercial expansion of the Aegean and Athenian dominance, and globalization as a transfer of capital. My typology suggests that cycles of expansion can be typologized on the basis of the circulation of cultural, political, and economic capital.

these societies political and economic activities were embedded within cultural institutions, because those activities were permeated with kinship and religious meaning. These were "moral order" societies (Redfield, 1953) and "multifunctional societies" (Diamond, 1977 in Rossi et al., 1977; Diamond and Belasco, 1980 in Rossi, 1980). The notion of multifunctionality entails that a given activity had simultaneously what we call a religious, kinship, economic, and political significance. In aboriginal cultures communal rituals and traditions provided the moral justification and the social standards for activities related to social order and the production and distribution of goods (Firth, 1936, 1965). The exchange of economic goods had at times a ceremonial meaning (the Kula Ring, for instance) and it was always governed by kinship ties and religious values. The ownership of cultural and strategically important items was controlled by the community as a whole. The governing functions were carried out in an egalitarian setting through the council of elders, and communal tasks were performed under situational and rotational leadership. Anthropologists have amply discussed intersocietal linkages among aboriginal cultures in the form of the exchange of marriage partners and exchange of goods (e.g., the well-known case of the Kula Ring; – Malinowski, 1922/1961). We can perhaps mention also the "Segmentary Lineage System" as an intertribal mechanism (Sahlins, 1961). However, because the rudimentary technology of aboriginal societies limited the number of social groups that could come in contact with each other, we cannot speak of transsocietal ties across the world. At that stage of societal development we had what I call transcultural ties of a preglobal nature.

Contemporary examples of cultural societies are Islamic theocracies, although, of course, they have a differentiated institutional structure with strong political and economic institutions. They would, certainly, like to base the course of globalization on religious foundations.

State Societies and the Advent of Political Globalization

With the advent of civilization, some egalitarian and rank societies were transformed into state societies; the latter were characterized by the emergence of the centralized (suprakinship) authority of the king or emperor and the emergence of social classes with the ruling classes having economic and political power over lower classes. Typically, centralized authority controlled the economic resources and favored the development of religion to provide justification for the centralization of power; hence, religious and economic institutions were subordinated to political institutions. Cultural anthropologists use the term "political economies" to refer to societies where the production and distribution of goods and services is controlled by a centralized authority (Bodley, 2000: 179). E. Wolf (1982) asserts that state societies were based on "tributary production" or on the extraction of surplus from the self-supporting peasantry; the prevalent economic activity in this type of society consisted of agricultural production that was totally controlled by the political class. The classic civilizations of Mesopotamia, Hindu, China, Mesoamerica, Andes, all had state forms of political systems, and eventually all collapsed, with the exception of China; the latter is a clear example of a civilization surviving political collapse. War, environmental, and ideological factors were related to the downfall of state societies. A critical factor seems to have been the centralization of the wealth in the hand of a growing political elite that was unable to sustain its lifestyle and military needs through the labor of an overworked and impoverished working class (Yoffee & Cowgill, 1988). State society took different forms, including decay and decentralization during feudal times, until in 12th century England a monarchy emerged (Duicker & Spielvogel, 2001: 329) that shared power with the nobility.

Because of the preeminence of political institutions and the control (and ownership) of economic goods by the elite (king and nobility), these societies can be called *political societies*. Besides agricultural activities, market and trade were already known in tribal societies and, to even a greater extent, in state societies and in high civilizations. As already mentioned, some protocapitalistic practices were present in ancient civilizations (Roman Empire, Greek city-states, the Hellenistic period, and classic Islamic civilization), in the city-states of the early Middle Ages, and in the commercial capitalism of the High Middle Ages; but in all these societies the main intersocietal linkages were of a political nature.

The ideal type "political society" is not synonymous with the modern "state", but with a stratified and centralized society, the first one of which emerged with civilization. Hence, the ideal type of political society entails the following elements: (a) predominance of law, order, domination, and conquest as societal functions; (b) the control by a small elite of legal, military, and economic resources; political centralization can take various forms, such as king, emperor, absolute monarch, or fragmented forms such as the feudal ones. In these societies we have a *political economy,* because the production and distribution of the wealth is always and exclusively in the hands of the rulers and used to protect and enhance their position in power.

It seems undeniable that in the period of strong empires political (and legal) ties provided the framework for the commercial transactions among the societies that composed the empires. These intersocietal ties were taking place mostly and preeminently within the political boundaries of the empire (that is, within a single state society) and were controlled by the elites who exploited intersocietal transactions for their own benefit. Moreover, the flow of trade was slower than the flow of military networks.

Cultural ties were also important, as Table 1.2 suggests; in fact, the unity provided by the ancient civilizations of the Middle East, Greece, Rome, and by Christianity and other universal religions is referred to by some authors as "proto-globalization" (Cohen & Kennedy, 2000: 42). Some authors (Hopkins, 2002: 4) use the term "archaic globalization" to encompass all forms of globalization that appeared before industrialization.

With the decay of state authority came the period of deglobalization and vernacularization of the Middle Ages. This era was characterized by the following traits: weak states and fluid territorial borders; presence of both universal (Hindu,

Islam, Buddhist, Christian) and local affiliations; free movement of ideas with the Arabic and Muslim community providing the common framework of interaction; respect for cultural and religious diversity; coordination rather than assimilation or standardization as a strategy of expansion; such modern features as the importance of cities, migrants, and diaspora, global division of labor, and universal aspirations of belief systems. During this period the universalism of Hinduism, Christianity, transcontinental civilizations (Hindu, Chinese, and Islam) provided major linkages, especially in societies with weak political authority. During this phase of archaic globalization transsocietal networks were produced by kings, warriors, religious wanderers, and merchants; among priced goods traded were exotic herbs and spices, coffee, cotton, iron, woods, silk, printed fabric, bullion, firearms, and Arabian horses. However, globalization was circumscribed (p. 6) because it did not reach America and Australasia; the size of the market was limited by the division of labor and limited technology. The following ideologies influenced consumers and producers: cosmic kinship (Chinese universal rule with a mandate from heaven), universal religion, holistic understanding of land (p. 50). (Hopkins, 2002: 56). Important world religions and transcontinental civilizations were based on Hinduism, Confucianism, and Islam.

Civilizations provided transnational linkages in the absence of strong political ones. Around 1400 China and India controlled most of the trade that linked the Far East, Middle East, North Africa, and Europe (Genoa, Venice, and Bruges). This was also the era of a global trade network when societies were still feudal. China withdrew from external trade in 1400; Japan filled a bit of the vacuum left by China.

Societies with weak political authority experienced a transitional phase of globalization. In these societies cross-societal integration was mostly a matter of commercial ties within a large geographical area delimited by an ideological and intercivilizational framework.

Economic Societies and Capitalist Globalization

(1) With the advent of commercial capitalism in the 12th and 13th centuries, Europe experienced a protoindustrialization and protocapitalism in the form of competitive enterprises by merchants who invested in risky ventures or joint stock companies. Merchants could rely on banks, letters of exchange (that were equivalent to our checks), accounting brokerage houses, insurance against transportation risks, and on such instruments as bills of books and letters of credit. All these elements point to rationality as the key characteristic of commercial capitalism (McKay et al., 2004: 387) way before the 15th and 16th century capitalism that is usually considered the beginning of capitalism as a modern phenomenon.

A significant concomitant phenomenon was the advent of the private ownership of economic resources by the emergence of a middle class and rich mercantile elite. Towns (where trading companies, banks, and bourgeoisie resided) began to share political power with the monarchy and the church. Up to 1400 A.D.

most business activities were small and family owned so that the capital was controlled by the state and prominent families (Robbins, 2005: 67). Commerce was the new economic force that slowly overtook the agricultural wealth of the church, king, and landed aristocracy. The monopoly of wealth by the king (and the church) was seriously challenged as the wealth of the society began to switch from the hands of the monarchy and landed aristocracy to the hands of the bourgeoisie that began to control capital and technology and purchased labor for economic production. All these are characteristics of an economic society where cross-societal links were mostly based on commercial activities. Hence, with economic society emerged *commercial globalization*, that is, one subtype of capitalist globalization, where the word "capitalist" indicates the crucial role of finance capital in commercial activities.

Economic societies are characterized by changes in the source of wealth; for instance, an increased role of global trade and craft production in addition to agricultural production. Economic societies are characterized also by changes in ownership; as already mentioned, the third estate emerged with the ownership of new sources of wealth that slowly became the driving factors of socioeconomic development (Bodley, 2000: 308); eventually, the total cultural system became organized by impersonal market forces (op. cit.: 21).

The term "eventually" is of particular importance. I do not claim that as soon as a new social form (or a principle of organization) emerges, it quickly transforms the entire society and becomes the dominant principle of social organization that supersedes all the previous ones. Social transformations are usually very slow, and sometimes undergo reverse processes. What is important is that a qualitatively new social form has emerged and it has sown the seeds of societal transformation. An ideal type is not based on statistical frequencies of certain events, but on the detection of transformative principles of social organization. It goes without saying that a given transformative principle stretches out and overlaps more than one type of society; this is the same as saying that more than one transformative principle can be present in a given type of society, although only one transformative principle characterizes a given historical period either as a qualitatively new principle of societal organization (in its emerging phase) or as the qualitatively and quantitatively dominant principle of social organization (in its mature phase). For instance, in the medieval Italian city-states all three principles of social organization (the cultural, the political, and the economic principles) were co-present in the form of three estates, respectively, the clergy who attended to the principle that society should be guided by spiritual ends (Duiker & Spielvogel, 2001: 375), the nobility who provided security and justice functions, and the peasants and merchants. We can say that during the Italian city-states the first two estates had a "statistical predominance," so to speak, but the merchants were the qualitatively new minority that put into motion processes that in latter periods placed them in a position of "statistical" dominance over the other two estates.

Let us briefly attend to one example of a gradual evolution of a transformative principle. I claim that the origins of economic society began with the commercial capitalism of the medieval Italian city-states, where bankers, merchants, and other entrepreneurs did not belong to dominant estates and were involved in making, buying, and selling things; these activities were largely obscure at that time and frowned upon. However, "in the construction of Western society these men (and a few women) were as important as the canniest monarchs and emperors" (King, 2003: 294).

In the 11th century the Italian merchants had ships up to 40 meters long, commercial contracts (with lawyers and notaries), and business partnerships (King, 2003: 319 ff): in true partnerships the partners contributed capital and shared in the risks and profits in proportion to the capital invested. The 13th and 14th century Florentine capitalists owned privately or corporately the means of production, had some monopolies on certain goods, charged interests on loans, and were thrifty, industrious, and careful planners (Kagan et al., 1983: 395).

Taking off from Arab models (King: 319), in the Italian city-states of the early Middle Ages a new method to keep track of revenues and expenditures emerged, double-entry bookkeeping. This permitted business people to have a quick and complete picture of the financial state of the company; the earliest preserved double-entry books are from 1340 in Genoa. The first published accounting work was written in 1494 by the Venetian monk Luca Pacioli (1450–1520).

This form of commercial capitalism was truly transformative, although, until the end of the monopoly by craft guilds, capitalism expanded mostly in the form of domestic capitalism ("putting out system"): entrepreneurs purchased raw materials, gave them to craftsmen to work in cottages; craftsmen were paid for their product that was sold to the market for profit. This commercial production remained limited until the advent of the machine and factory system in the late 18th, and early 19th century (Harrison & Sullivan, 1980: 337–38).

(2) Modern capitalism represents another subtype of economic society: monarchs used merchants and bankers to increase their power at the expense of the nobility (Harrison & Sullivan, 1980: 338). In the 16th century the trade of slaves and spices as well as piracy tripled the silver and increased the gold stocks by 20% in Europe. This heavy monetarization contributed to the collapse of feudalism and the full swing of capitalism: the lords could not control the serfs any more and the merchants bypassed the guilds (Stavrianos, 1999: 324). Joint-stock companies emerged in Western Europe during the 17th and 18th centuries to further trade with the East Indies. The companies, which had varying degrees of governmental support, grew out of the associations of merchant adventurers who voyaged to the East Indies (King, 2003: 450). Unlike the partnerships of medieval merchants, joint-stock companies were comprised of hundreds and even thousands of individuals. The company had an identity independent of the partners (shareholders), had its own bureaucracy and security force, and sold its shares on the stock market (1531 in Antwerp, 1613 in Amsterdam). These companies pushed for trade privileges and were given charters by their respective governments, which authorized them to acquire territory and to exercise in the

acquired territory various functions of government, including legislation, the issuance of currency, the negotiation of treaties, the waging of war, and the administration of justice.

Among the most notable Western European companies were the English East India Company which was chartered in 1600 and was granted a monopoly of trade in Asia, Africa, and America, with the formal restriction that it might not contest the prior trading rights of "any Christian prince." The Dutch East India Company was incorporated in 1602; at the peak of its power, in 1669, the Dutch company had 40 warships, 150 merchant ships, and 10,000 soldiers. Between 1602 and 1696 the annual dividends that the company paid were never less than 12% and sometimes as high as 63%. The charter of the company was renewed every 20 years, in return for financial concessions to the Dutch government. The French East India Company was established in 1664 and the Danish East India Company was chartered in 1729.

We can see here that political functions were delegated to business companies and we see also that business companies and private capital were essential mechanisms for the wealth of the state and for the state to win the competition for international trade (witness the competition among Holland, France, and England). Definitely, at this point in history, we no longer had a political economy where political authority owned the factors of production and determined the way production ought to be done as well as the way goods and services were to be distributed (Bodley, 2000: 179, 301). In this sense, the welfare of the whole society began to depend more and more on the market forces and on finance capital. (For an excellent discussion of the importance of finance capital in economic or capitalist society, see Arrighi & Silver, 2001). In contraposition to the political economy of political societies, I call capitalism a market economy, because the trend has grown stronger and stronger toward the control of ownership, production, and distribution of goods by the economic actors (entrepreneurs, buyers, sellers, financiers) that make up the marketplace. There were, of course, as there are today, episodes of wars and long wars, but most of the long-term efforts and orientation of capitalist society have been toward a strengthening of market expansion and global economic competitiveness.

There is no institutional reductionism in this thinking. Capitalism is not a mere economic principle of societal organization with the total exclusion of the political and cultural principles of organization. Randall Collins has shown (1980) that there was a set of ultimate and intermediate conditions that led to modern Western capitalism. Among the cultural elements listed in his causal chain are the remote conditions of Greek civic cults, Judaic prophecy, Christian proselytization, Reformation sect, church law, and bureaucracy. These remote cultural conditions are linked to the intermediate cultural conditions of a methodical nondualistic economic ethic. Randall Collins also lists remote political conditions (literate administrators, disciplined army, centrally supplied weapons) together with remote economic conditions (transportation and communication innovations, record-keeping, and coinage (monetarization). These remote political conditions are linked to the intermediate conditions of a bureaucratic state, citizenship, and calculable law. In turn, the intermediate political conditions (calculable law, bureaucratic state, citizenship) and cultural conditions (methodical ethics) accounted for rationalized capitalism, that is, the entrepreneurial organization of capital, rationalized technology, free labor, and unrestricted markets.

I underline certain points in this conceptualization: (1) capitalism does not consist of just economic factors (capital, market, labor, technology, unrestricted markets), but also of cultural ones (entrepreneurial organization and rationalized technology) and political ones (such as calculable law and a bureaucratic state). According to Table 1.2 political and cultural principles of organization are present also in economic societies. As a matter of fact, cultural and political antecedents contributed to the emergence of the capitalist form of producing wealth. Eventually, the new economic form became the dominant principle that transformed all aspects of the society. (2) The new sociocultural economic form evolved gradually over long periods of history (at least partially) from religious capitalism to economic capitalism both in the West and in Japan. Capitalism is a transformative principle of social organization with cultural, political, and economic elements interacting with each other to transform the whole society.

Rightly, Randall Collins in his 1997 article on the Weberian explanation for the origins of capitalism in Japan insists on the "sustained innovativeness of self-transforming capitalism which expands to mass markets and proliferates market niches and new products" (Collins, 1997: 843). The self-transforming characteristic is missing in coercive agrarian societies.[3] What makes capitalism self-transforming, according to R. Collins, is its very essential characteristics: markets for goods, labor, capital, and land; entrepreneurial combination of factors of production; and disciplined, calculating economic ethic (op. cit.: 845). These are a combination of cultural and economic characteristics, with the support of the bureaucratic state. The latter must at the very least provide a legal apparatus for the recognition and protection of property rights and market transactions.

When a society becomes an economic society it does not lose political institutions. As a matter of fact, throughout human history, the political principle has always interacted with novel economic principles. As we have seen, during the Middle Ages monarchs used the merchants and towns to fight the nobility. Yet, political power transformed itself under the impact of the clergy, nobility, and townspeople to produce an innovative political principle, the Magna Charta in England (1215), that secured the rights of the three estates against autocratic kings. Later on, the economic principle became transformed with the chartered statutes offered by the state to trading companies. We can also add that in 1886 the U.S. Supreme Court recognized the private corporation as a natural person, having the same rights extended by the Bill of Rights to people (Robbins, 2005: 95).

---

[3] The term "coercive agrarian society" strikes very close to my type of "political or centralized society". I realized this after the first draft of my essay. Not only the anthropologist Bodley, but also the sociologist R. Collins uses a threefold typology—of cultures in the case of Bodley—of economies in the case of Collins.

These are just a few high points of a self-transforming capitalism that has been all along fueled by finance capital.

(3) With the advent of the modern age we had the age of explorations and the expansion of capitalism. The forces that produced the globalization of capitalism were a strong support by the state, and new technological innovations and business practices, especially by trading companies. Historians have referred to the period from 1600–1800 in Europe, Asia, and part of Africa as the early modern global society (Hopkins, 2002: 56). This period was marked by notable political, economic, and cultural advances: a reconfiguration of the state system into national monarchies (Spain, England, and France), growth of finances, services, and preindustrial manufacturing; Muslim and Christian states strengthened links among territory, taxation, and sovereignty without quite attaining the monopoly of loyalties. Parallel commercial and political developments occurred in Islam, Christianity, and China. From 1760 England began the commercial expansion and imperial acquisitions aided by improved technologies of transportation. There was a convergence of goods sought and traded: bullion, sugar, tobacco, coffee, and opium. Meanwhile, the "green revolution," the plantation system, and slavery flourished (ibid. 6, 56).

The remarkable phenomenon was that in the 16th century a world economic system became possible without a centralized political authority (Wallerstein, 1974, 1990) that was the dominant institution in political societies. In my formulation this was the period of extended (colonial) commercial globalization, another subtype, if you will, of capitalist globalization. In fact, the entire geographical world as known at that time, became interlinked through the commercial activities of trade companies with the backing, as we have seen, of political powers: so it was primarily a capitalist (commercial) globalization and secondarily a political one, as predicted in Table 1.2 for economic societies.

Important cultural revolutions were also the hallmarks of the modern age, chiefly the scientific revolution and the Enlightenment. Notably, the Enlightenment put forth the notion of a universal market (see Smith, 1776/1994) and of universal democracy, a forerunner of cosmopolitanism that is nowadays a highly debated aspect of cultural globalization. Philosophers of the Enlightenment, such as A. R. J. Turgot, J. G. Herder, and M. de Condorcet were interested in the history of mankind as a whole and in the social unity of the world.

(4) The advent of 18th century industrial capitalism began with the textile industry and the factory system. The major events of this period were the following: old imperialism and mercantilism (up to 1870); the global wars between France and England; the new imperialism from 1871 (Franco–Prussian war) to World War I; and the Bill of Rights and free speech extended to the corporation.

From mid-1800 to 1918 the following types of events must be noted: (1) political ones, such as the rise of state, national identity, expanded colonialism, property as a foundation of sovereignty, and assimilation and association as control strategies; (2) economic ones, such as the spread of industrialization and concomitant economic integration; (3) cultural ones, such as individualism, equalitarianism, rationality, and acquisitive spirit. Western industrial societies centered their success on the capitalist economy and the success of the bourgeoisie.

The period of industrial globalization was supported by the ideologies of nationalism (and colonialism), capitalism, democracy, and consumerism. During colonial capitalism there was an expansion of national capitals for foreign investments: the British capital investments abroad averaged 4.6% of GDP between 1870 and 1913, a level that was not reached again subsequently. Correspondingly, the percentage of savings remaining within the country was lower between 1880 and 1910 than in any other subsequent period (Wolf, 2001). The world production that is traded on global markets is not that much higher today than it was in the years leading up to World War I. In 1910 the ratio of trade (merchandise exports plus imports) to GDP hit record highs in several of the advanced economies: it was 11% of the GDP.

Importantly, the level of pre-World War I migration of labor was never equaled since. Some people suggested that from an economic point of view, the period from 1915 to 1945 was a period of deglobalization, because of the progressive closing of the movement of capital, people, and goods. This view is, of course, based on a prevalently economic and political perspective on globalization. The same authors argue that a politically determined deglobalization indicates that new (and cheaper) technologies of communication and transportation are not sufficient by themselves to increase the integration of economies; the political factors can by themselves block economic globalization (Wolf, 2001).

World War II brought about the end of colonialism and the transition from internationalization to postcolonial globalization: (a) a liberalization of capital flows began in a few advanced countries during the 1950s and 1960s, but intensive liberalization did not start until the late 1970s across industrialized countries and much of the developing world, and not until the 1990s in the former communist countries. In post-World War II we achieved a lower integration of capital than with the 19th century economic integration; (b) The total amount of global production that was traded worldwide grew from about 7% in 1950 to more than 20% by the mid-1990s. Most advanced economies experienced a sharp increase in trade rate as a percentage of GDP from 1910 to 1995: from 44% to 57% in the United Kingdom, from 35% to 43% in France, from 38 to 46% in Germany, from 11% to 24% in the United States; the latter is the greatest increase, whereas that in Japan decreased; (c) production has become nowadays more integrated: since the 1970s, national economies have broken down and tend to be rearranged more and more into a single global production system (Robinson 2004, Dicken 2003, Castells 2000). National capitals become disembedded more and more from their national places and interpenetrate with other cross-border capitals in a transnational capital. The states do not control the capitalist economy as capitals seek out nations where there are favorable taxation, environmental regulations, and low labor costs. The state and labor organizations have difficulties dealing with outsourcing; (d) short-term capital today is much more mobile than ever before. Moreover, long-term flows now are somewhat differently constituted than in the earlier period. Investment in the early 20th century took the form of tangible assets rather than intangible ones. Portfolio flows predominated over direct investment in the earlier period (that trend has been reversed since World War II); within portfolios, stocks have increased in relative importance to roughly equal bonds today. Finally, before 1914, direct investment was undertaken largely by companies investing in mining and transportation, whereas today multinational companies predominate, with a large proportion of their investment in services; (e) the trend toward financial crises remained constant. In monetary policy, the biggest change has been the move from the gold standard of the 1870–1914 era to the floating currencies of today. The long-run exchange-rate stability inherent in the gold standard promoted long-term capital flows, particularly bond financing, more efficiently than does contemporary currency instability. Today's vast short-term financial flows are not just a consequence of exchange-rate instability, but one of its causes; (f) yet governments' control over the movement of people in search of employment has tightened virtually everywhere since 1915. With the exception of the free immigration policy among members of the European Union (EU), immigration controls are generally far tighter now than they were a hundred years ago; (g) the policy change that has most helped global integration to flourish is the growth of international institutions since World War II. Just as multinational companies now organize private exchange, so too do global institutions organize and discipline the international face of national policy. Institutions such as the World Trade Organization (WTO), the International Monetary Fund (IMF), the World Bank (WB), the EU, and the North American Free Trade Agreement (NAFTA) require cooperation among states and consolidate their commitments to liberalize economic policy. The 19th century was a world of unilateral and discretionary policy. The late 20th century, by comparison, was a world of multilateral and institutionalized policy. Others, however, still prefer to talk of a growing internationalization.

With the collapse of colonialism, we had the end of political hegemonies and, after World War II, the triumph of global capitalism. The survival of national economies heavily depends on their successful link to the policies of the International Monetary Fund and other intergovernmental organizations (IGOs). More and more the nations of the world share a common destiny, because of their economic interdependence. Economic activities have taken a much more preeminent transnational character: the organization of geographically dispersed economic activities is functionally integrated ("globalized" according to Dicken, 2003: 12). National economies cannot prosper without and are heavily conditioned by transnational capital and by a transnational capitalist class that does not know of national loyalties (Robinson, 2004; see also Sklair's essay in this book).

Since 1985 we had a tremendous financial expansion and witnessed the advent of financial globalization, another subtype of capitalist globalization. Financialization, in the sense of a rapid flow of a large amount of financial capital, is a later development of commercialization. This is evident in the dramatic increase of foreign direct investments, especially in the late 1990s, and in the fact that two thirds of the world trade in 1998 was initiated by the TNCs and was among TNCs.

As I mentioned, my periodization of capitalist globalization in commercial, industrial, and financial subtypes does not imply that these are qualitatively different types of modern capitalism; they are variations and moments of the economic process that have been all along propelled by expanding financial capital. Arrighi and Silver (2001) have well documented how the financialization of capital has been a central feature of capitalism since the 16th century; I have extended this notion to the role of business partnership before the 16th century, when joint companies emerged. Hence, my reference to the recent prominence of financial globalization does not refer to a new phase of capitalism, but to a dramatic increase in volume, velocity, and complexity of financial capital (or the centrality of finance capital, as Arrighi and Silver say). My descriptive classification of subtypes of capitalist globalization is based on the dominant instrument of capital accumulation: commodities in commercial capitalism, industrial products in industrial capitalism, and financial capital in the recent phasis of capitalism. Arrighi and Silver offer an excellent analysis of four cycles of material expansion and four cycles of financial expansion.[4]

Finally, one can argue that the cheapened cost of communication and transportation has made the cross-border circulation of capital and products more aggressive and difficult to control. There is an emerging gap between the structures setup in the 1950s (IMF, WB, GATT) and the emerging new structures outside state control; this is another way to explain globalization. (For a critical appraisal of this period in terms of the uneven development between the North and South see Arrighi's essay.)

I do not want give the impression to the reader that what mostly matters for understanding globalization as an historical process are economic trends. In this part of the chapter I have elaborated on this aspect because the focus of the discussion has progressed from cultural to political to economic societies. I have repeatedly referred to the importance of cultural, religious, ideological, and civilizational linkages among political societies. The advent of digital communication and the related information revolution has accelerated and magnified, not only economic processes, but also political and cultural processes: the digital technological medium has created an instantaneous global network of communications and exchanges (see Knorr Cetina, chapter 2 and my conclusion), and has facilitated the spreading of consumerism as the leading ideology of contemporary capitalism (see Sklair, chapter 3). Another strong cultural aspect is the much-debated cosmopolitanism (Beck, 2000). Culture has played a role in economic societies (as predicted in Table 1.2), so that there is no programmatic economic bias in my presentation; as a matter of fact, civilizational conflicts and the nature and impact of digital communication have a preeminent role in the second part of this chapter and in my concluding essay.

At the end of this brief historical excursus the question arises as to what the forces behind globalization are. Raymond Grew correctly states in his chapter that some authors prefer to treat globalization as an outcome of capitalism and the

---

[4] I thank Giovanni Arrighi for calling my attention to the fundamental role of financial capital throughout what I call subtypes of capitalist globalization.

play of market forces (Wallerstein, 1989; Chase-Dunn, 1989), whereas other authors discuss it as a result of international politics and escalating power play (Bright & Geyer, 1987, 1995, 1996, 2002; Modelski, 1987; Kennedy, 1987); sometimes the two approaches are combined. Finally, there are a few authors who make technological development and the ever-increasing exchanges of knowledge the engine of change.

As we show shortly, I have incorporated all these elements in an integrated fashion. In Table 1.2, I have shown that we can identify cultural, political, and economic societies on the basis of the dominance, respectively, of the cultural or political or economic principle of organization. In Table 1.2, I have presented a typology of cross-societal linkages that tend to prevail in cultural, political, and economic societies. Historians will be able to identify a lot of exceptions that do not fit into my schemes; this is to be expected as with most of theorizing that uses sociohistorical material. However, ideal types are tools to detect deep trends in history, and not descriptive summaries and much less evolutionary types of historical periods. Raymond Grew tells us in his essay that we lack adequate theories and methodologies to raise deep structural questions. Rightly so, but we will never make much progress if we do not begin to challenge hardnose historians with provocative schemes, as inchoate as they may be.

Having formulated some tentative hypotheses about globalization as an historical process, I now turn my attention to our global present. Having just been admonished by Raymond Grew on facile theorizing, I immediately revert to it with another round of theoretical schemes: one of the intents is to formulate a globalization framework that enables the reader to see how the diverse contributions of this book touch on different and complementary dimensions of contemporary globalization. To empower the reader with such an holistic understanding of it, the framework must identify and link micro and macro, intra- and intersocietal, historical/structural and sociopsychological perspectives in the study of globalization.

Contemporary Globalization as a Dialectic Process

The Conflictuality of the Global

According to Table 1.2 economic societies are characterized by the dominance of economic (capitalist) institutions, by typically weaker political institutions (see, for instance, the weak power of the United Nations (UN)), and by even weaker cultural institutions (see, for instance, the debated notion of cosmopolitanism and the controversies surrounding the "Universal Declaration of Human Rights"). Most nations recognize their economic dependence on the world economy; see, for instance, their membership in the World Trade Organization. On the other hand, contemporary societies are in strong competition with each other for world markets and sources of energy. In the absence of a strong politically (see Archer's essay) and culturally unifying framework (neoliberalism is opposed by nationalism and fundamentalism), the world situation is often said to be risky (Beck) or evolving as a web of self-organizing and unpredictable systems (see Urry's chapter). Yet, I argue that the world's situation is not inherently chaotic or necessarily hopeless. Some authors appear ready to state that we have in place a normative framework that facilitates a transnational understanding of issues and serves as a mechanism for negotiated solutions. Boli and Thomas (1997) have concluded that as many as 5983 nongovernmental organizations (NGOs) base their activities and philosophy on five principles they share in common: universalism, individualism, rational voluntaristic authority, human purposes of rationalizing progress, and world citizenship (universal human rigths). These principles are shared also by sovereign states and by intergovernmental organizations in dealing with international issues; in effect these five principles function as world-cultural principles.

But it is immediately evident that the principles of universalism, individualism, rational progress, and universal human rights have some sort of remote roots in the Greek and Judeo-Christian traditions, and more recent roots in the Renaissance, Enlightment, and liberalism. Obviously, these civilizational, religious, and intellectual traditions have shaped Western civilization. At the same time, it is also well known that Confucianist, Hindu, Islamic, and African cultural traditions are based on the opposite values of particularism (and familism), collectivism, and social hierarchy (Samovar & Porter, 2003).

Isn't it, then, legitimate to raise the question of whether these five so-called "world cultural principles" are understood in the same way by all societies of the world, many of which are based on different civilizational traditions? The "World Values Surveys" published by the University of Michigan show that newly developing countries have been modernizing along distinct civilizational paths, such as Confucian, South Asian, Islamic, Historically Protestant, Historically Catholic, Historically Communist, and African (Inglehart & Baker, 2000). Robertson and Khondker (1998: 29) argue that culture is a "crucial" aspect of globalization, and that cultural clashes and conflicts are major factors constituting the world as "a single place," a place where particularistic variations of universalistic themes interplay (1998: 29). We can agree that cultural and, we also show, political and economic conflicts make the world one conflictual arena, an arena, therefore, incapable of agreeing on such fundamental issues as the nature of democracy, human rights, and the role of religion in political affairs.

Lechner and Boli (2005: Ch. 1) have recently argued that we have a world polity that they define as follows: "The world polity is the conceptual vision of the world as a single social system, an encompassing "society" involving all "humanity" in extensive webs of interaction and flow of goods, ideas, money, values, and so on, among other social units (individuals, association, companies, ethnic groups, states, nations, I.G.O., etc.)." I suggest that we can clarify the issue by separating the components of this definition as follows: beliefs, values, norms, and the discourse about beliefs, values, and norms of different societies. Beginning from the international discourse, we certainly seem to have developed a common language, at least in the official discussions held at the UN agencies and other IGOs. However, someone could argue that this is a question of a "routinized" international discourse that does not necessarily entail an acceptance of underlying value premises that are typically Western in nature. An important question is whether there are universal and deeply shared cultural principles among world societies. I theorize that the commonality rapidly decreases when we move from beliefs to values to norms (and ethical and political systems). Certainly, across cultures we all share much of the scientific, technological, and medical knowledge; to some extent we also share similar knowledge of each other's history and civilizational encounters (with variations of interpretations, of course); we have a common pool of philosophical knowledge and social philosophies; we know, presumably, each other's philosophy, political, and religious systems (or, at least, we should). Therefore, we know our differences and the more we interact, the more we realize that there are real and legitimate differences.

I concur with Joana Breidenbach and Ina Zukrigl (2000) that cultural globalization is a two-pronged process: first, globalization contributes to cultural differentiation by exposing societies to new ideas and lifestyles that are interpreted according to one's own cultural framework; secondly, globalization helps in developing a common framework, set of standards, and a symbolic system of references (quoted in Lechner & Boli, 2005: 35). In Lechner and Boli's paraphrase, "global culture helps them (people) to bridge and to articulate differences." "World culture is not the opposite of diversity; rather it organizes diversity and stimulates difference" (ibid. 36).

However, differences seem to be more and more accentuated, even within the western hemisphere, where national heritages are, at times, invoked and even underlined in support of political and economic goals. In the case of Islamic theocracy and of Islamic fundamentalism, in general, the global discourse seems to augment misunderstandings and increase animosities. In this respect Immanuel Wallerstein is correct: "Culture is both a weapon of the powerful and a tool of resistance of the weak" (Wallerstein, 1991).

Yet, John Meyer (1998) emphasizes important communalities of world culture. For him, besides, economic and political interdependence,

> globalization means the expanded interdependence of expressive culture, through intensified global communication. . . . Globalization [also] means the expanded flow of instrumental culture around the world. Put simply, *common models of social order become authoritative in many different social settings*. . . . The world society creates, increasingly, common models of national state identity and purpose [models] having to do with socioeconomic development or welfare, and individual justice, rights, and equality.

We also have the spreading of common models of socioeconomic development and associated policies of investments and population control. J. Meyer asserts that we also see the spreading of common models of human rights and policies toward minorities, similar educational curricula, and standard models of organization.

I would, however, underline the strongly "instrumental" and imposed nature of the widespread adoptions of socioeconomic-organizational models; in fact, these models are all too often adopted because they are imposed by the IGOs, for instance, as conditions of admission in the WTO and for securing WB and IMF loans. Ultimately, because advanced technology and financial capital are mostly in the hands of industrialized nations, developing countries have only one option: to play the game according to the rule (and the language and practices) of the West. But, when we come down to concrete policies and implementations of agreements and clauses, great differences of interpretation and conflicts emerge. Scholars from the Third World countries strongly deplore the deleterious impact of economic conditionalities that destroy local institutions without effective replacement (Hoppers, 2000). This means that all too often the taunted communalities of development models is for developing countries a forced choice or a precondition to link to mechanisms of (hoped) economic development. Developing countries would prefer to formulate development strategies that are consistent with their own cultural and political institutions. For instance, the trend toward democracy is spreading among contemporary world nations, but Islam, Russia, or even Japan and the societies of the ASEAN organization have different conceptions of democracy (see the "World Value Surveys" on the cross-national opinions about the role of the state, strong leadership, and democracy). There is no agreement on the ultimate rules and logic for resolving international conflicts: witness the criticism of Western biases leveled against the system of international justice by the proponents of Sharia law.

The technological (and military) superiority of one or few nations that adjudicate for themselves the role of world policemen does not add up to a peaceful and united world either. The overwhelming evidence is that competing international actors favor the interpretation and implementation of the international normative principles that best serve their own national interests (witness the attitude of industrial nations within the IMF, WB, WTO: see Stiglitz, 2002): the stronger the nations' economic (and military) power is, the more convincing their logic becomes in international relations. This realization is not alien to the accelerating race toward nuclear armaments and international terrorism. It is no wonder, then, that other authors argue that today's world is characterized by a clash of civilizations (Huntington, 1997), "Clash of Fundamentalisms" (Ali, 2002), inherent political instability (see Archer's chapter) and unpredictable complexity (see Urry's chapter).

Yet, other authors argue in favor of the opposite thesis: the world is moving toward cultural homogenization (Beck, 2000), "deep" economic integration (Dicken, 2003: 12; Chase-Dunn and Jorgensen, chapter 7 in this book), and the interactive construction of a world culture (Lechner & Boli, 2005).

We need a framework that explains these apparently contradictory statements about our "global age" (Albrow, 1997).

A Multidimensional and Dialectic Perspective of Globalization

To understand the interaction among different societies, we must understand, first, the nature of modern societies. We can visualize the societal system along a horizontal and a vertical parameter (Table 1.3): (a) the horizontal parameter refers to the interaction (and conflict) among cultural, political, and economic principles

TABLE 1.3. Principles of social organization at different levels of societal concerns (a Western-centric perspective).

Societal Concerns	Principles of Social Organization		
	Cultural	Political	Economic
Local (ethnic, religious)	1	2	3
National	2	1	3
International	3	2	1

1 = Most dominant principle of social organization.
3 = Least dominant principle of social organization.
———————▶ = Primary integrating process.
- - - - - - - - -▶ = Secondary integrating process.

Modified from "Nationalism and Social Identity" by Ino Rossi, in *The Millennium Haze: Comparative Inquiries about Society, State and Community.* M. Toscano and V. Parrillo, eds. 2000. Milan (Italy): Franco Angeli (p. 101).

of social organization within each one of the three levels of societal concerns; in fact, the relative importance of the cultural, political, and economic principles is not agreed upon by the various social groups; (b) the vertical parameter refers to the interaction (and conflict) among the local, national, and international levels of societal concerns.

I make the argument that a dialectic understanding (Rossi, 1983, 1993) of the interactions among cultural, economic, and political principles of social organization within each level of societal concerns and among the three levels of societal concerns is a sine qua non to understand global relations. This is so for a substantive reason and for methodological reasons: (a) substantively, global relations occur among nations that are at different levels of development, as I have already mentioned. There is also a conflictuality internal to nations that is related to the spread of education, digital communication, and democratic aspirations. Different age and social groups within industrializing and industrialized nations assimilate modernization trends with varying degrees of intensity and speed; as a result, there is no consensus on national priorities, because, for instance, some groups push ethnic and religious agendas ahead of agendas that are important to the nation as a whole; (b) the theoreticomethodological usefulness of this dialectic framework is demonstrated by the following additional considerations: first, the dialectic approach helps explain not only intercivilizational processes but also microprocesses, such as identity formation in different types of societies (see Table 1.4 below).

Hence, the dialectic approach enables the reader to see the interrelationship between the micro- and the macrolevels of analysis; second, when the interface between the micro- and macroanalysis of globalization is operationalized through the interaction of place and space, agency, and open systems, one can tackle with reasonable clarity some of the most difficult issues in globalization theory. I discuss these analytical payoffs in my conclusive essay. Let us discuss now the various facets of the dialectical framework.

Levels of Societal Concerns

The upward direction of the solid arrow at the right end of the table indicates that the contemporary phase of capitalistic globalization issues of international economy tend to be the ultimate determinants (or at least the conditioning factor) of societal welfare and survival. This was the case for the downfall of communist Russia, and it may well be the ultimate reckoning for Cuba, Iran, and North Korea. (Communist China seems capable to cope with the pressure of international economic forces, but history will tell the final story on the evolution of its political system). The downward dotted arrow on the left of the table indicates the decreasing importance of local ethnic and religious concerns at the level of national sovereignty and even more decreasing at the level of concerns with issues related to the international economy.

A Western-centric perspective permeates the logic of this table. In fact, from the point of view of the Iranian theocracy, for instance, the far left downward arrow should, perhaps, be a solid arrow and the far right upward arrow should be a dotted one; the obvious reason is that in the Iranian society religious considerations control politics at the local, national, and international levels of societal concerns. This means that Table 1.4 provides a useful tool to understand present international conflicts stemming from a confrontation between Western nations endorsing an economic (and secular) perspective, on the one hand, and nations endorsing a theocratic society.

Another implication of Table 1.4 is that to find the solution to our global conflicts we should think in terms of "to-be-negotiated" principles of world order rather than of "presumably" universally accepted and understood principles. The international framework—to the extent that it really exists—must be continuously interpreted and applied via the interactive negotiation among nations that differ in civilizational perspective, political traditions, economic development, and national resources.

Economic Development, Cultural Pluralism, and Conflicts Within Nations and Among Nations

Let us first provide some evidence on the existence of a threefold level of societal concerns. The world's nations are at different stages of socioeconomic development, and, consequently, they are characterized by great social heterogeneity as documented by the "World Value Surveys" carried out during the last 20 years in 85% of the world societies by the University of Michigan under the directorship of Ronald Inglehart.

Industrial societies moved from an industrial phase of economic development (capital intensive and predominantly oriented to the manufacturing of goods) to a postindustrial phase (where the service sector prevails). From an emphasis on technical and rational bureaucracy during the industrial phase, Western societies moved to a postindustrial society that emphasizes, among other things, autonomous/ professional competence. Having secured issues of economic survival (with industrialization), the emphasis has shifted toward self-expressive values, subjective well-being, quality of life, and a preference for occupations that are psychologically fulfilling; these are the postmodern values typical of postindustrial societies. Concomitantly, there was a shift away from absolute and rigid attitudes (that prevailed during the industrial phasis) to attitudes of tolerance and social trust (that tend to be characteristics of postindustrial societies) (Inglehart & Baker, 2000).

Cross-national surveys (for instance, Inglehart & Norris, 2003) show that similar cultural changes accompany the economic developments of newly developing nations; they develop an orientation toward modern values first, and toward postmodern values next, as they move respectively from an industrial to a postindustrial level of development; traditional values, however, are not rejected or replaced, as we shortly discuss.

Huntington (1996) argued that the world is divided into eight major civilizations or "cultural zones" that are historically linked to major religious traditions; these civilizations keep their cultural distinctiveness despite the impact of modernization. On the basis of people's responses to cross-national surveys Inglehart and Norris (1993) identify the following cultural/civilizational heritages or tracks: historically Protestant, historically Catholic, Orthodox, Islamic, African, Latin American, South Asian, and Confucian, (pp. 29, 36). Differences on basic values among people belonging to different religious-civilizational tracks (let us say, Protestant, Catholic, Muslims) are clearly documented; however, the differences among Protestant and Catholics living within given societies are relatively small (Inglehart & Baker, 2000: 36). The inference is that historico–national experiences and institutions (education, mass media, etc.) produce modifications on how religious–civilizational traditions are transmitted. In fact, national heritages are shaped by intercultural contacts, conquest, trade, and economic development that have an impact on how civilizational traditions are transmitted to future generations.

Cross-national surveys that have been conducted over the last 20 years or so in 85% of world societies indicate that contemporary societies have a threefold cultural layer: (a) a common (intersocietal) modern and postmodern framework (in which I include the normative framework imposed by the IGOs); this framework can be analytically located at the level of "international societal concerns" in Table 1.4; (b) national traditions that interpret and modify civilizational heritages (national traditions can be analytically located at the "national level" of societal concerns in Table 1.4); and (c) national traditions are, in turn, deeply rooted in ethnic/religious/civilizational traditions that are modified by national historical experiences, but that continue to be the core of traditional heritages. (Traditional heritages can be analytically located at the level of ethnic and religious concerns in Table 1.4.)

The complexity of our global age derives from the three-way interaction among the different cultural traditions, the different national traditions, and the different levels of economic development. As a result, the world's nations have different cultural, political, and economic priorities. While holding on tight to their civilizational or religious and national traditions, developing nations aspire toward economic and technological development, but at their own pace and according to their national characteristics and civilizational heritages. Forms of nationalism and fundamentalism in developing countries mobilize their national and civilizational resources in reaction to the hegemonic pressures of industrial nations. Within modernizing societies there are rampaging ethnic, religious, and class conflicts that are often attributed to colonial experiences and introduce further uncertainties in international transactions. Finally, there exists a cross-national perception that industrial nations succeed in their economic agenda at the expense of deteriorating poor countries (if not of entire continents). These cultural, political, and economic conflicts within nations and among nations are the engines of globalization.

Before pursuing the issue of an additional element of conflictuality, the impact of digital communication, let us briefly touch upon a microglobal issue: what kind of identity is possible in a world of sharply different and conflicting cultural traditions? In fact, the concerns with the survival of cultural identity are at the core of the literature on globalization.

Psychosocial Processes of Identity in Our Age of Conflictual Globality

The interface among the three levels of societal concerns (and the three corresponding cultural layers: ethnic-religious, national, cross-national) within nations is reflected in the socialization process through the development of a threefold level of psychosocial identity. I have argued elsewhere (see Rossi, 2000) that social identity has a cognitive, interactional, and occupational component: "cognitively" identity is produced by the selective assimilation of cultural meanings that accompany one's own life experience; "interactionally" identity is developed by mastering interactional skills; "occupationally" identity derives from a socially recognized competence in performing one's own occupational role. Table 1.4 indicates that the impact of the cultural, political, and economic principles of societal organization on identity formation is specifically different at each level of societal concern.

Ethnic conflicts are often referred to as socially disruptive; yet, in strong democracies internal cultural conflicts lead to increased social participation, and, hence, to the mobilization of societal resources. The importance of the cultural capital at the level of ethnic-religious concerns fosters ethnic identity; the preeminence of patriotism and nationalism at the level of national sovereignty fosters national identity; the needed transnational skills at the level of international economy is a major factor fostering the development of global awareness.

TABLE 1.4. Identity formation at the three levels of societal concerns.

Levels of Societal Concerns	Dominant Principles of Social Organization		
	Cultural	Economic	Political
Local	1	2	3
	[Ethnic identity]		
National	2	1	3
		[National identity]	
International	3	2	1
			[Global awareness]

1 = Most dominant social institution.
3 = Least dominant social institution.
⟶ = Primary integrating process.
◄--------- = Secondary integrating process.

However, we must keep in mind that ethnic identities become accentuated also through cross-border linkages with other ethnic groups. The interaction of multiple ethnic identities, national identity, and global awareness can foster the development of differentiated and multicultural competent forms of identity (Rossi, 2000a).

Intersocietal linkages are developed also on the basis of gender and occupation. These cross-border linkages often contribute to the internal opposition against state power and to the strengthening of global civil society against arbitrary forms of globalization. These multiple and conflictual processes can fuel corrective countertrends to arbitrary forms of capitalist globalization, as we show later on.

Having discussed the systemic dimensions of world conflictuality in Table 1.4 I turn to the analysis of how this conflictuality plays out at the level of global interaction among global (and local) actors with different civilizational and political frameworks.

The Dialectics of Globalization and Digital Communication

Communication entails a transaction between transmitters and receivers of messages, and both transmitters and receivers interpret messages according to their own cultural orientation. Hence, a thorough understanding of the cultural, economic, and political framework within which the communication is transmitted and received is essential to ascertain the nature of communication and its impact on global communication. In particular, we must understand who controls the media of the transmitters of news and messages, and what are the content, form, and purpose of the messages that are transmitted. Because most of the communication media are under the control of wealthy nations, typically the virtual sender transmits from and imposes the ideological framework of dominant nations. Similarly, the virtual receiver interprets and reacts to messages from his or her national and local viewpoint, or, at least, attempts to do so. This is the reason why no local action and reaction can be understood independently of what people call "global action," and vice versa. "Virtual places," or communication encounters via digital media, are very effective in sustaining at the local level communication networks and in delivering instantaneous and ideologically embedded messages to counteract the ideologies from the above: see the massive antiwar protests mobilized via cell phones and radio communications; see the countless "places" interactively created by academicians, terrorists, news groups, discussion groups, music and downloading aficionados, drug users, and antiglobalization groups throughout the world.

The instantaneous co-presence of social actors who belong to geographically distant and culturally different contexts generates conflicts and "distances" between senders and receivers of messages. *Distance* or the *distancing effect* of digital communication refers to the tendency to pull further apart people with competing interests or worldviews. Various authors have pointed out that globalization is both dividing and uniting (for instance, Bauman, 1998). Clifford Geertz (1998) states that the world is "growing both more global and divided, more thoroughly interconnected and more intricately partitioned at the same time" (1998: 107). Giddens (1999/2002) talks about distant cultures colliding and about a cosmopolitan tolerance that embraces cultural complexity; yet, cosmopolitan tolerance is opposed by fundamentalists who take refuge in purified traditions. Barry K. Gills (2000) talks about the tension between neoliberal economic globalization (that seeks to expand the freedom of market and private capital), and movements of social resistance (that seek to protect and redefine community and solidarity). Paradoxically, global communication makes cultural and political resistance an inevitable and central characteristic of a globalizing world. Digital communication activates, and at the same times, weakens, the forces of social resistance.

In global communication, we do not have a mere juxtaposition of heterogeneous and conflictual worlds, but rather we have the production and/or accentuation of divisions (conflicts and exclusions) by the instantaneous (digital) "presence to each other" of actors from nations (or organizations or social groups) with different agendas and uneven power. The simultaneous and instantaneous confrontation of conflicting messages produces a distance and/or an amplification of already existing differences among social actors who identify themselves with different civilizational and national interests.

We can detect several moments in the dialectics of global communication:

1. *The thesis moment*: the distantiation or disuniting effect produced by digital communication at many levels and for many different reasons:
   a. First of all, some distancing of co-presentialized cultures is produced by the dematerializing and objectifying character of digital communication.

We show in the concluding essay that the instant and worldwide inter-connectivity of digital communication is based principally on cognitive and visual messages and that the sensory concreteness of the aural/tactile dimensions of communication is lost. We call this loss a de-materi-alization of "things," the production of "non-things" (or visualized and decontextualized things). Furthermore, an objectification of communi-cation often occurs that consists in the separation of the content of mes-sages from the protagonists or producers of the messages (social actors).

b. Secondly, digital communication depersonalizes people, because it relates people to each other as virtual actors and on the basis of cross-cultural competences, and not on the basis of personal and culturally-specific traits.

c. Thirdly, digital communication is a decultured medium, because it tends to emphasize the legal, economic, and political aspects of transnational interactions, leaving behind the other aspects of culture. What Geertz calls "thick culture" is left behind.

d. Fourthly, digital communication presents a dematerialized (decultured or diminished) impression of Western culture as a set of idealized principles of universalism, instrumental efficiency, and rationality. Other cultural and organizational elements that are at variance with these principles are ignored.

e. Because digital communication is controlled by industrialized nations, universalistic, rational, and impersonal criteria form the prevailing com-munication framework. The spiritual (mystical), familistic, collective, and empathy-based qualities of traditional Eastern, Islamic, African, and Latin American cultures tend to be ignored in electronic-based communication. This produces a twofold phenomenon: non-Western cultural experiences are misunderstood by Westerners and non-Western actors reject Western-imposed criteria. The first phenomenon is produced by a mistranslation of cultures for two reasons: cultures are interpreted from a Western framework and the intuitional, communal, and religious meanings of traditional cul-tures are decontextualized and dematerialized, that is, experientially lived systems of meaning are left behind; the bypassing of local and lived expe-riences seems to be an inevitable byproduct of globalizing (digital) processes.[5] The digitalized rendition of the inner core of traditional cul-tures within the international normative (Western) framework often amounts to intercivilizational and intercultural misrepresentations.

For one or more of the above-mentioned reasons, a breakdown of communication is the likely outcome of the instant presentialization (and confrontation) among actors with different cultural frameworks, especially when one (the Western) is in a position of domination over the others.

---

[5] I qualify this conception in my concluding essay.

Is there any evidence that the international normative framework is a Western dominated framework?

A careful study of the structure, purposes, and operations of 5983 INGOs has shown that the ideologies and structures of the INGOs are based on "five basic world-cultural principles: *universalism, individualism, rational voluntaristic authority, human purposes of rationalizing progress, and world citizenship (universal human rights)*" (Boli & Thomas, 1997). *Universalism* is defined as follows: "humans everywhere have similar needs and desires, can act in accordance with common principles of authority and action, and share common goals. . . . Most INGOs stress the uniformity of human actors" (ibid. 180). How can these values be reconciled with the views of Confucianism, Eastern Mysticism, and the African universalism Ubuntu that emphasizes humanness, care, understanding, empathy, and sharing (Hoppers, 2000: 114)? "Most INGOs accept as members" only individuals or associations of individuals. Individuals are the only "real" actors; collectivities are essentially assemblages of individuals" (ibid. 181). Yet, collective, cooperative, interdependent orientations prevail not only in Africa, but also in the traditional cultures of most of the non-Western world. Fukuyama speaks about the family-centrism of East Asian societies, and the same can be said of Muslim countries, Africa, and Latin America. In this sense Serge Latouche is correct in claiming that the universalizing drive of Western civilization is opposed to the survival of diverse (and local) cultures (Tomlinson, 1991: 190). Latouche refers not to the spread of culturally and geographically specific institutions, but to Western deterritorialized cultural principles, that is "machine, impersonal, soul-less, and nowadays master less, which have impressed mankind into its service" (Tomlinson op. cit.: 96: xii, 3).

f. There is a sixth dimension of distantiation besides the five already discussed: the imposed normative framework of IGOs and NGOs. The principles of universalism and instrumental efficiency are imposed as the preeminent platform of global interaction: as a result, a Western-biased normative framework in international relations prevails with a consequent distantiation, dematerialization, and marginalization of actors and nations that are already distanced by different cultural heritages.

g. I would add a seventh dimension of distantiation that consists of an ideological manipulation: IGOs and industrial nations spread the creed of neoliberal ideology (the principles of market economy and liberal democracy) as the only path for the world to follow. Samir Amin (1996), a prominent thinker on the nature of capitalism and North–South relations, argues that ethnicity and fundamentalism are preeminent forces because the ruling elites in the South have not succeeded to change the unequal terms of the imposed globalization. He rejects the polarizing form or simplistic formula equating development with market expansion.

My formulation is consistent with the notion of polarization that one encounters in the literature on globalization. For instance, various writings document the fierce opposition to neoliberalism in the Northern and Southern hemispheres. Examples of opposition from the Web sites of antiglobalization movements from around the world (global civil society) abound: see, for instance, the Filipinos, American Indians, and South Americans' perception of our imperialism. There is a deep meaning in the notion that we do not understand "local lives" without the "distant ties" (Eade, 1997).

The abstract and Westernized nature of globalizing spaces renders opaque the confrontational and alienating nature of international relations. Perhaps, this opaqueness helps to explain the fact that industrial nations continue to talk about endless economic growth, whereas poor nations and lower social strata experience the opposite. The asymmetrical power relations between industrialized and industrializing nations is a key intervening variable: what is excluded or hidden in the digitally mediated communications and transactions are the needs, interests, and perspectives that are specific to industrializing nations and to developing countries; the latter cannot compete on a worldwide scale with the cultural, economic, and political interests that prevail in global exchanges of communication, most of which are controlled by industrial nations. It is no wonder that the spreading of democracy activates the reaction of marginalized societies and fuels forms of ethnonationalism (Chua, 2003).

2. *The antithesis moment*: the antihegemonic thrust. The unilateral and asymmetrical imposition of Western principles of normative order produces the reaction of the "local, especially from the Global South"; this is the second phase (antithesis) of the dialectics of globalization. Grassroots global civil society wants to recapture the familistic, particularistic, and religious traditions that tend to be lost in transnational transactions.

   Next, we discuss how this second moment of the dialectics can provide important directions for the global future.

3. *Can this dialectic framework generate strategies for a possible resolution of global confrontations?* How is a movement toward an equitable global future possible?

   The best starting point is to develop an enlightened global awareness (see the lower right-end corner of Table 1.5) of the consequences of global confrontations to which most nations, directly or indirectly contribute. We need to achieve an acute sense of global problems that are related to international confrontations and competing national interests: ecological degradation, health crises, and widening cross-national inequalities (see Arrighi, chapter 8). The plight of newly developing nations is aggravated by the replacement of imported commodities from developing countries with products manufactured with the technologies of industrialized countries (see Schaffer, chapter 9). We need to achieve an adequate knowledge of the marginalization of entire continents, and an acute awareness of the dangers of the militarization

TABLE 1.5. Dominant structures and related identity at the local, national and international levels of societal concerns.

Societal concerns	Dominant structure /&/ [identity]		
	Cultural	Political	Economic
Local	1	2	3
	Cultural instit/&/ [Ethnic identity]		
National	2	1	3
		Political instit/&/ [National identity]	
International	3	2	1
			IGO's/&/ [Global awareness]

1 = Most dominant social institution and [identity type].
3 = Least dominant social institution and [identity type].
———————▶ = Primary integrating process.
◀--------- = Secondary integrating process.

and nuclearization of the world as well of proxy wars and privatized warfares (Mamdani, 2005). This line of thinking has affinity with a two-pronged argument made by Mohammed A. Bamyeh (2000): globalization produces massive disjunctions among the cultural, economic, and political logics at a world scale; on the other hand, these disruptions possess the potential to free human capabilities that were restrained by nation-state and other traditional institutions. (This is an important counterargument to that proposed by Archer's chapter.)

But who will start this process of an enlightened awareness about the roots of our global problems? Repeated warnings from international institutions, such as the UN, and from the heads of strong states and religious leaders do not seem to be effective to steer the course of international events. In the absence of world institutions with adequate coercitive power, the only avenue for a long-term solution is to bring individual nations to an acute awareness of their responsibility for inaction or for adopting all-out confrontational strategies on issues and problems that affect the whole world. Obviously, local and national leaders and grass-roots social actors should have a key role in this process, but they are influenced by the larger social structure. The first crucial step is for social actors (especially grass-roots leaders) to understand, and to make their followers understand, the exploitative structures of their own society. In a second moment, and as a result of this first step, leaders and other social actors must understand international structures as replications of exploitative national structures.

4. *The role of social actors toward an increased national and cross-societal awareness of structural inequalities.* The analysis of the link of social actors to social structure is a logical development of the institutional perspective that I have adopted in this chapter. "Institution" refers to the set of values and norms that govern the activities of people operating in the cultural, political, and economic spheres of society. We have seen that patterns of interaction give origin to microglobal structures (see Knorr Cetina's chapter), first, and macrostructures, next (see Rosenau's chapter). As explained above, social actors develop from and contribute to cultural, political, and economic structures via the interactive process of identity formation. Table 1.5 shows that cultural, political, and economic structures facilitate the formation of respectively ethnic, national, and global identity and awareness; in turn, sociocultural identity contributes to the further dynamics of social structures.

At this micro–macro level of analysis we clearly realize that social structures are the sources of psychosocial maladjustment and societal malfunctioning at both the national (intrasocietal) and international (cross-societal) levels. A fundamental premise of my argument is that cultural, political, and economic structures are present at each level of societal concern, but cultural structures have a particular salience at the level of local concerns where issues of ethnic and religious identity formation are of paramount importance. In turn, political structures have salience at the level of national concern, and so on. This hierarchy of structures is responsible for social order (and integration), but also for social distortions and related psychosocial maladjustments. As I have previously mentioned, nobody will deny that cultural (ethnic and religious) priorities often are not reflected in national priorities. Conflicts and tensions among cultural, political, and economic structures are present in almost any society; in a capitalist society economic structures have a steering control and tend to be the ultimate conditioning factor of the effectiveness of the other structures. The economic overdeterminance of capitalist societies puts strains on the political and cultural agendas of other nations (to adopt a cross-societal level of analysis); it puts also stress on the ethnic, national, and global dimensions of psychosocial identity (to adopt an intrasocietal level of analysis). Social actors quickly realize that the emphasis by their own nations on economic agendas is very often consistent with and sustaining the global emphasis on economic priorities and on capital accumulation. This trend tends to occur regardless of whom will bear the social costs of capital accumulation.

Equipped with an interdisciplinary perspective, the reflexive human agency is capable of stretching back to the humane and equalitarian warmth of cultural societies that David Sapir defined as "genuine cultures" (1924) or Robert Redfield "moral order" societies (1953). Yet, because of historical developments, the differential weight of cultural, political, and economic structures are here to perpetuate intrasocietal and cross-societal inequalities. Yet, we have to reestablish a balance among social structures within nations and among nations. Operationally, cultural structures encompass the realm of Civil Society (the so-called third sector), whereas political structures refer to the State (the public sector), and economic structures refer to the business sector (or private sector).

A short parenthesis on the debated notion of civil society is in order at this point. The definition of civil society has changed throughout history concomitantly with the dominant ideologies of the time. Contemporary competing ideologies produce different notions of civil society. For rightists and libertarians (for instance, F. Hayek) civil society refers to the need of replacing some state power with intermediate institutions based on voluntarism. For liberals, civil society refers to social movements and local politics (beyond the state). In actuality, the term civil society encompasses different sociocultural elements for different authors. Because space does not allow an extended discussion, I mention two positions based on quite different reference points. Jeffrey Alexander uses capitalism as the reference point to differentiate civil society from other societal sectors (at least in his essay on the history of the concept, 2001). On the other hand, Charles Taylor defines civil society as a network of institutions independent of the state. These institutions unite citizens around the principle of common solicitude. The foundation of this principle is neither the state nor the market, but a social or public sphere that is autonomous from both the state and the market. Civil society is a network of nongovernmental organizations and associations, which can exist besides the state (and the market, my addition) and can organize the life of the people (Taylor, 1996: 70). Fukuyama also uses the state as a reference point of differentiation to define civil society. He states the following,

> If a democracy is in fact liberal, it maintains a protected sphere of individual liberty where the state is constrained from interfering. If such a political system is not to degenerate into anarchy, the society that subsists in that protected sphere must be capable of organizing itself. Civil society serves to balance the power of the state and to protect individuals from the state's power.

Perhaps the only element of agreement among authors is that civil society differs from the public (state) and the private (business) sectors. The dispute is about the constituent elements and, relatedly, about the boundaries among the three sectors. These boundaries cannot be easily drawn on the basis of the membership of social actors in one or another of the three sectors. For instance, Johns Hopkins University's Web site refers to the civil society sector "which encompasses private, nonprofit and nongovernmental organizations; [organizations that] are self-governing; people are free to join or to leave [them]. [They are] private organizations that work for the common good, often in collaboration with government and business" (http://www.jhu.edu/~ccss/). Not only do the three sectors cooperate at times and on certain issues, but members of the one sector can be active members of another sector.

The distinction among the three sectors is an analytical one, namely the principles (values, norms, rules) of civil society are not political/legal principles or the logic of market forces. Because the ground rules for civil society are not derived from political or economic institutions, they must be grounded, of course, in the remaining realm of culture, which gives us a residual definition of civil society: civil society derives its principles from cultural values, social ethics, and sociopolitico-philosophical ideologies that are not institutionalized in the government and business sectors.

In a stratified society, different social classes and different interest groups have different cultural, political, and economic priorities. The negotiation among different interest groups is what makes the dynamics of civil society. The analytic boundaries of its operative logic seem to be drawn from the negotiated quest of the common good or the welfare of the society as a whole. The negotiation takes place among different interest groups whose leaders (agency) must find a socially acceptable compromise. We go back to the basic notion that dialectics is embedded within the cultural, the political, and the economic realm of society and this is true at the local, national, and international levels of societal concern. The dynamics of civil society is embedded in the agency–structure dialectics.

The reflexivity of the human agency is nurtured by the interface with cultural structures that are sources of meaning and identity (see first row and first column of Table 1.5). However, human agency realizes that political structures may have to mediate the interface between cultural and economic priorities. In fact, the historical role of the state was to help entrepreneurs, trade companies, and TNCs, and it was the capitalist state that established the Bretton Woods pact and continued to support the IGOs and propound the doctrines of neoliberalism and free market as universal panaceas. (On this point see Kellner's chapter.) The state has also introduced various regulations to protect workers and mitigate excesses of the profit motive (Kiely, 1998). Recently, the developmental role of the state has been emphasized (for instance, in East Asian countries) and its social welfare function as well.

This intrasocietal analysis can be extrapolated to the cross-societal level of analysis. Human agencies operating at the global level have to foster some sort of dialogue or compromise for the co-existence of different forms of political structures: capitalist state, welfare state, developmental state and statism (in East Asian countries), autocratic state (Russia), and dictatorial state (Iran, North Korea, Cuba, some Middle Eastern states).

The references to theocracy and communism bring the attention back to civilizational and ideological divides. Theocratic and communist dictatorships are fed by religious doctrines and ideologies that are fundamentally opposite to the prevailing Western ideology, at least in their fundamentalist versions. Hence, cultural actors have the crucial role to make political actors realize that civilizational, religious, and ideological differences underlie different conceptions of political processes, legal systems, and social economies. We are back to the fundamental role of cultural structures in relationship to political structures, and to the role that cultural and political structures must play to rein in economic structures. The interface among cultural, political, and economic structures is a three-way street mediated by the reflexive human agency.

Hence, the future of globalization and the very survival of our civilization depends on the constructive engagement of social actors with their social structures, intrasocietally, and cross-societally. Cultural actors must make political actors realize the internal and international consequences of unregulated economic agendas (see Rodni's position) and the need to develop policies that balance economic profit and human development (Kiely, 1998). Without this balance in national and global agendas, there is no hope for a constructive dialogue among nations. For this reason a right globalization begins from home and it is rooted in the critical awareness of the structural inequities of one's own nation.

What is the analytical link among national and global structures and their respective agencies? The three intrasocietal structures have parallels at the cross-societal level: (a) Global Civil society is a major cultural agency that is fueled by a large variety of local civil societies, both in the Global North and in the Global South. As Nicanor (2003) states, civil society now joins the State and the Market as the third key institution shaping globalization. Global civil society can mediate the interface between the economic and political IGO. This activity is a reflection and continuation of the role that local civil society can play intrasocietally in partnership with the government and the business sector to chart a different and sustainable kind of globalization. Based on the model of the Philippines Agenda 21 (pcsd.neda.gov.ph/pa21.htm), Nicanor shows how civil society and progressive individuals and agencies in government and business are effectively working to ensure that globalization benefits the poor, societies, and nature. (Nicanor Perlas is president of the Philippines' Center for Alternative Development Initiatives (CADI); (b) Political IGOs (UN, International Court/ Tribunal, etc.) are the global counterparts of national governmental agencies; (c) economic IGOs (WB, IMF, WTO, etc.) are the global counterparts of the private business sector within nations.

Today we have examples of societies where cultural and political institutions are predominant (see first row, columns 2 and 3 in Table 1.6). Islamic theocracy certainly falls in the first category because of the dominance of religion on the rest of society. Communist dictatorships seem to fit the category of predominantly political societies (see second row, columns 3 and 4 of Table 1.6). The predominance of capitalist institutions in economic societies can be conceptualized descriptively in terms of economic IGOs or, in critical key, in terms of IGOs as submissive to a transnational state, TNS (Robinson, 2004); global economic

TABLE 1.6. Dominant structure and agency in cultural, political, and economic societies.

Types of societies	Dominant institutions					
	Cultural		Political		Economic	
	Structure	Agency	Structure	Agency	Structure	Agency
Cultural	Religious institutions	Ayatolla				
Political			Dictatorship	Communist Leaders		
Economic					TNS (1)/IGOs	Hegemonic Leaders/ TNC (2)

(1) TNS = Transnational state; (2) TNC = Transnational class.

leadership (agency) has been conceptualized as a transnational class, TNC (see Sklair's chapter and Robinson, 2004).

The key to a viable global future is to have interaction and mutual understanding among the three types of leadership; cultural, political, and economic. The heuristic value of Table 1.6 is twofold: it enables social actors to realize that the three types of transnational leadership reflect upon and respond to the pressure of their respective transnational structures. Hence, exercising an impact on these structures from below, from national agencies and structures is of crucial importance; in addition, Table 1.6 enables the social actor's realization that different political and economic systems are at times rooted in different civilizational or ideological traditions. Therefore, the pretense of economic societies to impose on noneconomic societies their own economic and political logics is an historical and cultural nonsequitur destined to fail. Again, the right path toward globalization can begin only from home, namely from the critical examination of reflexive agencies on their local and national structures. I may add that there is here no implicit or explicit advocacy of a socialist form of globalization, or it is excluded. The ILO Report on the "Social Dimensions of Globalization" (www.ilo.org/public/english/fairglobalization/report) could be another platform for such a dialogue and the "Social Democratic Alternative to the Washington Consensus" by David Held (www.lse.ac.uk/collections/pressAndInformationOffice/publications/books/Global_Covenant.htm) still another. These are just two examples of many initiatives developed by Global Civil Society.

I have barely mentioned the raw elements of an "agency and structure" framework that provides analytical tools for an intercivilizational and cross-societal negotiation of the global future. It is an understatement that this framework remains to be worked out in detail. Suffice here to say that we have both classical and novel tools for dealing with micro and macro global processes and their conflictuality. Perhaps, the awakening of the human agency in our technological society is the major tool we have to avoid the quagmire of chaos theory. I develop this alternative perspective in the concluding chapter.

References Cited and Bibliography

Albrow, M. (1996, 1997). *The global age: State and society beyond modernity*. Stanford, CA: Stanford University Press.

Alexander, J. C. (2001). "The past, present, and future prospects of civil society." In B. A. Schemmon (Ed.), *Civil society, citizenship, and learning*. M. Hamburg, Munster.

Ali, T. (2002). *The clash of fundamentalisms: Crusades, jihads and modernity*. London/New York: Verso.

Amin, S. (1996). *Capitalism in the Age of Globalization: The management of contemporary society*. New York: St. Martin's.

Arrighi, G., & Silver, B. (2001). "Capitalism and world (dis)order 2001," *Review of International Studies, 27*, 257–279.

Bamyeh, M. A. (2000). *The ends of globalization*. Minneapolis: University of Minnesota.

Bauman, Z. 1998. Globalization: the human consequences. Cambridge, UK: Polity Press.

Beck, U. (2000). *What is globalization?* Cambridge, U.K.: Polity Press.

Bodley, J. H. (2000). *Cultural anthropology: Tribes, states, and the global system.* 3rd ed. Mountain View, CA: Mayfield.

Boli, J., & Thomas, G. M. 1997. "World culture in world polity: A century of international non Governmental organization," *American Sociological Review, 62(12),* 171–190.

Breidenbach, J., & Zukrigl, I. (2000). *Tanz der Kulturen: Kulturelle Identitat in einer Globalisierten Welt (Dance of Cultures: Cultural Identity in a Globalized World).* Reinbek bei Hamburg: Rowolt Taschenbuch Verlag.

Bright, C., & Geyer, M. (1987). "For a unified history of the world in the twentieth century," *Radical History Review, 39,* 69–91.

—— (1995). "World history in a global age," *American Historical Review, 100(4),* 1034–1060.

—— (1996). "Global violence and nationalizing wars in Eurasia and America: the politics of war in mid-nineteenth century," *Comparative Studies in Society and History, 38(4),* 617–657.

—— (2002). "Where in the world is America?" In T. Bender (Ed.), *Rethinking American history in a global age.* Berkeley: University of California Press, pp. 63–99.

Castells, M. (2000). *The rise of network society.* 2nd ed. Malden, MA: Blackwell.

Chase-Dunn, C. (1989). *Global formation: Structures of the world-economy.* Cambridge, UK: University of Cambridge Press.

Chua, A. (2003). *World on fire: How exporting free market democracy breeds ethnic hatred and global instability.* New York: Doubleday.

Cohen, R., & Kennedy, P. (2000). *Global sociology.* New York: New York University Press.

Collins, R. (1980). "Weber's last theory of capitalism: a systematization," *American Sociological Review, 45(December),* 925–942.

—— (1997). "An Asian route to capitalism: religious economy and the origins of self-transforming growth in Japan," *American Sociological Review, 62(December),* 843–865.

Diamond, S. (1977). "Primitive society in its many dimensions." In I. Rossi, J. Buettner-Janusch, & D. Coppenhaver (Eds.), *Anthropology full circle.* New York: Praeger, pp. 418–424.

Diamond, S., & Belasco, B. (1980). "The anthropological study of complex-societies." In I. Rossio (Ed.), *People in culture.* pp. 568–596.

Dicken, P. (1992/2003) (4th ed.). *Global shift: The internationalization of economic activity.* London: Paul Chapman/Guilford.

Duiker, W. J., & Spielvogel, J. J. (2001). *World History. Vol. 1 and 2.* 3rd ed. Belmont, CA: Wadsworth.

Eade, J. (Ed.) (1997). *Living in the global city: Globalization as a local process.* London and New York: Routledge.

Firth, R. (1936/1957). *We, the Tikopia.* New York: Barnes and Noble.

—— (1965/1975). *Primitive Polynesian economy.* New York: Norton.

Geertz, C. (1998). "The world in pieces: Cultures and politics at the end of the century," *Focaal: Tijdschrift voor Antropologie, 32,* 91–117.

Giddens, A. (1999/2002). *Runaway world: How globalization is reshaping our lives.* BecaRaton, Fr: Routledge.

Gills, B. K. (Ed.) (2000). *Globalization and the politics of resistance.* London: Macmillan.

Harrison, J. B., & Sullivan, R. E. (1980). *A short history of Western civilization.* 5th ed. New York: Knopf.

Held, D., & McGrew, A. (Eds.) (2000). *The global transformations reader: An introduction to the globalization debate.* Cambridge, UK: Polity Press/Blackwell.

Held, D., McGrew, A., Goldblatt, D., & Perraton, J. (1999). Global transformation: politics, economics, and culture. Stanford, CA: Stanford University Press.

Hopkins, A. G. (Ed.) (2002). *Globalization in history*. New York: Norton.

Hoppers, C. A. O. (2000). "Globalization and the social construction of reality: affirming or unmasking the inevitable?" In N. P. Stromquist, & K. Monkman (Eds.), *Globalization and education: Integration and contestation across cultures*. Lanham, MA: Rowman and Littlefield, pp. 99–119.

Huntington, S. P. (1993). "The clash of civilizations?" *Foreign Affairs, 72(3)*, 22–49.

—— (1996/1997). *The clash of civilizations and the remaking of world order*. New York: Simon and Schuster.

Inglehart, R., & Baker, E. W. E. (2000). "Modernization, cultural change and the persistence of traditional values," *American Sociological Review, 65 (February*: 19–51).

Inglehart, R., & Norris, P. (2003). "The true clash of civilizations," *Foreign Policy*, March/April 2003.

Kagan, D., Ozment, S., & Turner, F. M. (1983). *The western heritage. Vol. 1 and 2*. New York: MacMillan.

Kennedy, P. M. (1987). *The rise and fall of the great powers: Economic change and military conflict from 1500 to 2000*. New York: Random House.

Kiely, R. (1998). *Industrialization and development*. London: University College London Press.

King, M. L. (2003). *Western civilization: A social and cultural history*. 2nd ed. Upper Saddle River, NJ: Prentice-Hall.

Lechner, F. J., & Boli, J. (2005). *World culture: Origins and consequences*. Malden, MA: Blackwell.

McKay, J. P., Bennett, H. D., John, B., & Buckley, E. P. (2004). *A history of world societies. Vol. I*. 6th ed. Boston: Houghton Mifflin.

Malinowski, B. (1922/1961). *Argonauts of the western Pacific*. New York: Dutton.

Mamdani, M. (2005). *Good Muslim, bad Muslim: America, the cold war, and the roots of terror*. New York: Doubleday.

Meyer, J. W. (1998). "Globalization: Sources and effects on national states and societies." Prepared for the *Conference on globalizations: Dimensions, trajectories, prospects, Stockholm*. (*http://www.yale.edu/ccr/meyer2.doc*).

Modelski, G. (1987). *Long cycles in world politics*. Seattle: University of Washington Press.

Nicanor, P. (2003). *Shaping globalization: Civil society, cultural power and threefolding*. Cabriola Island, BC, Canada: New Society Publishers.

Osterhammel, J., & Peterson, N. P. (2005). *Globalization: A short history. translated by Dona Geyer*. Princeton, NJ: Princeton University Press.

Redfield, R. (1953). *The primitive world and its transformation*. Ithaca, NY: Cornell University Press.

Robbins, R. H. (2005). *Global problems and the culture of capitalism*. 3rd ed. Boston: Pearson.

Robertson, R. (1992). *Globalization: Social theory and global culture*. Newbury Park, CA: Sage.

Robertson, R. (2003). *The three waves of globalization: A history of a developing global consciousness*. London: Zed.

Robertson, R., & Khondker, H. H. (1998). "Discourses of globalization: Preliminary considerations," *International Sociology, 13(1)*, 25–40.

Robinson, W. I. (2004). *A theory of global capitalism: Production, class, and state in a transnational world*. Baltimore, MD: Johns Hopkins University Press.

Rossi, I. (Ed.). (1974). *The unconscious in culture: The structuralism of Claude Levi-Strauss in perspective*. New York: Dutton.

Rossi, I (Ed.). (1980). *People in culture: A survey of cultural anthropology*. New York: Praeger.

—— (1983). *From the sociology of symbols to the sociology of signs: Toward a dialectic sociology* (translated in Japanese). New York: Columbia University Press.

—— (1993). *Community reconstruction after an earthquake: Dialectical sociology in action*. Westport, Ct: Praeger.

Rossi, I. (2000). "Globalism, nationalism and social identity." In M. A. Toscano., & V. N.. Parrillo (Eds.), *Millenium haze: Comparative inquiries about society, State, and Community*. Milan (Italy): Franco Angeli, pp. 101–112.

—— (2000a). "The human in the cultural, the cultural in the global: intercultural dialogues and the humanization of global processes." In *Proceedings of the International Conference on "Globalization and Latin humanism" organized by the World Latinist Union*. Treviso, Italy: Cassamarca Foundation, 2000, pp. 23–35.

Rossi, I., Buettner-Janusch, J., & Coppenhaver, D. (1977). *Anthropology full circle*. New York: Praeger, pp. 418–424.

Sahlins, M. (1961). "The segmentary lineage: An organization expansion," *American Anthropologist, 63(2, pt 1)*, 322–345.

Samovar, L. A., & Porter, R. E. (2003). *Intercultural communication*. 10th ed. Belmont, CA: Wadsworth.

Sapir, D. (1924). "Culture, genuine and spurious," *American Journal of Sociology, 29(4)*, 401–429 (reprinted in Rossi 1977).

Scholte, J. A. (2000). *Globalization: A critical introduction*. New York: St. Martin's.

Smith, A. (1776/1994). *The wealth of nations,* edited by Edwin Cannan. New York: Modern Library.

Stavrianos, L. S. (1999). *A global history: From prehistory to the 21st century*. 7th Ed. Upper Saddle River, N.J.: Prentice-Hall.

Stiglitz, J. E. (2002). *Globalization and its discontents*. New York: W.W. Norton.

Taylor, P. J. (1996). *The way the modern world works: World hegemony to world impasse*. Chichester: Wiley.

Tomlinson, J. (1991). *Cultural imperialism*. Baltimore, MD: Johns Hopkins University Press.

Wallerstein, I. (1974). *The modern world system: Capitalist agriculture and the origins of the European world economy in the sixteenth century*. New York: Academic.

—— (1989). *The modern world-system, III: The second era of great expansion of the capitalist world-economy, 1750–1840s*. New York: Academic.

—— (1990). "Culture as the ideological battleground of the modern world system," *Theory, Culture and Society, 7*, 31–55

—— (1991). "The national and the universal: Can there be such a thing as world culture?" In A. D. King (Ed.), *Culture, globalization and the world system*. Binghamton, NY: State University of New York.

Wolf, E. R. (1982). *Europe and the people without history*. Berkeley: University of California Press.

Wolf, M. (2001). "Will the nation-state survive globalization?" *Foreign Affairs (Jan/Feb), 80(1)*.

Yoffee, N., & Cowgill, G. L. (1988). *The collapse of ancient states and civilizations*. Tucson: University of Arizona Press.

2
Microglobalization[1]

KARIN KNORR CETINA

Introduction

What is microglobalization? In this chapter, I draw on earlier studies of global financial markets and of the new global terrorism to suggest that global configurations may be based on microstructures: on forms of connectivity and coordination that combine global reach with microstructural mechanisms that instantiate self-organizing principles and patterns. The basic intuition that motivates the concept of a global microstructure is that genuinely global forms, by which I mean fields of practice that link up and stretch across all time zones (or have the potential to do so), need not imply further expansions of social institutional complexity. In fact, they may become feasible only if they avoid complex institutional structures. Global financial markets, for example, where microstructures have been found, appear too fast and change too quickly to be contained by institutional orders.[2] Global systems based on microstructural principles do not exhibit institutional complexity but rather the asymmetries, unpredictability, and playfulness of complex (and dispersed) interaction patterns, a complexity that

---

[1] This chapter draws on material published in Knorr Cetina (2005). Microstructures can also be analyzed in terms of complexity concepts, a perspective I do not pursue in this chapter.

[2] The new terrorism involves different mechanisms, but it also has so far consistently outrun the capacity of state intelligence agencies and their "vast, lumbering bureaucracies" (Silberman and Robb, 2005) to counter its threat or track and identify its challenges.

65

results, in John Urry's terms, from a situation where order is not the outcome of purified social processes and is always intertwined with chaos (2003: 106, 17–38; see also Thrift, 1999). More concretely, these systems manifest an observational and temporal dynamics that is fundamental to their connectivity, autoaffective principles of self-motivation, forms of sourcing, and principles of amplification that substitute for the principles and mechanisms of the modern complex organization.

If the basic intuition is correct, microsociology—and the methodology of qualitative research—provide significant resources for the study of global systems. In other words, it is not correct to assume, as social scientists sometimes do, that global forms simply outstrip the capacity of the social sciences to study such forms empirically. In fact, the analysis of global microstructures helps to collect and assess empirical evidence for the architecture of the global structural forms of a world society. It also suggests a theory of microglobalization, the view that the texture of a global world becomes articulated through microstructural patterns that develop in the shadow of (and perhaps liberated from) national and local institutional patterns. Although I illustrate microglobalization by global forms that are disembedded from national societies and that exhibit a level of global integration, microglobalization is not limited to such forms. Microstructures are likely to come into play in what has been called "response-presence-based social forms," in which participants are capable of responding to one another and common objects in real-time without being physically present in the same place (Knorr Cetina & Bruegger, 2002). Response-presence-based social forms tend to be bound together by information technologies, the arteries of global and transnational connectedness through which the interactions flow. Response-presence-based forms have to be distinguished from situations of physical co-presence, which is what microsociologists have focused on in the past. But microstructures may also come into play when seemingly small changes have global effects, a phenomenon that may be explained by the emergence of microstructural connectivities among distantiated elements that lead to disproportional amplification effects. One example is the near breakdown of the Capital Management Fund, which has been attributed to the emergence of a microstructure (MacKenzie, 2005). Such microconnectivities may be of particular interest to the understanding of global systems that may experience more massive consequences of structural instabilities and phase transitions than local forms. The general point here is that microstructures can "carry" globalization and the patterns of a world society. They specify densities and time warps within the vast texture of a global world.

What Are Global Microstructures?

I have conceptualized microglobalization as being based upon structures of connectivity and integration that are global in scope but microsociological in character. I now want to emphasize four characteristics of global microstructures: they are "light," institutionally speaking, as implied before; they appear to facilitate a certain non-Weberian effectiveness; they cannot simply be reduced to networks; and they tend to be temporal structures: the resulting systems exhibit flow characteristics.

Let us first consider lightness. By "lightness" I mean that the mechanisms and structures involved suggest a reversal of the historical trend toward formal, rationalized (bureaucratic organizational) structures whose beginning appears to date back to the medieval church (Lancaster, 2005). Thus although microstructures are on some level organized or coordinated systems, the coordinating elements involved are not of the kind we associate with formal authority, complex hierarchies, rationalized procedure, or deep institutional structures. In fact, the mechanisms involved may be akin to those we find in face-to-face situations, but at the same time they hold together distantiated arrangements and distributed systems (they are based on response-presence rather than physical co-presence). The notion *micro*structures is intended to capture this quality of the mechanisms involved.

A second characteristic of global microstructures pertains to the relationship between institutional lightness and the achievement of effects. Weber's notion of rationalization was radical in that it postulated a particular organizing structure composed of legitimate authority, formal expertise, and rational instrumental procedure as an effective agent of modernization. The structure underlies not only the effectiveness of capitalist production economies, but also that of public service sectors and nation-state administrations. Postmodern consumer society also owes its success to a significant degree, it is plausibly argued, to the presence and proper functioning of such rationalized systems (e.g., Ritzer, 1994, 2002). Rationality, authority, expertise, and formalized procedures were interiorized in such systems. Global microstructures do not correspond to Weberian ideals of highly rationalized systems, yet they appear nonetheless effective. Their effectiveness derives at least in part from external support structures that amplify and augment a system's effectiveness and provide for the conditions of its success. In other words, global microstructures may derive disproportionality benefits from decoupling internal operations from support structures that provide for the conditions under which operations can remain light. Sourcings of this kind point away from the inclusive notion of an internally rationalized system. To put it in economic terms, it is the systematic and reflexive use of externalities that helps account for the success of global microstructures.

The notion of "sourcing" here can perhaps be seen as the global equivalent of rootedness (and belonging). Sourcing relationships link microglobal structures with their environment and context without the localizing connotations of roots; that is, without the idea that the system supported by the source growth out of the latter, links its identity to the source, or is deeply embedded in it. Yet source–system relationships should not be cast merely as economic alliances. In global foreign exchange markets, almost the entire work of world making, of creating, on screens, the informational reality within which traders move, is outsourced to provider firms such as Reuters, Bloomberg, and Telerate. Clearly in this case the sources shape the core of trading. Also, source (e.g., Reuters) and system (e.g., electronic over-the-counter markets, see below) co-evolved over the last 20–30 years in a near-symbiotic relationship. Sources are not just financially and instrumentally, but also symbolically (e.g., through patterns of communication) connected to systems. This is perhaps more apparent when one considers the new terrorism that relies on an Islamic diaspora as its source (see section on "Scopic Media and the Information Societies of the New Terrorism"). In any case, amplification and augmentation strategies such as the ones exemplified by sourcing relationships exploit the potential for disproportionalities between input and output or effort and effect, and they can overcome disproportionalities between actors who pursue conflicting goals (see also Cohen & Stewart, 1994; Urry, 2003: 7). Disproportionality effects can also be distilled from the working and use of media of various kinds that amplify and multiply system results. And they can be distilled, for example, from the use of technology and from scientific and other innovations. Finally, lightness may emerge in response to de- or underregulation that creates the space for an adaptive and adaptable self-organization.

A third characteristic of global microstructures is that they are not simply networks, although they may comprise a variety of relational arrangements. Networks are sparse social structures (e.g., Fligstein, 1996: 657); they essentially consist of channels or "pipes" (Podolny, 2001) through which information and resources flow between nodes. What flows through the channels carries much of the burden of explaining outcomes, as does participants' selection of network channels over other means of distribution or coordination. But more is going on in global social forms than transfers between actors.[3] For example, it would seem to be difficult to understand Al Qaeda, which can be viewed as a global microstructure, without taking into account the spiritual influence of Islamist religious representations, or its family structure and self-reproducing mechanisms. Although global microstructures tend to be flat rather than hierarchically organized systems, they are at the same time highly textured systems. The specific textures respecify and may in fact contradict assumptions about network structures (e.g., Knorr Cetina, 2003). The term "microstructure" is intended to point to the richness and diversity of elements and practices that layer global social forms. It is also intended to suggest that relational connectivity may not be enough to effectively organize complex systems.

Thus although all elements may play a role in organizing or integrating a microstructure, I want to specifically point to *scopic media* (see section on "Scopic Systems") as mechanisms of coordination on a global scale. Scopic media enable flow architectures that are not territorially bound, but the specific character of these architectures varies greatly across microstructured domains. For example, global institutional currency markets, which can be seen as global microstructures and which are entirely electronic markets, include a level of intersubjectivity that derives from the character of these markets as reflexively observed by participants in temporal continuity, synchronicity, and immediacy. The observation is enabled by global reflex systems (GRS) that assemble and project the reality of these markets. As a consequence, these markets are communities of time, but in a different sense than the terrorist groups for which disconnections and "structural holes" are a characteristic of operative practice.

The time aspects just illustrated are a fourth characteristic of global microstructures that I would like to emphasize here. There is more than one temporal dimension that is of interest, but I want to specifically note that global microstructures appear to be time-based and work with time in ways that transcend temporal patterns in more local configurations. One suggestion here is that time articulation

---

[3] Consider how much of Al Qaeda one can explain by simply doing a network analysis of known participants, as has been attempted (e.g., Sageman, 2004).

and time mechanisms substitute for the loss of spatially differentiated stability and articulation in global systems. In some respects, spatially stabilized configurations can be made more productive when they become part of a temporal stream. To again take the example of financial markets, spatially dispersed currency markets, that is, interests in trading and knowledge about prices have become integrated, since the 1980s, into a temporal stream of activities made possible by electronic information and dealing systems that connect participants across locations and time zones (for the details see Knorr Cetina, 2003). This development eliminated arbitrage as a form of transaction that exploits the geographical separation of buying-and-selling interests. Yet the transformation of a spatial system into a temporal stream of sequentially connected activities also arguably increased the liquidity and innovativeness of market transactions and contributed to the growth, global power, and reproduction of financial markets.[4] Similarly, Foucault and Lepenies argue that premodern spatial arrangements and categories of knowledge were replaced by a temporal approach as knowledge became "historical" at the turn of the 19th century, a move that transformed the speed of knowledge production and the growth of knowledge (cited in Jokisch, 1996: 184–194).[5]

There is a second idea that is relevant here and it is based on Luhman's notion of the "temporalization of complexity" (1984: 76–81). This is the idea that what is temporal in a "temporalized" system are its components; they are unstable, changing, even transient. The argument here is that temporally unstable components increase the complexity and thereby the stability of the larger system, because nonenduring components change in response to the irritations of an (always more) complex environment and help the larger system cope with external factors.[6] In the language used here, it is "lightness" in the sense of nonentrenched, "nervous," degenerating elements that exemplify microstructuration and that carry the system forward. Another way to put it is that continual disintegration on the microlevel creates the space for successor elements and this increases the complexity and the chances of survival of the overall system (see also Zeleny, 1981: 4–17). Note that this notion is in contrast to network notions that see strong and expanding rates of relatedness between units whose identity is unproblematically

---

[4] The rise in volumes of trading has to do with the increased availability of investment money (e.g., Bank for International Settlement, 2005), but finance theorists (e.g., Crane et al., 1995) also point to market internal factors, such as the elimination of information barriers and the possibility of increased risk taking and risk diversification on a global scale.

[5] We may also consider a counter-example, cultures. Cultures tend to be geographically distributed and they are separated by various boundaries. Participants tend to divide themselves up along ethnic, religious, corporate, professional, and other lines spatially, socially, and symbolically. In fact, the notion of culture is widely used to capture the idea of local patterns and traditions that emerge within a culturally differentiated landscape. What would it imply if a group of cultures transformed into a global stream? Clearly diversity would suffer and potentially disappear. Would cultural learning and change increase, as it sometimes appears to do when corporate cultures merge?

[6] One illustration here is the transition, in physics, from the idea of elementary particles as simple, spotlike, nonreducible elements to the transitory, decaying subatomic processes of today. In today's physics, it is the nonidentity, fluidity, and speed of transformation of the basic units of matter that is of interest (see also Jokisch, 1996: 195–198).

assumed as a guarantee of success.[7] The contrasting assumption here is that fluid, or, in Luhmann's parlance, temporalized elements lead to a continual change of patterns of relatedness, and this is a causal factor in the successful reproduction of the system. These concepts refer back to the notion that autopoetic systems are emergent and do not have (stable) "foundations" (see also Urry, 2003: 51).

For Luhmann, temporalized complexity, as he termed it, was simply a way to theorize process in systems theory. According to his reasoning, all social systems display temporalized complexity by virtue of the fact that system elements, which he took to be actions, are temporally limited events rather than stable enduring structures. But this is a formal definition that does not allow us to pin down and evaluate differences between spatial structures and flow structures. Nor does it allow us to conceptualize flow concretely as something more specific than process and the character of social reality when seen from an action perspective. In other words, it is useful to reenter the question and ask which systems become time-based and what this means.

The two cases I consider in the following, global foreign exchange markets and the terrorist group Al Qaeda, exemplify the temporal characteristics described, but in different ways. I first discuss the scopic mechanism of coordination that enables the flow architecture of the financial markets discussed. I also address market intersubjectivity as a central feature identifying how these markets are microstructured and at the same time temporal systems. The scopic mechanism is important in that it provides an alternative to network coordination. It shows how infrastructural electronic connections may be instantiated, in practice, by nonnetwork forms of coordination. Scopic projections also play an important role in the new terrorism of Al Qaeda, to which I turn next. Here I propose a different sort of temporality, transcendent time, to account for Al Qaeda's parallel structure of living and a level of global symbolic integration. I also use the example of Al Qaeda to say more about the role of sourcing and the fluid and mobile components of a microstructure, Al Qaeda's cells. Within the confines of this chapter I can only provide selective illustrations of these cases.[8] But these fragments are important in that they illustrate the feasibility of a microglobalization research program and some of its results.

Microglobalization I: The Virtual Societies of Global Currency Markets

Unlike other financial markets, the foreign exchange market is not organized mainly in centralized exchanges but derives from interdealer transactions in a global banking network of institutions; it is what is called an "over-the-counter"

---

[7] Actor-network theory provides an example of an approach that postulates such an effect.
[8] For a full version of the analysis of Al Qaeda based on secondary literature, Web material, and news reports see Knorr Cetina (2005). For the analysis of financial markets see, for example, Knorr Cetina & Bruegger (2002) and Knorr Cetina (2003).

market (for descriptions of bond, stock, and other financial markets see, for example, Smith, 1981, 1999; Baker, 1984; Abolafia, 1996; Hertz, 1998). Over-the-counter transactions are made on the trading floors of major investment firms and other banks. On the major trading floors of the global banks where we conducted our research in Zurich and New York, between 200 (Zurich) and 800 (New York) traders were engaged in stock, bond, and currency trading involving various trading techniques and instruments. Smaller floors in Sydney, Zurich, and New York featured between 40 to 80 traders. Up to 20% of these traders will deal in foreign exchange at desks grouped together on the floors. The traders at these desks in interbank currency markets take their own "positions" in the market in trying to gain from price differences while also offering trades to other market participants, thereby bringing liquidity to the market and sustaining it, if necessary, by trading against their own position. Foreign exchange deals via these channels start at around several hundred thousand dollars per transaction, going up to a hundred million dollars and more. The deals are made by investors, speculators, financial managers, central bankers, and others who want to profit from expected currency moves, or who need currencies to help them enter or exit transnational investments (e.g., in mergers and acquisitions). In doing deals, traders on the floors have a range of technologies at their disposal: most conspicuously, the up to six computer screens that display the market and serve to conduct trading. When traders arrive in the morning they strap themselves into their seats, figuratively speaking, they bring up their screens, and from then on their eyes will be glued to these screens, their gaze captured by it even when they talk or shout to each other, their bodies and the screen world melting together in what appears to be a total immersion in the action in which they are taking part. The market composes itself in these produced-and-analyzed displays to which traders are attached.

Scopic Systems

The terminals deliver much more than just windows on physically distant counterparties. In fact, they deliver the reality of financial markets, the referential whole to which "being in the market" refers, the ground on which traders step as they make their moves, the world that they literally share through their shared technologies and systems. The thickly layered screens laid out in front of traders provide the core of the market and most of the context. They come as close as one can get to delivering a standalone world that includes "everything" (see below) for its existence and continuation: at the center the actual dealing prices and incoming trading conversations, in a second circle the indicative prices, account information, and some news (depending on the current market story), and further headlines and commentaries providing a third layer of information. It is this projection of a world assembled and drawn together onscreen in ways that make sense and allow navigation and accounting that requires further explanation. What make this world possible, I suggest, are scopic systems.

The term "scope", derived from the Greek *scopein*, to see, when combined with a qualifying notion, means an instrument, and the like for seeing or observing, as in "periscope". Social scientists tend to think in terms of mechanisms of coordination, which is what, for example, the network notion stands for: a network is an arrangement of nodes tied together by relationships that serve as conduits of communication, resources, and other coordinating instances which hold the arrangement together by passing between the nodes. Cooperations, strategic alliances, exchange, emotional bonds, kinship ties, personal relations, and forms of grouping and entrenchment can all be seen to work through ties and to instantiate sociality in networks of relationships. But we should also think in terms of reflexive mechanisms of observation and projection, which the relational vocabulary does not capture. Like an array of crystals acting as lenses that collect light, focusing it on one point, such mechanisms collect and focus activities, interests, and events on one surface, from whence the result may then be projected again in different directions. When such a mechanism is in place, coordination and activities respond to the projected reality to which participants become oriented. The system acts as a centering and mediating device through which things pass and from which they flow forward. An ordinary observer who monitors events is an instrument for seeing. When such an ordinary observer constructs a textual or visual rendering of the observed and televises it to an audience, the audience may start to react to the features of the reflected represented reality rather than to the embodied prereflexive occurrences.

In the financial markets studied, the reflexive mechanism and "projection plane" is the computer screen; with the screen come software and hardware systems that provide a vast range of observation, presentation, and interaction capabilities sustained by information and service provider firms. Given these affordances, the prereflexive reality is cut off and replaced; some of the mechanisms that we take for granted in a lifeworld, for example, its performative possibilities, have been integrated into the systems, and others have been replaced by specialized processes that feed the screen. The technical systems gather up a lifeworld while simultaneously projecting it. They also "apresent" (bring near, see Schutz & Luckmann, 1973) and project layers of context and horizons that are out of reach in ordinary lifeworlds; they deliver not only transnational situations, but a global world spanning all major time zones. They do this from trading floors located in global cities (Sassen, 2001) which serve as the bridgehead centers of the flow architecture of financial markets. Raised to a level of analytic abstraction, the configuration of screens, capabilities, and contents that traders in financial markets confront corresponds to a global reflex system, or GRS, where R stands for the reflexively transmitted and reflexlike (instantaneously) projected action and other capabilities of the system and G stands for the global scopic view and reach of the reflex system. The term is intended to denote a reflexive form of coordination that is flat (nonhierarchical) in character while at the same time being based on a comprehensive summary view of things, the reflected and projected global context and transaction system. This form of coordination contrasts with network forms of coordination which, according to the present terminology, are prereflexive in character: networks are embedded in territorial space, and they do not suggest the existence of reflexive mechanisms of projection that aggregate, recontextualize, and augment the relational activities within new frameworks that are analytically relevant to understanding the continuation of activities. With the notion of a GRS system, I am offering a simplifying term for the constellation of technical, visual, and behavioral components packaged together on financial screens that deliver to participants a global world in which they can participate on a common platform, that of their shared computer screens. On a technological level, the GRS mechanism postulated requires that we must understand as analytically relevant for a conception of financial markets not only electronic connections, but computer terminals and screens—the sorts of teletechnologies (Clough, 2000: 3) that are conspicuously present on trading floors and the focus of participants' attention—as well as the trading floors themselves, where these screens cluster and through which markets pass.

Sequential Markets and Communities of Time

Scopic systems of the kind discussed are comprehensive innovations. In the case considered, they enabled the transition from network-based markets to a global market. Over time (it took time to develop this particular, highly customized scopic system)[9] they transformed spatially dispersed interests in trading and knowledge about prices into a temporal stream that connected participants across locations and time zones (Knorr Cetina, 2003). Let us first consider the temporal part of this transformation. As indicated, the emergence of GRS eliminated arbitrage as a form of transaction that exploits the geographical separation of buying and selling interests. Geographical separation had meant information barriers, which disappeared with the transparency of a common market. Reuters, the main developer of GRS at the time with respect to currency markets, assembled and pooled the information for this market. The firm projected, through its terminals and software, an identical market (dealing and indicative prices as well as contextual information) to all participants connected. But for the present market to emerge, more was necessary than the transparency that ensued. Dispersed parallel interests in trading had to become ordered sequentially according to price levels, a task originally accomplished through the presentation, on screen, of lists of prices that indicated what prices particular banks and traders were potentially willing to pay. This kind of successive ordering is now done by algorithms that are built into electronic broker systems (see Muniesa, 2003). As a

---

[9] Screens began to present a dispersed and dissociated matrix of interests more directly only in 1973, when the British news provider Reuters first launched the computerized foreign exchange system "Monitor," which became the basis for this electronic market (Read, 1992). Monitor still apresented the market only partially, however, because it, too, only provided indicative prices. Nonetheless it did, from the beginning, include news. Actual dealing remained extraneous to screen activities and was conducted over the phone and telex until 1981, when a new system also developed by Reuters, one which included dealing services, went live to 145 institutional customers in nine countries. The system was extended within a year to Hong Kong, Singapore, and the Middle East, resulting in a market with a worldwide presence (Read, 1992: 283 ff., 310–311).

consequence of this sort of sequential ordering any participant could buy or sell at the universally best price within the common global market. The best price was a present price; such a price is valid only at a given point in time, and at any one time, only one deal could be performed globally. Time and price became inseparably locked together, and time-price changes became the pulsating beat of these markets. The principle of only one deal at a time implies a second sequence, that of the succession of done deals and traded prices. This sequence of deals is indicated on screen; it articulates and defines a streaming market. As best prices are selected in dealing and recognized by the system, the price of a financial instrument at which a deal was done constrains and potentially selects (one also has to figure in volume) the next price.

One needs to appreciate the full force of this transformation. A world of parallel goings on (trading, information processing) as it occurs in spatially dispersed markets has been eliminated and replaced by a strict sequence of activities that are frequently separated only by split seconds. As a result, sequential changes have become not only the pulse, but also the personal memory, common history, and projected future of the streaming market. The present in this sequence is now "metastable", to use a term borrowed from physics; it lasts potentially long enough for human intervention to occur, but not longer. Time itself would seem to have been transformed; the global market moves at accelerated, intensely punctuated speed. We may also say that the spatial cultures of trading linked by arbitrageurs have been transformed into a flow culture.

The argument just presented links scopic systems to the emergence of a flow market and explains the sequentialization of a streaming market. I now want to add a further conceptual level to the argument that (some) global social fields are microstructured by turning to the participants involved, that is, to traders. A global reflex system may enable market unification and sequentialization in the sense described, but there is also the question whether the participants involved, market-making traders, remain isolated atomized individuals as postulated by economic theory or whether we can assume a level of integration in global fields. To put this differently, a test case for the microsociological argument I offer is whether microsociological concepts allow us to go beyond the notion of atomized economic actors. The question is also whether they suggest an alternative to the sociological view which is that atomistic actors need to be seen as embedded in networks of social relationships that define the sociological component of these markets (Granovetter, 1985). Perhaps the concept most relevant to microsociological thinking when it comes to social binding is that of intersubjectivity. But ideas about intersubjectivity have been pitched at a fundamental level of social reciprocity that occurs in a small space; intersubjectivity "belongs," one might say, to the territory of the face-to-face situation. Can we maintain that a level of intersubjectivity also obtains between individuals who are globally spread out in space? What passes between territorially separated individuals who may never share the same space on the levels of consciousness, interpretation, cultural orientation? Markets and in particular spot markets are purportedly classic examples of anonymous discrete exchanges ruled by supply and demand adjustments rather than by intersubjectivity (Williamson, 1975, 1985; Powell, 1990). Can we nonetheless assume that a certain level of connectedness (intersubjectivity) is characteristic of some markets? In this section, I submit that participants' reciprocal observation of markets on screens—enabled by scopic systems—may constitute a basis for a form of intersubjectivity and integration of some global spheres. I discuss this by drawing on Schutz's idea of a "We-relation", a term that captures a community of time and can be related back to the temporal character of global foreign exchange markets (e.g. 1964, vol. II: 25–26).

Schutz's analysis of intersubjectivity can be summarized by considering two examples. The first is a situation where two individuals are oriented to each other in the face-to-face situation (Schutz, 1964, vol. II: 27–33; Natanson, 1962: 13). In his analysis of this situation, Schutz bracketed out the question why a particular interaction occurs and what individuals explicitly communicate to each other in order to focus on the more primordial nonverbal interaction that occurs; he described very vividly the "interlocking of the glances" and the "thousand-faceted mirroring of each other" which he saw as a unique feature of face-to-face situations (1967: 169–70). These mirrorings, he maintained, make another person's presence and consciousness accessible to an actor and define the situation as an intersubjective situation. The second example to which Schutz linked his analysis of intersubjectivity is not of two individuals facing each other, but two subjects watching a third object, a bird flying. In analyzing this situation, Schutz arrived at another idea which became central to his conception, that of temporal coordination. As one of his followers put it, "The reciprocal interlocking of the time dimension is for Schutz the core phenomenon of intersubjectivity" (Zaner, 1964). Why did Schutz associate intersubjectivity with time, a connection not commonly made in sociology? Schutz took the objects observed to be things that move or change over time. The experience of such events is temporal in that it is constituted step by step as the event unfolds. Two persons watching the same event are brought into a "state of intersubjectivity," so to speak, by their experience evidently changing in similar ways, in response to what unfolds. The basis of this sort of we-experience, for Schutz, was the temporal immediacy of events. Temporal immediacy allowed one to recognize and follow another person's experience of the bird in flight as contemporaneous with one's own experience.

Schutz attempted a number of formulations of temporal coordination, always associating it with sequential aspects of consciousness rather than with any content. He spoke of the coordination of "phases of consciousness," of the "synchronization of two interior streams of duration," and of the fact that during this synchronization, "we are growing older together" (1964, vol. II: 24–26). The point for us is that in emphasizing temporal coordination, Schutz moved away from any attempt to base social relatedness on the assumption of the shared content of experience or on any real understanding of other minds. Instead, he left things with the subject recognizing the other as a fellow human being here and now, evidently paying attention to the same event. What turned this experience into a "We-relation" as he called it, was the contemporaneousness of an event, one's experiencing it, and the indications of the other's attentiveness to it: "Since we are growing older together during the flight of the bird, and since I have evidence, in my own observations, that you were paying attention to the same event, I may say that we saw a bird in flight" (1964, vol. II: 25).

It is his avoidance of any requirement of real understanding and his shift from two subjects engaged with each other to subjects engaged with a third object who notice this engagement that makes Schutz' ideas useful for conceptualizing the sociality of global fields, as a level of intersubjectivity and integration that obtains before any concrete relationship is entered into and before any economic transaction has been performed. To illustrate this in regard to financial markets we can start with the question what the "same events" might be that could plausibly be construed as globally observed in the same binding fashion in which events are observed in the face-to-face situation. These events are delivered, I want to argue, by the knowledge-created phenomena onscreen and the content of the supplemental channels to which traders are oriented. In other words, the bird that traders watch together around the clock is "the market," as it is assembled in identical (price actions, market analyses, news descriptions, etc. furnished by global information providers), overlapping (information exchanged through personal relationships), and coordinated fashion in the many windows and channels to which participants are attached. In these windows and channels the "same" market has a vivid presence; it speaks out to participants and demands their connected continuous attention and action. This action component is implicated in a second requirement associated with the We-relation, that of *reciprocity*: it must somehow be noticeable that others are watching the same events and that they are attuned to one another's presence. For Schutz, observing the other observe was crucial for any interlocking of subjectivities to come about; his emphasis was on nonverbal expressions as signals of the other's attention and attunement to the situation. On the global plane, this attention and attunement to the market— comprising price action, economic context, and a set of market participants—is presupposed and hardly needs to be expressed. One assumes that no professional trader or salesperson can survive financially if he or she pays no attention to the market, and that floor managers watch over participants' attention signals. Nonetheless, there is a variety of indicators of others' active interest in the market that traders observe: most notably the deal requests they make, the messages they send, and the price movements they trigger. Through these signals, absent market participants have what Goodwin (1995: 260) once called a "mediated" presence on screen. Market activities can be considered as signals not only of economic opinion but also of social connectedness of participants' reciprocal awareness of others' presence and constitutive involvement in an unfolding market situation.

The reciprocity just indicated marks the current context as also involving what Schutz called the "interlocking of motives characteristic of interaction in the We-relation" (1964: 55), the possibility of one's "in-order-to" motive becoming the other's "because" motive. A trader selling a currency in order to take a profit may trigger trading responses in others because of what he or she has done. Here reciprocity points to the fact that global financial markets are fields of interaction: at any point in time all traders watch the same events and one another, but some also interact (trade), and in interacting they may add new levels of reciprocity and reflexivity (see Soros, 1994). But we should turn now to the third feature on which Schutz based the We-relation, that of temporal coordination (see also Zerubiavel, 1981). First, traders, salespeople, and others on trading floors located within a particular time zone share a *community of time*. They watch the market as it comes into view in the morning and builds up during the day virtually continuously in synchronicity and immediacy during their working (and waking) hours.[10] All three aspects are important here: synchronicity refers to the phenomenon that traders and salespeople observe the same market events simultaneously over the same time period; continuity means they observe the market virtually without interruption, having lunch at their desk and asking others to watch when they step out; and temporal immediacy refers to the immediate real-time availability of market transactions and information to participants within the appropriate institutional trading networks. Local news is also transmitted on screen "live" when the events are scheduled at a particular time (e.g., announcements of economic indicators), or they are transmitted with as little delay as possible. Traders, investors, and others attempt to gain advance knowledge of special developments, but these pursuits presuppose rather than undercut the community of time which obtains with respect to the market.

Time coordination also involves, second, a temporal division of labor across time zones, to the effect that the community of time extends around the clock. As an example take the trading instrument of an option to buy or sell a currency at a particular point in the future, at an agreed price. In contrast to the instantaneously completed on the spot sales and purchases of currencies discussed so far, options expire weeks or months after the deal was made; hence unlike a spot trader's accounts, an option trader's accounts cannot be closed every night. One way to organize such long-term transactions globally is to pass on a desk's option accounts every evening to the same bank's option traders in the next time zone, who will manage the accounts and add deals during their working hours. The "option book" that circles the globe indicates global financial cooperation: one extends the surveillance of the "bird in flight," the market, through the eyes of others, when it threatens to disappear from view during the night. As a result, the

---

[10] As Harvey has argued (1989: 239–259), increasing time-compression is a characteristic of the whole process of modernity and of postindustrialization. A similar argument had been advanced by McLuhan (1964: 358), who proposed that electricity establishes a global network of communication that enables us to apprehend and experience media-transmitted events nearly simultaneously, as in a common central nervous system (see also Waters, 1995: 35; Giddens, 1990:17–21). These views anticipate global integration by means of a common (media) culture or consciousness rather than by means of economics, in contrast to other approaches (Waters, 1995: 33–35; Wallerstein, 1974, 1980). Yet what I am after here is something much less general in scope (most of the world is excluded from traders' screen world) and more microlevel in character: a form of time coordination that penetrates all of the participants' interactions and involves dozens of small mechanisms of binding participants into the same timeframe.

coordination of consciousness Schutz discussed becomes more inclusive, encompassing groups that are not simultaneously present but that take turns sequentially and overlapping in observing and acting on the market: traders coordinate trading intentions and philosophies with the next and the previous desk in time in evening and morning phone calls and emails, and the book remains on their mind (and available on their screens) while it is out of their hands. In other words, the circling book can be seen as an attempt to weave together the consciousness of those attending to it in different time zones, with the effect of creating an around-the-clock synchronization of observation and experience.

A third aspect of time coordination beyond this attempted global contemporaneity brings into view market *calendars* and *schedules*: dates and hours set for important economic announcements and for the release of periodically calculated economic indicators and data. These calendars and schedules structure and pace participants' awareness and anticipation. They create an atmosphere of collective anticipation and preparation for specific events that pace and interrupt the regular flow of market activities. Temporal structures of this sort recurrently focus a global field of watchers on possible changes of direction of the "bird in flight." They bind the field to specific timeframes around which global attention is heightened and in relation to which expectations build up. The ordinary temporal flow of synchronous and sequential time-zone observation is thus punctuated regularly by potentially trend-changing occurrences. The scheduled character of these events not only synchronizes experience on a collective and global level, but adds to it a measure of emotional arousal. Durkheim thought such arousals to be central to bringing about a feeling of "solidarity": he maintained that the We-experience arises when a group becomes excited. One should note that the Durkheimian "force field" (Wiley, 1994: 106, 122) of social solidarity is energized by feeling or sentiment but it also entails the unity of something shared. With Durkheim, this something shared was either moral or semantic, that is, a unity of meaning. In the present case, the unity of meaning has much to do with knowledge, with the punctuation of existing trends by new information.

The question that lies at the core of the notion of a response-presence-based social form that extends across global distances is: what are the possibilities of its inherent connectivity and integration as the key to overcoming the geographical separation between participants? I introduced the notion of a global we-relationship that is based on temporal coordination to suggest that a level of microintegration, or intersubjectivity, is possible in global fields. Other micro-structures illustrated elsewhere for these markets include linkages through global conversations, the structural use of interaction means to maintain order, the form response-presence takes in the face-to-screen situation and ways of bodily anchoring that show how electronically mediated markets as collective disembodied systems nonetheless penetrate and reflect the bodily experience of participants (see Knorr Cetina & Bruegger, 2002). The point about selecting the phenomenon of Schutzean intersubjectivity as a mechanism of integration to be illustrated for the purpose of this chapter is that it also casts light on the temporal makeup of microglobalized domains. One should note that the community of time discussed emerged in connection with the transformation of a spatial market into a flow market that circles the globe continuously with the sun: these time registers overlap, but they are nonetheless, distinctive. In Al Qaeda's case, to which I now turn, and which allows me to illustrate a different microstructure, time dimensions are also central, but they are of a different type than the ones discussed. I use Al Qaeda's case also to provide an example of sourcing and to illustrate the continued relevance of scoping systems.

Microglobalization II: The New Terrorist Societies

The new terrorism, as the 9/11 Commission Report of the U.S. Congress and President terms it, is sophisticated, patient, disciplined, and lethal (Kean & Hamilton, 2004: xvi, 47 ff.; see also Hall, 2004). The 9/11 attack was a complex international operation that could not have been mounted by just anyone in any place. Such an operation required, the Commission states at the end of a long and detailed investigation, a logistics network able to manage the movement of operatives and money. It had to find and transport resources, and it had to have reliable communication between coordinators and operatives, a command structure, planning, the ability to test plans, recruitment, and training (Kean & Hamilton, 2004: 365–366). And yet it is clear that Al Qaeda is not an omnipotent evil empire, a massive multinational corporate structure, or a military-industrial complex. The Commission speaks of the active support of "thousands" of young Muslims for Bin Laden's message, not of millions (Kean & Hamilton, 2004: 362). It also states that the group of conspirators which brought off the attacks was at the same time fragile, dependent on a few key personalities, and occasionally left vulnerable by the marginal unstable people often attracted to such causes (Kean & Hamilton, 2004: 364).

How, then, are we to conceptualize sociologically this "hydra of destruction" which is simultaneously no more than a marginal group of conspirators that makes mistakes, whose tradecraft is not especially sophisticated, and which lives by donations? The new terrorism would seem to be a major exemplifying case for a global microstructure; for example, it exemplifies a lack of institutional form, self-organizing, emergent structures, and a surprising interactional effectiveness when it launches its attacks. What are the social morphologies of groups that operate on a global scale and are capable of such asymmetry effects? Modern industrial society created "complex" forms of organizations that managed uncertainty and task fulfillment through interiorized systems of control and expertise. But complexity was institutional complexity; it meant sophisticated multilevel mechanisms of coordination, authority, and compensation that assured orderly functioning and performance. Al Qaeda does not exhibit this sort of interiorized complexity. Instead it seems to lean toward a different form of complexity; one emanating from more microstructural arrangements and the rise of mechanisms of coordination akin to those found in interaction systems.

Transcendent Time: A Structure of Parallel Living

Although the Muslim belief system of Al Qaeda clearly has many aspects, I want to discuss it in terms of the lived time that potentially connects the members of the group. This may help to understand the character of Al Qaeda terrorism as a parallel world disjoined from the world of the host societies in which Al Qaeda volunteers live. A useful approach in this regard is to go back to early Christian communities and the way they lived time, according to Heidegger (2004; see also Guignon, 2000 and Ciborra, 2004: 23 ff.). Heidegger reconstructs the temporality of these communities from St. Paul's letter to the Thessalonians. According to St. Paul, at the beginning of primal Christian spirituality lies the Annunciation as an experience that shapes religious life at the time and is, for the individual and the community, a moment of transformation. St. Paul refers to the "having become" that characterizes Christians after the Annunciation. In early Christian religiosity there is also the prospect of the "second coming" and the burning question of when this event will happen. St. Paul addresses the question by indicating how one should live the situation of waiting: it is not a matter of simply awaiting this future occurrence but instead of "running forward" toward it by living every moment in a distinctive way. In this 'living-forward' one is resolute in assuming a context shaped by having become a Christian in order to be prepared for the Event which is already happening. Life becomes simplified in a certain manner as it is "brought into the simplicity of its fate" and pulled back from "the endless multiplicity of possibilities which offer themselves" (Guignon, 2000: 88–89). As the later Heidegger states, the world "does not become another in its content, nor does the circle of others get exchanged for a new one." Rather the transformation pertains to the "form" of everyday activity, leaving the content of the world unchanged (Dreyfus, 1993: 321f.). Thus, those who "have become" will still go about the business of everyday life and attend to what is demanded of them. But they will do so in a different mode; what has changed, to use a term borrowed from Williams (1977: ch. 9), is a structure of feeling, and the living of time.

I propose that such a "futural" mode of living based on a "having become" can also be seen to characterize the new religious terrorism. Like the early Christians confronting an eschatological promise, many members of Al Qaeda would seem to similarly ground their life in "moments" of transformation. They also appear to be pulled into living-forward toward the end, a parallel life that has been delivered over to a new temporality and commitment while it is at the same time participating in the business of ordinary life. In the terrorist case, the new temporality appears to actively confront if not embrace the possibility of personal death, as a transitional occurrence en route to a promised and visually pictured personal paradise But it also runs forward toward an imagined and ecstatic success of "jihad" as "holy war" beyond personal death and toward the future of the community in whose history one's own death is enmeshed. These more collective ideas run counter to the Heideggerian concept of time as individual being-toward-death. Thus, the lived time of terrorism appears "transcendent" in regard to personal life, and it transcends ordinary time by "shadowing" it with a second future that embeds everyday activities within a new meaning structure.

The assumption of a second transcendent temporal structure of terrorism is important in the following respects. First, it grounds modes of affectivity that appear to have served Al Qaeda in the past: two characteristic aspects of these activities have been patience and preparedness: the patience to wait for the right situation to strike while at the same time resolutely preparing for specific attacks, and the patience to call off projects and accept backlashes while simultaneously reorganizing and living forward toward the goal of an Islamic state. The members of Al Qaeda are not improvisers who act on the spur of the moment or in response to fleeting circumstances. But neither are they given to the strict schedules and modes of control that characterize rationalized systems of planning. As analysts have noted, Al Qaeda has shown a surprising degree of patience, sometimes giving itself years of meticulous preparation without indication of any hurry or deadline pressure (9/11 Report; Kean & Hamilton, 2004: ch. 5.2). At the same time, participants have undergone extensive preparatory training, often for concrete tasks (e.g., Gunaratna, 2003: 10–12); in other words, they resolutely assumed the context of becoming a fighter for a cause in order to be prepared for demands when they call. Second, this sort of temporality would also appear to bind together an otherwise dispersed and diverse community whose members derive endurance, tension, and lived significance from the act of giving themselves over to transcendent time.

Al Qaeda membership cuts across national, cultural, and language boundaries, and it includes and liaises with different Muslim religious orientations. Osama bin Laden has continually stressed the need for Muslims of different orientations to unite in the fight against Americans and "the degradation and disbelief which have spread in Muslim lands."[11] Temporal coordination alleviates the problem of constructing unity from diversity and the problem of "other minds," that is, of closely coordinating and shaping individuals' thinking. It suggests that a level of intersubjectivity may develop among participants that live different daily lives and have experienced various cultural upbringings and national situations. For this argument to be plausible one needs to consider that transcendent time involves more than time reconstructed in terms of a new beginning and end. As in the case of financial markets, it also implies time structuring, a temporality punctuated by events that include widely communicated historical experiences and references (such as the Afghan war against Russia), successful terrorist attacks, public summons (fatwas), sermons and television appearances (e.g., Bin Laden's appearance before the U.S. election of November 2004). Thus transcendent time would appear to be structured in terms of an historical sequence to which participants are oriented and which contextualizes individual time and effort. The sequence provides not only for a collective memory of the group, it also situates the collective project that is continually reinstantiated, extended, and reshaped as events are incorporated into the historical sequence. Time, here, may have to be thought of

---

[11] Al Qaeda recruitment video cited in Gunaratna (2003: 72).

as a "punctuated flow" (punctuated by a sequence of occurrences) into which individual participants are absorbed and feel integrated, a flow that runs on in the shadow of everyday time and the temporal orders of host cultures.

One implication of the temporal coordination postulated is that globality becomes possible as spatial mechanisms of coordination based on geographic closeness, routine face-to-face contacts, national political knowledge, and the like lose their importance. Another implication is that—as a form of coordination—the temporality postulated fulfills some of the functions Weber associated with rational authority structures. In other words, the theoretical argument here is that time structuring affords a form of coordination that can take the place of institutional control and social authority structures. We have thus given a first illustration of how the new terrorism is a microstructure that operates on a global scale. Transcendent time is the equivalent of the Schutzean intersubjectivity postulated for the financial markets considered. But temporal coordination here is less tightly woven. What is missing is the synchronicity, continuity, and temporal immediacy that locked together participants and activities in the global market.

Scopic Media and the Information Societies of the New Terrorism

The punctuated flow I postulated can only emerge and have integrative effects if the relevant events are widely transmitted. In this section, I want to consider the teletechnologies (Clough, 2000: 3) that accomplish the transmission. In Al Qaeda's case, TV channels, the Web, videotapes and audiotapes, and their producers can be seen as the components of a dispersed scopic system through which the collective terrorist project becomes assembled and channeled. These media provide sensorily rich records and projection planes for the transmission of images, speeches, commentary, and events. The technical systems are "apresentational" in the sense indicated before; they bring near to receivers distant situations that are out of reach for ordinary lifeworlds. They are also a-representational, by which I mean that the content of the televised items should not be primarily decoded in a representational idiom. Although the representational truth of these items may be invoked, the contents tend to be media productions by TV stations and by authors such as religious leaders aiming at a range of performative effects.

The teletechnological media and media contents correspond to a scopic system that fills transcendent time with collective content, structures time in terms of events, and give concreteness and substance to the temporal coordination I have postulated. Many of the broadcast events are also intentionally moral and performative in the sense of "calling" the audience to particular forms of actions. These calls, exemplified by Bin Laden's declaration of war against the Americans of February 1998 or his and Ayman al-Zawahiri's "messages" of warning and threat in 2002, are not of the same order as the exchanges that coordinate concrete plans of action. But they may well have coordinating force on another level: that of reiterating and extending the transcendent project to which the audience is committed, that of renewing an affective community, and that of creating for this community a background world that grounds their activities and experiences. In other words, one assumes that the images and messages have a binding effect on prepared participants, as these select and interpret the content within the framework of already existing commitments to a transcendent project. One also assumes that for those "having become" and regularly drawing on scopic presentations, the sequences of occurrences begin to constitute something of a referential world, a thick context that situates individual activities, provides frameworks of interpretation for further events, and is a venue for the renewal of emotional dedication. When scopic systems are systematically used they have "world-making" (Goodman, 1978) effects.

The world involved is informational rather than "natural" or "material." This is implied by the notion of scopic systems and the mediated character of the communities they create. In communicating distant occurrences in identical fashion to distributed diasporic audiences, scopic systems are information systems, and Al Qaeda is part of the contemporary information society in that it uses its means and mechanisms. The informational makeup of this world is also apparent in its processual character. Most of our world notions imply that the world is a place (however extended) or perhaps a totality of objects (e.g., the physical universe) "wherein" we live, and "in" which factual (e.g., globalization) and symbolic processes can be said to take place. In comparison, the parallel world of Al Qaeda appears to be fluid, processual, and a-territorial. It is neither presupposed nor given, but constructed-in-going-along. As the flow of events into which Al Qaeda members are plugged is continuously reiterated, updated, and extended, the various temporal and other coordinates of this world are continuously articulated and changed as operational goals are adopted, religious commentary and messages are interpreted, new decrees are issued, and the activities of various "enemies" are observed and decoded. The very accoutrements of this noninstitutional timeworld change as new events take place and become food for imagined new scenarios and works. If the image I used in the section on "Transcendent Time: A Structure of Parallel Living" of Al Qaeda "running forward" toward the future by living every moment in a distinctive way is plausible, then it implies that Al Qaeda's world is dynamic and quickly changing rather than static and in a state of equilibrium. This dynamism has a correlate in the mobility of participants. We know from various records and descriptions that Al Qaeda members themselves, and their camps, cells, and other bases, are extremely mobile. Participants travel, move, and change identity frequently. Cells are equally mobile, and the membership, leadership, and operational structure of the group also change. The mobility of Al Qaeda surely is a strategic element in its success; but it also points to the "placeless" character of the Al Qaeda microstructure, its floating, scapelike (Appadurai, 1996: ch. 2) form and the readiness of participants to interlock with any territory for specific purposes but to share none.

Cells and Diasporas

So far I have introduced two major elements of the global microstructure of Al Qaeda: transcendent time as a structure of orientation constitutive of parallel living, and scopic systems that deliver the "mediated presence" of remote participants and update interpretations and events. The two elements enable a floating global microstructure to emerge and fuel its dynamics. I now address a last element, the organizational form of Al Qaeda. Central to the discussion is the distinction between its cells and a religiously defined Arabic diaspora on which Al Qaeda relies for external support. Several theoretical arguments can be linked to this organization. One is that the organizing principles invoked are microstructural; they involve trust, the analogy of family relationships, and a cellular organization. The second line of arguments brings up sourcing as a way to account for some of Al Qaeda's disproportional effects. The dual organization described offers an argument for how lightness of structure can be combined with enhanced effectiveness through strategies of amplification and augmentation. I also show, in this section, that lightness of structure amounts to more than a lack of formal, rationalized institutional structures. It implies a transition to a temporal complexity of a kind where system stability depends on and arises from the fluidity and instability of components.

Consider first the roles of amplification and augmentation in relation to Al Qaeda's organization. In the last section, I cited scopic media as a constitutive feature of the global microstructure of terrorism. Yet some of the most important of these media are not managed or "owned" by Al Qaeda but are independent agents (e.g., television channels) that broadcast to a wide and predominantly nonterrorist audience. The television channel Al Jazeera records and broadcasts terrorist messages and images, and it produces, in the eyes of observers, inflammatory programs that have disturbed not only Washington but also Arab governments. Yet it clearly also caters to the broad concerns of nonterrorist clienteles (it reaches an audience of 30 million to 50 million), it prides itself on being independent and impartial, and it is subsidized by and operates out of Qatar, the American-friendly state and U.S. ally in the Persian Gulf. Terrorist microstructures incorporate and use some teletechnological media, but they also draw on outside systems that are independent of their communities. The issue this raises is the dual organization of Al Qaeda: some functions are interiorized within its framework of organization, whereas others are outsourced to external agents and units not controlled by the Al Qaeda leadership and not directly engaged in its projects. These external components may not live transcendent time, that is, partake in Al Qaeda's parallel mode of living. They are nonetheless implicated in its projects, which they enable and support. In fact, Al Qaeda's lightness of structure can at least partially be explained by the externalization of some crucial components. Al Qaeda practices a form of sourcing: it delegates tasks to outside agents, and it takes advantage of outside agents' willing or unintentional promotion of its cause. For example, it takes advantage of media channels that broker communications and meanings to a wide audience of spectators, it sources much of the recruitment process to sales agents, the radical religious leaders who propagate relevant interpretations of Islam and head religious schools, and it has externalized much of its financing to independent NGOs, Islamic charity organizations, specific churches, and the like (for detailed overviews, see Gunaratna, (2003: ch. 3) and the 9/11 Report (Kean & Hamilton, 2004: XVIII).

Al Qaeda's sources can be understood in terms of what one may call, follow-ing Ho (2004), a "diaspora" of Islamic agencies and people. Ho describes the long existence of a diaspora of Arabs from Hadramawt, Yemen, across the Indian Ocean, and its confrontations with the British Empire from the 16th century onward. A diaspora, in this parlance, is not understood as a homogeneous group that spreads out across territories but is a composite; for example, the Hadrami in their movement throughout the Indian Ocean became natives anywhere, inter-married with the local population, and their offspring assimilated or developed a mixed creole identity. Ho extends his model to the current situation, arguing that Bin Laden is a member of the Hadrami diaspora, and his operations, spreading from East Africa to the Philippines, take place in an old theater of Arab diasporic mobility and activity. These geographical parallels mean that for viewers in South and Southeast Asia, the events unfolding on the television screen have deep historical resonances (2004: 234 ff.).

The notion of diaspora, then, recaptures the idea of a religious commitment introduced in the beginning but it gives it breadth and historical depth: it draws attention to a long-standing and persistent confrontation between a religiously defined Arabic diaspora and various Western empires. To be sure, the diaspora can no longer be regarded as limited to the Indian Ocean. America is not a colo-nial power, although it may come close to one in the diasporic imagination. Potential historical continuities of the sort implied are accomplished rather than simply given. The point I want to make by bringing up these historical references is not that the present confrontation echoes past ones precisely or that it is in fact identical with them. It is rather that Al Qaeda's global reach and microstructural effectiveness is easier to understand if we not only assume the existence of "sympathizers," but an historically anchored movement of Islamic people—with overlapping religious beliefs and a tradition of confrontation with non-Islamic powers—of whom a portion remains connected to the Arab and Islamic world. Awareness of the historical continuities and specific characteristics of such a dias-pora may account for Al Qaeda's success in its global support and recruitment efforts. The dual organization I postulated captures the role of this diaspora in providing Al Qaeda with an external belt of potential capital: financial, social, cultural, and political capital. According to estimates by the CIA, Al Qaeda can draw on the support of some 6 to 7 million Muslims worldwide, of which 120,000 are potential recruits for its violent projects (cited in Gunaratna, 2003, p. 95). Al Qaeda's "few thousand" active members are augmented by millions of support-ers that are linked to it by a diasporic history and imagination. In this sense Al Qaeda can maintain its lightness of structure, while at the same time mustering disproportional effectiveness with regard to selected outcomes.

If the existence of an historical diaspora provides a belt of potential resources, what is inside the belt? In other words, how are we to think of the other leg on which Al Qaeda stands, the second component of its dual organization? The con-sensual answer (for which I draw here on the summary account by Gunaratna, 2003, ch. 3) is that Al Qaeda is organized in terms of a cellular structure. Cells are units of 2 to 15 members placed in various settings to prepare for certain tasks, or they emerge in a certain place as recruits living in a particular area become committed to Al Qaeda. Several defining characteristics of this cellular structure can be indicated. The first is that cells are independent and self-contained. Gunaratna (2003, p. 97) recounts that Al Qaeda's structure remains close to that of Egyptian terrorist groups, whose cells were called *anguds*, which is Arabic for a bunch of grapes. If a grape is plucked from a grapevine, its disappearance does not affect the others. Thus cells appear to have independent bank accounts, and their members may only know of their own role in a project and not that of other cells. A second characteristic, continuous with the first, is that cells are productive units. For example, cells or their members may come up with their own proposals for terrorist attacks, find ways of assembling the necessary materials and knowledge, carry out relevant research, and even take charge of financing part of the preparatory work and of their own expenses. Third, cells are mobile in regard to location and flexible in regard to membership. New members may join teams, previous members may transfer to other locations, teams may disband, and cells may relocate. Although the cell nodes are regional, regional nodes do not have a fixed abode. For example, after Al Qaeda relocated from Sudan to Afghanistan in 1996, its European and North American bureau moved to Turkey and Yemen, and the Turkish bureau moved again, to Spain, after the arrest of a key figure in Europe in 1998.[12] Fourth, the system of communication that links cells to leaders appears fractal and mutational, an apparent advantage when it comes to preventing transparency and leaks. There were some cell members among those involved in the 9/11 attacks who communicated directly with leaders in Afghanistan, but most cells appear to have been coordinated through "agent-handlers" who lived near the target location or in the "hostile zone" of Europe and America, and they reported only to them. This also implies that cell structure is decentralized and without formal hierarchy or system of governance. What substitutes for a formal hierarchy is a family structure in which "older brothers" may play a greater role than the others. "Family" frequently stands for nationality. Fifteen of the hijackers of the 9/11 attacks were from Al Qaeda's "Saudi family," which, perhaps in continuity with Ho's account of the Hadrami diaspora, appears to play a dominant role in Al Qaeda. Families function regionally, but individuals from different national "families" may also be "handpicked" and cross-posted outside their regions (Kean & Hamilton, 2004: 98).

Al Qaeda's family organization responds to problems posed by cultural and linguistic barriers in a global organization; Anderson's imagined communities are put to specific uses here (1983). It is worth mentioning that high energy physicists, in conducting their large-scale experiments staffed by participants from many regions of the world, also frequently team people up according to national origin. But the metaphor of "family," like the metaphor of brotherhood ingrained in Islam, also appeals to trust and sentiment and suggests the constitution of community, at least

---

[12] Some of these movements and the travels of Al Qaeda members are recounted in great detail in Gunaratna (2003: ch. 3).

potentially. In other words, cells and families and the modes of diasporic assistance and affiliation they assume invoke microstructural principles of connectivity and integration. However, I also want to emphasize temporal complexity here. The characteristics of the cell structure I have outlined, in particular the mobility, flexibility, and mutability of cells with regard to membership and location, as well as their relative autonomy and planned disintegration, all point to the temporal nature of cells. Cells are not durable units but changing implementations of short-term projects sequentially replaced by new projects: they are units that their creators plan from the outset to abolish, abandon, and recreate as nonidentical units at a different location. Paradoxically, perhaps, it is this instability and nervous irritability of the components of a system associated, in the section on "What Are Global Microstructures?", with a complexity based on time that serves the stability and successful continuation of the whole group. The bureaucratically organized intelligence agencies and military machines that have been mobilized to fight Al Qaeda rely on elaborate interiorized systems of rules, authority, and control that offer legitimacy and transparency of procedure. What they do not offer is Al Qaeda's lightness of being manifest here in its sequentially recreated mode of functioning and nonidentical cellular structure.

Time-based complexity, one should emphasize, is continuous with the fluidity concepts some writers have discussed (e.g., Abbott, 2001; Urry, 2000; Bauman, 2000; DeLaet & Mol, 2000). Yet the distinction added here between the flexibility and fluidity of the component level of a system and its overall stability is an important one to make; it provides a particular angle on emergence, implies sequential learning on a microstructural level and refers us back to transcendent time, as a binding mechanism on a global level. A second distinction emphasized previously in this chapter is also important: that between a spatial arrangement where stability resides in fixed categories and traditions distantiated from one another and temporal cultures that integrate things into a global stream. The natural history approach, according to Foucault and others, was a spatial arrangement of knowledge. Molecular biology (or experimental systems within it) appears today to be integrated global streams of processing superimposed on any remaining spatial logic (see Jokisch, 1996: 184–194). Al Qaeda distinguishes itself from all other terrorist groups that are nationally based by the appearance it gives of having become such a global stream. Transcendent time as described in the section on "What Are Global Microstructures?" lies at the heart of this stream. Sustained and extended by the scopic transmission of media content, it provides for a level of bindingness and integration of the terrorist project beyond the coordination of operational performance and mission planning. Beyond the level, that is, of the ever-decaying, ever-regenerated cellular structure. In the case of foreign exchange markets, the ever-regenerated structure is actorial; agency resides with individual market makers, as illustrated elsewhere.[13] The market case also showed how sequential, time-based systems may result from a particular historical transformation, from the development and use of a scopic system that came to provide a special global world.

---

[13] See Knorr Cetina and Bruegger (2002: 913–114).

Some Implications for Globalization Research

Microglobalization implies that the micro (in the sense of microprinciples of patterning) and the macro (in the sense of global scope and extension) should not be seen as two levels of empirical reality that stand in contrast to each other. Rather, the micro in the form indicated instantiates the macro; microprinciples enable and implement macroextension and macroeffects. The hallmark of microsociology in the past was not the connection to the macro, but the separation from it. For example, Goffman called the interaction order relatively autonomous, and not prior to, fundamental to, or constitutive of, macroscopic phenomena (Goffman, 1983: 9; Collins, 1981; Knorr Cetina, 1981; Alexander & Giesen, 1987). This argument also came with an understanding of the microworld as situational: as tied to the concrete social setting and the social occasion, which were thought to be governed by principles and dynamics not simply continuous with or deducible from macrosocial variables (Goffman, 1972: 63; Alexander, 1987).[14] Yet these assumptions, which have characterized much microsociological thinking in the past—that of the relative autonomy of microorders and that of their confinement to the physical setting—are theoretically no longer adequate in a world in which interaction can also be disembedded from local settings, in which space may be separated from place, as Giddens put it (1990: 18), and in which "situations" may link participants who are physically located in different continents and timezones.[15] Both assumptions were, from the present viewpoint, less analytical necessities than political moves: they had much to do with how macrosociology had been perceived earlier in social theory, as given to unrealistic abstractions and as losing sight of the human element in society. Early microsociologists attacked these tendencies. Goffman and others shifted the discussion away from the attacks and refocused it on the task of charting the territory for qualitative field work on areas of real life that had hitherto been ignored by sociologists (Collins, 1988: 380–384). What appears necessary today is that we rechart the territory of microsociology once again in ways that include distantiated spatial

---

[14] Goffman defined the situation as "any physical area anywhere within which two or more persons find themselves in visual and aural range of one another" (1981: 84; 1972: 63). Ethnomethodologists have expressed similar ideas through the notion of the "local accomplishment" of social order, where local has meant "witnessable," through seeing or hearing, in contrast to imputed or inferred. Ethnomethodologists have not restricted themselves to the physical setting through their definitions in quite the same sense in which Goffman did, placing greater emphasis on accomplishment, as, for example, in the observation that "witnessed settings" also have an accomplished sense (of objectivity, familiarity, and the like; Garfinkel, 1967: 9; Atkinson, 1988; Drew & Heritage, 1992). Yet this shift in emphasis leaves intact the tendency of ethnomethodological studies to equate fundamental reality with that which is highly focused in a small space, which lies in talk rather than writing, and which points to the nanoworld of the nonverbal signals that accompany such exchanges (Goodwin, 1981).

[15] Giddens (1990: 21–29) used the notion "disembedding" to refer to the "lifting out of social relations from local contexts." In this chapter, we are concerned with how interaction principles traditionally associated with local contexts shape global domains.

configurations. This chapter argues for an extension of microviewpoints that are pitched at the level of the local, and the situation as the prime social reality, to larger settings. If the hallmark of microsociology in the past was its emphasis on local social forms, one should now open the door to corresponding research on genuinely global forms.

Some microsociological notions such as that of the face-to-face situation will lose force in the process. They need to be replaced, I suggest, by the notion of response-presence and in some contexts by that of the face-to-screen situation. Some fundamental concepts we all share, such as that of a social actor, may acquire different connotations. My suggestion here is the increasing relevance of the notion of an observer. Meaning, with such a move, no longer simply resides in the minds of actors (in their intentions) but is in fact contextual. It becomes relocated in the strategies, distinctions (as in Luhmannian sociology, Luhmann, 1984; see also White, 1981), and perspectives (as in the sociology of knowledge) of third agents who observe (as financial analysts do) particular situations. Another concept that may become relevant and that I discussed in this chapter is that of global microstructures. Such microstructures specify cultures in which interlocking time dimensions and forms of embeddedness in time substitute for the loss of spatial rootedness and stabilization. Streaming markets, and the terrorist time warps discussed, provide examples of such time-based cultures. The flows implied demand methodological strategies and further concepts that pay attention to their decay, regeneration, and asymmetries and to underlying processes of information.

References

Abbott, A. (2001). *Chaos of Disciplines*. Chicago and London: University of Chicago Press.

Abolafia, M. (1996). *Making Markets: Opportunism and Restraint on Wall Street*. Cambridge, MA: Harvard University Press.

Alexander, J. (1987). Action and Its Environments. In J. Alexander, B. Giesen., R. Münch, & N. Smelser (Eds.), *The Micro–Macro Link* (pp. 289–318). Berkley: University of California Press.

Alexander, J., & Giesen, B. (1987). From reduction to linkage: The long view of the micro–macro link. In J. Alexander, B. Giesen, R. Münch, & N. Smelser (Eds.), *The Micro–Macro Link* (pp. 1–44). Berkeley: University of California Press.

Anderson, B. (1983). *Imagined Communities. Reflections on the Origin and Spread of Nationalism*. London: Verso.

Appadurai, A. (1996). Disjuncture and difference in the global cultural economy. In A. Appadurai (Ed.), *Modernity at Large: Cultural Dimensions of Globalization* (pp. 27–47). Minneapolis: University of Minnesota Press.

Atkinson, P. (1988). Ethnomethodology: A critical review. *Annual Review of Sociology*, 14, 441–465.

Baker, W. (1984). The social structure of a national securities market. *American Journal of Sociology*, 89 (4), 775–784.

Bank for International Settlements (2005). *Triennial Central Bank Survey. Foreign Exchange and Derivates Market Activity in 2004*. Basel: Bank for International Settlements.

Bauman, Z. (2000). *Liquid Modernity*. Cambridge: Polity.

Bodie, Z., & Merton, R. (1995). The informational role of asset prices. The case of implied volatility. In D. Crane et al. (Eds.), *The Global Financial System* (pp. 197–224). Boston: Harvard Business School.

Ciborra, C. (2004). *Labyrinths of Information*. Oxford, UK: Oxford University Press.

Clough, P. (2000). *Autoaffection: Unconscious Thought in the Age of Technology*. Minneapolis: University of Minnesota Press.

Cohen, J., & Stewart, I. (1994). *The Collapse of Chaos*. Harmondsworth: Penguin.

Collins, R. (1981). Micro-translation as a theory-building strategy. In K. Knorr Cetina & A. Cicourel (Eds.), *Advances in Social Theory and Methodology. Toward an Integration of Micro- and Macro-Sociolgies* (pp. 81–108). London: Routledge & Kegan Paul.

Collins, R. (1988). *Theoretical Sociology*. San Diego: Harcourt Brace Jovanovich.

Crane, D. et al. (Eds.) (1995). *The Global Financial System: A Functional Perspective*. Boston: Harvard Business School Press.

De Laet, M., & Mol, A. (2000). The Zimbabwe bush pump: Mechanics of a fluid technology. *Social Studies of Science*, 30 (2), 225–263.

Drew, P., & Heritage, J. (1992). *Talk at Work: Interaction in Institutional Settings*. Cambridge, UK: Cambridge University Press.

Dreyfus, H. (1993). *Being-in-the-World: A Commentary on Heidegger's Being and Time, Division I*. Cambridge: The MIT Press.

Fligstein, N. (1996). Markets as politics. A political–cultural approach to market institutions. *American Sociological Review*, 61, 656–673.

Garfinkel, H. (1967). *Studies in Ethnomethodology*. Englewood Cliffs, NJ: Prentice Hall.

Giddens, A. (1990). *The Consequences of Modernity*. Stanford, CA: Stanford University Press.

Goffman, E. (1972). The neglected situation. In P.P. Giglioli (Ed.), *Language and Social Context*. Harmondsworth: Penguin.

Goffman, E. (1981). *Forms of Talk*. Philadelphia: University of Philadelphia Press.

Goffman, E. (1983). The interaction order. *American Sociological Review*, 48, 1–17.

Goodman, N. (1978). *Ways of Worldmaking*. Indianapolis: Hackett.

Goodwin, C. (1981). *Conversational Organization*. New York: Academic.

Goodwin, C. (1995). Seeing in depth. *Social Studies of Science*, 25, 237–274.

Granovetter, M. (1985). Economic action and social structure: The problem of embeddedness. *American Journal of Sociology*, 91, 481–510.

Guignon, C. (2000). Philosophy and authenticity: Heidegger's search for a ground for philosophy. In M. Wrathall & J. Malpas (Eds.), *Heidegger, Authenticity and Modernity: Essays in Honor of Hubert L. Dreyfus*, Vol. 1 (pp. 79–1002). Cambridge, MA: MIT Press.

Gunaratna, R. (2003). *Inside Al Qaeda. Global Network of Terror*. Berkeley, CA: Berkeley Publishing Group.

Hall, J. R. (2004). Apocalypse 9/11. In P. Lucas, & T. Robbins (Eds.), *New Religious Movements in the Twenty-First Century. Legal Social and Political Challenges in Global Perspective* (pp. 25–82). London: Routledge.

Harvey, D. (1989). *The Condition of Postmodernity: An Inquiry into the Origins of Cultural Change*. Oxford: Blackwell.

Heidegger, M. (2004/1920–21). *The Phenomenology of Religious Life*. Bloomington: Indiana University Press.

Hertz, E. (1998). *The Trading Crowd. An Ethnography of the Shanghai Stock Market*. Cambridge, UK: Cambridge University Press.

Ho, E. (2004). Empire through diasporic eyes: A view from the other boat. *Society for Comparative Study of Society and History*, 10 (4175), 210–246.

Jokisch, R. (1996). *Logik der Distinktionen. Zur Protologik einer Theorie der Gesellschaft*. Opladen: Westdeutscher Verlag.

Kean, T. H., & Hamilton, L. H. (2004). *The 9/11 Report. The National Commission on Terrorist Attacks upon the United States. With Reporting and Analysis by the New York Times*. New York: St. Martin's Press.

Knorr Cetina, K. (1981). Introduction. In K. Knorr Cetina & A. Cicourel (Eds.) *Advances in Social Theory and Methodology. Toward an Integration of Micro- and Macro-Sociologies* (pp. 1–47). London: Routledge & Kegan Paul.

Knorr Cetina, K. (2003). From pipes to scopes. *Distinktion, Special Issue on Economic Sociology*, 7, 7–23.

Knorr Cetina, K. (2005). Complex global microstructures. The new terrorist societies. In J. Urry (Ed.), *Theory, Culture and Society, Special Issue on Complexity*, Vol. 22, No. 5, 213–234.

Knorr Cetina, K., & Bruegger, U. (2002). Global microstructures: The virtual societies of financial markets. *American Journal of Sociology*, 107 (4), 905–995.

Lancaster, R. (2005). *The Office of St. Peter. The Bureaucratization of the Catholic Church, 1050–1250*. (Doctoral dissertation, Northwestern University, 2005).

Luhmann, N. (1984). *Soziale Systeme. Grundriss einer allgemeinen Theorie*. Frankfurt: Suhrkamp

MacKenzie, D. (2004). Social connectivities in global financial markets. *Environment and Planning D. Society and Space*, 22, 83–101.

MacKenzie, D. (2005). How a superportfolio emerges: Long term capital management and the sociology of arbitrage. In K. Knorr Cetina & A. Preda (Eds.), *The Sociology of Financial Markets* (pp. 62–83).Oxford: Oxford University Press.

McLuhan, M. (1964). *Understanding Media*. New York: American Library.

Muniesa, F. (2003). *Des Marchés Comme Algorithmes. Sociologie de la Cotation Electronique à la Bourse de Paris*. Paris: Ecole Nationale Supèrieure des Mines (Dissertation).

Natanson, M. (1962). Introduction. In A. Schutz (Ed.), *Collected Papers I* (pp. XXV–XLII). The Hague: Nijhoff.

Podolny, J. (2001). Networks as the pipes and prisms of the market. *American Journal of Sociology*, 107 (1), 33–60.

Powell, W. (1990). Neither market nor hierarchy: Network forms of organization. *Research in Organizational Behavior*, 12, 295–336.

Read, D. (1992). *The Power of News. The History of Reuters*. Oxford: Oxford University Press.

Ritzer, G. (1994). *The MacDonaldization of America*. Thousand Oaks: Pine Forge Press.

Ritzer, G. (2002). *The Globalization of Nothing*. Thousand Oaks: Pine Forge Press.

Sageman, M. (2004). *Understanding Terror Networks*. University of Pennsylvania Press.

Sassen, S. (2001). *The Global City: New York, London, Tokyo*. Princeton, NJ: Princeton University Press.

Schutz, A. (1964). *Collected Papers II. Studies in Social Theory*. The Hague: Nijhoff.

Schutz, A. (1967). *The Phenomenology of the Social World*. Evanston, IL: Northwestern University Press.

Schutz, A., & Luckmann, T. (1973). *The Structures of the Life-world*. Evanston, IL: Northwestern University Press.

Silberman, L., & Robb, C. (2005). *Commission on the Intelligence Capabilities of the United States Regarding Weapons of Mass Destruction*. Report to the President (www.wmd.gov/report).

Smith, C. W. (1981). *The Mind of the Market*. Totowa, NJ: Rowman & Littlefield.

Smith, C. W. (1999). *Success and Survival on Wall Street. Understanding the Mind of the Market.* New York: Rowman & Littlefield.

Soros, G. (1994). *The Alchemy of Finance.* New York: Wiley & Sons.

Thrift, N. (1999). The place of complexity. *Theory, Culture and Society,* 16, 31–70.

Urry, J. (2000). *Sociology Beyond Societies.* London, Routledge.

Urry, J. (2003). *Global Complexity.* Cambridge, UK: Polity Press.

Wallerstein, I. (1974). *The Modern World System.* New York and London: Academic.

Wallerstein, I. (1980). *The Modern World-System II: Mercantilism and the Consolidation of the European World-Economy, 1600–1750.* New York: Academic.

Waters, M. (1995). *Globalization.* London: Routledge.

White, H. (2002). *Markets from Networks: Socioeconomic Models of Production.* Princeton, NJ: Princeton University Press.

Wiley, N. (1994). *The Semiotic Self.* Chicago: University of Chicago Press.

Williams, R. (1977). Structures of feeling. In R. Williams (Ed.), *Marxism and Literature* (pp. 128–135). Oxford: Oxford University Press.

Williamson, O.E. (1975). *Markets and Hierarchies: Analysis and Antitrust Implications.* New York: The Press.

Williamson, O.E. (1985). *The Economic Institutions of Capitalism, Firms, Markets, Relational Contracting.* New York: Free Press.

Zaner, R. (1964). *The Problem of Embodiment.* The Hague: Nijhoff.

Zeleny, M. (1981). What is autopoiesis? In M. Zeleny (Ed.), *Autopoiesis: A Theory of Living Organization* (pp. 4–17). New York and Oxford: North Holland.

Zerubiavel, E. (1981). *Hidden Rhythms: Schedules and Calendars in Social Life.* Berkeley, CA: University of California Press.

3
A Transnational Framework for Theory and Research in the Study of Globalization

Leslie Sklair

Introduction

The continuing popularity of globalization as a motif for the social sciences and humanities is little short of astonishing. Introduced in the print media around 1960, the term first started to be used systematically by scholars and journalists in the 1980s, and by the turn of the millennium it was to be found everywhere, and applied to almost everything.[1] Attempts to survey the field vary widely in their interpretations of the term. Nevertheless, most agree (often compounding conceptual confusion) that globalization represents a serious challenge to the state-centrist assumptions of most previous social science. This explicit or implicit critique of state-centrism has aroused many sceptics, some of whom announce the myth of globalization. Globalization, in the words of some populists, is nothing but globaloney.

I argue here that globalization as a sociological concept has always been too frail to sustain the theoretical and substantive burdens loaded on to it. In the

---

[1] There are few ideas in the social sciences that have spawned textbooks of several hundred pages so soon after they have been announced. See, for example, Scholte (2000) and dozens of collections, notably Lechner and Boli (2003). There is a useful account of the origin of the term in the social sciences in the first, short textbook, Waters (1995, Chap. 1). The present chapter borrows from my own contributions, Sklair (2001, 2002).

language (though not the spirit) of so-called postmodernism, it needs to be deconstructed. In order to do this I propose to distinguish three modes of globalization in theory and practice, what we may term "the silent qualifiers" of globalization, namely:

Generic globalization
Capitalist globalization
Alternative globalizations

Globalization in a generic sense needs to be distinguished from its dominant type, namely capitalist globalization, and both of these have to be confronted in theory and research if we are to have any grasp of the contemporary world and, in particular, the prospects for alternative forms of globalization. This can be done in the context of what I have termed global system theory. The global system can best be analyzed in terms of transnational practices and in this way alternatives to capitalist globalization can be conceptualized. In order to reach this stage in the argument it is necessary to identify and assess three competing approaches that have dominated the study of globalization: inter-nationalist (state-centrist), transnationalist (globalization as a contested world-historical project with capitalist and other variants), and globalist (capitalist globalization as a more or less completed and irreversible neoliberal capitalist project). This is where the construction of a new framework for the study of globalization might profitably begin.

Competing Approaches to Globalization

What distinguishes competing approaches to any phenomenon is that they utilize different units of analysis. There are three types of units of analysis that different (competing) groups of globalization theorists and researchers take to define their field of inquiry. First, the inter-national (state-centrist) approach to globalization takes as its unit of analysis the state (often confused with the much more contentious idea of the nation-state). The hyphen in "inter-national" is deliberate, emphasizing the fact that globalization is seen as something that powerful states impose on weaker states, and something that is imposed by the state on weaker groups in all states. This line of argument is similar to older theories of imperialism and colonialism and more recent theories of dependency. The idea that globalization is the new imperialism is common among radical critics of globalization, by which they often mean (but do not always say) capitalist globalization. This view can be rejected on the grounds of theoretical redundancy and empirical inadequacy. It is theoretically redundant because if globalization is just another name for internationalization and/or imperialism, more of the same, then the term is redundant at best and confusing at worst. State-centrist approaches to globalization offer no qualitatively new criteria for globalization and, paradoxically, appear to offer at least nominal support to those who argue that globalization is a myth. The literature on globalization is strewn with lapses into state-centrism.

The globalist approach is the antithesis of the state-centrist thesis. Globalists argue that the state has all but disappeared, that we have already entered a virtually borderless world, and that globalization, by which is meant invariably capitalist globalization, is irreversible and nearing completion. The central concerns of globalists are the global economy and its governance, and they are said to be driven by nameless and faceless market forces, the globalist unit of analysis. Globalism of this variety is often referred to as neoliberal globalization. Whereas the inter-nationalist approach exaggerates the power of the state, the globalist approach fails to theorize correctly the role of the state and the interstate system under conditions of capitalist globalization. Globalists (like state-centrists) are unable to analyze adequately the changing role of state actors and agencies in sustaining the hegemony of capitalist globalization. In particular, as I argue below, globalists and state-centrists both fail to conceptualize the state as a site of struggle and to probe adequately the relations among the state, its agents and institutions, and the transnational capitalist class.

The transnational approach to globalization is the synthesis of the collision of the flawed state-centrist thesis and the flawed globalist antithesis. I consider this to be the most fruitful approach, facilitating theory and research on the struggle between the dominant but as yet incomplete project of capitalist globalization and its alternatives. My own version of this synthesis proposes transnational practices (TNPs) as the most conceptually coherent and most empirically useful unit of analysis. Within the familiar political economy categories—economy, politics, and (somewhat less familiar) culture-ideology—we can construct the categories of economic, political, and culture-ideology TNPs and conduct empirical research to discover their characteristic institutional forms in the dominant global system (manifestation of globalization). This approach is developed in more detail below. Despite the fundamental differences between the inter-national, globalist, and transnational approaches, they all stem from a real phenomenon, generic globalization.

Generic Globalization

The central feature of all the approaches to globalization current in the social sciences is the conviction that many important contemporary problems cannot be adequately studied at the level of nation-states, that is, in terms of national societies or inter-national relations, but need to be theorized—more or less—in terms of globalizing (transnational) processes, beyond the level of the nation-state. For state-centrists, remember, it is the state (or usually the most powerful states) that drives globalization. However, because the dominant form of globalization in the world today is clearly capitalist globalization there is much confusion in the literature due to the inability of most theorists and researchers to distinguish adequately between generic globalization and its historical forms, actual and potential.

Generic globalization can be defined in terms of four new phenomena that have
become significant in the last few decades, moments in both the chronological
and social forces sense:

1. The electronic moment, notably transformations in the technological base
   and global scope of the electronic mass media and to most of the material
   infrastructure of the world today[2]
2. The postcolonial moment[3]
3. The moment of transnational social spaces[4]
4. Qualitatively new forms of cosmopolitanism[5]

Although the first and second of these, the electronic and postcolonial moments,
have been the subject of an enormous amount of research in recent decades, the
third, the moment of transnational social spaces, is of more recent origin and opens
up some new lines of theory and research. The fourth, new forms of cosmopolitanism, is in a different category. The idea of cosmopolitanism is quite ancient and
had its most important modernist reincarnation in the proposal of Kant at the end
of the 18th century for the achievement of perpetual peace through the construction of a cosmopolitan society. However, this left many questions about the relations among democracy, capitalism, and human rights unanswered, and these have
to be urgently asked in this transformed world of the 21st century. Thus, any new
framework for globalization theory and research requires systematic inquiry into
the prospects for new forms of cosmopolitanism for our times.

These four new phenomena—the electronic revolution, postcolonialism,
transnational social spaces, cosmopolitanism—are the defining characteristics of
what I term globalization in a generic sense. In the absence of global catastrophe
these four moments are irreversible in the long run because the vast majority of
the people in the world, rich or poor, men or women, black or white, young or
old, able or disabled, educated or uneducated, gay or straight, secular or religious,
see that generic globalization could serve their own best interests, even if, in a
system dominated by capitalist globalization, it is not necessarily serving their
best interests at present. This is the world most people live in, big landlords as
well as subsistence farmers in villages, corporate executives as well as laborers in
sweatshops in major cities, well-paid professionals as well as informal workers in
tourist sites, comfortable manual workers as well as desperate migrants in transit

---

[2] See, for example, from rather different political perspectives, Castells (2000) and Herman
and McChesney (1997).

[3] Although, of course, a first great wave of political decolonization took place in Latin
America during the 19th century, I would argue that postcolonialism is a product of the
second great wave from the middle of the 20th century in Asia, Africa, and the Caribbean.
See Castle (2001), Lazarus (1999), and Krishnaswamy and Hawley (forthcoming).

[4] Worked out in different ways in Faist (2000), Basch et al. (1994), and Smith and Guarnizo
(1998).

[5] For a range of views, see, for example, Esteva and Prakash (1998), Beck (1999), and
Vertovec and Cohen (2002).

in the hope of better lives. There is a multitude of theory and research on how capitalist globalization works, who wins and who loses as it conquers the globe and transforms communities, cities, regions, whole countries and cultures, however, there is relatively little theory and research on globalization as a generic phenomenon, thought about and even on occasion practiced outside its historical container of globalizing capitalism.

This is not surprising. We live in a world of generic globalization but this is also a world of actually existing capitalist globalization. So, the dominant global system at the start of the 21st century is the capitalist global system. The most fruitful way to analyze and research it is in terms of its transnational practices.

Capitalist Globalization

My theory of capitalist globalization is based on the concept of transnational practices, practices that cross state boundaries but do not originate with state institutions, agencies, or actors (although they are often involved). This conceptual choice offers, as it were, the tools with which to construct a series of working hypotheses for the most keenly contested disagreements between globalization theorists and their opponents. These would certainly include the debates over whether and to what extent (i) capitalism is the central issue for globalization theory and research; (ii) the transnational capitalist class really is the main driver of capitalist globalization; (iii) capitalist globalization is synonymous with "Westernization" and/or "Americanization"; (iv) globalization induces homogenization or hybridization or both at the same time; (v) the state is in decline relative to the forces of capitalist globalization; (vi) the culture-ideology of consumerism is central to the system; and (vii) alternatives to capitalist globalization are possible within the conditions of generic globalization.

Analytically, transnational practices operate in three spheres, the economic, the political, and the cultural-ideological.[6] The whole is what I mean by the global system. The global system at the beginning of the 21st century is not synonymous with global capitalism, but the dominant forces of global capitalism are the dominant forces in the global system. To put it simply, individuals, groups, institutions, and even whole communities, local, national, or transnational, can exist, perhaps even thrive as they have always done outside the orbit of the global capitalist system but this is becoming increasingly more difficult as capitalist globalization penetrates ever more widely and deeply. The building blocks of global system theory are the transnational corporation, the characteristic institutional form of economic transnational practices, a still-evolving transnational capitalist class in the political sphere, and in the culture-ideology sphere, the culture-ideology of consumerism.

---

[6] What follows is a brief summary of the theoretical and substantive place of transnational practices in the global system theory elaborated in my own work (Sklair, 2002). However, the idea of transnational practices has been used in globalization studies in a variety of ways.

The Transnational Capitalist Class

The transnational capitalist class (TCC) is transnational in the double sense that its members have globalizing rather than or in addition to localizing perspectives; and it typically contains people from many countries who operate transnationally as a normal part of their working lives.[7] The transnational capitalist class is composed of fractions, the corporate, state, technical, and consumerist, as follows.

1. Those who own and control major TNCs and their local affiliates (corporate fraction)
2. Globalizing state and interstate bureaucrats and politicians (state fraction)
3. Globalizing professionals (technical fraction)
4. Merchants and media (consumerist fraction)

This class sees its mission as organizing the conditions under which its interests and the interests of the system can be furthered in the global and local context. The concept of the transnational capitalist class implies that there is one central transnational capitalist class that makes systemwide decisions and that it connects with the TCC in each locality, region, and country. Although the four fractions are distinguishable analytic categories with different functions for the global capitalist system, the people in them often move from one category to another (sometimes described as the revolving door between government and business).[8]

Together, these groups constitute a global power elite, ruling class, or inner circle in the sense that these terms have been used to characterize the class structures of specific countries.[9] The transnational capitalist class is opposed not only by those who reject capitalism as a way of life and as an economic system but also by small capitalists who are threatened by the monopoly power of big business under conditions of capitalist globalization. Some localized, domestically oriented businesses can share the interests of the global corporations and prosper, but many cannot and many have perished. Influential business strategists and management theorists commonly argue that to survive, local businesses must globalize. Although most national and local state politicians (aided by their administrators) fight for the interests of their constituents, as they define these interests, government bureaucrats, politicians, and professionals who entirely reject globalization and espouse extreme nationalist ideologies are comparatively rare, despite the recent rash of civil wars in economically marginal parts of the world. And although there are anticonsumerist elements in most societies, there are few cases of a serious anticonsumerist party winning political power anywhere in the world.

---

[7] For a book-length treatment of the issues raised in this section, see Sklair (2001). For a useful survey of the literature on this concept, introduced in the first edition of my *Sociology of the Global System* in 1991, see Carroll and Carson (2003).

[8] For a constructive critique of this apparent inflation of the class concept, see Embong (2000).

[9] Preglobalization capitalist class theory, for which see Scott (1997), does not necessarily exclude the globalizing extension proposed here.

In direct contrast to proponents of the state-centrist approach to globalization, who assume that the globalization process is driven by businesses and their supporters in government and the state on the basis of the national interest, the transnational approach to globalization sets out to demonstrate that the dominant mode of the capitalist class is now transnational. Thus, the transnational capitalist class can be said to be transnational in the following respects.

1. The economic interests of its members are increasingly globally linked rather than exclusively local and national in origin. Their property and shares and the corporations they own and/or control are becoming more globalized. As ideologues, their intellectual products serve the interests of globalizing rather than localizing capital. This follows directly from the shareholder-driven growth imperative that lies behind the globalization of the world economy and the increasing difficulty of enhancing shareholder value in purely domestic firms. For some practical purposes the world is still organized in terms of discrete national economies, however, the TCC increasingly conceptualizes its interests in terms of markets, which may or may not coincide with specific states, and the global market, which clearly does not. I define domestic firms as those serving an exclusively sovereign state market, employing only local co-nationals, whose products consist entirely of domestic services, components, and materials. If you think that this is a ridiculously narrow definition for the realities of contemporary economies then you are more than halfway to accepting the transnational approach to globalization and the importance of the concept of transnational practices to analyze it.

2. The TCC seeks to exert economic control in the workplace, political control in domestic and international politics, and culture-ideology control in everyday life through specific forms of global competitive and consumerist rhetoric and practice. The focus of workplace control is the threat that jobs will be lost and, in the extreme, the economy will collapse unless workers are prepared to work longer and for less in order to meet foreign competition. This is reflected in local electoral politics in most countries, where the major parties have few substantial strategic (even if many rhetorical and tactical) differences, and in the sphere of culture-ideology, where consumerism is rarely challenged.

3. Members of the TCC have outward-oriented globalizing rather than inward-oriented localizing perspectives on most economic, political, and culture-ideology issues. The growing TNC and international institutional emphasis on free trade and the shift from import substitution to export promotion strategies in most developing countries since the 1980s have been driven by alliances of consultancies of various types, indigenous and foreign members of the TCC working through TNCs, government agencies, elite opinion organizations, and the media. Some of the credit for this apparent transformation in the way in which big business works around the world is attached to the tremendous growth in business education since the 1960s,

particularly in North America and Western Europe, but increasingly all over the world.

4. Members of the TCC tend to share similar lifestyles, particularly patterns of higher education (increasingly in business schools) and consumption of luxury goods and services. Integral to this process are exclusive clubs and restaurants, ultraexpensive resorts on all continents, private as opposed to mass forms of travel and entertainment, and, ominously, increasing residential segregation of the very rich secured by armed guards and electronic surveillance in gated communities all over the world, from Los Angeles to Moscow, from Manila to Beijing.

5. Finally, members of the TCC seek to project images of themselves as citizens of the world as well as of their places of birth and are widely publicized as devoted to the pursuit of profit and corporate aggrandizement above all else wherever the opportunity arises. Leading exemplars of this phenomenon have included Jacques Maisonrouge, French-born, who became in the 1960s the chief executive of IBM World Trade; the Swede Percy Barnevik who created Asea Brown Boverei, often portrayed as spending most of his life in his corporate jet; the German Helmut Maucher, former CEO of Nestlé's far-flung global empire; David Rockefeller, once said to have been one of the most powerful men in the United States; the legendary Akio Morita, the founder of Sony; and Rupert Murdoch, who actually changed his nationality to pursue his global media interests. Today, major corporate philanthropists, notably Bill Gates and George Soros, embody the new globalizing TCC.

Men such as these (and a small but increasing number of women and other "minorities" who have fought their way to the top against formidable odds) move in and out of what has been termed the inner circles of big business around the world. The inner circle of the TCC gives a unity to the diverse economic interests, political organizations, and cultural and ideological formations of those who make up the class as a whole. As in any social class, fundamental long-term unity of interests and purpose does not preclude shorter-term and local conflicts of interests and purpose, both within each of the four fractions and between them. The culture-ideology of consumerism is the fundamental value system that keeps the system intact, but it permits a relatively wide variety of choices, for example, what I term emergent global nationalisms as a way of satisfying the needs of the different actors and their constituencies within the global system. The four fractions of the TCC in any region, country, city, society, or community, perform complementary functions to integrate the whole. The achievement of these goals is facilitated by the activities of local and national agents and organizations connected in a complex network of global interlocks.

This is a crucial component of this integration of the TCC as a global class. Virtually all senior members of the TCC—globally, regionally, nationally, and locally—will occupy a variety of interlocking positions, not only the interlocking directorates that have been the subject of detailed studies for some time in a variety of countries, but also connections outside the direct ambit of the corporate sector, the civil society as it were, servicing the statelike structures of the corporations. Leading corporate executives serve on and chair the boards of think tanks, charities, scientific, sports, arts and culture bodies, universities, medical foundations, and similar organizations in the localities in which they are domiciled. Those actors known in the terminology of network theory as "big linkers" connect disparate networks, and in the case of the leading members of the transnational capitalist class this frequently crosses borders and takes on a global dimension. But this global dimension invariably also connects with national and local organizations and their networks. In these ways the claim that "the business of society is business" connects with the claim that "the business of our society is global business." Globalizing business, usually but not exclusively big business, and its interests become legitimated beyond the global capitalist system simply as an economic imperative into the global system as a whole. Business, particularly the transnational corporation sector, then begins to monopolize symbols of modernity and postmodernity such as free enterprise, international competitiveness, and the good life and to transform most, if not all, social spheres in its own image.

Alternatives to Capitalist Globalization

The literature on globalization is suffused with a good deal of fatalism, popularly known as the TINA ("there is no alternative") philosophy. Even some progressive academics, popular writers, and political and cultural leaders seem to accept that there is no alternative to capitalist globalization and that all we can do is to try to work for a better world around it (see Giddens, 2000). Although I cannot fully develop the counterargument to this fatalism here, it seems to me to be both morally indefensible and theoretically short-sighted. Capitalist globalization is failing on two counts, fundamental to the future of most of the people in the world and, indeed, to the future of our planet itself. These are the class polarization crisis and the crisis of ecological unsustainability. There is mounting evidence to suggest that capitalist globalization may be intensifying both crises.[10] Nevertheless, generic globalization should not be identified with capitalism, although capitalist globalization is its dominant form in the present era. This makes it necessary to think through other forms of globalization, forms that might retain some of the positive consequences of capitalism (insofar as they can exist outside capitalism) while transcending it as a socioeconomic system in the transition to a new stage of world history. There have been, of course, many alternatives to capitalism historically and there are many alternatives to it today, but none of them appears viable. In order to articulate possible alternatives to capitalist globalization we have to be prepared to think ourselves out of the box of capitalist

---

[10] These two crises of capitalist globalization are elaborated in Sklair (2002: 47–58 and *passim*). For a research-rich attempt to connect these crises in terms of radical geography see O'Brien and Leichenko (2003).

globalization. To do this it is necessary to reclaim generic globalization, and in doing this we find that there may be many alternatives, one of which is outlined briefly below as a suggestion for further theory and research.[11]

One path out of capitalism that is clear to some but quite unclear to most, takes us from capitalist globalization (where we are), through what can be termed co-operative democracy (a transitional form of society), to socialist globalization (a convenient label for a form of globalization that ends class polarization and the ecological crisis).[12] One strategy to achieve such a transformation involves the gradual elimination of the culture-ideology of consumerism and its replacement with a culture-ideology of human rights. This means, briefly, that instead of our possessions being the main focus of our cultures and the basis of our values, our lives should be lived with regard to a universally agreed system of human rights and the responsibilities to others that these rights entail. This does not imply that we should stop consuming. What it implies is that we should evaluate our consumption in terms of our rights and responsibilities and that this should become a series of interlocking and mutually supportive globalizing transnational practices.

By genuinely expanding the culture-ideology of human rights from the civil and political spheres, in which capitalist globalization has often had a relatively positive influence, to the economic and social spheres, which represents a profound challenge to capitalist globalization, we can begin seriously to tackle the crises of class polarization and ecological unsustainability. But political realism dictates that this change cannot be accomplished directly, it must proceed via a transitional stage. Capitalism and socialism, as can be seen in the case of market socialism in China, are not watertight categories. Capitalist practices can and do occur in socialist societies (for example, making workers redundant to increase profits) just as socialist practices can exist in capitalist societies (for example, trying to ensure that everyone in a community enjoys a basic decent standard of living). The issue is hegemony, whose interests prevail, who defends the status quo (even by reforming it), who is pushing for fundamental change, and how this is organized into effective social movements for change globally.

The transition to socialist globalization will eventually create new forms of transnational practices. Transnational economic units will tend to be on a smaller and more sustainable scale than the major TNCs of today; transnational political practices will be driven by democratic coalitions of self-governing and co-operative communities, not the unaccountable, unelected, and individualistic transnational capitalist class. And cultures and ideologies will reflect the finer qualities of human life not the desperate variety of the culture-ideology of consumerism. These sentiments might appear utopian, indeed they are, and other alternatives are also possible, but in the long term, muddling through with capitalist globalization is not a viable option for the planet and all those who live on it.

---

[11] The following paragraphs are based on Sklair (2002: Chap. 11).
[12] I am, of course, well aware of all the negative baggage that the term "socialist" carries today and hope that others will find new ways to characterize alternative forms of globalization that achieve similar ends.

Thus, although the discourse and practice of capitalist globalization would seem to suggest that it is a force for convergence, the inability of the transnational capitalist class, the driver of the processes of capitalist globalization, to solve the crises of class polarization and ecological unsustainability makes it both necessary and urgent to think through alternatives to it. This implies that capitalist globalization contains the seeds of divergence. The globalization of economic and social human rights leading to what can (but need not necessarily) be termed socialist globalization is certainly one, if presently rather remote, alternative, and there are many others. Communities, cities, subnational regions, whole countries, multicountry unions, and even transnational co-operative associations could all in principle try to make their own arrangements for checking and reversing class polarization and ecological unsustainability. It is likely that the 21st century will bring many new patterns of divergence before a global convergence on full human rights for all is established. This is unlikely to occur in a world dominated by transnational corporations, run by the transnational capitalist class, and inspired by the culture-ideology of consumerism.

A New Framework for Globalization Studies

My proposal for a new framework for the study of globalization explicitly connects the theoretical and the substantive. Concepts, if they are doing their job properly, ask questions about empirical reality, however flimsy and/or difficult to represent that might turn out to be under the scrutiny of the trained researcher. But they do more than this, they direct attention to how certain aspects of reality fit into the totality that the theory is attempting to conceptualize and organize. Global system theory is based on a central concept as its fundamental unit of analysis, transnational practices. The question that this asks about empirical reality is precisely: how can we best organize our investigation of how transnational practices explain aspects of the totality, the global system. This entails theoretical (really analytical) choices; in this case the choices are the economic, the political, and the culture-ideology spheres as the most fruitful complexes within the totality of empirical reality for the purposes of this research.

But how does this analytical framework direct us to the most appropriate parts of empirical reality in order to carry out substantive research? In my formulation the answer to this question lies in the characteristic institutional forms for economic, political, and culture-ideology transnational practices that we actually find in the contemporary capitalist global system. These are the transnational corporations for economic TNPs, the transnational capitalist class for political TNPs, and consumerism for culture-ideology TNPs. Operationalizing each of these is difficult, not entirely without controversy, but not so difficult and controversial as to paralyze any attempt to proceed.

As I argued above, these conceptual choices offer tools with which to construct a series of working hypotheses for the central disputes between globalization theorists of different persuasions and between them and their opponents. I identified seven major debates and will briefly outline a research program for each of them. It is important to note that all of these debates are about "whether and to what extent" a phenomenon is dominant or exists, and how it fits into the totality of the global system.

1. *Capitalism as the central issue for globalization theory and research.* This idea, although still controversial, is much less so now than it was before 1990, the dissolution of the Soviet Union, and the system that it supported in eastern Europe and beyond. Even those cultural theorists who see globalization as primarily a set of issues around local and/or national cultures and the retention of cultural identity routinely acknowledge that capitalist globalization plays an increasingly important role in these processes. The research agenda of a transnational approach to globalization would focus on how culture (or, more precisely, culture-ideology) practices are organized, for example, within specific communities (class, gender, age, ethnic, religious, occupational, etc.) and how this relates, if at all, to the totality of capitalist globalization. Clearly, the logical possibilities are that every cultural practice relates entirely to the totality (that is, all cultural practices have become TNPs in my meaning of the term), or has no relationship at all to it, or that some do to a greater extent than others. The transnational approach to globalization would predict that over the last few decades more and more cultural practices have become TNPs, and that the culture-ideology of consumerism as driven by the transnational capitalist class and mediated through the activities of the transnational corporations, is the root cause of this. In my own work such issues have been substantively researched in the cases of health and nutrition, specifically infant formula, pharmaceuticals, and cola beverages (and this could easily be extended to food in general), and the culture of smoking (Sklair, 1998). These are cultural practices in the broad sense; in the narrow sense, for example, music, art, and literature, similar projects could be designed to assess the extent of the transnationalization of cultural practices. My current research on "iconic architecture in globalizing cities" focuses on how some architectural practices have become increasingly globalized and attempts to explain this in terms of the interests of the transnational capitalist class in general and the role of its four fractions in the architecture industry in particular (Sklair, 2005).

2. *The transnational capitalist class as the main driver of capitalist globalization.* This may be the most controversial of the claims, because not only does class itself have less resonance in the social sciences than was once the case but also the idea of a transnational class appears counterintuitive to many theorists. Research to identify the members and networks of the inner circle of what might be a transnational capitalist class has begun, but its exact power and influence have yet to be determined. Although its existence in what has come to be known as world or global cities has proved a fruitful

line of research, there is still a great deal of work to be done in establishing transnational linkages and/or networks and investigating how these work. Even if it can be shown to exist, issues about the fundamental long-term unity of interests and purpose of a transnational capitalist class cannot simply be assumed. It is anticipated that the best way to approach these questions will be by the case study method, and here the idea of the state as a site of struggle will be central. Here, it is important to appreciate the range of political programs under which capitalist globalization can thrive, from extreme neoliberalism where the state apparatus really is shrunk in physical and policy terms all the way to welfare state capitalism where the state is more deliberately used to subsidize the business of major corporations on a global scale. Research on these issues can fruitfully focus on how those who own and control major corporations operate, their patterns of investment around the globe, their relationship to legislation in the national and global context (for example, their influence on the creation and activities of the main international financial institutions and the World Trade Organization), and their links with members of the other three fractions (state, technical, and consumerist). As indicated above, study of the impact that members of the TCC have on nonbusiness (notably cultural, educational, and charitable) networks is already advanced, but there is always room for more. Research on topics such as these is necessary to provide evidence for or against the thesis that a transnational capitalist class does exist and that it exerts an influence beyond the world of big business.

3. *The state in decline relative to the forces of capitalist globalization.* This is probably the fiercest debate in and around globalization, but it misses the point. The point is not whether the state is in decline but, on the contrary, the extent to which the globalizers—expressing the interests of the transnational capitalist class of which they constitute the state fraction—or the localizers—expressing the interests of national capitalists or some other group—have seized control of the state and its agencies. It is in this very specific sense that the state can be conceptualized as a site of struggle in the transnational approach to globalization. Global system theory predicts that under normal circumstances the globalizers will prevail in issues where the state still has some freedom of decision making, making decisions that generally serve the interests of the transnational capitalist class. However, in exceptional cases the outcome of such struggles may be difficult to assess in the short and medium terms. The most important recent example, the invasion of Iraq in 2003 led by the Bush administration in the United States, does not appear to be a simple case of the exercise of power by the state fraction of the transnational capitalist class. Indeed, my own analysis of the evidence suggests that the invasion and the subsequent economic, political, cultural, and military consequences have so far (Summer 2007) proved to be against the interests of the TCC, whose main interest lies in stability and conditions under which the culture-ideology of consumerism can flourish. The state and, in this case, the interstate system was certainly a site of

struggle and it is apparent that only the most powerful state in the system in terms of military power could have prevailed against the interests of the transnational capitalist class. The fact that the U.S. state continues to be led by groups that have ample and varied reasons to personalize the conflict points in my, admittedly unfashionable, view to the epiphenomenal nature of party politics. If correct, this interpretation of events shows that the will of the transnational capitalist class does not always prevail in the short run, but forthcoming events may show that it lives to fight another day, for example, in the struggles over the contracts to rebuild Iraq.

4. *Capitalist globalization as synonymous with "Westernization" and/or "Americanization and:"*

5. *Globalization inducing homogenization or hybridization or both at the same time.* Although not identical, these debates are very much linked by the twin facts that corporations domiciled in the United States and Western Europe dominate the global market for many everyday consumer products and that the world's mass media are likewise dominated by the culture-ideology of consumerism. However, this does not necessarily mean that capitalist globalization is synonymous with "Westernization" and/or "Americanization." The research project implied by the apparently competing theses that capitalist globalization produces homogenization (elimination of differences) or hybridization (celebration and maximization of differences) or both is a promising entry point into this complex area. The transnational approach to globalization would predict that as capitalists are primarily interested in profits rather than destroying or sustaining particular cultural identities, capitalist globalization will encourage homogenization where this appears to be the most profitable path and hybridization where this does. These are eminently researchable hypotheses, and the findings from such research in almost any sphere will be of value in the context of the following.

6. *The culture-ideology of consumerism as central to the system.* A central argument for this theoretical framework to study capitalist globalization is that the culture-ideology holding the system together and providing its global rationale is consumerism. This is implicit in all that has gone before insofar as big business, indeed most business is dependent on satisfying induced wants much more than basic needs (even expanding this category to give a generous benefit of the doubt to those with a decent standard of living), and the four fractions of the transnational capitalist class work tirelessly to reproduce the conditions for ever-increasing consumerism on a daily basis. However, this does not mean that everyone on the planet is only interested in consuming. For the proposition to be true and for the framework to be supported it means only that enough people operate enough of the time as if they were driven by the culture-ideology of consumerism to sustain the system and, crucially, to give it the appearance of immutability by associating it with some vague notion of consumerism as an integral part of human nature. Research on this range of questions is vitally important, not only to explain in detail how the culture-ideology of consumerism operates in capitalist

globalization but, even more vitally, how it can be transcended within alternative globalizations.

7. *Alternatives to capitalist globalization within the conditions of generic globalization.* This attempt to flesh out the research framework of the transnational approach to globalization has focused mainly on capitalist globalization because that is where we are at now. As argued above, the twin crises of class polarization and ecological unsustainability, crises that capitalist globalization intensifies and cannot resolve, make it essential to start thinking about alternatives. (These crises, of course, are hypotheses within global system theory, and research on them proceeds apace.) A summary of a program for research on socialist globalization was presented above and it only remains to say that explicit historical, abstract, and contemporary research on economic, political, and culture-ideology transnational practices within socialist (or, indeed, any other viable alternative) globalization is urgently required. The focus of any new radical framework for globalization theory and research—in contrast to a supine social science that limits its task to describing the status quo—is clearly to elaborate such alternatives within the context of genuinely democratic forms of globalization. But we have little chance of successfully articulating such forms unless we understand what generic globalization is and how capitalist globalization really works.

References

Basch, L. G., Schiller, N. G., & Blanc, S. (Eds) (1994). *Nations unbound: Transnational projects, postcolonial predicaments, and deterritorialized nation-states.* Luxembourg: OPA.

Beck, U. (1999). *World risk society.* Cambridge: Polity.

Carroll, W., & Carson, C. (2003). "The network of global corporations and elite policy groups: a structure for transnational capitalist class formation," *Global Networks* 3/1: 29–58.

Castells, M. (2000). *The rise of the network society.* Oxford: Blackwell.

Castle, G. (Ed) (2001). *Postcolonial discourses: An anthology.* Oxford: Blackwell.

Embong, A. R. (2000). "Globalization and transnational class relations: Some problems of conceptualisation," *Third World Quarterly* 21/6: 989–1000.

Esteva, G., & Prakash, M. S. (1998). *Grassroots postmodernism.* London: Zed.

Faist, T. (2000). *The volume and dynamics of international migration and transnational social spaces.* Oxford, UK: Oxford University Press.

Giddens, A. (2000). *The third way and its critics.* Cambridge: Polity.

Herman, E., & McChesney, R. (1997). *The global media.* London: Cassell.

Krishnaswamy, R., & Hawley, J. (Eds) (forthcoming). *The postcolonial and the global.* Minneapolis: University of Minnesota Press.

Lazarus, N. (1999). *Nationalism and cultural practice in the postcolonial world.* Cambridge, UK: Cambridge University Press.

Lechner, F., & Boli, J. (Eds). (2003). *The globalization reader*, second edition. Oxford: Blackwell.

O'Brien, K., & Leichenko, R. (2003). "Winners and losers in the context of global change," *Annals of the Association of American Geographers* 93/1: 89–103.

Scholte, J. A. (2000). *Globalization: A critical introduction.* London: Macmillan.

Scott, J. (1997). *Corporate business and capitalist class.* Oxford: Oxford University Press.

Sklair, L. (1991). *Sociology of the global system.* Baltimore, MD: The Johns Hopkins University Press.

Sklair, L. (1998). "The transnational capitalist class and global capitalism: the case of the tobacco industry," *Political Power and Social Theory* 12: 3–43.

Sklair, L. (2001). *The transnational capitalist class.* Oxford: Blackwell.

—— (2002). *Globalization: Capitalism and its alternatives.* Oxford: Oxford University Press.

—— (2005). "The transnational capitalist class and contemporary architecture in globalizing cities," *International Journal of Urban and Regional Research,* 29/3: 485–500.

Smith, P., & Guarnizo, L. (Eds) (1998). *Transnationalism from below.* Brunswick, NJ: Transaction.

Vertovec, S., & Cohen, R. (Eds) (2002). *Conceiving cosmopolitanism.* Oxford: Oxford University Press.

Waters, M. (1995). *Globalization.* London: Routledge.

4
Global Systems, Globalization, and Anthropological Theory

JONATHAN FRIEDMAN

The project of a global anthropology had its beginnings in the 1970s. It began as a confrontation between the assumed nature of society as a closed entity that can be studied and understood in its own right, and a global reality that seemed to falsify that assumption. Although the assumption of social closure was taken for granted in anthropology and reinforced very much by the fieldwork tradition itself, the stringent definitions of structuralist Marxism made it easier to see just what was wrong. This is because of the centrality of the concept of social reproduction as the framework of analysis, rather than institutional arrangements or cultural meanings. The former insists on understanding social form as constituted by socially organized processes of production, distribution, and consumption, the basic framework within which a population reproduces itself over time. Social reproduction is a process of self-constitution of social form over time, and in the particular approach that we advocated in the 1970s, the more static proposals of "structural Marxism" as well as the more orthodox materialist models were eliminated. The only adequate account of a particular social form was to be found in the way it comes into existence historically. The concept of reproduction, thus, implies both systematicity and historical transformation. There was no interest in reducing social form and cultural structure to material conditions, whether they be organizations of production, technologies, ecological adaptations, or levels of population density. The positive intentional organization of social reproduction was conceived as a social and, by implication, a cultural phenomena. The so-called material determinants of the reproductive process were interpreted as constraints and potential contradictions with respect to the dominant strategies of social life rather than positive determinants in the sense of having any causal/organizational effect. On the contrary, most of the constraints at any historical moment were conceived largely as the product of the historical operation of the social system itself. Constraints were conceived in our version of structuralist Marxism (Friedman, 1974) as limits of functional compatibility between the different operative logics included within a system of social reproduction. Such limits were equivalent to what could be called internal contradictions of a system. Similar notions were developed by Godelier in his important and inspiring early works (Godelier, 1972). Phenomena such as carrying capacity or limit ratios of fictitious to real capital accumulation can be included in this notion.

From a framework based on social reproduction the movement in the direction of a global systemic anthropology was relatively simple. One can even reduce this to a question of method. One need simply ask whether the population in question reproduces itself based on its own resources or whether its reproduction is part of a larger regional or even wider set of relations and flows (Friedman, 1976). This conclusion became a concrete ethnographic and historical issue in the 1970s when it appeared that societies assumed to be totalities turned out to be loci within larger processes. Kajsa Ekholm's fieldwork in northern Madagascar was crucial in this respect. These societies could only be understood in terms of the articulation of the local social world with the larger Indian Ocean economy and with the politics of the French, British, and Arabs in the Indian Ocean arena over a half a millenium (Ekholm 1976, Ekholm and Friedman 1980). Although the global framework was rejected in anthropology as in other disciplines in this period, a number of common projects were established with historians, archaeologists, geographers, and political scientists in which a long-term global systemic approach was firmly established (e.g., Ekholm 1997, 1980, 1987; Ekholm & Friedman, 1979, 1980; Rowlands et al., 1987; Frank & Gills, 1993; Denemark et al., 2000).

The shift toward the global was clearly marked by the publication of Wallerstein's first volume of *The Modern World System* in 1974. This was paralleled in anthropology by the important work of Eric Wolf (1980). These works were primarily concerned with the history of the modern world (i.e. from the 15th century on) and the very notion of world system was limited to the modern era. Our own approach stressed the long-term historical continuity of capitalist forms of accumulation, however varied, and the structural continuities in larger systems. This was taken to its limits in the work of Frank and Gills who claimed that the last 5000 years could be characterized in terms of a single world system.

Globalization

In anthropology the emergence of a discourse on cultural globalization is very much associated with related developments in cultural studies and especially in what are called postcolonial studies. The two are, of course, related and have emerged more as tendencies in other disciplines than as disciplines in themselves. The names of sociologists and anthropologists such as Roland Robertson, Arjun Appadurai, and Ulf Hannerz are associated with this approach although there are significant differences among them. For all of these, although to a lesser degree for Robertson, the field of globalization is a culturally autonomous field. It is generally assumed that globalization is a new phenomenon in history and it is understood in evolutionary terms. Much of the approach is part of a larger focus of interest in fields from business economics and geography to literature, from "global reach" to the "global village." It has often been proclaimed that we are entering a new world. The world is now one place, there is a world culture, and people, information, money, and technology all flow around the globe in a rather chaotic set of disjunctive circuits that somehow bring us all together.

There are two essential differences between the globalization and the global systemic approach and they are logically dependent on each other. In the global systems approach, the global refers to the total social arena within which social life is reproduced, and the global systemic refers to the properties of the complex cycles of global social reproduction, the way in which they constitute local institutional forms, identities, as well as economic and political cycles of expansion and contraction. The local is always part of the global in this framework, but this does not mean that the local is produced by the global. On the contrary, the global is not something other than the local, inhabiting a higher plane. The global simply refers to the properties of the systemic processes that connect the world's localities, and this includes their formation as more or less bounded places. There is no global space floating above the local. The global is a purely structural concept.

Globalization is a phenomenon that occurs within already existent global systems (Friedman, 1994), and it may even, in the right conditions, give rise to a consciousness of the global that may not have existed previously. In our approach the global is not new, nor is globalization. The global is at least as old as commercial civilizations and, in structural terms, it is arguable that it is as old as human social organization. We try to demonstrate that the isolated "tribes" of anthropological mythology are not leftovers from the paleolithic, but historical products of larger processes. This argument (Ekholm and Friedman 1980) has been increasingly vindicated by historical, anthropological, and archaeological studies (Wilmsen, 1989; Gordon, 1992; Rowlands et al., 1987). Now this is not the same kind of argument as that of the globalization approach. The latter is in our terms, empiricist and behavioral. It is about contact, movement of people and things, and about diaspora formation, and about global internet communication and CNN (Figures 4.1 and 4.2).

It is about things that are strikingly apparent, not about the underlying structures that generate their appearance and even their disappearance. We might suggest here that there is a significant difference in this sense among the work of Saskia Sassen and David Harvey and the work of the globalization school. Sassen suggests a model of global transformation in which the globalization of capital plays a central role. Harvey provides a model of the globalization of capital that includes as instrumental the technological increases in speed that lead to "time–space-compression."

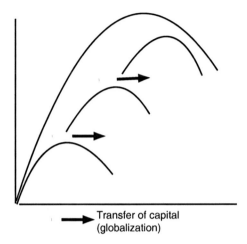

FIGURE 4.1. Globalization as a cyclical phenomenon.

For Sassen globalization relates to what she sees as the collapse of the geographical differentiation of center and periphery into the singular space of the global city.
For Harvey, time–space compression is the latest in an historical process that has
decreased the size of the world arena rather than expanding the self into that arena.
This geographical concentration might thus be understood as the localization of the
world arena. These latter approaches are not about the emergence of the global
but about its transformation. Globalization for these researchers is not a question
of a stage of world history but a reconfiguration of an already existent world arena.
For most other globalization "theorists" the phenomenon is usually understood as
something new, described as a new connectivity whose existence is simply an
empirical fact that needs no explanation. It is also defined as a set of observable
interactions in the usual structural functionalist framework.

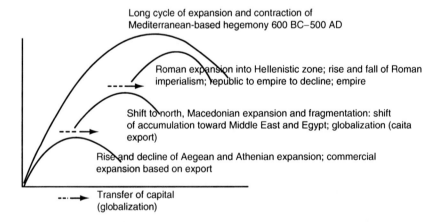

FIGURE 4.2. Cycles of hegemony in the Hellenistic world.

We have argued following other researchers, such as Arrighi, that the last round of globalization at the turn of the 19th century is quite comparable to the current round. There was a huge diffusion of capital from Britain to other parts of the world, with levels at least as elevated as today. There was mass migration, a focus on technological change, and speedup just as today. And the entire process went into reverse in the 1920s. Globalization was thus followed by deglobalization. Because much of the cultural globalization discourse focuses on border crossing it is important to note that this, as well, has occurred before. Migration in percentage terms in the period from the 1880s to the 1920s was as great or greater than today and global and multicultural consciousness was also a major issue in this era of mass immigration to the United States, when concepts of cultural pluralism and "transnationalism" were employed in contemporary debates (Kallen, 1924; Bourne, 1916). But if we look more closely at history we find similar forms of consciousness as far back as the Hellenistic world and Rome when cosmopolitanism and localism were also common and where problems of immigration and multiethnicity were significant issues (Friedman, 2005). In the above graphics we outline the way in which globalization in Braudelian terms can be understood as a world systemic phenomenon, related to hegemonic decline. This process can be related to hegemonic shifts in European hegemony as Arrighi has suggested, but it might also be applied to similar phenomena in the ancient world. It was a very pleasant surprise to us to find, some years ago, that a group of illustrious researchers in political science, economics, sociology, and history had joined in the development of a science of world historical systems. This group, the world historical systems group of the International Studies Association, has published a number of volumes and has made a concerted effort to establish cooperation among a number of disciplines (Frank & Gills, 1993; Denemark et al., 2000).

Global systemic anthropology is about the history of the human species, the forms of its social life and culture, understood in terms of the logics of social reproduction that have guided its trajectories. This framework encompasses the study of cultural forms, of symbolic structures of ritual practices, and of everyday strategies of life. It does not aim to replace them, but to contextualize them. It is this that allows for a transdisciplinarity that reaches out to all subjects that deal with one or another aspect of the human condition.

Ethnography and the Global System

The array of approaches to the global life of the species includes both the analysis of political economic structures and processes and the phenomenology of everyday life. It is in its foundation existential, but understands that the conditions of human life are bound up with processes that are profoundly nonhuman and even inhuman. The concept of culture in this endeavor lies somewhere in between. It lies in the specificities of human existence, in the different products that are generated by different lives. But it is nowhere the central problem for an anthropology that never heeded the powerful critique proffered by Radin against the false abstractions that became the basis of much of the subject (Radin, 1987). The cultural anthropology

that takes rituals as texts, that focuses on cultural products rather than lived existence, is a field that has lost contact with human life. It becomes a collector's science: texts, objects, commodities, symbols, and meanings that take on a
"reifiedganic" existence, a false reality that has become the tangible object of much
anthropology. Much of the cultural globalization discourse is based on such
assumptions that lead to a truly impoverished understanding of human life. Culture
flows, mixes, hybridizes, and does things that it didn't use to do when it was more
bounded in an imaginary past, when the world was still a cultural "mosaic." That
all of these concepts are related to the way people in the complex relations of power
in their social lives bind, unbind, fix, disintegrate, and move meanings is eliminated
and replaced by a magical quality of culture as a dynamic substance in its own
right, culture-as-Subject. This is no mere error in anthropological thinking. It is a
pervasive reality of anthropological practice, of a world of assumptions concerning
the nature of the world itself. The culture concept as a set of discrete and relative
texts has become, for many, central to the entire construction of the discipline.
Radin's critique is not just a timely corrective. It is an expression of that which was
marginalized in the very foundation of the subject, the notion that anthropology
was about lived existence rather than its more tangible products. All of those
aspects of life that have been reduced to culture harbor the risk of taking the life
out of anthropology. It is, of course, true that cultural things are much easier to
study than life itself, the life within which such *cultural things* take on existential
meaning, but this challenge remains central to any self-respecting anthropology.

Now this is not, of course, meant as a characterization of all of anthropology.
On the contrary there have always been examples of attempts and even systematic programs that have focused on the concrete forms of social existence. These
are characteristic of all the more phenomenologically oriented approaches in the
field, especially those that have delved into the nature of sociality, but they are
also fundamental aspects of an older pretexual anthropology. They range from
recent developments in cognitive anthropology (Strauss & Quinn, 1994), to the
work of anthropologists such as Kapferer and Csordas and many others. Even
Geertz has sometimes grappled with such problems in discussing the varying
nature of personhood, but he has most often fallen back on the textual models that
have turned his insights into cultural objects. A crucial misunderstanding in this
respect is what is assumed to be the extreme objectivism found in the work of
Lévi-Strauss. It might well be argued that this is not at all the case. The latter was
perfectly conversant with the problem of the relation between the lived and the
structural which he understood as different aspects of a single reality. The most
interesting example of this kind of analysis can be found, strangely enough, in
that most maligned and celebrated, *La Pensée Sauvage* (1962), and specifically in
his discussion of the "totemic operator," a combinatorial model that he used to
analyze the relation between the concrete categories of cosmology and the identification of the person. The model is one that begins with a series of totemic
species and then divides them into subgroups followed by a further breakdown
into body parts. As one descends from the cosmic species toward the individual,
the different parts and subgroups are recombined to finally coalesce in the forma-

tion of an individual identity. This is a logic that can account for the specific individuality of the person as well as the fact that he or she is entirely an expression of the larger group. The characteristics of the individual's life, his personality, his exploits, and his physical appearance can be rendered meaningful with respect to the more encompassing categories of the group without erasing his individuality. Although this is certainly not a phenomenological analysis, it is an attempt to gain purchase on a structure that organizes the specificity of a kind of sociality. For Lévi-Strauss, structure is never to be understood as an abstract reality but as the organization of the properties of concrete lived reality which is always the fundamental object of understanding.[1]

"la praxis . . . constitue pour les sciences de l'homme la totalité fondamentale"
Lévi-Strauss (1962). *La Pensée Sauvage.* Paris: Plon p 173

Ethnography in the global context is not simply a question of expanding the horizons of the anthropological gaze. It requires, from our point of view, a reorientation that in itself has nothing to do with the global but with the general perspective of field research. This is particularly important because there is a tendency that we noted for globalizing anthropology to distance itself increasingly from the question of social existence and to transform the field into a collectors domain: local, global, and hybrid objects defined and interpreted entirely by the observer. In one sense, then, ethnography of the global need not imply increasing complexity of perspective. If the global is not a place but merely a set of properties that informs the local then nothing in the fieldwork situation need change other than the perspective on what we are looking at and the need to understand that world processes work through a number of different places simultaneously. But this has always been the case insofar as social life has always been globally enmeshed. Multisited ethnography should have always been part of ethnography, because the world has always been organized in global/local articulations. And it might be argued that ethnography has always had a multisited component. The current infatuation with going beyond borders and with assuming that today's world challenges such borders because everyone is on the move, is a middle-class mirage, an interesting object of analysis in its own right. If only 1.7% of the population of the world is on the move today, then we have reason to suspect that the globalizing visions are based exclusively on the experiences of the academics and other movers who so identify. This does not mean, as it might for globalizers, that the large majority of the world is not part of a larger systemic reality. On the contrary, we have insisted on the way the local has always been produced in local–regional–global articulations.

The challenge for the kind of global systemic anthropology that we have struggled to develop is precisely in the combination of the analysis of the structural articulations of the global and the local, all of which are embedded in a deeper understanding of people's lives, of their conflicts, their joys, and their pains. The cultural in this

---

[1] Lévi-Strauss, of course, has never argued for the primacy of the emotional over the cognitive, but this is because he assumes that the emotional is structured within the cognitive which is its specificity.

approach can be understood to either include the existential as well as the objectified products of life processes insofar as it focuses on the specific properties of life forms, or to limit the use of the cultural to the objectified as opposed to the lived-experiential. The understanding of witchcraft in the Congo, as personal disintegration and the loss of control over the components of the self is only comprehensible in terms of the specificity of Congolese constitutions of personal experience. A fuller understanding of this experience requires that we look at the way it became what it was or is as well as the conditions, local, regional, and global that orchestrate its appearance and reproduction. Similarly, the formation of Hawaiian "endosociality," in which the outside world is rejected, in which Hawaiians face each other and have their backs to the world, can be understood in historical transformational terms but it is still a form of sociality whose ramifications cannot be reduced to a set of rules, principles, or other form of objectified culture. It is a way of being in the world that in its turn conditions the generation of local cultural products and objectifications (see Methodological Implications below).

Global System Versus Globalization

The global systemic does not refer to a theory, but to a perspective or framework of understanding that has always been potentially available in the civilization that we inhabit. It does not always appear obvious, however, as the early reception of this research demonstrates. The notion that "society" is not an adequate unit of analysis because it is reproduced within a larger regional system was met with more than mere skepticism. On the left it was seen as a renegade attempt to deny the importance of class struggle. From liberal social scientists it was a jolt to a comfortable position with respect to local social totalities that had been taken for granted. In both cases, the systemic nature of the argument was seen as dangerous. Society was the unit of analysis; it was a unit under control, easy to map, and reinforced by the fieldwork paradigm.

In the early years of the 1970s we made two kinds of arguments in favor of the global. The first was that local social forms were constituted in larger historical–geographical processes. The second was that such forms were only reproduced within such larger processes. This was not an argument that there was a global sphere above the local, but that the relations between localities were systemic and that they were also constitutive of particular local forms. The global is always about interlocal relations, not about a supralocal organism. The latter is an abstraction, that is, the structural properties of such relations. Any global approach that assumes that the global is an empirical field in its own right is a victim of misplaced concreteness. Unfortunately this is precisely the nature of much of the globalization literature. The notion that the global is somehow postnational or transnational is precisely this kind of error. It is one harboring its own evolutionary bias; once we were local but now we are global. In a global systemic approach, on the contrary, the global is not an empirical unit or space, but a set of properties of the reproduction of any locality, not just now, but always.

There is an interesting parallel here with the structural functionalist versus structuralist position in anthropology. For the former, the local is primary, the descent group or even the on-the-ground resident group. Relations are then established with other such groups in a process that builds ever new levels of sociocultural integration (Steward, 1955). There is an interesting linkage between structural functionalism and evolutionism here, one that moves from simple to complex, from primary units to relations between such units, to relations between relations and so on, until we get to the global. The common property of these understandings is that relations are links between already constituted entities, that is, entities that by definition exist previous to the relations that connect them. This conflates complexity with scale as if it were a mere effect of addition. The structuralist approach, as suggested above, is that larger structures always constitute smaller ones, and that alliance structures generate the specific form of descent groups, or at least that descent groups are constitutive elements of larger alliance structures rather than preexisting units (Dumont 1967). This is not to say that descent can be deduced from alliance, but that alliance and descent form a single reproductive process in which the exchange relation is dominant. It is the core of Lévi-Strauss' concept of the atom of kinship. His argument against the nuclearity of Radcliffe-Brown's nuclear family was based on his argument that the group, as an exogamous unit, could only reproduce itself via a social relation to another group, thus the necessity of including the wife-giver (or husband-giver) in the elementary structure. Descent only becomes salient where exogamy is random, neither repetitive, nor structured in any other way. In more general terms structuralism postulates that the relation constitutes its units which are, thus, inseparable from the latter. Rather than seeing relations as an addition of something in between units, it seeks to understand the unit as an aspect of the larger relation.

Another way of understanding this is in terms of the logic of wholes and parts, expressed in Hegel, Marx, and Lévi-Strauss. It states that the world never begins with parts that somehow come together into larger wholes. Rather the wholes, or structures, are already immanent in their parts, and the parts can have no autonomous existence. A lineage is a mere aspect of a larger structure of kinship-organized reproduction. A factory is a localization of larger processes of capital investment, labor recruitment, and the formation of a production process that can only exist because the products themselves can be realized and thus converted back into the production process itself.

Just as an alliance structure does not create a new social place, global relations do not create a global place separate from lineage space, not unless a higher function is associated with such an encompassing unity, as in the formation of a chiefdom or state. The self-defined citizen of the world belongs to the world, not to an in-between place, but to the world as a whole, that is, as a single place. All notions of globalization are dependent on prior notions of bounded political units that can be transcended. The global systemic perspective is based on the hypothesis that the bounded entities are themselves generated by the larger global process within which they exist and reproduce themselves. This is not to say that nations and other political units are mere products of global subdivision, because the globe as such is not a system. Rather, political units are constituted in larger relations within the global, and the global is that structured field, rather than an entity in its own right. This is the basic principle of structuralist analysis. The global does not generate the local. It is rather the field whose processes are necessary and sufficient for understanding the formation of the local. And the local is not a common global product or concept, spread by diffusion or generated from "above," as in Robertson and Appadurai. Localization may be a global process, but the local is always an articulation between a specific historical, cultural, and localized set of practices and a larger field of forces and conditions of reproduction. Papua New Guinea may well be a nation state defined in terms of globalized political institutions that shape conditions of naming and formalizing particular organizational spheres, but PNG is organized more directly by specific (i.e., cultural) structures of political practice that are very unlike those found in Western European nation states. To call them hybrid is to misconstrue and even mystify the real relations of articulation involved. In other words, it is not a question of mixture and formation of a new product but of a field of tensions and contradictions, a combination of opposing forces rather than a cultural pea soup.

The properties of global processes are what we have called global systems. They are not visible behavioral relations, but the properties of such visible forms and relations. These properties are explored in terms of notions such as expansion and contraction, the formation and demise of center–periphery relations, and the cyclical and dialectical relations between cultural identity and global hegemony. "Systemic properties" are hypotheses about the dynamics of global systems. They are no more visible in immediate terms than the properties of business cycles. Only their effects are visible. Now this ought not to appear strange nor even especially sophisticated. It is the basis of any scientific approach in which the behavioral or the directly observable is what is to be explained and has no explanatory value in itself. Thus, a particular imperial organization is not a global system but the product of such a system in a particular historical situation. Its specific or cultural properties cannot be accounted for in global systemic terms, but its more general properties are deducible from those of the system (Friedman, 1994).

There is indeed an apparent paradox in discussions of global versus local. Attempts to address this issue by using words such as "glocal" is a symptom of this paradox which is itself an outcome of misplaced concreteness and its objectification within globalizing identities. The paradox exists because of the fact that at any one particular time there are populations organized into political units and separated by boundaries that are penetrated by transborder organizations and processes. At any one point in time the question of local versus global is a question of that which is internal as opposed to external or in between. But from the global systemic point of view, both the internal and external are products of the bounding process itself which is a global phenomenon, not in the sense of a process that lies outside the local, but in the sense of a process that simultaneously constitutes both the inside and outside. The notion of "glocalization" (Robertson, 1992: 177–78) which comes from Japanese marketing discourse, concerns the globalization of the local (e.g., the making of home abroad (for the Westerner) in international hotels), but is applied to phenomena such as fundamentalism that seem to have become global forms, just as indigenous movements, nationalisms, even democracy. It is assumed that these are forms have diffused and have become global institutions of local processes.

But aside from planned glocalization as in the establishment of colonial regimes, it would pay to look more closely at the conditions under which phenomena such as fundamentalisms emerge. Christian fundamentalism, Islamic communalism, and religious revival may indeed be related within the global system as "identity" movements, but to account for them in terms of the globalization of a single form of activity or cultural paradigm is superficial, completely ignoring the specificities of the processes involved. Christian fundamentalism, we would argue, is structured differently and arises in different circumstances than the new Islamic movements. If there are similarities they are at the very general level of the emergence of identity politics and are not a question of diffusion or formation of a globalized phenomenon (Robertson, 1992: 178). The particular forms of identity politics in the world are the outcome of articulations between local lives and global processes within which those lives are lived and reproduced. They are practices that develop in larger arenas of interaction and not simply packages of ideas that circulate around the world.

Because the global is embedded in real lives, although its properties may not necessarily be experienced directly in those lives, it is not another place or level of reality, but an aspect of the same social reality, and thus, ethnographically accessible. There can be no ethnography of the global as such, because there is no such place, because the global only exists in its local effects. The fact that ethnographic understanding of a phenomenon may require multisited fieldwork does not detract from this understanding. If the global is not a new place, it is certainly a particular perspective on social reality. If it is not something that has suddenly occurred, it is at least an insight into the organization of the world. There are certainly ethnographic and institutional realities that are global: from transnational corporations and international institutions to ethnic diasporas. These are not new phenomena in world history, however, and their historical vicissitudes are central to any analysis of the global.

One of the most salient aspects of what is often called globalization is, in fact, the intensification of localization that results from time–space compression. The world is localized to living rooms, to television sets, and to computer screens. Access to the world has not globalized anything other than access itself. And this implies the converse, that is, that globalization is really a form of radical localization. People, some people, can stay home and access all points of the globe without moving. And, likewise the movement of some people in the world has led to local concentrations of migrants from distant origins. The implosion of the urban has led to the extension of its sources beyond those regions that were common in the past. This is the basis of so-called global consciousness, not movement as such, but an informational and, even more important, an awareness implosion. The process of globalization is clearly expressed in certain key phenomena.

1. The access to the wider world that results from the development of the media
2. The movement of things and people around the world at a greater velocity than ever before and at lower costs
3. The standardization of global places under the aegis of global capital or even local adaptations to the global
4. The formation of global institutions and organizations

Now these phenomena which are the framework for most discussions of globalization are not the results of research. They are, rather, present in the everyday lives of those who are continuously bombarded with media images of these phenomena. One can, that is, know all of this without going anywhere. And for those who only circulate among global nodes, the same images are available everywhere and no new information need intrude on the weary global traveler, not unless he or she ventures farther into the hinterlands of local social relations. It is here that even the state apparatus appears as something other than a glocalization, because presidents may also be vampires and bureaucracies may be clan hierarchies. National and regional identities may prove to be very different than what one would expect if they were merely glocal. The term creolized or hybridized may spring to mind, but such terms obfuscate the details which are not mere mixtures, but specific articulations. The offices of government may have formal Western titles, but what goes on in and between the offices may be of an entirely different character than the ideal type would have us expect. This is not a mere question of "quasi-states" or corruption (Jackson, 1990; Bayart, 1989), but of an assimilation of the global to local strategies. It is this articulation that must be understood. It is perhaps the case, for example, that what we perceive as corruption is nothing other than the assimilation of Western political categories to local strategies, but we need to go much further in our understanding of such phenomena. Potlatching with sewing machines does not turn the former into a practice that is half Western and half Kwakiutl. It is instead, an appropriation of the foreign within a local form of sociality.

And then, finally, one must ask, whose globalization is it; globalization for whom? And whose hybridity? Can one be a cultural hybrid without knowing it? We would argue that hybridity is only meaningful as an identity term, that is, in the identification of different origins as part of one's own identity. And it is only meaningful socially if it has a social effect. If anthropologists and others, in a new-found diffusionist discourse, itself a product of the turn to roots in the global system, busy themselves with discovering where things come from and showing how they become combined in particular urban places, this need not have anything to do with real social lives other than their own as observers. This conflation of the emic and the etic is a hierarchical and ethnocentric vision that was the hallmark of the colonial project of classification that gave rise to terms such as hybridity and creolization in the first place. The latter terms are products of the global gaze, and are part of the world of the observer. They are ways of identifying the experience of multiplicity at a distance.

Globalization, as we stated above, is one process within global systems and depends upon the prior existence of such systems. The absence of this understanding among proponents of cultural globalization is, in our approach, a fatal error that results in the array of problems that we have detailed here: the assumption of evolution from local to global, the renaissance of diffusionism, and the focus on strange combinations that become a new kind of exoticism, hybrid cultures of Coca Cola, Dallas, and "traditional" rituals. This new self-identified diffusionism has a clear ideological component.

> Diffusionism, whatever its defects and in whatever guise, has at least the virtue of allowing everyone the possibility of exposure to a world larger than their current locale. (Appadurai, 1988: 39)

Diffusionism, no matter what its virtues, is not so much a theory as a preoccupation with the geneaology of objects, rather than with their integration into a larger social context. Even the celebrated archaeologist Gordon Childe understood that diffusion was embedded in larger systems of exchange. And American cultural anthropology has always been concerned to stress that culture is not about the origins of cultural elements but of their structuration into larger schemes of life. It is significant that it is precisely this tendency to practice coherence and structuration of local life that is questioned by these New Diffusionists (Hannerz, 1992: 218).

Methodological Implications

The study of global systems necessitates a set of quite different methods, due to its different kinds of properties, from the macro- to the microphenomena of everyday existence. The issues involved can be stated succinctly as follows.

1. First, the very question of the existence of global relations is related to analysis of the circuits of social reproduction themselves. The question, "How does this population reproduce itself," is the starting point of any such inquiry. This is further subdivided as follows.
   a. If the population reproduces itself materially via a larger network of flows then these are part of any understanding of the dynamic relations of that society and even its very constitution.
   b. If the population is self-reproductive, then one must also ask whether this is an historical constant or the result of material reproductive isolation. There are innumerable examples of such historical processes that are generally related to marginalization, whether self-willed or not.

2. The analysis of macroproperties of global systems is one that must be historical, focusing on long- and short-term processes, the discovery of cycles of expansion and contraction, the nature of accumulation of wealth, and the

distribution of conditions of accumulation within the larger arena that has also to be delimited in empirical terms.

3. The analysis of process is also an investigation of the conditions of action within the arena. Its properties must be analyzed/discovered hypothesized in a dialectic of theory and falsification.

4. Within this arena there are numerous phenomena that can be investigated in ethnographic terms. But even here there is no reason why statistical techniques cannot also be used to map out problems. The lifeworlds constituted in relation to class relations, political structures and strategies, and local lives are all susceptible to classical ethnographic techniques. But we should like to stress the need for a phenomenologically based approach in order to discover the logics of structuration, in different domains, the tendencies to consistency as well as to disorder. Many global systemic phenomena are quite different from those associated with globalization: the emergence of social movements, new identities, state formation, and the like are local articulations of global processes rather than the movement of models and ideas around the world (as in Robertson, 1992; Meyer et al., 1997: 144–181).

5. Phenomena typical of globalization such as migration, diasporization, ethnic formations, and transnational class formations can all be studied in themselves, as they often are in the field, but they must also be placed within the larger context of the global arena in order to gain a fuller understanding. Migration, for example, need not lead to the formation of transnational identities. This is all a question of practices in specific historical conditions. Whether populations are largely integrated or even assimilated to host societies depends on numerous interactions and articulations that are often historically specific. We have suggested that diaspora formation is typical for periods of hegemonic decline in which immigrants cannot be integrated economically and where conflicts are easily ethnicized. Periods of hegemonic expansion often have the converse effect, a strong tendency to territorial integration. These different situations are also reflected in interpersonal, generational, and other microrelations. Similarly research on the proliferation of indigeous identities has detailed the way in which the latter has accelerated since the mid-1970s in the Western-dominated sectors of the world increasing the ethnic fragmentation of nation-states at the same time as the tendency to strong integration and even homogenization has been characteristic of East Asia.

6. The term multisitedness was introduced by George Marcus quite a few years ago in an argument against the assumed community studies bias of ethnography. If the world arena contains processes that make any understanding of a particular locality impossible without access to the larger social field, then it is obvious that ethnography must adapt to this situation. Fieldwork in a contemporary Hawaiian fishing village requires fieldwork in surrounding populations, in the tourist "industry," and the state sector in order to gain a complete understanding of the realities involved in village life. But this has always been the case and not a few anthropologists have dealt with such problems in their own research (e.g., the urban anthropology of Oscar Lewis, the Manchester School, etc.). However, it should be noted that the issue of

the quality of ethnography is easily passed over in stressing multisitedness. We argue that the in-depth analysis of lifeworlds requires more than quick interviews and the collection of objects and texts while one is in transit to the next site. This implies that multisited ethnography must take a good deal more time than is usually allotted for standard fieldwork.

7. The importance of ethnographic depth should be evident in the discussion above of the problems of diffusionism. An orientation to objects in circulation may easily blind us to the need to understand the way in which objects enter into lifeworlds and are integrated within particular cultural projects. Diffusion in itself is a false objectification and abstraction from the context of movement itself, one that ignores, moreover, the nature of exchange relations. For example, the "diffusion" of European cloth into Africa is not a mere issue of flow but of the way in which cloth was a significant prestige good that was valued locally precisely as foreign and thus of high status, entering into a regional system of exchange that produced chiefs as well as slaves in terms of locally specific categories and social relations. Diffusion is not a process in itself, but a product of already existing strategies and relations in novel circumstances.

Predicaments of Globalization: The Not So Hidden Agenda

We have indicated the importance of understanding the emergence of discourses of globalization in global systemic terms. We suggested that such discourses were socially positioned and could be understood as a particular experience-based perspective of new global elites. This is expressed in the growing interest, often normatively framed, in the transnational.

The concern with the translocal which has fast become something of a cult, expressed as transnational, border-crossing, postnational, is more indicative of the immediate orientation of the authors of such terms than of their referents in the real world. It is, as we have stressed, a classificatory or interpretative device of intellectual observers rather than a product of research into the emic-intentional and nonintentional realities of the global/local arena. The approach has virtually nothing to say of the way in which borders and boundaries are constituted (Sahlins, 1999). After all, one cannot cross boundaries unless they already exist. Transnational communities can only abide in the presence of national entities. This is trivial but equally easily forgotten or ignored by those who have invoked the prophecy of a new postnational world.

There is an evolutionary assumption that seems to function as the doxa for much of this discourse. This is the notion that we move from the local to the global as if to a higher stage of world history. Just as with the older notion of civilization, those who belong to the global are truly *évolué*. They have left the "rednecked" masses behind and have entered the new world of the cosmopolitan, a world, not a position, in which all the values of humanism, democracy and human rights, cultural pluralism and hybridity, catchwords of global organizations from CNN to UNESCO, have been adopted by what we would characterize as a new organic intellectual class. For the new centrists (e.g., New Labour, Third Way) the *Neue Mitten* as it is so aptly called in Germany, for whom the most serious problems in the world are in their own downwardly mobile national populations who are becoming so terribly local, and even xenophobic, the older term *classes dangereuses* is returning to common usage, at least by implication. There are indeed other voices here who have tried to promote another more grass-roots transnationalism, one that is critical to the received culturalist and elitist version, one that in fact harks back to the internationalism of the left earlier in this century. Such visions may prove important in the future but they are not for the time being a real alternative and they don't speak to the overwhelming majority of the world's populations that are not on the move. And yet they are as much a part of the global system as the globalizing elites who gaze upon their disordered lives from above. The discourse of cultural globalization has a strong ideological component, what might be referred to as a global vulgate (Friedman, 2002).

The latter consists of an assault on the family of terms that convey closure, boundedness, and essence, of all expressions of the same basic problem related to the assumed Western nature of such categories. The root metaphor is the category of the nation-state itself. The latter is represented as a closed unit, whose population is homogeneous and whose mode of functioning is dominated by boundedness, by territoriality, and thus, by exclusion. The notions of national purity, ethnic absolutism, and all forms of essentialism are deducible from the root metaphor. But in order for this metaphor to work, the nation-state has first to be reduced to a culturally uniform totality. Now even Gellner's notion of the homogeneity of the nation-state was not about cloning, but about the formation of shared values and orientations, primarily related to the public sphere. When this notion is culturalized it suddenly implies total cultural homogenization, that is, the formation of identical subjects. It is via the essentialization as well as the individualization of the culture concept that the latter is transformed into a substance that is born of or at least possessed by people. The subject is, in this sense, filled with culture. And this substance can be pure or mixed, monocultural, or multicultural. Multiculture here is a mixture of substances within the same human receptacle that fuse into a single creole or hybrid body. The reduction of culture to substance is curiously like earlier metaphors of race defined as kinds of blood, and the solution to the problem of racism is simply mixture. This is not a critique of essentialism but an extreme form of the latter. And as in a certain biological individualism, culture is shared to the degree that individuals are filled with the same or different cultural substance; that is, the collective is a product of the similarity of its individuals. This is clearly a replication of 19th century racialism (Young, 1995). It is why biracial and mixed race movements in the West, which are clearly based on racialist categories, have been understood as progressive by constructivist postcolonial intellectuals.

The new critique, which seeks to unbound the old categories consists largely of inserting the prefix "trans-" into all such formerly closed terms. Thus: translocal, transcultural, and transnational all stress the focus on that which is beyond borders, all borders. The core of all of this vocabulary may well be located in a certain identity crisis among a specific group of intellectuals, as it is expressed in its purest form in the work of Judith Butler (1993) and her discourse of postgender. This hyperconstructivist discourse is premised on the notion that the only personal reality consists of acts, such as sexual acts, and that gender classifications are externally imposed political categories. It is power that creates gender identity and our politics must therefore be directed against this power so that we may be truly liberated. As a mode of orientation this position expresses a desire to transgress the boundaries of embodied identity which is conceived as an act of imposition. If the gendered body is so victimized, then what of all other identities?[2]

Trans-X discourse consists largely of deconstructing supposedly pure or homogeneous categories in order to reveal their artificial nature. In this practice there is a logical relation between the trans- and the hybrid or even the creole. The latter terms are used to describe social realities that are culturally mixed or plural, a plurality that results from the movement of culture throughout the world. The misrepresentation of the nation-state as a homogeneous entity thus hides its true heterogeneity. There are two models of this "true situation." One that is partially suggested by Homi Bhabha is that hybridity was the condition of the world before the Western colonial imposition of principles of national uniformity. The period of modernity, also the era of colonialism, was an era of homogeneity imposed from above.[3] With the decline of colonialism the true hybridity of the world is again appearing in the postcolonial era. The other model, most prominent in anthropology, is that the world was indeed once a mosaic of separate cultural units, but that with globalization these units have been opened up and culture is today flowing throughout the world creating a process of mixture referred to as hybridity or creolity, what I have referred to as a leaky mosaic (Friedman, 1994). In this latter approach, the terms trans-X + hybridity + globalization form a conceptual unity.

There is a certain convergence in this conceptual clustering of postcolonial and globalization discourses in anthropology. It is said that globalization has changed the world profoundly. It has destroyed our old categories of place, locality, culture, and even society. The contemporary world is one of hybridity, translocality, movement, and rhizomes. Is this an intellectual development, the realization that the world has really changed (i.e., before we were local but now we are global), or is it the expression of the experience of those who themselves move from conference to conference at increasing velocities and are otherwise totally taken with the facility of Internet communication with their colleagues across the world? I have argued that this latter situation may be the true explanation of this new development, the experience of academic elites, traveling intellectuals, and a variety of global movers, an experience that is presaged by the representations of CNN and other internationalized media as well as in the spontaneous representations of international networks of media managers, politicians, diplomats, and "high-end" NGOs.

---

[2] It is worth noting that the desire to transcend all categories also contradicts the existence of categories such as multiculture and hybridity as all cultural categories.

[3] The notion of a precolonial hybridity appears in works as diverse as Bhabha (1994), Mamdani (1997), and even Amselle (1999), who uses the term *logiques métisses* to refer to the openess and flexibility of precolonial sociopolitical categories rather than what is usually understood as hybridity. In his new introduction to *Logiques Métisses* he is quite critical of these new intellectual tendencies that reinforce the kind of racialism that they may have hoped to surpass (1999: I–XIII).

This discourse is thus, positioned, the class conciousness of frequent travelers (Calhoun, 2003). It is the discourse of globalizing elites whose relation to the earth is one of consumerist distance and objectification. It is a birds-eye view of the world that looks down upon the multiethnic bazaar or ethnic neighborhood and marvels at the fabulous jumble of cultural differences present in that space. Hybridity is thus the sensual, primarily visual, appropriation of a space of cultural difference. It is the space below that thus becomes hybridized, even if, for the people who occupy that space, reality is quite different. The hybrid space is a space for the observer, or rather for the consumer/appropriater of that space. This is the perspective that generates the identification of a Papua New Guinea war shield painted with a beer advertisement as a hybrid object (Clifford, 1997). It may be hybrid for us but in the street or the village, things are otherwise.

To ascertain that there is a clear political or ideological content to this discourse we have only to look at some of the texts produced by people so identifying. First there is the apocryphal statement by Appadurai, "We need to think ourselves beyond the nation" (1993: 411) which is elaborated upon in the context of an article in *Public Culture* in which both native Fijians and Hawaiians are taken to task by the anthropologist John Kelly:

> Across the globe a romance is building for the defense of indigenes, first peoples, natives trammeled by civilization, producing a sentimental politics as closely mixed with motifs of nature and ecology as with historical narratives. . . . In Hawaii, the high water mark of this romance is a new indigenous nationalist movement, still mainly sound and fury, but gaining momentum in the 1990's. . . . This essay is not about these kinds of blood politics. My primary focus here is not the sentimental island breezes of a Pacific romance, however much or little they shake up the local politics of blood, also crucial to rights for diaspora people, and to conditions of political possibility for global tansnationalism. (Kelly, 1995)

More recently he has gone somewhat further in the affirmation of transnationalism. Citing an Indian Fijian member of Parliament as saying, "Pioneering has always been a major element in the development of resources for the good of mankind ... " (Kelly, 1999: 250) the latter chimes in with

> People who move inherit the earth. All they have to do is keep up the good work, "in search for better opportunity. " (ibid)

Lisa Malkki, another adherent of this ideology, has gone to some lengths in her monograph on Burundian refugees in Tanzania to argue for a dichotomy between those who stay in the refugee camp and cultivate their Hutu nationalism and others, who make it to town (for what reason we might ask?) and identify out of the group.

> In contrast (to the nationalists in the camps), the town refugees had not constructed such a categorically distinct, collective identity. Rather than defining themselves collectively as "the Hutu refugees," they tended to seek ways of assimilating and of manipulating multiple identities – identities derived or "borrowed" from the social context of the township. The town refugees were not essentially "Hutu" or "refugees" or "Tanzanians" or "Burundians" but rather just "broad persons" (Hebdige, 1987: 159). Theirs were creolized, rhizomatic identities – changing and situational rather than essential and moral (Hannerz, 1987, Deleuze & Guattari, 1987: 6, 21). In the process

of managing these "rootless" identities in township life, they were creating not a heroized national identity but a lively cosmopolitanism. (Malkki, 1997: 67–68)

Despite the fact that she cites no ethnographic evidence for her dichotomization, the thrust of the article is clear. Camp refugees are dangerous nationalists because this rooted identity can only lead to violence, whereas those who have adapted and given up that identity to become "broad people" point the way for the rest of us, toward a cosmopolitan hybridity. This is an extraordinary piece of doctored ethnography made to fit a simple ideological scheme; good guys versus bad guys, essentialist, nationalist, refugees longing for their imagined homeland, versus hybrid cosmopolitans adeptly adapting to their current circumstances. Her message to the refugee camps is to forget their identities and get on with the process of adapting to the current situation. Deleuze and Guattari are borrowed here to argue that arboreal metaphors, typically Western, have only caused suffering. It is time to switch to rhizomes. In this metaphoric space the evil is easy to spot. If national identity is dangerous, indigeneity is positively deadly. She, more cautious than Kelly, does not venture a critique of indigenous politics but instead displaces her critique to Western supporters of such movements who would wed them to green politics.

That people would gather in a small town in North America to hold a vigil by candlelight for other people known only by the name of "Indigenous" suggests that being indigenous, native autochthonous, or otherwise rooted in place is, indeed, powerfully heroized (op.cit. 59)

Are people "rooted" in their native soil somehow more natural, their rights somehow more sacred, that those of other exploited and oppressed people? And, one wonders, if an "Indigenous Person" wanted to move away to a city, would her or his candle be extinguished. (op.cit.)

This distinction is explicitly designed to criticize the ideological association between ecology and native peoples as romantic and basically reactionary, as becomes clear in her own celebration of cosmopolitanism. It is part of the error of conflating "culture and people," "nation and nature" (op.cit.). "Natives are thought to be ideally adapted to their environments" (op.cit.). These are understandings that entail that natives "are somehow *incarcerated*, or confined, in those places" (Appadurai, 1988: 37). But is this really the case? Who has argued for such a model of reality? Is it perhaps the fact that people do adapt to their environments and develop social and cultural worlds around specific places that is the problem? When indigenous peoples "romanticize" their territories is this not because they maintain some practical and spiritual relation to them. Does this contradict the equally obvious fact that people also move, that the history of global systems has been one of massive displacement as well as the emergence of dominant global elites? I fail to see the problem. But there is, clearly, a real conflict for these new globalizers. If, as argued by Gordon, Wilmsen and others, the Bushmen of the Kalahari have a long history of integration and marginalization within the Western world system, does this eliminate their identification with their territories? Even more striking in Malkki's version is the reduction of the entire issue to one of individual preferences. What if some individuals move to town, she asks, as if this were relevant to the situation of indigenously identified populations. Perhaps, as she seems to imply, they should all move to town and rid themselves of their reactionary rootedness. One senses a categorical disenchantment with what was perhaps an assumed anthropological authenticity, just as among many inventionists (as in "the invention of tradition") who in their disillutionment have taken to criticizing "natives" for having invented unauthentic traditions for political reasons.

Anthropological Versions of Jihad and MacWorld

The most recent publications in the above vein have extended the metaphor to one of global flows versus local identity. Flows of culture, are the normal state of affairs in a globalized world, flows of people, things, culture, and money. This is difficult to accept for anthropologists with their model of bounded units and so they may tend to deny the truth. Meyer and Geschiere in their edited volume (1999) argue that closure is a reaction to flows, to the experienced, if not real, loss of control over conditions of existence. This is not a new idea of course. It is clearly stated as the Jihad versus McWorld thesis. The difference between this more recent approach and some of the earlier writings is that there is less optimism about the new globalized world. On the other hand globalization seems to be accepted as a fact of nature. The Comaroffs (1999) suggest that South Africa today has developed a modern or post-colonial "occult economy" in which magic and witchcraft accusations are rampantly intertwined with real violence, all a result of the integration of the area into the new globalized economy where there is so much to buy and so little income with which to buy it. Now this isn't the first time that such an argument has been suggested. It is arguably a transformation, even an inversion, of the older structural functionalist explanations of Marwick (1965) and others into the new postcolonial discourse. The earlier situation was one in which colonial markets offered opportunities for accumulation that contradicted the control exercised by elders over the distribution of wealth. The recent one, which is several decades old, is one in which wealth accumulation is increasingly impossible in relation to desire for consumption, in which the market is flooded with goods that are inaccessible for most people. But that this should generate witchcraft accusation can never be explained by the circumstances alone. Globalization is understood by these authors as a thing in itself, an evolutionary reality, composed of intensifying flows. A global systemic perspective would allow for such flows as well, but would see them as generated by specific conditions of capital accumulation, as articulations between local conditions and global relations of which globalization is only one possibility. Thus although disaster and social disintegration characterize much of Africa (and this is not the first time), East Asia has become increasingly integrated in conditions of rapid growth.

It is, paradoxically, the limited character of the transnational approach, its obsession with the closure of the local, that leads its practitioners to criticize those who talk of bounding and territorialization inasmuch as such terms are thought to be old fashioned, even reactionary. Unfortunately social reality would seem to be mistaken as well!

> . . . anthropologists' obsession with boundedness is parallelled by the ways in which the people they study try to deal with seemingly open-ended global flows. (Meyer and Geschiere 1999 p.3)

But if people are doing this thing called bounding and closure and essentializing, should this not be recognized as a real social phenomenon rather than shunned as a terrible mistake? Everything from the New Right to African witchcraft must now be accounted for in terms of the production of locality, an apparent reaction to globalization itself. And, of course, it must be asked, who is it that produces locality. Are there any agents, any subjects in this process of conversion of flow into place. Could it be that people have been local all the time and did not simply land from the global jet stream to construct locality? Could it be that the local is indeed a structure of the global, but not by way of the application of an idea diffused around the world. Couldn't it be that the local is a relation of interlocality, thus not a cultural representation but a social and cultural practice within a larger arena?

We have suggested that the transnationalist trend or perhaps urge in anthropology and neighboring disciplines is more than just intellectually flawed. It is an agenda that seeks to morally reform the discipline. Otherwise it is difficult to understand why the obsessive attack on just boundedness. It is true that there have been tendencies to treat societies as closed units, especially in the heyday of structural functionalism. In fact the very starting point of our own global systemic anthropology, as we have indicated, was a critique of the tendency to treat societies as isolates and explanatory totalities. But this was not an issue of culture, nor of nationalism. Nor was it argued that this was the case because societies were now finally joined together in a single globalized world. On the contrary, we argued that regional systems were as old as humanity and that if there were cases of more or less isolated societies that they most often were societies that became isolated in the global historical process.

Similarly this approach entails that the production of culture is interwoven with such systems of relations, rather than a product of the circulation of ideas or cultural elements. The fact that people occupying a particular place and living and constructing a particular world are in their entirety integrated into a larger system of relationships does not contradict the fact that they make their world where they are and with the people that are part of their local lives. But not so for transnational/globalization approaches to the subject. For the latter globalization is behavioral, as structure was for Radcliffe-Brown. It is about people, things, and ideas in transit, as if such movement implied something systemic in itself. For the globalizers, the introduction of new objects into former strategies implies total rupture, as we said of potlatching with sewing machines. That if witchcraft representations include Whites that come from far off places, if underage children are now targeted instead of maternal uncles, then we are in a new ball game called "modernity". If this is the argument then Latour's suggestion that "We have never been modern," begins to make all the more sense.

Marshall Sahlins has made some important suggestions concerning this so-called "afterology" (Brightman, 1995). Where, he asks, are the classical anthropologists that maintained a view of culture as bounded and homogeneous, as essentialized? Sahlins argues to the contrary.

> They could even speak of "the fallacy of separation": the mistaken idea that because cultures are distinctive they are closed. (Sahlins, 1999: 404)

He describes at several junctures how the cultural relativists stressed that cultures were constantly undergoing change, and he cites Herskovits himself on the issue of homogeneity.

> "To think in terms of a single pattern for a single culture is to distort reality . . . for no culture is (so) simple (as not) to have various patterns." (op.cit. 405)

Of course there are deeper patterns that anthropologists attempt to discover, but this is not a question of homogeneity it is a question of coherence, which is not the same thing.

This is not, as we have suggested, a mere question of misrepresenting reality including the way the discipline of anthropology has perceived its own ethnographic world. It is also a positioned discourse that is the product of a particular historical conjuncture, one that coincides with real globalization but which participates in that globalization as actor and that is fully identified with the latter. I have suggested elsewhere and above that globalizing discourse occurs in the rising globalizing elites of the world system. It is their identity but it has hegemonic pretentions insofar as it claims to represent everyone's reality. The discourse is not new in itself, but it does become salient in certain historical periods. These are periods in which declining hegemony, increasing class polarization, mass migration, and the globalization of capital coincide, where class polarization produces a confrontation between indigenizing downwardly mobile classes and new cosmopolitanizing elites. The latter identify with the world rather than with their nation states which are declassified as dangerously racist. This is a discourse that supports global control and global governance, which has even strived to transcend the demos in democracy in favor of a new autocracy of respectability, in which democracy is embodied in political personalities rather than the political arena, a discourse that logically entails the emergence of new dangerous classes, the enemies of the new merging of left and right.

> The Neue Mitte manipulates the Rightist scare the better to hegemonize the "democratic" field, i.e. to define the terrain and discipline its real adversary, the radical Left. Therein resides the ultimate rationale of the Third Way: that is, a social democracy purged of its minimal subversive sting, extinguishing even the faintest memory of anti-capitalism and class struggle. The result is what one would expect. The populist Right moves to occupy the terrain evacuated by the Left, as the only "serious" political force that still employs an anti-capitalist rhetoric – if thickly coated with a nationalist/racist/religious veneer (international corporations are "betraying" the decent working people of our nation). At the congress of the Front National a couple of years ago, Jean-Marie Le Pen brought on stage an Algerian, an African and a Jew, embraced them all and told his audience: "They are no less French than I am—it is the representatives of big multinational capital, ignoring their duty to France, who are the true danger to our identity!" In New York, Pat Buchanan and Black activist Leonora Fulani can proclaim a common hostility to unrestricted free trade, and both (pretend to) speak on behalf of the legendary desaparecidos of our time, the proverbially vanished proletariat. While multicultural tolerance becomes the motto of the new and privileged "symbolic" classes, the far Right seeks to address and to mobilize whatever remains of the mainstream "working class" in our Western societies. . . . In this uniform spectrum, political differences are more and more

reduced to merely cultural attitudes: multicultural/sexual (etc.) "openness" versus traditional/natural (etc.) "family value". (Zizek, 2000: 37–38)

References

Amselle, Jean-Loup (1990). *Logiques métisses: Anthropologie de l'identité en Afrique et ailleurs*. Paris: Payot.
Appadurai, A. (1988). "Putting hierarchy in its place," *Cultural Anthropology* 3(1): 36–49.
Appadurai, A. (1993). "Patriotism and its futures," *Public Culture* 5: 415–40.
Bayart, Jean-Francois (1989). *L'Etat en Afrique: La politique du ventre, L'Espace du politique*. Paris: Fayard.
Bhabha, H. (1994). *The location of culture*. New York: Routledge.
Bourne, R. (1916). "Transnational America," *Atlantic Monthly* 118: 86–97.
Brightmann, R. (1995). "Forget culture: Replacement, transcendence, relexification." *Cultural Anthropology*, 10: 509–46.
Butler, J. (1993). *Bodies that matter: On the discursive limits of sex*. New York: Routledge.
Calhoun, C. (2003). "The class conciousness of frequent travellers: Toward a critique of actually existing cosmopolitanism," *South Atlantic Quarterly* 101(4): 869–97.
Clifford, J. (1997) *Routes*. Cambridge, MA: Harvard University Press.
Comaroff, J. and J. (1999). "Occult economies and the violence of abstraction: Notes from the South African postcolony," *American Ethnologist* 26(2): 279–303.
Deleuze, G., and Guattari, F. (1987). *Thousand plateaux*. Chicago, Illinois: Chicago University Press.
Denemark, R., Gills, B., & Modelski, G. (2000). *World system history: The social science of long term change*. London: Routledge.
Denemark, R., Friedman, J., Gills, B., & Modelski, G. (2000). *World system history: The Science of long term change*. London: Routledge.
Dumont, L. (1967). "Homo hierarchicus, essai sur le système des castes," *Bibliothèque des sciences humaines*. [Paris]: Gallimard.
Ekholm, K. (1976). "Om studiet av det globala systemets dynamik," *Antropologiska Studier* 14: 15–23.
—— (1977). "External exchange and the transformation of Central African social systems," in Friedman & Rowlands (Eds), *The evolution of social systems*, London.
—— (1980). "On the limitations of civilization: The structure and dynamics of global systems," *Dialectical Anthropology*.
—— (1987). "The study of risk in social systems: An anthropological perspective," in Sjöberg (Ed), *Risk and society: Studies of risk generation and reactions to risk*, London.
Ekholm, K. & Friedman, J. (1979). "'Capital', imperialism and exploitation in ancient world systems," in M. T. Larsen (Ed,), *Power and propaganda: A symposium on ancient empires*, Copenhagen.
—— (1980). "Towards a global anthropology," with Jonathan Friedman, in Blussé et al. (Eds,), *History and underdevelopment*, Leiden and Paris.
Frank, A. G., & Gills, B. K. (1993). *The world system: Five hundred years or five thousand?* London: New York: Routledge.
Friedman, J. (1974). "Marxism, structuralism and vulgar materialism," *Man* 9: 444–469.
Friedman, J. (1976). "Marxist theory and systems of total reproduction," *Critique of Anthropology* 7: 3–16.
Friedman (1994). *Cultural identity and global process*. London: Sage.
—— (2002). "From roots to routes: Tropes for trekkers," *Anthropological Theory* 2: 21–36.

—— (2005). "Plus ça change: on not learning from history," in J. Friedman., & C. Chase-Dunn (Eds.), *Hegemonic declines: Past and present*. Boulder, CO: Paradigm. 89–114.

Godelier, M. (1972). *Rationality and irrationality in economics*. London: NLB.

Gordon, R. J. (1992). *The bushman myth: The making of a Namibian underclass, conflict and social change series*. Boulder, CO: Westview.

—— (1992). *Cultural complexity*. New York: Columbia University Press. 546–59.

Hannerz, U. (1987). "The world in Creolization," *Africa* 57. *Cultural complexity*. New York: Columbia University Press, p. 546–549.

Hebdige, D. (1987). *Cut 'n' Mix*. London: Methuen.

Jackson, R. (1990). Quasi-states: Sovereignty, international relations and the third world. *Cambridge studies in international relations; 12*. Cambridge [England]; New York: Cambridge University Press.

Kallen, H. (1924). *Culture and democracy in the United States*. New York: Arno.

Kelly, J. (1995). "Diaspora and world war, blood and nation in Fiji and Hawaii," *Public Culture* 7(3): 475–97.

Kelly, J. (1999). "Time and the global: Against the homogeneous, empty communities in contemporary social theory," in B. Meyer., & P. Geschiere (Eds.), *Globalization and identity: Dialectics of flow and closure*. Oxford: Blackwell.

Lévi-Strauss, C. (1962). *La pensée sauvage*. Paris: Plon.

Malkki, L. (1997). "National geographic: the rooting of peoples and the territorialization of national identity among scholars and refugees," *Cultural Anthropology* 7(1): 24–44.

Mamdani, M. (1997). *Citizen and subject: Contemporary Africa and the legacy of colonialism*. Princeton: Princeton University Press.

Marwick, M. (1965) *Sorcery in its social setting: A study of the Northern Rhodesia Cave*. Manchester: Manchester University Press.

Meyer, B., & Geschiere, P. (Eds.) (1999). *Globalization and identity: Dialectics of flow and closure*. Oxford: Blackwell.

Meyer, J. W., Boli, J., Thomas, G. M., & Raminez, F. (1997, July). "World society and the nation state," *American Journal of Sociology* 103: 144–181.

Radin, P. (1987). *The method and theory of ethnology: An essay in criticism*. South Hadley, Mass.: Bergin & Garvey.

Robert, B. (1995). "Forget culture: Replacement, transcendence, relexification," *Cultural Anthropology* 10: 509–46.

Robertson, R. (1992). *Globalization: Social theory and global culture*. London: Sage.

Rowlands, M. J., Larsen, M. T., & Kristiansen, K. (1987). *Centre and periphery in the ancient world, new directions in archaeology*. Cambridge [Cambridgeshire] & New York: Cambridge University Press.

Sahlins, M. (1999). "Two or three things that I know about culture," *Journal of the Royal Anthropological Institute* 5: 399–421.

Steward, J. H. (1955). *Theory of culture change; The methodology of multilinear evolution*. Urbana: University of Illinois Press.

Strauss, C., & Quinn, N. (1994). A cognitive/cultural anthropology, in R. Borofsky (Ed.), *Assessing cultural anthropology* (pp. 284–300). New York: McGraw Hill.

Wallerstein, I. M. (1974). The modern world-system: Capitalist agriculture and the origins of the European world-economy in the sixteenth century. Text ed, *Studies in social discontinuity*. New York: Academic.

Wilmsen, E. N. (1989). *Land filled with flies: A political economy of the Kalahari*. Chicago: University of Chicago Press.

Wolf, E. (1980). *Europe and the people without history*. Berkeley: University of California Press.

Young, R. (1995). *Colonial desire: Hybridity in theory, culture, and race*. London: Routledge.

Zizek, S. (2000). "Why we all love to hate Haider," *New Left Review* 2: 37–38.

5
The Eigenstructures of World Society and the Regional Cultures of the World

RUDOLF STICHWEH

Introduction: Eigenstructures of World Society

World society is the only societal system that presently exists in the world. This statement formulates a highly improbable hypothesis. First of all one will ask questions about the concept of society. Is it not true that the concept of society has primarily been conceived by looking to small social systems comprising a few hundred or at most a few thousand members? How can we apply the same concept to tribal social systems as well as to a potential world society? One part of the answer will point to the concept of communication and to connectedness. Society is based on communications as its most elementary events. Communications are connected to other communications and the historical limits of connectivity seem to function as the boundaries of society. Another important part of the answer is to be found in the tradition of sociological systems theory established by Talcott Parsons and Niklas Luhmann. Parsons as well as Luhmann came close in their understanding of society to the Aristotelian tradition: society is understood as the highest order social system that encloses all relevant social structures and processes into its purview. What distinguishes society from other social systems in this understanding is "self-sufficiency".[1] If one applies the concept of self-sufficiency to the contemporary situation there are good reasons to be

---

[1] For a more detailed argument that concentrates on the significant interpretive differences between Parsons and Luhmann, cf. Stichweh, (2005f) (Luhmann, 1997; Parsons, 1961b, 1966, 1971).

found that only world society can be conceived to be a sufficiently autonomous social entity to be called a self-sufficient social system.[2]

In historical terms we have to deal with a highly unusual circumstance. The history of human societies was always characterized by the coexistence of at least hundreds, or more probably thousands of societies that had some contact with one another, but were mainly independent from one another. In this sense they were closed towards one another. The same is true of the civilizational empires of the last three- to four-thousand years which should be conceived as self-sufficient societies with occasional exchanges and occasional contacts with other societies. Besides these civilizational empires (Mesopotamia, Egypt, China, Hellenistic Greece) there again existed thousands of small and local societies that were only loosely coupled to the civilizational empires. Insofar it can be said that the rise of the European-Atlantic societal system, since approximately the 15th century, and the incorporation of the whole of the remaining world in this system, which was never unified in a political sense,[3] brings about a singularity into the history of human societies. Never before in human history was there only one societal system on earth.

Global inequality, global conflict, and national and international wars have to be analyzed as structures of world society. Their prominence and frequency are not arguments against world society. Instead they have to be understood as formative moments of a global societal system.[4] Although it still bears significant characteristics of its Western origin, the system of world society as it is today absorbed the multiplicity of empires and societies from the ancient and medieval world.

The question this chapter focuses on is how this unique system of society succeeds in this improbable achievement: absorbing differences and reconstituting conflict lines. Looking for an answer, there are two positions prominent in the present literature on globalization. The first of these two analytical options conceives world society as a unifying force that systematically reduces behavioral and cultural differences. This thesis has sometimes been called McDonaldization,[5] a name which already seems to be dated as it comes from a time a few years ago when McDonald's was perceived to be a much more potent marketing machine

---

[2] As is well known Parsons himself did not come to this conclusion but there are numerous caveats in his writings that consider the possibility of a world society. See, for example, Parsons, 1961a, Fn. 14, p. 44.

[3] The permanent absence of political unification is the criterion for the existence of a world-system Immanuel Wallerstein added to the discussion (Wallerstein, 1974).

[4] There is an interesting story in a book by two Australian filmmakers about the discovery of the population of the highlands of New Guinea in the 1930s (these highlands had thought to be uninhabited until then). When the authors of the book interviewed the highlanders in the 1960s about their experience of first contact, many of these now old men were decorated with their war medals from Australia. That is only a few years after having had their first encounter with a world unknown to them until they had been involved as soldiers for the state of Australia in World War II (Connolly & Anderson, 1988).

[5] Ritzer (1993) and Ritzer (2002).

than it is now. A second proposal postulates the conservation and maintenance of pre-existing diversity in the system of world society. This thesis is best known under the title of "multiple modernities" and it is closely connected to the writings of Shmuel N. Eisenstadt.[6] Both of these theories are probably wrong as they postulate too much continuity in the emergence of world society. This continuity is either caused by world society being a homogenizing force which always neutralizes historical differences or it is guaranteed by the maintenance and extension of pre-existing cultural differences.

This chapter tries to establish a third, completely different argument. It looks to structural patterns germane to world society. Insofar as these are new structural patterns it points to discontinuities and not to continuities. The structural patterns in question I call Eigenstructures of world society thereby making use of a term well established in mathematics but not yet in sociology. Eigenstructures reproduce pre-existent cultural diversity and push it back at the same time, creating new social and cultural patterns of their own.

This argument is based on a cumulative model of social structure that does not describe social change as a substitution of new structures in place of old structures. Instead it hypothesizes plural levels of structure formation in social systems which means that new structures overlay old structures but do not extinguish them. They rather reduce the informational relevance and the frequency of activation of the structures they push back over very long stretches of historical time.[7]

The following argument makes it clear that the Eigenstructures of world society are not to be seen as recent inventions. Some of them are structural patterns going back to antiquity and to the European Middle Ages. But this only points once more to the fact that world society itself is a system with a long history of at least five- to six-hundred years. And these Eigenstructures are related to World Society via reciprocal intensifications. They advance the emergence of world society to the degree they themselves are articulated. On the other hand they are privileged by the emerging system of world society as structural patterns compatible with it.

Differentiation of Function Systems

The first and probably most important candidate on my list of Eigenstructures is the function system. World society does not arise via the encounter and conflict of the great civilizations of the world—this last point seems to be the position of Samuel Huntington[8]—as it does arise via the emergence of functional differentiation. By this is meant that thematically specialized function systems come about as global communication complexes. Examples of global function systems are the

---

[6] Eisenstadt (2000).
[7] Cf. some remarks on a cumulative model of social structure in Stichweh (1994b).
[8] Huntington (1997).

world economy or world science or world law or finally world literature. All of these global systems somehow undermine the autonomy of the regional cultures of the world without attacking these cultures directly. This offers a good illustration of how a new structural pattern overlays an older one without these two layers necessarily coming into conflict with one another.

An interesting contemporary case study of this could be the ongoing integration of the Islamic economy into the world economy. There is a corpus of Islamic economic law (Shari`ah Law) which is incompatible with many practices considered normal in the Western world: sale of alcohol; pork-related products; conventional financial services (banking, insurance); entertainment (hotels, casinos/gambling, cinema, pornography); tobacco manufacturing; defense and weapons companies. On the other hand, the last few years saw numerous unification tendencies based on instruments that try to enhance the comparability between different Islamic investments and between Islamic and non-Islamic investments. Among these instruments one can count the implementation of numerous "Islamic Market Indexes" by Dow Jones, indexes that only list securities compatible with Shari`ah Law (this compatibility is certified by a council of Islamic scholars) and which then allows one to compare investments into these securities with alternative investments.[9] Another important instrument is the "Islamic Financial Services Board" founded in Malaysia in 2002 which tries to control the fragmentation of financial services in the Islamic countries by creating unified standards for Islamic banking and thereby building up a critical mass of uncontroversial financial products with a global reach.[10] An interesting development is to be seen in the fact that meanwhile even medium-scale German cities issue bonds that are shaped according to Islamic standards and which in this way are addressed to Islamic investors. All these institutions are characterized by a highly technical character specific of financial markets, and therefore they can coexist without obvious collisions with ideological languages that try to postulate rigid barriers between the Islamic and the Western world. And furthermore these developments document the ability of the economy to internalize most heterogeneous value patterns (e.g., ecological values, Islamic values) as long as a measure can be found that compares the results obtained in an evaluative language specific for the economic function system.

The same force attributed here to the economy as a global function system can be seen in all the other function systems of modern society. Obviously, there exist a significant number of them: religion, law, the world polity, science, the arts, the global system of intimate relations and families, education, the global health system, the sports, mass media, and tourism.[11] They all are not only structures differentiating a certain functional aspect of communication. Additionally all of them are producers of global semantics. And as such they do not only realize

---

[9] Cf. http://www.djindexes.com

[10] Cf. http://www.ifsb.org

[11] See for a short historical overview of the differentiation of function systems and for different stages in this process Stichweh (2005a).

Eigenstructures of world society but are also constituting Eigencultures of the function systems which can in no way be reduced to the traditional regional cultures of the world. Looking again to the economy, brands are an interesting aspect of such a global Eigencultures of a function system and they are a remarkable case of penetrating most improbable regions of the world.[12]

How and why do these function systems acquire the globalizing impetus characteristic of them? The most important features seem to be the binary codes on which function systems are based. By this I mean binary distinctions such as truth/falsity (science), to pay/not to pay (economy), powerful/subject to power (polity), and other such codes that are universal mechanisms of information processing by which nearly everything in the world can be classified according to a specific functional point of view.[13] From the perspective of such a binary code there is no reason to be seen why it should be of only national or regional significance. Binary codes have no endogenous reasons for accepting spatial or territorial restrictions on their relevance. Such restrictions if they occur always are constraints deriving from the concurrent universal relevance of other binary codes. These binary codes generate a dynamics that is always a global dynamics. The concepts interpreted by the codes are generalized symbols that bring about a disembedding of the respective function from other social contexts. This disembedding can also be described as a kind of purity negating any admixture with points of view coming from other functional points of view.[14] From these arguments one can derive that in a first approximation the theory of world society is nearly identical with the theory of functional differentiation, and this in a double sense: first, one cannot imagine function systems that do not inherently tend to be global communication complexes; second, a system of world society seems to be inconceivable that is not based on the autonomous dynamics of global function systems.

The Career of Formal Organizations

The second candidate on my list of Eigenstructures is the formal organization which is an invention that derives from the secular and spiritual organizations of the late Middle Ages.[15] Historically the formal organization is related to the genesis of the function system. Early functional specifications in stratified societies were prepared in functionally specified corporations. These corporations were allowed to incorporate a principle—horizontal heterogeneity—which was not yet acceptable on the level of primary societal differentiation.[16] Among the early

---

[12] Cf. Friedman (1994) on Africa and the constitution of local identities via the famous brands of French *haute couture* (pp. 105–108).

[13] Cf. on binary codes Luhmann (1986).

[14] Cf. on disembedding Granovetter (1985) and on purity Abbott (1981).

[15] On the genesis of the formal organization, Coleman (1990, esp. Ch. 20).

[16] Cf. on this Stichweh (1991, esp. Ch. II).

corporations of medieval Europe were monastic orders, universities, incorporated cities, trading companies, and guilds of craftsmen.

Even in early modern Europe one could easily observe the globalizing force due to the principle of formal organization. Among the monastic orders the Jesuits are a significant example as they succeeded in a few decades between their foundation in 1540 and 1620 in covering Europe and parts of Asia and the Americas with a dense network of educational and ecclesiastical organizations. The celibacy which partially dissolved the link between the members of the order and their families and the free transferability of the personnel of the order (normally they were transferred to another often far distant place every three years) were probably the most important enabling conditions for the global penetration of the Jesuit order.[17]

If one looks at modern organizations one finds similar circumstances as conditions of their relevance for global society. First of all, they are successful in effecting internal transfers of personnel. These internal transfers of personnel allow the neutralizing of political boundaries that are not so easily crossed by other types of migrants who cannot rely on membership status in a global organization.[18] Secondly, organizations are effective machines for the internal transfer of knowledge of which it is often said that global markets for knowledge are very inefficient. In evolutionary economics there exists some evidence for the hypothesis that the inefficiency of knowledge transfers between organizations is the main reason for the rise of the multinational enterprise as a mechanism for the internalization of knowledge transfers.[19] Thirdly, organizations often combine the global connectedness in a worldwide network of branches with an intensive local situatedness of the individual subsidiary.[20] Today there are many types of global organizations. But what is remarkable in looking at most of them is this compatibility of globality and locality, of global connectedness and local situatedness.

Among the different types of global organizations three should especially be mentioned. There are first of all the so-called IGOs (international governmental organizations) which are the organizational structures in which the thematically specified cooperation of the multiple nation-states of the world are realized. There are then the INGOs (international nongovernmental organizations) of which there are at least 25,000 today[21] and which together with the IGOs may be described as the basic structures of an emerging world government. And we should mention again the MNEs (multinational enterprises) which represent the most significant case of a function system based in global organizations with a clear functional layout. Looking at this we are referred back to function systems as something being closely interrelated with those organizations with which they share their functional primacy.

---

[17] Cf. Meier (2000).
[18] Cf. Stichweh (2005d, Ch. 8).
[19] Kogut and Zander (1993) and Scaperlanda (1993).
[20] Cf. Das (1993).
[21] This number in Boli & Thomas (1997: p. 174).

The Delocalization of Networks

Network is one of the most prominent metaphors of present-day society. It is a remarkable convergence that the term is as well used for the technical infrastructures of societal communication (energy networks, electrical networks)[22] as well as for the structures of communication itself, and that finally the term even entered the self-description of the lifeworld. Members of society without possessing any knowledge of sociology nowadays often describe themselves as doing networking.

But in social science the network terminology is a comparably recent phenomenon although networks as social structures are much older than organizations as they do not depend on complicated legal instruments as is the case with organizations. Networks build up and decompose in social space seemingly without preconditions.

For a long time the study of networks was primarily a concern of social anthropologists[23] who were interested in relatively self-contained local communities. Communities of Norwegian fisherman were a characteristic subject of study.[24] But, of course, in looking back in history you will find networks in kinship, friendship and patron–client-relations. On the other hand, networks seem to be a dramatic case of a social form that only finds its adequate context of expansion in world society. What are the reasons for this elective affinity between networks and world society?

First of all, networks are based on abstracting completely from the material content of the social relations going into them. Any kind of entity, and that means very heterogeneous entities, can be connected via networks. This distinguishes networks from autopoietic social systems that depend on homogenized elements by which they constitute themselves and it distinguishes networks from function systems that are autopoietic systems, of course.[25] But a network can function as the material infrastructure of an autopoietic system and of many other types of social relations, too. The abstract character of networks is an important enabling condition for the very heterogeneous patterns of system formation in contemporary society. For example, networks can be indifferent towards the distinction of personal and impersonal social relations which is so characteristic of and innovative in modern society in other respects.

A second important point regards individualization. Individual personalities must have the freedom to enter into network relations without being unnecessarily hindered by social controls and they must have the freedom to be content with weak ties.[26] The social acceptability of weak ties is essential for the potential global extension of network relations. Only on the basis of weak ties can the extensive

---

[22] Cf. Baedeker (1999).
[23] Historians who are much more interested in persons do *prosopography* instead.
[24] Barnes (1954).
[25] Cf. on autopoietic social systems Luhmann (1984).
[26] On the concept of "weak tie", Granovetter (1983).

personal networks of 1000–1500 acquaintances which are supposed to be typical of present-day society[27] be managed by individuals with a limited capacity for information processing. Furthermore networks are lateral and nonhierarchical, which is again a circumstance dependent on modern values and legitimations. Finally networks are evolutionary. That is, they are based on point-to-point relations which can be changed locally by continually adding and losing network ties. This can more easily be done with weak ties that can be dissolved quickly than it can be done on the basis of strong ties. All these characteristics seem to establish a strong affinity of networks to global social relations. This is to be seen, too, in the fact that some of the prominent terms of network theory—connectivity, connectedness, interrelatedness—are at the same time core concepts in globalization theory.

The rise and prominence of the social form network changes the stability of boundaries of organizations and the chances of control in organizations. Even organizations have to fit into networks transcending the individual organization. It seems to be characteristic, for example, of economic organizations today that one condition of their success consists in their understanding that they can only control a small part of the value chain related to their products. A McKinsey study in 1998 found out that the total sales volume of Microsoft—then the biggest enterprise in the world in terms of market capitalization—only amounted to 4% of the whole business volume related to the core Microsoft products (software and services related to Windows).[28] This need of adaptation to a value chain one is only a part of has to be distinguished from the explicit cooperative ventures agreed by an individual enterprise, although the variety and flexibility in forming alliances is an important part of the adaptation to network structures in modern society. For a global software firm a number of five to seven hundred of such explicit cooperative alliances seems to be a characteristic number, which may demonstrate that organizational networks have an order of magnitude comparable to the acquaintanceship networks of natural persons. Whereas these cooperative alliances are established on the basis of formal agreements among organizations, they are dissolved in a much more informal way. They simply peter out which is one indicator of the informality of the network economy. Resuming these arguments it can be said that business networks offer their participants a good chance of significant influence on markets as long as these participants are willing to accept a certain loss of control potentials.

The interrelationship of networks and world society and the attendant delocalization of networks is most easily seen in the fast growing literature on *small worlds*.[29] Small worlds are so-called "scale-free networks" that are able to incorporate a significant number, even billions, of knots or members. Locally they can be characterized as clusters of members closely linked with one another. Via

---

[27] Cf. Wellman (1992). Laumann (1989) even speaks of 2000 to 6000 acquaintances.
[28] Del Vecchio & Trigg (2000).
[29] Cf. on this Kochen (1989), Watts and Strogatz (1998), Barabási (2003, 2005), and Bray (2003).

some individual members who possess extensive links to addresses outside of the local cluster these clusters open up towards macrosocial environments.[30] From this coupling of local clusters with a certain number of external linkages derives the special capability of small worlds in which even if there is a huge number of members each individual member can be connected to any other member in a small number (around five to six) of steps. From this results the surprise that one can approach precise addresses in distant regions of the social world and that one can do it in fewer steps than one would have surmised.

Regarding world society such an approach towards the network analysis of small worlds does not imply that world society is *one* small world. Such a reductive hypothesis would not allow an adequate picture of the internal and functional differentiation of world society. Instead world society probably consists of a multiplicity of such small worlds (e.g., function systems and their subsystems, the Internet, etc.). Each of these small worlds presumably has millions or even billions of elements (e.g., inclusion addresses, Web sites).[31] Regarding the interrelations of these small worlds among one another one should make use of sociological systems theory. Small worlds will then be analyzed as autopoietic systems that can only irritate one another. Furthermore one will look for other types of interference and for structural couplings among small worlds.[32]

Epistemic Communities and the Globalization of Knowledge

Organizations and networks have to be distinguished from epistemic communities. Epistemic communities are based on strong cognitive and normative commitments, something that organizations do not need as they are based on membership rules and on organizational goals, and something that networks cannot achieve as they often consist of informal and weak ties and are too fluid for consolidating strong commitments. Epistemic communities were again to be observed in the history of European society for a number of centuries. The most important types since late medieval Europe were professional communities such as clerics, medical doctors, and lawyers, and secondly scientific and disciplinary

---

[30] The term *scale-free* means that the network cannot be characterized by a modal number of ties typical for most members; instead there are many members with only a few (local) ties and few members distinguishing themselves by extensive linkages with even far-flung regions of the social world. These few members are the "hubs" of the respective small world.
[31] Cf. McCue (2002) who makes use of the concept of sampling in characterizing the selectivity constitutive of small worlds. Obviously this approach is another way of making allowance for functional differentiation.
[32] *Structural coupling* is again a term from systems theory which takes into account the closure of systems towards one another but points to the possibility that (autonomous) structure formation in a system is influenced by the permanent proximity of the structures of an environmental system. Cf. Luhmann (1993, Ch. 10).

communities such as physicists and philologists which only in 19th-century society were clearly separated from professional communities.[33]

Often epistemic communities are strongly embedded into the structural requirements of a specific function system. Sometimes they are directed by contravening values. A very interesting contemporary example that illustrates the originality of epistemic communities as an Eigenstructures of world society is the global community of Linux developers. In the case of this community it is obvious that it can neither be conceived as an organization nor as a network. Furthermore we have here a case in which the autonomy of the epistemic community towards a specific function system (the economy) is easily seen. The community mainly consists of software developers who in their day job work for organizations in the economy.[34] On the other hand they try to develop a product that is understood as a public good, the core of which one therefore tries to withdraw from any possibilities of private appropriation. That is, the commitment to Linux is primarily meant to block out any possibilities of private economic usage, and a further observation shows that there is no other function system either which guides this epistemic community. This points to the autonomy of this knowledge system towards the imperatives of all the function systems.

The global inclusion of competent and interested experts into the respective epistemic community goes without saying in the case of Linux and other epistemic communities. And this kind of epistemic community is completely independent of the cultural imperatives of the traditional regional cultures of the world. Epistemic communities therefore well illustrate that tendency in present-day global society which motivates observers to speak of a knowledge society. By this is meant that in a number of different domains of communication there arise global communities of experts that govern relevant forms of knowledge which are no longer necessarily scientific or academic forms of knowledge. That is, the knowledge basis of world society is to be seen in the orthogonality of knowledge itself towards the principle of functional differentiation.[35] Nearly in all function systems important forms of knowledge are to be observed today and never again will one of the function systems be able to claim a societal primacy for the production of knowledge. The epistemic community is insofar that form of societal structure formation which at its beginnings in the European Middle Ages was limited to the small number of knowledge systems that gave rise to autonomous professions. Epistemic communities rarely occurred as systematic knowledge was restricted to small domains of societal activity. But in present-day society the

---

[33] On this separation see Stichweh (1994a, esp. Part III), and cf. Haskell (1984b), especially the essay by Haskell himself on the disinterestedness of professional communities (Haskell, 1984a).

[34] In the first years it was characteristic that in their day jobs they could not do any work on Linux (see Gomes, 1999). This has changed because organizations such as IBM massively invest in Linux. On recent transformations in the Linux community, occasioned among others by patent disputes, see Lohr (2004).

[35] Cf. on this hypothesis Stichweh (2004) and Stichweh (2005c).

epistemic community functions as that form of structure formation which is the best representation of the pluralization and diversification of knowledge in the process of the emergence of world society.

World Events as Spatiotemporal Representations of World Society

The world event is our next candidate on the list of significant forms of structure formation that function as Eigenstructures of world society. A decisive aspect of its relevance distinguishing it from the other Eigenstructures is the reflexive constitution of world by world events. That is, world events include descriptions and representations of the world and of world society and then they identify a role for themselves via these reflexive representations.

At least two types of world events have to be distinguished. The first type consists of those events that are post hoc identified as world events. Nobody ever plans these events. Only after they have happened historians and other observers retrospectively attribute to them the character of a world historical event. The French Revolution is an apt example for this kind of world event. This example illustrates at the same time that the identification of something as an event is an artifact of the respective observers who reduce a long-time process to which a kind of directionality cannot necessarily be ascribed to one single historical moment to which they attribute a dramatic historical importance.

But it is not this type of retrospectively identified world historical event that deserves closer attention in our context. Much more important for us are planned world events that are tied to a specific place and a specified time. That is, they show clearly demarcated spatial and temporal boundaries. Normally they take a few days or at most a few weeks. Often these events are repeated in a certain cycle with fixed intervals, and this happens either at changing or at permanently fixed places. They ensure their status as world events by specializing in a specific subject and by recruiting a global circle of participants relevant for the subject in which they specialize. Besides this globally recruited circle of active participants[36] many world events address a global public of (passive) observers most of whom are attained via mass media. This public consists of consumers of the performances of the active participants who are engaged in the system in achievement roles.[37] Even in the production of such a planned world event the reflexive identification of world is very important. The events ascribe to themselves world significance—and they choose names that give an expression to this claim—and they continuously try to validate this by the way the events are organized.

---

[36] It is optimal if this circle of participants includes everyone who bears a global reputation in the subject matter in question.

[37] On the distinction of "achievement roles" and "public roles" cf. Stichweh (2005d) and cf. Nadel (1957) and Luhmann (1981).

Presumably the World Exhibitions that have regularly taken place since 1851 were historically the first example for the second type of world event just described in abstract terms. Looking at the world exhibitions in the 19th and in the early 20th centuries there is easily to be seen an achievement that the world exhibitions of the last few decades did not succeed to reproduce. At the early world exhibitions the elites of the different function systems of modern society— politics, science, the economy—really met one another. They had not been able to do this before and this experience made the concept of worldwide interrelations available to them in an unforeseen way. Since 1896 the Olympic Games were added as a second successful kind of planned world event. Until today they have been unsurpassed in their importance for the differentiation of sports as a 20th-century function system of its own. In the following decades of the 20th century new examples of world events were invented: summit conferences, world conferences in every functional domain, world championships, trade fairs, the global tours of world stars from different domains (rock stars, the pope, etc.)[38], and finally the most recent invention in the catalogue of world events: the terrorist world event which is known to us at least since September 11, 2001.[39] The basic structural feature of all these world events is always the same: unification of the world in concentrating performers and observers on one worldwide response focus.[40] And it is easily seen that the enormous pluralization and diversification of world events since the invention of this structural form only 150 years ago follows the main lines of functional differentiation of world society. From this derives the decline of the world exhibitions that invented the form but today can no longer take account of the global fact of functional differentiation.

Markets as Self-Similar Social Structures

One may be surprised to find the market on a list of the structures specific to world society. To make this plausible one needs a sociological concept of the market and this has to be a sufficiently abstract concept that thanks to this abstractness is not immediately restricted to economic contexts. One finds a good example of such an abstract concept of markets in Harrison White's metaphor of the market as a mirror in which the participants of a market observe one another reciprocally.[41] This seems to be a remarkable insight that uncovers the market as a self-contained way of structure formation in society. It is not based on ties (as in networks) or on norms and rules (as in organizations) or on the value commitments characteristic of epistemic communities. Instead it only needs the incessant mutual observations of all the participants in a market and the operational consequences of these

---

[38] In this case the whole tour with its spatially and temporally distributed performances functions as one world event. One even has a "never ending tour" (Bob Dylan since 1988).
[39] Cf. Stichweh (2005b).
[40] The concept of response focus was invented by Erving Goffman (Goffman, 1983).
[41] White (1981).

observations. The commonality of one market then is a presupposition made by these observations. Harrison White furthermore adds the mathematical concept of self-similarity which means an independence of the basic properties of a market from the order of magnitude on which a market operates.[42] That is, very small, local social systems and seemingly very big, global systems do not differ from each other as long as both of them are constituted as markets.[43] This indifference of constitutive properties of a system towards the order of magnitude or level of social reality on which the system operates is once more a potent force in globalization processes. In such self-similar systems you may easily be able to transit from local to global levels and then go back to a local set of relevancies.

Further Forms of Structure Formation in World Society

The list of Eigenstructures can be prolonged and it has to remain an open list as research on this subject is only just beginning and the further history of world society obviously cannot be foreseen. I only mention some candidates. There is first of all the *World War* as a new form of military conflict that first arose in 1914 from a conflict which all participants intended and began as a regional event. A world war implies a polarization of the world along the conflict lines that motivate ever more states to enter into this conflict in which they perhaps were not as much interested in the beginning.

Furthermore one may think of the *World Public Sphere* which is an addressee of communications one can invent as an addressee as soon as global mass media are available. By postulating and addressing such a world public sphere one discloses the reach one wants to give to one's own communications.[44]

Finally, one could mention the *World City*, a hypothesis which is to be found in many variants. In a first variant, which is close to the typical self-observations of urban and metropolitan settings, the main point is that everything which happens in a (world) city has to be conceived and evaluated from the point of view of its world-relevance or cosmopolitan relevance. That is, there is always the expectation of the self-transcendence of the local towards world-relevance. World cities that observe themselves from this kind of perspective are probably the best places for the organization of world events. Whereas world events are primarily limited in a temporal sense, the world city always functions as a spatially bounded representation of world society.

---

[42] Some scattered but interesting remarks on self-similarity can be found in White (1992), especially Ch. 1.

[43] One implication seems to be that all these markets have a characteristic median number of participants—perhaps around six to eight—which may point to inherent oligopolistic tendencies on markets. Another relevant distinction is proposed by Ronald S. Burt: on markets one either establishes oneself as a "player" or one retreats into the "scenery" (Burt, 1992). Perhaps this can explain oligopoly.

[44] Cf. Stichweh (2003).

There is at least a second significant variant of the idea of a world city. This new variant does not look to self-observations and self-descriptions of urban settings. Instead it analyzes world cities as places of the spatial concentration of the communicative centers of function systems. In a further regard it then investigates the transnational interconnectedness of these centers as a kind of condensation of world society.[45] This hypothesis favors the classical urban centers of cities such as New York and Tokyo. One can doubt that this is still adequate today; there frequently arise communicative centers in function systems (e.g., Santa Clara County in California which is Silicon Valley) that are not connected to classical urban centers. For world society it may be a more representative statement that it nearly exclusively consists of quasi-urban spaces of an infinite variety[46] and that in relation to this the remaining nonurban spaces (rural spaces, the high mountains) are becoming peripheries of society, unless they are claimed by tourism. It will be very interesting to investigate how these new, quasi-urban spaces[47] reflect the concept of the world and to see if they acquire the self-understanding and the organizational capacities to become a place for the organization of world events.

The Delocalization of Diversity

The catalogue of Eigenstructures of world society presented in this chapter obviously is a provisional and hypothetical one. All the cases of structure formation mentioned should be a subject of empirical, historical, and conceptual research. From this research may result a picture that shows how these Eigenstructures are related towards world society via reciprocal intensification. They become ever more prominent in the history of world society, and on the other hand world society can only arise together with their progressive articulation. This makes it plausible that the global social system does not at all eliminate the regional cultures of the world via homogenizing tendencies. Instead it superimposes new levels of structure formation on traditional and as such regional (national, local) social structures. These new levels of structure formation push back—but they do not eliminate—the informational relevance of regional cultures and they substitute for them new sources of diversity.

Perhaps the most important insight derived from this is that the synonymy of diversity and locality which is to be observed as an implicit or explicit presupposition in most present-day globalization literature is not valid at all. Local contexts of the production of social structure are not the guarantor of social and cultural diversity. Instead all the forms of structure formation we introduced into our discussion are producers of diversity (e.g., the differentiation of function systems, the multiplication of organizations, the multiple sampling of the world by

---

[45] Sassen (1994) and Sassen (2001).

[46] Cf. on this with the apt title *Stadtland Schweiz*, Eisinger and Schneider eds. (2003).

[47] See very interesting "edge cities," by Garreau (1991) and more general on cities and globalization, Stichweh (2005e).

small-world networks, the pluralization of epistemic communities, the functional differentiation of world events, the multilevel structure of markets, etc.). In all these cases of newly arising processes of production of diversity one will never experience the diversity to be observed as a local phenomenon. All those things that are still legitimately called "local" as well as the repetitiveness of "everyday life"[48] as well as certain features of "interaction systems"[49] may possibly be rather homogeneous phenomena. But all the Eigenstructures of world society obviously are production machines of nonlocal diversity.

References

Abbott, A. (1981). Status and status strain in the professions. *American Journal of Sociology* 86: 819–835.

Baedeker, H. (1999). Lokalität und Translokalität. Vom Mythos des Transports. *Soziale Systeme* 5, no. 2: 363–384.

Barabási, A. L. (2003). *Linked. How Everything Is Connected to Everything Else and What It Means for Business, Science and Everyday Life*. New York: Plume.

—— (2005). Network theory – The emergence of the creative enterprise. *Science* 308, no. 5722: 639–641.

Barnes, J. A. (1954). Class and committees in a Norwegian island parish. *Human Relations* 7: 39–58.

Boli, J., & Thomas, G. M. (1997). World culture in the world polity: A century of international non-governmental organization. *American Sociological Review* 62, no. 2: 171–190.

Bray, D. (2003). Molecular networks: The top-down view. *Science* 301: 1864–1865.

Burt, R. S. (1992). *Structural Holes. The Social Structure of Competition*. Cambridge, MA: Harvard University Press.

Coleman, J. S. (1990). *Foundations of Social Theory*. Cambridge, MA: Harvard University Press.

Connolly, B., & Anderson, R. (1988). *First Contact: New Guinea's Highlanders Encounter the Outside World*. London: Penguin.

Das, G. (1993, March–April). Local memoirs of a global manager. *Harvard Business Review* 71, no. 2: 38–47.

Del Vecchio,V. J., & Trigg, M. (2000). What the next Microsoft will look like. Available from http://www.fool.com/news/2000/msft001205.htm.

Eisenstadt, S. N. (2000). *Die Vielfalt der Moderne*. Weilerswist: Velbrück.

Eisinger, A., & Schneider, M. (Eds.) (2003). *Stadtland Schweiz. Untersuchungen und Fallstudien zur räumlichen Struktur und Entwicklung in der Schweiz*. Basel: Birkhäuser.

Friedman, J. (1994). *Cultural Identity and Global Process*. London: Sage.

Garreau, J. (1991). *Edge City: Life on the New Frontier*. New York, London, Toronto, Sydney, Auckland: Doubleday.

Goffman, E. (1983). The interaction order. *American Sociological Review* 48, no. 1: 1–17.

---

[48] Cf. Klüver (1988).
[49] In Goffman's terms "forms of face-to-face life are worn smooth by constant repetition" (Goffman, 1983: p. 9).

Gomes, L. (1999). Puffins take H-P on alien mission to build on beloved Linux system. *The Wall Street Journal Europe* 19, no. 3: 4.

Granovetter, M. (1983). The strength of weak ties: A network theory revisited. *Sociological Theory* 1: 203–233.

——(1985). Economic action and social structure: The problem of embeddedness. *American Journal of Sociology* 91: 481–510.

Haskell, T. L. (1984a). Professionalism versus capitalism: R. H. Tawney, Emile Durkheim, and C. S. Peirce on the disinterestedness of professional communities. In T. L Haskell (Ed.), *The Authority of Experts – Studies in History and Theory*. Bloomington: Indiana University Press, pp. 180–225.

Haskell, T. L. (Ed.) (1984b). *The Authority of Experts – Studies in History and Theory*. Bloomington: Indiana University Press.

Huntington, S. P. (1997). *Der Kampf der Kulturen. The clash of civilizations. Die Neugestaltung der Weltpolitik im 21. Jahrhundert*. München: Europaverlag.

Klüver, J. (1988). *Die Konstruktion der sozialen Realität Wissenschaft: Alltag und System*. Braunschweig/Wiesbaden: Vieweg.

Kochen, M. (1989). *The Small World*. Norwood, NJ: Ablex.

Kogut, B., & Zander, U. (1993). Knowledge of the firm and the evolutionary theory of the multinational corporation. *Journal of International Business Studies* 24, no. 4: 625–645.

Laumann, E. O. (1989). Monitoring the AIDS epidemic in the United States: A network approach. *Science* 244: 1186–1189.

Lohr, S. (2004). R.I.P.: The counterculture aura of Linux. *The New York Times*, 25.5.

Luhmann, N. (1981). *Politische Theorie im Wohlfahrtsstaat*. München Wien: Günter Olzog. Available from: http://www.nytimes.com/2004/05/25/technology/25linux.html?ei=5007& en=6b641915e.

——(1984). *Soziale Systeme: Grundriß einer allgemeinen Theorie*. Frankfurt a.M.: Suhrkamp.

——(1986). Distinctions directrices: Über Codierung von Semantiken und systemen. In F. Neidhardt (Ed.), *Kultur und Gesellschaft. Sonderheft 27 der KZfSS*. Opladen: Westdeutscher Verlag, pp. 145–161.

——(1993). *Das Recht der Gesellschaft*. Frankfurt a.M.: Suhrkamp.

——(1997). *Die Gesellschaft der Gesellschaft*. Vol. 1–2. Frankfurt a.M.: Suhrkamp.

McCue, B. (2002). Another view of the "small world". *Social Networks* 24: 121–133.

Meier, J. (2000). *"... usque ad ultimum terrae" – Die Jesuiten und die transkontinentale Ausbreitung des Christentums 1540–1773. (Studien zur Außereuropäischen Christentumsgeschichte: Asien, Afrika, Lateinamerika, Band 3)*. Göttingen: Vandenhoeck und Ruprecht.

Nadel, S. F. (1957). *The Theory of Social Structure*. London: Cohen & West.

——(1961a). An outline of the social system. In T. Parsons., E. Shils., K. D. Naegele., J. R. Pitts (Eds.), *Theories of Society*. Glencoe, II: Free Press, pp. 30–79.

Parsons, T. (1961b). Order and community in the international social system. In J. N. Rosenau (Ed.), *International Politics and Foreign Policy*. Glencoe, II: Free Press, pp. 120–129.

——(1966). *Societies: Evolutionary and Comparative Perspectives*. Englewood Cliffs, NJ: Prentice Hall.

——(1971). *The System of Modern Societies*. Englewood Cliffs, NJ.: Prentice Hall.

Ritzer, G. (1993). *The McDonaldization of Society: An Investigation into the Changing Character of Contemporary Social Life*. Thousand Oaks, CA: Pine Forge.

——(Ed). (2002). *McDonaldization: The Reader*. Thousand Oaks, CA: Pine Forge.

Sassen, S. (1994). *Cities in a World Economy*. Thousand Oaks, London, New Delhi: Pine Forge.

——— (2001). *The Global City. New York, London, Tokyo*. 2nd Ed. Princeton, NJ, Oxford: Princeton University Press.

Scaperlanda, A. (1993). Multinational enterprises and the global market. *Journal of Economic Issues* 27, no. 2: 605–616.

Stichweh, R. (1991). *Der frühmoderne Staat und die europäische Universität. Zur Interaktion von Politik und Erziehungssystem im Prozeß ihrer Ausdifferenzierung (16.–18. Jahrhundert)*. Frankfurt a.M.: Suhrkamp.

——— (1994a). *Wissenschaft, Universität, Professionen: Soziologische Analysen*. Frankfurt a.M.: Suhrkamp.

——— (1994b). Soziologische Differenzierungstheorie als Theorie Sozialen Wandels. In Miethke, Jürgen and Klaus Schreiner (Eds.) *Sozialer Wandel im Mittelalter. Wahrnehmungsformen, Erklärungsmuster, Regelungsmechanismen*, Sigmaringen: Jan Thorbecke, pp. 29–43.

——— (2003). The genesis of a global public sphere. *Development* 46: 26–29.

——— (2004). Wissensgesellschaft und Wissenschaftssystem. *Schweizerische Zeitschrift für Soziologie* 30, no. 2: 147–165.

——— (2005a). Das Konzept der Weltgesellschaft: Genese und Strukturbildung eines globalen Gesellschaftssystems. In Schulte, Martin and Rudolf Stichweh (Eds.), *Weltrecht*. Berlin: Duncker & Humblot.

——— (2005b). Der 11. September 2001 und seine Folgen für die Entwicklung der Weltgesellschaft: Zur Genese des terroristischen Weltereignisses. In Bonacker, Thorsten and Christoph Weller (Eds.), *Konflikte der Weltgesellschaft* Akteure-Strukturen-Dynamiken. Frankfurt a.M.: Campus.

——— (2005c). Die Universität in der Wissensgesellschaft. Ms. Luzern.

——— (2005d). *Inklusion und Exklusion. Studien zur Gesellschaftstheorie*. Bielefeld: Transcript.

——— (2005e). Zentrum/Peripherie-Differenzierungen und die Soziologie der Stadt: Europäische und globale Entwicklungen. In Lenger, Friedrich and Klaus Tenfelde (Eds.), *Die europäische Stadt im 20. Jahrhundert. Wahrnehmung – Entwicklung – Erosion*. Köln, Weimar: Böhlau.

——— (2005f). Zum Gesellschaftsbegriff der Systemtheorie: Parsons und Luhmann und die Hypothese der Weltgesellschaft In: B. Heintz et al. (Eds.), Weltgesellschaft. Theoretische Zugänge and empirische Problemlagen (Zeitschrift für Soziologie. Special issue). Stuttgart: Lucius & Lucius, pp. 174–185.

Wallerstein, I. (1974). *The Modern World-System: Capitalist Agriculture and the Origins of the European World-Economy in the Sixteenth Century*. New York: Academic.

Watts, D. J., & Strogatz, S. H. (1998). Collective dynamics of small-world networks. *Nature* 393: 440–442.

Wellman, B. (1992). Men in networks: Private communities, domestic friendships. In P. M. Nardi (Ed.), *Men's Friendships*. Newbury Park: Sage, pp. 74–114.

White, H. C. (1981). Where do markets come from? *American Journal of Sociology* 87: 517–547.

——— (1992). *Identity and Control: A Structural Theory of Social Action*. Princeton, NJ: Princeton University Press.

6
Global Complexities

JOHN URRY

The Growth of The Global

The 1990s has seen the growth of the Internet with a take-up faster than any previous technology, with one billion users soon worldwide. The dealings of foreign exchange that occur each day are worth $1.4 trillion, sixty times greater than the amount of world trade. Communications "on the move" are being transformed with new mobile phones more common in the world than conventional landline phones. There are over 700 million legal international journeys each year, a figure soon to pass 1 billion. Three million people across the world receive the same total income as the richest 300. Globally branded companies have budgets greater than most individual countries. Images of the blue earth from space or the golden arches of McDonald's are ubiquitous upon the billion TV sets across the world. New technologies are producing "global times" with distances between places and peoples "dematerializing" it seems.

Various commentators have tried to understand these global changes. Giddens described modern social life as being like a driverless out-of-control "juggernaut" (1990), Bauman describes speeded-up "liquid modernity" (2000), Castells elaborates the growth of an "internet galaxy" (2001), Hardt and Negri suggest that nation-state sovereignty is being replaced by a single system of power, of "empire" (2000), Rifkin analyzes the implications of the "new physics" for the study of capitalist property relations (2000: 191–193), and over one hundred authors a year elaborate the "globalization" of economic, social, and political life.

These debates transform existing controversies, such as the relative significance of social structure and human agency. However, there is no single and agreed-upon thesis that deals with this new global order/disorder. I suggest there are five main theories, based respectively upon the concepts of structure, flow, ideology, performance, and complexity (see Urry, 2003: Ch. 1).

It is the last of these that concerns me here because the systemic features of globalization are not yet appropriately theorized. Globalization is often taken to be both cause and effect. It is worth examining whether the complexity sciences may provide concepts and methods that illuminate globalization as a series of co-evolving self-organizing systems (see Capra, 2002).

The U.S.-based *Gulbenkian Commission on the Restructuring of the Social Sciences*, chaired by Wallerstein and including nonlinear scientist Prigogine, advocates breaking down the division between "natural" and "social" science through seeing both as characterized by "complexity" (Wallerstein, 1996). The Commission recommends that scientific analysis "based on the dynamics of non-equilibria, with its emphasis on multiple futures, bifurcation and choice, historical dependence, and . . . intrinsic and inherent uncertainty" should be the model for the social sciences and this undermines any clear-cut division between social and natural science (Wallerstein, 1996: 61, 63).

Strangely this Commission is silent on the study of globalization although the global level is surely characterized by complex processes that are simultaneously social and natural. Indeed most significant phenomena that the so-called social sciences now deal with are hybrids with no purified sets of the physical or the social. These hybrids include health systems, technologies, global brands, the environment, the Internet, automobility, extreme weather events, global violence, and so on.

Complexity and Social Theory

I begin briefly with structure and agency (Giddens, 1984). Giddens developed the "duality of structure" in order to overcome the limitations of the structure–agency divide. Important here is the recursive character of social life. He examines the temporal processes by which "structures" are both drawn on to generate actions, and then are the unintended outcome of countless recursive actions by knowledgeable agents. So rather than a dualism between structure and agency there is seen to be a "duality" in which structure and agency are bound up together and co-evolve over time. This structurationism breaks with linear notions because it sees the rules and resources of systems both being drawn upon by knowledgeable agents and then feeding back through actions to reproduce system rules and resources. There are not fixed and separate entities that happen to possess variable characteristics (see critique in Abbott, 2000).

However, Giddens insufficiently examines the "complex" and "systemic" character of these structure–agency processes that are better understood through "iteration" rather than "recurrence." Because of iteration the tiniest of "local" changes can generate, over billions of repeated actions, unexpected, unpredictable, and chaotic outcomes, sometimes the opposite of what agents thought they were trying to bring about. Events are not "forgotten" within systems. Such complex changes have little to do with agents seeking to change their world but stem from how agents respond to local configurations. Such agents may conduct what appear to be the same actions involving a constant imitation of the actions of others. But because of what can be tiny adaptations of other agents, iteration can result over time in transformations in even large-scale structures. Iteration can produce through dynamic emergence, nonlinear changes and the sudden branching of large structures. Change can occur without a determining "agency."

The character of such iterative social interactions have been likened to walking through a maze whose walls rearrange themselves as each new step is taken (Gleick, 1988: 24). And as one walks new steps have to be made in order to adjust to the changing location of the surrounding walls. Complexity investigates systems capable of adapting and evolving, each of which is self-organizing over time (Prigogine, 1997: 35).

There are various characteristics of what we can call a "complex" relationality (see Dillon, 2000). First, the very large number of elements makes systems unpredictable and lacking finalized "order." Systems are thus seen as "on the edge of chaos." Order and chaos are in a kind of balance where the components are neither fully locked into place but yet do not dissolve into anarchy. Chaos is not complete anarchic randomness but there is an "orderly disorder" present within all such dynamic systems.

Second, these systems interact dissipatively with their environment, islands of order in a sea of disorder. Any such system operates under conditions that are far from equilibrium, partly because each element only responds to "local" sources. Interactions are complex, rich, and nonlinear. Elements at one location have very significant time–space effects elsewhere through multiple connections and trajectories (see Cilliers, 1998).

Third, there are multiple negative and, more significantly, positive feedback loops with patterns of increasing returns and path-dependency (see Arthur, 1994). The notions of path dependence emphasizes the importance over time of the ordering of events or processes. (Mahoney, 2000: 536). Causation can flow from contingent minor events to hugely powerful general processes that through increasing returns get locked in over lengthy periods of time; "history matters" in the processes of path-dependent development (North, 1990: 100). Systems possess a history that irreversibly evolves and where past events are never "forgotten."

Fourth, points of bifurcation may be reached when the system branches. If a system passes a particular threshold with minor changes in the controlling variables, switches may occur and the emergent properties turn over. Thus a liquid turns or tips into a gas; relatively warm weather suddenly transforms into an ice age (Byrne, 1998: 23). Nicolis summarizes how in a nonlinear system: "adding two elementary actions to one another can induce dramatic new effects reflecting the onset of cooperativity between the constituent elements. This can give rise to unexpected structures and events whose properties can be quite different from those of the underlying elementary laws" (1995: 1–2).

Fifth, there is no consistent relationship between cause and effect. Rather relationships between variables can be nonlinear with abrupt switches occurring, so the same "cause" can in specific circumstances produce quite different kinds of effect. "Nonlinear phenomena dominate much more of the inanimate world than we had thought, and they are an essential aspect of the network pattern of living systems" (Capra, 1996: 122). A further consequence of this flowingness of time is that minor changes in the past produce potentially huge effects in the present. Such small events are not "forgotten." Chaos theory in particular rejects the common-sense notion that only large changes in causes produce large changes in effects (Gleick, 1988).

Sixth, the emergence of patterning within any given system stems from co-evolution and mutual adaptation. An emergent complex system is the result of a rich interaction of simple elements that "only respond to the limited information each is presented with" (Cilliers, 1998: 5). Agents act in terms of the local environment but each agent adapts, or co-evolves, to local circumstances "within an environment in which other similar agents are also adapting, so that changes in one agent may have consequences for the environment and thus the success of other agents" (Gilbert, 1995: 148). Each co-evolves, demonstrating a "capability to 'orientate' to macro-level properties" so paradoxically bringing into being certain emergent properties (Gilbert, 1995: 151).

Seventh, thus nothing is fixed forever. Abbott maintains that there is "the possibility for a pattern of actions to occur to put the key in the lock and make a major turning point occur" (Abbott, 2001: 257). Such nonlinear outcomes are generated by systems moving across turning or tipping points. Tipping points involve three notions: that events and phenomena are contagious, that little causes can have big effects, and that changes can happen not in a gradual linear way but dramatically at a moment when the system switches. Gladwell describes the consumption of fax machines or mobile phones, when at a moment every office needs a fax machine or every mobile person needs a mobile. Wealth derives not from scarcity as in conventional economics but from abundance (Gladwell, 2000: 272–273).

Complexity and The Global

In *Global Complexity* (2003) I argue there are two main forms of global hybrids. First there are global networks such as that characterizing McDonald's with a tightly coupled network consisting of complex, enduring, and predictable connections between peoples, objects, and technologies across multiple and distant spaces and times (Murdoch, 1995: 745; Law, 1994: 24). Relative distance is a function of the relations between the components comprising that network. The invariant outcome of a network is delivered across its entirety in ways that often overcome regional boundaries. Things are made close through these networked relations. Such a network of technologies, skills, texts, and brands—a global hybrid—ensures that the same "service" or "product" is delivered in more or less the same way across the entire network. Such products are predictable, calculable, routinized, and standardized. Many "global" enterprises organized through such networked relations, such as McDonald's, American Express, Coca Cola, Microsoft, Sony, Greenpeace, Manchester United, and so on (Ritzer, 1998; Klein, 2000).

Second, there are various global fluids, such as world money, automobility, digitized information, the Internet, social movements, international terrorism, travelling peoples, and so on. Global fluids travel along various scapes but they may escape, rather like white blood corpuscles, through the "wall" into surrounding matter and effect unpredictable consequences upon that matter. Fluids move according to certain novel shapes and temporalities as they break free from the linear, clock-time of existing socioscapes, but they cannot go back spatiotemporally. Such fluids result from people acting upon the basis of local information but where these local actions are, through countless iteration, captured, moved, represented, marketed, and generalized, often affecting upon hugely distant places and peoples. Such fluids demonstrate no clear point of departure, just deterritorialized movement, at certain speeds and at different levels of viscosity with no necessary end-state or purpose. This means that such fluids create over time their own context for action rather than being seen as "caused" by such contexts.

One such global fluid is the Internet, in a kind of way invented in 1990 and which has developed into an irreversible autopoeitic system, especially following the "chance" invention of the first Web browser in 1993/4. Plant argues that:

> No central hub or command structure has constructed it. . . . It has installed none of the hardware on which it works, simply hitching a largely free ride on existing computers, networks, switching systems, telephone lines. This was one of the first systems to present itself as a multiplicitous, bottom–up, piecemeal, self-organizing network which . . . could be seen to be emerging without any centralized control (1997: 49).

The Web possesses what Morse describes as an "elegant, non-hierarchical rhizomatic global structure," based upon lateral, horizontal hypertext links that render the boundaries between objects as fluid (1998: 187).

Thus global complexity is comprised of many different "islands of order" within a sea of disorder. There are global networks and global fluids; and there are also national societies, diasporas, "supranational states," global religions or "civilizations," international organizations, international meetings, NGOs, and cross-border regions (Habermas, 2001: Ch. 4). Any single society thus finds diverse self-organizing networks, fluids, and "polities" seeking to striate its space. States have shifted away from governing a relatively fixed and clear-cut national population resident within its territory and constituting a clear and relatively unchanging community of fate, what I used to call "organized capitalism" (Urry, 2000: Ch. 8). Shifts towards global networks and fluids transform the space

beyond each state that they have to striate. Habermas argues " 'globalization' con-
jures up images of overflowing rivers, washing away all the frontier checkpoints
and controls, and ultimately the bulwark of the nation itself" (2001: 67). States thus
act as a legal, economic, and social regulator, or gamekeeper, of practices and
mobilities that are predominantly provided by, or generated through, the often
unpredictable consequences of many other entities. Social regulation is both
necessitated by, and is made possible through, new computer-based forms of
information gathering, retrieval, and dissemination (Power, 1994).

Thus the intensely fluid and turbulent nature of global complexity means that
"the role of the state is actually becoming more, rather than less, important in
developing the productive powers of territory and in producing new spatial configurations" as with the U.S.-led global coalition against terrorism (Swyngedouw,
1992: 431). There has been an "enormous expansion of nation-state structures,
bureaucracies, agenda, revenues and regulatory capacities since World War II,"
in order to deal with multiple and overlapping global fluids that move across borders through time–space in dizzying, discrepant, and transmutating form (from
students to tourists to terrorists). States are not converging in a uniform powerless
direction but becoming more diverse, such as the United States, the European
Union, and the Taliban (Weiss, 1998: Ch. 7).

Power and Complexity

Much thinking about power in the social sciences has been focused upon the
interrelationships between agents or subjects. Power is conceptualized as an
attribute of agents, through observing two or more human agents and seeing in
what ways, and to what degree, the actions of one are influenced by those of the
other.

However, complexity transcends the division between free will and determinism and hence between agency and structure. It transcends the characteristic way
in which power has been located, as agency. So what then would constitute a
complexity approach to power? Power would not be regarded as a thing or a possession. It is something that flows or runs and it has become increasingly
detached from specific territory or space and especially noncontiguous. Bauman
outlines a "post-panoptical" conception of power (2000: 10–14). Power is not
necessarily exercised through real co-presence as one agent gets another to do
what the other would otherwise not have done through interpersonal threat,
force, or persuasion. But also power no longer necessarily involves the imagined
co-presence of "others" within a literal or simulated panopticon.

Rather the prime technique now of power is that of "escape, slippage, elision
and avoidance," the "end of the era of mutual engagement" (Bauman, 2000: 11).
The new global elite, according to Bauman, can rule: "without burdening itself
with the chores of administration, management, welfare concerns," even involving
developing disposable slave-owning without commitment (2000: 13; see Bales,
1999, on "disposable peoples"). Travelling light is the new asset of power. Power

is all about speed, lightness, distance, the weightless, the global, and this is true both of elites and of those resisting elites, such as antiglobalization protestors or bioterrorists. Power runs in and especially jumps across different global networks and fluids. Power is hybridized and is not purely social but material.

First, such power is enormously technologized with the development of vision machines, tens of thousands of satellites, bugs, listening devices, microscopic cameras, CCTV, the Internet, and new computerized means of sharing information (see Lyon, 2001, on the post-September 11th surveillance effects). Second, everyday life also increasingly involves speed, lightness, and distance, with the capacity to move information, images, and bodies relatively unnoticed through extensively surveilled societies (such bodies transmutating from student to tourist to terrorist back to student and so on). Resistance to power is also mediated and highly fluidlike. Third, such mediated power functions like an attractor. Within the range of possibilities, the trajectories of systems are drawn to "attractors" that exert a gravity effect upon those relations that come within its ambit. The global media exert such a gravity effect, with almost the whole world both "watching" and being seduced into being "watched" (as with the videos of Bin Laden).

And fourth, such power is mobile, performed, and unbounded. This is its strength and its vulnerability. Attempted ordering by the most powerful can result in complex unintended effects that take the system away from equilibrium. In such unpredictable and irreversible transformations, mediated power is like sand that may stay resolutely in place forming clear and bounded shapes with a distinct spatial topology (waiting, say to be arrested or bombed) or it may turn into an avalanche and race away sweeping much else in its wake. And correspondingly, challenging that power is also hard because bombing certain nodes of power cannot destroy the "lines of flight" that simply flow like "packets" in email systems and follow different routings and get around destroyed nodes.

Empires and Multitudes

Many argue that there is a more "liquid" character to contemporary global relations, with the dematerializing of information and the unpredictable and sped-up character of networked and fluid relationships. Key, it seems, to examining the global are the wide array of global networks and global fluids that occupy complex, contradictory, and irreversible relationships with each other.

Why does the increasingly "liquid" character of the global world not mean that relationality is unproblematic? Why does not "liquid modernity" generate mobile solutions to system "failings"? The answer is that those mobilities connecting the local and global always depend upon multiple stabilities. Deterritorialization presupposes reterritorialization. The complex character of such systems stems from the multiple time–space fixities or moorings that enable the fluidities of liquid modernity to be realized. Thus "mobile machines," such as mobile phones, cars, aircraft, trains, and computer connections, all presume overlapping and varied time–space immobilities (see Graham & Marvin, 2001).

This relationality between mobilities and immobilities is a typical complexity characteristic. There is no linear increase in fluidity without extensive systems of immobilities. Thus the so far most powerful mobile machine, the airplane, requires the largest and most extensive immobility, of the airport-city employing tens of thousands of workers (see Pascoe, 2001, on the complex nature of such multiple "airspaces"). It is this that produces the strange ways in which chaos and order are combined in global systems.

I illustrate this through a rereading of *Empire*. Hardt and Negri argue that the concept of "empire" or "imperial sovereignty" has replaced that of nation-state sovereignty or "society". By "empire" they mean the emergence of a dynamic and flexible systemic structure articulated horizontally across the globe, a kind of "governance without government" that sweeps together all actors within the order as a whole (Hardt & Negri, 2000: 13–4). Empire is the sovereign power, a "smooth world", the single logic of rule that now governs the world. This new sovereignty is deterritorialized and decentered, with a merging and blending of a "global rainbow" (Hardt & Negri, 2000: xiii). There is no center of power and no fixed boundaries or barriers. The "age of globalization is the age of universal contagion" (Hardt & Negri, 2000: 136). "Empire" crucially generates its opposite, what they describe as "the resistances, struggles and desires of the [mobile] multitude" that constitutes the "other" to empire (Hardt & Negri, 2000: xvi, 398).

What would complexity say about *Empire*? Hardt and Negri do not examine the systemic relations within empire and especially how empire operates in conditions far from equilibrium. Theirs is an undynamic account of self-reproducing global relations. They say, for example, that empire "is emerging today as the center that supports the globalization of productive networks" (2000: 20). Empire here is conceived of almost functionally; it does not sufficiently capture the dynamic properties of global relations that only in part can be characterized as "a sovereign power that governs the world" (Hardt & Negri, 2000: xi). Although Hardt and Negri conceptualize "empire" as decentered and deterritorialized, they do not examine the interdependent fluid global hybrids that both make up and problematize their claim that "there is world order" (2000: 3).

Rather I would argue the concept of "empire" does not characterize global relations as a whole. Empire is an attractor; all societies could be said to be becoming more like empires. Contemporary societies increasingly possess a visible center, with icons of power such as buildings, landscapes, and brands. However, beyond the center there is a spreading of effects outwards with a relative weakness of some borders. And within such empires there are emergent inequalities rather than, as in at least welfare societies, an attempt to create citizenship rights common throughout the territory. In particular, societies are drawn onto, attracted to, the world's stage, showing off their trophies, competing with each other for the best skyline, palaces, galleries, stadia, infrastructures, games, skilled workforce, and so on. And societies as empires seek to avoid mediatized scandal and risk. Societies are endlessly drawn into this attractor. This remakes them as "empires," the United States being the most powerful and dominant of such societal empires currently strutting the world's stage. The United States possesses a number of exceptional centers (New York, Los Angeles, and Washington), many icons of power (Pentagon, Wall Street, Hollywood, ivy league universities, Texan oil wells, Silicon Valley, MOMA), a porosity of certain borders (see Davis, 2000, on the United States's Latinization) and huge "imperial" economic and social inequalities. It is the paradigm case of "society as empire." Thus rather than there being a single "empire," global complexity suggests that each society is drawn into the attractor of "empire".

And each society qua empire produces its opposite, its other, its rebellious multitude. The events of September 11th seem to have unpredictably emerged from one of the very poorest countries in the world, and yet it is said to have irreversibly changed many parameters structuring economic, social, and political life. September 11th demonstrates the complexity of "asymmetric threats," that "wars" are increasingly fought between formally unequal powers with the apparently weak able to inflict massive blows on the apparently powerful (see Gunaratna, 2002). It is almost the secular equivalent of "The first shall be last, and the last shall be first." The mightier is the power of society as empire, the greater the harm that can be inflicted.

Global complexity can thus be seen in the power of the powerless to inflict harm upon the institutions of imperial power, especially those buildings, institutions, and people that symbolize the intense condensation of imperial power. The United States, is the paradigm case of "society as empire." And it is the New York skyline that most graphically symbolizes its imperial power.

Moreover, huge transformations are taking place in the very production of "empire-and-multitude" across the globe. Indeed one effect of global markets is to generate "wild zones" of the increasingly dispossessed. In parts of the former USSR, sub-Saharan Africa, the Balkans, Central America and central Asia are zones are places of absence, of gaps, of lack. Such zones possess weak states with very limited infrastructures, no monopoly of the means of coercion, barely functioning economies often dependent upon commodifying illegal materials, an imploded social structure, and a relatively limited set of connections to the global order.

In analyses of the West, sociospatial inequalities have often been largely invisible. There is a "splintering urbanism" with the invisibility of the "other" taken to extreme lengths in the "gated" cities of North America (Graham & Marvin, 2001). The gates of the "camps" separate out the safe zones from the wild and dangerous zones. But increasingly the time–space edges of the safe and the wild are coming into strange and dangerous new juxtapositions even or perhaps especially, in the West. The flows from the wild zones of people, risks, substances, images, and so on, increasingly slip under, over, and through the safe gates, suddenly and chaotically eliminating the invisibilities that had kept the zones apart. Through money laundering, the drug trade, urban crime, asylum seeking, people smuggling, slave trading, and urban terrorism, the spaces of the wild and the safe are chaotically juxtaposed (what Bauman sometimes refers to as the "boomerang" effect).

In systems of global complexity wild and safe zones have become highly proximate through the curvatures of space–time. There is "time–space compression," not only of the capitalist world but also of the terrorist world. Wild zones are now only a telephone call, an Internet connection, or a plane ride away. Capitalist markets have brought the whole world closer and this is especially and paradoxically true of those bent on its violent destruction and especially on destroying the dominance of the "American empire" within the global order.

I have thus suggested that rather than there being an "Empire" with its multitude, there is a new attractor, societies as empires. Societies across the world are being drawn into developing as empire. And as they are drawn into such an attractor new unstable and unpredictable multitudes arise, seeking to topple those empires and their icons. Societies as empires are developing strange new practices as systems develop to deal with the nonlinear multitudes that are increasingly in their very midst.

Conclusion

John Gray describes the current state of the globe as "an intractably disordered world" (2001). I have tried to show that complexity provides some metaphors, concepts, and theories essential for examining such intractable disorderliness. Relations across that world are complex, rich, and nonlinear, involving multiple negative and, more significantly, positive feedback loops. There are ineluctable patterns of increasing returns and long-term path-dependencies. Such global systems are characterized by unpredictability and irreversibility; they lack finalized "equilibrium" or "order," pools of order that heighten overall disorder. They do not exhibit and sustain unchanging structural stability. Complexity elaborates how there is order and disorder within all physical and social systems. Following Gray we can see how there is a complex world, unpredictable and irreversible, disorderly but not simply anarchic.

In such systems components are irreversibly drawn towards various attractors that exercise a gravity effect. Such components within any system operate under conditions that are far from equilibrium, partly because each responds to local sources of information. But components at one location have substantial time–space effects elsewhere through multiple connections and awesome trajectories. Such systems possess an unpredictable history which then irreversibly evolves and where past events are not forgotten.

Points of bifurcation are reached when the system branches because causes and effects are disproportionate. There are nonlinear relationships between them with the consequence that systems can move quickly and dramatically from one state to another. Systems reach "tipping points" when what seem like stabilities flip over into their apparent opposite (Gladwell, 2000), such as the collapse of the Soviet empire, the astonishing growth of the Internet, the spread of mobile phones, the overnight emergence of global terrorism, the combination of intense mobility and multiple gates/camps, and so on.

References

Abbott, A. (2001). *Time matters*. Chicago: University of Chicago Press.

Arthur, B. (1994). Summary remarks, in G. Cowan, D. Pines, and D. Meltzer (eds.), *Complexity, metaphors, models and reality*. Santa Fe Institute: Studies in the Sciences of Complexity Proceedings, vol. 19.

Bales, K. (1999). *Disposable people*. Berkeley: University of California Press.

Bauman, Z. (2000). *Liquid modernity*. Cambridge: Polity.

Byrne, D. (1998). *Complexity theory and the social sciences*. London: Routledge.

Capra, F. (1996). *The web of life*. London: Harper Collins.

—— (2002). *The hidden connections*. London: Harper Collins.

Castells, M. (2001). *The Internet galaxy*. Oxford: Oxford University Press.

Cilliers, P. (1998). *Complexity and post-modernism*. London: Routledge.

Davis, M. (2000). *Magical urbanism*. London: Verso.

Dillon, M. (2000). Poststructuralism, complexity and poetics, *Theory, Culture and Society*, 17: 1–26.

Giddens, A. (1984). *The Constitution of Society*. Cambridge: Polity.

—— (1990). *The Consequences of Modernity*. Stanford: Stanford University Press.

Gilbert, N. (1995). Emergence in social simulation, in N. Gilbert and R. Conte (eds.), *Artificial Societies*. London: UCL.

Gladwell, M. (2000). *Tipping points: How little things can make a big difference*. Boston: Little, Brown.

Gleick, J. (1988). *Chaos*. London: Sphere.

Graham, S., & Marvin, S. (2001). *Splintering urbanism*. London: Routledge.

Gray, J. (2001). The era of globalization is over, *New Statesman*, 24th September.

Gunaratna, R. (2002). *Inside Al-Qaeda: Global networks of terror*. New York: Columbia University Press.

Habermas, J. (2001). *The postnational constellation*. Cambridge: Polity.

Hardt, M., & Negri, T. (2000). *Empire*. Cambridge, MA: Harvard University Press.

Klein, N. (2000). *No logo*. London: Flamingo.

Law, J. (1994). *Organizing modernity*. Oxford: Basil Blackwell.

Lyon, D. (2001). Surveillance after September 11, *Sociological Research Online*, 6(3).

Mahoney, J. (2000). Path dependence in historical sociology, *Theory and Society*, 29: 507–48.

Morse, M. (1998). *Virtualities*. Bloomington: Indiana University Press.

Murdoch, J. (1995). Actor-networks and the evolution of economic forms: Combining description and explanation in theories of regulation, flexible specialisation, and networks, *Environment and Planning A*, 27: 731–57.

Nicolis, G. (1995). *Introduction to non-linear science*. Cambridge, UK: Cambridge University Press.

North, D. (1990). *Institutions, institutional change and economic performance*. Cambridge, UK: Cambridge University Press.

Pascoe, D. (2001). *Airspaces*. London: Reaktion.

Plant, S. (1997). *Zeros and ones*. London: Fourth Estate.

Power, M. (1994). *The audit explosion*. London: Demos.

Prigogine, I. (1997). *The end of certainty*. New York: Free Press.

Rifkin, J. (2000). *The age of access*. London: Penguin.

Ritzer, G. (1998). *The McDonaldization thesis*. London: Sage.

Swyngedouw, E. (1992). Territorial organization and the space/technology nexus, *Transactions, Institute of British Geographers*, 17: 417–33.

Urry, J. (2000). *Sociology beyond societies*. London: Routledge.
—— (2003). *Global complexity*. Cambridge, UK: Polity.
Wallerstein, I. (1996). *Open the social sciences. Report of the Gulbenkian commission on the restructuring of the social sciences*. Stanford, CA: Stanford University Press.
Weiss, L. (1998). *The myth of the powerless state*. Cambridge, UK: Polity.

Part 2
Economic and Political Processes

7
Trajectories of Trade and Investment Globalization

CHRISTOPHER CHASE-DUNN AND ANDREW JORGENSON

Introduction

Since the 1980s the term "globalization" has become a popular buzzword that has been used to describe allegedly recent and important changes in the world economy. In the received discourse globalization refers to changes in technologies of communication and transportation, increasingly internationalized financial flows and commodity trade, and the transition from national to world markets as the main arena for economic competition. These ostensible changes have been used to justify economic and political decisions such as deregulation and privatization of industries, downsizing and streamlining of work forces, and dismemberment of the welfare services provided by governments. We propose a conceptualization of structural globalization as several interrelated dimensions of the expansion and intensification of interaction networks (Chase-Dunn & Jorgenson, 2003).

Our research examines the actual historical trajectories of two important types of structural globalization. Did the globalized world economy arrive all at once in a rapid and recent transition from national to global economic networks? Or are the processes of international economic integration long-term trends that have been going up for centuries only to be noticed recently because they have reached such a high peak? Or, alternatively, is globalization a cyclical phenomenon in which the world economy alternates between periods of national autarchy followed by periods of international economic integration?

This chapter discusses research that is designed to examine the historical trajectory of structural globalization as an attribute of the whole world-system.

The real trajectories of different kinds of globalization over the last two centuries are knowable only if we gather comparable data over time. Studies of recent decades do not answer the question of the shape of long-term trajectories. Our project improves upon data for the 19th century and splices earlier cruder measures with later, more refined, and complete data series.

The two main objectives of our research are:

To determine the trajectories of trade and investment globalization
To empirically examine the relationship between these and several other world-system variables that have been hypothesized to cause international economic integration

The trajectories of different types of globalization have important implications for our understanding of the processes of development in the modern world-system. In this chapter we present new results on the trajectory of investment globalization.

Both the popular and the academic discourses about globalization contain great confusion and disagreement regarding the meaning and connotations of this contested term. We contend that the scientific study of globalization can move forward by making a clear distinction between globalization as greater integration and interdependence of the world-system, on the one hand, and the political discourses that employ ideas about global integration and competition to justify actions and policies (McMichael, 1996).

Our research will distinguish between:

Globalization as ideology
Globalization as objective structural trends of spatial integration

Our main focus is on different types of structural globalization, but we are also interested in understanding changes in the ideologies that are used to legitimate the actions of the powerful. Giovanni Arrighi is researching the transition from Keynesian theories of national development to the neoliberal "Washington Consensus." Phillip McMichael (1996) describes the emergence of what he calls the "globalization project," a revitalized glorification of market mechanisms as allegedly efficient antidotes to rent seeking and the "vampire state." The "globalization project" emerged with Thatcherism and Reaganism in the 1980s, and has swept around the world as a justification for attacking and dismantling welfare states and labor unions following the demise of the Soviet Union. Although this is an interesting and consequential phenomenon, it is not the main focus of the research here proposed.

Rather, we intend to determine the real temporal trajectories of structural dimensions of global integration over the past 200 years. We understand structural globalization as composed of different interrelated dimensions of expanding and intensifying interaction networks, especially political, economic, and cultural globalization (Chase-Dunn, 1999). We specifically reject the notion that these dimensions constitute completely different aspects of social reality that should be studied separately by different academic disciplines, but we contend that it is useful to distinguish among them in order to understand how they have affected one another (Jorgenson & Kick, 2003).

Our research has already shown that trade globalization is primarily a cyclical phenomenon, although the most recent upsurge has reached a level that is significantly higher than the level reached at earlier peaks (Chase-Dunn, Kawano, & Brewer, 2000). In this chapter we determine the trajectories of investment globalization: the extent to which international capital flows and investments increase (or decrease) in relationship to the size of the world economy.

In the future, we propose to determine the trajectories of political globalization: the degree to which the multicentric international system has moved toward centralization, integration, and hierarchy. The quantification of political globalization will require measures of the relationship between the power and sizes of large and small political and military organizations in the world-system. We propose to operationalize these characteristics of the whole world-system over the past 200 years in order to compare their temporal trajectories with that of trade globalization, and to examine their hypothesized causes.

We define structural globalization as the increasing spatial scale and intensity of interaction networks. Charles Tilly (1995: 1–2) proposes a similar definition of globalization as "an increase in the geographic range of locally consequential social interactions, especially when that increase stretches a significant proportion of all interactions across international or intercontinental limits." If both national level and global networks increase in intensity at the same rate, this approach would not see an increase in the globalization of interaction. Globalization in the structural sense is increasing integration and interdependence. As with other efforts to measure globalization (e.g., Chase-Dunn, Kawano, & Brewer, 2000), the estimation of a global characteristic needs to take account of the changing size of the system as a whole. Of course there are more transnational interactions now than there were in the 19th century. There are also more within-nation interactions because the world population and the world economy have become larger. It is the ratio of these that must be studied.

Human interaction networks have been increasing in scale and intensity for millennia as transportation and communications technologies have made regular trade and interaction over greater distances possible (Chase-Dunn & Hall, 1997). It is obvious that the railroad and the steamship facilitated a massive increase in the spatial scale of interaction networks. Ideally we would like to trace the relative degrees of interaction integration at several levels. Households exchange goods and ideas with other households. Neighborhoods and towns exchange with other neighborhoods and towns, cities with cities and so on. But such a study is not feasible at the present for two reasons: our unit of analysis is the world-system as a whole (meaning all the countries of the world), and we want to examine trends over the past 200 years. It might be possible to examine local and regional inter-action networks for a particular country or for a few core countries in recent decades. But in order to study the whole system over two centuries we must nec-essarily use data on the units that have been the main data-gatherers in this period of human history, the national states.

By this decision we do not mean to imply that national states are the only, or even the most important, actors in the world-system. We recognize the impor-tance of transnational relations emphasized by political scientists 30 years ago (Keohane & Nye, 1970; and more recently by Sklair, 1995, 2001). The world-systems perspective has long pointed out that the interstate system—the system of sovereign national states—is only one institutional structure of the global polit-ical economy. The world-system is composed of individuals, households, towns, cities, regions, firms, classes, states, and other nongovernmental and international organizations. It is not simply a matter of "international relations." The world-system is the whole system, not just relations among states. Transnational rela-tions occurring across state boundaries among all these social actors are not a new, or a recent, phenomenon. Intersocietal migrations and trade among individ-uals, families, and firms have been important aspects of small, medium, and large world-systems for thousands of years. There was never a time in which the members of different societies did not importantly interact with one another (Chase-Dunn & Hall, 1997). But the spatial scale of both societies and intersoci-etal interactions has grown. And intersocietal integration only became global in the sense of linking every region of the Earth into a single network in the 19th century. The unit of analysis we study in this research is the modern Europe-centered system as bounded by the system of allying and conflicting states. It was during the 19th century that the states' systems of East Asia and Europe became linked by political/military interaction, although they had long been linked by the exchange of prestige goods.

If we think of the world economy as a system, the phenomenon of globaliza-tion should represent increases in the intensity of global interaction networks rel-ative to the intensity of local interaction networks. If both local and global interactions increase at the same rate it would be mistaken to say that the system is becoming more globalized. It is when global interactions increase at a greater rate than local interactions that the system *qua* system is more integrated at the global level. In order to study globalization in this sense we need to measure the intensity of both global and local interactions.

This study focuses on variable characteristics of the world-system as a whole. The questions we are asking here are about the continuities and changes at the level of the whole system, and so our empirical strategy is to construct measures of how this single larger system changes over time. For this reason we have only one "case," although we can utilize the method of time series analysis to test proposi-tions about the relationships among variables in this single case (Chase-Dunn, 1998: Ch. 15).

Internationalization of finance and investment, the growth of international trade as a proportion of all economic interaction, and the organization of production on a global scale by transnational corporations have undoubtedly increased in the last two decades. There are potentially a large number of different indicators of economic globalization and they may exhibit similar patterns with respect to change over time.

Trajectories of Trade and Investment Globalization

We have constructed an improved measure that shows that there have been three waves of trade globalization since the early 19th century. Our new measure of trade globalization extends yearly data further back in time and greatly improves the time resolution relative to the widely spaced estimates that had been previously available. Our new measure of "average openness" trade globalization estimates the world level based on averages of country ratios of GDP to imports. Because both GDP and imports are available in country currencies (e.g., francs, pesos, etc.) we are able to estimate trade globalization without resorting to the problematic assumptions involved in converting country currencies into a single currency (e.g., U.S. dollars), and we do not have to convert the current values into constant values using estimates of inflation and deflation. The results of our study were published in the *American Sociological Review* (Chase-Dunn et al., 2000).[1] Our study of trade globalization shows that it is a cyclical phenomenon, as well as containing a long-term upward trend based on the comparison of the peaks of the cycles (see Figure 7.1).

It is possible that investment globalization behaves in a similar way, but we do not know for sure. Existing estimates of investment globalization (e.g., Bairoch, 1996) are even more intermittent than estimates of trade globalization were before we undertook our ASR study. It would be desirable to have a better understanding of the relationship between investment and trade globalization and to be able to study the causes of both.

The Trajectory of Political Globalization

We conceptualize political globalization analogously to our understanding of economic globalization as the relative strength and density of larger versus smaller interaction networks and organizational structures. Much has been written about the emergence and development of global governance and many see an uneven and halting upward trend in the transitions from the Concert of Europe to the League of Nations and the United Nations toward the formation of a protoworld state. The emergence of the Bretton Woods institutions (the International Monetary Fund and the World Bank) and the more recent restructuring

---

[1] The appendix to our *ASR* article contains the aggregate trade globalization data as well as the results of comparison of our average openness measure with the traditional world totals approach. This is available at http://www.irows.ucr.edu/cd/appendices/asr00/asr00app.htm

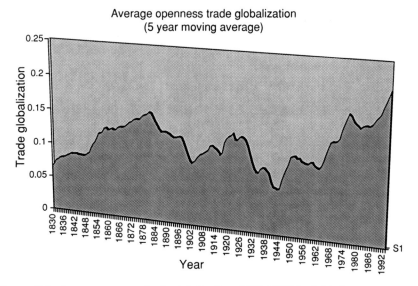

FIGURE 7.1. Average openness trade globalization, 1830–1992 (weighted).

of the General Agreement of Tariffs and Trade as the World Trade Organization, and the visibility of other international fora (the Trilateral Commission, The Group of Seven [Eight], the Davos meetings, etc.) support the idea of emerging global governance. The geometric growth of international nongovernmental organizations (INGOs) is also an important phenomenon of global governance and the emergence of global civil society (Murphy, 1994; Boli & Thomas, 1999).

All world-systems go through cycles of political centralization and decentralization with occasional leaps toward new and higher levels of political integration (Chase-Dunn & Hall, 1997). In the modern world-system the cycle for the last 400 years has taken the form of the rise and fall of hegemonic core states. Some claim that this hegemonic sequence is now morphing into a new structure of core condominium (Goldfrank, 1999). We intend to study both the hegemonic sequence and emerging global governance. Although these might be combined into a more general concept of political globalization, we contend that it is important to keep them separate because hegemonic rise and fall is an old feature of the world-system, whereas political globalization is arguably much more recent. Political globalization can be analytically reduced to the question of the relative strength of larger versus smaller political and military organizations (including also the functionally "economic" ones (IMF, World Bank, WTO) mentioned above.[2]

---

[2] Our conceptualization of political globalization needs to include regional international organizations such as NATO, the Warsaw Pact, COMECON, the European Community, NAFTA, ASEAN, MERCOSUR, and others.

There is a single size distribution of political/military organizations in the world-system. We plan to operationalize three different parts of this size distribution, as well as the whole thing. Our conceptualization of political globalization is analogous to our understanding of economic globalization: a ratio of the size and importance of global and international organizations versus the sum of size and importance of national (and multinational) states. But we also operationalize the hegemonic sequence by examining changes in the distribution of economic and military power among the core states using the research of Modelski and Thompson (1996). And we study the changing shape of the whole system of states as well, taking into account the processes of colonization and decolonization (Bergesen & Schoenberg, 1980), the incorporation of the peripheral and semiperipheral regions into the interstate system, and changes in the distribution of economic and political/military power in the whole system of states. We also combine political globalization, hegemonic rise and fall, and state power stratification into a single overall measure of the distribution of power among state and protostate institutions. This latter we call "overall global political/ military inequality."

Measuring Investment Globalization

We have assembled an annotated bibliography on sources of information about international investments since 1800.[3] In principle, investment globalization is the proportion of all invested capital in the world that is owned by nonnationals (i.e., "foreigners"). In practice we cannot easily measure the sum total of all invested or loaned capital (or the amount of domestically owned capital) over the desired time period, so we use the total of all the national GDPs to estimate the economic size of the world economy. World GDP serves as the denominator of our "world totals" estimate of investment globalization.

The numerator includes most, but not all, international capital flows, ownership claims, and debts. We do not include transfer payments made by individuals to their families in other countries because these are not economic investments of the kind we want to study. We do not include payments for imported or exported goods; these are the basis of our measure of trade globalization. Nor do we include foreign reserves held by central banks in order to support their currencies in the world money market. But we do include loans and direct equity investment, profits (repatriated or not), and intrafirm transfers that cross state boundaries regardless of whom the parties to the transactions are. The transacting parties may be individuals, firms, banks, or governments. In principle we want to measure all of the international financial transactions that involve claims of ownership, control or debt irrespective of who the parties are. And ideally we would like to systematically distinguish among these different kinds of international capital flows and obligations to see how they are similar or different in their geographical and temporal distributions.

---

[3] Our investment globalization annotated bibliography is available at [http://irows.ucr.edu/research/globres/globbib.htm]. We want to thank Carol Bank for her work on this.

This latter desideratum is only possible for the period after World War II. Before that we find different combinations of the several types of international capital flows and obligations in the available data and we need to be careful about how we combine and splice data series that contain different components. For example, for early periods it is easier to get data on loans made to governments, than to find information on loans made to private firms or individuals within a country. Whenever possible we continue the less inclusive measures into periods in which more comprehensive and decomposable information is available and we overlap less complete indicators with more complete ones. This enables us to splice different data series in a more sophisticated way than simply switching from one to another as more complete data become available.[4]

We also need to pay close attention to the important distinction in international capital data between *stocks* and *flows*. Stocks are the total accumulation of debts or the book value of foreign investments at a particular point in time, and flows are the amount of moneys that flowed in (or out) over a short period, usually one year.

We are pursuing two different strategies for constructing long-term measures of investment globalization. These are loosely analogous to the "world totals" and "average openness" strategies that we describe in our *ASR* study of trade globalization. The first involves gathering data on the main investing countries, (e.g., Britain, France, Germany, the United States, the Netherlands, Belgium, and Switzerland) on both the outflows and the accumulated values of foreign loans and investments. This is the strategy that has been employed in earlier studies. It assumes that the great bulk of foreign capital comes from these countries and so efforts are concentrated where they reap the greatest informational returns. The disadvantage is that the number of countries with significant capital outflows increases over time and it is difficult to know how the missing cases might be affecting the estimate of the value of international capital. This method also requires the problematic assumptions involved in converting values into a single currency unit for purposes of comparison of different countries, and converting current into constant units for comparing over time.

Nevertheless we propose to upgrade the currently available estimates that use this approach by adding data from more investing countries. Suter (1992: Appendix (f)) has compiled the most complete long-run data series on the value of international capital holdings. We propose to improve upon Suter's compilation by adding data from additional investing countries and splicing the early series to a series compiled from more complete data after 1950. We also disaggregate the "net" figures used by Suter whenever possible for the countries that

---

[4] Economists typically assume that the slopes of least squares regression lines of two data series are the same in order to merge one series with the other. This would be a risky approach when we are dealing with variables that are known to be cyclical in nature. We use a measurement error strategy that weights the different indicators according to our best guesses of how closely they measure the underlying concept. In practice this usually means that the more recent series will be given greater weight than the earlier series.

he did cover. Net figures are the balance of credits and debits. In most previous studies of changes in the level of foreign investment net values have been used (e.g., Suter, 1992). The problem here is that a country may have large amounts of capital invested abroad and large investments from abroad and these will cancel each other when net values are used.[5]

Our second strategy is similar to the "average openness" approach we developed for studying trade globalization. This involves estimating "investment dependence" for each country, the ratio of the foreign debt to the national income (GDP), and then taking the weighted average of these as our indicator of world investment globalization. The advantage of this approach is that it does not require converting into a single currency and computing constant from current values. We already have the country currency GDPs (national income estimates) from Mitchell (1992, 1993, 1995) that we used for our measure of average openness trade globalization. For our new "average investment dependence" measure of investment globalization we collect estimates of inflows and accumulated stocks and debts of foreign capital in country currencies for each country.[6] With complete data these indicators would be equivalent to the total sum of international capital flows and obligations divided by the world GDP. But as with average openness, we do not have complete data for the years before 1950. This is a "sampling" problem in which the sample is biased because we have more core than peripheral countries. This indicator is compared with the results of our first strategy discussed above.

Analyses

The first task of analysis is to use the new data we have coded on international capital flows and obligations to construct several new indicators of investment globalization. Then we show how these relate to one another and study their temporal trajectories in comparison to what we have found for trade globalization. We expect that investment globalization will show a similar cyclical pattern, but it may not. We also consider the question of a long-term trend in investment globalization, much as we did in our study of trade.

We have coded and analyzed data on nonnet British foreign investment flows from 1865 to 1914 that were not available to Suter (Stone, 1999), and we have coded several measures of investment globalization from 1938 to 1999. A discussion of British foreign investment flows in the 19th century is included in Appendix A (http://irows.ucr.edu/cd/appendices/globworld/globworldapp.htm).

---

[5] Whenever possible we compare the net figures with the credit figures to estimate how much error there is in the net figures. Christian Suter is serving as a consultant to our project. We also intend to improve our measures of trade globalization by adding information on East Asian interstate trade during the 19th century (Hamashita, 1994).

[6] This means collecting data on country debits. We also collect data on credits in country currencies and construct an analogous "average investment dominance" measure based on these.

Investment Globalization, 1938–1999

These measures are based on credits and debits on investment income coded from
the International Monetary Fund *Balance of Payments Yearbooks*. Investment
income includes the repatriated profits on direct investment and dividends on portfolio investment. "Credits" means that such was earned from abroad. "Debits"
means that investors abroad were paid profits and dividends by their holdings in the
country.[7] In principle, if we had data on the whole world, the sum of credits should
equal the sum of debits. But of course we do not have complete data until very
recent years, so it is useful to compare credits with debits to see how our "sample"
of countries may be biasing our estimates of this variable characteristic of the whole
world economy (investment globalization).

Investment income has been used as a proxy for estimating the total book value
of foreign investment, because there is a general profit rate that averages around
10% and so the profit can be used as a proxy.[8] And the amount of profit and
dividends produced by foreign investment are also of interest in their own right.

We coded investment income debits and credits for all available countries from
the IMF *Balance of Payments Yearbooks* from 1938 to 1999. We found that the
CD ROM datasets made available from the IMF do not always include all the
information that was published in the original *Balance of Payments Yearbooks*
and so it is important to use both the printed volumes and the CD ROM.

Our new measures of "average investment dependence/dominance" investment
globalization estimate the world level based on averages of country ratios of GDP
to credits and debits of investment income. Because both GDP and investment
income are available in country currencies (e.g., francs, pesos, etc.) for many
countries we are able to estimate investment globalization without resorting to the
problematic assumptions involved in converting country currencies into a single
currency (e.g., U.S. dollars). Exchange rates vary because of monetary regulation
regimes such as the Bretton Woods agreements, and because of speculative activities of money traders. And we do not need to convert the current values into constant values using estimates of inflation and deflation. Removal of the error
introduced by exchange and inflation rates provides superior estimation of investment globalization.[9] Another advantage of using the IMF *Balance of Payments
Yearbook* data is the avoidance of net values. In our analysis of balance of
payments data we examine both credits (the returns received by a country for
investments abroad), and debits (the amounts paid out to foreign investors).

---

[7] Investment income is the major component of net factor income paid abroad, which is the
difference between gross national product (GNP) and gross domestic product (GDP). GNP
is calculated by deducting (or adding) net factor income from GDP.

[8] Of the course the profit rate varies over time and across countries, so the proxy is problematic. Economists contend that the profit rate in noncore foreign investments is higher
than in the core because of additional risks.

[9] Unfortunately, country currency values were not available for some countries, especially
in more recent years as the IMF began reporting in U.S. dollars.

In order to estimate the world level of investment globalization we need to weight the country values. Treating large and small countries equally produces an average that overvalues the information from small countries. We weighted the investment ratios for each country by the ratio of the country's population size to the world population. The weighted and unweighted averages were compared to make sure that our weighting did not produce strange results. The problem is that the sample of countries upon which we are estimating the world level of investment globalization changes over time. Usually, we have more complete data on core countries than on noncore countries in earlier time periods,[10] but the number of countries does not rise in a nice even trend. Figure 7.2 shows the changes in the number of countries for which we have estimates for debits of investment income since 1938.

Notice that in Figure 7.2 the number of countries for which we have information on debits on investment income decreases during the 1970s. Researchers at the IMF have been unable to explain to us why the availability of data decreases in that period. Notice also that the data availability decreases after 1995. This is because some countries are tardy in reporting their international financial statistics. The pattern of availability is almost exactly the same for investment income credits.

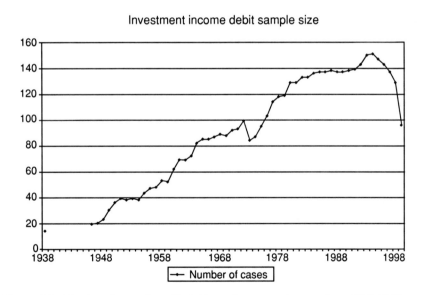

FIGURE 7.2. Number of countries with debits on investment income data, 1938–1999.

---

[10] Our division of countries into core and noncore categories for the IMF data analysis is shown in Appendix B http://irows.ucr.edu/cd/appendices/globworld/globworldapp.htm.

We present the results of our study using three different indicators from the IMF *Balance of Payments Yearbooks*: total investment income, direct investment income, and portfolio investment income. Total investment income is the sum of direct investment income, portfolio investment income, and "other" investment income. The definitions of these current account items are as follows.

Investment income covers receipts and payments of income associated, respectively, with holdings of external financial assets by residents and with liabilities to nonresidents. *Investment income* consists of direct investment income, portfolio investment income, and other investment income. The direct investment component is broken down into income on equity (dividends, branch profits, and reinvested earnings) and income on debt (interest), portfolio investment income is broken down into income on equity (dividends) and income on debt (interest), other investment income covers interest earned on other capital (loans, etc.) and, in principle, imputed income to households from net equity in life insurance reserves and in pension funds (Balance of Payments Statistics Yearbook, 2001).[11]

We have coded the three subcategories of investment income because we are interested in the differences between foreign direct investment and portfolio investment. Direct investment involves organizational control, as when a transnational corporation invests in its subsidiary. Portfolio investment does not involve direct organizational control. The purchase of stocks of firms or of bonds by foreigners is considered portfolio investment. The subcategories are available for many fewer cases and for only recent years. Nevertheless we are interested in comparing direct and portfolio investment globalization.

Figure 7.3 shows the weighted average investment income debit ratios for 1938–1999. Recall that investment income debits include the profits, interest, and dividends earned by foreigners within a national economy. Not surprisingly this estimate of worldwide investment globalization goes up over this 40-year period. But the yearly data enable us to examine the exact temporality of the rise.

The results in Figure 7.3 show the averages for all the countries for which we have data (the number of which increases greatly over time as shown in Figure 7.2), for just the core countries and for the noncore countries. The changes in Figure 7.3 are partly due to changes in the level of worldwide investment globalization and partly due to changes in the availability of data over time. In order to take out the part due to changing N we use the method of constant groups, looking at a set of countries for which we have data over the whole span of time. In Figure 7.3 the constant group includes eleven countries (Australia, Canada, Denmark, Finland, Ireland, Italy, the Netherlands, Norway, Sweden, United Kingdom and the United States). The close similarity between the results for the constant group and for the core is due to the fact that the core countries are the ones for which we have the most data further back in time.

---

[11] IMF accounting conventions have changed over the period we are studying. For an overview of these changes see http://irows.ucr.edu/research/globres/definitions/accountdef.html.

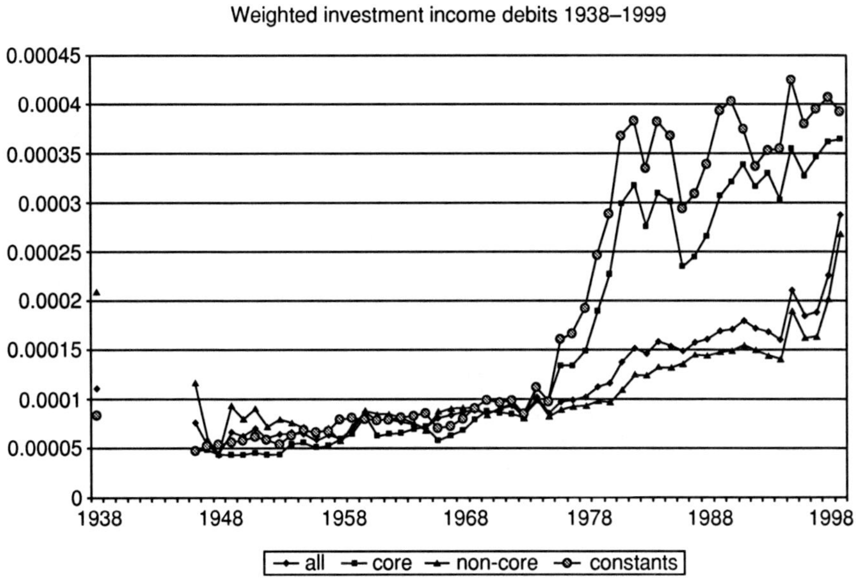

Weighted investment income debits 1938–1999

FIGURE 7.3. Weighted total investment income debits, 1938–1999.

The trajectory of investment globalization indicated by including all the countries for which we have data on debits on investment income shows that there was a decrease between 1938 and 1946, and that was followed by a slowly accelerating upward trend. The 1938 level was not reached again until 1979, but the level reached by 1999 was almost three times higher than the 1938 level. Thus the perception that the world economy experienced a wave of investment globalization in recent decades is confirmed by our results using our new "average investment dependence" estimator based on debits on investment income.

Figure 7.3 also shows that the trajectory has been rather different for the core and the noncore. In 1938 the noncore countries were more than twice as dependent on foreign investment as were the core countries and the noncore declined from this high level until the late 1950s, whereas the core began a new ascent from 1946 on. In 1975 the core began a sharp upturn in payments out on investment income, whereas the noncore was experiencing a much slower increase. This indicates that investment globalization occurred much earlier and to a much greater extent for the core countries than for the noncore.

Now let us examine the credit component of investment income. This is composed of the profits, interest, and dividends taken in by countries as a result of their investments abroad, a feature we call "average investment dominance." Figure 7.4 shows the weighted trends since 1938 for the same groups studied in Figure 7.3.

The results in Figure 7.4 are similar in most respects to Figure 7.3, except that the upward trend for the whole world and for the noncore countries is much

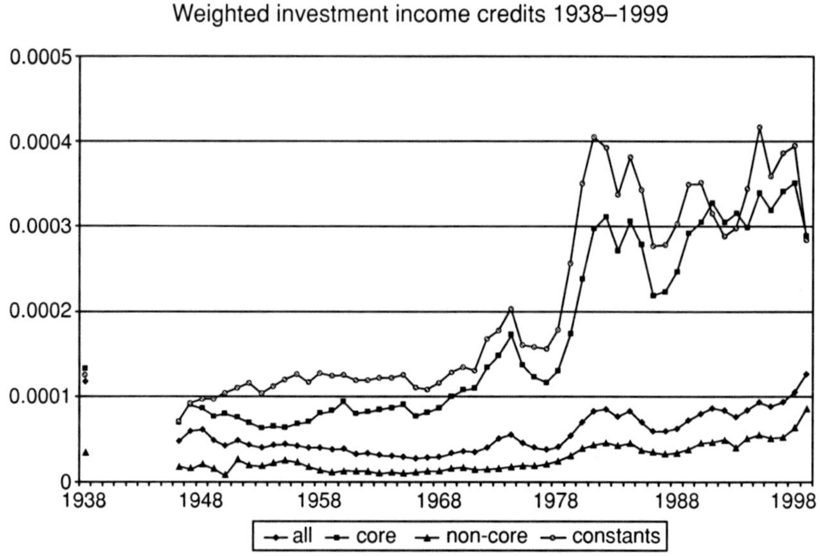

Weighted investment income credits 1938–1999

FIGURE 7.4. Credits on total investment income, 1938–1999.

weaker.[12] Credits on investment income have gone up mainly for the core, and this acceleration is temporally similar to the results for core debits shown in Figure 7.3. The other difference is that core credits were already higher than noncore credits in 1938. This is just the opposite of the pattern for debits. Core countries are the main global investors and this difference between core and noncore has increased over time despite all the talk of emerging markets and transnational corporations based in the semiperiphery.

Figure 7.5 compares two of the components of investment income debits with the total investment income debits for the core countries.

Figure 7.5 shows some interesting differences for the core countries across different kinds of investment income debits. The total investment income trajectory is the same as that shown in Figure 7.3 above. Average weighted direct investment income debits for the core countries do not show an upward trend. The upward trajectory shown by total investment income debits is entirely due to the increase of payments out on portfolio investment and on "other" investment income (not shown).[13] "Other" investment income primarily includes items that can be considered as parts of international investment.[14] Thus the increase in core investment globalization as indicated by debits on investment income appears to be largely due to the rise of portfolio investments corresponding to the financialization of the

---

[12] The constant cases for credits in Figure 7.4 are the same as in Figure 7.3 plus India.

[13] The sum of direct, portfolio, and other investment income equals total investment income.

[14] "Other" investment income does not include transfer payments such as remittances of guest workers to their families back home.

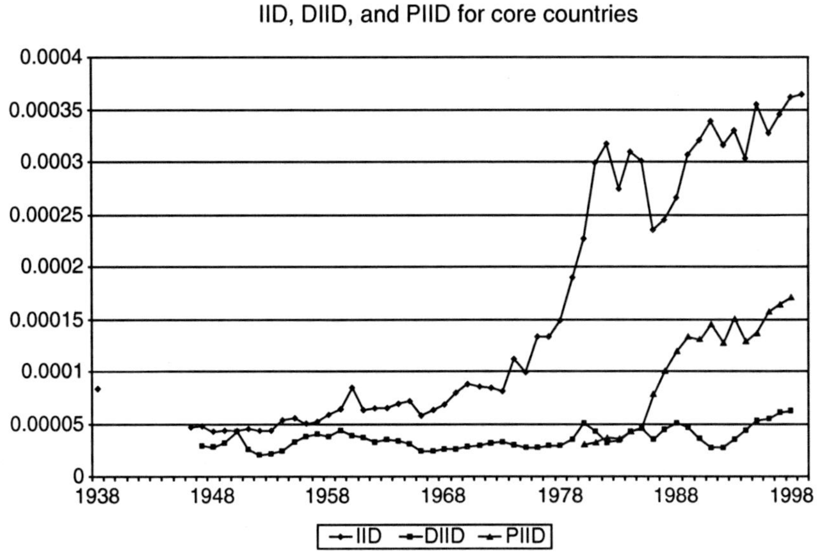

IID, DIID, and PIID for core countries

FIGURE 7.5. Total, direct, and portfolio investment income debits, core countries.

world economy that has accompanied the ideological hegemony of neoliberalism since the 1970s. Debits on direct investment income in the core appear to have remained flat relative to the size of the world economy in this period, meaning that the amount of profit paid out by core countries resulting from the activities of subsidiaries of transnational corporations has apparently not increased.

Let us now examine the trends for the subtypes of credits on investment income. Figure 7.6 shows the credits categories corresponding to those shown in Figure 7.5.

Figure 7.6 shows a very similar pattern to Figure 7.5. The trend in total investment income credits for core countries is the same as in Figure 7.4 above. As in Figure 7.5, direct investment globalization is flat, whereas portfolio investment globalization shows a strong rise since the late 1970s. But some of the trend in Figure 7.6 is due to changes in the cases. Figure 7.7 shows the results when we hold the cases constant for each of the subtypes.

Figure 7.7 indicates that the flatness of the trend in direct investment credits shown in Figure 7.6 may be due to the addition of cases as we move through time. When we hold the cases constant, direct investment credits show a modest upward trend.[15]

---

[15] The constant cases for each of the subtypes in Figure 7.7 are different, depending on available data for each. This explains why the trajectories do not appear to add up to the total investment income credits.

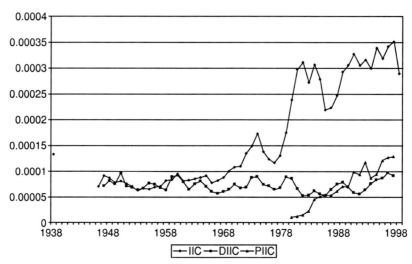

FIGURE 7.6. Total, direct, and portfolio investment income credits, core countries.

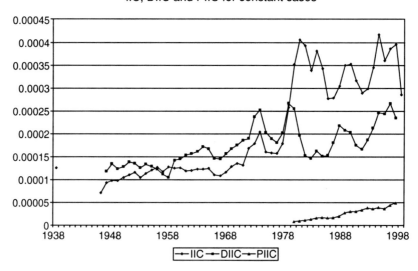

FIGURE 7.7. Credits on total, direct, and portfolio investment income for constant cases.

Conclusion

The conclusions suggested by our study of investment globalization from 1938 to 1999 are as follows. There was indeed an upward trend of investment globalization during this period but it began after a decline during World War II. The big rise began in the late 1970s corresponding with the abandonment of the Bretton Woods regulations over international investment and the deregulation of international monetary arrangements. There were important differences between the core and the noncore with regard to investment globalization. The core did it earlier and rose to a much higher peak. Portfolio investment was a major contributor to the big wave of investment globalization that occurred after the late 1970s. This corresponded to the shift of capital accumulation away from investment in production and trade and into finance capital. We hope to compare these current findings with those for the forthcoming analyses of political globalization as well as previous results for our study of trade globalization.

References Cited and Bibliography

Aglietta, M. (1979). *A theory of capitalist regulation: The U.S. experience*. London: New Left.

Amin, S. (1998). *Capitalism in the age of globalization*. London: Zed.

Bairoch, P. (1996). Globalization myths and realities: one century of external trade and foreign investment. In R. Boyer & D. Drache (Eds.), *States against markets: The limits of globalization*. London and New York: Routledge.

Banks, A. S. (1975). *Cross-national time series data archive*. Binghamton, NY: Center for Comparative Political Research, Binghamton University (ICPSR 7412).

Bergesen, A., & Fernandez, R. (1998). Who has the most Fortune 500 firms? A network analysis of global economic competition, 1956, 1989. In V. Bornschier, & C. Chase-Dunn (Eds.), *The future of global conflict*. London: Sage.

Bergesen, A., & Schoenberg, R. (1980). Long waves of colonial expansion and contraction 1415–1969. In A. Bergesen (Ed.), *Studies of the modern world-system*. New York: Academic, pp. 231–278.

Blanton, R. G. (1999). Structure and behavior in the world trading system. *International Interactions* 25, 2: 119–144.

—— (1999). Trading blocs and the capitalist world-economy: insights and evidence. *Sociological Inquiry* 69, 2: 187–215.

Boli, J., & Thomas, G. M. (1997, April). World culture in the world polity. *American Sociological Review* 62, 2: 171–190.

—— (Eds.). (1999). *Constructing world culture: International nongovernmental organizations since 1875*. Stanford, CA: Stanford University Press.

Bornschier, V. (1996). *Western society in transition*. New Brunswick, NJ: Transaction.

Borrego, J. (1998). Twenty-fifty: The hegemonic moment of global capitalism. In V. Bornschier, & C. Chase-Dunn (Eds.), *The future of hegemonic rivalry*. London: Sage.

Boswell, T., & Sweat, M. (1991, June). Hegemony, long waves and major wars. *International Studies Quarterly* 35, 2: 123–150.

Boyer, R., & Drache, D. (1996). *States against markets: The limits of globalization*. London: Routledge.

Casson, M. (Ed.). (1983). *The growth of international business*. London: Allen and Unwin.

Chase-Dunn, C. (1990, April). World state formation: historical processes and emergent necessity. *Political Geography Quarterly* 9, 2: 108–30

—— (1998). *Global formation: Structures of the world economy*. Lanham, MD: Rowman and Littlefield.

—— (1999). Globalization: a world-systems perspective. *Journal of World-Systems Research* 5, 2: 176–198.

Chase-Dunn, C., & Grimes, P. (1995). World-systems analysis. *Annual Review of Sociology* 21: 387–417.

Chase-Dunn, C., & Hall, T. D. (1997). *Rise and demise: The comparative study of world-systems*. Boulder, CO: Westview.

Chase-Dunn, C., & Jorgenson, A. K. (2003). Regions and interaction networks: A world-systems perspective. *International Journal of Comparative Sociology* 44: 1–18.

Chase-Dunn, C., Kawano, Y., & Brewer, B. (2000, February). Trade globalization since 1795: Waves of integration in the world-system. *American Sociological Review*, Special Millennial Issue.

Dunning, J. H. (1983). Changes in the level and structure of international production: The last one hundred years. In M. Casson (Ed.), *The growth of international business*. London: Allen and Unwin, pp. 84–139.

Feis, H. (1930). *Europe, the world's banker 1870–1914*. New Haven, CT: Yale University Press.

Freeman, J. R. (1983). Granger causality and the time series analysis of political relationships. *American Journal of Political Science* 27: 327–358.

Goldfrank, W. L. (1999). Beyond hegemony. In V. Bornschier, & C. Chase-Dunn (Eds.), *The future of global conflict*. London: Sage.

Goldstein, J. (1988). *Long cycles: Prosperity and war in the modern age*. New Haven, CT: Yale University Press.

Gordon, D. (1994). The global economy: new edifice or crumbling foundation? In D. Kotz, T. McDonough, & M. Reich (Eds.), *Social structures of accumulation*. Cambridge: Cambridge, UK: University Press, pp. 292–306.

Grimes, P. (1996). Economic cycles and mobility. (Ph.D. dissertation, Johns Hopkins University, Department of Sociology).

Hamashita, T. (1994). The tribute trade system and modern Asia. In A. J. H. Latham, & H. Kawakatsu (Eds.), *Japanese industrialization and the Asian economy*. London: Routledge, pp. 91–107.

Harvey, D. (1995). Globalization in question. *Rethinking Marxism* 8, 4: 1–17.

Held, D., McGrew, A., Goldblatt, D., & Perraton, J. (1999). *Global transformations: Politics, economic and culture*. Palo Alto, CA: Stanford University Press.

Hirst, P., & Thompson, G. (1996). *Globalization in question: The international economy and the possibilities of governance*. Cambridge, UK: Polity Press.

Hopkins, T. K., & Wallerstein, I. (1982). Cyclical rhythms and secular trends of the capitalist world economy. In T. K. Hopkins, & I. Wallerstein (Eds.), *World-systems analysis: Theory and methodology*. Beverly Hills, CA: Sage, pp. 104–120.

International Monetary Fund. *Balance of Payments Statistics Yearbook* 2001.

Jorgenson, A. K., & Kick, E. (2003). Globalization and the environment. *Journal of World-Systems Research* 9: 195–203.

Junne, G. (1999). Global cooperation or rival trade blocs? In V. Bornschier, & C. Chase-Dunn (Eds.), *The future of global conflict*. London: Sage.

Keohane, R. O. (1984). *After hegemony: Cooperation and discord in the world political economy*. Princeton, NJ: Princeton University Press.

Keohane, R., & Nye, J. (Eds.) (1970). *Transnational relations and world politics.* Cambridge, MA: Harvard University Press.

Krasner, S. D. (1976). State power and the structure of international trade. *World Politics* 28, 3: 317–347.

—— (Ed.) (1983). *International regimes.* Ithaca, NY: Cornell University Press.

Kravis, I. B., Heston, A., & Summers, R. (1982). *World product and income: International comparisons of real gross product.* Baltimore, MD: Johns Hopkins University Press.

Kremple, L., & Pluemper, T. (1999). International division of labor and global economic processes: an analysis of the international trade of cars with world trade data. http://www.mpifgkoeln.mpg.de/~lk/netvis/globle/.

Lewis, C. (1945). *Debtor and creditor countries: 1938, 1944.* Washington, DC: The Brookings Institution.

Lipietz, A. (1987). *Mirages and miracles: The crises of global fordism.* London: Verso.

Maddison, A. (1995). *Monitoring the world economy, 1820–1992.* Paris: OECD.

Mandel, E. (1975). *Late capitalism.* London: New Left.

Manning, S. (1999). Introduction to special issue on the future of globalization. *Journal of World Systems Research* 5, 2: 1–5. http://csf.colorado.edu/wsystems/jwsr.html.

Markoff, J. (1996). *Waves of democracy: Social movements and political change.* Thousand Oaks, CA: Pine Forge.

McKeown, T. J. (1983). Hegemonic stability theory and 19th century tariff levels in Europe. *International Organization* 37, 1: 73–91.

McMichael, P. (1996). *Development and social change: A global perspective.* Thousand Oaks, CA: Pine Forge.

Meyer, J. W. (1996). The changing cultural content of the nation-state: A world society perspective. In G. Steinmetz (Ed.), *New approaches to the state in the social sciences.* Ithaca, NY: Cornell University Press.

Mitchell, B. R. (1992). *International historical statistics: Europe 1750–1988* (3rd Edition). New York: Stockton.

—— (1993). *International historical statistics: The Americas 1750–1988* (2nd Edition). NY: Stockton.

—— (1995). *International historical statistics: Africa, Asia, & Oceania 1750–1988* (2nd Edition). NY: Stockton.

Mittelman, J. H. (Ed.) (1996). *Globalization: Critical reflections.* Boulder, CO: Lynne Rienner.

Modelski, G., & Thompson, W. R. (1996). *Leading sectors and world powers.* Columbia, SC: University of South Carolina Press.

Murphy, C. (1994). *International organization and industrial change: Global governance since 1850.* New York: Oxford.

Navarro, V. (1998). Neo-liberalism, 'globalization,' unemployment, inequalities, and the welfare state. *International Journal of Health Services* 28, 4: 607–682.

Pfister, U., & Suter, C. (1987). International financial relations as part of the world-system. *International Studies Quarterly* 31, 3: 239–272.

Polanyi, K. (1957). *The great transformation.* New York: Beacon.

Robertson, R. (1992). *Globalization: Social theory and global culture.* London: Sage.

Robinson, W. I. (1996). *Promoting polyarchy: Globalization, U.S. intervention and hegemony.* Cambridge, UK: Cambridge University Press.

Ross, R., & Trachte, K. (1990). *Global capitalism: The new leviathan.* Albany: State University of New York Press.

Russett, B. (1993). *Grasping the democratic peace.* Princeton, NJ: Princeton University Press.

Sachs, J., & Warner, A. (1995). Economic reform and the process of global integration. *Brookings Papers on Economic Activity* 1: 1–118.

Sassen, S. (1998). *Globalization and its discontents*. New York: New Press.

Sklair, L. (1995). *Sociology of the global system*. Baltimore, MD: Johns Hopkins University Press.

—— (2001). *The transnational capitalist class*. Malden, MA: Blackwell Publishers.

Soros, G. (1998). *The crisis of global capitalism*. New York: Pantheon.

Stone, I. (1999). *The global export of capital from Great Britain, 1865–1914: A statistical survey*. New York: St. Martin's Press.

Su, T. (1995, Summer). Changes in world trade networks: 1938, 1960, 1990. *Review* XVIII, 3: 431–459.

Suter, C. (1992). *Debt cycles and the world-economy: Foreign loans, financial crises and debt settlements, 1820–1990*. Boulder, CO: Westview.

Taylor, P. (1996). *The way the modern world works: World hegemony to world impasse*. New York: Wiley.

Thompson, W. R. (2000). *The emergence of the global political economy*. London: Routledge.

Tilly, C. (1995). Globalization threatens labor's rights. *International Labor and Working-Class History* 47: 1–23.

United Nations (1994). *World investment report 1994: Transnational corporations, employment and the workplace*. New York.

—— (1999). Human Development Report 1999. New York: United Nations Development Project. http://www.undp.org/hdro/report.html.

Wallerstein, I. (1974). *The modern world-system*. vol. 1. New York: Academic.

Webb, M. C., & Krasner, S. 1989. Hegemonic stability theory: An empirical assessment. *Review of International Studies* 15: 183–198.

Woytinski, W. S., & Woytinski, E. S. (1955). *World commerce and governments*. New York: Twentieth Century Fund.

World Bank (I.B.R.D). (1980). *World tables* (2nd Edition). Baltimore, MD: Johns Hopkins University Press.

—— (1998). *World development indicators*. http://www.worldbank.org/html/extpb/wdi98.htm.

8
Globalization and Uneven Development

GIOVANNI ARRIGHI

"Globalization" as Historical Process and as Ideology

The term globalization became fashionable in the late 1980s and early 1990s both as a description of an historical process of increasing world economic and societal integration, which we may call "structural globalization" and as a prescription of policies allegedly dictated by that process, which we may call "ideological globalization" (cf. Chase-Dunn, 1999). As many commentators have pointed out, structural globalization has been going on with ups and downs for centuries. After the Second World War the process experienced a new major upswing that resulted in an unprecedented degree of global economic and societal integration. Moreover, as in previous upswings of the same kind, the great expansion of world trade and production of the 1950s and 1960s gave rise in the 1970s to a worldwide intensification of competitive pressures on businesses and governments. At least initially, this intensification of competition more negatively affected Northern countries including and especially the United States than Third World countries. Indeed, throughout the 1970s many Third (and Second) World countries benefited from the higher prices for natural resources (oil in particular) and/or the abundant supply of credit and investment at highly favorable conditions generated by the intensification of competition among Northern countries (Arrighi, 2002).

What eventually turned the tide to the advantage of Northern countries (or at least some of them) was not structural globalization as such but ideological globalization. As it materialized since circa 1980, ideological globalization consists of two closely related but distinct prescriptions: a domestic prescription, which advocated the liquidation of the legacy of the New Deal in the United States and of the welfare state in Western Europe; and an international prescription, which advocated the liquidation of the developmental state in the Third (and Second) Worlds. Both prescriptions drew ideological inspiration from Margaret Thatcher's (in)famous slogan "There Is No Alternative" (TINA). Politically and economically, however, they became a global reality under the impact of U.S. policies and actions.

The domestic prescription was first put into practice at the end of the Carter administration, but it gained ideological and practical momentum only under Reagan. Under the banner of "supply-side economics," the money supply was cut drastically, interest rates were raised sharply, taxes for the wealthy and corporate capital were reduced, and capitalist enterprise was granted increasing freedom of action. The immediate result was a deep recession in the United States and in the world at large on the one side, and a U.S.-led escalation of interstate competition for capital worldwide on the other. TINA was thereby turned into a self-fulfilling prophecy. Whatever alternative to cut-throat competition for increasingly mobile capital might have existed before 1980, it became moot once the world's largest and wealthiest economy led the world down the road of ever more extravagant concessions to capital. This was especially the case for Third (and Second) World countries which, as a result of the change in U.S. policies, came to experience a sharp contraction both in the demand for their natural resources and in the availability of credit and investment at favorable conditions.

It was in this context that the domestic prescription of ideological globalization came to be supplemented by the international prescription. This component refers to the sudden switch in the early 1980s of U.S. thought and action from promotion of the "development project" launched in the late 1940s and early 1950s to promotion of the "globalization project" under the neoliberal Washington Consensus of the 1980s and 1990s (McMichael, 2000). As a result of the switch, the U.S. government, directly or through the IMF and the World Bank, withdrew its support from the "statist" and "inward-looking" strategies (such as import-substitution industrialization) that most theories of national development had advocated in the 1950s and 1960s, and began instead to promote capital-friendly and outward-looking strategies, most notably macrostability, privatization, and the liberalization of foreign trade and capital movements.[1]

---

[1] As Toye (1993) has argued, the turnabout amounted to a true "counterrevolution" in economic thought about development. As Singer (1997) has pointed out, the description of development thinking in the postwar era as statist and inward-looking is correct, but neither characterization had the derogatory implications they acquired in the 1980s. Indeed, even within the neoliberal Washington Consensus, the initial antistatist bias was superseded in the 1990s by an emphasis on "good governance" (see, in particular, World Bank 1989, 1992, and 1993). Nevertheless, the essence of the "good governance" advocated by the U.S. government and the Bretton Woods institutions remained the promotion of macrostability, privatization, and the liberalization of foreign trade and capital movements.

As World Bank economist William Easterly has acknowledged, the "sea-change beginning around 1980 towards market-friendly economic policies" by governments of low- and middle-income countries was associated not with an improvement but with a sharp deterioration in their growth performance, the median rate of growth of the per capita income of these countries falling from 2.5% in 1960–1979 to 0% in 1980–1998. Easterly does not blame the new policies for this disappointing outcome. Because similar policies had previously been associated with good performance, he suggests two possible reasons for their failure to deliver on their promises after 1980. One is that "good" policies may be subject to decreasing returns. When they are pursued beyond a given threshold by a particular country, or are pursued simultaneously by a growing number of countries, they may cease to yield their "good" results. "While you may grow faster than your neighbor if your secondary [school] enrollment is higher, your own growth does not necessarily increase as your (and everyone else's) secondary enrollment ratios rise." In addition, he went on to suggest that the new policies may have not yielded the expected results because of a deterioration in the global economic environment. In his words, "Worldwide factors like the increase in world interest rates, the increased debt burden of developing countries, the growth slowdown in the industrial world, and skill-biased technical change may have contributed to the developing countries stagnation" (Easterly, 2001: 135–145, 151–155).

As we show in the next section of the chapter, the idea that certain policies and actions may be subject to decreasing returns has a far greater bearing on developmental issues than Easterly seems to realize. For now, however, let us notice that the second reason he gives for the disappointing results of neoliberal policies in low- and middle-income countries ("that is, the deterioration of the global economic environment") was part and parcel of the neoliberal turn. As noted above, the hike in world interest rates, the increased debt burden of low- and middle-income countries, and the growth slowdown in Northern countries, were all provoked or made worse by the domestic (U.S.) component of ideological globalization. The deterioration of the global economic environment, in other words, was no accident. Rather, it was an integral aspect of the dynamic of ideological globalization, partly an effect of the neoliberal turn in the United States, and partly a cause of the adoption of neoliberal policies by Third (and Second) World countries.

Industrial Convergence and the Persistence of the North–South Income Divide

Easterly's suggestion that "good" policies may be subject to decreasing returns implicitly challenges one of the most widely held beliefs in the theory and practice of national development. This is the belief that policies and actions yield similar developmental results regardless of how many countries undertake them. Easterly's illustration of policies that may contradict this belief (an increase in secondary school enrollment) is somewhat misleading, because a generalized increase in secondary school enrollment is in itself a desirable development even if it does not speed up economic growth, an issue to which I return in the conclusion of the chapter. A far more appropriate and compelling illustration of the contradiction in question is the failure of North–South industrial convergence to bring about North–South income convergence.

From the very beginning of their development efforts, Third World governments have eagerly promoted the industrialization of their national economies as the generally prescribed means of catching up with the per capita income of First World countries. Manufacturing activities were thought to have higher productivity than both agricultural and service activities (see especially Clark, 1957; Baumol, 1967). Industrialization was therefore expected to bring about an acceleration in the rate of growth of Third World economies, and the widely anticipated "coming of post-industrial society" (Bell, 1973) was expected to bring about a deceleration in the rate of growth of First World economies. The general expectation, in other words, was that industrial convergence would be accompanied by income convergence.[2]

This expectation was so entrenched across theoretical (and ideological) divides as to turn industrialization into a synonym of development, and thus an end in itself. As Dean Tipps (1973: 208) noted, the ambivalence towards modern industrial society that characterized the writings of Marx, Weber, and Durkheim became conspicuous by its absence in modernization and development thinking.[3] Little attention was paid to the accumulating evidence that in reality industrial convergence was not bringing income convergence in its train. A comparison of Tables 8.1 and 8.2 clearly demonstrates the discrepancy.

Leaving aside for now the extreme unevenness of the trends among the world's regions, Table 8.1 shows that the degree of industrialization of the Third World as a whole (measured by the proportion of GDP produced in manufacturing) first caught up with, and then overtook the degree of industrialization of the First World as a whole. In 1960 the degree of industrialization of the Third World was 74.6% of that of the First World, however, in 1980 it was virtually the same (99.4%), and in 2000 it was 17.1% higher. At least by this measure, the continuing designation of the North as industrial and of the South as nonindustrial (or less industrial) has become wholly anachronistic.

---

[2] See, among others, Walt Rostow's canonical text (1960). Income convergence was also the expectation of neoclassical theories of growth (see, especially, Solow, 1956). These theories, however, did not deal explicitly with industrialization.

[3] This was as true of dependency and Marxist theories as of mainstream modernization theories. See, especially, Cardoso and Faletto (1979) for dependency theory and Warren (1980) for Marxist theories. In both texts industrialization and development are treated as equivalent terms. In the late 1980s and early 1990s, the ambivalence of classical social theory towards modern industrial society reemerged with a vengeance in the postmodernist critique of modernization and development theories (see, especially, Escobar, 1995 and the contributors to Sachs, 1992). This current of thought has been an important corrective to the acritical acceptance across the ideological spectrum of development/industrialization as a generally beneficial pursuit. Nevertheless, in rejecting the alleged benefits of development and industrialization, postmodernist critics have tended to treat the two terms as equivalent, just as did those whom they criticized.

In sharp contrast to the tendency of the South to catch up with and then overtake the North in degree of industrialization, Table 8.2 shows that the income gap between the same two groups of countries has remained virtually the same, the gross national product (GNP) per capita of Third World countries as a proportion of that of First World countries being 4.5% in 1960, 4.3% in 1980, and 4.6% in 2000. In this respect there was no catching up. Against all expectations, 40 years of relatively successful industrialization left the South as poor relative to the North as it was at the start.[4]

The particular indicator I am using here to measure the North–South income gap does not in itself enable us to take a position on the issue of whether intercountry income inequality (measured by summary indicators such as the Gini or Theil coefficients) has been rising or declining. This remains a highly controversial issue that admits of conflicting answers, depending on which data are used and on how they are elaborated (see, among others, Wade, 2004; Ravallion, 2004). For our present purposes, however, all the summary indicators used in gauging intercountry income inequality have two fundamental shortcomings. For one thing, they provide no indication of changes in the position of countries or group of countries (such as North and South) within the global distribution of income.[5] Moreover, and partly related to the above, they do not tell us anything about the relationship between structural transformations (such as industrialization) of Southern countries and changes in relative incomes, which is what concerns us here.

In this regard, the failure of industrialization to bring in its train income convergence suggests that the relationship between industrialization and economic growth is subject to a "composition" or "adding up" effect. As long as relatively few countries (or countries accounting for a small proportion of world population) had succeeded in industrializing, the economic benefits of industrialization were positive and significant. But when an increasing number of countries (or countries accounting for a growing proportion or world population) industrialized in an attempt to increase their national wealth, competition in the procurement of

---

[4] In calculating the manufacturing share of GDP we have weighted countries by their total GDP and in calculating GNP per capita we have weighted countries by their population. The particular indicator used for industrialization and the use of income data at actual exchange rates (FX-based data) rather than at purchasing power parity (PPP-based data) increases the contrast between industrial convergence and income nonconvergence. Nevertheless, the contrast persists regardless of which particular indicator and data we use. Moreover, the aggregate combination of North–South industrial convergence without income convergence is not the spurious result of heterogeneous national experiences, that is, of countries that experienced a narrowing of both the industrialization and income gaps and countries that did not. Rather it is the result of the absence of any positive correlation between industrial and income performance (Arrighi, Silver & Brewer 2003: 11–12, 15–16).

[5] Thus, owing to the property of the indicators in question known as "anonymity" or "symmetry" axiom, all Northern countries could swap places in the global distribution of income with a group of Southern countries of equal demographic weight without having any impact whatsoever on the Gini or Theil measurements of inequality (cf. Ravallion, 2004: 19).

TABLE 8.1. Region's percentage of GDP in manufacturing as percentage of First World.

Region	1960	1970	1980	1990	2000
Sub-Saharan Africa (w/SA)	53.0	63.0	71.1	88.1	77.8
Latin America	97.1	94.8	115.3	113.1	94.6
West Asia and North Africa	37.7	43.0	41.1	70.4	74.8
South Asia	47.9	51.2	71.2	81.6	84.3
East Asia (w/o China and Japan)	48.5	67.9	95.4	115.3	133.7
China	81.8	106.6	165.8	149.5	185.9
Third World (w/China)*	**74.6**	**78.3**	**99.4**	**108.1**	**117.1**
Third World (w/o China)*	**73.9**	**76.2**	**94.6**	**102.9**	**102.2**
North America	95.9	87.5	88.0	84.4	90.4
Western Europe	101.5	101.3	97.0	96.8	100.4
Southern Europe	90.6	91.8	111.3	99.7	105.4
Australia and New Zealand	87.1	86.0	80.3	68.3	67.5
Japan	119.5	127.4	119.5	127.6	116.8
First World**	**100**	**100**	**100**	**100**	**100**

Source: Calculations based on World Bank (1984, 2001, 2004 for 2000 figures).

*Countries included in Third World:

Sub-Saharan Africa: Benin, Botswana, Burkina Faso, Cameroon, Central African Republic, Chad, Congo Dem. Rep., Congo Rep., Cote d'Ivoire, Gabon, Ghana, Kenya, Lesotho, Malawi, Mali, Mauritania, Mauritius, Niger, Nigeria, Rwanda, Senegal, South Africa, Tanzania.

Latin America: Argentina, Brazil, Chile, Colombia, Costa Rica, Dominican Republic, Ecuador, El Salvador, Guatemala, Honduras, Jamaica, Mexico, Nicaragua, Panama, Paraguay, Peru, Uruguay.

West Asia & North Africa: Algeria, Egypt Arab Rep., Morocco, Oman, Saudi Arabia, Tunisia, Turkey **(No Oman in 2000).**

South Asia: Bangladesh, India, Pakistan, Sri Lanka.

East Asia: Hong Kong, Indonesia, Malaysia, Philippines, Singapore, South Korea, Thailand.

China

**Countries included in First World:

North America: Canada, United States.

Western Europe: Austria, Belgium, Denmark, Finland, France, Luxembourg, Netherlands, Norway, Sweden, United Kingdom **(No Netherlands in 1970).**

Southern Europe: Greece, Italy, Portugal, Spain.

Australia & New Zealand: (No New Zealand in 1960 and 1970).

Japan

industrial inputs and disposal of industrial outputs in world markets intensified, and the economic benefits of industrialization were sharply reduced.

As argued in detail elsewhere (Arrighi & Drangel, 1986; Arrighi et al., 2003: 16–23), this interpretation is consistent with Joseph Schumpeter's theory of competition under capitalism and Raymond Vernon's closely related theory of the "product cycle." According to Schumpeter, the main determinant of the intensity of competition under capitalism is neither the number of units nominally competing with one another, nor restrictions to entry imposed or enforced by governments, as economists generally assume. Rather, it is the process of

TABLE 8.2. GNP per capita for region as percentage of First World's GNP per capita.

Region	1960	1970	1980	1990	2000
Sub-Saharan Africa (w/SA)	5.2	4.4	3.6	2.5	2.0
Latin America	19.7	16.4	17.6	12.3	13.7
West Asia and North Africa	8.7	7.8	8.7	7.4	8.3
South Asia	1.6	1.4	1.2	1.3	1.6
East Asia (w/o China and Japan)	5.7	5.7	7.5	10.4	10.0
China	0.9	0.7	0.8	1.3	3.0
Third World*	**4.5**	**3.9**	**4.3**	**4.0**	**4.5**
Third World (w/o China)*	**6.4**	**5.6**	**6.0**	**5.2**	**5.4**
North America	123.5	104.8	100.4	98.0	121.1
Western Europe	110.9	104.4	104.4	100.2	85.8
Southern Europe	51.9	58.2	60.0	58.7	56.2
Australia and New Zealand	94.6	83.3	74.5	66.2	65.9
Japan	78.6	126.1	134.1	149.4	135.9
First World	**100**	**100**	**100**	**100**	**100**

Source: Calculations based on World Bank (1984, 2001, 2004 for 2000 figures).

*Countries included in Third World:

Sub-Saharan Africa: Benin, Botswana, Burkina Faso, Burundi, Cameroon, Central African Republic, Chad, Rep. of Congo, Congo Dem. Rep., Cote d'Ivoire, Gabon, Ghana, Kenya, Lesotho, Madagascar, Malawi, Mauritania, Mauritius, Niger, Nigeria, Rwanda, Senegal, South Africa, T.

Latin America: Argentina, Bolivia, Brazil, Chile, Colombia, Costa Rica, Dominican Republic, Ecuador, El Salvador, Guatemala, Haiti, Honduras, Jamaica, Mexico, Nicaragua, Panama, Paraguay, Peru, Trinidad and Tobago, Uruguay, Venezuela.

West Asia & North Africa: Algeria, Arab Rep. of Egypt, Morocco, Saudi Arabia (2002 used for 2003), Sudan, Syrian Arab Rep., Tunisia, Turkey.

South Asia: Bangladesh, India, Nepal, Pakistan, Sri Lanka.

East Asia: Hong Kong, Indonesia, South Korea, Malaysia, Philippines, Singapore, Taiwan (not included in 2000 and 2003), Thailand.

China

"creative destruction" generated by major clusters of profit-oriented innovations, defined broadly to include the introduction, not just of new methods of production, but also of new commodities, new sources of supply, new trade routes and markets, and new forms of organization (Schumpeter, 1954: 83). These major clusters of innovations are the main direct and indirect source of gains and losses in the economy at large (Schumpeter, 1964: 80). They throw "to a small minority of winners" spectacular "prizes much greater than would have been necessary to call forth [their] particular effort." But they propel "the activity of that large majority of businessmen who receive in return very modest compensation or nothing or less than nothing, and yet do their utmost because they have the big prizes before their eyes and overrate their chances of doing equally well" (Schumpeter, 1954: 73–74).

A similar logic is at work in Vernon's product cycle model (1966; 1971: Ch. 3). In this model, the diffusion of innovations is a spatially structured process that originates in the more "developed" (i.e., wealthier) countries and gradually involves poorer, less "developed" countries. The spatial diffusion of innovations, however, goes hand in hand with their routinization, that is, with their ceasing to be innovations in the wider global context. As a result, by the time the "new" products and techniques are adopted by the poorer countries they tend to be subject to intense competition and no longer bring the high returns they did in the wealthier countries. Worse still, both product and process innovations originate under the conditions of high incomes, abundance of capital, and shortage of labor typical of wealthy countries. As they diffuse to poorer countries, they introduce patterns of consumption and techniques of production that aggravate the shortage of capital and the overabundance of labor typical of poor countries.

The logic that underlies Vernon's product cycle model is operative not only at the level of individual industries but also at the level of the manufacturing sector as a whole. That is to say, opportunities for economic advancement through industrialization, as they present themselves successively to one country after another, do not constitute equivalent opportunities for all countries. As countries accounting for a growing proportion of world population attempt to catch up with First World standards of wealth through industrialization, competitive pressures in the procurement of industrial inputs and disposal of industrial outputs in world markets intensify. In the process, Third World countries, like Schumpeter's "majority of businessmen," tend to underrate their chances of becoming the losers in the intense competitive struggle engendered by their very success in industrializing. As we show, there have been winners as well as losers among Third World countries, and even the countries that lost out in the competition drew some benefits from industrialization. Nevertheless, on average, 40 years of relatively successful industrialization has left Third World countries in the global hierarchy of wealth more or less where they were at the start.

Globalization and World Politics

The foregoing interpretation of the lack of income convergence in spite of industrial convergence may lead to two unwarranted conclusions. One is that the reproduction of the North–South income divide under conditions of generalized Southern industrialization has little to do with globalization, either structural or ideological. And the other is that Southern countries are powerless in their attempts to overcome the North–South divide.

The first conclusion is unwarranted because generalized Southern industrialization played a critical role in shaping the trajectory of structural globalization, and was in turn affected decisively by ideological globalization. Structural globalization is often identified with export-oriented industrialization (EOI) in contrast with import-substitution industrialization (ISI). In reality, there is a fundamental unity and complementarity between these two kinds of industrialization. Suffice it to mention that the more successful Southern ISI is, the fewer the imports that can be easily and advantageously replaced by domestic production. The smaller the population, natural resources, and domestic market of the countries engaging in ISI, and the more capital- and energy-intensive their industrialization, the sooner and the more compellingly would that limit be reached. Sooner or later, however, all rapidly industrializing countries are bound to find it more advantageous to seek through exports the means of payments necessary to increase their imports, rather than substitute domestic production for an increasing number and variety of imports. The very success of Southern ISI in the 1950s and 1960s was thus creating the conditions for its supersession by one form or another of EOI, thereby strengthening the cross-border interdependence of economic activities that constitutes a major aspect of structural globalization.

The tendency of Southern ISI to be superseded by EOI unfolded in conjunction with the tendency towards "financialization" that in the 1970s began to characterize the United States and other Northern economies. As Krippner (2002) has shown for the United States, heightened international competition (especially in trade-intensive activities such as manufacturing) induced corporations to divert a growing proportion of their incoming cash flows from investment in fixed capital and commodities to liquidity and accumulation through financial channels. In a sense, this diversion was a continuation of the logic of the product cycle by other means. The logic of the product cycle for the leading capitalist organizations of a given epoch is to ceaselessly shift resources from market niches that are becoming overcrowded (and therefore less profitable) to market niches that are less crowded (and therefore more profitable). When escalating competition reduces drastically the actual and potential availability of relatively empty and highly profitable niches in the commodity markets, the epoch's leading capitalist organizations have one last refuge where to retreat and from where to shift competitive pressures onto others. This last refuge is the world's money market, the market that, in Schumpeter's words, "is always, as it were, the headquarters of the capitalist system, from which orders go out to its individual divisions" (1961: 126).

Throughout the 1970s, financialization did not actually help Northern capital in shifting competitive pressures onto Southern countries. On the contrary, it seemed to make capital so abundant as to be almost a free good. Thus, in the mid-1970s real long-term interest rates in the United States fell below zero. It was also at this time that, as previously noted, Northern capital flowed to Third (and Second) World countries at very favorable conditions. Initially, therefore, the financialization of Northern capital strengthened the tendency towards the relocation of industrial activities from North to South, as well as the tendency of Southern ISI to be superseded by EOI (Arrighi, 1994: Ch. 4).

Had this situation persisted, Southern industrialization and structural globalization might have proceeded along a different trajectory than the one that materialized after the United States embraced the neoliberal creed and the TINA doctrine. It is impossible to tell what this alternative trajectory would have been. But we do know which particular alternative trajectory the United States was reacting against when it embraced the neoliberal creed and the TINA doctrine. This alternative trajectory was one of Third World empowerment and U.S. disempowerment.

The empowerment of the Third World in the 1970s was first and foremost a political fact. Its main landmarks were the U.S. defeat in Vietnam, Portuguese defeat in Africa, Israeli difficulties in the 1973 War, and the accession of the PRC in the Security Council of the United Nations. But the politics and the economics of the situation affected each other. Thus, the first and second oil shocks were integral to the political empowerment of the Third World. And so was the growth of North–South flows of capital, both private and public. Third World demands for a New International Economic Order (NIEO) sought to increase and at the same time institutionalize the ongoing redistribution of resources and power (cf. Krasner, 1985). Initially, First World countries seemed to yield to Third World pressures (see especially Brandt Commission, 1980), even pledging 1% of their GNP in aid to Third World countries. While these pledges were being made, however, the neoliberal turn in the United States resulted in a sudden turnaround.

The main reason why the United States promoted such a turnaround is that Third World empowerment was accompanied by a sharp decline in U.S. power and prestige. The decline reached its nadir in the late 1970s with the Iranian Revolution, the second oil shock, the Soviet invasion of Afghanistan, and a serious crisis of confidence in the U.S. dollar. Control over the world's money seemed to be slipping from U.S. hands, directly and indirectly disempowering the United States not just vis-à-vis the Third World but also vis-à-vis the USSR and Western Europe. It was in this context that the United States decided that the slide in its power and prestige could be reversed only by embracing the neoliberal creed, both at home and abroad. In this respect, the neoliberal turn in U.S. thought and action was a counterrevolution, not just in development theory as Toye (1993) maintains, but in world politics as well.

The main reason why the neoliberal counterrevolution succeeded in reversing the decline in U.S. power beyond the rosiest expectations of its perpetrators is that it brought about a massive rerouting of global capital flows towards the United States and the U.S. currency. To be sure, this massive rerouting transformed the United States from being the main source of world liquidity and foreign direct investment, as it had been in the 1950s and 1960s, into the world's main debtor nation and absorber of liquidity in the 1980s through the present.[6] Increases in indebtedness of this order cannot be sustained indefinitely. For 20 years, however, an escalating foreign debt enabled the United States to achieve through financial means what it could not achieve through political and military means: defeat the USSR in the Cold War and contain the empowerment of the South.

For massive borrowing from abroad, mostly from Japan, was essential to the escalation under Reagan of the armament race well beyond what the USSR could

---

[6] The extent of this rerouting can be gauged from the change in the current account of the U.S. balance of payments: in the five-year period almost half (46%) of the total surplus of G7 countries. In 1970–1974, the surplus contracted to $4.1 billion and to 21% of the total surplus of G7 countries. In 1975–1979, the surplus turned into a deficit of $7.4 billion. After that the deficit escalated to previously unimaginable levels: $146.5 billion in 1980–1984; $660.6 billion in 1985–1989; falling back to $324.4 billion in 1990–1994 before swelling to $912.4 billion in 1995–1999. By the end of 2004 the deficit in the U.S. current account was approaching $2 billion a day, that is, almost four times its average in the 1995–1999 period (calculated from International Monetary Fund various years).

afford economically. Combined with generous support to Afghan resistance against Soviet occupation, the escalation forced the USSR into a double confrontation, neither of which it could win and both of which it eventually lost: the one in Afghanistan, where its high-tech military apparatus found itself in the same difficulties that had led to the defeat of the United States in Vietnam; and the one in the armament race, where the United States could mobilize financial resources that were wholly beyond the Soviet reach.

At the same time, the massive redirection of capital flows to the United States turned the "flood" of capital that Southern countries had experienced in the 1970s into the sudden "drought" of the 1980s. First signaled by the Mexican default of 1982, this drought was probably the single most important factor in shifting competitive pressures from North to South and in provoking a major bifurcation in the fortunes of Southern regions in the 1980s and 1990s. As we show presently, the impact of the neoliberal counterrevolution was especially catastrophic for sub-Saharan Africa and Latin America in the 1980s and for the former USSR in the 1990s. But insofar as the Third World as a whole is concerned, these catastrophes were partly counterbalanced in the 1980s, and more than counterbalanced in the 1990s, by the significant economic advance of East Asia (especially China) and the less significant advance of South Asia (see Table 8.2). There is, of course, no way of knowing what would have happened to the North–South income divide in the absence of the neoliberal counterrevolution. But the very unevenness of the Southern experience can provide some insights into what enabled some regions to do better than others and what might have been done to avoid or alleviate the African and Latin American catastrophes.

Globalization and Uneven Development

As Table 8.2 shows, insofar as the overall North–South income divide is concerned the neoliberal counterrevolution made little difference one way or another. It did nonetheless make a big difference for the individual regions of the South. Some regions (most notably East Asia) succeeded in taking advantage of the increase in U.S. demand for cheap industrial products that ensued from U.S. trade liberalization and the escalating U.S. trade deficit. These regions tended to benefit from the redirection of capital flows towards the United States, because the improvement in their balance of payments lessened their need to compete with the United States in world financial markets, and indeed turned some of them (most notably China) into major lenders to the United States. Other regions (most notably sub-Saharan Africa and Latin America), in contrast, did not manage to compete successfully for a share of the North American demand. These regions tended to run into balance of payments difficulties that put them into the hopeless position of having to compete directly with the United States in world financial markets. Either way, the United States benefited economically and politically, because U.S. business and governmental agencies were best positioned to mobilize in the global competitive struggle the cheap commodities and credit that

Southern "winners" eagerly supplied, as well as the assets that Southern "losers" willy-nilly had to alienate at bargain prices. As a result, the United States reversed its economic decline vis-à-vis most world regions, and the gains and losses of Southern regions relative to the North balanced each other, thereby leaving the North–South income gap in 2000 roughly where it was in 1960 and 1980.

The question then arises as to whether it would have been possible (or might be possible in the future) to avoid Southern losses while retaining Southern gains so as to achieve a significant narrowing of the North–South income divide. The main institutional promoters of ideological globalization, most notably, the World Bank, the IMF, the U.S., and U.K. Treasuries, backed by opinion-shaping media such as *The Financial Times* and *The Economist* have championed the view that the main reason why some Southern countries have done better than others since 1980 is that they followed more closely the prescriptions of ideological globalization.[7] This view flies in the face of the fact that, comparatively speaking, the three world regions that have performed worst (sub-Saharan Africa and Latin America in the 1980s and the former USSR in the 1990s) are also the regions that willy-nilly were subjected more extensively or intensively to the structural adjustment or shock therapy advocated by the promoters of ideological globalization. In light of this basic fact, James Galbraith wonders whether we should continue to consider the 1990s a "golden age of capitalism" rather than "something closer to a golden age of reformed socialism in two places (China and India)" alongside an age of disasters for those who followed the prescriptions favored by *The Economist*. "In truth," he goes on to claim, "countries that followed the IMF–World Bank prescriptions to the letter" Argentina, say, or Russia in the early 1990s "have seen catastrophes worse in every way than the Great Depression of the 1930s was for us" (Galbraith, 2004).

It may be legitimate to question Galbraith's claim that China and especially India are practicing "reformed socialism" rather than some variant of capitalism. But whatever we may want to call what these countries have been practicing, it is hard to question Galbraith's claim that neither country did well since 1980 because it adhered to the prescriptions of ideological globalization more closely than the countries that did badly. If anything the opposite is true. "Both China and India steered free from Western banks in the 1970s, and spared themselves the debt crisis. Both continue to maintain capital controls to this day, so that hot money cannot flow freely in and out. Both continue to have large state sectors in heavy industry to this day." Moreover, China "continues to be run by the Communist Party, which is not the institution most noted in history for devotion to the free market." And so, we may well ask, if China and India have on the whole done well, is it because of their reforms or because of the regulations they continued to impose? "No doubt", claims Galbraith, "the right answer is: Partly to both" (Galbraith, 2004).

---

[7] For the latest critical survey of these claims, see Wade (2004).

I would reformulate and qualify this claim as follows. First, India and especially China fully participated in the process of structural globalization by opening up their economies and by putting greater emphasis on EOI than they had done before the mid-1980s. By so doing they took advantage of the benefits of operating in a wider and comparatively wealthier economic space. Nevertheless, they did so on terms and at conditions that suited their own national interests, rather than the interests of Northern countries embodied in U.S.-promoted ideological globalization. Among other things, this meant a slower and more selective process of deregulation and privatization than occurred in countries and regions subjected to the shock therapies and structural adjustments advocated by ideological globalization.

Second, India's and China's greater capacity to participate in structural globalization on terms that suited their own national interests was undoubtedly due in part to the fact that, as Galbraith suggests, through the 1970s both countries had become far less dependent on foreign capital than Latin America or Africa. Foreign capital never comes for free; and even when it comes at very favorable conditions, as it did in the 1970s, it may establish "addictions" that subsequently constrain the capacity to pursue the national interest. In 2003 China surpassed the United States as the world's largest recipient of foreign direct investment. But China's increasing dependence on foreign capital has been more than counterbalanced by increasing U.S. dependence on cheap Chinese commodities and credit, so that its capacity to dictate, rather than being dictated to, the terms of much of this investment has not lessened.

Third, India's and China's greater capacity to participate in structural globalization on their own terms has not been solely due to the fact that they have remained far less dependent on foreign capital than sub-Saharan Africa or Latin America. Equally important is another peculiarity of India and China, namely, the fact that they are no mere national states but continent-sized states, each with a population considerably larger than that of Latin America or Africa. Moreover, both countries had a long history of highly diversified production and market exchanges within their boundaries and with the surrounding regions, a history that has endowed them with a huge supply, not just of comparatively skilled and versatile labor, but also of micro- (and not so micro-) entrepreneurship. As a result of this legacy and of considerable infrastructural investment in domestic transport and communication, India and China have been far better positioned than economically and politically fragmented Latin America or Africa in combining the advantages of EOI and foreign investment with those of an informally protected and substantively self-reliant domestic economy.

Finally and partly related to the above, China appears to have an additional advantage in industrialization, whether of the ISI or the EOI variety. Contrary to a widely held belief, this advantage is not low wages, at least not low wages as such. Rather, as a recent cover story in *The New York Times* magazine entitled, "The Chinese Century," has underscored, it is the widespread deployment of techniques of production that substitute as much as possible inexpensive educated labor for expensive machines and managers. The experience of Wafeng automotive factory outside Shanghai illustrates the point. In that factory "there is not a single robot in sight." Instead, hundreds of young recruits from China's expanding technical schools man the assembly lines "with little more than large electric drills, wrenches and rubber mallets." Engines and body panels, instead of moving from station to station on automatic conveyors (as they would in a Western, Korean, or Japanese factory) are hauled by hand and hand truck. The company is not using multimillion-dollar machines; it is using highly skilled workers whose yearly pay is less than the monthly pay of new hires in Detroit. That is the reason why Wanfeng can sell its handmade luxury versions of the Jeep (mostly to buyers in the Middle East) for $8000 to $10,000 (Fishman, 2004).

Moreover, Chinese businesses are substituting inexpensive educated labor, not just for expensive machinery, but for expensive managers as well. For a self-managed labor force "keeps management costs down too." By Western standards, the ranks of managers "are remarkably thin. Depending on the work, you might see 15 managers for 5,000 workers, an indication of how incredibly well self-managed they are" (Fishman, 2004). It is hard to tell how widespread the use of these machine-and-manager-saving techniques actually is. But if it is as wide-spread as Ted Fishman suggests, it constitutes an important antidote to the previ-ously noted tendency of innovations originating in wealthy countries to absorb scarce capital instead of abundant labor in the poorer countries.

In any event, the substitution of inexpensive educated labor for expensive machines and managers is not inimical to more mainstream, applied industrial development and innovation. On the contrary, last year China spent $60 billion on research and development, considerably less than the $282 billion spent by the United States. But again, because China's engineers and scientists usually make one-sixth and one-tenth what Americans do, "the wide gaps in financing do not necessarily result in equally wide gaps in manpower or results. The U.S. spent nearly five times what China did, but had less than two times as many researchers (1.3 million to 743,000)" (Fishman, 2004). In this respect too, therefore, a large supply of inexpensive educated labor is a crucial enabling condition for a Southern country to participate in processes of structural globalization on its own terms rather than on the terms dictated by the interests of Northern countries.

Implications for Future Research

The foregoing analysis has three main implications for future research. First, the con-tention that China and India have benefited from structural globalization because they did not subject themselves to the prescriptions of ideological globalization is no more than a hypothesis. In order to assess its plausibility, countries must be classi-fied as rigorously as possible by the degree of their participation in structural glob-alization on the one side, and by the extent to which they have subjected themselves to the prescriptions of ideological globalization. Such a classification would provide us with a more precise idea than we have at the moment of differences among coun-tries in the way in which they have related to structural and ideological globalization.

It would thus enable us to investigate whether and how these differences have affected economic performance, and can themselves be traced to country-specific social, historical, and geographical characteristics.

Second, our analysis also suggests that demographic size matters. The huge populations of China and India have provided them with developmental options (such as the formation and preservation of a coherent national economy even when pursuing EOI) that may well be beyond the horizon of most other Southern countries. And yet, rapid demographic growth has often been associated with a deterioration rather than an improvement in the capacity of Southern countries to benefit rather than lose from greater integration in the global economy. The question then arises of how demographic growth affects, and is in turn affected, by economic performance. In dealing with this question, special attention should be paid to the possibility that some Southern countries have been caught in a "low-level equilibrium trap," that is, a situation in which tendencies towards an increase in rates of economic growth call forth increases in demographic growth that provoke stagnation in per-capita income. By carefully comparing cases of this kind of entrapment with cases of escape from it, as well as with cases of stagnant or falling relative income associated with a stagnant or declining population, we will be able to endogenize demographic growth within a sociological explanation of the North–South income gap and thus avoid crude Malthusian generalizations.

Third, and for present purposes last, it has been my contention that, contrary to the TINA doctrine, there were and there still are alternatives to the kind of cutthroat competition for capital advocated by the promoters of ideological globalization. One such alternative is for governments to compete, not in making ever more extravagant concessions to capital, but in providing the education, health, and quality of life that would make their citizens more productive. As Fishman suggests, a large supply of inexpensive educated labor has probably been the greatest of China's competitive advantages, not just in production, but in research and development as well. Also this contention is for now simply a hypothesis. In order to assess its validity, we need first of all more comprehensive evidence in support of Fishman's contention concerning China's competitive advantage. We then need to compare this evidence with the experience of other Southern countries to gauge differences in the extent to which they have resorted to strategies of economic advancement that relied more heavily on the provision of incentives to capital than on the improvement of the health, education, and well-being of their populations. With some luck, this comparative analysis will provide us with the information necessary to determine (1) which strategy has been more productive in terms of national wealth and welfare, and (2) which particular combination of social, historical, and geopolitical conditions has been conducive to the adoption of one strategy or the other.

Sustained research along these directions would greatly advance our understanding of the relationship between globalization and uneven development. For what we know this may well result in a greater "pessimism of the intelligence." But it may not, and in any event it will, it is hoped, dispel the present confusion between ideological and structural globalization and undermine the groundless self-assurance of the TINA doctrine.

References

Arrighi, G. (1994). *The long twentieth century: Money, power and the origins of our times.* London: Verso.

—— (2002). The African crisis: World systemic and regional aspects. *New Left Review* 15: 5–36.

Arrighi, G. & Drangel, J. (1986). The stratification of the world-economy: An exploration of the semiperipheral zone. *Review* (Fernand Braudel Center) X: 9–74.

Arrighi, G., Silver, B. J., & Brewer, B. D. (2003). Industrial convergence and the persistence of the North–South Divide. *Studies in Comparative International Development* 38: 3–31.

Baumol, Willian J. (1967). Macroeconomics of unbalanced growth: The anatomy of urban crises. *American Economic Review* 57: 415–26.

Bell, D. (1973). *The coming of post-industrial society.* New York: Basic.

Brandt Commission (1980). *North–South: a program for survival.* London: Pan.

Cardoso, F. H., & Faletto, E. (1979). *Dependency and development in Latin America.* Berkeley: University of California Press.

Chase-Dunn, C. (1999). Globalization: A world-systems perspective. *Journal of World-Systems Research* 5: 176–198.

Clark, C. (1957). *The conditions of economic progress.* 3rd ed. London: Macmillan.

Easterly, W. (2001). The lost decades: Developing countries stagnation in spite of policy reform 1980–1998. *Journal of Economic Growth* 6: 135–157.

Escobar, A. (1995). *Encountering development: The making and unmaking of the third world.* Princeton, NJ: Princeton University Press.

Fishman, T. (2004). The Chinese century. *The New York Times* (Magazine), July 4.

Galbraith, K. (2004). Debunking *The Economist* Again. Available at http://www.salon.com/opinion/feature/2004/03/22/economist/print.html.

International Monetary Fund

—— *Balance of Payments Statistics Yearbook* 2001.

—— (various years). *International financial statistics yearbook.* Washington, DC: International Monetary Fund.

Krasner, S. D. (1985). *Structural conflict: The third world against global liberalism.* Berkeley: University of California Press.

Krippner, G. (2002). What is financialization? Paper presented at the annual meeting of the American Sociological Association, Chicago, IL, 16–19 August.

McMichael, P. (2000). *Development and social change: A global perspective.* 2nd ed. Thousand Oaks, CA: Sage.

Ravallion, M. (2004). Competing concepts of inequality in the globalization debate. *World Bank Policy Research Working Paper* 3243 (March).

Rostow, W. (1960). *The stages of economic growth: A non-communist manifesto.* Cambridge, UK: Cambridge University Press.

Sachs, W. (Ed.) (1992). *The development dictionary.* London: Zed.

Schumpeter, J. (1954). *Capitalism, socialism & democracy.* London: Allen & Unwin.

—— (1961). *The theory of economic development.* New York: Oxford University Press.

—— (1964). *Business cycles: A theoretical, historical, and statistical analysis of the capitalist process.* New York: McGraw Hill.

Singer, H. (1997). The golden age of the Keynesian consensus – The pendulum swings back. *World Development* 25: 293–295.

Solow, R. M. (1956). Contribution to the theory of economic growth. *Quarterly Journal of Economics* 70: 65–94.

Tipps, D. C. (1973). Modernization theory and the study of national societies: A critical perspective. *Comparative Studies in Society and History* 15: 199–226.

Toye, J. (1993). *Dilemmas of development. Reflections on the counter-revolution in development economics.* 2nd ed. Oxford: Blackwell.

Vernon, R. (1966). International investment and international trade in the product cycle. *Quarterly Journal of Economics* 80 (2): 190–207.

—— (1971). *Sovereignty at bay: The multinational spread of U.S. enterprises.* Harmondsworth, UK: Penguin.

Wade, R. (2004). Is globalization reducing poverty and inequality? *World Development* 32 (4): 567–589.

Warren, B. (1980). *Imperialism, pioneer of capitalism.* London: New Left.

World Bank (1984). *World tables.* Vols. 1 & 2. Washington D.C.: World Bank.

—— (1989). *Sub-Saharan Africa: From crisis to sustainable growth. A long-term perspective study.* Washington, DC: World Bank.

—— (1992). *Governance and development.* Washington, DC: World Bank.

—— (1993). *The East Asian miracle: Economic growth and public policy.* A World Bank policy research report. New York: Oxford University Press.

—— (2001). *World development indicators.* CD-ROM. Washington, DC: World Bank.

—— (2003). *World development indicators.* CD-ROM. Washington, DC: World Bank.

—— (2004). *World development indicators.* CD-ROM. Washington, DC: World Bank.

9
Globalization and Disintegration: Substitutionist Technologies and the Disintegration of Global Economic Ties

Robert K. Schaeffer

One of the most significant developments associated with contemporary globalization has been the dramatic fall in prices for "primary commodities," the mineral products and agricultural goods produced in the periphery and exported to consumers in the core. Prices have collapsed because commodity supplies in the periphery have increased and because demand for these goods in the core has constricted, in large part because new "substitutionist" technologies invented in the core have made it possible for producers and consumers there to replace peripheral goods with products originating in the core. The substitution and "dematerialization" of peripheral commodities—processes first theorized by environmental scholars associated with the sociology of agriculture school (Goodman et al., 1987: 2–4, 580)—has adversely affected producers, workers, and states where primary goods are produced. Moreover, they have contributed to the disintegration of long-standing, structural economic ties between core and periphery. These developments suggest that economic relationships may be weakening as a result of technological innovation, which is the opposite of what most theories of globalization predict, and challenge the assumption, common in the literature, that globalization is everywhere and always a force for economic integration.

Commodity Price Deflation

Since 1980, the prices primary producers in the periphery received for the goods they export have fallen precipitously. Using a price index of 100 in 1980, price levels in 2001 stood at 72 for oil, 30 for coffee, 30 for sugar, and 40 for cocoa, the four most valuable raw materials traded on the world market (Lea, 2002: 244, 113, 311, 95). On average, the price of the top 17 primary commodities fell by nearly half—to 53.6 of 1980 levels—by 2001.

But the story is actually worse than price index figures suggest for two reasons. First, most commodities are traded on world markets in dollars. So a devaluation of the dollar reduces the real value of dollar-denominated goods, when measured against other currencies. Since 1980, the dollar has twice been devalued. The first devaluation, in 1985–1988, reduced the dollar by half against the yen and most Western European currencies. The second, since 2001, has reduced the dollar about 30 percent against the euro, although not the yen. If the price index for coffee was 30 in 2001, its real value in nondollar currencies is probably about 10 (the 1985 devaluation reduced it from 30 to 15, and the 2001 devaluation reduced it from 15 to 10), a 90% decline since 1980. Of course, dollar devaluations have different meanings in different regions. In Latin America, where countries sell primary goods in dollars and import manufactured goods from the United States, paying for them in dollars, dollar devaluations have relatively little impact. But in Africa or Asia, where countries sell goods in dollars and then import manufactured goods from Western Europe or Japan, paying for them in euros or yen, dollar devaluations have an adverse impact because it weakens the terms of trade with their primary trading partners.

Second, prices for manufactured goods in the core have increased in this same period, which means that the terms of trade have also deteriorated. During the Great Depression, raw material prices fell, but so too did prices for manufactured goods. But during the last 20 years, while raw material prices fell, prices for manufactured goods rose, so the money primary producers earned for their goods bought less than it did before. In real terms, conditions for primary producers are much worse than they were during the Great Depression (Maizels, 1993: 27–29).

Writing in the 1950s, the Latin American economist Raul Prebisch predicted that prices for primary goods would fall over the long term and argued that the secular decline in the terms of trade was "not casual or accidental, but deeply ingrained in the world trading system itself" (Maizels, 1993: 105–106). Events have demonstrated the accuracy of his predictions. Prices and terms of trade for primary producers fell between 1950 and 1970, rose during the 1970s, then fell, and fell, and fell again. But although Prebisch and other "dependency" theorists anticipated some of these developments, the decline since 1980 has occurred for reasons they did not theorize or expect. Dependency theorists thought that efforts to increase the scale and/or productivity of mining and agricultural industries would increase the supply of primary goods. They assumed that demand for these goods would grow, but at a slower pace, so that increasing supplies would glut markets and force down prices. This has been an ongoing problem. But in the 1980s, something new occurred. The demand for many primary products contracted because new substitutionist technologies made it possible to replace or reduce raw material inputs from the periphery. In the current period of globalization, it is important to appreciate both the changing character of peripheral supplies, which was appreciated by dependency theorists, and of core demand, which was not well understood.

Growing Supplies

Supplies of primary commodities have increased significantly during the last 30 years, although for different reasons at different times. During the 1970s, the OPEC oil embargo and food shortages in the Soviet Union drove up commodity prices. Rising prices encouraged primary producers to expand production, and they used borrowed money from Eurodollar markets and global financial institutions to finance their expansion (Schaeffer, 2003: 95–118). Oil production expanded in the North Sea and Mexico, increasing world supplies, coffee production grew from 3.8 million tons in 1970 to 4.9 million tons in 1979, world cotton production grew from 11 to 14 million tons, and world sugar production increased from 585 to 754 million tons in the same period (Dinham & Hines, 1983: 189, 193). To maintain high prices as supplies increased, many primary producers banded together to form commodity cartels to manage supplies and allocate market shares among their members. OPEC was the most famous of these cartels, but there were others for coffee, sugar, cocoa, coconuts, rubber, and tin.

But although high prices and debt stimulated the expansion of commodity supplies in the 1970s, a different set of developments contributed to growing supplies during the 1980s and 1990s. In the early 1980s, the U.S. Federal Reserve increased interest rates in an effort to slow inflation (Schaeffer, 2003: 95–118). Rising interest rates then triggered a debt crisis for producers and states that had used borrowed money to finance the expansion of commodity production. To manage debt, the International Monetary Fund imposed structural adjustment programs in many peripheral states. These programs typically required indebted states to expand the production of export commodities so they could earn the foreign exchange needed to repay their debts.

At the same time, core countries and international lending agencies took steps to reduce their dependency on single sources of supply and weaken commodity cartels by "diversifying" sources of supply. Perhaps the most striking example of supply diversification was in Vietnam, where World Bank financing expanded the area of land devoted to coffee production from 20,000 hectares in 1980 to 300,000 hectares in 1998, a 15-fold increase. Vietnam produced one million bags of coffee by 1990 and 13 million bags by 2000, making it the world's second largest coffee producer, behind Brazil and ahead of Columbia (Forero, 2001: W1; Gonzales, 2001: A3).

Core efforts to diversify supplies were largely successful. The subsequent adoption of new free trade agreements in the early 1990s (WTO, NAFTA) consolidated these gains by establishing rules making supply-management practices by commodity cartels subject to retaliatory action (Schaeffer, 2003: 220). Of course, although governments in the core have devoted considerable effort to weakening commodity cartels in the periphery, they have done nothing to reduce the monopoly and monopsony power of transnational corporations (TNCs) in commodity markets, excluding antitrust provisions from the new free trade agreements (Schaeffer, 2003: 238–240).

Unfortunately, the expansion of commodity supplies in the periphery in the 1980s occurred at a time when demand in the core was weak, a result of the recession caused by high interest rates in the United States. Because supplies grew faster than demand, prices began to fall from the levels reached in the 1970s. But when the recession in the core ended in the 1990s, the demand for primary goods did not significantly expand, as one might have expected. To understand why it did not, it is necessary to look at the growing role played by new substitutionist technologies and changing consumer preferences in the core during the 1980s and 1990s.

Technology, Consumers, and Changing Demand

In the late 1980s, scholars studying the sociology of agriculture made an important theoretical observation. Goodman et al. (1987: 2–4) found that new agricultural technologies being developed in the core allowed producers to replace agricultural products made in the periphery with products originating in the core, a process of "substitutionism." Goodman and Redclift (1991: 91–92) later predicted that substitutionist technologies would enable producers to "dematerialize" some primary products.

This theoretical framework can usefully be conceptualized as two related processes: substitution and dematerialization. *Substitutionist* technologies are those used to replace one raw material input with another, high fructose corn sweetener (HFCS) for cane sugar. *Dematerialist* technologies are those that reduce raw material inputs through conservation, waste reduction, recycling, repair, remanufacture, and reuse. This elaboration of their theory is useful, I think, for two reasons: it facilitates the application of their theory to minerals, which their work does not examine; and it allows one to appreciate the different consequences of technological change. If, for example, HFCS technology enables producers to substitute corn for sugar in sweeteners, there is little net dematerialization (cane sugar is dematerialized, but corn is materialized). If, on the other hand, producers recycle metals, there is a real net reduction in the demand for mined ore. Used in this manner, dematerialization occurs when fewer raw materials are needed to produce the same quantity of goods. So, the reduction of waste, what is called muda in Japan, made it possible for producers there to consume in 1984 "only 60 percent of the raw materials required for the same volume of production in 1973," clearly an instance of "dematerialization" (Hawken et al., 2001: 125).

Technological innovations are not the only developments that have altered core demand for peripheral products. Changing consumer preferences in the core have also played an important role. Of course, many scholars have argued that consumer "demand" is largely shaped by corporate design, because corporations use media technologies and mass marketing to persuade consumers to "demand" particular goods and brands. From this perspective, consumer demand is less an expression of consumer preference than it is an expression of producer preference. This may be partly true, however, it is important to recognize that consumers are not simply passive subjects but also agents, who can sometimes change the structure of demand in the market. Changing dietary preferences for organic, fair trade, heart-healthy, low-carbohydrate, low-fat, low-sugar, decaffeinated, low-chloresterol foods are a good example. Growing consumer demand for foods with these characteristics was not an expression of producer preferences, indeed, producers often opposed their introduction or ridiculed them. Instead, demand for these goods was developed first by consumers and consumer advocacy groups. Only later, and slowly, did producers create products to meet these demands. This suggests that consumers possess some agency and autonomy. But although changing consumer preferences, either as an expression of corporate design or consumer choice, can alter the structure of demand for peripheral products, neither producers nor consumers have appreciated the impact of dietary changes in the core on primary producers and their diets, an issue that becomes evident when we look at the consequences of change.

To appreciate the growing importance of substitutionist and dematerialist technologies and changing consumer preferences, it is useful to describe briefly the changes that have affected the structure of demand for primary goods from the periphery, looking first at the four most valuable commodities, in rank order, that are traded on the world market—pertroleum, coffee, sugar, and cocoa—and then examining other important primary products.

Petroleum (selling in 2001 at 72% of 1980 price). High oil prices during the 1970s accelerated the invention and diffusion of myriad substitutionist and dematerialist technologies designed to reduce the demand for oil in transportation, residential and business heating, cooling, and lighting, and consumer appliances. These collective improvements were described by some scholars as a *nega* watt revolution (Flavin & Lenssen, 1994: 71–72).

In transportation, new technologies reduced vehicle weight and friction, improved engine efficiency and safety, and increased car and truck mileage. More recently, new hybrid technologies are increasing mileage and dematerializing oil, and research on hydrogen and other fuel substitutes is being developed.

During the 1980s, architects and engineers developed new construction technologies that have dematerialized oil for residential and commercial buildings. The development of Owens-Corning fiberglass insulation is probably the most recognizable technology of this sort, but weatherproofing, high-efficiency lighting, photovoltaic cells, solar heating and cooling technologies, often assisted by government tax-credit and subsidy policies (which should be regarded as financial technologies) reduced the demand for oil in shelter. Western Europe and Japan promoted these technologies more aggressively than the United States, and Japan "now generates half the world's solar power" (Belson, 2003: C1). In 2002, the European Union announced plans to obtain "22 percent of its electricity and 12 percent of all energy from renewable sources by 2010" (Belson, 2002: D1).

Refrigerators use one-sixth of the electricity produced in the United States. But new dematerialist technologies reduced energy consumption in refrigerators by 75% between 1987 and 1997 (Hawken et al., 2001: 105; Renner, 2004: 107–108).

When oil prices were high between 1973 and 1985, new technologies made it possible for core countries to grow substantially without increasing their demand for oil (Hawken et al., 2001: 253). Although the dematerialization of oil now proceeds at a slower pace, new technologies, changing consumer preferences, and government policies will eventually have a significant impact on the demand for oil.

Coffee (30% of 1980 price). Between 1975 and 1991, per capita consumption of coffee in the United States dropped by one-third. Demand fell because consumers switched to caffeinated beverage substitutes (soda pop) and because they reduced caffeine as part of health-conscious diets. When they did switch to coffee substitutes, they turned increasingly to higher caffeine sodas and "energy drinks," which are very high in caffeine. (Red Bull's 8-ounce can has as much caffeine as one cup of coffee and twice as much caffeine as a 12-ounce Coke), and other "energy-enhancing" ingredients such as ginseng and taurine (a compound extracted from bull's testicles). "We think energy drinks are the new coffee," argues Scott Moffit of SoBe, a substitutionist beverage technology. "It delivers the pick-me-up that coffee does. But it tastes better and it's better for you. It has a better image and it's more portable. You can't throw a cup of coffee into your backpack" (Day, 2004: B4).

Among those who still drank coffee, consumers increasingly preferred "more subtle, high-quality arabica coffees," which are lower in caffeine than robusta varieties (Brown & Tiffen, 1992: 32). This shift has increased the demand for arabica coffees produced in Latin America, but reduced demand for robusta from Africa, where it is the principal variety. But whether they are abandoning coffee or embracing coffee substitutes, changing consumer preferences have simultaneously dematerialized coffee and shifted the structure of demand for coffee produced in different regions.

Sugar (30% of 1980 price). In the 1960s and 1970s, scientists developed technologies that enabled producers to replace cane and beet sugars with agricultural and chemical substitutes. The most important of these was the development of enzymes that produced fructose sugar from the starch in corn, resulting in HFCS. During the 1980s, HFCS replaced cane and beet sugar in many food products. The 1983 decision by Coke and Pepsi to use HFCS in their beverages was a turning point. Within two years, per capita consumption of HFCS doubled from 29.8 to 60 pounds (Dinham & Hines, 1983: 189, 193). HFCS now accounts for 55% of the sweetener market (Brody, 2004: D7).

Scientists also developed dietary sweetener technologies—saccharin, aspartame, acesufamed-k, sucralose, thaumatin, and xylitol—that are many times sweeter than sugar and provide taste without the calories in sugar (Squires, 2004: D8). Not surprisingly, diet-conscious consumers have increased their consumption of dietary substitutes, which have captured about 13% of the sweetener market. Altogether, substitutionist sweetener technologies now make up about 70% of the market for sweeteners. Cane and beet sugars make up only 30% of the market, down from 90% just a few decades ago (Borrell & Duncan, 1993: 24). Of course, some new beverage technologies replace multiple primary products, so Coke might be though of as a substitutionist technology that replaces both coffee and cane sugar.

Cocoa (40% of 1980 price). Cocoa, the primary ingredient in chocolate, has only recently been subjected to substitutionist technology and government policy. In the late 1990s, the European Union announced plans allowing chocolate producers in Europe to replace up to 5% of the cocoa fats in chocolate with noncocoa vegetable fats (see role of temperate oil seeds as substitutes for other primary products below). This development will allow producers to introduce substitutionist temperate oils into chocolate manufacture, a small but significant development for cocoa producers (Lea, 2002: 88).

The introduction of substitutionist technologies has also been an important development for the producers of other agricultural commodities. Temperate oil seeds (soybean and rapeseed) produced in the core have been used increasingly as substitutes for coconut oil (45% of 1980 price). Soybean, cottonseed, and sunflower oils are replacing groundnuts (59% of 1980 price) in many uses. A variety of industrial and herbal beverages are used as substitutes for tea (70% of 1980 price), much as they are for coffee. The 1988 decision by food processors in the United States to discontinue using oil palm (49% of 1980 price) in the manufacture of food and candy because it is high in saturated fat and cholesterol, and replace it with temperate oil seeds and hydrogenated oils that are low in cholesterol, has had a huge impact on demand for this oil and other tropical oils (coconut and groundnut). In all of these cases, changing consumer preferences have encouraged and rationalized the substitution process.

In a related development, new genetically modified (GM) corn technologies, assisted by government subsidy programs in the United States, are being exported to the periphery, where they undersell non-GM, indigenous corn varieties, which are grown without comparable government subsidy assistance. The substitution of GM for indigenous corn is different from the other cases examined here because peripheral countries do not typically export their corn but instead sell and consume it locally. In Mexico, for instance, GMO corn from the United States now accounts for one-quarter of the Mexican market, with important consequences for the "15 million Mexicans who depend on corn for their livelihood" (Weiner, 2002: A4). HFCS produced in the United States is having much the same impact in Mexico. In this context, U.S.-GMO corn is being used as a substitute both for corn and for sugar in the periphery.

In the case of mineral, and of agricultural commodities such as rubber, the introduction of substitutionist and dematerialist technologies have weakened core demand for many periphery products.

Copper (75% of 1980 price). A series of technologies has undermined core demand for copper, a metal used for electrical applications and plumbing. In the 1970s, the development of fiber optic cables enabled phone companies to use it as a replacement for copper wire in telephone lines. The subsequent adoption of wireless technologies further reduced the demand for copper in telecommunications. Meanwhile, PVC plastic pipe replaced copper in plumbing fixtures. Finally, recycling technologies made it possible for producers to reuse copper rather than purchase it from primary producers. By 1985, producers in the United States obtained one-half of all the copper they needed from recycled copper scrap, a development that significantly dematerialized copper (Mikesell, 1988: 56).

Gold (30% of 1980 price). Even gold is not immune to substitution. For millennia, gold was seen as a repository of value, the "ultimate form of payment" (Fuerbringer, 1999: C1). But starting in the 1970s, officials in the United States, at the IMF, and at private financial institutions and central banks in the core have worked to "demonetize" gold, first by severing the connection between gold and the dollar, and then by using monetary technologies (securities, stocks, bonds, hedge funds, mutual funds, money market funds, derivatives) to provide investors with financial substitutes for gold (Lea, 2002: 146–148; Ferguson, 2001: 325–326). This substitution has been so effective that central banks in core states have been selling off their stocks of gold by the ton. U.S. gold reserves have fallen from 701 to 261 million ounces, a level indicative of U.S. disinterest in gold as a financial instrument (Ferguson, 2001: 326).

Nickel (95% of 1980 price). Unlike most primary products, prices for nickel have remained high (Lea, 2002: 215; Simon, 2004: W1). But if core states impose battery recycling laws, which are designed to reduce the toxic waste associated with battery disposal, then recycling would dematerialize nickel, and also cadmium, much as they have copper. And if producers replace nickel with chromium in the manufacture of stainless steel, this cheaper substitute could drive down the price of nickel.

In general, new recycling technologies are increasingly being used to "mine" the metals in computers, electronics, automobiles, and appliances. In Japan, for example, technology used to recover metals for 16,000 cell phones yielded 0.4 pounds of gold, 2.6 pounds of silver, 255.7 pounds of copper, 0.2 pounds of palladium, 205 pounds of steel, and 83 pounds of aluminum (Belson, 2002: D1).

Rubber (41% of 1980 price) Although rubber is not a mineral, it can be recycled, like metals, although its usefulness degrades in the process. Nike has used dematerialist technologies to "downcycle" old sneakers, converting outsole rubber into surface material for running tracks, playgrounds, and carpet padding (Renner, 2004: 108).

Of course, it has taken some time for technological innovations and changing consumer preferences to affect the structure of demand for peripheral products. But ongoing research and development, supported by public and private research infrastructures in the core and by government patenting systems and trade laws that reward the invention of substitutionist and dematerialist technologies, will contribute in coming years to an ongoing process of substitution and dematerialization. And if commodity prices rise, as they have recently for oil and some metals, even temporarily, the pace of technological change will likely accelerate. So technology now acts to keep prices "in line" at historically low levels and discourage efforts by primary producers to raise them.

It is equally evident that consumer, health, and environmental movements have played an important role in the adoption and diffusion of these technologies. Movements have persuaded producers and consumers in the core to reduce their demand for many peripheral products, arguing that new technologies and conservation practices benefit consumers and the environment. Some environmental scholars have urged core governments to adopt policies that would encourage the provision of a given volume of goods and services with one-tenth as much material input, what they call a "Factor 10" approach to resource and energy conservation (Renner, 2004: 102).

But environmental proponents of resource conservation typically ignore the impact that new technologies have on resources, people, states, and the environment in the periphery. In the same way, consumer groups often fail to appreciate the impact that changing dietary preferences have on primary producers and their diets. By reducing their consumption of foods high in chloresterol, saturated fat, sugar, and caffeine, consumers in the core can improve their diets. But at the same time, falling demand for palm oil, coconut oil, goundnuts, cane sugar, coffee, and tea has contributed to lower prices, falling income, and deteriorating diets for agricultural producers in the periphery.

To appreciate these developments, let me briefly describe the impact that falling prices have had on people in the periphery and on the structural economic relations between core and periphery.

Consequences for Producers, Workers, and States

When prices fall, high-cost producers are affected first. They may have higher costs because they have poorer soils, lower-grade ores, or deeper mines than others, or because they have weak or expensive infrastructures (roads, old railways, shallow ports), or because they have higher labor costs. As prices decline and profits are squeezed, these producers go out of business. Their exit often results in a shift in the geography of production. So, for example, the production of copper has shifted from high-cost producers in Africa and Latin America to low-cost producers in Australia, a core country where high levels of investment in technology and infrastructure have created economies of scale that producers elsewhere cannot match (Gaylord, 2002: W1). Likewise, coffee production has shifted from Africa to Vietnam and also to Latin America. Of course, when prices fall to historically low levels, producers everywhere are driven from field and mine.

Falling prices lead to bankruptcy for large-scale producers (who grow tea, rubber, cotton, and sugar on plantations, and also most mineral producers), small-scale producers (who grow coconuts, coffee, groundnuts, cocoa, and oil palm), and the workers employed by producers large and small. Once you know that 50 million people work in sugar production worldwide, 25 million grow coffee, and 15 million grow corn in Mexico, the impact of falling prices becomes evident

(Smith, 2003: W1). By comparison, relatively few people are employed in mining industries, mostly because they are much more capital intensive than agriculture. But those who do are skilled, highly paid workers, whose economic role in poor countries is much greater than their numbers alone would suggest. In South Africa, for example, the number of workers employed in the gold mines fell from 514,000 to 180,000 in the last decade (McNeil, 1998: B1, B4; Swarns, 1999: B1, B3). For producers and workers, falling commodity prices have led to falling incomes and massive unemployment.

For states in the periphery, falling prices have created a series of problems. Producer bankruptcy and worker unemployment in the primary goods industries have lowered tax revenues, which contributes to budget deficits and cuts in social spending. As their export earnings decline, states are unable to secure the foreign exchange they need to repay debt, purchase essential goods (oil, medicine), or import the manufactured goods from the core that are necessary for their economic development.

Disintegration

Falling prices, the introduction of substitutionist and dematerialist technologies, and changing consumer preferences in the core have been extremely disruptive, leading to the "disintegration" of long-standing economic ties between core and periphery. Recall that core countries established sugar production in their Caribbean and American colonies 450 years ago. Producers in the periphery have been growing cocoa, coconut, coffee, groundnut, oil palm, rubber, tea, and wool since the 19th century, and mining gold, copper, nickel, and tin for at least as long. The economic relations established between core and periphery survived the Great Depression, world war, and decolonization. But they may not long survive globalization, not in their present form.

Of course, Schumpeter argued long ago that the introduction of new technologies and the consequent destruction of "obsolete" industries was a healthy and normal kind of "creative destruction." In the face of this, some effort has been made by peripheral states to develop export manufacturing or tourism as alternatives to declining primary goods industries (Schaeffer, 2003: 134–36). But they are not realistic alternatives in most settings, for reasons that are easy to discern. China is fast becoming the center of low-level export manufacturing in the world, at the expense of "maquila" producers across the periphery. Tourism can provide an alternative in a few places, but the willingness of worker-tourists from the core to travel to peripheral destinations is increasingly problematic, as the perceived risks from disease, poverty, violence, and terror rise (Siano & Connelly, 2003: C9). There are some new agricultural industries in the periphery—fresh flowers, specialty vegetables, shrimp—that produce commodities for export. But they are specialty crops for limited markets and they employ relatively few people. Moreover, they are subject to many of the same problems—supply gluts, falling prices, technological innovation, and changing consumer preferences—that plague other primary producers (Thompson, 2003: A1, A27). Under these circumstances, it is naïve to imagine that the "destruction" of primary goods industries in the periphery will have a "creative" or beneficial impact. Instead, long-standing economic relations between core and periphery are disintegrating, and there are few new productive activities that will replace lost ties or establish new relations that would integrate core and periphery.

Theoretical Frameworks: Old and New

Using a theoretical framework derived from world-system theory (particularly the relation between core and periphery) and operational concepts from the sociology of agriculture (particularly substitutionism and dematerialization) to analyze the contemporary period of globalization (1970–2000), this chapter examines the impact that new technologies, changing consumer preferences, and state policies in the core have had on primary producers in the periphery. I have synthesized the two schools because the world-system could benefit from a greater appreciation of technology as a force for change, which the sociology of agriculture provides, and because environmental-agricultural scholars could benefit from a wider understanding of the import of technological change for global structures, which the world-system perspective provides. Using these theories, I have analyzed why supplies of primary commodities from the periphery have grown, why demand for primary products in the core has weakened, and why these developments have undermined long-standing ties between core and periphery. These developments have important implications for theories of dependency, environment, and globalization.

Dependency Theory. In recent years, producers in the core have introduced technologies that replace or reduce the need for many goods from the periphery, consumers in the core have altered their consumption patterns, and states in the core have taken steps to undermine the bargaining power of producers in the periphery. As a result it is now the core that practices "import-substitution", making it less dependent on the periphery than it was before. This reversal turns dependency theory on its head. Recall that Prebisch and other dependency theorists that urged peripheral states to adopt import-substitutionist industrialization policies to reduce peripheral dependence on the core.

In the era of globalization, the problem for the periphery is no longer its "dependency" on the core. Instead, the disintegration of its economic ties with the core and the marginalization and exclusion that this entails creates a new problem, one of "in-dependency." But this should not be confused with self-reliance, autonomy, self-determination, or "independence" in the traditional sense. Because there are few economic alternatives to primary commodity production, because investment by the core in the periphery has not been forthcoming, because populations in the periphery have little education, possess few skills, are burdened with chronic and epidemic disease, and are ruled by states that are incapable of providing the services and institutions that could help them overcome these disadvantages, marginalization or "in-dependency" will likely result in banditry and anarchy in collapsed states across much of the periphery. Indeed, marginalization may result in exclusion from the world economy, so that in-dependent regions would no longer be counted even as part of the "periphery", but instead become, in the language of world-systems theory, part of an "external arena."

Environmental Theory. Environmental theorists (Hawken, Lovins, and Lovins; contributors to the *State of the World* annuals) have praised new substitutionist and dematerialist technologies because they reduce global demand for the earth's finite and renewable resources. They have praised efforts to promote "greater regional self-sufficiency" in the core as part of a more "sustainable" development program (Hawken et al., 2001; Renner, 2004). And they have urged consumers to demand "less" of the world, an approach expressed by injunctions to "eat locally" and "travel locally," rather than eat foods imported from distant places or vacation in distant exotic locales.

But these theorists have failed to appreciate the impact of new technologies and changing consumer preferences on people in the periphery, making them vulnerable to critics who have long argued that environmentalists are indifferent to the fate of the world's poor (Tucker, 1982: 25, 34, 80). Moreover, the assumption by environmental theorists that new technologies and regional self-sufficiency are universally "good", can be faulted by postmodern critics because these developments can be shown to benefit some (rich consumers in the core) but disadvantage others (poor producers in the periphery), which calls into question the "universalism" implicit in such claims.

This perspective has also been challenged by environmentalists in Alternative Trading Organizations (ATOs). Instead of demanding technological substitutes, activists promoting "fair trade" have urged consumers to demand that the market deliver "natural" products from the periphery (cane sugar, coffee) not "synthetic" products from the core (HFCS, Coca-Cola, and Red Bull). They have urged consumers to pay a higher price for these products and/or insist that a greater share of the final price go to pay primary producers, not transnational intermediaries. In return, environmentalists have asked primary producers to employ environmentally sound farming practices, using organic and shade-grown methods to produce their goods. Although this approach avoids the problems associated with the uncritical embrace of substitutionist technologies, its success depends on persuading consumers and transnational corporations based in the core and producers based in the periphery to change their behavior and redistribute wealth along commodity supply chains (Brown & Tiffen, 1992: 142). They have had some success at the margins, but have as yet persuaded only a small number of consumers, corporations, and producers in niche markets to change.

Globalization Theory. The disintegration of long-standing economic relations between core and periphery calls into question theories that see globalization as a force for "integration." The growth and spread of investment, production, trade, and technology are seen by globalization theorists, both its proponents and its critics, as contributing to global integration, which is said to make the world a smaller and more homogeneous place (Schaeffer, 2003: 1–16). For many, technology is seen as a particularly important force for integration, as electronic, computer, and communications technologies knit people together in global networks and compress time and space.

By contrast, the argument here is that technology can also play a very different role, one that disrupts existing economic and social networks. Moreover, the globalization literature's emphasis on communications technologies may be misplaced, insofar as more prosaic agricultural and mineral technologies arguably have more dramatic consequences, and for millions more people, than the Internet. The argument here is that theoretical expectations about the role of technology and globalization as forces for integration need to be revised to appreciate the ways in which technology contributes to disintegration and deglobalization in some regions.

In this context, world-systems theory may be useful because its proponents have argued that the world economy only recently became a global structure, and that it long had an external arena that was not part of it. The disintegration of ties between the core and regions in the periphery may again be creating a new external arena in which the logic of globalization does not apply. The result could be theorized as a shrinking world economy that is becoming more integrated, and a growing external arena made up of the postperiphery. Although this is awkward language, it might be useful to recall that the globalizing European world economy in the 17th century had a global footprint, one that touched on nearly every continent, but it did not tread on the vast hinterlands in the interior of each continent (Wallerstein, 1974: 300–345).

There is a second implication here for theories of globalization. Many theorists have argued that globalization is a homogenizing process and that the development associated with it have uniform consequences for people in different settings. By contrast, the argument here is that the development of new technologies does not necessarily have uniform consequences, but has instead diverse and contradictory meanings for people in different settings. So, for example, the technologies deployed to improve the diets of consumers in the core have also undermined the diets of producers in the periphery. This accords with postmodern theorists who are critical of the universalist claims made by environmental and globalization theories. It also accords with world-system theorists, who have argued that the capitalist world economy is based on processes that differentiate core from periphery and produce different outcomes for people located in each.

The argument here does not imagine that global change has a singular, universal social meaning. Instead, global change is conceptualized as having diverse social meanings. By analogy, picture a Weather Channel satellite view of a low-pressure system in the Pacific as it approaches North America. Then scroll it forward. As the low-pressure system sweeps across the continent, it has very different meteorological consequences for people living along its path. It brings fog to people on the coast, rain to people in the interior, snow to people in the mountains, and drought to people in the high desert beyond. So it is with the economic, political, and technological changes that have swept across the contemporary global landscape. Global change has had different social consequences and meanings in different settings. This chapter examined the "storm" of change associated with new agro-industrial technologies, arguing that it has wreaked different kinds of havoc on people around the world.

Future Research

This approach suggests several avenues of research in future. First, given the complex impact of substitutionist and dematerialist technologies on economic relations between different regions of the world economy, it would make sense to undertake a wider, more critical analysis of the role technology plays in contemporary globalization. Technology is widely assumed in the literature to be a force for integration. But this work suggest that this assumption is incorrect or, at least, incomplete.

Second, if substitutionist and dematerialist technologies contribute to the disintegration of relations between core and periphery, it would be useful to examine other developments that contribute to the disintegration of global economic, political, and cultural ties. In political terms, civil and ethnic conflict in some regions has contributed to the collapse of states (Somalia, Liberia, Congo) and the exit of people in these peripheral regions from the interstate system and the world economy. At the same time, migration, job transfers, and terrorism have contributed to economic "protectionism" and political "isolationism" in the core. These developments should be examined to assess their impact on globalization generally and identify the contradictions associated with or inherent in contemporary globalization. It may be that globalization will continue to be a force for integration, despite these developments. But it is important nonetheless to weight these other countertendencies in the balance.

Endnotes

1. David Goodman, Bernardo Sorj, and John Wilkinson, *From Farming to Biotechnology: A Theory of Agro-Industrial Development* (London: Blackwell, 1987), pp. 2–4, 580.
2. David Lea, ed., *Agricultural and Mineral Commodities Year Book* (London: Europa Publications, Taylor and Francis, 2002), pp. 244, 113, 311, 95.
3. *Ibid.* There were, of course exceptions. In 2001, the index price was 95 for nickel, 125 for tin, and 101 for sisal. But most commodities lost ground.
4. Dollar devaluations have somewhat different meanings. In Latin America, where countries sell primary goods in dollars and import oil and manufactured goods from the United States, paying for them in dollars, the devaluations have had little impact. But in Africa or Asia, where countries sell goods in dollars and then import manufactured goods from Western Europe or Japan and pay for them in euros or yen, dollar devaluations have an adverse impact because it weakens the terms of trade with their primary trading partners.
5. Alfred Maizels, *Commodities in Crisis: The Commodity Crisis of the 1980s and the Political Economy of International Commodity Policies* (Oxford: Clarendon, 1993), pp. 27–29.
6. *Ibid.*, pp. 105–106.

7. Robert K. Schaeffer, *Understanding Globalization: The Social Consequences of Political, Economic and Environmental Change, Second Edition* (Lanham, Md.: Rowman and Littlefield, 2003), pp. 95–118.

8. B. Dinham and C. Hines, *Agribusiness in Africa* (London: Earth Resources, 1983), pp. 189, 193.

9. Schaeffer, 2003, pp. 95–118.

10. Juan Forero, "The Caprice of Coffee: World Glut Takes Toll on Latin American Economy," *New York Times*, November 8, 2001; David Gonzales, "A Coffee Crisis' Devastating Domino Effect in Nicaragua," *New York Times*, August 29, 2001.

11. Schaeffer, 2003, p. 220.

12. *Ibid.*, 238–240. Three to six transnational corporations control 85–90 percent of the world market in wheat, corn, coffee, and tobacco exports and 90 percent of forest exports, giving them enormous leverage over prices.

13. Goodman, Sorj, and Wilkinson, 1987, pp. 2–4.

14. David Goodman and Michael Redclift, *Refashioning Nature: Food, Ecology & Culture* (London: Routledge, 1991), pp. 91–92. Although substitutionism is not an entirely new development—coal tar distillates were used early in the 20th century to create industrial dyes that replaced mineral and vegetable dyes; synthetic rubber replaced natural rubber in many uses—the invention and adoption of a new set of technologies in the 1970s and 1980s set the stage for the widespread displacement of many important peripheral products.

15. Paul Hawken, Amory Lovins, and L. Hunter Lovins, *Natural Capitalism: Creating the Next Industrial Revolution* (Boston: Little, Brown, 2001), p. 125.

16. C. Flavin and N. Lenssen, "Reshaping the Power Industry," in L. Brown, ed., *State of the World 1994* (New York: W. W. Norton, 1994), pp. 71–72.

17. Of course, technological innovation slowed after 1985 as oil prices fell and consumers persuaded themselves to abandon high-mileage cars and purchase low-mileage minivans, light trucks, and SUVs.

18. The capacity of solar panels in Japan increased from 10 megawatts in 1994 to 250 megawatts in 2002, a 25-fold increase. Ken Belson, "With Sun on Roof, More Yen in the Pocket," *New York Times*, July 29, 2003.

19. Ken Belson, "Mining Cellphones, Japan Finds El Dorado," *New York Times*, February 28, 2002.

20. Hawken, Lovins, and Lovins, 2001, p. 105. In Europe and Asia, the adoption of new "extended producer responsibility policies," which require companies to take back appliances at the end of the useful life and then recycle, repair, or remanufacture component parts would essentially dematerialize the metals used in their manufacture. Michael Renner, "Moving Toward a Less Consumptive Economy," in Brian Halweil and Lisa Mastny, eds., *State of the World 2004* (New York: W. W. Norton, 2004), pp. 107–108.

21. Hawken, Lovins and Lovins, 2001, p. 253.

22. Sherri Day, "Energy Drinks Charm the Young and the Caffeinated," *New York Times*, April 4, 2004.

23. Micahel Barratt Brown and Pauline Tiffen, *Short Changed: Africa and World Trade* (London: Pluto, 1992), p. 32.

24. Dinham and Hines, 1983, pp. 189, 193.

25. Jane E. Brody, "In an Obese World, Sweet Nothings Add Up," *New York Times*, March 9, 2004.

26. Sally Squires, "Corn Syrup is Feeding Obesity Epidemic in the U.S." *Manhattan Mercury*, March 23, 2004.

27. B. Borrell and R. C. Duncan, "A Survey of World Sugar Policies," in S. V. Marks and K. E. Maskus, eds., *The Economic and Politics of World Sugar Policies* (Ann Arbor: University of Michigan, 1993), p. 24.

28. Lea, 2002, p. 88.

29. Tim Weiner, "In Corn's Cradle, U.S. Imports Bury Family Farms," *New York Times*, February 26, 2002.

30. R. F. Mikesell, *The Global Copper Industry: Problems and Prospects* (London: Croom Helm, 1988), p. 56.

31. Fuerbringer, 1999.

32. Lea, 2002, pp. 146–148; Niall Ferguson, *The Cash Nexus: Money and Power in the Modern World, 1700–2000* (New York: Basic, 2001), pp. 325–326.

33. *Ibid.*, p. 326. If Auric Goldfinger, the fictional villain in the James Bond movie returned to plunder Fort Knox today, he would find much of the gold already gone.

34. Lea, 2002, p. 215; Bernard Simon, "Metal Prices Fall; 'Froth' Is Blown off Market," *New York Times*, April 30, 2004.

35. Belson, 2002.

36. Renner, 2004, p. 108.

37. *Ibid.*, p. 102.

38. Becky Gaylord, "Australia Is Riding Its Own Cycle," *New York Times*, March 6, 2002.

39. Tony Smith, "Difficult Times for Coffee Industry, Growers Seek Relief From Falling Prices and Demand," *New York Times*, November 25, 2003.

40. Donald G. McNeil, Jr., "Gold Breaks Its Promise to Miners of Lesotho," *New York Times*, June 16, 1998; Rachel L. Swarns, "A Bleak Hour for South African Miners," *New York Times*, October 10, 1999.

41. During the 1980s, Latin American countries reduced their purchases of manufactured goods from the core, mostly from the United States, by nearly $400 billion. Bill Orr, *The Global Economy in the 90s: A User's Guide* (New York: New York University Press, 1992), p. 150.

42. As Peter Drucker has argued, "The primary products economy has become 'uncoupled' from the industrial economy." Peter F. Drucker, "The Changed World Economy," *Foreign Affairs*, (Spring, 1986), p. 768.

43. Schaeffer, 2003, pp. 134–136.

44. *Ibid.*, p. 134.

45. Joseph Siano and Marjorie Connelly, "America Most Beautiful," *New York Times*, February 23, 2003. There are some new agricultural industries in the periphery— fresh flowers, specialty vegetables, shrimp and fish farming—that produce commodities for export. But they are specialty crops for limited markets and they employ relatively few people. Moreover, they are subject to many of the same problems— supply gluts, falling prices, new technologies, and changing consumer preferences— that plague other primary producers. Georgia Thompson, "Behind Roses' Beauty, Poor and Ill Workers," *New York Times*, February 13, 2003.

46. As Peter Drucker has argued, "For if primary products are becoming of marginal importance to the economies of the developed world, tradition development [and dependency] theories and policies are losing their foundations." Drucker, 1986, pp. 774–775.

47. Hawken, Lovins, and Lovins, 2001; Renner, 2004; Brian Halweil and Danielle Nierenberg, "Watching What We Eat," in Halweil and Mastny, 2004.

48. Renner, 2004.

49. William Tucker, *Progress and Privilege: America in the Age of Environmentalism* (Garden City, N.Y.: Anchor, 1982), pp. 25, 34, 80.
50. Brown and Tiffen, 1992, p. 142.
51. Schaeffer, 2003, pp. 1–16.
52. Immanuel Wallerstein, *The Modern World-System: Capitalist Agriculture and the Origins of the European World-Economy in the Sixteenth Century* (New York: Academic, 1974), pp. 300–345.
53. Lawrence Summers has argued that "The laws of economics, it is often forgotten, are like laws of engineering. There's only one set of laws and they work *everywhere* [emphasis added]." Duncan Green, *The Silent Revolution: The Rise of Market Economies in Latin America* (London: Cassell, 1995), p. 27. George Ritzer's McDonaldization thesis is another expression of this same view.

References

Belson, K. (2002, February 28). Mining cellphones, Japan finds El Dorado. *New York Times*.

—— (2003). With sun on roof, more Yen in the pocket. *New York Times*.

Borrell, B., & Duncan, R. C. (1993). A survey of world sugar policies, in S. V. Marks., & K. E. Maskus (Eds.), *The economic and politics of world sugar policies*. Ann Arbor: University of Michigan.

Brody, J. E. (2004). *In an obese world, sweet nothings add up*. New York Times.

Brown, M. B., & Tiffen, P. (1992). *Short changed: Africa and world trade*. London: Pluto.

Day, S. (2004). Energy drinks charm the young and the caffeinated. *New York Times*.

Dinham, B., & Hines, C. (1983). *Agribusiness in Africa*. London: Earth Resources.

Drucker, P. F. (1986, Spring). The changed world economy. *Foreign Affairs*.

Ferguson, N. (2001). *The cash nexus: Money and power in the modern world, 1700, 2000*. New York: Basics

Flavin, C., & Lenssen, N. (1994). Reshaping the power industry, in L. Brown (Ed.), *State of the World 1994*. New York: W. W. Norton.

Forero, J. (2001). The caprice of coffee: World glut takes toll on Latin American economy. *New York Times*.

Fuerbringer, J. (1999). An icon's fading glory. *New York Times*.

Gaylord, B. (2002). Australia is riding its own cycle. *New York Times*.

Goodman, D., & Redclift, M. (1991). *Refashioning nature: Food, ecology & culture*. London: Routledge.

Goodman, D., Sorj, B., & Wilkinson, J. (1987). *From farming to biotechnology: A theory of agro-industrial development*. London: Blackwell.

Gonzales, D. (2001). A coffee crisis' devastating domino effect in Nicaragua. *New York Times*.

Green, D. (1995). *The silent revolution: The rise of market economies in Latin America*. London: Cassell.

Halweil, B., & Nierenberg, D. (2004). Watching what we eat, in B. Halweil and L. Mastny (Eds.), *State of the world*. New York: W.W. Norton.

Hawken, P., Lovins, A., & Lovins, H. L. (2001). *Natural capitalism: Creating the next industrial revolution*. Boston: Little, Brown.

Lea, D. (Ed.). (2002). *Agricultural and mineral commodities year book*. London: Europa, Taylor and Francis, 2002.

Maizels, A. (1993). *Commodities in crisis: The commodity crisis of the 1980s and the political economy of international commodity policies*. Oxford, UK: Clarendon Press.

McNeil, D. G. Jr. (1998). Gold breaks its promise to miners of Lesotho. *New York Times*.

Mikesell, R. F. (1988). *The global copper industry: Problems and prospect*. London: Croom Helm.

Orr, B. (1992). *The global economy in the '90s: A user's guide*. New York: New York University Press.

Renner, M. (2004). Moving toward a less consumptive economy, in B. Halweil, & L. Mastny (Eds.), *State of the World 2004*. New York: W.W. Norton.

Schaeffer, R. K. (2003, 2nd Edition). *Understanding globalization: The social consequences of political, economic and environmental change*. Lanham, Md.: Rowman and Littlefield.

Siano, J., & Connelly, M. (2003). America most beautiful. *New York Times*.

Simon, B. (2004). Metal prices fall: 'froth' is blown off market. *New York Times*.

Smith, T. (2003). Difficult times for coffee industry, growers seek relief from falling prices and demand. *New York Times*.

Squires, S. (2004). Corn syrup is feeding obesity epidemic in the U.S. *Manhattan Mercury*.

Swarns, R. L. (1999). A bleak hour for South African miners. *New York Times*.

Thompson, G. (2003). Behind roses' beauty, poor and ill workers. *New York Times*.

Tucker, W. (1982). *Progress and privilege: America in the age of environmentalism*. Garden City, N.Y.: Anchor.

Wallerstein, I. (1974). *The modern world-system: Capitalist agriculture and the origins of the European world-economy in the sixteenth century*. New York: Academic.

Weiner, T. (2002). In corn's cradle, U.S. imports bury family farms. *New York Times*.

10
Social Integration, System Integration, and Global Governance

Margaret S. Archer

Introduction

What differentiates globalization from the world-system that developed after the 16th century?[1] Not every element of the new is necessarily novel nor does all that is solid always melt into air, as those keen to proclaim "new ages" and to carve out "new eras" like to suppose. Instead, the distinctive feature of the globalization process is held to lie in its penetration and penetrative potential. The combined consequence of those economic, political, and cultural changes, which constitute globalization, is that they affect everyone on the planet. Progressive penetration means that we all become denizens of one world; the problem is that we have not become "citizens" of it.

Specifically, the problem raised by globalization concerns guidance and participation. The absence of guiding agencies has been highlighted by sociologists in terms of the "runaway society"[2] or the "risk society." The lack of participatory mechanisms has been captured by the concept of "exclusion." If participation means "having a say" and channels through which to say it, then the human family is worse off in these respects and becoming more so, although the costs are unequally distributed around the globe. To be affected by globalization,

---

[1] As advanced most notably by Wallerstein, I. (1974–1989). *The modern world system*, 3 vols. New York & San Diego: Academic Press.
[2] Beck, U. (1986, 1992). *Risk society: Towards a new modernity*. London: Sage.

without any ability to exert a countereffect, is the lot of the vast majority of the
world's population. It means that global penetration is negatively related to participation. Not only is it unaccompanied by new forms of government and governance, it systematically disempowers those previous and hard-won agencies for
guidance and participation—representative democracy, the institutions of civil
society, trade unionism, and citizenship—which, until now, were associated with
development. That is the truly novel consequence of early globalization.

To some sociological commentators, all that had seemed solid had melted, into
the ether. What globalization left was a gaping void between free-floating global
networks and the atomized individual, the two connected only by the Internet. One
of the results was an alarm call for the immediate generation of new sociological
perspectives. Sociology, as a product of modernity, had followed its contours until
the last few years. In particular, this meant that the nation-state was equated with
society, that different nation-states constituted different societies, and that any international organizations (first of all the UN), alliances (NATO and the Warsaw Pact),
or supranational organizations (EEC), the latter having some quasi-federal features,
were quite properly studied internationally. "The global shift changed all that, and
much of the theoretical alignment of sociology today flows from the challenge of
globality to modernity."[3]

Too often, sound-bite concepts substituted for sustained analysis and too frequently a discursive *mésalliance* was forged with postmodernism, despite the
irony of global commentators supplying the proponents of virtual reality with
their repudiated metanarrative. Although the two should not be elided, their joint
impact was to inflate the hegemony of discourse, imagery, and artistic license
over *La Misère du Monde*.[4]

Analysis is indispensable; it cannot be replaced by epistemic "takes" on reality, which accentuate only the most observable changes, to the detriment of
underlying causal processes, and privilege the vantage point of academic elites in
the Western world. Moreover, generic analytical concepts cannot be discarded in
the same way as substantive concepts, linked to particular social formations at
particular times (such as "the deferential voter" or the "affluent worker"). Instead,
this chapter is based upon harnessing one of the most fruitful generic frameworks
of the analysis of globalization, its impacts upon prior social configurations and
its consequences for posterior ones.

This framework rests upon the distinction between "system integration", the
orderly or disorderly relations between the institutional parts of society, and
"social integration", the orderly or disorderly relations between members of
society.[5] The point of sustaining this distinction is twofold. These two elements

---

[3] Albrow, M. (2002, July). "The global shift and its consequences for sociology", paper
presented at the 13th World Congress of Sociology, Brisbane.
[4] Bourdieu, P. et al. (1999). *La Misère du Monde*, Ed. du Seuil, Paris.
[5] Lockwood, D. (1964). "Social integration and system integration," in Zollschan, G. K.,
and Hirsh, W. (Eds.), *Explorations in social change*. Boston: Houghton Mifflin.

of social reality possess different properties and powers from each other; systemic integration can vary from contradiction to complementarity, whereas social integration can vary from antagonism to solidarity. In addition, they may vary independently of one another and it is thus their combination that accounts for different patterns of stability and change in society. Social regularity results *caeteris paribus* when both are high and societal transformation, when both are low. These are only two out of the four possible combinations, but they are the pair with the most strikingly different outcomes. This framework, which has been applied to premodern formations such as patrimonial bureaucracy, and to modern variants such as state socialism, should also be able to reveal what combination of social and systemic integration characterized the developed democracies in late modernity and what new combination of them is induced by globalization. On the most macroscopic scale, it is maintained that two types of combinations between social and system integration do characterize successive phases of recent world history, although this is to use broad brushstrokes that inevitably overgeneralize.

Firstly, in the period that can be called Late Modernity, both forms of integration had slowly been rising because of their mutual dependence within the nation state. Such dependence underlay the growing responsiveness of the system to society and vice versa. When this reached the point of their mutual regulation, then its emergent causal power was simultaneously to foster further increments in social and systemic integration. Such societies were far from being fully good, fully fair, or fully consensual. Nevertheless, their stability and regularity was an achievement: supplying plural and legitimate channels for their own reshaping, a relatively stable context for institutional operations, and a relatively secure environment for individual life-projects. However, this configuration was intolerant of disturbance from outside. Thus, at the climacteric of the nation-state in the 20th century, the world wars always entailed "national reconstruction." External disruption was precisely what globalization represented, and it entirely undermined the configuration upon which the developed democracies depended for their existence. The emergence of what is termed Nascent Globality, meant that both forms of integration plummeted to such a low level that they were incapable of regulating each other as key institutions moved beyond national confines, onto the world stage, after the 1980s.

Following the Second World War, these successive phases represented the disjunctive transition from the mutual regulation between system and society in Late Modernity to their precise opposite, a configuration working for mutual deregulation in Nascent Globality. It is the speed of their succession and their juxtapositioning that fueled the call for a new sociological perspective to grasp this *rerum novarum*. There is no dispute here that a new phenomenon had come about with globalization. However, I defend the ability of our generic framework, with its ontological depth and distrust of observable surface features, to provide a better analytical purchase upon its causes and consequences than any of the current popular forms of rhetorical impressionism.

This defence can be evaluated by the leverage it provides on the big question of governance, by its ability to answer the question, "What made governance relatively unproblematic in Late Modernity and so very problematic within Nascent Globality?" Moreover, this framework enables the question about future governance to be posed with some analytical specificity, namely, "Can the process of mutual deregulation between the systemic and the social be overcome at world level?"

Late Modernity—The Mutual Regulation of the Systemic and the Social

The predominance of the nation-state made the national subsystem more important than the world-system, although there were more internal institutional linkages and dependencies within the nation than ones outside it. For example, this social configuration was characterized by a national labor market, upon which the national economy was heavily dependent; a national legal system, whose definition of rights and duties constituted membership of the *pays légale*; a national educational system, the validity of whose credentials was largely restricted to the country (and its dependencies); and a national demarcation between the powers of state and church. Such was the magnitude of these differences that they fostered the development of comparative sociology as a comparison of nation-states.

The developed democracies, which finally emerged in the mid-20th century, after 200 years of struggle in the West and 80 years of consolidation in Japan, were distinctive societal configurations. These nation-states were characterized by a relatively smooth dovetailing of their component institutions and the less smooth, but nevertheless successful, integration of their populations into a citizenship that took the revolutionary edge off enduring class divisions.[6] In short, they had achieved a rising level of system integration in conjunction with a growing level of social integration. This common underlying configuration was attributable to internal processes, particular to each country, as is underlined by the fact that it did not preclude warfare between them. Certainly, the stress placed upon internal processes should not underplay the significance of colonialism or neocolonialism as sources of wealth, means of off-loading surplus production, and a method for controlling migration and immigration to national advantage. Nevertheless, there was never one uniform colonial adventure because patterns of external incursion were specific to each nation-state and accommodated to nationally defined aims and objectives.[7]

Because the conjunction between rising systemic integration and growing social integration cannot be attributed to a hidden hand or to automatic functional adaptation, because the process itself was tense, conflict-ridden, and haunted by

---

[6] Marshall, T.H. (1963). "Citizenship and social class," in *Sociology at the Crossroads*. London: Heinemann.
[7] Hence, for example, the huge difference between British and French colonial rule: the one direct and the other indirect; the former structurally antiassimilationist and the latter assimilating through the export and imposition of its educational and legal systems, and so on.

the specter of revolution, what accounted for it in such different countries? A causal mechanism needs to be identified because the Russian revolution *inter alia* shows that there are important instances where it was lacking.

The mechanism advanced here consists of the successful if stressful emergence of mutual regulation between the systemic and the social. First, the necessary but not sufficient conditions for mutual regulation are rooted in the nation-state itself. When state boundaries also defined the outer skin of society, then the necessary interplay between the systemic and the social within the same territorial confines ineluctably meant that the state of the one mattered to the state of the other. This is an ontological statement about interdependence, which is itself independent of either the institutional elites or the popular masses knowing it, and articulating it, let alone getting it right. Indeed, the case of Tsarist Russia illustrates the actuality of getting it wrong.

However, the sufficient, although nonetheless contingent, condition for the emergence of mutual regulation from mutual dependence was fundamentally cultural. It depended upon the vanguards of the system and of society both finding "voice". Historically, overwhelming emphasis has been placed on the systemic side of this equation, for institutional elites undoubtedly found their voice first. Thus, burgeoning nationhood was presented as "the great age of ideology." What this age fundamentally involved was the (attempted) legitimation of the system to society, entailing the crucial recognition that the state of society mattered to systemic stability. (A recognition that was signally lacking in Russia after the "enlightened" attempts of Catherine the Great.) However, the emergence of mutual regulation is not built upon protracted false consciousness. For such regulation to supersede mutual dependence, it was equally important that the third estates should find their own voice in the counterideologies of republicanism, political philosophy, socialism, or the volkgeist, pressing for representation and redistribution within the system. Their common denominator was the simple message that the state of the system was intolerable to society, and the warning that this state of affairs mattered so much that society threatened to overthrow and recast the system.

In fact, such ideological conflict was the precursor of mutual regulation itself. This is because as ideology and counterideology lock horns, the predominant effect is not to promote extremism (or synthesis) but the progressive argumentative elaboration of both doctrines and their successors.[8] Because charge was met by countercharge and riposte by counterriposte on both sides, the two increasingly defined each other's agendas. What emerged represented victory for neither but, rather, much more sophisticated and refined versions of both, as I have illustrated elsewhere for classical political economy versus socialist economics in late 19th century England.[9] The unintended consequence was that two corpuses of

---

[8] See Archer, M.S. (1988). *Culture and agency.* Cambridge, UK: Cambridge University Press, which takes up Imre Lakatos's notion of progressive and degenerating paradigm shifts and applies them, as he suggested was possible for any form of argumentation, to ideological elaboration (pp. 239–242).

[9] Ibid, pp. 248–253.

ideas were elaborated in opposition to each other, unintentionally mutual regulation had been instituted. In this process, with neither winners nor losers, the result was that both sets of ideas became socially embedded and assured the other's continued salience in society precisely because of their enduring opposition. This was their *effet pervers mais positif* for each other. In other words, mutual regulation depends neither upon a growing consensus between people nor upon compatibility between ideas. It is only a matter of co-presence and ideational engagement between the "parties" involved. (Significantly, it is precisely the absence of co-presence that explains the efforts directed to *concientización*—in the old usage of the term— within Latin America, as a precondition of effective movements for justice and equality.)

The same two elements—co-presence and engagement—also underpinned the emergence of mutual regulation between system and society at the institutional level. What is different is that these were explicit attempts at two-way regulation. This was most obvious in political institutions, with elites attempting to use restricted participation in order to be able to regulate the people and the popular classes seeking to extend democratic access and rights in order to regulate the elites. But the same scenario was enacted throughout the array of increasingly interconnected institutions and was largely responsible for their growing interconnectedness. Thus, in the British economy, the entrepreneurs sought to control wage rates, working conditions, work hours, housing, shopping, and eventually the religious denomination and definition of appropriate instruction, in order to regulate their workforce. The workers responded with Luddism, unionization, and direct and indirect political action, to regulate their bosses, and co-operative retailing as well as independent secularized education to offset the regulative incursions of capitalism. Again in the law, whereas the institutional elites sought to buttress social control through the workhouse, asylum, experimentation with imprisonment, and by linking legal participation tightly to property-holding, radical elements worked to undermine the legal privilege definitive of or associated with privilege itself.

The educational scenario is particularly revealing of how systemic interconnectedness grew out of the struggle over mutual regulation. If reform could be introduced from above, as with the Napoleonic *Université Impériale*, the new political elite could immediately make it an institution subserving State requirements, by dispossessing owners of previous networks of their schools, controlling their right to teach, and limiting *lycée* access to socially appropriate pupils. Yet the resistance of the traditional religious educators combined with the insistence of the new industrialists and also with resurgent republicanism meant that in the second half of the 19th century the state educational monopoly was both cut and regulated by *liberté d'enseignement* (religious freedom to [re-]open schools), by *éducation spéciale* (geared to industry and commerce), and by *gratuité* (opening it to the people). Conversely, if reform was introduced from bottom-upwards, as in England, strong private networks were developed in a competition to serve their respective owners and regulate the rest of the population through spreading their particular definitions of instruction. First and foremost was the Anglican

Church's network, second that of the alliance between entrepreneurs and religious dissenters (what we would now call the Free Churches), and last and least numerous by that of the working class, represented by secular Mechanics Institutes, in resistance to the first two networks. When this market competition in schooling ended in educational stalemate, by the mid-19th century, the next 50 years witnessed the formation of a state educational system (1902) through the incorporation of these diverse institutions for regulation, counterregulation, and resistance to regulation.

Thus, in both countries, the 100-year conflict resulted in State Educational Systems[10] that also serviced diverse sectors of society, an unintended consequence in each case. The two educational systems epitomized mutual regulation between the State and civil society, which had given them their 20th century form and content. Equally, both educational systems were now intimately interconnected with a plurality of other social institutions, thus increasing overall systemic integration, and both were approaching universal enrollment, thus simultaneously extending overall social integration.

This is not quite the end of the story in those countries where the analytical key has been held to lie in the mutual regulation achieved between high systemic and high social integration. In fact, the storyline continues with their collective endorsement and enactment of the "postwar formula" (social democracy + neocapitalism + welfare state) and runs on past it.

First, systemic integration could be extended beyond the boundaries of the nation-state, as the working of the European Union shows in various institutional domains. What is significant here is that the mutual regulation of system and society expanded correspondingly. For example, even individual nationals availed themselves of this new systemic apparatus for the regulation of national society. Cases of gender discrimination against female employees, initially dismissed at home, were often sustained at the European Court of Justice, whose rulings finally became established as "good practice" back home in the national society.

Second, there remained considerable scope for increasing social integration within the nation-state by incorporating a growing number of sectional interest groups, which were previously marginalized and subjected to discrimination. From the 1960s, the lead given earlier by the lower classes was passed like a baton to other interest groupings that had not engaged in large-scale collective action, developing neither articulate aims nor organizing for their pursuit. Gender and ethnic groups became the new collective agents of the western world. Pursuant of their interests, each eventually made the political and institutional breakthroughs that spelled fuller social incorporation. In turn, increased civil rights; changes in social security entitlements; in terms of employment; and especially the variety of antidiscrimination laws, procedures, and protocols introduced, also represented new modalities through which new sections of society could play a part in regulating the system.

---

[10] For a detailed account of this protracted conflict, see Archer, M.S. (1979). *Social origins of educational systems*. London & Berverly Hills: Sage.

In the quarter of a century following the Second World War, the developed democracies were characterized by the robust nature of mutual regulation prevailing between their institutional orders and social orders, between the parts of society and its members. These societies were far from being fair, egalitarian, or fully democratic. Nevertheless, the two-way regulation established between system and society was better than it had been throughout modernity. This conjuncture held the promise of intensifying mutual regulation, such that fairer societies might be progressively and peacefully negotiated; ones where guidance and participation were increasingly interlinked. All of that promise depended upon the nation-state remaining co-extensive with society.

However, no final balance sheet can be presented because these remained unfinished stories. They were cut short by the structural and cultural transformations of the 1980s, which spelled nascent globalization, slicing through national boundaries as the outer skins of societies and demolishing their hard-won, if cosy, internal settlements between the system and the social. The key structural dynamic was the rise of multinational enterprises and finance markets, whose nongeocentric interests were epitomized in the abandonment of foreign exchange regulations in 1980. The central cultural dynamic was the invention of the World Wide Web in 1989, severing most of the link between intellectual property and its geo-local ownership. It is common to add the fall of state socialism to this list, in the sense that the end of the Cold War brought down the barriers between the first and second worlds, opened up new markets, enhanced free communication, and fostered population movements. All of that was important and contributory. However, for the present argument, the significance of the ending of state socialism also lay in showing the nontransferability of the formula for mutual regulation between systemic and social integration. Eastern European countries lacked both features and therefore the regulative relationship between them. With nascent globalization, they could never even try to consolidate (unlikely as its prospects seemed) that which the developed democracies were themselves about to lose.

Nascent Globality—Reducing Systemic and Social Integration

The sociocultural effects of globalization were registered as a simultaneous decline in the relatively high levels of systemic and social integration that had slowly and quite recently been achieved in the developed democracies. The simultaneity of their decline served to reinforce the fragmentation of each other. As this occurred, their mutually regulatory relationship was a necessary casualty. The process of its demise repays attention, because pinpointing what was lost enables us to question the prospects of it being regained on a world scale.

Where systemic integration is concerned, the downsizing of the nation-state's powers was the prime consequence of economic and financial operations bursting through national boundaries, at the same time and in synergy with the means of communication and cultural distribution. Specifically, "its regulatory ability is challenged and reduced."[11] The challenge to the state is obvious; so many economic activities, previously subject to government controls, now escaped governmental jurisdiction, and so many information flows, previously amenable to national restriction, now floated free in the ether. But the reduction in the regulatory ability of the nation-state is more complex. When leading elements of the structural and cultural systems re-(or de-)located themselves globally, then other institutions could no longer operate primarily within national confines. To take education as an example; "transferable skills" then became more important than learning national history, professional training for law or accountancy surpassed mastery of the local "black letter" or competence in dealing with the IRS or Inland Revenue, and in academia, Mannheim's free-floating intelligentsia was finally in its element. All of this was readily observable in Britain and, ironically, at precisely the time that government (both parties) attempted to exert unprecedented control over curriculum, teaching, and research.

At its simplest, such institutions were confronted by new "markets" and by pressure from their clients to prepare them for these new outlets, which precluded supine responsiveness to governmental regulation. Instead, institutional leaders had to respond with innovation, making their best guesses about best new practice, where national guidelines no longer constituted the best information. As they did so, each in a real sense went its own way, no longer constrained by old institutional interrelations and interdependencies. In sum, "once culture, economy, even politics were de-linked from the nation state, there followed more general de-linkage of each from the other, and of all from society."[12]

The delinking of system from society is vital. It has been argued that the ultimate source of mutual regulation lay in the fact that the state of society mattered to the working of the system and vice versa. This was decreasingly the case as can be seen most clearly for the economic elites. Because they are no longer dependent upon one (largely) national population, their concern vanishes about whether multinational practices receive endorsement from within any nation, which in the past had meant accepting conciliatory regulation. Instead, enterprises move parts of their operations to employ "suitable" personnel throughout the world. Thus, corporate management looses itself from the constraint that the need for legitimation had previously imposed upon it, because now there is no determinate population of employees, indispensable to its activities, who are also its national legitimators. Social consensus therefore becomes irrelevant to the exercise of institutional power. Institutional power has less and less need to seek to transform itself into authority. Instead, what is important is temporary local amenability, which, if wanting, is not met by durable concessions but by the transfer of operations. Although most marked in the multinational corporations, nonlegitimation and unconcern about it is the new institutional rule; our universities are largely indifferent to where their students come from or what they study, as long as they come

---

[11] Held, D. (1995). *Democracy and the global order.* Cambridge, UK: Polity.
[12] Albrow, M. (2002, July). "The global shift and its consequences," Ibid., p. 8.

in growing, fee-paying numbers. Of course, the one institution that cannot be indifferent to legitimacy (and cannot substitute among its subjects) is the downsized state itself. Yet, the delegitimization of the state is also a victim of the loss of mutual regulation between system and society.

This is because, where social integration is concerned, the state of the national system matters less and less to the national population. As public recognition grows that national institutions, but especially the state, are incapable of regulating the major players and issues, thus having a shrinking role in determining the life-chances of the nation's people, they are progressively deserted. This is indexed by the progressive drop in voter turnout across Europe, especially among the young, the fall in political party membership, and the rapid shrinkage in trade union members. The message is simple: "If these institutions can no longer perform their regulatory role on behalf of society, then why bother with them?" But it is compounded by the fall in social integration itself.

Sociologists have accentuated two features as responsible for a reduction in social integration, whose effects fall upon distinct sections of the population, generating different responses to the state of the national system. Respectively, these pick out those unconcerned about and those impotent in relation to systemic regulation by the social at the national level.

In the first place, the effect of increasing affluence in the developed democracies—one that reached down to benefit a substantial proportion of working class males in steady employment—has long been held to be associated with their "privatization."[13] This phenomenon predated Nascent Globality. The "affluent worker" takes an instrumental orientation to his work, as a source of pay rather than a relation to production defining his social identity. Affluence enables his family unit to focus upon privatized concerns: upon home ownership, house improvement, holidays, and material acquisitions. In some interpretations, it heralded an *embougeoisement* that would actually foster social integration by diminishing class antagonism and neutralizing the workplace as the prime site for the expression of class conflict. At the time, that thesis proved contentious but new forms of "privatization" have advanced under Nascent Globality, whose accompanying depoliticization and self-preoccupation augment indifference to the systemic and the social alike.

In an important book, Teune and Mlinar[14] maintained that as sources of innovative ideas became concentrated within the (cultural) system, rather than distributed across different parts of society (as with early industrial inventions and the technological innovations of modernity), this induced a different pattern for their assimilation. Instead of a process of collective social interaction (between management and unions, for example) being necessary for the appropriation and application of "variety," its concentration within a single system, free from local

[13] Goldthrope, J.H. et al. (1968). *The affluent worker: Industrial attitudes and behaviour.* Cambridge, UK: Cambridge University Press.
[14] Teune H., & Mlinar, Z. (1978). *The development logic of social systems.* London & Beverly Hills: Sage.

gatekeepers, prompted transaction between the systemic source and those units who saw benefits to be derived from it.[15] This abstract analysis became more vivid when concretized in the new quotidian transactions taking place between the "net" and its users.

The "privatization thesis" was recast as (an exaggerated) "individualization" and explicitly accentuated the reduction in social integration involved. In Beck's version, because individualization was induced by the free flow of information and media representation, traditional categories for self-direction, such as class and status or norms and values were superseded by new notions of "living a life of one's own," personal reinvention, familial experimentation, and biographical revision.[16] This preoccupation with the individualized "life of one's own," negotiated and renegotiated among our new "precarious freedoms," was held to underpin various strands that contributed to the major reduction in social integration, for example, the loss of intergenerational solidarity, demise of the traditional family, the reduced salience of class, indifference to party politics, and the absenting of normative consensus.

In the second place, the growing social exclusion of significant tracts of the population pointed to another source of plummeting social integration. In this case, it arises from the impotence rather than the indifference of this collectivity, who can make common cause neither vertically, with employed workers, nor horizontally with one another. Whether this collectivity is correctly identified as the underclass, its members are rightly termed the subjects of social exclusion; this highlights their radical displacement from the hierarchies of remuneration, representation, and repute, rather than placing them at the bottom of the old continuum of social stratification. Moreover, their very heterogeneity as a collectivity— single mothers, the homeless, asylum seekers, unemployed youth, drug users, the handicapped and the old—is a diversity that divides, precluding social solidarity and collective action alike.

As such, the excluded are passive agents, incapable of combination, which might allow them some regulative role in the system. Instead, they are people to whom things happen, rather than those who can assume some say over their own lives or the systemic structures that exclude them. Moreover, members of this collectivity, the new poor of Nascent Globality, are more reflexively concerned with their differences than their similarities. And these differences generate social antagonism. Generational differences divide the young unemployed from the old-aged, as two of the largest portions of the new poor. The old live in fear of street mugging and barricade themselves indoors, thus intensifying their isolation. Ethnocentrism raises another barrier to cohesion, as racism provides scapegoats as the cause of "poor white" grievances. Simultaneously, the inner cities are minutely partitioned by the turf wars of the street-corner drug barons.

---

[15] For discussion of this concept, see Archer, M.S. (1988). *Culture and agency*. Cambridge, UK: Cambridge University Press.
[16] See Beck, U. & Beck-Gersheim, E. (2002). *Individualization*. London: Sage.

The disintegrative consequences, for system and society alike, of the loss of mutual regulation between them are not confined to the developed democracies. Were these effects predominantly internal, then concern about them could be restricted to them. Instead, these disintegrative dynamics are exported into the global arena, with the same repercussions for all parts of the world. What is now being witnessed is how the deregulated system, assuming world proportions, simultaneously undermines the conditions for its own regulation by world society.

Disintegrative Dynamics at World Level

The main argument about the developed democracies was that the decline in mutual regulation between system and society, entailed reduced integration for both system and society thus weakening the conditions for any reestablishment of two-way regulation between them. It is now argued that precisely the same scenario has been precipitated at world level. In general, this new configuration of low systemic and low social integration is ripe for radical transformation, often entailing violent disruptions.

In part, the global structural consequences derive from neoliberalism succeeding where traditional liberalism had failed. In the birthplaces of capitalism, liberal political economy had strenuously repudiated state intervention or any other institutionalized interference with the free play of market forces. But in precisely those countries, society had progressively been able to enforce greater accountability because economic enterprise could not remain indifferent to the populations upon whom it depended. Globalized neoliberalism was under no such constraint. It shifted from being merely a strong proponent of noninterventionism to itself becoming a strong and active deregulator.

Specifically, the multinationals could seek out cheap labor markets and weak states, unable to impose regulation as the price for external investment. Because enterprises were indifferent to any given population, the global possibilities of substitution meant that any attempted regulation was met by moving on. Both prospectively and retrospectively, the effect was to amplify deregulation. Countries seeking to attract the multinationals knew the terms of the deal; those deserted by them, or increasingly in hock to them, inherited a debt burden whose servicing weakened their already frail powers of state guidance over societal development. Equally, unregulated labor markets deprived civil society of the main agency whose participation could temper the state. The unreeling of institutionalized corruption in government and the (almost inevitable) extension of the informal sector in society were the consequences of conjoint reductions in systemic and social integration. This is, of course, a combination that is mutually reinforcing, carrying these societies ever farther away from the possibility of mutual regulation between them. Prospects for the effective internal governance of these countries declined accordingly. The inane and corrupt populism of Mugabe represents only a particularly extreme case of more general consequences.

In part, the disintegrative effects are as much cultural as structural, although the two tend to amplify each other. However, although the impact of the globalized economy and finance markets were registered locally as damage to whatever fragile systemic integration existed, the impact of global information technology was more deleterious for indigenous social integration. This works in several distinct ways.

First, the other face of the consolidation of cheap, deregulated labor markets throughout the world is the emergence of a cosmopolitan elite drawn from everywhere. The very rich kids from the very poor countries are its mainstay. The minority of extremely wealthy parents in the Third World readily exchanges its local monetary capital for a globally convertible cultural capital embodied in its offspring, where it becomes immune from seizure. Hence the emergence of the "globobrat," the multilingual, cybersmart, frequent flyer, who is typically educated in three countries and often emerges with that emblematic qualification, the MBA. In Britain, our independent boarding schools could not survive without them and they can represent half of a University's postgraduate enrollment. Take "Raphael," the charmingly urbane son of a Thai judge: schooled privately in England, first degree in law from Bangkok, followed by another from the United Kingdom, vacations spent in Japan acquiring the language to extend the family firm's clientele, and currently surfing the net for American law schools. He can tell a real from a fake Rolex at a glance, carries multiple international phone cards, and is the campus guru on software. His proudest achievement is teaching his father that Highland malt is superior to the most expensive blended whisky. "Raphael" is a cosmopolitan; he has much less in common with the people of Thailand than is the case for his father, let alone his mother.

Thus, the emergence of this hi-tech cosmopolitan elite depresses indigenous social integration by increasing the cultural gulf within the home country. UNDP statistics show that although the OECD countries had 19% of the world population, they accounted for 91% of Internet users.[17] What "Raphael" stands for is one embodiment of that small but influential 9%. Others overtly damage social integration. The expansion of cybercrime and the application of information technology to drug dealing and arms trading serves to consolidate a globalized criminal elite whose activities augment the underclass in the First World and increase corruption in the Third World.

Finally, the global divide induces social antagonism from areas retaining preglobal sources of social integration, especially religion and ethnic "tribalism." The effects of intensified religious fundamentalism are often registered as terrorism that dangerously increases social antagonism at world level.

> There is . . . an explosion of fundamentalist movements that take up the Qu'ran, the Bible, or any holy text, to interpret it and use it, as a banner of their despair and a weapon of their rage. Fundamentalisms of different kinds and from different sources will represent the most daring, uncompromising challenge to one-sided domination of informational, global capitalism. Their potential access to weapons of mass extermination casts a giant shadow on the optimistic prospects of the Information Age."[18]

---

[17] UNDP (1999). Human Development Report 1999. Oxford, UK: Oxford University Press. Inside front cover.
[18] Castells, M. (1998). *End of millennium*. Oxford: Blackwell.

However, the inward effects of religious fundamentalism also amplify internal social antagonism. This is because its accentuation exacerbates indigenous ethnic divisions, which could otherwise have slowly lost their social salience, Bosnia and Afghanistan being the most recent examples.

Global Order or Divided World?

The dynamics of Nascent Globaility have been analyzed to account for the precipitous worldwide decline in both systemic and social integration. It follows that overcoming this divisive scenario that now affects us all, without our being able to effect it, ultimately depends upon the prospects of establishing a completely new relationship of mutual regulation between the systemic and the social at world level.

The major systemic barrier consists of the lack of a single agency for global governance. The absence of any framework for accountability means that no shift from growing dependence to growing regulation can take place, which would parallel the histories of the developed democracies. Pessimistic commentators accentuate two negative factors. First, existing international institutions (the UN, NATO, the IMF, and WTO) are decentered and delinked, working independently of one another in a manner that simultaneously epitomizes and intensifies low systemic integration, and most would resist the introduction of any tighter linkage between them. Second, the feasibility of increasing global governance is also cast in doubt by the resilient nationalism of the world's sole superpower. Instances include the United States' recent repudiation of international agreements (for example, Kyoto), insistent pursuit of its own Star Wars program, and its recent willingness to dispense with a UN mandate before declaring war.

Optimism hangs on a single thread, but one that can only become stronger, unless burned through by world conflagration. This is the fact that, like it or not, globalized dependence has already come about, indeed been brought about by the very decentered nature of worldwide institutional operations. Its name is global finitude;[19] resources are finite, ecological ruin has begun, and nuclear proliferation can complete it. Nothing prevents the end of the world as (and because) the vultures fight over its dying spoils. However, the hope remains that nascent forms of globalized social integration can overcome systemic malintegration, transforming dependency into mutual regulation. Here, the ethical face of global finitude is the secular recognition of one people in one world, of "humanity" and our common interests, rights and obligations (contra those sociologists whose gaze is riveted upon the process and practices of "individualization").

---

[19] This was first elaborated upon by Albrow, M. (2002, July). "The global shift and its consequences for sociology," paper presented at the 13th World Congress of Sociology, Brisbane.

In the new social movements—new because they do not originate in the institutions of national civil society—rests the frail hope of a global networking that could counterbalance resilient nationalism, resurgent fundamentalism, multinational malpractice and the deregulative force of international finance markets. Certainly, some of these movements hold up the wrong banner, reading "antiglobalization," but they can also be seen as an ideological expression of and search for a global society. Thus, those

> seeking to advance greater equity throughout the world's regions, peaceful dispute settlement and demilitarization, the protection of human rights and fundamental freedoms, sutainability across generations, the mutual acknowledgement of cultures, the reciprocal recognition of political and religious identities, and political stability across political institutions are all laying down elements essential to a cosmopolitan democratic community.[20]

Two factors distinguish this notion of resurgent social integration from optimistic idealism.

On the one hand, information technology facilitates new forms of social integration just as it enables the unregulated expansion of institutional activities. The co-ordination of protest is no longer confined to the slow building up of international organizations, as was the case with the Campaign for Nuclear Disarmament and its late development in Europe. The swift build-up of the new movements is ironically because they are, at least initially, postorganizational. However, it is possible to point to concrete instances of their regulative impact, although their contribution defies quantification. For example, the antiapartheid movement received some credit for Mandela's victory (and the Western universities fellover one another to shower him with honorary degrees). Equally, Greenpeace claims credit for inducing greater responsiveness to calls for nuclear restraint and the responsible disposal of nuclear waste. Perhaps, more significant—because mutual regulation has clearly engaged when it becomes self-reflexive—multinational enterprises have begun to take much more seriously the issues of sustainable development, environmental protection, and contribution to the local communities housing their installations. Correspondingly, the supermarket chains and local authorities have responded by the voluntary provision of recycling facilities.

However, what does seem grossly overoptimistic is the *laissez-faire* approach that appears to hold that the transition from mutual dependence to mutual regulation can be left to the cultural influence of the new social movements. This appears to rest on two fallacies: that unorganized social protest can properly master decentered institutions, still operating as forces for deregulation, and the fallacy of aggregate individualism, namely that changes in public opinion alone spell the control of the social over the system. I believe these to be fallacious in relation to free-floating social movements for several reasons.

First, these movements frequently provide no sustained critique or follow-through, given their reliance upon media attention (their effect is ephemeral). For example,

---

[20] Held, D. (1995). *Democracy and the global order.* Cambridge, UK: Polity. Ibid., p. 281.

humanitarian crises are forgotten as soon as their photographic immediacy fades: does world society still show active concern for those Romanian teenagers who made headlines as orphaned babies in the early 1990s? Second, the movements responses tend to be mainly expressive, rather than furnishing in-depth analyses (their effect is superficial). For example, the anticapitalist demonstrations grew in participants but became increasingly fixated on the "quick fix" of debt remission for the poorest countries. Third, the inspiration fueling some movements is highly vulnerable to systemic takeover (their effect is undermined by incorporation). For example, marketing products as "green," "organic," or "vegetarian" have simply become profitable big business; in what way does the bold sticker on my box of muesli, proclaiming it "green" and "suitable for vegetarians" do anything for either ecology or animal rights? Fourth, these movements are often impotent when resilient nationalism deliberately mobilizes and maximizes enduring sources of social antagonism (their effect is limited). For example, resurgent racism was harnessed by the European Union at Seville to press through its depressing prime concern, the collective restriction of immigration.

In short, these diverse movements do witness to genuine global concerns that transcend localized or sectional vested interests. However, to be effective in exerting consistent regulative pressure on world affairs they need to be relinked to the processes of decision making. Yet there is no cosmopolitan democracy in which their members can participate. They are self-conscious members of the new global order, who cannot yet be "citizens" of it. As such, they are like the *sans culottes* prior to the formation (and experimentation) of the Revolutionary Assemblies. At most, they can be seen as laying down new building blocks as components of a new civil society. In their most institutionalized forms, agencies such as OXFAM, Amnesty, and *Médecins sans Frontières,* represent a new humanitarian consciousness engaged in cosmopolitan action. Nevertheless, they are not the basis upon which the social can regulate the world system. This is because other, equally novel components of the global civil society in formation—the cosmopolitan elites, management of the multinationals, finance-market players, protagonists of fundamentalism—do not collectively stand in anything approximating a state of social integration. And, without that, "the social" can play no concerted regulatory role in relation to "the system."

Therefore, the alternative is attractive, namely to hope that the existing quasi-global organizations can develop an institutional framework that increases systemic integration at world level. Here, the equivalent building blocks are the new institutions, such as the International Criminal Court, the proliferating NGOs, and encouragingly effective bodies like FIFA, institutionalizing world football. Nevertheless, like every proposal to extend the governance of the United Nations, the stumbling block is that these are all international organizations. They are at the mercy of enduring national and regional interests and their authority can be repudiated by the strongest remaining power of the nation-state, legitimate command over its armed forces.

That, Weber regarded as definitive of the nation-state. Because we confront low systemic and low social integration at the global level, perhaps the key to moving from mutual dependence to mutual regulation between system and society lies precisely there, in controlled national demilitarization. This would be good in itself and the process would result in necessary global institution building for world peacekeeping, control of arms dealing, and of the drug trade. Yet, is there not something contrary in identifying the main current stumbling block to regulation of the world system with the engine that could begin the upward spiral towards increased systemic integration? Moreover, from where is the impetus for demilitarization to come? Paradoxically, a possible answer seems to be "from war itself."

With the war in Iraq, for the first time, huge sections of world society were more concerned to express outrage at this nonmandated act than to take sides in it. The six classic conditions for a just war, which were not met in this case, appear to be acquiring a seventh, that "justness" must be determined by a world forum, rather than unilaterally by a protagonist. With this, heightened social integration makes its diffuse protest against the malintegration of the international system and lodges its first significant plea for increased systemic regulation. Of equal importance is the fact that the majority of nation-states endorsed it. Even the (shifting) rhetoric of the war started to be heedful; we heard less and less about "liberating a people" and more about provisions to avoid "humanitarian crises." The superpower knew its Achilles' heel; it was aware that even September 11th would not exculpate it from another Mai Lai, and that is a completely new regulative tug, however inchoate it may be.

Conclusion

If there is anything in the broad-brush analysis presented, it has an important implication for the diagnoses and prognoses for globalization that have been proffered by political science. The foregoing discussion has highlighted the relatively sudden and conjoint development of low social and low systemic integration at global level, always a combination with explosive potential, but never one whose outcome can laconically be regarded as necessarily issuing in a higher and beneficial level of adaptation. Indeed, despite the tendency for political concepts to be endlessly recycled and re-presented, the one belief that seems beyond resuscitation is in any form of hidden hand that would automatically foster global adjustment.

Instead, two distinct tendencies can be detected in the avalanche of literature forthcoming from political science. Significantly, these two trends focus respectively upon the problems of low global social integration, as and of low global systemic integration, examined above. What is significant about this is that neither tendency gives a sustained analysis of the other side of the equation. In consequence, these two predominant strands of thought necessarily fail to address the question of how the restoration of mutual regulation between the social and the systemic might come about.

There are the advocates-cum-apologists of "global civil society," whose preoccupation is fundamentally with the social. Basically, their message is that the state of global social integration is really much better than I have painted it, if only we can be imaginative enough to (re)conceptualize its new fluid, dynamic, distanciated, syncretic, and elaborative forms. Here, John Keane's recent *Global Civil Society?*[21] is emblematic. Basically, it is a rhetorical peon to the character I called "Raphael," to his mobility, associations, networks, and especially to his contribution to global plurality and his "newfound" ethical tolerance of pluralism. Yet, "Raphael," whose existence is indubitable, symbolises the new globalised elite; what of the rest of the world's population and their state of social integration? Again and again, the cat is let out of the bag; everyone else is affected by the global institutional complex, but they are not integrated with it. This is quite overt in Keane's ideal type of global civil society, which, he states, "properly refers to a *dynamic non-governmental system of interconnected socio-economic institutions that straddle the whole earth, and that have complex effects that are felt in its four corners.*"[22] Being affected without having a reciprocal say in the matter is exactly where we came in.

Yet, if we turn to this author's discussion of "systemic integration," particularly the development of what he calls "cosmocracy," as a new type of polity, we find that those very features associated with all "having a say" are admittedly absent. This is equally the case for public accountability, universal access, effective steering mechanisms, regular forums, recognized channels for the expression of opinion, and any basis for citizenship. Keane himself is quite ready to acknowledge these profound shortcomings of "global systemic integration": "cosmocracy also chronically lets global civil society down. It does not bring peace and harmony and good government to the world, let alone usher in calm order. Its hotch-potch of rules and institutions produce negative—disabling and destabilising effects."[23] Precisely; the whole argument hangs upon a perceived increase in "global social integration"—underpinning the burgeoning "global civil society" as presented—whereas the other side of the equation is admitted to be disastrous and to hold within it the potential for nuclear disaster. The book is honest in its conclusions; the two forms of integration can and indeed do vary independently of each other. Yet, in the absence of mutual regulation "cosmocracy" does not merely let global society "down," it has the potential to annihilate it, along with the rest of the world.

On the other hand, does the second strand of political science thinking grasp both sides of the equation any better than the first? This is the approach that foregrounds the problems of "global systemic integration" by its exploration and advocacy of some version of "cosmopolitan democracy." Here, David Held's book, *Democracy and the Global Order*[24] can serve as a good representative, especially given its

---

[21] Keane, J. (2003). *Global civil society?* Cambridge, UK: Cambridge University Press.
[22] Ibid., p. 8.
[23] Ibid., p. 112.
[24] Held, D. (1995). *Democracy and the global order*. Cambridge, UK: Polity.

subtitle, *From the Modern State to Cosmopolitan Governance*. Unlike the first tendency just examined, this approach to "embedded utopianism" is indeed preoccupied with defining the institutional conditions under which "all can have a say." Held painstakingly redesigns existing political organizations into a new multilevel polity— operating at transnational, regional, national, and local levels and involving political actors such as INGOs, NGOs, and social movements—which would inaugurate a new form of "high systemic integration." He is greatly exercised, unlike the first approach, that those social forms having effects upon everyone should correspondingly be open to being affected by all. Consequently, for example, the extensive

> use of referenda, and the establishment of the democratic accountability of international organizations, would involve citizens in issues which profoundly affect them but which—in the context of the current lacunae and fragmentation of international organizations—seem remote. These mechanisms would help contribute, thereby, to the preservation of the ideal of a rightful share in the process of governance. . . .[25]

What would turn this ideal into a new working form of governance? Fundamentally, the answer given is the implementation of cosmopolitan democratic law, whose Kantian categorical imperative would be to ensure the rights of all to autonomy. Yet, how is this lynchpin of the new Global Order compatible with the existing low level of social integration? At one point, Held acknowledges this problem:

> the notion that "rights" advance universal values and are, accordingly, human rights—intrinsically applicable to all—is open to doubt. It is clear, for example, that many nations and peoples do not necessarily choose or endorse the rights that are proclaimed often as universal. . . . The tension between the claims of national identity, religious affiliation, state sovereignty and international law is marked, and it is by no means clear how it will be resolved.[26]

This seems indisputable.

If it is beyond dispute, one would then expect Held to produce a sustained analysis of the problems presented to cosmopolitan democracy by the (contra Keane) manifestly low level of social integration, and a discussion of how it might be overcome. On the contrary, the whole question of "the social" receives remarkably short shrift throughout the book. Perhaps that should have alerted one to his otherwise amazing conclusion, "A cosmopolitan democratic community does not require political and cultural integration in the form of a consensus on a wide range of beliefs, values and norms."[27] Why not? The answer is because democracy is about the public settlement of differences within the (world) community. That is its attraction, the possibility of pursuing various notions of the "good life" as defined under free and equal conditions of participation. Then, "the resolution of value conflicts becomes a matter of participating in public deliberation and negotiation"[28] and the whole problem surrounding the absence

---

[25] Ibid., p. 273.
[26] Ibid., p. 223.
[27] Ibid., p. 282.
[28] Idem.

of global social integration evaporates. The drawback, as Held does recognize, is that his whole argument is premised upon (developing) value-consensus throughout the world on the value of democracy itself. In fact, social integration in this vital respect is the predicate of increased systemic integration, represented by cosmopolitan democratic law and leading to global order. Yet the predicate is lacking; democracy is not valued the world over. The high level of global systemic integration envisaged is simply incompatible with the prevalent low level of social integration.

I do not presume to have any solution to offer to the dangers presented to the world by the existence and endurance of the conjunction between low social integration and low systemic integration. What I would conclude from the above argument is that no solution can be proffered that effectively eliminates either the systemic or the social from consideration, in relation to the other. If this chapter has contributed anything at all, it is the suggestion that the key to global order is more likely to be found by exploring the conditions under which the social and the systemic might once again come to stand in a mutually regulatory relationship, at world level. What increases the likelihood of this possibility, without in any way guaranteeing its outcome, is the objective fact and growing subjective recognition of the forces of finitude.

I started by arguing that the development of mutual regulation between the system and the social had taken two hundred years of struggle to accomplish in the Western democracies. Throughout this discussion, the only certainty is that we do not have another 200 years in which to achieve cosmopolitan solidarity in a global system.

References

Albrow, M. (1996). *The global age*. Oxford: Polity Press.
—— (2002). "The global shift and its consequences for sociology," paper presented at the 13th World Congress of Sociology, Brisbane.
Archer, M. S. (1979). *Social origins of educational systems*. London & Berverly Hills: Sage.
—— (1988). *Culture and agency*. Cambridge, U.K.: Cambridge University Press.
Beck, U. (1986, 1992). *Risk Society: Towards a new modernity*. London: Sage.
Beck, U. & Beck-Gersheim, E. (2002). *Individualization*. London: Sage
Bourdieu, P. et al. (1999). *La misere du monde*, Ed. du Seuil, Paris.
Castells, M. (1998). *End of millennium*. Oxford: Blackwell.
Giddens, A. (1990). *The consequences of modernity*. Cambridge: Polity Press.
Goldthrope, J. H., et al. (1968). *The affluent worker: Industrial attitudes and behaviour*. Cambridge: Cambridge University Press.
Held, D. (1995). *Democracy and the global order*. Cambridge: Polity.
Keane, J. (2003). *Global civil society?* Cambridge: Cambridge University Press.
Lockwood, D. (1964). "Social integration and system integration," in Zollschan, G. K., and Hirsh, W. (Eds.), *Explorations in social change*. Boston: Houghton Mifflin.
Marshall, T. H. (1963). "Citizenship and social class," in *Sociology at the crossroads*. London: Heinemann.

Teune, H., & Mlinar, Z. (1978). *The development logic of social systems*. London & Beverly Hills: Sage.

UNDP (1999). Human development report 1999. Oxford, UK: Oxford University Press.

Wallerstein, I. (1974–1989). *The modern world system*, 3 vols. New York & San Diego: Academic.

11
Globalization, Terrorism, and Democracy: 9/11 and Its Aftermath

DOUGLAS KELLNER

Globalization has been one of the most hotly contested phenomena of the past two decades. It has been a primary attractor of books, articles, and heated debate, just as postmodernism was the most fashionable and debated topic of the 1980s. A wide and diverse range of social theorists has argued that today's world is organized by forms of globalization, which are strengthening the dominance of the world capitalist economic system, supplanting the primacy of the nation-state by transnational corporations and organizations, and eroding local cultures and traditions through a global culture. Contemporary theorists from a wide range of political and theoretical positions are converging on the position that globalization is a distinguishing trend of the present moment, but there are fierce debates concerning its nature, effects, and future.[1]

For its defenders, globalization marks the triumph of capitalism and its market economy (see apologists such as Fukuyama, 1993; Friedman, 1999 & 2005 who perceive this process as positive), whereas its critics portray globalization as negative (see Mander & Goldsmith, 1996; Eisenstein, 2004; Robins & Webster, 1999). Some theorists highlight the emergence of a new transnational ruling elite

---

[1] Attempts to chart the globalization of capital, decline of the nation-state, and rise of a new global culture include the essays in Featherstone (1990), Giddens (1990), Robertson (1991), King (1991), Bird et al. (1993), Gilroy (1993), Arrighi (1994), Lash and Urry (1994), Wark (1994), Featherstone et al. (1995), Axford (1995), Held (1995), Waters 1995; Hirst and Thompson (1996), Albrow (1996), Cvetkovich and Kellner (1997; Kellner 1999, 2002), Friedman (1999), Held et al. (1999), Lechner and Boli (2000), Hardt and Negri (2000, 2004), Steger (2002), and Stiglitz (2002).

and the universalization of consumerism (Sklair, 2001), and others stress global fragmentation of "the clash of civilizations" (Huntington, 1996). Driving "post" discourses into novel realms of theory and politics, Hardt and Negri (2000 & 2004) present the emergence of "Empire" as producing evolving forms of sovereignty, economy, and culture that clash with a "multitude" of disparate groups, unleashing political struggle and an unpredictable flow of novelties, surprises, and upheavals.

Discourses of globalization initially were polarized into pro or con "globophilia" that celebrates globalization contrasted to globophobia that attacks it. For critics, globophilia provides a cover concept for global capitalism and imperialism, and is accordingly condemned as another form of the imposition of the logic of capital and the market on ever more regions of the world and spheres of life.[2] For defenders, globalization is the continuation of modernization and a force of progress, increased wealth, freedom, democracy, and happiness. Its champions thus present globalization as beneficial, generating fresh economic opportunities, political democratization, cultural diversity, and the opening to an exciting new world. Its globophobic detractors see globalization as harmful, bringing about increased domination and control by the wealthier overdeveloped nations over the poor underdeveloped countries, thus increasing the hegemony of the "haves" over the "have nots". In addition, supplementing the negative view, globalization critics assert that it produces an undermining of democracy, a cultural homogenization, and increased destruction of natural species and the environment.

There was also a tendency in some theorists to exaggerate the novelties of globalization and others to dismiss these claims by arguing that globalization has been going on for centuries and there is not that much that is new and different. Some imagine the globalization project—whether viewed positively or negatively—as inevitable and beyond human control and intervention, whereas others view globalization as generating new conflicts and new spaces for struggle, distinguishing between globalization from above and globalization from below (Brecher, Costello, & Smith, 2000).

I sketch aspects of a critical theory of globalization that undercuts the opposing globophobic and globophilia discourses in order to discuss the fundamental transformations in the world economy, politics, and culture in a dialectical framework that distinguishes between progressive and emancipatory features and oppressive and negative attributes. This requires articulations of the contradictions and ambiguities of globalization and the ways that globalization is both imposed from above and yet can be contested and reconfigured from below in ways that promote democracy and social justice. I argue that the key to understanding globalization critically is theorizing it at once as a product of technological revolution and the global restructuring of capitalism in which economic, technological, political, and cultural features are intertwined. From this perspective, one should avoid both

---

[2] What now appears as the first stage of academic and popular discourses of globalization in the 1990s tended to be dichotomized into celebratory globophilia and dismissive globophobia. For an excellent delineation and critique of academic discourses on globalization, see Steger (2002).

technological and economic determinism and all one-sided optics of globalization in favor of a view that theorizes globalization as a highly complex, contradictory, and thus ambiguous set of institutions and social relations, as well as involving flows of goods, services, ideas, technologies, cultural forms, and people (see Appadurai, 1996; Kellner, 2002).

To illustrate my approach, I argue that the September 11 terrorist attacks and the subsequent wars in Afghanistan and Iraq put on display contradictions and ambiguities embedded in globalization that demand critical and dialectical perspectives to clarify and illuminate these events and globalization itself. Showing the ways that globalization and a networked society were involved in the 9/11 events and subsequent wars in Afghanistan and Iraq, I argue that the terror attacks and ensuing Terror War show contradictions in the nature of globalization that require dialectical analysis and critique.[3] I conclude with some reflections on the implications of September 11 and the subsequent Terror War for critical social theory and democratic politics, envisaging a new global movement against terrorism and militarism and for democracy, peace, environmentalism, and social justice.

September 11, Terrorism, and Globalization

The September 11, 2001, terrorist attacks and subsequent Bush administration military response in Afghanistan and Iraq have dramatized once again the centrality of globalization in contemporary experience and the need for adequate conceptualizations and responses to it. The terrorist acts on the United States on September 11 and subsequent Terror War dramatically disclose the downsides of globalization, the ways that global flows of technology, goods, information, ideologies, and people can have destructive as well as productive effects. The disclosure of powerful anti-Western terrorist networks shows that globalization divides the world as it unifies, that it produces enemies as it incorporates participants. Globalization links people together and brings new commonalties into experience just as it differentiates them and produces new inequalities. Likewise, although it connects and brings into global networks parts of the world that were isolated and cutoff, it ignores and bypasses other regions. The events disclose explosive contradictions and conflicts at the heart of globalization and that the technologies of information, communication, and transportation that facilitate globalization can also be used to undermine and attack it, and generate instruments of destruction as well as production.[4]

---

[3] I am using the term "Terror War" to describe the Bush administration's "war against terrorism" and its use of unilateral military force and terror as the privileged vehicles of constructing a U.S. hegemony in the current world (dis)order (see Kellner, 2003).

[4] I am not able in the framework of this chapter to theorize the alarming expansion of war and militarism in the post-9/11 environment. For my theorizing of these topics, see Kellner 2003.

The experience of September 11 points to the objective ambiguity of globalization, that positive and negative sides are interconnected, that the institutions of the open society unlock the possibilities of destruction and violence, as well as democracy, free trade, and cultural and social exchange. Once again, the interconnection and interdependency of the networked world was dramatically demonstrated as terrorists from the Middle East brought local grievances from their region to attack key symbols of American power and the very infrastructure of New York. Some saw terrorism as an expression of "the dark side of globalization," whereas I would conceive it as part of the ambiguity and contradictions of globalization itself that simultaneously creates friends and enemies, wealth and poverty, and growing divisions between the "haves" and "have nots." Yet, the downturning of the global economy, intensification of local and global political conflicts, repression of human rights and civil liberties, and general increase in fear and anxiety certainly undermined the naïve optimism of globophiles who perceived globalization as a purely positive instrument of progress and wellbeing.

The use of powerful technologies as weapons of destruction also discloses current configurations of power and emergent forms of terrorism and war, as the new millennium exploded into dangerous conflicts and interventions. As technologies of mass destruction become more available and dispersed, perilous instabilities have emerged that have elicited policing measures to stem the flow of movements of people and goods across borders and internally. In particular, the U.S.A. Patriot Act has led to repressive measures that are replacing the spaces of the open and free information society with new forms of surveillance, policing, and repression, thus significantly undermining U.S. democracy (see Kellner, 2003b).

Ultimately, however, the abhorrent terror acts by the bin Laden network and the violent military response by the Bush administration may be an anomalous paroxysm whereby a highly regressive premodern Islamic fundamentalism has clashed with an old-fashioned patriarchal and unilateralist Wild West militarism. It could be that such forms of terrorism, militarism, and state repression would be superseded by more rational forms of politics that globally criminalize terrorism, and that do not sacrifice the benefits of the open society and economy in the name of security. Yet the events of September 11 may open a new era of Terror War that will lead to the kind of apocalyptic futurist world depicted by cyberpunk fiction.

In any case, the events of September 11 and their aftermath have promoted a fury of reflection, theoretical debates, and political conflicts and upheaval that put the complex dynamics of globalization at the center of contemporary theory and politics. To those skeptical of the centrality of globalization to contemporary experience, it is now clear that we are living in a global world that is highly interconnected and vulnerable to passions and crises that can cross borders and can affect anyone or any region at any time. The events of September 11 also provide a test case to evaluate various theories of globalization and the contemporary era. In addition, they highlight some of the contradictions of globalization and the need to develop a highly complex and dialectical model to capture its conflicts, ambiguities, and contradictory effects.

Consequently, I argue that in order to properly theorize globalization one needs to conceptualize several sets of contradictions generated by globalization's combination of technological revolution and restructuring of capital, which in turn generate tensions between capitalism and democracy, and "haves" and "have nots." Within the world economy, globalization involves the proliferation of the logic of capital, but also the spread of democracy in information, finance, investing, and the diffusion of technology (see Friedman, 1999, 2005; Hardt and Negri, 2000, 2004). Globalization is thus a contradictory amalgam of capitalism and democracy, in which the logic of capital and the market system enter into ever more arenas of global life, even as democracy spreads and more political regions and spaces of everyday life are being contested by democratic demands and forces. But the overall process is contradictory. Sometimes globalizing forces promote democracy and sometimes inhibit it, thus either equating globalization and capitalism with democracy, or simply opposing them, are problematical.

The processes of globalization are highly turbulent and have generated new conflicts throughout the world. Benjamin Barber (1995) describes the strife between McWorld and Jihad, contrasting the homogenizing, commercialized, Americanized tendencies of the global economy and culture with traditional cultures that are often resistant to globalization. Thomas Friedman (1999) makes a more benign distinction between what he calls the "Lexus" and the "Olive Tree." The former is a symbol of modernization, of affluence and luxury, and of Westernized consumption, contrasted with the Olive Tree that is a symbol of roots, tradition, place, and stable community. Barber, however, is overly dualistic and negative toward McWorld and Jihad, failing to adequately describe the democratic and progressive forces within both. Although Barber recognizes a dialectic of McWorld and Jihad, he opposes both to democracy, failing to perceive how both what he describes as McWorld and Jihad generate their own democratic forces and tendencies, as well as opposing and undermining democratization. Within the Western democracies, for instance, there is not just top-down homogenization and corporate domination, but also globalization from below and oppositional social movements that seek alternatives to capitalist globalization.[5]

---

[5] Barber's recent *Fear's Empire* (2003) sharply criticizes the Bush administration policy of "preemptive strikes" and "preventive wars" as an unilateralist militarism, destructive of international law, treaties, alliances, and the multilateral approach necessary to deal with global problems such as terrorism, a critique with which I would agree (see Kellner, 2003, 2005). I also am in accord with Barber's position that both bin Laden's terrorism and Bush militarism promote a politics of fear that is counter to building a strong democracy. Hence, although I find Barber's general categorical explication of globalization problematically dualistic and his categories of McWorld and Jihad too homogenizing and totalizing, I am in general agreement with his criticism of Bush administration policy.

Friedman, by contrast, is too uncritical of globalization, caught up in his own Lexus high-consumption lifestyle, failing to perceive the depth of the oppressive features of globalization and breadth and extent of resistance and opposition to it. In particular, he fails to articulate contradictions between capitalism and democracy and the ways that globalization and its economic logic undermine democracy as well as circulate it. Likewise, especially in his 1999 study, he does not grasp the virulence of the premodern and Jihadist tendencies that he blithely identifies with the Olive Tree and the reasons why globalization and the West are so strongly resisted in many parts of the world.

Hence, it is important to present globalization as a strange amalgam of both homogenizing forces of sameness and uniformity, and heterogeneity, difference, and hybridity, as well as a contradictory mixture of democratizing and antidemocratizing tendencies. On one hand, globalization unfolds a process of standardization in which a globalized mass culture circulates the globe creating sameness and homogeneity everywhere. But globalized culture makes possible unique appropriations and developments all over the world, thus proliferating hybridity, difference, and heterogeneity.[6] Every local context involves its own appropriation and reworking of global products and signifiers, thus proliferating difference, otherness, diversity, and variety (Luke & Luke, 2000). Grasping that globalization embodies these contradictory tendencies at once, that it can be both a force of homogenization and heterogeneity, is crucial to articulating the contradictions of globalization and avoiding one-sided and reductive conceptions.

My intention is to present globalization as conflictual, contradictory, and open to resistance and democratic intervention and transformation and not just as a monolithic juggernaut of progress or domination as in many discourses. This goal is advanced by distinguishing between globalization from below and the globalization from above of corporate capitalism and the capitalist state, a distinction that should help us to get a better sense of how globalization does or does not promote democratization. "Globalization from below" refers to the ways in which marginalized individuals and social movements resist globalization and/or use its institutions and instruments to further democratization and social justice.

Yet, one needs to avoid binary normative articulations, because globalization from below can have highly conservative and destructive effects, as well as positive

---

[6] For example, as Ritzer argues (1993, 1996), McDonald's imposes not only a similar cuisine all over the world, but circulates processes of what he calls "McDonaldization" that involve a production/consumption model of efficiency, technological rationality, calculability, predictability, and control. Yet as Watson et al. (1997) argues, McDonald's has various cultural meanings in diverse local contexts, as well as different products, organization, and effects. Yet the latter goes too far toward stressing heterogeneity, downplaying the cultural power of McDonald's as a force of a homogenizing globalization and Western corporate logic and system; see Kellner (2003).

ones, whereas globalization from above can help produce global solutions to problems such as terrorism or the environment. Moreover, as Michael Peters argues (2005), globalization itself is a kind of war and much militarism has been expansive and globalizing in many historical situations. Yet, on the other hand, antiwar and peace movements are also increasingly global, hence globalization itself is marked by tensions and contradictions.

Thus, although on one level, globalization significantly increases the supremacy of big corporations and big government, it can also give power to groups and individuals that were previously left out of the democratic dialogue and terrain of political struggle. Such potentially positive effects of globalization include increased access to education for individuals excluded from sharing culture and knowledge and the possibility of oppositional individuals and groups to participate in global culture and politics through gaining access to global communication and media networks and to circulate local struggles and oppositional ideas through these media. The role of information technologies in social movements, political struggle, and everyday life forces social movements and critical theorists to reconsider their political strategies and goals and democratic theory to appraise how new technologies do and do not promote democratization (Kellner, 1997, 1999; Best & Kellner, 2001).

In their book *Empire*, Hardt and Negri (2000) present contradictions within globalization in terms of an imperializing logic of "Empire" and an assortment of struggles by the multitude, creating a contradictory and tension-full situation. As in my conception, Hardt and Negri present globalization as a complex process that involves a multidimensional mixture of expansions of the global economy and capitalist market system, information technologies and media, expanded judicial and legal modes of governance, and emergent modes of power, sovereignty, and resistance.[7] Combining poststructuralism with "autonomous Marxism," Hardt and Negri stress political openings and possibilities of struggle within Empire in an optimistic and buoyant text that envisages progressive democratization and self-valorization in the turbulent process of the restructuring of capital.

---

[7] While I find *Empire* an impressive and productive text, I am not sure, however, what is gained by using the word "Empire" rather than the concepts of global capital and political economy, or the use of "multitude" in place of traditional class and sociological categories. While Hardt and Negri combine categories of Marxism and critical social theory with poststructuralist discourse derived from Foucault and Deleuze and Guattari, they frequently favor the latter, often mystifying and obscuring the object of analysis. I am not as confident as Hardt and Negri that the "multitude" replaces traditional concepts of the working class and other modern political subjects, movements, and actors, and find the emphasis on nomads, "New Barbarians", and the poor as replacement categories problematical. Nor is it clear concerning what forms their poststructuralist politics would take. The same problem is evident in an earlier decade's provocative and post-Marxist text by Laclau and Mouffe (1985), who valorized new social movements, radical democracy, and a postsocialist politics without providing many concrete examples or proposals for struggle in the present conjuncture.

In *Multitude* (2004), Hardt and Negri valorize the struggles of masses of people against Empire. Many theorists, by contrast, have argued that one of the trends of globalization is depoliticization of publics, the decline of the nation-state, and end of traditional politics (Boggs, 2000). Although I would agree that globalization is promoted by tremendously powerful economic forces and that it often undermines democratic movements and decision making, one should also note that there are openings and possibilities for both a globalization from below that inflects globalization for positive and progressive ends, and that globalization can thus help promote as well as destabilize democracy.[8] Against capitalist globalization from above, there has been a significant eruption of forces and subcultures of resistance that have attempted to preserve specific forms of culture and society against neoliberal and homogenizing globalization, and to create alternative forces of society and culture, thus exhibiting resistance and globalization from below. Most dramatically, peasant, populist, and guerrilla movements in Latin America, labor unions, students, and environmentalists throughout the world, and a variety of other groups and movements have resisted capitalist globalization and attacks on previous rights and benefits.[9] Several dozen people's organizations from around the world have protested World Trade Organization policies and a backlash against globalization is visible everywhere. Politicians who once championed trade agreements like GATT and NAFTA are now often quiet about these arrangements.

Globalization involves both a disorganization and reorganization of capitalism, a tremendous restructuring process, which creates openings for progressive social change and intervention as well as highly destructive transformative effects. On the positive ledger, in a more fluid and open economic and political system, oppositional forces can gain concessions, win victories, and effect progressive changes. During the 1970s, new social movements, emergent nongovernmental organizations (NGOs),

---

[8] I am thus trying to mediate in this paper between those who claim that globalization simply undermines democracy and those who claim that globalization promotes democratization like Friedman (1999 and 2005). I should also note that in distinguishing between globalization from above and globalization from below, I do not want to say that one is good and the other is bad in relation to democracy. As Friedman (1999 and 2005) shows, capitalist corporations and global forces might very well promote democratization in many arenas of the world, and globalization-from-below might promote special interests or reactionary goals, so I am criticizing theorizing globalization in binary terms as primarily "good" or "bad". Although critics of globalization simply see it as the reproduction of capitalism, its champions, such as Friedman, do not perceive how globalization undercuts democracy. Likewise, Friedman does not engage the role of new social movements, dissident groups, or the "have nots" in promoting democratization. Nor do concerns for social justice, equality, and participatory democracy play a role in his book.

[9] On resistance to globalization by labor, see Moody (1988, 1997); on resistance by environmentalists and other social movements, see the studies in Mander and Goldsmith (1996).

and novel forms of struggle and solidarity emerged that have been expanding to the present day (Hardt and Negri, 2000, 2004; Burbach, 2001; Best & Kellner, 2001; Foran, 2003).

But not only the anticorporate globalization movement of the 1990s emerged as a form of globalization from below, but also Al Qaeda and various global terror networks intensified their attacks and helped generate an era of Terror War. This made it difficult simply to affirm "globalization from below" while denigrating "globalization from above," as clearly terrorism was an emergent and dangerous form of globalization from below that was a threat to peace, security, and democracy. Moreover, in the face of Bush administration unilateralism and militarism, multilateral approaches to the problems of terrorism called for global responses and alliances to a wide range of global problems (see Kellner, 2003b; Barber, 2003), thus demanding a progressive and cosmopolitan globalization to deal with contemporary challenges.

Furthermore, the present conjuncture is marked by a conflict between growing centralization and organization of power and wealth in the hands of the few contrasted with opposing processes exhibiting a fragmentation of power that is more plural, multiple, and open to contestation. Both tendencies are observable and it is up to individuals and groups to find openings for progressive political intervention, social transformation, and the democratization of education that pursue positive values such as democracy, human rights, literacy, equality, ecological preservation and restoration, and social justice, while fighting poverty, ignorance, terror, and injustice. Thus, rather than just denouncing globalization, or engaging in celebration and legitimation, a critical theory of globalization reproaches those aspects that are oppressive, while seizing upon opportunities to fight domination and exploitation and to promote democratization, justice, and a forward-looking reconstruction of the polity, society, and culture.

From September 11 to Terror War

Momentous historical events, such as the September 11 terrorist attacks and the subsequent Terror War, test social theories and provide a challenge to give a convincing account of the event and its consequences. The Bush administration has expanded its combat against Islamic terrorism into a policy of Terror War where they have declared the right of the United States to strike any enemy state or organization presumed to harbor or support terrorism, or to eliminate "weapons of mass destruction" that could be used against the United States. The right wing of the Bush administration seeks to promote Terror War as the defining struggle of the era, coded as an apocalyptic battle between good and evil and has already mounted major military campaigns against Afghanistan and Iraq, with highly ambiguous and unsettling results.

Social theories generalize from past experience and provide accounts of historical events or periods that attempt to map, illuminate, and perhaps criticize dominant social relations, institutions, forms, trends, and events of a given epoch. In turn, they can be judged by the extent to which they account for, interpret, and critically assess contemporary conditions, or predict future events or developments. One major theory of the past two decades, Francis Fukuyama's *The End of History* (1993), was strongly put into question by the events of September 11 and their aftermath.[10] For Fukuyama, the collapse of Soviet communism and triumph of Western capitalism and democracy in the early 1990s constituted "the end of history." This signified for him "the end point of mankind's ideological evolution and the universalization of Western liberal democracy as the final form of human government." Although there may be conflicts in places such as the Third World, overall for Fukuyama liberal democracy and market capitalism have prevailed and future politics will devolve around resolving routine economic and technical problems, and the future will accordingly be rather mundane and boring.

Samuel Huntington polemicizes against Fukuyama's "one world: euphoria and harmony" model in his *The Clash of Civilizations and the Remaking of World Order* (1996). For Huntington, the future holds a series of clashes between "the West and the Rest." Huntington rejects a number of models of contemporary history, including a "realist" model that nation-states are primary players on the world scene who will continue to form alliances and coalitions that will play themselves out in various conflicts. He also rejects a "chaos" model that detects no discernible order or structure. Instead, Huntington asserts that the contemporary world is articulated into competing civilizations that are based on irreconcilably different cultures and religions. For Huntington, culture provides unifying and integrating principles of order and cohesion, and from dominant cultural formations emerge civilizations that are likely to come into conflict with each other, including Islam, China, Russia, and the West. On Huntington's model, religion is "perhaps the central force that motivates and mobilizes people" and is thus the core of civilization.

Although Huntington's model seems to have some purchase in the currently emerging global encounter with terrorism, it tends to overly homogenize both Islam and the West, as well as the other civilizations he depicts. As Tariq Ali argues (2002), Huntington exaggerates the role of religion, while downplaying

---

[10] Fukuyama's 1993 book was an expansion of a 1989 article published in the conservative journal *The National Interest*. His texts generated a tremendous amount of controversy and were seen by some as a new dominant ideology proclaiming the triumph of Western ideals of capitalism and democracy over all of their opponents. With a quasi-Hegelian gloss, Fukuyama proclaimed the victory of the Ideas of neo-Liberalism and the "end of history", and his work prompted both skepticism ("it ain't over,'til its over") and impassioned critique. If terrorism and the Bush administration militarism soon pass from the historical scene and a neoliberal globalization driven by market capitalism and democracy returns to become the constitutive force of the new millennium, Fukuyama would end up being vindicated after all. But in the current conflictual state of the world, his views appear off the mark and put in question by the present situation.

the importance of economics and politics.[11] Moreover, Huntington's model lends itself to pernicious misuse, and has been deployed to call for and legitimate military retribution against implacable adversarial civilizations by conservative intellectuals such as Jeane Kirkpatrick, Henry Kissinger, and members of the Bush administration, as well as, in effect, to give credence to Al Qaeda and Jihadist attacks against the "corrupt" and "infidel" West.

In sum, Huntington's work provides too essentialist a model that covers over contradictions and conflicts both within the West and within Islam. Both worlds have been divided for centuries into dueling countries, ethnic groups, religious factions, and complex alliances that have fought fierce wars against each other and that continue to be divided geographically, politically, ideologically, and culturally (see Ali, 2002). Moreover, Huntington's ideal type that contrasts East and West, based on conflicting models of civilization, covers over the extent to which Arab and Muslim culture preserved the cultural traditions of the Greece and Rome during the Middle Ages and thus played a major role in constituting Western culture and modernity. Huntington downplays as well the extent to which Western science and technology were importantly anticipated and developed in the Middle and Far East.[12]

Furthermore, Islam itself is a contested terrain and in the current situation there are important attempts to mobilize more moderate forms of Islam and Islamic countries against Osama bin Laden's Al Qaeda terror network and Islamic extremism (see Rashid, 2003). Hence, Huntington's binary model of inexorable conflict between the West and Islam is not only analytically problematic, but covers over the crucial battle within Islam itself to define the role and nature of religion in the contemporary world. It also decenters the important challenge for the West to engage the Islamic world in a productive dialogue about religion and modernity and to bring about more peaceful, informed, and mutually beneficial relations between the West and the Islamic world. Positing inexorable conflicts between civilizations may well describe past history and present dangers, but it does not help produce a better future and is thus normatively and politically defective and dangerous.

Globalization includes a homogenizing neoliberal market logic and commodification, cultural interaction, and hybridization, as well as conflict among corporations, nations, blocs, and cultures. Leading dualistic theories that posit

---

[11] Ali also notes (2002: 282f) that after the September 11 attacks, Huntington modified his "clash of civilization" thesis to describe the post-Cold War era as an "age of Muslim wars," with Muslims fighting each other, or their specific enemies (see Huntington essay in *Newsweek*, Special Davos Edition (December–January 2001–2). As Ali maintains, besides being a highly questionable overview of the present age, it contradicts his previous model, reducing Huntington's thought to incoherency. Hardt and Negri (2004: 33f) mock Huntington as a *Geheimrat* (i.e., "secret adviser of the sovereign") and indicate how his discourse had been rejected by many neoconservatives in the Bush administration.

[12] Critical scholarship has revealed the important role of Islam in the very construction of modernity and globalization; see Rahman (1984), Ali (2002) and Simons (2003).

a fundamental bifurcation between the West and Islam are thus analytically suspicious in that they homogenize complex civilizations and cover over differences, hybridizations, contradictions, and conflicts within these cultures. Positing inexorable clashes between bifurcated blocs à la Huntington and Barber fails to illuminate specific discord within the opposing spheres and the complex relations between them. These analyses do not grasp the complexity in the current geopolitical situation, which involves highly multifaceted and intricate interests, coalitions, and conflicts that shift and evolve in response to changing situations within an overdetermined and constantly evolving historical context. As Tariq Ali points out (2002), dualistic models of clashes of civilization also occlude the historical forces that clashed in the September 11 attacks and the subsequent Terror War.

Consequently, the events of September 11 and their aftermath suggest that critical social theory needs models that account for complexity and the historical roots and vicissitudes of contemporary problems such as terrorism rather than bifurcated dualistic theories. Critical social theory also needs to articulate how events such as September 11 produce novel historical configurations while articulating both changes and continuities in the present situation.[13] It requires historical accounts of the contemporary origins of Islamic radicalism and its complicity with U.S. imperialism. The causes of the September 11 events and their aftermath are highly multifaceted and involve, for starters, the failure of U.S. intelligence and the destructive consequences of U.S. interventionist foreign policy since World War II and the failure to address the Israeli–Palestinian crisis; U.S. subversion of Middle Eastern regimes deemed "socialist" and support of authoritarian regimes deemed friendly to U.S. interests, which among other things, led to take-over in Iran by Islamicist forces; U.S. policies since the late 1970s that supported Islamic Jihadist forces against the Soviet Union in the last days of the Cold War; and the failure to take terrorist threats seriously and provide an adequate response. In other words, there is no one cause or faction responsible for the 9/11 terror attacks, but a wide range of responsibility to be ascribed and a complex historical background concerning relations between the United States and radical Islamic forces in the Cold War and then conflicts starting with the 1990–1991 "crisis in the Gulf" and subsequent Gulf War (see Kellner, 1992 & 2003). In the next section, I want to suggest how these events have been bound up with the trajectory of globalization.

Globalization and 9/11: What Has Changed?

In the aftermath of September 11, there was a wealth of commentary arguing that "everything has changed," that the post-September 11 world is a different one, less innocent, more serious, and significantly altered, with momentous modifications in the economy, polity, culture, and everyday life. There were some doubters such as historian Alan Brinkley who stated in a interview: "I'm

---

[13] I provide my own historical and theoretical account of the background to the events of September 11 in Kellner (2003).

skeptical that this is a great rupture in the fabric of history."[14] Time alone will tell the depth of the magnitude of change, but there are enough significant shifts that have occurred already to see September 11 as a transformational event that has created some dramatic alterations in both the United States and global society, signaling reconfigurations and novelties in the current world.

In the context of U.S. politics, September 11 was so far-reaching and catastrophic that it flipped the political world upside down, put new issues on the agenda, and changed the political, cultural, and economic climate almost completely overnight. To begin, there was a dramatic reversal of the fortunes of George W. Bush and the Bush administration. Before September 11, Bush's popularity was rapidly declining. After several months of the most breathtaking hard-right turn perhaps ever seen in U.S. politics, Bush seemed to lose control of the agenda with the defection of Vermont Republican Senator Jim Jeffords to the Democratic Party in May 2001. Jeffords' defection gave the Democrats a razor-thin control of Congress and the ability to block Bush's programs and to advance their own (see Kellner, 2001: Ch. 11). Bush seemed disengaged after this setback, spending more and more time at his Texas ranch. He was widely perceived as incompetent and unqualified, and his public support was seriously eroding.

With the terror attacks of September 11, however, the bitter partisanship of the previous months disappeared and Bush was the beneficiary of a extraordinary outburst of patriotism. Support for the Bush administration was strongly fueled by the media that provided 24/7 coverage of the heroism of the firemen, police, and rescue workers at the World Trade Center. The response of ordinary citizens to the tragedy showed American courage, skill, and dedication at its best, as rescue workers heroically struggled to save lives and deal with the immense problems of removing the Trade Center ruins. New York City and the country pulled together in a remarkable display of community, heroism, and resolve, focused on in the ongoing media coverage of the tragedy. There was an explosion of flags and patriotism and widespread desire for military retaliation, fanned by the media (see Gitlin, 2006).

The U.S. media's demonizing coverage of bin Laden and his Al Qaeda network of terrorists and constant demand for strong military retaliation precluded developing broader coalitions and more global and less militarist approaches to the problem of terrorism. The anthrax attacks, unsolved as I write in Fall 2007, fueled media hysteria and mass panic that terrorism could strike anyone at any time and any place. Bush articulated the escalating patriotism, vilification of the terrorists, and the demand for stern military retaliation, and a frightened nation supported his policies, often without seeing their broader implications and threat to democracy and world peace.

There was a brief and ironical ideological flip-flop of Bush administration policy, in which it temporarily put aside the unilateralism that had distinguished its first months in office in favor of a multilateral approach. As the Bush administration

---

[14] Brinkley elaborated his position in a forum at Columbia University on October 5, 2001; see http://www.columbia.edu/cu/news/01/10/historical_reflection_9_11.html

scrambled to assemble a global coalition against terrorism with partners such as Pakistan, China, and Russia, that it had previously ignored or in the case of China even provoked, illusions circulated that the United States would pursue a more multilateral global politics. Yet ultimately the United States largely chose to fight the Afghanistan war itself, depending on U.S. Special Forces and Afghan war lords, rather than a significant multilateral coalition. One could indeed argue that the failures of the Afghan intervention to capture bin Laden, Mullah Omar, and other top Al Qaeda and Taliban leadership was a result of the United States choosing a largely unilateral military policy rather than a more multilateral approach (see Kellner, 2003).

In any case, the September 11 events dramatized that globalization is a defining reality of our time and that the much-celebrated flow of people, ideas, technology, media, and goods could have a downside as well as an upside, and expensive costs as well as benefits. The 9/11 terror attacks also call attention to the complex and unpredictable nature of a globally connected networked society and the paradoxes, surprises, and unintended consequences that flow from the multidimensional processes of globalization. Al Qaeda presented an example of a hidden and secretive decentered network dedicated to attacking the United States and their Afghanistan base represented what theorists called "wild zones" or "zones of turmoil" that existed out of the boundaries of "safe zones" of globalized metropoles such as Wall Street and Northern Virginia (see Mann, 2001; Urry, 2002). Globalization thus generates its Other, its opponents, just as it destroys tradition and incorporates ever more parts of the world and forms of life into its modernizing and neoliberal market.

For the first time, the people of the United States were obliged to perceive that it had serious enemies throughout the globe and that global problems had to be addressed. No longer could the United States enjoy the luxury of isolationism, but was forced to actively define its role within a dangerous and complex global environment. Moreover, the terror attacks of 9/11 put in question much conventional wisdom and forced U.S. citizens and others to reflect upon the continued viability of key values, practices, and institutions of a democratic society. In particular, the events of September 11 force the rethinking of globalization, technology, democracy, and national and global security. 9/11 and its aftermath demonstrate the significance of globalization and the ways that global, national, and local scenes and events intersect in the contemporary world. The terror spectacle also pointed to the fundamental contradictions and ambiguities of globalization, undermining one-sided pro- or antiglobalization positions.

9/11 was obviously a global event that dramatized an interconnected and conflicted networked society where there is a constant worldwide flow of people, products, technologies, ideas, and the like. September 11 could only be a megaevent in a global media world, a society of the spectacle (Debord, 1970), where the whole world is watching and participates in what Marshall McLuhan (1964) called a global village. The 9/11 terror spectacle was obviously constructed as a media event to circulate terror and to demonstrate to the world the vulnerability of the epicenter of global capitalism and American power.

Thus, September 11 dramatized the interconnected networked globe and the important role of the media in which individuals everywhere can simultaneously watch events of global significance unfold and participate in the dramas of globalization. Already, Bill Clinton had said before September 11 that terrorism is the downside, the dark side, of globalization, and after 9/11 Colin Powell interpreted the terrorist attacks in similar fashion. Worldwide terrorism is threatening in part because globalization relentlessly divides the world into haves and have nots, promotes conflicts and competition, and fuels long-simmering hatreds and grievances as well as bringing people together, creating new relations and interactions, and new hybridities. This is the objective ambiguity of globalization that both brings people together and brings them into conflict, that creates social interaction and inclusion, as well as hostilities and exclusions, and that potentially tears regions and the world apart while attempting to pull things together. Moreover, as different groups gain access to technologies of destruction and devise plans to make conventional technologies, such as the airplane, instruments of destruction then dangers of unexpected terror events, any place and any time proliferate and become part of the frightening mediascape of the contemporary moment.

Globalization is thus messier and more dangerous than previous theories had indicated. Moreover, global terrorism and megaspectacle terror events are possible because of the lethality and power of new technology, and its availability to groups and individuals that previously had restricted access. In a perverted distortion of Andrew Feenberg's theory of the reconstruction and democratization of technology (1995, 1999), terrorist groups seek technologies of mass destruction in the past monopolized by the state and take instruments of mass transportation and communication run by corporations and the state, such as airlines and mail delivery, and reconvert these instruments into weapons of mass destruction, or at least of mass terror. I might parenthetically note here the etymology of the term terrorism, which, according to most scholars, derives from the Latin verb *terrere*, "to cause to tremble or quiver." It began to be used during the French Revolution, and especially after the fall of Robespierre and the "reign of terror," or simply, "the Terror" in which enemies of the revolution were subjected to imprisonment, torture, and beheading, the first of many modern examples of state terrorism.

It is clear from September 11 that the new technologies disperse power, empowering angry disempowered people, leveling the playing field and distributing the use and application of information technology and some technologies of mass destruction. Many military technologies can be obtained by individuals and groups to use against the superpowers and the access to such technology produces a situation of asymmetrical war where weaker individuals and groups can go after superpowers. The possibility of new forms of cyberwar, and terrorist threats from chemical, biological, or nuclear weapons, creates new vulnerabilities in the national defense of the overdeveloped countries and provides opportunities for weaker nations or groups to attack stronger ones. Journalist William Greider, for instance, author of *Fortress America: The American Military and the Consequences of Peace*, claims that "A deadly irony is embedded in the potential of these new technologies. Smaller, poorer nations may be able to defend themselves on the cheap against the intrusion of America's overwhelming military strength," or exercise deadly terrorism against civilian populations.[15]

Hence, the United States discovered that it is vulnerable domestically to terrorist attack. Likewise, it is becoming clear that the more technologically advanced a society is, the more vulnerable it is to cyberwar. There are now, of course, serious worries about the Internet and cyberterrorism disrupting the global economy and networked society. It is somewhat surprising that terrorist groups have not, in fact, gone after the Internet, and attempted to shut it down since they were obviously attempting to disrupt global business by attacking the World Trade Center and airlines industry. Already Paul Virilio evoked the frightening possibility of the collapse of the Internet through a major technological "event" that would cause its shutdown, disruptions previewed by hacker attacks, worms, and viruses over the past years.[16]

Rather, the Al Qaeda terror network used the Internet, as it used globalization, to move its communication, money, people, propaganda, and terror. Curiously, then, 9/11 dramatizes that all of the most positive aspects of globalization and new technology can be turned against the United States, or, in general, positive aspects of globalization can turn into their opposite. This situation illustrates Horkheimer and Adorno's (1972) "dialectic of Enlightenment," in which reason, science, technology, and other instruments of Enlightenment turned into their opposites in the hands of German fascism and other oppressive social groups. Airplanes, for example, can be instruments of terror as well as transportation. Indeed, globalization makes possible global terror networks as well as networks of commerce and communication. The circulation of commodities, technologies, ideas, money, and people can facilitate networks of terror, as well as trade and travel. The Internet makes possible the spreading of hate and terror, as well as knowledge and culture. Computers can be an integral part of a terror network just as they are part of businesses everywhere and many of our own everyday lives. And biotechnology, which promises such extravagant medical advances and miracles, can provide weapons of mass destruction, as well as medicines and healing forces.

Thus, September 11 and its aftermath exhibits the contradictions and ambiguities of globalization, the Internet, biotechnology, and technology in general in the contemporary age. Globalization has upsides and downsides, costs and benefits, which are often interconnected, and is consequently intrinsically ambiguous. New technologies can be used positively or negatively and in fact are at once potentially empowering and productive and disempowering and destructive, and are thus fraught with contradictions. Often, the positives and negatives of globalization and new technology are intertwined, as when the free and open society

---

[15] William Greider, cited at abcsnew.com, November 11, 1999.
[16] For Virilio (1998), every technology has its accident that accompanies it, so the airplane's accident is the crash, the automobile a wreck, and a ship its sinking. For Virilio, the accident the Internet faces is "the accident of accidents," as he calls it, the entire collapse of the global system of communication and information, and thus the global economy. On Virilio, see Kellner (1999).

enabled the open movement of terrorists; the open architecture of the Internet enabled terrorists to communicate, circulate money, and organize their terror attacks; and the networked society of globalization, with its dark sides, enabled terrorists to attack the very symbols of American global wealth and power.

Certainly bin Laden's Al Qaeda network represents bad globalization, most would agree, and the perverted use of technology. But in a sense the Al Qaeda Jihad is the reverse image of McWorld, which imposes its Jihad on tradition and local culture, wanting to create the world in its image. Just as Al Qaeda dreams of imposing a radical premodern Islam on the world, taking over and destroying Western infidel culture and imposing a homogenized Islamic fundamentalism, so too does McDonald's want to destroy local and traditional eating habits and cuisine and replace them with a globalized and universalized menu.

Hence, whereas theories of globalization, the Internet, and cyberculture tended to be on the whole one-sided, either pro or con, 9/11 and its aftermath showed the objective ambiguity and contradictions of globalization and need for a more dialectical and contextualizing optic. On one hand, the events showed the fundamental interdependence of the world, dramatizing how activities in one part of the world affects others and the need for more global consciousness and politics. The September 11 events exposed the dangers and weaknesses inherent in constructions of Fortress America, and the untenability of isolationism and unilateralist policies. They made evident that we are in a local/global world with local/global problems, which require a dialetic of local and global solutions.

As the Bush administration pursued increasingly unilateralist policies after seeming to make gestures toward a multilateralist response, the aftermath of 9/11 shows the limited possibilities for a single nation to impose its will on the world and to dominate the complex environment of the world economy and politics, as the turmoil evident by fall 2003 in both Afghanistan and Iraq and the continued turbulence in both countries reveal.

The 9/11 terror attacks also disclosed the failures of laissez-faire conservative economics, which claimed that there was a market solution to every problem. Just as the 2000 U.S. presidential election revealed the failure of voting technology, the voting registration process, the very system of voting, as well as the failure of the media and judicial system in the U.S system of democracy (see Kellner, 2001 and 2005), so too did September 11 reveal the massive failure of U.S. intelligence agencies, the National Security State, and the U.S. government to protect the people in the country, as well as cities and monuments, against terrorist attack. The privatization undergone by the airlines industry left travelers vulnerable to the hijacking of airplanes; the confused and ineffectual response by the federal government to the anthrax attacks uncovered the necessity of a better public health system, as well as more protection and security against terrorist attacks. Going after the terror networks disclosed the need for tighter financial regulation, better legal and police coordination, and an improved intelligence and national security apparatus. Rebuilding New York City and the lives of those affected by the terror attacks showed the need for a beneficent welfare state that would provide for its citizens in their time of need.

Thus, the 9/11 events should have ended the fantasies of Reagan–Bush conservative economics that the market alone can solve all social problems and provide the best mechanism for every industry and sector of life. The succeeding Enron and other corporate scandals also reveal the utter failures of neoliberalism and the need for a stronger and more effective polity for the United States to compete and survive in a highly complex world economy and polity (see Kellner, 2003b: Ch. 9). Yet the Bush administration has managed to keep neoliberal ideology alive despite its failures and the escalating problems of its economic policies that is producing skyrocketing federal deficits, growing global trade deficits and a fallen dollar, and a shaky economy.

On the whole, September 11 and its aftermath have made the world a much more dangerous place. Regional conflicts from the Israel–Palestine hostilities in the Middle East to the India–Pakistan conflict to discord in Africa, the Philippines, Columbia, and elsewhere have used Bush administration discourse against terrorism to suppress human rights, to legitimate government oppression, and to kill political opponents throughout the world. Bush administration unilateralism in pursuing the war against terror throughout the world, including against an imagined "axis of evil" not directly related to the Al Qaeda terror network, has weakened multilateral agreements and forces from NATO to the UN and has increased collective insecurity immensely. The Bush administration polarizing policy of "you are with us or against us" has divided alliances, is ever more isolating the United States and is producing a more polarized and conflicted world. The alarming build-up of U.S. military power is escalating a new militarism and proliferating enemies and resentment against the United States, now being increasingly seen as a rogue superpower. Finally, aggressive U.S. military action throughout the world, failed U.S public diplomacy (i.e., propaganda) in the Arab world, and what is perceived as growing U.S. arrogance and belligerence is producing more enemies in the Arab world and elsewhere that will no doubt create dangerous blowback effects in the future.

Not only has the Bush administration unilateralist foreign policy exposed the United States to new attacks and enemies, but Bush administration domestic policy has also weakened democracy, civil liberties, and the very concept of a free and open society. Draconian antiterror laws embodied in the so-called "USA Patriot Act" have immeasurably increased government powers of surveillance, arrest, and detention. The erection of military prison camps for suspected terrorists, the abrogation of basic civil liberties and legal rights, and the call for military trials undermines decades of progress in developing a democratic policy, producing among the most regressive U.S. domestic policies in history.

Bush administration economic policy has also done little to strengthen the "new economy," largely giving favors to its major contributors in the oil, energy, and military industries. Bush administration censorship of Websites, email, and wireless communication use of surveillance technologies to monitor domestic commnication, refusal to release government documents, and curtailment of the Information Freedom Act signals the decline of the information society and perhaps of a free and open democratic society. Traditional Bush family secrecy explains part of the extreme assaults on the open flow of information and freedom, but there are also signs that key members of the Bush administration are contemptuous of democracy itself and threaten to drastically cut back democratic rights and freedoms. After the failure to find "weapons of mass destruction" and in need of a new justification for its controversial invasion of Iraq, the Bush administration adopted a new ideology of "democracy on the march" in 2004 and promoted democratization as a foreign policy while undermining democratic institutions and traditions at home.

Consequently, Bush administration policy has arguably exploited the tragedy of September 11 for promoting its own political agenda and interests and threatens to undermine the United States and world economy and American democracy in the process. Still, many corporate and political interests and individual citizens pursue business as usual at the same time that significant conflicts and problems unfold in the economy and politics. There are, however, intelligent and destructive ways to fight global terrorism and such virulent global problems require global and multilateral solutions, demanding alliances of a complex array of countries on the legal, police, economic, and military fronts. In this global context, there are serious dangers that the Bush administration will make the problem of terrorism worse and will immeasurably weaken the United States and the global economy and polity in the process. In the name of containing terrorism, the Bush administration is both championing curtailment of civil liberties and the public sphere domestically and promoting military solutions to terrorism globally. These policies legitimate repressive regimes to suppress human rights and democracy and to themselves use military and police methods to deal with their respective regime's opponents and critics, as was evident in the India–Pakistan dispute, the intensification of the Israeli–Palestinian conflict, and numerous other actions around the world following the Bush administration Afghanistan intervention.[17] And the U.S.–U.K. Iraq intervention also arguably destabilized the Middle East and created more enemies for the West and new waves of terrorist violence. In this situation, it is now becoming increasingly important to seek local/global solutions to local/global problems, to defend democracy and social justice, and to criticize both militarism and terrorism.

For Democracy and Against Terrorism and Militarism

In conclusion, I want to argue that in the light of the Bush administration attacks on democracy and the public sphere in the United States and elsewhere in the name of a war against terrorism, there should be a strong reaffirmation of the basic values and institutions of democracy and a call for local/global solutions to problems that involve both dimensions. As noted, the Bush administration

---

[17] Human Rights Watch has released a report that has documented how a wide spectrum of countries have used the war against terrorism to legitimate intensified repression of its domestic opponents and military action against foreign adversaries. See http://www.hrw. org/press/2002/02/usmil0215.htm. In the past years Amnesty International, Human Rights Watch, and other organizations documented how Bush administration policies of prisoner abuse violated international law. See also Greenwald 2006.

adopted a discourse of democracy as a foreign policy goal to legitimate its failed Iraq invasion but it is an important goal of the present moment to argue for a more robust concept of democracy and democratization.

Progressive social movements should thus struggle against terrorism, militarism, and social injustice and for democracy, peace, environmentalism, human rights, and social justice. Rather than curtailing democracy in the naming of fighting terrorism we need to strengthen democracy in the name of its survival and indeed the survival of the planet against the forces of violence and destruction. Rather than absolve Bush administration domestic and foreign policy from criticism in the name of patriotism and national unity, as the administration's supporters demand, we need more than ever a critical dialogue on how to defeat terrorism and how to strengthen democracy throughout the world.

Democracy is in part a dialogue that requires dissent and debate as well as consensus. Those who believe in democracy should oppose all attempts to curtail democratic rights and liberties and a free and open public sphere. Democracy also involves the cultivation of oppositional public spheres and as in the 1960s on a global scale there should be a resurrection of the local, national, and global movements for social transformation that emerged as a reaction to war and injustice in the earlier era. This is not to call for a return to the 1960s, but for the rebirth of local/global movements for peace and justice that build on the lessons of the past as they engage the realities of the present.

In addition to reaffirming democracy, we should be against terrorism and militarism. This is not to argue for an utopic pacifism, but to argue against militarism in the sense that the military is offered as the privileged solution to the problem of terrorism and in which the military is significantly expanded, as in the Bush administration massive military buildup, and promotion of unilateral military action. Thus, although I would argue that military action against terrorism is legitimate, I would oppose U.S. unilateralist militarism outside the bounds of recognized military conventions and law, and would favor more multilateral action in the context of global law and coalitions.

Yet just as globalization from above and from below can both have positive and destructive dimensions and effects, likewise unilateralism is not per se bad and multilateralism is not itself good. Sometimes it is necessary for nation-states to undertake unilateral action, and often multilateral agreements and coalitions are deployed to exert power of the haves over the have nots, or for stronger states to suppress weaker ones. Yet in the context of current debates over terrorism and global problems such as the environment and arms control, certain multilateral and global solutions have become necessary and the Bush administration unilateralism has clearly shown its flaws and failures.

The debacle in Iraq, for example, discloses the fallacious assumptions upon which the Bush doctrine of preventive war was predicated. For preventive war to work, there must be solid intelligence upon which military action can be taken and the Iraq case revealed deep flaws in U.S. intelligence capabilities and or illicit "cherry picking" of intelligence by the Bush administration to promote their war arms against Iraq (Hersh, 2005). Secondly, launching preventive war requires that

U.S. military power is sufficiently superior to guarantee victory and minimize loses, while being able to secure the peace. The Iraq debacle however shows that U.S. military power does not ensure victory and that military power alone does not guarantee successful resolutions to difficult political problems.[18]

The Iraq case suggests that multilateral solutions are needed for global problems and that as with Bosnia, Kosovo, Haiti, and other recent political crises, global and multilateral alliances and forces were necessary. With Immanuel Wallerstein (2004), I would agree that this should not be taken as an endorsement of "weak multilateralism," defined as a U.S.-dominated system of alliances whereby the United States dictates to allies, controls the UN and global institutions, and imposes its will on the world. Such a form of "weak multilateralism" is top-down and not really multilateral, but conceals control and hegemony of the United States and global corporate domination.

This form of what I would call "neoliberal multilateralism" should be opposed to a strong or genuine multilateralism that is multipolar, involves autonomous partners and alliances, and is radically democratic. Such a democratic and global multilateralism would include NGOs, social movements, and popular institutions, as well as global institutions such as the UN. A democratic and multipolar globalization would be grounded philosophically in Enlightenment cosmopolitanism, democracy, human rights, and ecology, drawing on notions of a cosmos, global citizenship, and participatory democracy.[19]

The need for cosmopolitan multilateralism and globalization shows the limitations of one-sided antiglobalization positions that dismiss globalization out of hand as a form of capitalist or U.S. domination. Taking this position is admitting defeat before you've started, conceding globalization to corporate capitalism and not articulating contradictions, forms of resistance, and possibilities of democracy grounded in globalization itself. Rather, a U.S.-dominated or corporate globalization represents a form of neoliberal globalization which, interestingly, Wallerstein claims is "just about passé" (2004: 18). The argument would be that Bush administration unilateralism has united the world against U.S. policies, so that the United States can no longer push through whatever trade, economic, or military policies that they wish without serious opposition. Wallerstein points to the widely perceived failures of IMF and WTO policies, the collapse of 2003 Cancun and Miami trade meetings that ended with no agreement as strongly united so-called southern countries opposed U.S. trade policy, and, finally, global opposition to the Bush administration Iraq intervention. He also points to the rise of the World Social Forum as a highly influential counterpoint to the Davos

---

[18] This argument is made by Ivo H. Daalder and James M. Lindsay, "Shooting first. The preemptive-war doctrine has met an early death in Iraq" (Los Angeles Times, May 30, 2004: M1 and M6). The authors also argue that "Bush's conception of preemption far exceeded responding to an imminent danger of attack. He instead advocated preventive wars of regime change. The United States claimed the right to use force to oust leaders it disliked long before they could threaten its security."

[19] On cosmopolitanism, see Cheah and Robbins (1998). Cosmopolitics and special issue of Theory, Culture & Society on cosmopolis, Vol. 19, Nrs. 1–2 (February–April 2002).

World Economic Forum, which has stood as an organizing site for a worldwide anti-neoliberal globalization movement.

Cosmopolitan globalization thus overcomes the one-sidedness of a nation-state and national interest dominant politics and recognizes that in a global world the nation is part of a multilateral, multipolar, multicultural, and transnational system. A cosmopolitan globalization driven by issues of multipolar multilateralism, democratization, and globalization from below, would embrace women's, workers', and minority rights, as well as strong ecological perspectives. Such cosmopolitan globalization thus provides a worthy way to confront challenges of the contemporary era ranging from terrorism to global warming.

The Bush administration intervention in Iraq showed the limitations of militarist unilateralism and that in a complex world it is impossible, despite awesome military power, for one country to rule in a multipolar globe. The failures of the Bush administration policy in Iraq suggest that unilateralist militarism is not the way to fight international terrorism, or to deal with issues such as "weapons of mass destruction," but is rather the road to an Orwellian nightmare and era of perpetual war in which democracy and freedom will be in dire peril and the future of the human species will be in question.

Furthermore, we need to reflect on the global economic, social, environmental, and other consequences of promoting militarism and an era of warfare against terrorism. Evoking and fighting an "axis of evil" called for by the Bush administration is highly dangerous, irrational, and potentially apocalyptic. It is not clear that the global economy can survive the constant disruption of warfare. Nor can the environment stand constant bombardment and warfare, when ecological survival is already threatened by unrestrained capitalist development (see Kovel, 2002; Foster, 2003). To carry out continued military intervention, whether against an "axis of evil" or any country that is said to support terrorism by the Bush administration, risks apocalypse of the most frightening kind. Continued large-scale bombing of Iraq, Iran, Syria, or any Arab countries, especially after growing anger following the U.S.–U.K. war against Iraq in 2003, could trigger an upheaval in Pakistan, with conceivable turmoil in Saudi Arabia and other Moslem countries. It could also help produce a dangerous escalation of the Israeli–Palestinian conflict, already at a state of white-hot intensity, whose expansion could engulf the Middle East in chaos and flames.

Thus, although it is reasonable to deem international terrorism a deadly threat on a global scale and to take resolute action against terrorism, what is required is an intelligent multifaceted and multilateral response. This would require a diplomatic consensus that a global campaign against terrorism is necessary which requires the arrest of members of terrorist networks, the regulation of financial institutions that allow funds to flow to terrorists, the implementation of national security measures to protect citizens against terrorism, and the worldwide criminalization of terrorist networks that sets international, national, and local institutions against the terrorist threat. Some of these measures have already begun and the conditions are present to develop an effective and resolute global campaign against terrorism.

There is a danger, however, that excessive unilateral U.S. military action would split a potential coalition of liberal democratic countries against global terrorism, creating uncontrollable chaos that could destroy the global economy and create an era of apocalyptic war and misery such as Orwell (1961 [1948]) evoked in *1984*. We are living in a very dangerous period and must be extremely careful and responsible in appraising responses to the events of September 11 and other terrorist attacks bound to happen. This will require the mobilization of publics on a local, national, and global level to oppose both terrorism and militarism and to seek productive solutions to the social problems that generate terrorism, as well as to terrorism itself.

At this moment of history, the United States is confronted with the question of whether it wants to preserve its democratic Republic or attempt to expand its imperial Empire, a project likely to create new enemies and alienate old allies.[20] Global problems require global solutions and Bush administration unilateralism and its quest for Empire has arguably created new enemies, overextended U.S. military power, and weakened international alliances. These are frightening times and it is essential that all citizens become informed about the fateful conflicts of the present, gain clear understanding of what is at stake, and realize that they must oppose at once international terrorism, Bushian militarism, and an Orwellian police-state in order to preserve democracy and make possible a life worthy of a human being.

References

Ali, T. (2002). *The clash of fundamentalisms: Crusades, jihads, and modernity*. London and New York: Verso.

Albrow, M. (1996). *The global age*. Cambridge, UK: Polity.

Appadurai, A. (1996). *Modernity at large*. Minneapolis: University of Minnesota Press.

Arrighi, G. (1994). *The long twentieth century*. London and New York: Verso.

Axford, B. (1995). *The global system*. Cambridge, UK: Polity.

Barber, B. R. (1995). *Jihad vs. McWorld*. New York: Ballatine.

—— (2003). *Fear's empire*. New York: Norton.

Best, S., & Kellner, D. (2001). *The postmodern adventure*. London and New York: Routledge and Guilford.

Bird, J., et al. (1993). *Mapping the futures: Local cultures, global change*. London and New York: Routledge.

Boggs, C. (2000). *The end of politics*. New York: Guilford.

Brecher, J., Costello, T., & Smith, B. (2000). *Globalization from below*. Boston: South End.

---

[20] On the dangers of perpetual war and threats to the U.S. democratic republic in the expansion of Empire, see Vidal (2002, 2003) and Mann (2003). On the dangers of Bush administration unilateralist militarism and the need for global solutions to global problems, see Kellner (2003), Barber (2003) and Clark (2003). Clark warns that the Bush administration has planned a series of wars against the "axis of evil" to promote U.S. hegemony and to use U.S. military power to further a neoconservative agenda of control of the Middle East.

Burbach, R. (2001). *Globalization and postmodern politics from Zapatistas to high-tech robber barons.* London: Pluto.

Cheah, P., & Robbins, B. (1998). *Cosmopolitics.* Minneapolis: University of Minnesota Press.

Clark, W. (2003). *Winning modern wars: Iraq, terrorism, and the American empire.* Washington: Public Affairs Books.

Cvetkovich, A., & Kellner, D. (1997). *Articulating the global and the local. Globalization and cultural studies.* Boulder, Colorado: Westview.

Daalder, I. H., & Lindsay, M. J. (2004). Shooting first: The preemptive-war doctrine has met an early death in Iraq, *Los Angeles Times.*

Debord, G. (1970). *Society of the spectacle.* Detroit: Black and Red.

Eisenstein, Z. (2004). *Against empire: Feminism, racism, and the West.* New York: Zed.

Featherstone, M. (Ed.). (1990). *Global culture: Nationalism, globalization and modernity.* London: Sage.

Featherstone, M., Lash, S., & Robertson, R. (Eds.) (1995). *Global modernities.* London: Sage.

Feenberg, A. (1995). *Alternative modernity.* Los Angeles: University of California Press.

—— (1999). *Questioning technology.* London and New York: Routledge Press.

Foran, J. (Ed.). (2003). *The future of revolutions: Rethinking radical change in the age of globalization.* London: Zed.

Foster, J. B. (2003). *Ecology against capitalism.* New York: Monthly Review Press.

Friedman, T. (1999). *The lexus and the olive tree.* New York: Farrar, Straus, Giroux.

—— (2005). *The world is flat.* New York: Farrar, Straus, Giroux.

Fukuyama, F. (1993). *The end of history and the last man.* New York: Harper Collins.

Giddens, A. (1990). *Consequences of modernity.* Cambridge and Palo Alto: Polity and Stanford University Press.

Gilroy, P. (1993). *The black Atlantic: Modernity and double consciousness.* Cambridge, MA: Harvard University Press.

Gitlin, Todd. (2006). *The Intellectuals and the flag.* New York: Columbia University Press.

Greenwald, Glenn. (2006). *How would a Patriot Act? Defending American Values from a President Run Amok.* San Francisco: Working Assets Publishing.

Greider, W. (1998). *Fortress America: The American military and the consequences of peace.* New York: Public Affairs.

Hardt, M., & Negri, A. (2000). *Empire.* Cambridge, MA: Harvard University Press.

—— (2004). *Multitude: War and democracy in the age of empire.* New York: Penguin.

Held, D. (1995). *Democracy and the global order.* Cambridge and Palo Alto: Polity and Stanford University Press.

Held, D., McGrew, A., Goldblatt, D., & Perraton, J. (1999). *Global transformations.* Cambridge and Palo Alto: Polity P and Stanford University Press.

Hersh, Seymour. (2005). Chain of command: The to road 9/11 from Abu Graib. New York: Harper Perennial.

Hirst, P., & Thompson, G. (1996). *Globalization in question.* Cambridge, UK: Polity.

Horkheimer, M., & Adorno, T. W. (1972) [1948]. *Dialectic of enlightenment.* New York: Herder and Herder.

Huntington, S. (1996). *The clash of civilizations and the remaking of world order.* New York: Touchstone.

Kellner, D. (1992). *The Persian Gulf TV war.* Boulder, Co: Westview.

—— (1995). *Media culture: Cultural studies, identity, and politics between the modern and post modern.* London and New York: Routledge.

—— (1997). "Intellectuals, the public sphere and new technologies," in *Research in Philosophy and Technology*, Vol. 16. pp. 15–32.

—— (2001). *Grand theft 2000*. Lanham, MD: Rowman & Littlefield.

—— (2002). "Theorizing globalization," *Sociological Theory*, Vol. 20, Nr. 3, pp. 285–305.

—— (2003). *From 9/11 to terror war: Dangers of the Bush legacy*. Lanham, MD: Rowman and Littlefield.

—— (2005). Media spectacle and the crisis of democracy. Boulder, C: Paradigm.

King, A. D. (Ed.). (1991). *Culture, globalization and the world-system: Contemporary conditions for the representation of identity*. Binghamton: SUNY Art.

Kovel, J. (2002). *The enemy of nature: The end of capitalism or the end of the world*. London: Zed.

Laclau, E., & Mouffe, C. (1985). *Hegemony and socialist strategy: Towards a radical democratic politics*. New York and London: Verso.

Lash, S., & Urry, J. (1994). *Economies of signs and space*. London: Sage.

Lechner, F. J., & Boli, J. (2000). *The globalization reader*. Malden, MA and Oxford, UK: Blackwell.

Luke, A., Luke, C (2000). "A situated perspective on cultural globalization," in *Globalization and education,* edited by Nicholas Burbules and Carlos Torres. London and New York: Routledge. pp. 275–297.

Mander, J., & Goldsmith, E. (1996). *The case against the global economy*. San Francisco: Sierra Club Books.

Mann, M. (2003). *Incoherent empire*. London and New York: Verso.

—— (2001). "Globalization and September 11," *New Left Review 12*. pp. 51–72.

McLuhan, M. (1964). *Understanding media*. New York: Signet.

Moody, K. (1988). *An injury to one*. London: Verso.

—— (1997). "Towards an international social-movement unionism," *New Left Review* Vol. 22, Nr. 5, pp. 52–72.

Orwell, G. (1961). *1984*. New York: Signet.

Peters, M. (2005). "War as globalization and globalization as war: the 'education' of the Iraqi people education, the state, and globalization in an age of terror." *In Education, Globalization and the State in the Age of Terrorism*, Micheal Peters, (Eds.) Landam, Md: Rowman and Littlefield.

Rahman, F. (1984). *Islam and modernity*. Chicago: University of Chicago Press.

Rashid, A. (2003). *Jihad: The rise of militant Islam in central Asia*. New Haven, CT: Yale University Press.

Ritzer, G. (1993; revised edition 1996). *The McDonaldization of society*. Thousand Oaks, CA: Pine Forge Press.

Robertson, R. (1991). *Globalization*. London: Sage.

Robins, K., & Webster, F. (1999). *Times of the technoculture*. London and New York: Routledge.

Simons, T. W. (2003). *Islam in a globalizing world*. Palo Alto, California: Stanford University Press.

Sklair, L. (2001). *The transnational capitalist class*. Cambridge, UK: Blackwell Publishers.

Steger, M. (2002). *Globalism. The new market ideology*. Lanham, MD: Rowman and Littlefield.

Stiglitz, J. E. (2002). *Globalization and its discontents*. New York: Norton.

Urry, J. (2002). "The global complexities of September 11th," in *Theory, Culture, and Society*, Vol. 19, Nr. 4.

Vidal, G. (2002). *Perpetual war for perpetual peace: How we got to be so hated.* New York: Thunder Mouth Press/Nation Books.

Vidal, G. (2003). *Dreaming war: Blood for oil and the Cheney–Bush junta.* New York: Thunder Mouth Press/Nation Books.

Virilio, P. (1998). *The Virilio reader*, edited by James Der Derian. Malden, MA and Oxford, UK: Blackwell Publishers.

Wallerstein, I. (2004, February 2nd). "Soft multilateralism." *Nation.*

Waters, M. (1995). *Globalization.* London: Routledge.

Wark, M. (1994). *Virtual geography: Living with global media events.* Bloomington and Indianapolis: Indiana University Press.

Watson, J. L. et al. (1997). *Golden arches East: McDonald's in East Asia.* Palo Alto, California: Stanford University Press.

Part 3
Studying Globalization: Methodological Approaches

12
Finding Frontiers in Historical Research on Globalization

RAYMOND GREW

When historical analysis meets globalization, history gains the excitement of a hot topic and ideas of globalization gain the past often denied them. Although a past is not the dowry everyone wants globalization to have, the meaning of the term is shallow without it. Globalization studies that neglect history find frontiers (ones more useful for journalism than research) wherever they look, circularly defined by whatever established practices appear compelled to change. There are essentially three views of globalization, and all three rest on historical arguments. One sees it as a distinctively modern, indeed recent, phenomenon propelled by the synergy of developments in many aspects of contemporary life. With economics and technology as its most prominent engines, this view of globalization incorporates the expansive reach of political and military power but also even of ideas and culture in a dynamism that reaches around the world. The result is a new global consciousness and networks of global connections that mark our era as different from the past. This interpretation implies a decisive historical change; and unless that case is made, proclamations of newness advertise change but provide no way to measure it. A second view sees globalization as a process that may have its own internal momentum but that has a longer history connected to capitalism, state making, industrialization, and all the ideological and social components of modernity. In that perspective a great deal of historical research on the last several centuries comes into play, and not just passively as a source of relevant information. Such an understanding of globalization compels considerable rethinking of both past and present, aided by postmodern challenges to older conceptual frameworks, deconstructed for their (sometimes) hidden biases: Eurocentric, imperialistic, hierarchic, racial, and gendered. Historical analysis is central. A third approach considers globalization as a particular kind of historical process but one subject to ebb and flow, a rejection of teleology that allows historical examples from even a distant past potential relevance for revealing how this process comes about, creates resistance, and dissolves. It makes a difference, of course, whose history is being written (Wolf, 1982), and none of this means that only historians should address these issues, but it does mean that historical questions, evidence, and methods must play an important part in research on globalization (see Hülsemeyer, 2003; Waters, 2001).

On questions of newness, however, historians do have one homely advantage. Fond of the societies they have intently studied and devoted to uncovering complexity and change within them (even when from a distance those societies appear relatively simple and unchanging), historians are predisposed to distrust facile contrasts between the past and the present, however perceptive. Knowing that seers of other ages regularly declared their own times to be experiencing unprecedented change, historians carry antibodies resistant to fanfare about the transformations occurring today. They may of course be wrong; and in any case skepticism is hardly enough. Historians doing research on globalization will need, in addition to a certain openness of mind and the full panoply of their discipline's investigative tools, a serious engagement with the theories and data of economists, political scientists, sociologists, and anthropologists.

Historical research on globalization must also confront two classic historical (and philosophical) concerns: determinism and agency. The literature on globalization has a strong deterministic tendency, a result in part of the factors adduced in describing globalization: the constraints of environment and biology, responses to market opportunities as predictable expressions of human nature, and state policies necessitated by international competition. A deterministic aura arises as well from the rhetoric of rapid and relentless change useful to those more interested in predicting the future than analyzing the past. Historians, of course, will want to weigh assertions about current globalization against historical parallels, and they will look (from habit as much as methodology) for instances in which human agency made a critical difference. In doing so, they will encounter a troubling asymmetry. For the most part, agency is passed over in explanations of globalization but becomes prominent in descriptions of resistance to it (see Touraine, 1998). Historians will need to look closely on both counts. This is not to predict the outcome of their research. Historians could well conclude that the globalization we are experiencing today is fundamentally new (my guess is that a majority of them will), and many are likely to consider that the larger forces behind globalization have their own momentum and direction. Historical research and debates among historians are nevertheless needed to sharpen the concept of globalization, and they can, by identifying elements of globalization that occurred earlier and in other forms, contribute to a fuller understanding of how the processes of globalization function.

Seeking Global Histories

There are numerous ways in which historical research can seek out the interconnections that make for globalization (Iriye & Mazlish, 2005), and they can be grouped into four broad categories: the common experiences of humankind everywhere, the diffusion of ideas and techniques from one society to another, the building of durable connections, and the impact of cultural encounters. Some examples will suggest the range of fruitful historical investigation within each category. Common experience, the foundation of demography and the object of epidemiology, underlies much global history (and the problematic results of theories based exclusively on large-scale demographic findings also contain a cautionary note global historians should heed). So, increasingly, environmental history, with its attention to the impact of a specific ecology and available (ultimately limited) resources has become important to global and world history (McNeill, 2000; Environment and History, 2003). Historians have long attended to the global implications of the trade, treaties, and empires supported by fortifications, naval coaling stations, and military bases near oil fields that have been established for the purpose of exploiting water, land, coal, and oil. Societies also evolve elaborate customs, regulations, and institutions to maintain renewable resources (fisheries are the classic case) and these have been the subject of an extensive literature and important theoretical work (Ostrom, 1990). The understanding of globalization grows with historical research into the circumstances that lead from these responses to global relationships. Crucial if sometimes less tangible ties also build from global responses to common needs through the spread of religious charity, medical training, philanthropy, NGOs, and others. Insofar as such responses build networks and communication, they participate in globalization (Castells, 2000; Hewa, 2005).

Looked at closely, diffusion is a complex matter; technology, law, social behaviors, music, standards of human rights, fashions, and commodities may all spread differently to then be differently interpreted and incorporated. The diffusion of techniques, ideas, crops, and products, a major element in archaeology, anthropology, and world history, has obvious potential as a source of globalization (Salaman, 1949, is a classic; Kurlansky, 2002 shows the influence of modern global awareness). The effects of diffusion are not uniform, however, and thus study of globalization should include analysis of the habits and lore that accompany the diffusion of crops, language, printing, religion, cotton clothes, or cell phones. There is much more to be learned about the circumstances in which some diffusion leads to more and to further ties, thus paving the way for globalization. The thing diffused changes in the process and that process deserves subtle and sophisticated research. Nor is the process likely to be politically neutral (Adas, 1989); oddly, the importance of the Cold War in the diffusion of institutions and ideas tends to be overlooked (perhaps because globalization is so often associated with American capitalism). If the effects of globalization can be shown to be markedly different in different historical eras, that should weigh heavily both in debates about the periodization of globalization and in decisions about whether it has been a cyclical or a long-term process in the past (Becker, Hartmann, Huth, & Mohle, 2001).[1]

Most of all, descriptions of globalization point to visible connections that facilitate the flow of capital and goods around the world, as corporations (Gabel & Bruner, 2003), banks, and investment firms do. There is a huge literature to be tapped on transnational economic connections in all eras of history, including influential work on periods before Europeans went to the New World (Curtin, 1984; Abu-Lughod, 1989, have been particularly important in revealing earlier global connections). Trade across great distances can be found throughout history, and the argument for the distinctiveness of modern trade must be that the more recent qualitative increase has made a qualitative difference. That modern economic connections reach far beyond formal institutions has been powerfully demonstrated by writings on imperialism, on capitalist world systems, and on dependency in less developed countries (Wallerstein, 1974, 1979, 1980, 1989; Frank, 1967, 1978, 1998). Global ties are also woven by international organizations, religious political movements, and professional associations; and patterns of travel and migration may be as important as any institutional links (Hannerz, 1996). Each has its own history, but we have little analysis of when these various links actually contribute to globalization, although there is a recent and impressive model of human connectedness on a world-historical scale (McNeill & McNeill, 2003). Cities and the migration to them of people, techniques, and ideas are age-old phenomena; yet their enormous significance today cannot be obscured by the fact of earlier examples (Sassen, 2000, 2001). Historical examples can provide evidence of when such connections prove lasting and foster others; they do not in themselves negate claims that contemporary globalization is a new phenomenon. Establishing their historical importance for understanding globalization will require a firmer theoretical sense of globalization itself.

Cultural encounters, an essential element of globalization, have the longest history of all. The results are complex, usually more than borrowing (for culture rarely flows in just one direction) and often creative. There are periods, however, in which cultural encounters are geographically widespread and intensely engaged, involving a wide spectrum of knowledge and behaviors. Potentially, these are periods of globalization, even if the impetus for them comes from military force, religious proselytizing, or economic pressure (Featherstone, 1992; Roland Robertson, 1992; Yudice, 2003). Some caution is warranted, however. When Japanese statesmen adopted top hats or Parisian artists were influenced by Japanese prints, globalization was involved only if these encounters were related to many others and had lasting effects. The definition is circular. Historical research must therefore seek evidence that such encounters were part of a process with wider effects on, for example, Japanese and European institutions, art markets, journalism, and education. Such research needs to attend to more than mere

---

[1] Their proposal of analysis in terms of belief systems, actors, and culture (*Wahnehmungfaktoren, Akteur-faktoren, Kulturfaktoren*) as the three distinctive elements in globalization points to a quite different sort of analysis.

influence. Much of the creativity stimulated by cultural encounters emerges in practices and perceptions that are neither borrowed nor traditional but an integral part of continuing change within all cultures. Central to that is what can be called the Frantz Fanon phenomenon, the native educated in the metropolitan culture, the country boy or girl who becomes a journalist or artist, the Indonesian who writes novels in Dutch, the nationalist or radical outsider who, standing at cultural inter-sections, transforms cultural canons with a defense of the particular in universal terms (Anderson, 1983). Global and local influences intermix in complex ways (recent work in cultural and gender studies in particular deserve a larger place in studies of globalization; see Lacsamana, 2004), and historical research can probe the tensions and compromises that result from the extraordinary adaptability of individuals and societies in their capacity to sustain multiple identities and conflicting value systems (Friedman, 1994, 2003; Warnier, 2003; Iriye & Mazlish, 2005).

In practice, these four categories obviously overlap, and they invite historians to undertake an essentially empirical search for global relationships, reconsidering often familiar material in terms of ties and processes. A next step is then to establish the relevant global context. Can the relationships uncovered be understood as diverse responses to common challenges, forces, needs, or aspirations? Are there global patterns—in institutions, concerns, or policies—that are obscured because usually seen as locally contingent? The recent work of Charles Bright and Michael Geyer illustrates how analysis of the global context can bring new insight (and quite different interpretations) to well-plowed historical fields. Historians have long connected their study of the application of power and the formation of foreign policy to domestic politics and ideologies. Eighty years ago Robert Binkley noted something significant in the simultaneity of Italian and German uni-fication, the American Civil War, and the emancipation of Russian serfs; but there was little to follow up from that insight (Binkley, 1935). When given a global con-text, however, mere parallels become a powerful way of recognizing a more fun-damental interconnectedness that poses new questions about both international and domestic policies (Bright & Geyer, 1987, 1995, 1996, 2002).

These ways of exploring global relationships and establishing a global context currently come together most often when a group of scholars investigates the interaction of global history around a single selected topic. Many of the books on globalization are in fact collections of essays by specialists, who bring previous research to bear on issues of globalization, suggesting research agendas that could occupy scholars for decades. The New Global History group (of which I have been a part) is one example, having sponsored a number of conferences on the intersection of global history around a particular topic (Wang, 1997; Grew, 1999; Medal and Bruner, 2003; Morss, 2005; Childhood and globalization, 2005; Hewa, 2005). Promising beginnings, such efforts demonstrate that matters histo-rians have long investigated are fodder for new work on globalization once the appropriate questions are posed. They point to the possibilities for new research and for global histories that go beyond the recasting of previous work, although more often acknowledging the need for theoretical frameworks and formal hypotheses than meeting it.

On Method, Periodizations, and Scale

This historical research can test and refine particular claims about various aspects of globalization while adding to historical knowledge; but historians must also address globalization as a whole that is greater than the sum of its parts, both because that is the concept's central point and for methodological reasons. Globalization is a clear example of what Aviezer Tucker discusses as "underdetermination" in history (Tucker, 2000: 142–167). On some large, interesting, and important questions, competing theories cannot be resolved because the evidence is insufficient or the theory is too vague. Globalization is not quite a theory in itself, although explanations of it attach to theories of historical change. Its vagueness, however, is salient; and historians face the challenge of engaging theory while wrestling with specificity. Explanations of globalization cluster factors allowed to vary in importance from case to case. Because the utility of globalization as a concept requires that its boundaries remain unclear, theories with different emphases can always adduce different evidence. What Tucker calls adhoc theories can be brought to bear on specific elements of globalization (as in the search for global relationships discussed above). They can clarify discussion, prompt new questions, pose hypotheses, and usefully shape research agendas. They cannot eliminate differing overall views of globalization (consider the implications for more common suppositions of the comment that "ideological and political conflict had, in fact, achieved global scale before economic uniformities," (Bayly, 2004: 7). Such variety may be frustrating, but it effectively reflects the reality of global and indeterminate processes of historical change.

The currently preeminent approaches treat globalization in terms of large historical tendencies, as an outcome of capitalism and the play of market forces (Wallerstein, 1989; Chase-Dunn, 1989) or as a cumulative result of international politics and the escalating play of power (Modelski, 1987; Kennedy, 1987; Bright & Geyer, 1987, 1995, 1996, 2002), and sometimes the two are combined. Somewhat less frequently, technological development (or in Wolf Schäfer's useful term, technoscience) is made the engine of change, ecology its persistent restraint. Less commonly, ever-increasing exchanges of knowledge are cast in that role. Each of scores of works using these diverse approaches is subject to criticism both on theoretical grounds and in terms of specific cases, but collectively they constitute a distinctive approach to understanding historical change, and they challenge received opinions underlying a wide variety of historical interpretations. Even when theoretical assumptions remain suspect, research on globalization can bring new evidence and insight to many historical questions that have long concerned scholars in many disciplines.

Global histories have in common their effort to employ a larger framework that reaches beyond the boundaries (national and topical) of the historiography from which they work. In doing so, they bring to the fore issues fundamental to history as a discipline, including some classic issues of historical methodology. The problem of periodization is the most obvious. A particular obsession of historians, periodization is often treated as a problem of definition, which nearly always leads to a dead end and not just because "It is only possible to define something that has no history. All concepts in which an entire process is semiotically concentrated elude definition; only that which has no history is definable." (The quotation from Nietzsche's *The Geneology of Morals* is cited in Connelly, 2004: 411.) In the case of globalization, periodization is a tautology, a summary restatement of conclusions reached that directly depend on the questions asked, which in turn depend on the problem being addressed. Even within the group involved in the New Global History, preferences on periodization differ (Mazlish & Buultjens, 1993; and http://newglobalhistory.com). Bruce Mazlish, the leader of the group, considers globalization the term for a new historical era that opened in the 1970s (Mazlish, 1998). Concentrating on a changed consciousness about humankind's place in the universe, he finds evidence of fundamental change in the impact of space travel, ecological awareness, instant communication on the Internet, international corporations wealthier than many nations, and much more. Wolf Schäfer, who tracks global history from plate tectonics to the present, follows his emphasis on technoscience in considering the era of globalization to have begun in the late 19th century, essentially with the second industrial revolution and the new technologies that accompanied it (Schäfer, 2003). I prefer what can kindly be called flexibility when it comes to periodization. While accepting that the increasing extent and variety of global relationships is the central characteristic of our times, I see the *terminus ad quo* as jagged (earlier for trade and empire, later for communication and culture) and remain unwilling to embrace a teleology that would predict a *terminus ad quem*. If forced to choose one time as the beginning of the global era, I would pick the aftermath of the French Revolution, while noting an expanded global consciousness emerging with World War II and the new diplomatic, military, institutional, and economic ties established in the years afterward.[2] The point that matters more is that each periodization follows from a particular interpretation of the essence of globalization. A convenient heuristic device, useful in designing research, periodization cannot stand alone.

We can agree nevertheless that recognition of contemporary globalization raises issues that stimulate historical research not only on the modern era but also on previous ones, and with reciprocal benefit. Our contemporary awareness alerts us to new questions about globalizing processes in the past (where they can be seen more clearly and their outcome is known). That research in turn prompts further hypotheses requiring additional investigation about more recent processes. Many historians now see several historical waves of globalization. Roland Robertson sees six stages of globalization since the 15th century; Robbie Robertson finds three waves in the same period; A. G. Hopkins proposes four in all of world history (Robertson, 2003; Gunn, 2003; Hopkins, 2002). The periods most commonly cited are the 16th and 17th centuries (with the spread of

---

[2] Having in mind the Congress of Vienna, Latin American revolutions, the Monroe Doctrine, and the beginning of new colonialism; the industrial revolution, railroads, and expanding world trade; the spread of revolutionary and nationalist ideologies; and Christian missionary movements.

European empires and the Columbian exchange of crops), the industrial revolution, and the present. But many emphasize the importance of globalization in still earlier periods, carried out across the China Sea, Indian Ocean, and Mediterranean, along the silk road, or by the march of the Mongols. These broader chronologies raise issues of lasting effects and of what makes global connections spread or wither away. Processes of globalization may create resistance that checks their progress and even forces a retreat. (Bourdieu, 1998; O'Rourke & Williamson, 1999, suggest that happened between the two world wars.) Debates about periodization open important possibilities for research even though periodization remains underdetermined.

Another methodological issue is one of scale. Historical writing on globalization tends to combine broad claims (about many activities all over the globe) with single, often small, facts, tying large sweeps of time to moments. If the facts are piled high enough, the claim seems convincing. A further rationale is needed, however, for the selection of evidence when the proposition being supported is so grand that the potential evidence is nearly limitless. That rationale lies in a well-formulated historical problem that determines the relevance of particular evidence. The problem addressed, which is likely to arise from previous work, implies hypotheses that in the best of cases directly relate to theory (and on the need for theory, see Koselleck, 2002; Ch. 1 "On the Need for Theory in the Discipline of History"). In fact, writing on globalization contains large components of theory, but historians have a penchant for leaving underlying theories not quite stated. Despite a certain and obvious intellectual limpness, that is not always harmful. Theoretical assumptions as familiar as gravity are not necessarily more enlightening when made explicit. Nevertheless, research on globalization requires more than the constraints of narrative, and historians have much to gain from the other social sciences in giving systematic attention to theoretical underpinnings.

Although not quite a theory but redolent with theoretical implications, globalization is also a representation, a description presented as a developing reality. A way of conceiving changes shaping the modern world, it incorporates a particular view of change (recent, rapid, and spreading) and gives priority to certain of its striking characteristics (global markets and instant communication). Its rhetoric evokes images of irresistible forces and de-emphasizes political choices. Globalization presents itself as the future and universal in much the way that science and medicine do and that Marxists and liberals have sought to do. A silent selectivity thus accompanies much of the writing on globalization, for conceptual frameworks do not announce the things they tend to obscure. Subtler than bias (those who welcome globalization and those who denounce it tend to share the same limited view of what it is), this representation needs to be queried and problematized. One of the contributions of global history can surely be to establish that globalization needs to be conceived not as an external force imposed from outside but rather as a reciprocal process in which local, regional, and national changes interact with global changes, all of them reconstituted in continuing mutation. For that, history is especially useful, because study of similar processes in the past is the most accessible means of accomplishing it. Comparison is therefore important to the historical study of globalization, and its effective use is facilitated by keeping some simple points in mind. The unit of comparison need not be a state or any other political entity but can be an historical process, institution, social practice, or particular circumstance. Mere analogy, useful in starting comparison, is not enough. The historical problem at issue must establish the purpose of the comparison, and the cases compared (however different in other respects) must be shown to be relevant to that purpose. Comparison across time, although as valid as comparison between contemporary societies, is vulnerable to the misplaced reification that comes from assuming that a given category or term means the same thing in different periods and places. Historians avoid this danger more readily than other social scientists by dint of their preference for heavily contextualized case studies rather than abstract categories; and in undertaking comparison, they are aided by the fact that the examples compared need not be equal in the amount or quality of the research on which they rest. (Grew, 2006; for an example of how effective global comparison can be: Wong, 1997).

Concepts of globalization are in their origin and language intricately intertwined with conceptions of modernity, which is a source of philosophical richness and of analytic confusion. Presumptions about alienation, uprootedness, *gemeinschaft* and *gesellschaft*, rationality, capitalism, and freedom infiltrate discussions of globalization (Featherstone, Lash, and Robertson, 1995; Appadurai, 1996). When these historic intrusions are recognized, they can lead to compelling reflections; unrecognized they make a subliminal appeal to the partially hidden biases with which each of us faces the modern world. Because the literature on globalization tends to grant ideas little autonomous importance, it becomes all the easier for scholars to overlook reliance on conventional ideas of modernity (and modernization). Assumptions that globalization means homogenization and secularization are rooted in conceptions of modernity more than evidence. More careful consideration, however, leads to the recognition of multiple modernities and multiple globalizations (Eisenstadt, 2003, especially Chs. 20 and 21) and recognition that fundamentalism (Grew, 1997), universal religions, communism, and fascism can be agents of globalization along with American capitalism. Defining globalization too narrowly as a sharp break with the past or as merely economic gives rise to complications of the sort Reinhart Koselleck warns against in writing of history and "asymmetrical concepts" (Koselleck, 2004: Ch. 10). There is no automatic protection against unrecognized assumptions (far-reaching as they may be), no single method for embracing complexity while achieving analytic clarity; but more historical knowledge and careful comparison can help, by making inherited preconceptions apparent and noting historically important parallels and trends.

Some Potential Contributions from Global History

Historians wanting to place their research in a worldwide context have a considerable historiography on which to build (Manning, 2003, provides a comprehensive introduction to this literature). Although world history is hardly new, much recent work is clearly inspired by current ideas of globalization so that even with its broader scope it adds to the understanding of modern global change (Pomper et al., 1998). Sweeping from cosmology and the origin of human life, "big history" invites the kind of philosophical speculation associated with what was called universal history in the 18th and 19th centuries. Yet in its use of the natural sciences (bringing it close to environmental history), its aspirations to make the study of history more scientific, its emphasis on material history, and its determination to see the world (and even the universe) whole, this kind of history is in itself a product of a very modern global consciousness (Spier, 1996, 2005; Diamond, 1999; Christian, 2004). Christopher Bayly's book on modern history exemplifies how a study of globalization can, with the coherence of a skillful collage, put together current research on different parts of the world and on an impressive range of topics (Bayly, 2004).

There is no sharp demarcation between this sort of world history and global history, which is more explicitly rooted in contemporary attention to globalization, more analytic than narrative in style, and less comprehensive and more thematic in focus (on the developing distinctiveness of global history: Mazlish & Buultjens, 1993; Mazlish in Pomper et al., 1998: 41–52). Because their interest in globalization opens historical questions that reach beyond the history of globalization itself, global historians can pursue specific issues over a wide range of time. Much of that research will necessarily take place within established areas of research. The problems addressed become different, however, when conducted with attention to global frameworks and relationships; and those problems will be related to and cast light on problems critical to the analysis of contemporary globalization, for the historical process of globalization remains an ultimate concern of global history.

These various approaches to investigating the history of one world can be thought of as laying the groundwork for further historical study of globalization. All research creates its own frontiers, recognizable only when there has been some scouting of the terrain beyond. Forays thus far suggest some of the ways in which historical research is likely to engage the larger questions arising from the study of globalization. Theories of globalization will become better grounded in history, moving beyond selective incursions; by starting from cultivated fields, which after all are more productive than those cleared by slash and burn. By incorporating findings from all the social sciences (one hopes more systematically than ever before), historical studies will address many of the topics looming in the farther terrain now visible from where we currently stand. To illustrate that point, I will list just six big questions.

What difference do states make? In many interpretations the essence of globalization is the tendency of economic decision making (by corporate directors, traders, investors, and money managers) to operate beyond national boundaries, reaching around the world quite independently of governments, while deeply affecting society, patterns of consumption, and culture (Gabel & Bruner, 2003). Other scholars, however, note a centuries-long trend toward ever larger political entities, from city states to larger monarchies and to national states, a trend that may continue beyond the state as with the European Union (Kearney, 1992; Bellier & Wilson, 2002) and international bodies that take on roles in governance formerly reserved to states (Iriye, 1997; Kitching, 2001; Hirst & Thompson, 1999; Kroes, 2000; Iriye, 2002; Kühnhardt 2003). Globalization may also foster domestic movements that seek to limit the authority of the state or circumvent it through international ties. One can envision innumerable conferences and entire institutes working on globalization and the state.

What difference in practice does globality make? For most human beings during the last millennium or two, much of the content of their culture and many of the pressures shaping their lives have come from a distance greater than they could see or travel. It is reasonable to ask whether global influences are experienced differently from those that originate with unseen kings, markets far away, or unknown authors. Businesses have operated, empires spread, translated books crossed political boundaries and continents for centuries; and in that light globalization can seem merely a difference of scale. Or rather, perhaps critical decisions in business, law, and policy, in careers and family life are made differently and have different effects in the environment of globalization. The issue calls for a special kind of research.

What difference does global consciousness make? By global consciousness, two conditions seem to be meant: widely shared awareness that human beings are subject to many of the same circumstances and constraints (environmental, economic, and political) by dint of living on one planet; and a widely shared awareness of connectedness (through institutions, trade, disaster, disease, shared or conflicting values) that makes events and conditions on any part of the planet relevant everywhere else. This awareness usually includes a firm belief that historic changes are taking place, that their pace is picking up, and they are experienced by everyone, even if in different ways. If that is so, global awareness should affect behavior, causing political leaders to look farther afield for opportunities, dangers, and alliances; business people to plan beyond their customary scope; culture to function differently, and so forth. Analysis of the impact of global awareness has become a worthy if demanding object of research.

Does the content of communication change with ease, speed, and frequency? All interpretations of globalization, in whatever era it is said to occur, emphasize the importance of communication, and many scholars study the historic impact of the media, from printing to the Internet. The effect of globalization on the content communicated deserves a place on the research agenda. Perhaps Abraham Lincoln reading English classics by candlelight absorbed more of the culture that literature came from, more of its language and way of thinking than someone today with instant access to selected and decontextualized bits of information on any subject. Perhaps those young South Americans who read Auguste Comte imagined a world of reason and progress more powerfully than can someone regularly confronted with confusing glimpses of competing ideologies and of complex realities around the world. Time may permit new information to be swaddled in creative misunderstandings, allowing imported ideas and technology to be culturally filtered, socially integrated, and domesticated. The effects may be quite different when the vehicle carrying knowledge is capacious but coherent (a long book, some sermons, a magazine subscription) rather than arriving in continuing and more random streams of information (Ong, 1988). Ideologies and techniques disseminated rapidly may have less opportunity to shed the cultural baggage of the society that spanned them, and faster and more vivid communication (studies of newspapers, radio, film, television, and the Internet can test this) may disseminate more varied knowledge with more immediate impact. Reception theory and empirical research provide a lot on which to build fuller understanding of the changes that come with global communication.

Is globalization a source of global differences? Opposition to globalization is less studied than globalization itself. Although the one presents itself as a force and the other as a movement, they belong to a single historical process. Thus demonstrations against corporate practices, genetically engineered seeds, and IMF policies are as much a product of globalization as Wal-Mart; and they, too, use the networks commonly considered instruments of globalization. Contrasting responses increase social difference and political tension, and the resulting conflicts have much in common with other conflicts that erupted in peasant revolts, anticolonial uprisings, and nationalist movements (Scott, 1985; Paige, 1975). Something akin to participation in and resistance to globalization underlay the international labor movement and anarchism at the end of the 19th century, the antislavery movement earlier in that century, mercantilism and objections to empire before that. When social movements simultaneously develop global and local dimensions (Nader Sohrabi in Adams et al., 2005: 303–309), resistance strengthens among groups with limited power in one society that find external support by means of global connections (Commandante Marcos and Osama bin Laden are only extreme examples). As different sectors of society receive and respond to globalization differently, rapidly absorbed by some and quickly rejected by others, social divisions widen and take on new meanings. The clamorous attention to ethnic, religious, and regional identities prominent today may also be an element of globalization (King, 1997). Historical perspective joins current experience in inviting a broader view of what globalization is and its effects are (see Hülsemeyer, 2003), suggesting further questions for further research.

Is globalization a single process or the combination of many? Confusion over the meaning of globalization is currently a barrier to cumulative research, but barriers overcome can be transformed into permeable frontiers. The best descriptions see globalization as the intersection of many different spheres of activity, and as fluid and malleable without any single direction or final destiny (Bright & Geyer, 2002: 67–71). The complexity is daunting. A globalizing tendency locally adapted or appropriated, tends to become invisible, as coffee, costumes, or computers, once associated with a single region, come to be treated as if indigenous. That may lead to further globalization, but it may not. In short, the historical process of globalization might be better assessed in terms of multiple globalizations. Scholarly energy spent dispelling misimpressions about globalization could be saved by consistently recognizing from the first that globalizations differ according to when and where common experiences, diffusion, enduring connections, and cultural encounters develop; by postulating that the globalizations fostered by governments, corporations, NGOs, social movements, and cultural contacts may function independently of each other; and by accepting that globalizing trends not only intersect differently with different societies but within them are likely to point in different directions among the religious and the secular, have a different impact on formal institutions and informal society, and hold different meanings for rich and poor, young and old, urban and rural dwellers. To grant each globalization its own history, however (and historians can be expected to welcome the congenial particularity), makes establishing the linkages among multiple globalizations a critical step in analysis of the larger historical process.

A generation of work on the history of the world has revealed the importance of global connections barely visible in earlier accounts; recognized biology and ecology as historical sciences; and posed questions about Western dominance that exposed false premises and now seek to move beyond that issue. Historical research can be expected to temper the implied momentum within this troublesome term, showing that the changes globalization is meant to describe are incomplete, move in many directions, and construct barriers to their own expansion. Historians will remain attentive to concrete evidence (and therefore to the local), challenging many of the assumptions that have won globalization its popularity as a shibboleth; and research on contemporary globalization will raise new questions to be investigated in the past, in a fruitful cycle of sharper questions and more grounded theory. For all the difficulties and disagreements, there is reason to believe that through serious engagement with historical patterns and global processes the social sciences will deepen understanding of the modern world.

References

Abu-Lughod, J. (1989). *Before European hegemony: The world system A.D. 1250–1350.* New York: Oxford University Press.

Adams, J., Clemens, E.S., & Orloff, S. (Eds.) (2005). *Remaking modernity: Politics, history, sociology.* Durham, NC: Duke University Press.

Adas, M. (1989). *Machines as the measure of men: Science, technology, and ideologies of Western dominancez.* Ithaca, NY: University of Cornell Press.

Anderson, B. (1983). *Imagined communities: Reflections on the origin and spread of nationalism.* London: Verso.

Appadurai, A. (1996). *Modernity at large: Cultural dimensions of globalization.* Minneapolis: University of Minnesota Press.

Bayly, C.A. (2004). *The birth of the modern world, 1780–1914: Global connections and comparisons.* New York: Blackwell.

Becker, J., Hartmann, D.M., Huth, S., & Mohle, M. (2001). *Diffusion und globalisierung: migration, klimawandel und aids.* Wiesbaden, Westdeutscher: Verlag.

Bellier, I., & Wilson, T.M. (2002). *An anthology of the European Union: Building, imagining and experiencing the new Europe.* Oxford. Berg.

Binkley, R.C. (1935). *Realism and nationalism, 1852–1971.* New York: Harper & Brothers.

Bourdieu, P. (1998). *La misère du monde.* Paris, Éditions du Seuil.

Bright, C., & Geyer, M. (1987). "For a unified history of the world in the twentieth century," *Radical History Review*, 39, 69–91.

—— (1995). "World history in a global age," *American Historical Review*, 100: 4, 1034–60.

Bright, C., & Geyer, M. (1996). "Global violence and nationalizing wars in Eurasia and America: The politics of war in mid-nineteenth century," *Comparative Studies in Society and History*, 38: 4, 617–57.

—— (2002). "Where in the world is America?" In T. Bender (Ed.), *Rethinking american history in a global age*. Berkeley: University of California Press, 63–99.

Castells, M. (2000). *The rise of the network society*. Oxford, UK: Blackwell.

Chase-Dunn, C. (1989). *Global formation: structures of the world-economy*. Cambridge, UK: University of Cambridge Press.

Childhood and globalization (2005, Summer). Special issue of the *Journal of Social History*, 38: 4.

Christian, D. (2004). *Maps of time: An introduction to big history*. Berkeley: University of California Press.

Connelly, J. (2004). "A study of the idea of progress in Nietzsche, Heidegger, and critical theory, history and theory," *Review of Giuseppe Tassone*, 43: 3, October, 410–32.

Curtin, P.D. (1984). *Cross-cultural trade in world history*. New York & Cambridge, UK: University of Cambridge Press.

Diamond, J. (1999). *Guns, germs, and steel: The fate of human societies*. New York: W.W. Norton.

Eisenstadt, S.N. (2003). *Comparative civilizations and multiple modernities*. Leiden, Brill.

Environment and history. (2003). Theme issue 42 of *History and Theory* 42: 4 (December).

Featherstone, M. (Ed.). (1992). *Global culture: Nationalism, globalization and modernity*. London: Sage.

Featherstone, M., Lash, S., & Robertson, R. (Eds.) (1995). *Global modernities*. London: Sage.

Frank, A.G. (1967). *Capitalism and underdevelopment in Latin America*. New York: Monthly Review Press.

—— (1978). *World-accumulation 1492–1789*. New York: Monthly Review Press.

—— (1998). *Re-orient: Global economy in the Asian age*. Berkeley: University of California Press.

Friedman, J. (1994). *Cultural identity and global process*. London: Sage.

—— (2003). (Ed.) *Globalization, the state and violence*, Walnut Greek, CA: Altamira.

Gabel, M., & Bruner, H. (2003). *Globalinc: An atlas of the multinational corporation*. New York: New.

Grew, R. (Ed.) (1999). *Food in global history*. Boulder, CO: Westview.

Grew, R. (1997). "Seeking the cultural context of fundamentalisms." In M. Marty., & S. R. Appleby (Eds.), *Religion, ethnicity, and self-identity: Nations in transition*. Hanover, NH: University of New England Press, 19–34.

—— (1999). *Food in global history*. Boulder, CO: Westview.

—— (2006). "The case for comparing histories." In A. Yengoyan (Ed.), *Modes of comparison*. Ann Arbor: University of Michigan Press.

Gunn, G.C. (2003). *First globalization: The Eurasian exchange, 1500–1800*. New York: Rowman & Littlefield.

Hannerz, U. (1996). *Transnational connections: Culture, people, places*. London: Routledge.

Hewa, S. (2005). *Globalization, civil society and philanthropy*. New York: Kluwer Academic.

Hopkins, A.G. (Ed.). (2002). *Globalization in world history*. New York: W.W. Norton.

Hirst, P.Q., & Thompson, G. (1999). *Globalization in question: The international economy and the possibilities of governance*, (2nd ed.). Cambridge: Polity Press.

Hülsemeyer, A. (Ed.). (2003). *Globalization in the twenty-first century: Convergence or divergence*. London: Palgrave.

Iriye, A. (1997). *Cultural internationalism and world order*. Baltimore, MD: The Johns Hopkins University Press.

Iriye, A. (2002). *Global community: The role of international Organizations in the Making of the Contemporary World*. Berkeley: University of California Press.

Iriye, A., & Mazlish, B. (Eds.) (2005). *The global history reader*. New York: Routledge.

Kearney, R. (1992). *Visions of Europe: Conversations on the legacy and future of Europe*. Dublin: Wolfhound.

Kennedy, P.M. (1987). *The rise and fall of the great powers: Economic change and military conflict from 1500 to 2000*. New York: Random House.

King, A.D. (Ed.) (1997). *Culture, globalization and the world-system: Contemporary conditions for the representation of identity*. Minneapolis: University of Minnesota Press.

Kitching, G. (2001). *Seeking social justice through globalization: Escaping a nationalist perspective*. College Park: Penn State University Press.

Koselleck, R. (2002). *The practice of conceptual history: Timing history, spacing concepts*, Todd Samuel Presner et al., tr. Stanford, CA: Stanford University Press.

—— (2004). *Futures past: On the semantics of historical time*, Keith Tribe, tr. New York: Columbia University Press.

Kroes, R. (2000). *Them and us: Questions of citizenship in a globalizing world*. Urbana: University of Illinois Press.

Kühnhardt, L. (2003). *Implications of globalization for the raison d'être of European integration*, www.arena.u10.no/events/papers/Kuhnhardt.pdf

Kurlansky, M. (2002). *Salt: A world history*. New York: Penguin Group.

Lacsamana, A.E. (Ed.) (2004). *Woman and globalization*. Amherst, NY: Humanity.

Manning, P. (2003). *Navigating world history*. New York: Palgrave Macmillan.

Mazlish, B. (1998). Comparing global to world history, *The Journal of Interdisciplinary History*, 28: 3, 385–395.

Mazlish, B., & Buultjens, R. (Eds.) (1993). *Conceptualizing global history*. Boulder, CO: Westview Press.

Medal, G., & Bruner, H. (2003). *Global inc: An atlas of the multinational corporation*. New York. New.

Morss, E. (2005). *New global history and the city*. Available through the New Global History website http://www.newglobalhistory.com/publications

McNeill, J.R. (2000). *Something new under the sun: An environmental history of the twentieth-century world*. New York: W.W. Norton.

McNeill, J.R., & McNeill, W.H. (2003). *The human web: A bird's-eye view of world history*. New York: W.W. Norton.

Modelski, G. (1987). *Long cycles in world politics*. Seattle: University of Washington Press.

Ong, W. (1988). *Orality and literacy: The technologizing of the word*. London: Routledge.

Ostrom, E. (1990). *Governing the commons: The evolution of institutions for collective action*. Cambridge, UK: Cambridge University Press.

O'Rourke, K.H., & Williamson, J.G. (1999). *Globalization and history: The evolution of a nineteenth-century Atlantic economy*. Cambridge: M.I.T. Press.

Paige, J.M. (1975). *Agrarian revolution: Social movements and export agriculture in the underdeveloped world*. New York: Free Press.

Pomper, P., Elphick, R.H., & Vann, R.T. (Eds.). (1998). *World history: Ideologies, structures, and identities*. Malden, MA: Blackwell.

Robertson, R. (2003). *The three waves of globalization: A history of a developing global consciousness*. London: Zed.

—— (1992). *Globalization: Social theory and global culture*. London: Sage.

Salaman, R. (1949). *The history and social influence of the potato*. Cambridge, UK: Cambridge University Press.

Sassen, S. (2000). *Global networks, linked cities*. New York: Routledge.

Sassen, S. (2001). *The global city: New York, London, Tokyo*. Princeton, NJ: Princeton University Press.

Schäfer, W. (2003). "The new global history: Toward a narrative for Pangaea two," *Erwägen Wissen Ethik*, 14, 75–131.

Scott, J.C. (1985). *Weapons of the weak: Everyday forms of peasant resistance*. New Haven, CT: Yale University Press.

Spier, F. (1996). *The structure of big history: From the big bang until today*. Amsterdam: Amsterdam University Press.

—— (2005). *On David Christian, maps of time, History and Theory*, 44: 2, May, 253–64.

Touraine, A. (1998). *A return to the actor: Social theory in post-industrial society*. Minneapolis: University of Minnesota Press.

Tucker, A. (2004). *On knowledge of the past: A philosophy of historiography*. Cambridge, UK: University of Cambridge Press.

Wallerstein, I. (1974). *The modern world-system: Capitalist agriculture and the origins of the European world-economy in the sixteenth century*. New York: Academic.

—— (1979). *The capitalist world-economy*. Cambridge, UK: Cambridge University Press.

—— (1980). *The modern world-system, II: mercantilism and the consolidation of the European world economy, 1600–1750*. New York: Academic.

—— (1989). *The modern world-system, III: the second era of great expansion of the capitalist world economy, 1750–1840s*. New York: Academic.

Wang, G. (Ed.). (1997). *Global history and migrations*. Boulder, CO: Westview.

Warnier, J.P. (2003). *La mondialisation de la culture*. Paris: Éditions La Découverte.

Waters, M. (2001). *Globalization*. London: Routledge.

Wolf, E. (1982). *Europe and the peoples without history*. Berkeley: University of California Press.

Wong, R.B. (1997). *China transformed: Historiographical change and the limits of European experience*. Ithaca, NY: Cornell University Press.

Yudice, G. (2003). *The expediency of culture in the global era*. Durham, NC: Duke University Press.

13
Theoretical and Empirical Elements in the Study of Globalization

Saskia Sassen

This chapter develops theoretical and methodological elements for studying and interpreting a variety of dynamics that are part of globalization but are often, perhaps typically, not thought of as such. Critical among these are questions of place and scale because the global is generally conceptualized as overriding or neutralizing place and as operating at a self-evident global scale. I develop these elements through a focus on three particular components: places, scales, and the meaning of the national today. Each of these entails a specific research and theorization practice.

The first section develops the question of place as central to many of the circuits constitutive of economic globalization. This opens up the conceptualization of the global economic system to the possibility that it is partly embedded in specific types of places and hence subject to certain forms of state authority, and secondly, that the global economy is basically constituted through a variety of cross-border circuits rather than constituting a system. The second section develops some of these issues by focusing on an extreme case of this combination of the global and place: microenvironments with global span as might be a financial services firm but also the household of a global environmental activist. This, in turn, opens up our understanding of the local. These microenvironments may actually be oriented to other such microenvironments located far away, thereby destabilizing the notion of context, which is often imbricated with that of the local, and the notion that physical proximity is one of the attributes or markers of the local. These microenvironments can constitute horizontal types of globality, rather than the vertical globalities of supranational institutions. The third section concerns national states and how these are altered by the partial embeddedness of the global in the national described in the first two sections. This opens up our understanding of the global to the possibility that it gets partly constituted through the partial denationalization of what over the last century or more has been constructed as "national" (in the sense of "national state," not "national people") territories and institutional domains.

Place in a Global and Digital Economy

One of the organizing themes in much of my work on globalization is that place is central to the multiple circuits through which economic globalization is constituted. A strategic type of place for these developments, and the one focused on here, is the city (see also a variety of perspectives, e.g., Taylor, 2004; Brenner, 2004; Lloyd, 2005). Including cities in the analysis of economic globalization is not without conceptual consequences. Economic globalization has mostly been conceptualized in terms of the duality national–global where the latter gains at the expense of the former. And it has largely been conceptualized in terms of the internationalization of capital and then only the upper circuits of capital. Introducing cities in an analysis of economic globalization allows us to reconceptualize processes of economic globalization as concrete economic complexes situated in specific places. A focus on cities decomposes the nation-state into a variety of subnational components, some profoundly articulated with the global economy and others not. It also signals the declining significance of the national economy as a unitary category in the global economy. And even if to a large extent this was a unitary category only in political discourse and policy, it has become even less of a fact in the last fifteen years.

Why does it matter to recover place in analyses of the global economy, particularly place as constituted in major cities? Because it allows us to see the multiplicity of economies and work cultures in which the global information economy is embedded. It also allows us to recover the concrete, localized processes through which globalization exists and to argue that much of the multiculturalism in large cities is as much a part of globalization as is international finance. Finally, focusing on cities allows us to specify a geography of strategic places at the global scale, places bound to each other by the dynamics of economic globalization. I refer to this as a new geography of centrality, and one of the questions it engenders is whether this new transnational geography also is the space for the formation of new types of transnational political, social, cultural, and subjective dynamics. Insofar as my economic analysis of the global city recovers the broad array of jobs and work cultures that are part of the global economy though typically not marked as such, it allows me to examine the possibility of these new formations.

The Material Practices of Globalization

I think of the mainstream account of economic globalization as a narrative of eviction (Sassen, 1998: Ch. 1). Key concepts in that account—globalization, information economy, and digitization—all suggest that place no longer matters and that the only type of worker that matters is the highly educated professional. It is an account that privileges the capability for global transmission over the material infrastructure that makes such transmission possible; information outputs over the workers producing those outputs, from specialists to secretaries; and the new transnational corporate culture over the multiplicity of work cultures, including immigrant cultures, within which many of the "other" jobs of the global information economy take place. In brief, the dominant narrative concerns itself with the upper circuits of capital; and particularly with the hypermobility of capital rather than with that which is place-bound.

Massive trends towards the spatial dispersal of economic activities at the metropolitan, national, and global level are indeed all taking place, but they represent only half of what is happening. Alongside the well-documented spatial dispersal of economic activities, new forms of territorial centralization of top-level management and control operations have appeared. National and global markets as well as globally integrated operations require central places where the work of globalization gets done. Furthermore, information industries require a vast physical infrastructure containing strategic nodes with sharp concentrations of a variety of facilities. Finally, even the most advanced information industries have a work process, that is, a complex of workers, machines, and buildings that is more place-bound than the imagery of information outputs suggests.

Centralized control and management over a geographically dispersed array of economic operations does not come about inevitably as part of a "world system." It requires the production of a vast range of highly specialized services, telecommunications infrastructure, and industrial services. These are crucial for the valorization of what are today leading components of capital.

A focus on place and production produces an analysis that adds much unexpected empirical detail to the more typical focus on the power of large corporations over governments and economies, and the focus on the power of the new telecommunications. These forms of power are part of the story, but I argue there is also a story of work and place that is part of globalization. Work and place lead us to focus on the work and on the nonmobile structures necessary for the implementation and maintenance of a global network of factories, service operations and markets (see, for instance, Persky & Wievel, 1994; Peraldi & Perrin, 1996; Allen et al., 1999; Marcuse & Van Kempen, 2000; Sum, 1999). These are all processes only partly encompassed by the activities of transnational corporations and banks and by the new telecommunications.

One of the central concerns in my work has been to look at cities as production sites for the leading service industries of our time, and hence to recover the infrastructure of activities, firms, and jobs that is necessary to run the advanced corporate economy. I focus on the practice of global control: the work of producing and reproducing the organization and management of a global production system and a global marketplace for finance, both under conditions of economic concentration. This allows me to focus on the infrastructure of jobs involved in this production, including low-wage, unskilled manual jobs typically not thought of as being part of advanced globalized sectors.

Global cities are centers for the servicing and financing of international trade, investment, and headquarter operations (Sassen, 2001; Taylor, 2004; Yeung, 1996; Friedmann, 1995). There are today about 40 global cities, with considerable ranking; they are a key set of networked spaces for the global operations of firms and markets (Taylor et al., 2002). That is to say, the multiplicity of specialized activities present in global cities is crucial in the valorization, indeed overvalorization, of leading sectors of capital today. And in this sense they are strategic production sites for today's leading economic sectors. This function is reflected in the ascendance of such activities in the economies of these cities. Elsewhere (Sassen, 2001: Ch. 5) I have posited that what is specific about the shift to a service economy is not merely the much noticed growth in service jobs but, most importantly, the growing service intensity in the organization of the contemporary economy: firms in all industries, from mining to wholesale, buy more accounting, legal, advertising, financial, and economic forecasting services today than they did 20 years ago. Thus we see some of these trends also in cities that function as regional or national rather than global centers. Whether at the global or regional level, cities are adequate and often the best production sites for such specialized services. The rapid growth and disproportionate concentration of such services in cities signal that the latter have re-emerged as significant production sites after losing this role in the period when national mass manufacturing for national consumption was the dominant sector of the economy.

The extremely high densities evident in the downtown districts of cities with service production sites are the spatial expression of this logic. The widely accepted notion that agglomeration has become obsolete when global telecommunication advances should allow for maximum dispersal is only partly correct. It is, I argue, precisely because of the territorial dispersal facilitated by telecommunication advances that agglomeration of centralizing activities has expanded immensely. This is not a mere continuation of old patterns of agglomeration but, one could posit, a new logic for agglomeration. Information technologies are yet another factor contributing to the new logic for agglomeration. These technologies make possible the geographic dispersal and simultaneous integration of many activities. But the distinct conditions under which such facilities are available have promoted centralization of the most advanced users in the most advanced telecommunications centers (Castells, 1996; Graham, 1996; Rutherford, 2004).

A focus on the work behind command functions, on the actual production process in the finance and services complex, and on global marketplaces has the effect of incorporating the material facilities underlying globalization and the whole infrastructure of jobs typically not marked as belonging to the corporate sector of the economy. An economic configuration very different from that suggested by the concept information economy emerges. We recover the material conditions, production sites, and place-boundedness that are also part of globalization and the information economy. And we recover the broad range of types of firms, workers, work cultures, and residential milieux, which are part of globalization processes although never marked, recognized, valorized, or represented as such. In this regard, the new urban economy is highly problematic. This is perhaps particularly evident in global cities and their regional counterparts. It sets in motion a whole series of new dynamics of inequality (Sassen, 2001: Chs. 8, 9). The new growth sectors—specialized services and finance—contain capabilities for profit making vastly superior to those of more traditional economic sectors. The latter are essential to the operation of the urban economy and the daily needs of residents, but their survival is threatened in a situation where finance and specialized services can earn super-profits.

New Geographies of Centrality and of Marginality

The sharp polarization in the profit-making capabilities of different sectors of the economy has always existed. But what we see happening today takes place on another order of magnitude and is engendering massive distortions in the operations of various markets, from housing to labor. We can see this, for example, in the retreat of many real estate developers from the low- and medium-income housing market in the wake of the rapidly expanding housing demand by the new highly paid professionals and the possibility for vast overpricing of this housing supply.

What we are seeing is a dynamic of valorization that has sharply increased the distance between high profit-making sectors of the economy and medium or low profit-making sectors even when the latter are part of leading global industries. This devalorization of growing sectors of the economy has been embedded in a massive demographic transition toward a growing presence of women, African-Americans, and Third World immigrants in the urban workforce (Munger, 2002; Ehrenreich & Hochschild, 2003; Hondagneu-Sotelo, 2003).

We see here an interesting correspondence between great concentrations of corporate power and large concentrations of "others." Large cities are the terrain where multiple globalization processes assume concrete localized forms. A focus on cities allows us to capture, further, not only the upper but also the lower circuits of globalization. These localized forms are, in good part, what globalization is about. We can then think of cities also as one of the sites for the contradictions of the internationalization of capital. If we consider, further, that large cities also concentrate a growing share of disadvantaged populations, minoritized citizens, and migrants, then we can see that cities have become a strategic terrain for a whole series of conflicts and contradictions (Abu-Lughod, 1994; Sassen, 1998; Cordero-Guzman et al., 2001; Drainville, 2004; Dunn, 1994).

The global economy materializes in a worldwide grid of strategic places, uppermost among which are major international business and financial centers. We can think of this global grid as constituting a new economic geography of centrality, one that cuts across national boundaries and across the old North–South divide. It signals the emergence of a parallel political geography, a transnational space for the formation of new claims by global capital.

This new economic geography of centrality partly reproduces existing inequalities but also is the outcome of a dynamic specific to the current forms of economic growth. It assumes many forms and operates in many sectors, from the distribution of telecommunications facilities to the structure of the economy and of employment. It also operates at the level of whole cities. Thus global cities are sites for immense concentrations of economic power and command centers in a global economy, whereas cities that were once major manufacturing centers have suffered inordinate declines.

The most powerful of these new geographies of centrality at the interurban level binds the major international financial and business centers: New York, London, Tokyo, Paris, Frankfurt, Zurich, Amsterdam, Los Angeles, Sydney, and Hong Kong, among others. But this geography now also includes cities such as Sao Paulo, Buenos Aires, Bangkok, Taipei, and Mexico City (e.g. Gugler, 2004; Taylor, 2004). The intensity of transactions among these cities, particularly through the financial markets, transactions in services, and investment has increased sharply, and so have the orders of magnitude involved. At the same time, there has been a sharpening inequality in the concentration of strategic resources and activities between each of these cities and others in the same country.

The pronounced orientation to the world markets evident in such cities raises questions about the articulation with their nation-states, their regions, and the larger economic and social structure in such cities. Cities have typically been deeply embedded in the economies of their region, indeed often reflecting the characteristics of the latter; and mostly they still do. But cities that are strategic sites in the global economy tend, in part, to disconnect from their region. This conflicts with a key proposition in traditional scholarship about urban systems, namely, that these systems promote the territorial integration of regional and national economies. Alongside these new global and regional hierarchies of cities, is a vast territory that we need to specify or respecify theoretically and empirically.

But also inside global cities we see a new geography of centrality and marginality. The downtowns of cities and metropolitan business centers receive massive investments in real estate and telecommunications and low-income city areas are starved for resources. Highly educated workers see their incomes rise to unusually high levels and low- or medium-skilled workers see theirs sink. Financial services produce superprofits and industrial services barely survive. These trends are evident, with different levels of intensity, in a growing number of major cities in the developed world and increasingly in some of the developing countries that have been integrated into the global economic system.

A New Transnational Politics of Place

I have been particularly interested in the possibility of a new politics of traditionally disadvantaged actors operating in this new transnational economic geography. This is a politics that lies at the intersection of economic participation in the global economy and the politics of the disadvantaged; in this regard it would add an economic dimension, specifically through those who hold the other jobs in the global economy, from factory workers in export processing zones to cleaners on Wall Street. (See, e.g., *Indiana Journal of Global Legal Studies* 1996; Ehrenreich and Hochschild 2003).

The centrality of place in a context of global processes engenders a transnational economic and political opening in the formation of new claims and hence in the constitution of entitlements, notably rights to place, and, at the limit, in the constitution of "citizenship." The city has indeed emerged as a site for new claims:

by global capital which uses the city as an "organizational commodity," but also by disadvantaged sectors of the urban population, frequently as internationalized a presence in large cities as capital (Drainville, 2004; King, 1996; Machimura, 1998; Dunn, 1994; Eade, 1996; Low, 1999). This contributes to a denationalizing of urban space and the formation of new claims centered in transnational actors and involving contestation. The question then becomes, "Whose city is it?"

I see this as a type of political opening that contains unifying capacities across national boundaries and sharpening conflicts within such boundaries. Global capital and the new immigrant workforce are two major instances of this combination. Each is a transnationalized actor with unifying properties internally. But each finds itself in contestation with the other in the particular type of site that is the global city. Global cities are the sites for the overvalorization of corporate capital and professional workers, and the sites for devalorization of manufacturing capital and disadvantaged workers. The leading sectors of corporate capital are now global in their organization and operations. On the other hand, many of the disadvantaged workers in global cities are from groups that might not fully identify with the national-minoritized women, immigrants, and people of color generally. Both find in the global city a strategic site for their economic and political operations.

Is there a transnational politics embedded in the centrality of place and in the new geographies of strategic places, particularly the new worldwide grid of global cities? This is a geography that cuts across national borders and the old North–South divide. But also immigration is one major process through which a new transnational political economy is being constituted (Samers, 2002; Cordero-Guzmán et al., 2001; Iyotani et al., 2005; Ehrenreich and Hochschild, 2003), one that is largely embedded in major cities insofar as these contain the mix of resources and sizable groups allowing immigrants to be politicoeconomic actors. Understood this way, immigration is, in my reading, one of the constitutive processes of globalization today, even though not recognized or represented as such in mainstream accounts of the global economy.

I ground my interpretation of the new politics made possible by globalization in a detailed understanding of the economics of globalization, and specifically in the centrality of place in a context where place is seen as neutralized by the available capacity for global communications and control, as discussed in the prior section. My assumption is that it is important to dissect the economics of globalization in order to understand whether a new transnational politics can be centered in the new transnational economic geography. Secondly, I think that dissecting the economics of place in the global economy allows us to recover noncorporate components of economic globalization and to inquire about the possibility of a new type of transnational politics.

Sited Materialities and Global Span

There is a specific kind of materiality underlying the leading economic sectors of our era, notwithstanding the fact that they take place partly in electronic space. Even the most digitized and globalized sector, notably global finance, hits the ground at some point in its operations. And when it does, it does so in vast concentrations of very material structures. These activities inhabit physical spaces, and they inhabit digital spaces. There are material and digital structures to be built, with very specific requirements: the need to incorporate the fact that a firm's activities are simultaneously partly deterritorialized and partly deeply territorialized, that they span the globe, and that they are highly concentrated in very specific places. This produces a strategic geography that cuts across borders and across spaces yet installs itself also in specific cities.

There are three issues about locality and context that are illuminated by this configuration. One is the particular type of subeconomy this is: internally networked, partly digital, mostly oriented to global markets yet to a large extent operating out of multiple but specific sites around the world. The second is a more elusive, and perhaps purely theoretical issue—although I do not think so—which has to do with the point of intersection between the physical and the digital spaces within which a firm or, more generally this subeconomy operates. Here my concern is to understand this point of intersection not as a line that separates two different, mutually exclusive entities, but as a border zone, with its own specific features. The third is the matter of contextuality: in the local, in the sited, and in the contiguous. The particular characteristics of this networked subeconomy (partly deeply centered in particular sites, partly deterritorialized and operating on a global digital span), would seem to unbundle established concepts of context, of the relation to the surroundings (whether social, visual, operational, or rhetorical).

A Networked Subeconomy

To a large extent this sector is constituted through a large number of relatively small, highly specialized firms. Even if some of the financial services firms, especially given recent mergers, can mobilize enormous amounts of capital and control enormous assets, they are small firms in terms of employment and the actual physical space they occupy compared, for example, with the large manufacturing firms. The latter are far more labor intensive, no matter how automated their production process might be, and require vastly larger amounts of physical space. Secondly, specialized service firms need and benefit from proximity to kindred specialized firms, financial services, legal services, accounting, economic forecasting, credit rating and other advisory services, computer specialists, public relations, and several other types of expertise in a broad range of fields. The production of a financial instrument requires a multiplicity of highly specialized inputs from this broad range of firms.

Physical proximity has clearly emerged as an advantage insofar as time is of the essence and the complexity is such that direct transactions are often more efficient and cheaper than telecommunications (it would take enormous bandwidth and you would still not have the full array of acts of communications, the shorthand way in which enormous amounts of information can be exchanged among people in direct presence of each other). But, at the same time, this networked sector has global span and definitely operates partly in digital space, so it is networked also in a deterritorialized way, one not pivoting on physical proximity.[1]

The Intersection Between Actual and Digital Space

There is a new topography of economic activity, sharply evident in this subeconomy. This topography weaves in and out between actual and digital space. There is today no fully virtualized firm or economic sector. Even finance, the most digitalized, dematerialized, and globalized of all activities has a topography that weaves back and forth between actual and digital space. To different extents, in different types of sectors and different types of firms, a firm's tasks now are distributed across these two kinds of spaces; furthermore, the actual configurations are subject to considerable transformation as tasks are computerized or standardized, markets are further globalized, and so on. More generally, telematics and globalization have emerged as fundamental forces reshaping the organization of economic space (Graham, 2004; Rutherford, 2004; Allen et al., 1999). This reshaping ranges from the spatial virtualization of a growing number of economic activities to the reconfiguration of the geography of the built environment for economic activity. Whether in electronic space or in the geography of the built environment, this reshaping involves organizational and structural changes.

One question here is whether the point of intersection between these two kinds of spaces in a firm's or a dynamic's topography of activity is one worth thinking about, theorizing, and exploring. This intersection is unwittingly, perhaps, thought of as a line that divides two mutually exclusive zones. I would propose to open up this line into an "analytic borderland" that demands its own empirical specification and theorization, and contains its own possibilities for shaping practices and organizational forms. The space of the computer screen, which one might posit is one version of the intersection, will not do, or is at most a partial enactment of this intersection.

Admittedly, the question of this intersection is one that I have been somewhat obsessed with, and made only limited advances to its elaboration (Sassen, 2002; Latham & Sassen, 2005: Ch. 1). It is for me one instantiation of a broader condition that I see as pervasive in the social sciences: the dividing line as the unproblematized way of relating/separating two different zones (whatever they might be: conceptual, theoretical, analytic, empirical, of meaning, or of practice). What operations are brought in and what operations are evicted by putting a line there (Sassen, 1998: Ch. 1)? It is quite possible that these are analytic operations linked to the type of work I do and that they have little meaning for other types of inquiry and objects of study. They are certainly not an issue in conventional social science thinking.

---

[1] I examine some of these issues, particularly the future of financial centers given electronic trading and the new strategic alliances between the major financial centers, in Sassen, 2001: Ch. 7; for a full development of the interactions of digital and nondigital conditions see Sassen, 2006: Chs. 7 and 8.

What Does Contextuality Mean in This Setting?

A networked subeconomy that operates partly in actual space and partly in globe-spanning digital space cannot easily be contextualized in terms of its surroundings. Nor can the individual firms. The orientation is simultaneously towards itself and towards the global. The intensity of its internal transactions is such that it overrides all considerations of the broader locality or region within which it exists. On another, larger scale, in my research on global cities I found rather clearly that these cities develop a stronger orientation towards the global markets than to their hinterlands. Thereby they override a key proposition in the urban systems literature, to wit, that cities and urban systems integrate, and articulate national territory. Cities may have had such a function during the period when mass manufacturing and mass consumption were the dominant growth machines in developed economies and thrived on the possibility of a national scale for economic and political organization.

But it is not the case today with the ascendance of digitized and globalized, sectors such as finance. The connections with other zones and sectors in its "context" are of a special sort, one that connects worlds that we think of as radically distinct. For instance, the informal economy in several immigrant communities in New York provides some of the low-wage workers for the "other" jobs on Wall Street, the capital of global finance. The same is happening in Paris, London, Frankfurt, and Zurich. Yet these other zones and other workers are not considered to be part of the context, the locality, of the networked subeconomy I have been speaking of, even if, in my reading, they are. On the other hand, the immediate physical surrounding of the financial business district may be marked by attempts to do the now much in vogue contextual architecture and urban design. Yet from the type of research and analysis I have done, this would be a way of veiling, of hiding, the fact that the immediate physical surrounding is not a context for this networked subeconomy; there is, in fact, little if any direct connection.

What then is the "context," the local, here? The new networked subeconomy occupies a strategic geography, partly deterritorialized, that cuts across borders and connects a variety of points on the globe. It occupies only a fraction of its "local" setting, its boundaries are not those of the city where it is partly located, nor those of the "neighborhood." This subeconomy contains within itself the intensity of the vast concentration of very material resources it needs when it hits the ground and the fact of its global span or cross-border geography. Its interlocutor is not the surrounding, the context, but the fact of the global. Yet it is embedded, at least in one moment of its dynamic, in a set of very specific and material built environments.

I am not sure what this simultaneous embeddedness in physical sites and tearing away of the context (which comes to be replaced by the global) mean theoretically, empirically, and operationally. The strategic operation is not the search for a connection with the "surroundings," the context. It is, rather, installation in a strategic cross-border geography constituted through multiple "locals." In the case of the economy we can see that the old hierarchies of scale, typically shaped by some elementary criterion of size—local, regional, national, international—defined through specific national instantiations no longer hold for particular configurations exemplified by the networked subeconomy I have been discussing. Going to the next scale in terms of size is no longer how integration is achieved. The local now transacts directly with the global; the global installs itself in locals and the global is itself constituted through a multiplicity of locals.[2] In this sense, we see the forming of a geography that explodes the boundaries of contextuality and traditional hierarchies of scale.

Denationalized State Agendas and Privatized Norm-Making

States today confront a new geography of power. The changed condition of the state is often explained in terms of a decrease in regulatory capacities resulting from some of the basic policies associated with economic globalization: deregulation of a broad range of markets, economic sectors, and national borders, and privatization of public sector firms.

But in my reading of the evidence, this new geography of power confronting states entails a far more differentiated process than notions of an overall decline in the significance of the state suggest. We are seeing a repositioning of the state in a broader field of power and a reconfiguring of the work of states (for particular aspects see, e.g., Mittelman, 1996; Tabak and Chrichlow, 2000; Davis, 1999; Olds et al., 1999; Hall and Biersteker, 2002; Calabrese and Burgelman, 1999; Hardt and Negri, 2000). This broader field of power is constituted partly through the formation of a new private institutional order linked to the global economy (e.g., Cutler et al., 1999; Datz, 2007; Dezalay and Garth, 1996; Hall and Biersteker, 2002), and partly through the growing importance of a variety of institutional orders engaged with various aspects of the common good broadly understood, such as the international network of NGOs and the international human rights regime (e.g., Public Culture, 2000; Mittelman, 1996). This new geography of power also entails a more transformative process of the state than the notion of a simple loss of power suggests. The work of states or *raison d'e-tat*—the substantive rationality of the state—has had many incarnations over the centuries. Each of these transformations has had consequences. Today the conditionalities for and the content of specific components of the work of states have changed significantly compared to the immediately preceding period of the post-WWII decades. Some of these changes are typically captured with the image of the current neoliberal or competitive state as compared with the welfare state of the postwar era.

---

[2] I also see this in the political realm, particularly the kind of "global" politics attributed to the Internet. I think of it rather as a multiplicity of localized operations, but with a difference: they are part of the global network that is the Internet. This produces a "knowing" that re-marks the local. See, e.g., Sassen, 2000 and Sack, 2005.

In the larger research project I (2006) develop three arguments. I posit that the marking features of this new, mostly but not exclusively, private institutional order in formation are its capacity to privatize what was heretofore public and to denationalize what were once national authorities and policy agendas. This capacity to privatize and denationalize entails specific transformations of the national state, more precisely of some of its components. Furthermore, I posit that this new institutional order also has normative authority, a new normativity that is not embedded in what has been and to some extent remains the master normativity of modern times: *raison d'etat*. This new normativity comes from the world of private power yet installs itself in the public realm and in so doing contributes to denationalize what had historically been constructed as national state agendas. Finally, I posit that particular institutional components of the national state begin to function as the institutional home for the operation of powerful dynamics constitutive of what we could describe as "global capital" and "global capital markets." Thereby these state institutions contribute to reorient their particular policy work or, more broadly, state agendas towards the requirements of the global economy. This then raises a question about what is "national" in these institutional components of states linked to the implementation and regulation of economic globalization.

Geared towards governing key aspects of the global economy, both the particular transformations inside the state and the new emergent privatized institutional order are partial and incipient but strategic. Both have the capacity to alter possibly crucial conditions for "liberal democracy" and for the organizational architecture of international law, its scope, and its exclusivity. In this sense both have the capacity to alter the scope of state authority and the interstate system, the crucial institutional domains through which the "rule of law" is implemented. We are not seeing the end of states but, rather, that states are not the only or the most important strategic agents in this new institutional order and, secondly, that states, including dominant states, have undergone profound transformations in some of their key institutional components. Both of these trends are likely to add to the democratic deficit and to further strengthen the "legitimacy" of certain types of claims and norms.

One of the roles of the state vis-à-vis economic internationalization has been to negotiate the intersection of national law and the activities of foreign economic actors—whether firms, markets, or supranational organizations—in its territory as well as the activities of national economic actors overseas. This is not a new role, but it is a transformed and expanded one. In the case of the United States, the government has passed legislative measures, executive orders, and court decisions that have enabled foreign firms to operate in the United States. and markets to become international. Are there particular conditions that make execution of this role in the current phase distinctive and unlike what it may have been in earlier phases of the world economy?

Although this is in many ways a question of interpretation, I argue that there is indeed something distinctive about the current period. We have, the existence of an enormously elaborate body of law developed in good measure over the last hundred years that secures the exclusive territorial authority of national states to an extent not seen in earlier centuries, and, on the other hand, the considerable institutionalizing, especially in the 1990s, of the "rights" of non-national firms, the deregulation of cross-border transactions, and the growing influence/power of some of the supranational organizations. If securing these rights, options, and powers entailed an even partial relinquishing of components of state authority as constructed over the last century, then we can posit that this sets up the conditions for a transformation in the role of the state. It also signals a necessary engagement by national states in the process of globalization (e.g. Aman, 1998).

The next question, then, would concern the nature of this engagement and how it will vary for different types of state. Is the role of the state simply one of reducing its authority (e.g., as suggested with terms such as deregulation and privatization, and generally "less government") or does it also require the production of new types of regulations, legislative items, court decisions, in brief, the production of a whole series of new "legalities."

Furthermore, if it is in fact some states (i.e., the United States and the United Kingdom) that are producing the design for these new legalities, that is, particular aspects derived from Anglo-American commercial law and accounting standards, and are hence imposing these on other states given the interdependencies at the heart of the current phase of globalization, then this creates and imposes a set of specific constraints on participating states. Legislative items, executive orders, adherence to new technical standards, and so on, will have to be produced through the particular institutional and political structures of each of these states.

We generally use terms such as deregulation, financial and trade liberalization, and privatization, to describe the changed authority of the state when it comes to the economy. The problem with such terms is that they only capture the withdrawal of the state from regulating its economy. They do not register all the ways in which the state participates in setting up the new frameworks through which globalization is furthered, nor do they capture the associated transformations inside the state, precisely my two concerns.

Let me illustrate.

Central banks are national institutions that address national matters. Yet over the last decade they have become the institutional home within the national state for monetary policies that are necessary to further the development of a global capital market, and indeed, more generally, a global economic system. The new conditionality of the global economic system—the requirements that need to be met for a country to become integrated into the global capital market—contains as one key element the autonomy of central banks. This facilitates the task of instituting a certain kind of monetary policy, for example, one privileging low inflation over job growth even when a president may have preferred it the other way around, particularly at re-election time. Although securing central bank autonomy certainly cleaned up a lot of corruption, it has also been the vehicle for one set of accommodations on the part of national states to the requirements of the global capital market. A parallel analysis can be made of ministries of finance (or the Treasury in the United States) that have had to impose certain kinds of fiscal policies as part of the new conditionalities of economic globalization.

At the level of theorization, it means capturing/conceptualizing a specific set of operations that take place within national institutional settings but are geared to nonnational or transnational agendas where once they were geared to national agendas.

The accommodation of the interests of foreign firms and investors under conditions where most of a country's institutional domains have been constructed as "national" entails a negotiation. The mode of this negotiation in the current phase has tended in a direction that I describe as a denationalizing of several highly specialized national institutional components. My hypothesis here is that some components of national institutions, even though formally national, are not national in the sense in which state practice has constructed the meaning of that term since the emergence of the so-called regulatory state, particularly in the West. Although imperfectly implemented and often excluding national minorities, Keynesian policies aimed at strengthening the "national" economy, "national" consumption capacity, and raising the educational level of "national" workforces, are a good illustration of this meaning of the "national." There are, clearly, enormous variations among countries, both in terms of the extent to which such a national policy project existed and the actual period of time of its implementation.

Crucial to my analysis here is the fact that the emergent, often imposed, consensus in the community of states to further globalization is not merely a political decision: it entails specific types of work by a large number of distinct institutions in each of these countries. In this sense, that consensus partly shapes the actual work of states rather than being just a decision. Furthermore, this work of states has an ironic outcome insofar as it has the effect of destabilizing some aspects of state power. Thus the U.S. government as the hegemonic power of this period has led/forced other states to adopt these obligations towards global capital, and, in so doing, has contributed to strengthen the forces that can challenge or destabilize what have historically been constructed as state powers. In my reading this holds both for the United States and for other countries. One of the ways in which this becomes evident is in the fact that although the state continues to play a crucial, though no longer exclusive, role in the production of legality around new forms of economic activity, at least some of this production of legalities is increasingly feeding the power of a new emerging structure marked by denationalization in some of its components and by privatization in other of its components.

In this case the state can be seen as incorporating the global project of its own shrinking role in regulating economic transactions. The state here can be conceived of as representing a technical administrative capacity that cannot be replicated at this time by any other institutional arrangement; furthermore, this is a capacity backed by military power, with global power in the case of some states. Seen from the perspective of firms operating transnationally, the objective is to ensure the functions traditionally exercised by the state in the national realm of the economy, notably guaranteeing property rights and contracts. How this gets done may involve a range of options. To some extent this work of guaranteeing is becoming privatized, as is signaled for instance by the growth of international commercial arbitration and by key elements of the new privatized institutional order.

There is a set of strategic dynamics and institutional transformations at work here. They may incorporate a small number of state agencies and units within departments, a small number of legislative initiatives and of executive orders, and yet have the power to institute a new normativity at the heart of the state; this is especially so because these strategic sectors are operating in complex interactions with private, transnational, powerful, actors. This is happening to variable degrees in a growing range of states, even as much of the institutional apparatus of states remains basically unchanged. (The inertia of bureaucratic organizations, which creates its own version of path dependence, makes an enormous contribution to continuity.) I conceptualize this transformation as denationalization, more precisely, the incipient and partial denationalization of specific, typically highly specialized, state institutional orders and of state agendas. From the perspective of research I have argued that this entails the need to decode what is "national" (as historically constructed) about these particular specialized institutional orders inside national states, notably certain specific activities and authorities inside central banks and ministries of finance.

The mode in which this participation by the state has evolved has been towards strengthening the power and legitimacy of privatized and denationalized state authorities. The outcome is an emergent new spatiotemporal order that has considerable governance capabilities and structural power. This institutional order contributes to strengthen the advantages of certain types of economic and political actors and to weaken those of others. It is extremely partial rather than universal, but strategic in that it has undue influence over wide areas of the broader institutional world and the world of lived experience, yet is not fully accountable to formal democratic political systems. Although partially embedded in national institutional settings it is distinct from these. Because it is partly installed in national settings, identifying this institutional order requires a decoding of what is still national in what has historically been constructed as the national.

In brief, my argument is that the tension between (a) the necessary, although partial, location of globalization in national territories and institutions, and (b) an elaborate system of law and administration that has constructed the exclusive national territorial authority of sovereign states, has (c) been partly negotiated through (i) processes of institutional denationalization inside the national state and national economy, and (ii) the formation of privatized intermediary institutional arrangements that are only partly encompassed by the interstate system, and are, in fact, evolving into a parallel institutional world for the handling of cross-border operations. In terms of research this means, among other tasks, establishing what are the new territorial and institutional conditionalities of national states.

Conclusion

This chapter focused on a set of instantiations of the global that are actually sited in what are usually represented or thought of as national institutional orders and dynamics. These range from forms of globality centered on localized struggles and actors that are part of cross-border networks, through formations such as global cities, to specific types of state work geared towards accommodating global actors and their interests. Cutting across these diverse processes and domains is a research and theorization agenda. I have developed this agenda by bringing together different strands of a rapidly growing scholarship in several different disciplines, some focused on self-evidently global processes/conditions and others on local or national processes/conditions.

This agenda is driven by at least some of the following major concerns. At the most general level, a first key concern is establishing novel or additional dimensions of the spatialities of the national and the global. Specific structurations of what we have represented as the global are actually located deep inside state institutions and national territories. In turn, what has been represented (and to some extent reified) as the scale of the national contains a simultaneity of power relations, some pertaining to the national and others to the global.

A second major concern is with critical examinations of how we conceptualize the local and the subnational in ways that allow us to detect those instances—although these might be a minority of all instances—that are in fact multiscalar although represented and experienced as "simply local." The multiscalar versions of the local I focused on have the effect of destabilizing the notion of context, often imbricated in that of the local, and the notion that physical proximity is one of the attributes or markers of the local. Furthermore, a critical reconceptualization of the local along these lines entails an at least partial rejection of the notion that local scales are inevitably part of nested hierarchies of scale running from the local to the regional, the national, and the international. Localities or local practices can constitute multiscalar systems, operating across scales and not merely scaling upward because of new communication capabilities.

A third major concern is how to conceptualize the national, particularly the specific interactions between global dynamics and particular components of the national. The crucial conditionality here is the partial embeddedness of the global in the national, of which the global city is perhaps emblematic. My main argument here is that when specific structurations of the global inhabit/constitute what has historically been constructed and institutionalized as national territory, they engender a variety of negotiations. One set of outcomes evident today is what I describe as an incipient, highly specialized, and partial denationalization of specific components of national states. This type of focus allows us to capture the enormous variability across countries in terms of the incorporation/negotiation/resistance of globalization, because these are partly shaped by the specifics, both de facto and de jure, of each country. The understanding of globalization in this case would demand detailed studies of the particular ways in which different countries have handled and institutionalized this negotiation.

In all three instances the question of scaling takes on very specific contents in that these are practices and dynamics that, I argue, pertain to the constituting of the global yet are taking place at what has been historically constructed as the scale of the national or the subnational. One central task this brings up is the need to decode particular aspects of what is still represented or experienced as "national" whereas it may in fact have shifted away from what had historically been considered or constituted as national. This type of analysis also suggests a different—although by no means incompatible—research strategy from that which calls for transnational analyses as a response to methodological nationalism (e.g., Abu-Lughod, 2001; Brenner Beck, 2006). Transnational analysis is a response to the fact that the nation as container category is inadequate given the proliferation of transboundary dynamics and formations. I think of this as a crucial part of our large collective research agenda. But I want to distinguish it from the particular focus of this essay: the fact of multiple and specific structurations of the global inside what has historically been constructed as national. This is yet another type of emphasis in the (shared) critique of methodological nationalism.

There are conceptual and methodological consequences to this particular emphasis. Most importantly, it incorporates the need for detailed study of national and subnational formations and processes and their recoding as instantiations of the global. This means that we can use many of the existing data and technologies for research but need to situate the results in different conceptual architectures from those for which they were originally designed. We have some of these— transnational communities, global cities, postcolonial dynamics—but are they enough? I am not so sure. Furthermore, because the national is highly institutionalized and is marked by sociocultural thickness, structurations of the global inside the national entail a partial, typically highly specialized and specific denationalization of particular components of the national: is the analytic vocabulary of transnationalism, postcoloniality, and hybridity enough or adequate to map denationalized formations and denationalizing dynamics? Again, I am not so sure. There is much work to be done.

References

Abu-Lughod, J. L., (Ed.) (1994). *From urban village to "East Village". The battle for New York's Lower East Side.* Cambridge, MA: Blackwell.
——(Ed) (2001). *Sociology for the 21st century.* Chicago: University of Chicago Press.
Allen, J., Massey, D., & Michael, P. (Eds.) (1999). *Unsettling cities.* London: Routledge.
Aman, A. C., Jr. (1998). "The globalizing state: A future-oriented perspective on the public/ private distinction, federalism, and democracy." *Vanderbilt Journal of Transnational Law* 31 (4): 769–870.
Beck, U. (2006). *Cosmopolitan Vision.* Cambridge: Polity Press.
Brenner, N. (2004). *New state spaces: Urban governance and the rescaling of statehood.* Oxford: Oxford University Press.
Calabrese, A., & Burgelman, J. C. (1999). *Communication, citizenship, and social policy. Rethinking the limits of the welfare state.* Lanham, MD: Rowman & Littlefield.

Castells, M. (1996). *The rise of the network society*. Oxford: Blackwell.

Cordero-Guzmán, H. R., Smith, R. C., & Grosfoguel, R. (Eds.) (2001). *Migration, transnationalism, and race in a changing*. New York, Philadelphia: Temple University Press.

Cutler, C. A., Haufler, V., & Porter, T. (Eds.) (1999). *Private authority in international affairs*. Sarasota Springs, NY: SUNY Press.

Datz, G. (2007). "Global-National Interactions: Toward a Theory of Sovereign Debt Restructuring Outcomes" In *Deciphering the Global: Its Spaces, Scales and Subjects*. Edited by S. Sassen. New York and London: Routledge.

Davis, D. E. (Ed.) (1999). "Chaos and governance." *Political power and social theory*, Vol. 13, Part IV: Scholarly Controversy. Stamford, CT: JAI.

Dezalay, Y., & Bryant, G. (1996). *Dealing in virtue: International commercial arbitration and the construction of a transnational legal order*. Chicago: The University of Chicago Press.

Drainville, A. (2004). *Contesting globalization: Space and place in the world economy*. London: Routledge.

Dunn, S. (Ed.) (1994). *Managing divided cities*. Staffs, UK: Keele University Press.

Eade, J. (Ed.) (1996). *Living the global city: Globalization as a local process*. London: Routledge.

Ehrenreich, B., & Hochschild, A. (Eds.) (2003). *Global woman*. New York: Metropolitan.

Friedmann, J. (1995). "Where we stand: A decade of world city research". In Paul L. Knox and Peter J. Taylor (eds). 1995. *World Cities in a World-System*. Cambridge, UK: Cambridge University Press, pp 21–47.

Graham, S. (1996). *Telecommunications and the city: Electronic spaces, urban places*. London, New York: Routledge.

—— (Ed.) (2004). *The cybercities reader*. London, New York: Routledge.

Gugler, J. (Ed.) (2004). *World cities beyond the west: Globalization, development and inequality*. Cambridge, MA: Cambridge University Press.

Hall, R. B., & Biersteker, T. J. (Eds.) (2002). *Private authority and global governance*. Cambridge, UK: Cambridge University Press.

Hardt, M., & Negri, A. (2000). *Empire*. Cambridge, MA: Harvard University Press.

Hondagneu-Sotelo, Pierrette (Ed.) (2003) *Gender and U.S immigration: Contemporary trends*. Berkeley: University of California Press.

Indiana Journal of Global Legal Studies (1996, Fall). Special issue: *Feminism and globalization: The impact of the global economy on women and feminist theory*. Vol. 4, 1.

Iyotani, T., Sakai, N. and de Bary, B. (Eds.) (2005). *Deconstructing nationality*, Ithaca, NY: Cornell University East Asia Program.

King, A. D. (Ed.) (1996). *Representing the city: Ethnicity, capital and culture in the 21st century*. New York: New York University Press.

Latham, R., & Sassen, S. (Eds.) (2005). *Digital formations: IT and new architectures in the global realm*. Princeton, NJ and Oxford, UK: Princeton University Press.

Lloyd, R. (2005). *Neo Bohemia: art and commerce in the post industrial city*. London and New York: Routledge.

Low, S. M. (1999). "Theorizing the city." In Low et al. (Eds.) *Theorizing the city*. New Brunswick, NJ: Rutgers University Press.

Machimura, T. (1998). "Symbolic use of globalization in urban politics in Tokyo." *International Journal of Urban and Regional Research* 22 (2): 183–194.

Marcuse, P., & Van Kempen, R. (2000). *Globalizing cities: A new spatial order*. Oxford, UK: Blackwell.

Mittelman, J. (1996). *Globalization: critical reflections*. Boulder, Co: Lynne Rienner Publishers.

Munger, F. (Ed.) (2002). *Laboring under the line*. New York: Russell Sage Foundation.

Olds, K., P. Dicken, P.F. Kelly, L. Kong, Y.M. Yeung, & H. Wai-Chung (Eds.) (1999). *Globalization and the Asian Pacific: Contested territories*. London: Routledge.

Peraldi, M., & Perrin, E. (Eds.) (1996). *Reseaux productifs et territoires urbains*. Toulouse: Presses Universitaires du Mirail.

Persky, J., & Wievel, W. (1994). "The growing localness of the global city". *Economic Geography* 70 (2): 129–143.

Public Culture (2000, May). *Special Millenium Issue:* Globalization 12 (2).

Rutherford, J. (2004). *A tale of two global cities: Comparing the territoriality of telecommunications developments in Paris and London*. Aldershot: Ashgate.

Sack, W. (2005). "Discourse architecture and very large-scale conversations." In R. Latham, & S. Sassen (Eds.), *IT and new architectures in the global realm*. Princeton, NJ and Oxford, UK: Princeton University Press.

Samers, M. (2002, June). "Immigration and the global city hypothesis: Towards an alternative research agenda." *International Journal of Urban and Regional Research* 26, 2 (June): 389–402.

Sassen, S (1998). *Globalization and its discontents*. New York: New Press.

—— (2000). "Digital networks and the state: Some governance questions." *Theory, Culture & Society*. Special Section on Globalization and Sovereignty 17 (4): 19–33.

—— (2001). *The Global City: New York, London, Tokyo* (2nd Ed. originally published in 1991). Princeton, NJ: Princeton University Press.

—— (2002). "Towards a sociology of information technology." *Current Sociology* 50 (3), 365–388.

—— (2006). *Territory, authority and rights: From medieval to global assemblages*. Princeton, NJ: Princeton University Press.

Smith, D., Solinger, D., & Topik, S. (Eds.) (1999). *States and sovereignty in the global economy*. London: Routledge.

Sum, N. L. (1999). "Rethinking globalisation: Re-articulating the spatial scale and temporal horizons of trans-border spaces." In Olds et al. (Eds.), *Globalization and the Asian Pacific: Contested territories*. London: Routledge.

Tabak, F., & Chrichlow, M. A. (Eds.) (2000). *Informalization: Process and structure*. Baltimore, MD: The Johns Hopkins Press.

Taylor, P. J. (2000). "World cities and territorial states under conditions of contemporary globalization." *Political Geography* 19 (5): 5–32.

—— (2004). *World city network: A global urban analysis*. New York. Routledge.

——, Walker, D. R. F., & Beaverstock, J. V. (2002). "Firms and their global service networks." In S. Sassen (Ed.), *Global networks, linked cities*. New York: Routledge.

Yeung, Y. M. (1996). "An Asian perspective on the global city." *International Social Science Journal* 147: 25–32.

14
Three Steps Toward a Viable Theory of Globalization

JAMES N. ROSENAU

Notwithstanding the proliferation of inquiries into globalization and a continuing clarification of its various dimensions, synthesizing theories that combine different globalizing dynamics which, in turn, foster varied outcomes remain elusive. Students of international trade and their counterparts who analyze financial flows do proceed from a sound theoretical base, to be sure, but their studies are narrow in scope and limited to the economic dimension. Efforts to develop broad-gauged theory that explains the social, political, and cultural dimensions and how they interact with economic dynamics are conspicuously lacking. It is almost as if globalization defies the theoretical enterprise, being too amorphous and complex to allow for the framing and testing of incisive and empirical hypotheses. How, then, to begin to develop a viable theory of globalization that accounts for its underlying dynamics? How to free ourselves from conventional procedures and thereby possibly break through the barriers that make the task so difficult?

I am far from sure I can negotiate a breakthrough that facilitates surmounting the barriers and allows for a break from the conceptual and methodological jails that inhibit our analytic imaginations, but here I want to outline three possible and related steps that can be taken on the path to viable theory. One may seem outrageous at first glance, but it serves to facilitate movement down the other two.

The first step amounts to reversing the conventional links between theory and method. Ordinarily we employ methodology to affirm or reject theoretical propositions, but can this sequencing be altered, even reversed? Is it possible to employ a method that opens up previously unrecognized theoretical vistas? The section that follows offers at least a partial attempt to develop a positive response to these questions.

A First Step: From Method to Theory

If it is assumed (as I do) that all the dimensions of globalization are sustained by individuals at the microlevel as well as by diverse organizations at the macrolevel, one is faced by the enormous theoretical task of grasping how actors at the two levels shape each other's orientations and behavior. The task is enormous because a preponderance of the inquiries into globalization focuses almost exclusively on macrophenomena. Many of them include individual leaders and officials as central to globalizing processes, but they are included as heads of macroorganizations whereas the role of individuals who are not leaders—those innumerable people who contribute to the collective actions of publics—is ignored, or at least not regarded as theoretically relevant. In effect, therefore, attention to micro– macro interactions has yet to make its way into the globalization literature. Note may be taken of protest marches and counterrallies during times of turmoil and mass unrest, but even these micromanifestations are not built into theoretical formulations in the form of propositions that link them to the macro-actions or reactions of states and other organizations.

In short, it is arguable that there can be no viable theory without a micro–macro component. If it is assumed that people count—that all globalizing actions originate with individuals who may then form aggregate entities that engage in salient behavior—then it clearly follows that an adequate theory of globalization must perforce allow for micro–macro interactions. Put differently, the quick spread of the Internet and the advent of suicide bombers highlight the large degree to which world affairs have undergone transformations that accord ordinary people the capacity to meaningfully affect the course of events.

Of What Is This an Instance?

In order to generate theoretical insights that ensure the inclusion of microphenomena, I have long argued there is a powerful, six-word question that stimulates, even forces, us to proceed theoretically from the microlevel. The question is, of what is this an instance? The key word here is "this", as it refers to anything we observe, whether it be in personal, professional, political, or global life and irrespective of whether it occurs in our immediate environment, is read in print, or is seen on television. The question is powerful because it compels us to climb the ladder of abstraction to find a more encompassing phenomenon of which the observed "this" is an instance. Once we ask the question, in short, we have no choice but to engage in generalization and thus to undertake the first steps toward theory. The steps may be crude and ambiguous, but they nonetheless get us up to the rungs on the ladder where of necessity theory is constructed, if by "theory" we mean explanations of why clusters of phenomena cluster and behave as they do.

Yet, to cling precariously to the higher rungs on the ladder is not enough. There is no automatic connection between asking the of-what-is-this-an-instance question and the generation of micro–macro theoretical propositions. And it is here, in the link between the question and meaningful theoretical formulations, that a methodological procedure may be helpful.

A Journalistic Method

Strange as it may seem coming from a social scientist, the method I have in mind has its roots in journalism. Every newspaper in developed societies begins most of their stories with a paragraph or two descriptive of a microincident—an individual in trouble, a family divided, a community aroused—that is then used as an example of a more general situation, process, or institution. One can readily imagine a hardened newspaper editor saying to new cub reporters, "Be sure and start out your story with an account of particular circumstances that is illustrative of what you want to write about." Put in my terms, the editor is saying, "Make sure you go from the micro to the macro!" Such phrasing suggests methodology as a means of theorizing.

It is not, of course, an elaborate methodology and there is a lot about it that may not be reliable. It offers no means of checking on whether the move from the micro to the macro is accurate or whether the microsituation is typical of the macropattern it is claimed to exemplify. Nevertheless, it is a point of departure, a method that has the great virtue of getting students of globalization to cast their analyses in micro–macro terms before they move on to other concerns.

For analysts who are inclined to take microphenomena for granted and are thus disinclined to employ the method, starting with a journalistic technique will not be easy. One has to build up the habit of relying on the of-what-is-this-an-instance methodology for it to become a meaningful analytic tool. More accurately, one has to assume that individuals are illustrative of more encompassing processes and structures, not an assumption that can readily be developed into a habit by observers who have long assumed that states, international organizations, and other macrocollectivities are the entities that sustain and structure world affairs. On the other hand, it is a habit that quickly becomes engrained once one begins to pose the question and finds how clarifying it can be. For the question has no single answer when asked about any situation, nor any answer that is erroneous. There can be as many answers as one's knowledge and imagination can generate. If one's mind is alive, a microevent or action can be illustrative of a host of diverse macrosituations, thus enabling the analyst to differentiate between fruitful and fruitless theoretical lines of inquiry. Put more strongly, if one cannot come up with any responses to what a microevent is an instance of, then his or her conceptual jail is deeply incarcerating.

A simple example highlights the utility of this journalistic method. Suppose analysts have developed the of-what-is-this-an-instance habit and want to incorporate the cultural dimension into a comprehensive theory of globalization when they come upon the following brief newspaper story.

> After six months of tough negotiations with a group of Taiwanese investors, Barry Lewen, a real-estate broker, thought he was just two days from completing the $14-million sale of a building at 366 Madison Avenue when he was unexpectedly told there was one last detail.
>
> The investors insisted that before anything more was done, a Chinese mystic had to be flown from Taiwan to determine if the building's qi, or life force, was acceptable. "I thought they were joking," said Mr. Lewen. . . .
>
> A few days later, however, he anxiously watched as a practitioner of the ancient Chinese craft of feng shui paced the site for 30 minutes before giving his approval.
>
> "I wasn't sure if he was a witch doctor or what," Mr. Lewen said. "I can tell you there were a lot of sweaty palms."
>
> Long a tradition in the Far East, the millennia-old craft of feng shui (pronounced FUNG-shway) has begun to exert a subtle influence on the hard-edged world of real estate in America. Feng shui, which means "wind" and "water" in Chinese, is a blend of astrology, design and Eastern philosophy aimed at harmonizing the placement of man-made structures in nature.
>
> Driven by the influx of investors from Hong Kong, Singapore, Taiwan and China, the use of feng shui has surfaced in the design and marketing of projects from minimalls in Los Angeles to skyscrapers in Manhattan.[1]

A mind that is alive might view this microaccount as an instance of the macro-preeminence of commercial orientations. Or it might conclude this is an illustration of the complexity of commercial transactions. But such interpretations do not facilitate theorizing about the cultural dimension of globalization. However, if the instance is seen as indicating that cultural flows can move from west to east as well as east to west, globalization theorists can avoid the trap of assuming that globalization consists of the spread of American values and are thus in a better position to integrate the cultural dimension into their theoretical framework.

There is, of course, no magic in this journalistic method. It provides no guidance as to how the insight about cultural flows is best integrated into a theoretical framework. For this purpose a more encompassing micro–macro perspective is needed, one that combines the fruits of the what-is-this-an-instance question with a scheme that identifies the sources of globalization, generates hypotheses

---

[1]Ashley Dunn, "Ancient Chinese Craft Reshaping Building Design and Sales in U.S.," *New York Times*, September 22, 1994, p. 1.

as to how they might operate in a micro–macro context, and designs concepts that are suitable to analysis along these lines. What follows suggests two additional steps in this direction.

A Second Step: Eight Sources of Globalization

I conceive of globalization to consist of all those processes whereby flows expand across national borders: flows of goods, ideas, people, pollution, drugs, crime, disease, technology, and a host of other phenomena that are part and parcel of daily and national life. Given this perspective, the question becomes what are the prime sources that sustain the various flows? Again there is no standard response to this question. Analysts have to develop their own answer depending upon how they understand the dynamics of globalization. I have found it useful to specify eight sources, all of which have been set forth in Table 14.1. The entries in the cells of the 4 × 8 matrix are crude and untested hypotheses designed to illustrate the kinds of outcomes to which the various sources can give rise at the several levels of aggregation. They are intended to be suggestive and anything but definitive. Indeed, presumably a number of hypotheses can be developed for each of the 32 cells.

Is this to imply that the most we can hope for in developing a viable framework for theorizing about globalization is a 32-cell matrix, some cells of which may not be meaningfully linked to others? Not at all. The task is to evolve a scheme that specifies how each of the hypothesized outcomes in one of the rows contributes to the outcomes in the other cells in the row and then, eventually, how the outcomes in all the cells (including hypotheses not included) link to the postulated reactions listed in all the other cells. A formidable task, but one has to start somewhere. No one claims that a viable framework for the analysis of globalization will be parsimonious or simple to develop.

Elsewhere I have spelled out the phenomena encompassed by each of the eight sources of globalization, so that here it is sufficient to illustrate how the micro-foundations of three of the sources might be probed through the method outlined above. Of the sources listed, one, the skill revolution, derives entirely from micro-roots. It refers to a worldwide trend whereby analytically, emotionally, and imaginatively people are increasingly able to connect distant events to proximate circumstances. The reasons for these growing capacities are numerous, and they include some of the other sources listed in Table 14.1 such as the organizational explosion, the mobility upheaval, and authority crises. The operation of expanded skills can be initially probed by employing the journalistic method in such a way as to trace the ways in which specific individuals perceive and participate in collective actions (the third cell of the second row in Table 14.1).

The organizational explosion highlights a worldwide trend whereby new formal and informal organizations are being formed at every level of community and in every part of the world. The journalistic method can be used to trace this process by following how particular individuals are recruited to bring a specific

TABLE 14.1. Some Possible Sources of Fragmegration at Four Levels of Aggregation

Levels of Aggregation® / Sources of Fragmegration Δ	Micro	Macro	Macro–Macro	Micro–Macro
Skill Revolution	Expands peoples' horizons on a global scale; sensitizes them to the relevance of distant events; facilitates a reversion to local concerns	Enlarges the capacity of government agencies to think "out of the box," seize opportunities, and analyze challenges	Multiplies quantity and enhances quality of links among states; solidifies their alliances and enmities	Constrains policy making through increased capacity of individuals to know when, where, and how to engage in collective action
Authority Crises	Redirects loyalties; encourages individuals to replace traditional criteria of legitimacy with performance criteria	Weakens ability of both governments and other organizations to frame and implement policies	Enlarges the competence of some IGOs and NGOs; encourage diplomatic wariness in negotiations	Facilitates the capacity of publics to press and/or paralyze their governments, the WTO, and other organizations
Bifurcation of Global Structures	Adds to role conflicts, divides loyalties, and foments tensions among individuals; orients people toward local spheres of authority	Facilitates formation of new spheres of authority and consolidation of existing spheres in the multicentric world	Generates institutional arrangements for cooperation on major global issues such as trade, human rights, the environment, etc.	Empowers transnational advocacy groups and special interests to pursue influence through diverse channels
Organizational Explosion	Facilitates multiple identities, subgroupism, and affiliation with transnational networks	Increases capacity of opposition groups to form and press for altered policies; divides publics from their elites	Renders the global stage ever more transnational and dense with nongovernmental actors	Contributes to the pluralism and dispersion of authority; heightens the probability of authority crises
Mobility Upheaval	Stimulates imaginations and provides more extensive contacts with foreign cultures; heightens salience of the outsider	Enlarges the size and relevance of subcultures, diasporas, and ethnic conflicts as people seek new opportunities abroad	Heightens need for international cooperation to control the flow of drugs, money, immigrants, and terrorists	Increases movement across borders that lessens capacity of governments to control national boundaries

TABLE 14.1. (Continued)

Levels of Aggregation® Sources of Fragmegration Δ	Micro	Macro	Macro–Macro	Micro–Macro
Microelectronic Technologies	Enables like-minded people to be in touch with each other anywhere in the world	Empowers governments to mobilize support; renders their secrets vulnerable to spying	Accelerates diplomatic processes; facilitates electronic surveillance and intelligence work	Constrains governments by enabling opposition groups to mobilize more effectively
Weakening of Territoriality, States, and Sovereignty	Undermines national loyalties and increases distrust of governments and other institutions	Adds to the porosity of national boundaries and the difficulty of framing national policies	Increases need for interstate cooperation on global issues; lessens control over cascading events	Lessens confidence in governments; renders nationwide consensus difficult to achieve and maintain
Globalization of National Economies	Swells ranks of consumers; promotes uniform tastes; heightens concerns for jobs	Complicates tasks of state governments vis-à-vis markets; promotes business alliances	Intensifies trade and investment conflicts; generates incentives for building global financial institutions	Increases efforts to protect local cultures and industries; facilitates vigor of protest movements

organization into being which then mobilizes them to engage in protests against a specific community policy that, along with the protests of other like-minded organizations, undermines the viability of the community (any of the cells in the third row of Table 14.1) and amounts to an authority crisis for that community (any of the cells in the seventh row).

A Third Step: Focus on Relational Rather Than Possessional Phenomena

Still another step toward a viable theory of globalization is implicit in the possibility that micro–macro interactions can give rise to authority crises. Formulated in this way, the theory must allow for a focus on the links between those who exercise authority in the pursuit of goals and those toward whom the authority is exercised. At the core of a viable theory, therefore, are relational phenomena. But it is all too easy to let such a focus slip away in favor of a concern for the relative power at work in any situation. Theory that locates power at the center of the analysis is destined to be insufficient, even misleading. Why? Because power cannot be used as a verb. More than that, as far as I know, power cannot be used as a verb in any language. Actors can control others. They can influence each other. But they cannot power each other. Consequently, tempting as it may be to engage in power analysis, grammar drives us to treat power as a possession, as an attribute or commodity that people, organizations, states, or any collectivity have. This poses an insurmountable problem: power does not predict outcomes, and it is outcomes that interest us, provoke our curiosity, and clarify our understanding. To be sure, the power possessed by the actors in a situation contributes to its outcome, to whether resolution, stalemate, or postponement flows from their interactions. This is especially evident in situations where one actor possesses much greater power than the other has. As indicated by the outcome of the U.S. war in Vietnam, however, even a huge imbalance in the power possessed by adversaries may not foretell the outcome of a situation. Only if both possessional and relational factors are included in a theory of globalization are propositions derived from it susceptible to being upheld.

An appreciation of the distinction between possessional and relational phenomena is thus central to theorizing about globalization or, for that matter, any dynamic political–social process in which outcomes are the overriding concern. How, then, to resist the misleading lures of power analysis? One part of the answer has already been noted. It consists of recognizing that the power concept is driven by grammar to an exclusive focus on possessions and leads analysts either to ignore outcomes or to presume that evidence of them is embedded in possessional balances. Secondly, power analysis can be avoided by abandoning the concept of power and replacing it with two concepts, "capabilities" for the possessional factors and "control" for the relational factors. Such a conceptual adjustment ensures that the outcome of situations will be addressed and analyzed. It will enable observers to probe what possessions the parties to a situation bring to it and how the conduct of each party is founded not only on their relative possessions but also on the perceptions of the motives underlying each others' efforts to control the outcome of the situation.

Conclusion

In sum, to develop viable theories of globalization is to face a formidable challenge. Some might argue that a better strategy is to eschew a comprehensive theory that encompasses all the key dimensions of the subject and to settle instead for framing a theory for some of the prime dimensions. Such a strategy assumes that a theoretical linking of all the key dimensions is either not possible or too taxing. Such may be the case, but that can only be determined if an effort is first made to construct an overarching theory. The foregoing may demonstrate for some analysts that it is absurd to undertake such an effort. A conclusion along this line strikes me as premature. Or at least I am inclined to believe that a broad, all-encompassing theory is doable if one or, better, a team is dedicated to investing the time, energy, and creativity to pull it off.

15
Situating Global Social Relations

Martin Albrow

Ethnography and Globalization

Of all the long-established social science methodologies at first glance it is ethnography that faces the starkest challenge from all those processes summed up under the term "globalization". However defined, as the "intensification of world-wide social relations" (Giddens, 1990: 64), or "the compression of the world and the intensification of consciousness of the world as a whole" (Robertson, 1992: 8), or "the closer integration of the countries and peoples of the world" (Stiglitz, 2002: 9; reflecting far-reaching theoretical differences) globalization appears to be beyond the scope of ethnography's traditional concern to document the observable, even to confine its reports to the personal experience of the trained researcher of unmediated social processes.

As any ethnographer knows, it is difficult enough to identify, describe, and account for people's behavior in terms of kinship or neighborhoods. How on earth can we do this in terms of the globe? The requirement to exclude any evidence except that which is directly observed by the researcher makes social research austere and arduous, even when space and timeframes confine it to a household

Based on a paper originally presented at a conference, The Ethnography of Global Processes: Methodologies for Studying Local, National and Trans-National Linkages, May 12th, 2000, Center for International Studies, University of Chicago. I am grateful to the paper discussant, Axel Paul, for an extensive comment and for leading me to elaborate my argument on the centrality of social relations.

317

over a few weeks, let alone a nation over years. The globe over a century appears to break every scientific canon of observability.

Yet academic researchers contrive to write of globalization, and treat it as a social process, or better a set of contradictory processes, for which there is empirical evidence in the way people behave. Indeed, they do ethnographic research, even narrowly conceived, on globalization and thereby deepen our understanding of both methods and theory. Moreover, when they do, they engage with some of the key intellectual developments of our time.

There are also parallel developments in sociological theory that may broadly be called postmodern, and are particularly associated with an emphasis on actors' narratives, that are helpful in understanding globalization as lived experience. The shift in theoretical emphasis from class to identity, with its stress on the dependence of identity on recognition, has foregrounded social relations. We may take Craig Calhoun's volume *Social Theory and the Politics of Identity* (1994) as representative of this new genre and in it the paper by Margaret Somers and Gloria D. Gibson as a forceful and lucid expression of the viewpoint that by lodging identity in the narratives of relations we avoid essentialism and introduce space and time (Somers & Gibson, 1994: 69).

For the moment, the important point to make is that social relations are on our research agenda. The problem is that they have returned without owing too much to either of the main earlier traditions of thinking about social relations, the Marxist and the interactionist.[1] Marx uses social relations not only for face-to-face relations but also for relations at the workplace, the social relations of production, and also for the capital–labor relation: at his most provocative, "Capital, *also*, is a social relation of production" (Marx, 1977 [1849]: 212). The interactionists for their part entrenched the processes of the construction of social relations in the classic foundations of sociology in Chicago. Those two classic lines of sociological thought have never tied together properly which is partly why both have languished in recent years. The new politics of identity has effectively provided the new thematics that can bind them together.

So my first concern is with the way ethnography can and does successfully meet the challenge of globalization. In my view each heightens our understanding of the other; changes in the world on the one hand, and a research method. However, those are not the only outcomes. My second concern is for the theoretical payoff from the encounter. The self-denying modesty of ethnography as a method has always been matched, even warranted, by its fertility in promoting theoretical developments. In the case of the ethnography of globalization I propose that there is enough evidence already to suggest revisions and extensions to

---

[1] Although there are two other papers in the Calhoun volume, Norbert Wiley's (1994) "The Politics of Identity in American History" that usefully links the contemporary semiotic theory of identity with the pragmatist tradition and Mennell's (1994) "The Formation of We-Images: a Process Theory" that brings together an interactionist approach and Elias' (1978) figurational sociology. Elias' work represents an independent affirmation of social relations as central to sociology.

the theory of social relations that once assimilated can provide added impetus to further research.

In particular we can advance beyond one of the least critically developed central assertions of modern sociology, that social relations are of two general kinds, primary and secondary.

An ethnographic study of globalization will encourage us to consolidate global social relations in our basic vocabulary for the analysis of human society and to add, at the very least, tertiary to this old typology of social relations.

It also suggests new concepts that can grasp the immediacies of local social experience under globalized conditions. "Socioscape" and "sociosphere" may be better adapted to render the contemporary quality of social relations in a locality than community or even network. So my purpose here is not to redefine the scope of ethnography, but to affirm it not just as an appropriate method for researching globalization but also as a heuristic for the theory of global social relations.

Extracting Social Relations

Clifford Geertz's (1973a) "thick description" paper provides a classic statement of the relation of theory to ethnography. For a sociologist its value lies in the wonderfully adept course it steers between theory and observation and the emphasis it places on the necessity of taking "made in the academy concepts" such as "integration," "rationalization," "ideology," or "identity," and working them into the description of the meanings acts have for actors (Geertz, 1973a: 28). Following him we might likewise treat "social relations" as "made in the academy."

Yet, this opposition between academic theory and conceptual structures in our subjects' discourse is relative. These are poles at either end of a continuum and in the middle there are all kinds of mixes. Since Schutz (1972 [1932]), no one can think of everyday life as entirely untheoretical, or, indeed, not continually informed by encounters with science, even social science concepts. Think of the conceptual career of "charisma" in the 20th century from theology, through Weber (1968 [1921]), to sociology and political science, to journalism and finishing up variously as toilet article, racehorse, or sailing boat, to name just a few "Charismas" I've encountered.

There is a long history of academic commentary attached to "social relations." Famously Marx made social relations the key to avoiding the twin dangers of the abstract individualism of the political economists and the reification of society: "Society does not consist of individuals, but expresses the sum of the interrelations, the relations within which these individuals stand" (Marx, 1973 [1857–1858]: 265). He thus avoided imputing a fixed and bounded quality to society, through equating it with a country or an organized group, although he was quite happy to talk of countries as societies when it was appropriate.

We then need to be careful about the idea of reification. In older usage it equates reality with objects having fixed boundaries. Marx was quite clear that social relations were real; bounded entities such as countries were not, however, their only manifestation. The ultimate boundary was the world itself, the aggregate of all relations. In other words, keep the ideas of concreteness and fixity apart. As Appadurai (1996) persuades us: flows are real too. Social relations belong then to academic discourse, but that doesn't necessarily make them abstract or absent from everyday understandings. Indeed it is in order to emphasize their reality that the Marxist and later theorists have made them central in their accounts of society.

Geertz too follows this, in according social relations relative autonomy from culture. At the same time his formulations equivocate in a way that is symptomatic of another tendency of thought. Let us quote from one of his earlier essays on Java: "Culture is the fabric of meaning in terms of which human beings interpret their experience and guide their action; social structure is the form that action takes, the actually existing network of social relations. Culture and social structure are then but different abstractions from the same phenomena" (Geertz, 1973b: 145).

To paraphrase, culture is the meaning; structure is form of action. Yet we also find that structure, though form, actually *exists* as a network of social relations, and then that existence is only an *abstraction*.

I'm not scorning Geertz's conceptual maneuvers here. We none of us can avoid them when we have to accord primacy to description or analysis. In this case the phenomenon he abstracts from is the "concrete system of social action" that Parsons (1937) made famous, which for him includes the "hard surfaces of life – with the political, economic, stratificatory realities within which men are every-where contained"(Geertz, 1973a: 30). He is seeking, quite rightly, to get away from isomorphic functionalism, to which Parsons and others were prone, where culture and social structure are concentric and covary, to a frame of thought where they move independently of each other. As constraint, he even accords social structure more reality, at least in its effects, than culture.

But, in his terms, they are both abstractions: so how is one more real? Do we have to accept this? Well, in fact since the "cultural turn," few would allow culture to be less real than social relations. Communication, signs, language, media all exercise their constraints on what people can do, including, importantly, what social relations they can maintain. There are others who would even accord them more reality than social relations.

Part of our problem here is linguistic, in the use of the term "abstract". "Extract" would be better. If you "extract" culture and social relations from the "concrete system", rather than "abstract" them, you don't turn them into "abstractions". If we want to remain in "realspeak", then culture and structure are "elements" or "components", not "abstractions".

These days we have to view culture and social relations as elements of a greater unspecified nonessentialized, whole ("the world", "reality", "our time"), each moving relatively autonomously from state or ethnic boundaries. Not only culture and society, but political and economic spheres float relatively freely from them, and one from the other. This is part of the more general delinkages by which we can characterize our time, the origins of which I seek to explore in *The Global Age* (Albrow, 1996/1997).

It is in this new thoughtworld that I want to reassert the relative autonomy of social relations rather than of culture, (that now has advocates in plenty already) and to argue that globalization alerts us to dimensions of social relations concealed in the discourse of an old modern sociology, committed as it was to a certain view of community and social development. What concerns me here is to ensure that social relations have their rightful place in our accounts of globalization, not in order to revive Radcliffe-Brown's (1952) functionalism, nor even to celebrate Geertz's hard surfaces, but as dynamic elements in a changing world which ethnographers are well equipped to interpret and diagnose.

Inscribing the Globe

The political rationale of avoiding essentialism in a world of ethnic and religious conflict is quite as compelling as was the need to deconstruct state conflict in terms of class in Marx's time. The invitation to contextualize social relations in terms of time and space and material conditions effectively rejects the inevitability of conflict between irreconcilable and fixed worldviews, or a "clash of civilizations" (Huntington, 1996). Rather it treats each as constructed by the other in their ongoing exchanges and encounters.

Even as narratives, social relations are constructed realities, and as such they cannot be constructed simply as a matter of the narrators' own imaginations. They have to obey material and logical constraints. It is in the focus on narrative and on the constraints on and choices open to the narrator, whether researcher or the subjects of research, that the new ethnography has done most to open up the issues of time and space. It makes it possible for globalization to be an ethnographic research field.

To illustrate that ethnography is prepared for this I will take a study that appears to operate within even more limited confines than the traditional subject of the village community and does not breathe a word about globalization. John Law's *Organizing Modernity* (1994) begins as an ethnography of a scientific laboratory, weaves in with it a commentary on social theory, exposes the influence of politics, and confesses the personal experience of research, stories that for Law are inextricably connected. The personal and political then infuse the experience of time, space, and social relations, such that the boundaries of the laboratory are permeable and imprecise. Certainly it is physical space, or rather a network of different places, but these are full of different worlds, where the researcher has to get used to the fact of only being in one at a time, and never where the "real" action is.

But these constraints on the researchers are equally the constraints on the actors, and their work is the struggle each in their own way engages in to sustain an ordering that is not necessarily on the site of the laboratory at all. Just as Law interweaves into his ethnography social theory drawn from other times and places, so his laboratory workers bring their own conceptual baggage to the stories they tell. Inscribed in the materials and practices of the laboratory many worlds co-exist. If that is the case, why not globalization too?

As Geertz (1973a: 22) said, we don't study villages, we study in them. Law (1994: 40) acknowledged he was at a loss to say what a laboratory is, whether people, a set of plans, scientific results, or whatever else, but he declared he studied in it, and he focused on management. In a village too we can research anything from music-making to masculinity, from production to prejudice, from kinship to the globe. The globe? Well, yes, for if the stories in the village are as much sourced by what happens outside the village as what happens in, and if even in the village we are never where the action is, then the globe may as well feature as any other entity might in the ordering of daily events, and thus join the company of nations, peoples, and countries.

Both theory and ethnography have joined in an emphatic rejection of essentialism and of the privileging of one kind of account of social life that reifies the boundaries the state from time to time decrees. Stories of the globe belong as much within a village as they do within the boardroom. The nation has no prescriptive right to occupy a local space any more than a firm or a religion. The parallelism between this development in academic discourse and the rise of globalization in public discourse may of course suggest some intimate connection between the two. But that cannot be the premise of ethnographic work on globalization, rather it can be the topic for investigation. It would of course be an ironic outcome of those enquiries if they were to find that an intellectual movement that gives a hearing to and sympathetic understanding for minority voices of all kinds and posits diversity as an a priori of society has been impelled by a broader social transformation to which so many social scientists are opposed. It is exactly an ethnography of globalization that offers a way of exploring this Marxian contradiction or Weberian paradox of consequences and I won't prejudge that at this stage.

My colleagues and I at Roehampton in the mid-1990s undertook a series of explorations of globalization in the spirit of the new theory and ethnography. We worked and lived in Wandsworth in London, not a village, not even Gans' (1962) urban village, but more a network of urban villages. Much is contained in Eade's (1997) edited volume *Living the Global City: Globalization as Local Process*. We found the global inscribed in everyday life in London's docklands, in Carnival, in a working-class housing estate, in international phone calls. We didn't have to look hard, but we did have to speak differently and ask different questions. As Eade (1997: 127) says, we were challenging the rhetorical conventions that assume social practices are shaped by specific territories, in particular by the nation-state.

Of course, there were many different senses in which the globe was inscribed in practices. In the case of Docklands we explored aspects of the global city in Saskia Sassen's (1991) sense. In the beleaguered working-class estate we detected the global political economy at work with a crucial addition, a meaningful orientation to the globe as the focus of political consciousness (O'Byrne, 1997). With Carnival, we experienced the time–space compression of a universal diasporization, the localization of the global (Alleyne-Dettmers, 1997). As for international calls, the global equated with the deterritorialization that long distance communication achieves, but where failure to access technology is a new social exclusion (Fennell, 1997).

There were then multiple senses of globalization in that research. What bound them together was not some common core notion of the global, but an opposition to the national or the local as the territorial frame of meaning in which social practices are confined. For my purpose here of showing how globalization might lead us also to revise older conceptions of social relations we can take another paper in that collection, namely Laura Buffoni's "Rethinking Poverty in Globalized Conditions" (1997). She interviewed homeless and deprived persons who exhibited a direct awareness of their personal poverty relative to poverty in the rest of the world. These are the words of the seller of a street magazine, whose eligibility to sell it depended on being homeless:

> If we can get the homeless from other sites of the world to gather with the homeless of this country, then, maybe, those children together will have a better way of learn-ing about each other than I have had in learning about others. (Buffoni, 1997: 120)

Buffoni draws the conclusion that poverty as a global phenomenon means we have to rethink poverty locally. Basically this challenges all those attempts to measure poverty relative to national indices. Although you might say Buffoni's argument is "made in the academy," her respondent, Joseph, is emphatically thinking globally, orienting to unknown distant partners in poverty. He has a global social identity as a homeless person. Here, however, we should refer back to my earlier point about the continuum between the everyday and the academic: Buffoni finds that Joseph's words are redolent of the "think globally, act locally" slogan, itself a byproduct of counter-hegemonic intellectualism.

What's new? Is this not simply the incipient kind of consciousness of common fate across boundaries on which Marx founded his vain internationalist hopes of revolution? Yes it is, but it was also his association of internationalism with com-munism and misplaced political hopes built upon it that inhibited a deeper appre-ciation of the theoretical significance of transnational relations in social science. The wider social transformation of industrial production and class relations to which he responded prompted nationalism and led eventually to two World Wars. Minor collateral damage, but my main concern here, was the retreat of sociology into a fortress communitarianism that dominated through to the mid-1970s and has persisted in some forms to this day. We can find the seeds of this in the clas-sic period of sociology at the beginning of the 20th century, not just in the well-known form of Durkheim's sociology, in the German lament for *Gemeinschaft*, but also in the Chicago School's theory of social relations.

Tertiary Social Relations

Returning to the roots, let us take a classic textbook from the early years of the professionalization of sociology, Park and Burgess' *Introduction to the Science of Sociology* (1921) where we will find the distinction between primary and secondary social contacts, drawing on Charles Cooley's (1909) original emphasis on the vital importance for the individual of the primary group. The primary/secondary distinction survives through to widely used texts today such as John Macionis' *Sociology* (1997: 174–176), still citing Cooley, although it is my impression that these days we may have the first generation of students for whom it is no longer accepted doctrine, not so much because sociology textbooks have become more advanced, for Park and Burgess were more intellectually demanding than their current equivalents, but because theoretical groundings to introductory courses are no longer required pedagogy.

Park and Burgess aimed to build up an account of society on the basis of elementary, universal building blocks and this scientific strategy posited social contacts as the simplest form of interaction upon which primary and secondary groups were based. It facilitated the recognition of worldwide society in "the intricate and complex maze of relations created by competition and co-operation of individuals and societies within the limits of a worldwide economy" (Ibid: 281). In this way the breakfast coffee drinker was linked with the Java planter, the "pale-faced drug addict" with "dark skinned Hindu laborers." Similar images today underpin the work of every aid charity. In this way we have relations with people we don't know and who don't know us. Relations with intermediate links, are still relations.

They sum up these expanding spheres of social contacts in this way: first is one of "intimacy of sensory responses;" second there is a sphere of extended communication through media; and then there is a third involving worldwide interdependence. Now consider this in relation to Buffoni's Joseph. He knows through his own lived experience the homeless identity. He is actually as a newspaper seller involved in the sphere of extended communication. He is aware also of the worldwide existence of others like him. He relates to anyone who is homeless anywhere in the world. Buffoni calls this "global (class?) consciousness," and certainly it is the basis for the mobilization Marx expected from those who shared a position in the global economy. Joseph lived all three categories of Park and Burgess' social contacts simultaneously.

One might expect the third category of social contact, where they expressed their internationalism, to figure further in Park and Burgess' account of social relations. Theirs was not a cloistered national view of their discipline, and their account of worldwide contacts fits well with recent accounts of the period through which they lived, at least up to 1914, as an earlier age of globalization (Hirst & Thompson, 1996).

How, we might then ask, do we a few pages after this introduction to social contacts find their scope narrowed to primary and secondary? "Primary contacts are those of 'intimate face to face association'; secondary contacts are those of externality and greater distance" (Park & Burgess, 1921: 284), and the authors go on to cite the personal virtues Cooley lauded in his primary group as largely projections of family life, with the neighborhood and village as their natural area.

As is well known Park elaborated on the nature of secondary relationships in his account of city life, where people know each other only in one or two aspects of their lives, individuals become anonymous, and relationships become unstable. In this he was reflecting European thought on *Gemeinschaft* versus *Gesellschaft*, (as Nisbet [1966: 79] said of Cooley's distinction) and the third category, the worldwide, more strongly represented at the time in American social thought, had no place in this dichotomous account. But the emphasis on spatial ties was decisive in attenuating the scope of the Park and Burgess account, for they explicitly elaborate on these distinctions "in spatial terms" (Ibid: 282) and it is precisely to contrast village and city that they hold Cooley's primary group theory to be useful. The urban/rural territorial frame set the limit for sociological analysis and a silence descended on social relations of a world, or even national kind. A thousand pages of textbook fail to mention national elites or upper classes, where relations are both intimate and often widely dispersed geographically.

Park and Burgess' chapter on social contacts was theoretically rich, but, and perhaps consequently, replete with unresolved issues. Sensitized by globalization, we can be much more alert to the time and space assumptions built into their theory of primary and secondary relations. Primary for them means both prior in time and near; secondary means later and more distant. Primary is intimate and frequent presence, secondary is impersonal and normal absence. Primary is also emotional and secondary rational, and following this, sociology came to think of organizations as secondary groups in contrast to families or communities which are primary. But then the problem arises of friendship groups in organizations, dealt with in human relations theory as "informal" relations as opposed to "formal," a distinction long found to be wanting. Organization theory now acknowledges that the social relations of production can be face to face but mediated by technology, impersonal and emotional at one and the same time, irredeemably hybrid in primary/secondary terms (Albrow, 1997).

Park and Burgess were not unaware of these difficulties. They gave considerable space and attention to Simmel's (1908) essay on the stranger, who emphasized the hybridity of relations with the person from a strange place: the near is far and the far is near (Park & Burgess, 1921: 286). They also divided primary contacts into those of greater intimacy, family and friends, and those of lesser intimacy, acquaintances. But the key conjunction for them remained that between propinquity and emotional closeness and sociology has tended to stay with that idea to this day with the result that it still does not adequately render the fact that most of our time is spent with people to whom we are not emotionally close, and that our nearest and dearest are normally absent. And I am not talking just about our contemporary condition but about the human condition.

Perhaps the main exception to this is the condition of young children, though again probably most of them spend most of the time outside the presence of their parents. However insofar as mother/child care is the paradigm case for primary relations in our discipline we could say, with some exaggeration, that sociology has for generations existed in a state of infantilism, of arrested development. Absence is the *normal* condition of a human relationship, and without it we would not talk of relationships at all. Co-presence is only ever intermittent. Relationships only exist across time and space: the rest is the physics and chemistry of bodies. Michel de Montaigne (1991: 1103) four hundred years ago, proclaimed that "Loving affection, as I know, has arms long enough to stretch from one end of the world to another and meet" and he applauded the way absence strengthened the affections. What new communication technology does is to extend to new extremes the distances over which intimacy can be initiated and maintained.

As soon as we free ourselves from the temporal and spatial assumptions of the classic scheme we can bring our theory of social relations into closer conformity to experience. Let us consider Joseph and his homeless person anywhere in the world, with whom he identifies, can feel common cause, and for whom he may make sacrifices. In this case the hybridity of Simmel's stranger, the person of unknown identity in our presence, has a counterpart, namely the unknown person of known identity who is far away. Shared identity of this kind, real, imputed, or imagined, is not a marginal case, it is part of the fabric of everyday life.

We may, but don't have to, extend our frame of reference to the globe to begin to catalogue the identities known to us, to which we stand in a specific relation: sometimes singular, like the local mayor, the President, the movie star, sometimes categorical, other men, academics, Americans, refugees. With some we identify, as Joseph with other homeless, with some we are bonded by reciprocal ties (employers–employees), with others still our relations are mediated and indirect. To the extent that we call them global reflects either the degree of global consciousness or the extent of global markets. The interconnection between consciousness and dependency in global capital was a direct concern for Marx, for the identities of capitalist and worker were shaped by the worldwide realities of productive forces and markets.

The capital/labor relation is one where property and propertylessness can shape the relations two or more people may enter into anywhere in the world. What happens to the textile worker in Bangladesh is determined by the total relations of capital and labor worldwide, described by Marx as aggregate or social capital. Moreover this can be minutely documented, in text and deed, in the daily figures in the *Wall Street Journal* and prices in the shopping malls, even in Geertz's criterion for ethnographic description, microscopically.

At any one moment of time, the market will register the value of his output and of the capital employed in it in relation to labor and capital worldwide. This extraordinary human creation results in our being able to experience our relation with that worker, whom we do not know, through the shirt on our backs. It is this that often expresses itself in movements against globalization. The ethnography of the events in Seattle has to be a global ethnography. In a nontrivial sense nothing happened in Seattle; Seattle was a global event.

Identity relations are highly differentiated, very specific and activated on a daily basis. Our social competence is manifested in them as we accomplish innumerable interactions with an unspecified number of their representatives. This is no mass, or anonymous urban crowd. These relations are specific, in terms of politics, economics, or culture, and any description of wider society, beyond intimate groups and organizations, will largely focus on them. Parsons (1951) and his followers later tried to do justice to this complexity with role theory, but they went too far in specifying boundaries and expectations, bringing society within a communitarian frame.

The point of my account is to recover understanding of the worldwide potentiality of identity relations, and to suggest how globalization sensitizes us to them. Like class consciousness the relations of the homeless to each other are as much potential as actual. They would recognize their shared identity if they met. In this respect we can see class relations as a special case of identity relations, as indeed are stratification relations generally. Their potentiality for mobilization, enhanced by new forms of communication, is precisely why the politics of identity has replaced the politics of class.

The Ethnography of Society

What does this mean for ethnographic research? Let us first consider the spatial implications. Identity can be a clear marker of position in the village, town, region, or country, but equally in the globe. But affirmations of identity need have no specific territorial reference at all: "Anywhere on earth" is an old way of expressing this. What is to be American or Chinese or Kurdish is renegotiated continually through encounters in a global frame. And although they may have to resist local cultural definitions of gender and ethnicity, men and women, blacks and whites, can negotiate identities anywhere in the world that offer potential for common understandings, personal development and the basis of collective action.

What I have described as global or tertiary social relations depend on no particular idea of the globe, mainly because, as my account of the Roehampton work suggests, the globe enters in as a marker for a new rhetoric in a new time. The reference to the globe effectively denationalizes the modern frame, centered as it has been on the nation-state, and fulfills the need to find a positive replacement for the methodological nationalism that, as Martins (1974) argued, characterized most of mid-20th century sociology. Instead we have a global frame of cultural, economic, and political spheres, with countries, peoples, and movements, as the main agents enmeshed in a worldwide web of social relations.

For the ethnographer, the porosity of place means that not only community and national frames infuse the locality but also the global frame is instantiated repeatedly in everyday interactions. Thus the global reach of science is implicit in the daily work of Law's laboratory even if that is not the focus of his investigation. In this sense the very label tertiary is misleading, the spatial ordering implicit in the primary/secondary distinction itself reflecting a misconstruction of the spatiality of social relations. The primary, secondary, and tertiary are inscribed in daily relations in any place, and equally each has a potential global stretch. Our closest family may be thousands of miles away. There is no necessary time order for these relations either, in personal or historical experience. Whether the trained professional or the mother touches the infant first is a matter of record. We can't prioritize the species, tribe, or kinship group.

Taken to its full conclusion this is an argument for dropping the numerical ordering, primary, secondary, tertiary, with its implicit priorities, altogether. We retain it here only for maintaining the reference point in the older theory. But effectively we are considering a new conceptual scheme for social relations where there are three different orders, of intimacy, of instrumentality, and of identity. In each of these the intensity of feeling, frequency of contact, and degree of spatial separation can vary independently of each other and of the other orders.

When social theory allows for the everyday understanding that love can survive absences of years and distances of thousands of miles it will be better able to stipulate the conditions for the good society. Proximity relations with other people in a local space do not have to be forced into the dichotomy: either close/good or distant/bad. Anomie is not the only alternative to community. The prejudice in favor of this view is even older than the primary/secondary distinction. Here we can recall how Goffman (1971) led the way with his concepts of relations in public and civil inattention in demonstrating that trust in public spaces and institutions is not based on the growth of intimacy, but on a much wider framework of expectations in which tertiary relations will play a major part. He emphasized that the social arrangements he was analyzing could not be neatly attributed to a bounded social entity.

It would take us too far here to engage directly with the social capital approach to community, much celebrated after Putnam's (2000) work, but the implications of my account are that it is not only Marx scholars who should be interested in the global sense and scope of social capital. Ironically the development of social capital theory in recent years has sprung from ultra-individualistic origins in rational choice theory that has been impelled by its own logic to recognize the facticity of social relations: "social capital inheres in the structure of relations between persons and among persons"(Coleman, 1990: 302). Whether that facticity means they are real is perhaps best answered by observing their effects, on individuals, on the environment, and on culture. What is clear for our purposes is that there is no intrinsic necessity to link social capital, or the structure of social relations with community.

We cannot either allow the ethnography of local space to be dominated by the concept of community. Local spaces are inhabited by long-term residents, recent immigrants, workers, visitors, and strangers. They occupy them in co-presence, unequally, but in dynamic relations. Their local relations with each other are close or distant, but are mediated by their global relations. We need then a term to register the occupancy of a local space that does not prejudge the degree of social integration of the occupants, and certainly does not impute the necessary existence of community.

The proposal I have made elsewhere (Albrow, 1997a) is to use the term socioscape for the lived social relations of the occupants at any one time of a limited territorial space, be it street, ballpark, mall, suburb, or wider area. Only minimally does this include some of the census population of residents (at any moment many will be elsewhere). The socioscape comprises mainly the lived experience of the social relations of people in a locality, not just with others in their proximity (with whom they may equally have no contact) but also with those beyond, for the quality of social interaction of the moment is a function of all those other relations in which the actors are implicated. Place identities: Brooklyn, Soho, the Hamptons, owe as much to workers, visitors, and so on, and as much to the relations that residents and others have with the wider world as to the ties of residents with each other. Even when we do consider residency under globalized conditions a recent study by Savage et al. (2005) in the north of England suggests we have to understand attachment to place in terms of "elective belonging" rather than community, and the place itself becomes a source of chosen identity.

The wider relations of the occupants of the socioscape may conveniently be called sociospheres, again with no implicit wider organization or integration into a particular society.[2] Those are facts to be established through research and not to be taken for granted. Dürrschmidt (2000: 142) made effective use of the idea of sociospheres in his study of everyday life in London, proposing that it was the local intersection of sociospheres that formed the socioscape, "suggesting co-existence and overlap . . . but not necessarily their intermingling and fusion." Along with environmental realities, the socioscape generates the social atmosphere that qualifies these places as desirable or otherwise. It is a concept of the social adapted specifically to the professional skills of the ethnographer.

Socioscapes are located in but not determined by a particular territory. Sociospheres have no necessary specific location, but require space and material conditions for their activation. Both concepts contribute to the deconstruction of the communitarian, national, and territorial assumptions that older nation-state sociologies smuggled into the idea of society. They fit very well also with Dürrschmidt's (1997, 2000) notion of the extended milieu. Detached from localities, milieux such as the airport hotel, the gas station, Starbucks, are places that are familiar to the traveler, could be anywhere, and are vital to the journey.

In sum we have arrived at a more sophisticated account of the linkages between territory, material conditions, and social relations by basing it in the ethnographic study of globalization, and in so doing have recognized the relative autonomy of social relations from either. The weak point is that ethnography can study globalization effectively. The strong point is that it is through ethnographic research, for which globalization has been the catalyst, that we can advance theory to account for the emergent features of contemporary society, and indeed our understanding of society as such. This is a different conclusion from that John Urry (2000) has drawn in his account of mobilities where the erosion of the nation-state society tends to be equated with the obsolescence of the society concept.

It has become an almost standard postmodern challenge to conventional sociology to discard the concept of society because of its association with the

---

[2] "Socioscape" and "sociosphere" have evidently already proved useful to examiners as I can infer from the anxious email enquiry of a group of Maastricht students who complained to me that my 1997 paper and its concepts would come up in a forthcoming examination and their tutors gave them differing interpretations. I confirmed there was legitimate scope for further development and that there would be different nuances depending on observer's or participants' point of view. I was encouraged to receive the reply that the terms were now part of their everyday vocabulary: "Shall we cook together tonight"? "Good idea, I'll tell the socioscape". Thanks to Anne, Ben, Eloise and Astrid. Probably "sociosphere" lodged in my subconscious on reading and forgetting Toffler (1981: 42–46) where he writes of "socio-spheres" in contrast to "techno-" and "info-spheres".

statist project of modernity, even to regard society as a modern construct. This was a problem for Somers and Gibson (1994). It is not only the essentialism of identity they seek to leave behind. They want to escape society too. "Relational setting" is their preferred term, but they prefer it for reasons that to my mind are rhetorically incorrect. I hesitate to say "politically incorrect," because that is now incorrect, but I would say that if it hadn't changed its meaning to "fashionably censorious." It is both scientifically and politically important to retain the concept of society and we can do so if we provide a strong base in the theory of social relations.

The fluidity and negotiability of social relations should not be confused with fictitiousness, and the idea of society should not be equated with the self-definition of the nation-state. The relative decline of the nation-state should only encourage us to recognize the reality that it suppressed, namely that human society is worldwide and the only boundaries in social relations are the ones we make ourselves. In this respect the rhetoric of the global marks the real epochal divide from the modern period.

Discarding society removes a crucial base for counterfactual and critical explorations of injustice, exploitation and "man's inhumanity to man." For it is not through abstract notions of equality and freedom that we identify injustice, but in our explorations of real relations between people, of their dependence on each other, and their relative and absolute experiences of deprivation. Their engagement in and enjoyment of culture, economic well-being, and political freedom are conducted in and through ongoing social relations for which no better term than society has been invented.

References

Albrow, M. (1996, 1997a). *The Global Age: State and Society beyond Modernity.* Cambridge: Polity Press and Stanford: Stanford University Press.
—— (1997). *Do Organizations Have Feelings?* London and New York: Routledge.
—— (1997). Travelling beyond local cultures: Socioscapes in a global city. In J. Eade (Ed.), *Living the Global City* (pp. 37–55).
Alleyne-Dettmers, P. (1997). Tribal arts: A case study of global compression in the Notting Hill Carnival. In J. Eade (Ed.), *Living the Global City* (pp. 163–180).
Appadurai, A. (1996). *Modernity at Large: Cultural Dimensions of Globalization.* Minneapolis: University of Minnesota Press.
Buffoni, L. (1997). Rethinking poverty in globalized conditions. In J. Eade (Ed.), *Living the Global City* (pp. 110–126).
Calhoun, C. (Ed.) (1994). *Social Theory and the Politics of Identity.* Oxford: Blackwell.
Coleman, J. S. (1990). *Foundations of Social Theory.* Cambridge: Belknap.
Cooley, C. H. (1909). *Social Organization.* New York: Schocken.
Dürrschmidt, J. (1997). The delinking of locale and milieu: On the situatedness of extended milieux in a global environment. In J. Eade (Ed.), *Living the Global City* (pp. 56–72).
—— (2000). *Everyday Lives in the Global City.* London and New York: Routledge.
Eade, J. (Ed.) (1997). *Living the Global City: Globalization as Local Process.* London: Routledge.

—— (1997). Reconstructing places: Changing images of locality in Docklands and Spitalfieds. In J. Eade (Ed.), *Living the Global City* (pp. 127–145).

Elias, N. (1978). *What Is Sociology?* London: Hutchinson.

Fennell, G. (1997). Local lives–distant ties: Researching community under globalized conditions. In J. Eade (Ed.), *Living the Global City* (pp. 90–109).

Gans, H. (1962). *The Urban Villagers. Group and Class in the Life of Italian Americans.* New York: Free Press.

Geertz, C. (1973a). Thick description: Toward an interpretive theory of culture. In C. Geertz (Ed.), *The Interpretation of Cultures* (pp. 3–30). New York: Basic Books.

—— (1973b). Ritual and change: A Javanese example. In C. Geertz (Ed.), *The Interpretation of Cultures* (pp.143–169). New York: Basic Books.

Giddens, A. (1990). *The Consequences of Modernity.* Cambridge, UK: Polity.

Goffman, E. (1971). *Relations in Public: Microstudies of the Public Order.* New York: Basic Books.

Hirst, P., and Thompson, G. (1996). *Globalization in Question.* Cambridge, UK: Polity.

Huntington, S. P. (1996). *The Clash of Civilizations and the Remaking of World Order.* New York: Simon & Schuster.

Law, J. (1994). *Organizing Modernity.* Oxford, UK and Cambridge, MA: Blackwell.

Macionis, J. J. (1997). *Sociology* (International Edition). Upper Saddle River, NJ: Prentice-Hall.

Martins, H. (1974). Time and theory in sociology. In J. Rex (Ed.), *Approaches to Sociology.* London: Routledge & Kegan Paul.

Marx, K. (1973 [1857–8]). Tr. by M. Nicolaus, *Grundrisse: Foundations of the Critique of Political Economy.* Harmondsworth: Penguin.

—— (1977 [1849]). Wage labour and capital. In K. Marx and F. Engels (Eds.), *Collected Works Vol 9 1849* (pp. 197–230). London: Lawrence & Wishart.

Mennell, S. (1994). The formation of we-images: A process theory. In C. Calhoun (Ed.), *Social Theory and the Politics of Identity* (pp. 175–197).

de Montaigne, M. (1991). Tr. by M. A. Screech, *The Essays of Michel de Montaigne.* Harmondsworth: Penguin.

Nisbet, R. A. (1966). *The Sociological Tradition.* New York: Basic Books.

O'Byrne, D. (1997). Working class culture: Local community and global conditions. In J. Eade (Ed.), *Living the Global City* (pp. 73–89).

Park, R. and Burgess, E. W. (1921). *Introduction to the Science of Sociology.* Chicago: Chicago University Press. p. 284.

Parsons, T. (1937). *The Structure of Social Action.* New York: McGraw-Hill.

—— (1951). *The Social System.* Glencoe. Ill.: Free Press.

Putnam, R. (2000). *Bowling Alone.* New York: Touchstone.

Radcliffe-Brown, A. R. (1952). *Structure and Function in Primitive Society.* London: Cohen & West.

Robertson, R. (1992). *Globalization: Social Theory and Global Culture.* London: Sage.

Sassen, S. (1991). *The Global City.* Princeton, NJ: Princeton University Press.

Savage, M., Bagnall G., and Longurst, B. (2005). *Globalization and Belonging.* London: Sage.

Schutz, A. (1972 [1932]). *The Phenomenology of the Social World.* London: Heinemann.

Simmel. G. (1908). Excurs über den Fremden. In *Soziologie* (pp. 685–691). Tr. by R. Park & E. W. Burgess (1921), *Introduction to the Science of Sociology* (pp. 322–327). Leipzig: Duncker & Humblot.

Somers, M., and Gibson, G. D. (1994). Narrative and social identity. In C. Calhoun (Ed.), *Social Theory and the Politics of Identity* (pp. 37–99). Oxford: Blackwell.

Stiglitz, J. (2002). *Globalization and Its Discontents*. New York: Norton.

Toffler, A. (1981). *The Third Wave*. London: Pan.

Urry, J. (2000). *Sociology beyond Societies: Mobilities for the Twenty-First Century*. London: Routledge.

Weber, M. (1968 [1921]). In G. Roth and C. Wittich (Eds.), *Economy and Society*. New York: Bedminster.

Wiley, N. (1994). The politics of identity in American history. In C. Calhoun (Ed.), *Social Theory and the Politics of Identity* (pp. 131–149).

16
Toward a Framework for Global Communication: Durkheim, Phenomenology, Postmodernism, and the "Construction" of Place and Space

INO ROSSI

The chapters in this volume have documented contrasting dimensions of contemporary globalization: we have an an unprecedented cross-national interaction in terms of trade and circulation of financial capital (see Chapter 7 by Chase-Dunn and Jorgenson); on the other hand, we witness a severely curtailed migration of labor, unevenness of global development (see Chapter 8 by Arrighi) and economic marginalization of many nations because, among other reasons, of the superiority of Western technology (see Chapter 9 by Schaeffer). Digital interconnectedness accelerates the speed and magnifies the positive and negative impact of globalization. In fact, digital communication facilitates the financialization of the economy, the restructuring of production and distribution systems, the spreading of ideologies, and the intensification of global awareness. We have also seen that digital communication produces an instantaneous confrontation of geographically distant and socioculturally different societies; this confrontation accentuates old and recent conflicts and produces further distance and alienation among competing nations and civilizations. At the end of my essay on "Globalization as an Historical and a Dialectic Process" (Chapter 1) I pointed out that human agency can greatly contribute to a heightening of global awareness and to forging positive solutions to world affairs. Because human agency is heavily immersed in and formed through patterns of digitized interaction, I discuss in this chapter the nature of digital communication and the role of human agency in a digitally connected world.

Digital Communication in the Information Age

Digital media enable culturally, economically, and politically heterogeneous nations to interact as "one" ongoing totality at a given time (Castells, 2000). Social scientists have pointed out that digital media of communication have conquered geographical distances and chronological time through the phenomenon of time–space compression (Harvey, 1989). At the same time, an increased awareness of the problems of the world as a single place has been occurring; this subjective facet of globalization has been referred to with the terms of "globality" (Albrow, 1990) or "globalism" (Robertson, 1992). The role of digital communication in these processes and the kinds of global linkages it produces are matters of controversy. I start with some current controversies to outline the elements of a global communication framework that is based on the geographically and electronically based construction (and interaction) of "place" and "space." I also discuss the implications of the "constructionist" view of "place" for the analytical role of "meaning," "agency," and "structure."

Current Debates on the Time–Space Compression, the Disappearance of Time, and the Space of Flows

The claim has been made that during modernity (and classical capitalism) social relations were organized according to sequential, specific, contextualized time. Time was linear, sequential, measurable, and predictable; time dominated and defined space, because physical space was measured by the time needed to cover physical distances. With the advent of new information technologies, instant ("real") time dominates and displaces sequential time. For Anthony Giddens, time becomes differentiated from space, time becomes universalized (because one measure of time can be used across different localities) and time is stretched out across space. In a recent formulation posted on the Web site of the London School of Economics (LSE FAQs) Giddens states that distant events shape local events and vice versa; this process entails a "reduction of geographical, spatial and temporal factors as constraints to the development of society." On the contrary, I argue that digital communication enormously expands and diversifies global spatialization with the creation of new cultural forms. and systems of meaning. In Fredric Jameson's formulation, time has become a perpetual present, and, thus, spatial; this is what he calls a spatial turn or displacement of time. Space becomes the key to understand our place within the logic of late capitalism (2000). For Harvey (1990), the universalization of time means that space (physical space) is annihilated by time ("real" or digital time); space, then, becomes the key to understand our place within the logic of late capitalism.

I am not concerned with the subtle variations of these formulations, but rather with the implied notions of "place" and "space" and with the related notions of "meaning" and "agency." The definitions and interrelationships among these notions determine whether we have a deterministic view of digital communication (and global spacialization), or whether we have a human-centered, constructionist, and self-reflective view of this technological facilitator of globalization.

A cross-disciplinary probe has made it evident to me that philosophers, geographers, literary critics, anthropologists, and sociologists use these terms with different meaning. This is not surprising, given the great variations of theoretical perspectives among people, culture, and social structure. I start from the classical notion of space and time proposed by Durkheim to show that his static and cognitive categories must be complemented with the concrete notions of "place," subjectivity, and the materiality of the body; the latter notions have been recovered by phenomenologists and postmodernists. Drawing also on recent semiotic thinking, I show that electronic-based communication sustains two processes that are emphasized by two competing camps: dematerialized and disembodied informational spaces (flows, scapes); and the interactive construction of concrete "places," and their interconnectedness in global spaces. The real "global" story is that electronic media of information sustain selectively and interactively both of these kinds of processes.

On the Static Nature of the Durkheimian Categories of Time and Space

Here are a few quotes from the "Elementary Forms of Religious Life" (Durkheim 1961(1912):

> ... the first systems of *representations* [my italics] with which men have pictured to themselves the world and themselves were of religious origin ... Men owe to it [religion] not only a good part of the *substance* of their knowledge, but also the *form* in which this knowledge has been elaborated. At the roots of all our judgments there are a certain number of *essential ideas* which dominate all our *intellectual life*; they are what philosophers since Aristotle have called the *categories of understanding*: *ideas* of time, space, class, number, cause, substance, personality, etc. They correspond to the most *universal properties of things*. They are the solid frame which encloses all thought. It seems that we cannot *think of objects* that are not in time and space, which have no number ... (they are social, collective representations) ... (Op. Cit.: 21) (my italics).
>
> ... The *notion* or category of time ... is an *abstract and impersonal frame* which surrounds, not only our individual existence, but that of all humanity. It is like *an endless chart*, ... upon which all possible events can be located in relation to *fixed and determined guidelines*. ... Spatial representation consists essentially in a primary co-ordination of the data of *sensuous experience*. ... To dispose things spatially there must be a possibility of placing them differently, of putting *some at the right, others at the left, these above, those below, at the north of or at the south of*. ... Just as to dispose *states of consciousness* temporally there must be a possibility of localizing them at determined dates. That is to say that space could not be what it is if it were not, like time, divided and differentiated (Op. Cit.: 23).
>
> ... The function of the categories is to dominate and envelop all other concepts; they are *permanent moulds for the mental life*. ... The relations which they express exist in an implicit way in *individual consciousness*. The individual lives in time, and, as we have seen, he has a certain *sense of temporal orientation*. He is situated at a determined point in space, and it has even been held, and sustained with good reasons, that all *sensations* have something special about them (W. James). ... (p. 408). We also have the *sensation* of a certain regularity in the order of the succession of phenomena ... (p. 489).

The following characteristics of the Durkheimian social categories are evident from these quotes.

(a) Their *cognitive/intellectual* nature (the key terms are "ideas, notions, intellectual life, categories of understanding, thinking of objects, moulds for mental life"). Emmanuel Kant posited forms of sensibility and categories of understanding as constitutive of experience and knowledge, and Durkheim was influenced by Kantian thinking.

(b) Their essentialist, objective and static nature (Durkheim talks about essential ideas, categories as universal properties of things; categories as fixed guidelines).

(c) Their quasi-formalistic nature (categories are an abstract, impersonal frame that surrounds the whole of humanity).

(d) Their geographically or territorially linked nature: space enables one to locate things at the right of, at the left of, at the north of, at the south and so on.

Randall Collins responded to a conference presentation of mine, where I underlined the static nature of the Durkheimian time and space, as follows.

This may well be true in regard to the 'Elementary Forms' of a tribal society where a high mechanical solidarity prevails. Given that kind of social structure, the categories will be treated as absolute, as well as particularistic (the frame for the particular group in its social space); and given the lack of reflexivity in such a social structure, the categories are treated without self-consciousness, and reified. The more general Durkheimian argument is that the categories of thought reflect social morphology. A society of tightly bounded local networks (or "mechanical solidarity" or Mary Douglas' "high group") will have this concrete, reified view of time and space. With a different social morphology, the categories change to reflect that. Societies with a high division of labor, like differentiated modern societies, have a more abstract and reflexive collective conscience; Durkheim never worked this out specifically for time and space, but that would apply here. Also, in modern societies time and space become more abstract, and are viewed more reflexively. Thus, coming to globalizing spaces, the principle of social morphology would apply again: the dematerialized character of social relationships through electronic communication would thus bring about a corresponding shift in the categories of time and space. The hyper-relativizing of such concepts seems to me predictable from the logic of the Durkheimian theory (Personal correspondence, March 8, 2003).

Randall Collins may well be correct on the logical extension of the Durkheimian position. On the other hand, it is not a top secret that Durkheim was totally alien to the notion of "construction of social categories." For Durkheim, "time" and "space" are "given" social facts; even if one could predict that in societies with a high division of labor Durkheim would posit more abstract and reflexive categories, wouldn't he posit them as "given," as "social facts," consistent with the notion of a priori Kantian categories?

The central question here is the origin and nature of the categories used in electronic communication. Are they abstract, reflexive, dematerialized, and hyper-relativized categories, as some authors appear to suggest? What kind of sociocultural space do they presuppose or, rather, produce and sustain?

Contemporary geographers and phenomenologists are quick to differentiate themselves from the Durkheimian position. Michael Curry has discussed the notion of social space from an historical and epistemological perspective (Curry, 2002). According to him, Ptolemy imagined earth as a globe with an objective existence; every object is located in space which is absolute, immutable, and pre-exists things; the location of things in this absolute (that is, always the same and unchanging) space is contingent. This view implies that "place" is just that part of space that is taken up by the body. On the contrary, for the early Aristotle everything has its natural "place" in the universe that tends toward stasis; the universe is a universe of places (p. 12). In the 18th century the Ptolemaic view prevailed for the impact of Newton who upheld the notion of absolute space (p. 13). Leibniz countered this notion by arguing that space is just the order of coexistence of things, as time is the order of the succession of things. Hence, space and time consist only of relations. However, for both Leibniz and Newton space or place is abstract and formal without connection to everyday action; hence, both influential philosophers bypassed the notion of concrete (enacted and constructed) "place."

Durkheim echoes the abstract, formal, and absolute notion of Newtonian space; his conceptualizations seem to be consistent with what current phenomenologists (Casey, 2003) and geographers (Curry, 2002) refer to as the notion of "absolute space," space being "absolute" because it ignores the interactional activity that creates "place" and, as we explain latter on, "space."

"Place" as a Construction of Interactive Human Creativity; The Impact of the Phenomenological and Postmodernist Perspectives

We saw that Durkheim makes reference to sensuous experience, to the sensation of temporal orientation, to the temporal location of states of consciousness, and to the (individual) consciousness of temporal and spatial relations. But sensations and consciousness are taken as "data" that the mind arranges according to spatial and temporal coordinates; the categories are taken for given, as if they "exist out there," with no attention paid to the role of consciousness, experience, or interactional processes in the emergence of spatial and temporal coordinates. It was Heidegger (1977) who began reacting to the absolutist view of space to state that the "geographical" is contingent, because it emerges from the social and technological realms. Wittgenstein (1961) stated that "words only have meanings within the contexts of the individuals and groups that use them, in particular situations and particular places." Both Heidegger and Wittgenstein, then, took a deconstructive turn. Bachelard, Lefebvre, Certeau, and Foucault have greatly contributed to the role of people in the construction of places and other social formations.

Harvey (1990: 201) argues the following.

> I think it is important to challenge the idea of a single and objective sense of time and space, against which we can measure the diversity of human conceptions and perceptions . . . *we must recognize the multiplicity of the objective qualities which space and time can express, and the role of human practices in their construction.* Neither time nor space, the physicists now broadly propose, had existence (let alone meaning) before matter; . . . It is, however, by no means necessary to subordinate all objective conceptions of time and space to this particular physical conception, since it, also, is a construct (emphasis added) that rests upon a particular version of the constitution of matter and the origin of the universe. The history of concepts of time, space, and time–space in physics has, in fact, been marked by strong epistemological breaks and reconstructions. The conclusion we should draw is simply that neither time nor space can be assigned objective meanings independently of material processes, and that it is only through investigation of the latter that we can properly ground our concepts of the former. This is not, of course, a new conclusion (Harvey, 1990: 203–204).

Without denying the input of "material processes" one can hold a larger view of human practices in the construction of time and space. In modern times, there has been an interest in reflexivity and the role of the subject; Deleuze and Guattari are interested in *smooth places* of space of contact, small tactile, manual actions of contact rather than in the visual space of Euclidian space. Here, we see emerging the discourse on the *dematerialization* of signs as the distinguishing mark of the electronic-mediated communication. Some contemporary authors counter-oppose the tactile-based communication of pretechnological times and of concrete "places" to the visuallybased communication of electronic media; the implication of this counter-opposition is that in electronic communication the sign becomes detached from its material basis (it is "dematerialized"), the subject becomes fragmented, and meaning is lost; I return to this debatable point later.

For Scott Lash electronic media produce an "architecture of flows, of movement, encouraging real time relations over distances; it is an architecture of disembedding, of compression of time and space" (Lash, 2002: Chap. 1, p. 1–3). Scott Lash does not draw on Giddens, Harvey, Beck, and Castells, but on Virilio, Deleuze, Haraway, McLuhan, and Benjamin. Before the advent of electronic media, the medium of information was narrative, lyric, discourse, and painting. With the electronic media of communication, the information comes compressed in very short messages, in bytes. The medium is the message or the byte; *gone is the discourse, subjective meaning*, conceptual framework, propositional logic. We have a quasi-anarchy of information proliferation and flows, the symbolic violence of flow of bytes, the power of the immediacy of information and of dematerialized signs. For Lash the cultural is displaced into an immanent plane of actors attached or interlinked with machines; we experience culture as immanent things, as objects, and as technologies; we have an immanent plane of actor networks (humans, cultural objects, material objects) that are disembedded: actors, networks of nonhumans, and humans–machine interfaces, information is all disembedded (p. 8).

We can see postmodernists focusing on the materiality of practices and a dematerialized "bytelike" information.

The central question is how much of this analysis is derived from postmodernist epistemologies and how much of it is based on empirical evidence. A related question is whether the abstract, formal, absolute views of Durkheimian categories make us inevitably slip into conceptualizations of dematerialized signs and the loss of the subject. An affirmative answer would posit a definite disconnect between the cognitive/intellectual mode of social classifications à la Durkheim and, let us say, Levi-Strauss' concrete logic of aboriginal cultures—the cultures of concrete logic— the culture of communal and aboriginal "places." But, Levi-Strauss (1972) has demonstrated that an intellectual logic is embedded within the "concrete logic" of "Primitive Classifications."

These questions, then, must be examined: are Durkheim's "systems of representation" and "categories of understanding" disembedded because of the (presumed) dematerialized nature of electronic-based communication? If so, could we recapture that concreteness that is presumably lost in electronic-based communication? Would the recapturing of interacting people (both in terms of a reflexive "subject" and the "body") in the formation of spatial and temporal categories be a welcome corrective to the Durkheimian perspective?

The Multidimensional Richness of Virtual Connectivity

The Presumed Dematerialization of Virtual Connectivity

Communication in the virtual world occurs at a distance and primarily on the basis of the visual (and somewhat auditory) medium of communication. It is here that some authors introduce the discourse on the dematerialization of sign as the distinguishing characteristic of electronic communication. Some authors contrast the tactile-based communication of pretechnological times and of concrete "places" to the visually based communication of electronic media. In the latter, the sign presumably becomes detached from its material basis (it is "dematerialized"), and, for some people, the subject (and meaning) become fragmented into a sequence of signs. (Recollect the bytelike information à la Scott Lash above). For this reason fashionable modern thinkers à la French, such as Deleuze and Guattari, are interested in recovering "smooth places" or spaces of contact, small tactile and manual actions of contact, rather than being interested in the visual space of Euclides.

The Threefold Dimensionality of the Semiotic Function

The dematerializing notion of virtual communication emphasizes one side of the story. Experts from the field of semiotics and from art media argue that electronic media of communication sustain three semiotic functions. It is true that as we move from the iconic to the indexical to the symbolic communicative function, there is a progressively increasing distance between the sign and the physicality of the object. However, "informational technologies can and do develop on the three semiotic levels simultaneously: the expressive, the representational, and the signifying. . . ." (Cassirer quoted in Innis, 1999). In "expression" sign, meaning, object are indissolubly joined, so that "the sign is taken to participate existentially in its intended reality." "Word-magic and mythic consciousness are prime exemplifications of this stratum or form of consciousness" with its "affective configurations" and "physiognomic and qualitatively defined meanings." (Here, Geertz's definition of religion seems to be a good illustrative commentary and so Albrow's use of "thick" ethnography):

> In "representation" the relationship among sign, meaning, object moves to a higher level of *"abstraction."* "Whereas mythical consciousness works within the dimension of *"identity,"* representation introduces *"difference."* The word is not the thing; the image is not the imaged. Words and images, doing the "work" of representation, "articulate" the world without being a part of it. Language and art exemplify in clearest fashion this sense-function, albeit in rather different ways. They "grasp" the world (*begreifen*), upon *an intuitive* (*anschaulich*) base, to be sure, while not taking hold of it (*greifen*) in any material or magical fashion. "Signification" is the stratum of sense-functions farthest removed from sensory and intuitive supports; here, the concrete physical reality of the sign and its objects recedes. This meaning-space accesses, indeed constitutes, a world of events and their relations to one another, and not to our intuitional capacities. "Signification" is exemplified in modern mathematical physics and the notation systems that make it possible (as well as the various systems of pure mathematics and symbolic logic) (p. 1).

Information Technologies Do Not Impoverish or Distort the Concrete and the Experiential; They Have a Qualitative Feel of Their Own

> Abstraction is not by definition diminishing; it is rather enriching; this is one of the main lessons of semiotics. Information technologies are defined by their abilities to perform different types of abstraction. Rather than looking upon them as fundamentally distortive and disruptive, which seems to be infected with a kind of longing for immediacy, we should resolutely hold fast to the ineluctable universality of mediation, fateful as it is (Op. Cit.: 5–6). " . . . To be sure, inasmuch as all technologies, and technological artifacts, are perceived, they have an expressive or physiognomic dimension or qualitative 'feel'; the expressive function is the one experientially and affectively linking sign and object . . ." (Op. Cit.: 6).

Information Technologies Produce New Forms of Intelligibility and Partially Form the Information User

Information technology also

> . . . inscribes, a pattern of intelligibility upon the world, giving rise to "stamped forms" of every sort: from chipped stone to the "automatic" processes of modern computing systems (p. 2). This is what Levinson calls "process extending" informational technologies. . . . This is one of the main lessons of semiotics. Information technologies are defined by their abilities to perform different types of abstraction. . . .
>
> Modern "digital" technologies, which may be used primarily for 'aesthetic' purposes, are themselves made possible by notation systems that belong to the stratum of

signification. In this sense, "signification" makes possible distinctive forms of "expression" and "representation." . . . Such technologies [information technologies] function iconically, indexically, and symbolically. The information user is a multi-leveled percipient, a "topos" or place, defined by complex systems of affective, energetic, and intellectual or logical interpretants, understood as the proper significant effects of signs and sign systems. In this sense, we are the affective, actional, and conceptual "out-comes" of the mediating instruments in which we are embodied . . . (p. 8).

The information user is, at least partially, formed by the digital communication exchange, because she has to function at the affective (iconic communication), actional (indexical communication), and conceptual levels (symbolic communication).

The Dematerialization of "Signification" Does Not Inevitably Lead to the Fragmentation of Meaning and Subjectivity, but It Produces New Cultural Forms, New Cultural Logic, and New Electronic Places

Digital communication consists of the creation of new "places" through the exchanges of digital messages. The fact that digital communication transcends the physical and tactile dimension makes possible an enormous creativity of electronic exchanges, exchanges that produce new cultural forms. Moreover, the loss of tactile/olfactory aspects of communication can be compensated by the closeness and brightness of the visual and auditory dimensions of digital communication. Through a visually and auditorily sharpened focus on events, we can experience places that otherwise we would never experience. When we observe the digital images of the abuses on Iraqi prisoners of war, we can hardly conclude that dematerialized images cannot put us somewhat in touch with concrete subjects or that these images have a decontextualized meaning.

Digitization can provide messages and images with some sort of concrete, vivid, and emotional qualities of their own; this is very much the case, for instance, when political or economic agendas demand it. Facial expressions and tonal inflections can play out a whole range of arguments, ideals, symbols, and emotions; the emotionally laden messages are lived through, played out, and restaged in a million "local places." You cannot understand world politics at the macro-level (for instance, the impact of the U.S. military hegemony) without paying attention to the digital images of distraught, killed, or demonstrating Iraqis. Concrete human beings reappear and become preeminent at critical junctures produced by military events and disempowering economic forces.

The contemporary art media theorist from Austria, R. Braun, recognizes the increasing elimination of the sensual–physical in digital communication with related dematerialization and virtualization. He points at the process of disengagement of representation from social organization: texts, sounds, and images are sent out in the virtual world taken away from their contextual, embedded social matrix as "living dead" and capable of being revised, manipulated, and transformed into different contexts. Social time is converted into media time and the structure of media time is imposed on social life: "information rather than things itself is what counts" (2002).

However, Braun argues that these conditions do not lead to disintegration and decline because technologies of networked communication offer remedies to deracinated cultures of modernity; they are an "electropolis," a location where a new cultural logic is established. He goes on to argue that we have no more "place" understood as a symmetry of present, action, perception, and "social space" in which the subject takes up his place. Braun moves decidedly away from this old-fashioned view. It seems that the loss of the physical concreteness of the "places" is precisely what permits the creation of myriad instant electronic "places." R. Braun argues: "It is no longer about presentation or representation (both of which could be read or interpreted), but about activations, participation, circulation, and being hooked into the system (not just in the technical sense)." Which places and which territories and spaces could we be dealing with here? We must be aware that Braun speaks about media art and media art forms: he argues that there is a transition from object representation to artwork as an open field, as options of action, process constellations, and ambiguous possibilities of interpretations. He speaks also of conceptual spaces and formal spaces beyond physical spaces. Innis' notion that new forms of representations are made possible by digital media applies to the sociocultural realm in general. R. Braun offers another insight that it is applicable also in the sociocultural sphere: "the new spaces, public spaces are produced in and through the activities of the participants;" he speaks of cultural developments as "articulations of interlinked practices," sociocultural practices that produce "new cultural coordinates" and "new forms of appearance." The new spaces and "territories" have an ephemeral hold on matter, a tenuous position in space and a presence that "is measured in acts of participation rather than coincidence of location."

It is obvious that the global spaces R. Braun is talking about are not the absolute spaces à la Newton, but they are "places" validated by ongoing practices. In my view digital media have opened up new levels of creative and interactive places; they have also enriched the content and the geographical impact of traditional and geographically anchored "places." Let me summarize and clarify my position:

(a) The semiotic abstraction from the physicality (or the tactile dimension of "places") in digital communication fosters an enormous variety of electronic exchanges, and, therefore, the creation of new places.

(b) Digital communication supports the creation of new networks of interactive places, and, hence, of new cultural forms, as asymmetrical, unpredictable and semi-institutionalized as they might be (see Knorr Cetina's essay, Chapter 2).

(c) The loss of the tactile and olfactory in digital communication is compensated by the closeness and brightness of the visual and auditory representations. We can experience a visually and auditorily sharpened physicality of "places," places that otherwise we would never experience.

(d) The loss of spatiality is compensated also by what Knorr Cetina calls "time articulation" of microglobal structures. ". . . Digital communications are temporal streams of activities characterized by fluidity, lightness, temporal complexity . . . they are embedded in time, in substitution for loss of spatial rooted ness and stabilization." As microglobal structures are based on digital communication, they keep a recurring capacity to re-emerge in new ways.

(e) Electronic messages are perceived and interpreted not only through the slogans and prejudices of virtual culture, but also through one's own deep-rooted cultural orientations. This is clearly the case for today's international confrontations and fundamentalist movements. This is another facet of the ever-crucial importance of the culturally specific local; this is another reason why there is no "local" without "global" and vice versa (see below). In my opinion, this is a major reason why the micro is an instantiation of the macro. Knorr Cetina states elsewhere in this volume that "microstructures can carry globalization and the patterns of world society." How is this possible, if microglobal structures are fluid, temporal, and ephemeral? I argue that this is so because they are deeply rooted in cultural and ideological codes, so that they can emerge and re-emerge with new or modified patterns that adapt to new situations and issues.

(f) "Virtual places" are very effective in sustaining communication networks and in the delivery of instantaneous and "ideologically embedded" messages: see the massive antiwar protests recently mobilized via cell phone and radio communication; see the many "places" interactively created by academicians, terrorists, news groups, discussion groups, music and downloading aficionados, drug users, terrorists, and antiglobalization grass-root groups throughout the world. Economic and political ideologies are the core component—and the controlling one—of cultural exchanges. The ideological control of communication (by powerful nations and groups) is a major factor for the divisiveness of the dialectic nature of global communication, as I have argued in my previous essay.

(g) Local cultures are reinvented under transnational ideological impacts that are becoming more and more intrusive because of powerful digital media. This is an instance of the mutual reinforcing of the "global" and the "local."

(h) At the same time, the cultural and ideological awareness of the electronically connected individuals is enhanced. We frequently observe intense and instantaneous dialogues or confrontations and diatribes among contemporary world leaders who perform, as if it were, on the global digital theatre. One can hardly qualify these performances as consisting of dematerialized images, fragmented subjects, and decontextualized meanings. Digitization can be concrete, vivid, and emotionally powerful as a communication vehicle. The staging of facial expressions and tonal inflections can theatrically play out and give context to an whole range of arguments, ideals, symbols, and emotions; the emotionally laden messages are lived through, played out, and restaged in a million "local places."

(i) Finally, and importantly, individuals are engaged in multiform electronic interactions and, hence, they are capable of developing multiple identities as functions of their multiple performances, in as much as they must act out different roles in a variety of situations and multicultural contexts.

This is the "emergent" nature of the global: new cultural and social patterns are superimposed to transnational and local patterns (see Chapter 5 by Stichweh), and a multilayered civilizational consciousness emerges in individuals endowed with multiple identity and intercultural competences.

The Construction of "Places" as Building Blocks of Global Space

We must discuss the interactive processes through which virtual interactivity gives rise to emerging cultural forms. Quasi-Durkheimian formulations are still abundant. Giddens, for instance, states that "structure refers to rules and resources, or sets of transformation relations, organized as properties of space and time categories." Giddens refers to "the structuring properties allowing the binding of time and space in social systems. . . . Structuring properties make it possible for discernibly similar social practices to exist across varying spans of time and space" (*http://www.lse.uk/ Giddens/FAQs.htm*). This formulation seems to imply the notion of absolute space, inasmuch as no reference is made to the interactive encounters of actors with expanded consciousness and multiple identities that support these "structuring properties." Behavioral interaction consists of the construction of situation-specific sets of meaning; this is what we call "places." Giddens explains "time–space distantiation" as "disembedding (of traditional forms of relationships), as standard and abstract dimensions of space and time that come to order and rationalize activities in the place of local contexts" (*http://www.arasite.org/giddmod2.htm*). Isn't this similar to the abstract and static notion of space in Durkheim?

Against this background, it is significant that Edward J. Soja stresses that no adequate inquiry and theorization is possible without historicity, sociality, and spatiality; the latter was weakened by 19th century historicism and it must be reconstructed to provide an adequate social basis to history (1991: 133). We have to explore the way space was described and the meaning of the positions assigned within that space so that we can write a contextual rather than a linear and limited history.

But what is the relation between "place" and "space"? I have said that "place" is constructed by the interactive encounters of people and it does not have meaning independently of people's interaction, as much as words have no meaning separately from the contexts and particular situations where they are used by interacting individuals (Wittgenstein, 1961). Modern philosophers such as Wittgenstein, Heidegger, Lefebvre, Certeau, and Foucault have made us aware of the role of people in the construction of places, and other social arrangements. In the first chapter I explained how social identity is developed in social interaction; in this essay I said that in a multiculturally complex and digitally interacting world we have to develop multiple identities. Hence, "social interaction" entails the interactive construction of places, meaning, human agency, and multiple identity.

The interactional role of "places" is essential for understanding the dynamics of global spatialization. For this reason I find again that something important is missing in Giddens' notion that globalization entails "the reduction of geographical, spatial, and temporal factors as constraints to the development of society" (*http://www.LSE.ac.uk/Giddens/FAQs.htm*). Where is the production of new cultural forms in these formulations? Manuel Castells also bypasses "place" when he makes a distinction between the space of flows (simultaneous globalization) and the space of places (localization) (2000: 458). Place for him is a

> locale whose form, function, and meaning are self-contained within the boundaries of physical contiguity (op. cit.: 453). People do still live in places. But because function and power in our societies are organized in the space of flows, the structural domination of its logic essentially alters the meaning and dynamics of places. Experience, by being related to places, become abstracted power, and meaning is increasingly separated from knowledge. There follows a structural schizophrenia between two spatial logics . . . the dominant tendency is toward a horizon of networked, a-historical space of flows, aiming at imposing its logic over scattered, segmented places, increasingly unrelated to each other, less and less able to share cultural codes" (ibid. 458–459).

The notion of an a-historical space of flows is not much different from Durkheim's absolute categories. Worst, in Castells we are not dealing just with an epistemological absolute, but with an absolute power of the a-historical space of flows that imposes its own logic over a multitude of meaningless places, the places where human individuals live. My position is on the opposite side of the spectrum. Global space (or the space of global communication) is constructed by (and/or consists of) the interaction among the many electronic "places" and by the interface among digitally and geographically anchored "*places*." "Places" are the interactive encounters of individuals that give meaning to their existential situations, and "places" cluster in "spaces" along geographical, ethnic, occupational, ideological, and similar criteria. The centrality of interacting and meaning producing individuals is the reason why we can operate a critique of the structures of domination, as I shortly argue.

I made a distinction between a geographically based and a digitally based interaction. Geographical linkages and territorially based communication in Scholte's terminology (2000) remain valid as in the past and, at times, are even stronger; witness the territorially linked operations of Al Qaeda and other fundamentalist groups. However, with digital communication technologies, superimposed to territorial linkages are networks of instant spatializations. These networks, however, are not timeless spaces of flows with some sort of reified status. Cyberspace is not "out there" as an object existing prior to and independently of interacting people. We saw that such a view is attributed to Ptolemy who imagined the earth as a globe with its own objective existence, preexisting any event and as a surface where every event and object finds its location. On the contrary, globalization means the creation of digital spatialization or the simultaneous and instant connection via digital media among many actors interacting at a physical distance.

Paul Virilio argues that with the information superhighways we have "a duplication of sensible reality, into reality and virtuality" (1995: 2). On the contrary, the preceding analysis has shown that virtual communication selectively elaborates elements of sensible reality and produces new cultural forms. Virilio's indictment continues and grows ominous:

> A stereo-reality of sorts threatens. A total loss of the bearings of the individual looms large. To exist, is to exist *in situ*, here and now, *hic et nunc*. This is precisely what is being threatened by cyberspace and instantaneous, globalized information flows. . . . Together with the build-up of information superhighways we are facing a new phenomenon: loss of orientation (Ibid.).

In my opinion this kind of reified powerlessness is derived from a gratuitous epistemological posture. One can argue that the opposite is true: concrete individuals act both as physical and virtual individuals and through their virtual interaction construct new places and new sets of meanings. The interaction among "virtual" individuals is an interaction among individuals existing in the real place of "virtuality." Art, music, literature, and the Internet produce imagined or virtual realities; although not physical, virtual realities are "real" because they can have the "virtue" or capacity to produce real effects. The essential point is that virtual communication is started, interpreted, and elaborated by interacting individuals (physical or virtual) and that virtual communication produces new cultural forms and sustains and reinforces structures of domination. Hence, the latter are produced or sustained by individuals; therefore, they can only be dismantled by them through critical reflection.

"Reenter" Reflexive Human Agency

This interactive and person-centered view of global spatialization (interaction) rejects the epistemological view of an absolute "space" as if it were preexisting human interactivity. This person-centered view of global interaction provides a perspective that integrates various concepts and theoretical issues into a comprehensive framework for the analysis of global communication or virtual interactivity: (a) the relationship between the "global" and "local;" (b) the relationship between geographically based and digitally based interactivity; (c) the role of ideology; and (d) the role of structure in global interactive patterns.

(a) There is no global space without the interface among physically and electronically based "places," as much as there is no situational interaction (focused on geography, ideology, or ethnic, political, gender, or economic interests) that is not affected or stimulated by global cultural forms. Hence, the global–local polarity refers to two facets of the social interaction among nations, groups, individuals via digital communication media.

(b) Instant spatializations (social interactions) have the following characteristics: (1) they are locally rooted, namely they originate in and through geographically anchored "places;" (2) at times, they reinforce through visual digitations the salience of local factors; (3) they also produce liminal spaces or "nonplaces" (Ritzer, 2003), because certain elements of the physical and social world are not incorporated in the main stream content of digital communication. In fact, global communication and global spaces are formed on the basis of selective elements of the physical and social worlds. The items focused upon by digitally interacting social actors receive meaning and become "places," because they are "constructed" through meaningful interaction. The physical and social traits of the environment that are not directly focused on become "liminal" or interstitially located among the interactively "constructed" meaningful elements; these socially marginal elements are a sort of "nonplaces" (Auge', 2000).

Various chapters in this book make key contributions on the issue of the interface between geographically based interaction and digital communication, as well as on the nature of digital communication. Rosenau, Albrow, and Friedman's chapters clarify the notion of global relations and global system; Sassen's chapter deals with various operational dimensions of the interface between physical space and digital communication, and the interaction between the territorial (and national) and the global. Knorr Cetina's chapter elaborates on the asymmetrical, semi-institutional nature, complex and unpredictable nature, of microglobal structures: social order is not an outcome of purified social processes, but always connected with elements of chaos (see Chapter 6 by Urry). Microglobal structures entail a relational connectivity (see Chapter 14 by Rosenau) and demand an empirical and a structural (à la Friedman) level of analysis.

For Knorr Cetina microglobal structures are based not only on intersubjectivity, but also on "scopic structures" that may contradict new structures; scopic systems deliver the "mediated presence" of remote participants and update interpretations and events, which enable a floating global microstructure to emerge and fuel its dynamics.

I would like to mention an additional aspect of the unpredictability of microglobal structures. Diverse constituencies interpret the fragmented and partial information on which interactive structures are built; hence, novel and unpredictable microglobal structures are likely to emerge. In other words, we must not forget creativity as a factor of novelty and unpredictability; as a matter of fact, creativity is mentioned by Prigogine when he discusses the complexity of the world (see in Urry, 2002: v). However, I prefer to see "creativity" as a characteristic of human agency rather than as an element of fundamental natural trends.

(c) This is not to deny the importance of the ideological and structural framework within which global communication occurs. The efficacy and scope of ideological controls have been progressively increasing with the development of new information technologies. Electronic-based communication is the technological infrastratum that gives specificity to contemporary globalization processes; this is what Leslie Sklair calls "generic globalization," and I would call "basic globalization." There is no way to deny that the recent stages of societal development have been anchored on capitalism, mercantilism, conservativism, liberalism, nationalism, and recently neoliberalism. Currently, neoliberalism, fundamentalism, nationalism, and socialism are the dominant ideologies or "attractors" (à la Urry) for dominant strata and world leaders who seek to control the world's strategic resources.

I argue that dominant ideologies provide the anchors, loci, and "expanders" to the emerging structures, flows, and self-evolving systems of global transactions (if I must use other people's conceptualizations). The references to global ungovernability (Chapter 10 by Archer) and chaos (Chapter 6 by Urry) can be accepted only as intermediate analytic steps. The world contains inherent "risks" (Beck), but ultimately these risks are under the control or umbrella of dominant ideologies who are engaged in an all-or-none hegemonic struggle. In a sense, globalization is ultimately about a struggle of civilizations and ideologies. It is at this fundamental level that our steering mechanisms ought to become operative. As suggested in my previous essay, the only durable solution to global imbalances and global conflicts seems to be a critical reflection over dominant political, economic and cultural structures (including global civil society) by influential agencies. In fact, ideologies operate through human agencies and cultural, economic, and political structures.

(d) The concept of "structure" partially contributes to the understanding of the digitally based temporalities and spatialities that Knorr Cetina, Stichweh, Sassen, and others speak about in this volume; this is true no matter whether structural explanations are forged under the notion of emerging structures (Knorr Cetina, Stichweh), global system (either Marxist, Sklair's essay, or structural Marxist, Friedman's essay), flows (Lash, Castells), or self-evolving complex systems (Chapter 6).

As I have repeatedly stated, it is the continuous interaction among key actors (individuals, corporate, intergovernmental) as they critically reflect upon their social structures that produces the building blocks (or "places") of global communication and global space. This "constructionist" view provides a deeper understanding of global processes than the metaphors of megastructures, networks of flows (M. Castells), and scapes (Appadurai) can. I argue that "social actors"—be they individuals, corporate, governmental, intergovernmental (IGOs) and non-governmental (NGOs)—are key elements to understanding the structural tendencies of the global system and their ideological roots. Together "agency" ("actors" digitally interacting and constituting "places" via electronically mediated encounters) and structure (the hierarchically ordering of networks of "places") are key analytical concepts for societal analysis (see Rossi, 1983, 1993). A certain degree of democratization and universalization of digital communication provides access to instantaneous and worldwide exchanges of cultural, political, and economic nature to a greater number of individual and corporate actors than ever before. At the same time, it is true that the control of digital technologies makes the hierarchic ordering of micro- and macroglobal structures stronger. A penetrating sociological analysis of contemporary globalization rests on these two reciprocally constituted principles: the focus on digitally interacting actors as they reproduce hierarchically ordered networks of "places" under ideological and structural controls; and the critical reflection and counter-reaction of human agencies to these mechanisms of control. In my previous essay on globalization as a dialectic process I discussed the three main structures and related agencies existing within nations and also cross-nationally.

It is true that there exists an overload in the quantity and speed of information (hypermodernity), but these processes stimulate the selective orientation and the self-steering capabilities of social actors; these skills of social mastering are critical for survival. Self-reflection and critical capability are key features of global consciousness. Human agency has a new preeminent role in our digital time: to detect the ideological anchoring that perpetuates the unevenness and exploitative nature of global structures.

The continuous formation of new "places," meaning and identity, the growing reflexivity of global consciousness, and the ensuing tension among and interaction between agency and structure are all indispensable elements of globalization analysis.

References Cited and Bibliography

Albrow, M. (1990). "Globalization, knowledge and society: An introduction." In M. Albrow, & E. King (Eds.), *Globalization, knowledge and society*. London: Sage, pp. 3–16.

Auge', M. (2000). *Non-places*. Tr. John Howe. New York: Verso.

Braun, R. (2002). "Anomalous territories, an essay." http://devolve.aaeol.ca/online/rb-english.html

Casey, E. S. (2003). "Smooth spaces and rough-edged places: The hidden history of place," http://www.sunysb.edu/philosophy/faculty/papers/casey2.htm

Castells, M. (2000). *The rise of network society* (2nd edition). Malden, MA: Blackwell.

Curry, M. R. (2002). "Discursive displacement and the seminal ambiguity of space and place" in *The Handbook of new media*, eds. Leah Lierouw and Sonia Livingstone. London: Sage Publications.

Durkheim, E. (1961 (1912)). *Elementary forms of religious life*. New York: Collier.

Harvey, D. (1989/1990). *The condition of postmodernity*. Oxford: Blackwell.

Heidegger, M. (1977). "The age of the world picture." In Tr. L. Lovitt, *The question concerning technology and other essays*. New York: Garland, pp. 115–154.

Innis, R. E. (1999). "SRB insights: Cassirer's soft edge." *The semiotic review of books*, Vol. 10(1), pp. 10–12. See http://www.chass.utoronto.ca/epc/srb/srb/cassirer.html

Jameson, F. (2000). "Globalization and political strategy," *New Left Review*, 4, July–August. http://www.newleftreview.net/NLR23803.shtml

Lash, S. (2002). *Critique of information*. London: Sage.

Levi-Strauss, C. (1972). *Salvage mind*. Chicago: University of Chicago.

Ritzer, G. (2003). *The globalization of nothing*. London: Sage.

Robertson, R. (1992). *Globalization: Social theory and global culture*. Newbury Park, CA: Sage Publications.

Rossi, I. (1983). *From the sociology of symbols to the sociology of signs: Toward a dialectic sociology* (translated in Japanese). New York: Columbia University Press.

—— (1993). *Community reconstruction after an earthquake: Dialectical sociology in action*. Westport, CT: Praeger.

Scholte, J. A. (2000). *Globalization: A critical introduction*. New York: St. Martin's Press.

Soja, E. J. (1991). *Postmodern geographies: The reassertion of space in critical social theory.* Verso.

Urry, J. (2002). *Global complexity.* London: Polity Press.

Virilio, P. (1995). "Speed and information: cyberspace alarm!" in C Theory. http://www.ctheory.net/text_ file.asp?pick=72

Wittgenstein, L. (1961). *Tractatus logico-philosophicus,* Tr. D. F. Pears and Brian F. McGuinness. London: Routledge and Kegan Paul.

Part 4
Commentaries and Discussion

17
Globalization: In Search of a Paradigm

JANET ABU-LUGHOD

This book explores new terrain, as well as retraces well-trodden paths, in an effort to clarify the different definitions, theories, and research methods social scientists are deploying in search of the nebulous phenomena of globalization. One must admire the ecumenical courage of the editor who has assembled and given rough order to the chapters—some of which were papers presented in panels on the subject that he organized at various professional meetings—without forcing them into a consistent mold.

To do so would clearly have been premature, if not ultimately foolhardy. The provocative chapters trace approaches that are so diverse in their concepts and methods that, at the minimum, they throw into sharp relief the preparadigmatic state of the art. It may well be that, as Leslie Sklair suggests in his chapter, "Globalization as a sociological concept has always been too frail to sustain the theoretical and substantive burdens loaded on to it." Or as James Rosenau complains in his contribution, "It is almost as if globalization defies the theoretical enterprise, being too amorphous and complex to allow for the framing and testing . . . of empirical hypotheses." Or, more harshly put by Jonathan Friedman: any global approach that assumes that the global is an empirical field in its own right is a "victim of misplaced concreteness." So we have a real problem.

I personally do not believe that we shall ever reach agreement on a single paradigm. If anything, we have too many paradigms that follow from the preferred starting points of theoretical assumptions that currently co-exist in the social sciences and are not likely to be resolved. But these "too many notes" (what

353

Solieri accused Mozart's music as containing) are part of the excitement and promise of studies of globalization.

And yet, in this confusing landscape, one can discern clusters of agreement, often but not always related to the disciplines in which the authors work and the methods they use, and there are moments in which their paths cross in unexpected dialogues. First, one might call attention to areas of agreement. Underlying almost every chapter is the thesis that globalization is a process by which cultural groups, nations, and classes are drawn into greater interaction and interdependence. The major disagreements are over whether this is "new under the sun" or merely is an extension of past patterns, due to newer social and technological innovations. In addition, the authors evaluate the consequences of this process differently, some marveling that even moments of order can occur in a sea of chaos, others deploring the cruel inequalities that flow inevitably from advanced capitalism on a world scale. In what follows, I try to identify several clusters of approaches.

One such cluster draws its roots from Max Weber's seminal discussion of "Class, Status, Party,"[1] which gave us the threefold societal dimension of economic, cultural, and political organization and the basic problematics of how they are related in given societies. Although they make different uses of these Weberian categories, both Ino Rossi in Chapter 1 and Leslie Sklair in Chapter 3 frame their discussions of globalization in these terms, assuming that advanced capitalism drives the contemporary relationship.[2] Following Weber, they identify the emergent supremacy of the capitalist economy, now writ larger over more and more of the world's territory via its transnational class. Sklair is more critical of this hegemonic set of transnational operatives than is Rossi, not on the grounds of the "iron cage" but, as Sklair alleges, because of two negative consequences of its control, namely increasing class polarization and ecological degradation, which will doom it to fail.

To some extent, Rudolph Stichweh, following Weber's heir apparent Talcott Parsons, also falls into this structuralist–functionalist camp, although with greater sophistication. Although most of the authors in this cluster pay lip-service to the fact that the local and the global are not distinct entities but are jointly embedded in the same overarching system—what Stichweh refers to as the eigenstructure— all tend to make the global dominant, and minimize the interactions with and the reactions from "lower levels" of the system. This leads Stichweh into the uncomfortable position of positing culturally incompatible regionalisms, forcing him to

---

[1] See pp. 180–195 in *From Max Weber: Essays in Sociology*, translated by Gerth and Mills (New York: Oxford University Press, 1946). "Class" falls into economics, "status" groups into culture, and "party" is clearly the wrong word for Weber's intended meaning, the political factions or states.

[2] Rosenau is not satisfied that the issue is so easily resolved. He complains that global theory has failed to explain how the social, political and cultural dimensions of globalization interact with the economic dimension – the basic thrust of Weber's approach.

reluctantly agree with, but then deny Huntington's "clash of civilizations" thesis. Because all subsystems must be fitted into the "social system," which he claims is now dominant as a world system, there is a declining place for deviant social systems (i.e., the Islamic), as new structures overlay old structures but do not extinguish them.[3] Nor does he posit any possible reversal in the dominant eigenstructure via Wallerstein's anti-systemic movements or Sklair's hoped-for world socialism. The Thatcher slogan of "there is no alternative" (alluded to in Giovanni Arrighi's contribution) is a dismal prospect, especially inasmuch as Stichweh has already pointed out such negative attributes of the new period in world history as global inequality and national and international wars!

Margaret Archer, a British sociologist, sees some hope for achieving Parsonian systemic coherence through the development of world governance. Her discussion privileges the hard won congruence that European countries allegedly achieved between their institutional orders and their social orders. She fears that this coherence is being lost in the process of globalization with its "slicing through national boundaries, demolishing their internal settlements between the system and the social."[4] Unlike Sklair's dream of world socialism, she puts her faith in world government in which all can become world "citizens," participating in governance à la "Western" mode. She does not tell us how the poor can have a better voice in that participation.

A second cluster of authors seems to deny the overarching necessity for coherent eigenstructures or world government as prerequisites for "order." Two in particular try to grapple with the question of how microinteractions can fashion order out of chaos in at least parts of the global market. In their approach, they seem to contend that there is no overarching eigenstructure, or even a set of "masters of the universe," but only constant adjustments in flows. I doubt whether either would really want to go this far. Karin Knorr Cetina's fascinating description of the 24/7 process whereby exchange rates in financial markets are constantly set and reset by individual traders working simultaneously on computers around the world, posits "scopic concentration" as the new mechanism creating order of sorts, but one must recognize that this is a very narrow band of interactions with a narrow function. John Urry also hypothesizes that a fluid order of individual capitalist transactions can create some order out of inevitable chaos.[5] Both assume that no macroinstitutional system is in control, certainly an odd position, at least for Urry, whose earlier work with Scott Lash explored the consequences of *The End of Organized Capitalism*. And Knorr

---

[3] The parallel to Marx's discussion of the process whereby older social formations live on in later ones is obvious to this reader, although no citation to Marx appears.

[4] Could she mean mostly Great Britain before the massive immigration from dark-skinned former colonies? And there still remains the lack of "settlement" between indigenous religious groups in Northern Ireland. She also blames the "slicing of boundaries," in part, on the invention of the World Wide Web in 1989 (!), but surely these trends began much earlier.

[5] Shades of Adam Smith's invisible hand!

Cetina's ill-conceived leap, from her description of computer-driven financial markets and the single-minded concentration of their operators, which surely must have been based on fieldwork, to her amateur discussion of Al-Qaeda, as if its organization had no basis except in "light" information flows, is disappointing to say the least.[6] More attuned to reality is the small section on terrorism in Jonathan Friedman's wonderful and tendentious chapter, in which he points to the parallels with Christian (and he could have added Zionist) fundamentalism, organized through institutions, although obviously assisted by the Internet and other media developments.

The most coherent "school" of theorists engaged in empirical work is, of course, world-system scholars such as Christopher Chase-Dunn, Giovanni Arrighi, and Robert Schaeffer, even though their chapters in this volume sample only a small fraction of the rich empirical studies that have been generated under this paradigm.[7] Each, however, takes up a different part of the problematics posed by the historically embedded thesis pioneered in Wallerstein's seminal works, namely, to trace changing patterns in the ever unequal relations between hegemonic core regions and their semi-peripheries and peripheries.

Chase-Dunn and Jorgenson give a progress report on their ongoing empirical attempts to measure cycles in international trade over the past two centuries (more spiral than cyclical, I would contend) and financial investment–debt cycles over the past decades. To its credit, this chapter is the only one in the volume that tries to load empirical data on a model and that takes a longer historical approach to globalization as an ongoing process. Ideally, of course, they should be using flow data free from the confinement of national boundaries, but it is remarkable how much they can tell us within the limitations of existing data sets that can only measure intercountry transactions, a strange but unavoidable anomaly in a theory that stresses the openness of political conquests, unequal exchanges, and capitalist exploitation.

One notes the inevitable interdependence between theory and data, for without theory and "real world" political savvy, they would be hard-pressed to explain their findings. Particularly in their analysis of the post-1974 developments, their data reveal a shift from investment in production and trade into finance capital, which coincides with the abandonment of the Bretton Woods agreement and the deregulation of international monetary arrangements. This may just illustrate the primacy of politics over economics.

Their chapter raises the question of generic (or ideological) globalization, a topic taken up more systematically by Giovanni Arrighi. Both Chase-Dunn and

---

[6] *Editor's Footnote.* Knorr Cetina deals with Al Qaeda's communication networks as an example of microglobal structures rather than dealing with a systematic explanation of Al Qaeda as a form of global terrorism.

[7] One wishes that at least one analysis of commodity chains had been included in this volume. For a discussion of premodern commodity chains, see, for example, Terrence Hopkins and Immanuel Wallerstein, "Commodity Chains in the World-Economy," in *The Essential Wallerstein* (New York: The New Press, 2000), pp. 221–233.

Arrighi assume that the state, despite premature announcements of its death, remains the key actor in the global system. And it is the differential powers of states, between the core and other regions, that is the true eigenstructure within which international and class inequalities are produced and reproduced. It is institutional dominance by the "developed nations" that, by enforcing self-serving policies in such "international governance" bodies as the World Bank and the IMF, as well as national policy setters such as the U.S. and U.K. treasuries, account for the particular findings Arrighi explores in this chapter: the central issue of hegemony re-enters through the empirical door, even if the data are still aggregated at the country and regional levels. Comparing changes in the economic structures of the core (First World, sometimes now termed "the North") and various regions and levels of the "periphery" (increasingly, the preferred albeit imprecise term is now "the South") over the past four decades, he demonstrates an anomaly that cannot be explained except by their differential power. Thus, despite successful industrial developments in countries outside the core and the shift of manufacturing shares to the latter, except for a brief reversal in the 1970s, the gap in income and wealth between the core and the periphery has remained relatively constant. This suggests that powerful forces are operating to protect the West/North's hegemony.[8]

A second explanation for the major finding that poor countries remain behind, no matter what they do, is provided in Robert Schaeffer's factually rich proposition that in the core, the substitution of manufactured/synthetic products for the raw materials the periphery traditionally provided, as well as recycling and conservation (and we might add agricultural subsidies), have kept "natural" commodity prices artificially low. As an agricultural economist/historian, he does not include petroleum, for which no adequate substitute has yet been invented.[9] The current instability in the oil market, along with rising prices due to burgeoning demands by such "southern" giants as China and India, however, may yet change this. Is there vegetable/corn oil in our future?

Raymond Grew supports the attempts of the world-system political economists to incorporate historical trends in their analyses. His wise chapter makes a solid plea for the inclusion of history in the study of contemporary globalization, which makes his approach compatible with the theories if not the data of the foregoing authors. On the debate concerning whether today's globalization represents a quantum leap or merely an increase in scale and intensity facilitated by the enhanced annihilation of space by time, he comes out on the side of history, suggesting that the study of prior moments of integration (and disintegration) can yield important insights into present trends. Case studies of earlier times and different places can, at the minimum, deepen our perspectives on globalization.

---

[8] It is interesting to note that the themes of chaos and governance, associated with Urry and Archer, make their appearance in a recent collection edited by Arrighi and Silver. See their *Chaos and Governance in the Modern World System.*

[9] This, of course, explains the temporary reversal in the 1970s.

Although Saskia Sassen does not consider herself a world-system theorist, nor has she yet embedded her economic research in a longer historical framework (although she is heading that way), I see much in common between her work on world cities and the problematics addressed in world-system analysis. Like them, she sees geographic space as central to the structure of the world economy, but her ability to trace class differences within, as well as between, nations and cities, allows her to dissect the mechanisms of control and exploitation that are embedded (imbricated) in localities, whether these are countries, global cities, or in the headquarters of more transient transnational corporations. I should point out that the empirical work she has done on microstructures/actions,[10] unfortunately not presented in her more theoretical chapter in this volume, parallels the preoccupation of world-system's theorists with the causes and consequences of inequality. Her major thesis, however, that world cities are central to the process of strategic transnationalism, yields the same conclusion as theirs: money and power go together and their gain is at the expense of "peripheral" workers, whether abroad or in situ. In this she shares the world-system approach of political economy.

One of the themes that runs through most of the chapters in this collection is whether the global and the local can be considered separately or whether each can only be understood by integrating them, by studying both micro- and macrointeractions in real places and with real subjects who create meanings and experience global effects mediated by their experiences with them.[11] This may be a false dichotomy, because it depends upon the scale of the inquiry and the research question. We have seen that the world-system scholars, given their questions, fall on the side of the global focus, seeing localities in aggregate. That is not a complete story, however. Other researchers, not represented here but working within their general framework, have produced stunning case studies that trace how external forces interact with local structures. And as observed above, Sassen has done both, but in separate, more locationally specific sites. All these thinkers would resist the idea that the global and the local can be separated.

The anthropologists tend to dismiss the validity of macroanalyses that do not pay attention to how the global is actually received, interpreted, adapted, and given meaning. The prime interest of Martin Albrow and Jonathan Friedman, both of whom insist upon ethnographic methods of research, is in the interaction between external and internal, because only through the local does the global materialize and become visible. The most outspoken statement of this position is made by Friedman in, what I must confess, is my personal favorite in this volume. He baldly states that "the global is not something other than the local, on a higher plane. The global simply refers to the properties of the systemic processes that connect

---

[10] I am thinking here of her path-breaking ethnographic studies of informal labor in global cities.

[11] Or, in the case of Rosenau's more complex typology, see his table distinguishing four levels of scale in relation to eight sources of globalization, with little guidance to its operationalization.

the world's localities . . . and is at least as old as commercial civilizations. . . ."[12]
And later,

> [t]he global is always about interlocal relations, not about a supralocal organism. . .
> . Any global approach that assumes that the global is an empirical field in its own
> right is a victim of misplaced concreteness. The global is manifested in specific
> combinations with localities and is a product of a particular historical context.

Although he insists, along with Albrow, that contemporary ethnographies must attend to this interaction as their prime focus,[13] he is enough of a historian to admit that what can't be studied in place (dead people and disappeared cultures) can still be studied as a macroproblem, especially inasmuch as he insists that globalization is as old as commercial civilization.

Finally, most authors seem to be caught up in a debate over whether current patterns of globalization represent a new phenomenon or are merely a continuation of an ongoing process in world history. This strikes me as a completely unproductive argument. Advocates of "newness" stress recent technological innovations, especially in the means of communications, that have speeded up the velocity and extended the reach of potential connections in an unprecedented manner. Those whose inquiries enjoy a longer historical perspective do not deny that technological changes—in transportation as well as communication—mark critical turning points in the structure of global relations, but point out that in the past there have been equally dramatic revolutions speeding up and extending the reach of contacts. They do tend, however, to emphasize the unequal access to such innovations, not only in technologies of transport and communication but in social innovations that are part and parcel of what I have called the "shape of the world-system." So there is both continuity and newness. This, indeed, is the proper agenda for investigation.

I began my remarks by suggesting that not only do we not have a single paradigm but that I doubt we shall ever. This is not a defect in the study of globalization but actually one of its strengths. It is not unlike the old canard of blind men examining the elephant. Each partial view is both correct for what it observes but basically incomplete and therefore "biased" by its narrow focus and its preconceived theoretical assumptions. Each inquiry, when honestly conducted and devoid of ideological prejudgment, can contribute to our understanding of the most important contemporary questions of how the world works. That this volume captures some of the complexities and engages competing perspectives in dialogue is its true contribution to our ongoing search for

---

[12] In fact, the first time I came across the work of Friedman and Kajsa Ekholm was in the late 1970s when they were examining ancient world-systems, work that encouraged me to pursue my study of pre-Wallersteinian world-systems.

[13] One of my favorite illustrations of this methodology is Friedman's own description of the use of "degriefed" Parisian high fashion labels as decorations on the high stockings of competitive male dancers in Africa. See his *"The Political Economy of Elegance: An African Cult of Beauty"* (1990).

clarification and description in the fuzzy realm not only of globalization but of social science itself.

References Cited and Bibliography

Arrighi, Giovanni and Beverly J. Silver (1999). *Chaos and Governance in the Modern World System* Minneapolis: University of Minnesota Press.
Ekholm, Kajsa (1980). "On the limitations of civilization: The structure and dynamics of global systems," *Dialectical Anthropology* 5.
—— and Jonathan Friedman (1979). "'Capital,' imperialism and exploitation in ancient world systems," in M.T. Larsen, ed., *Power and Propaganda: A Symposium of Ancient Empires* (Copenhagen).
Friedman, Jonathan (1990). "The political economy of elegance: An African cult of beauty," *Culture and History* 7.
—— (1994). *Culture, Identity and Global Process.* Thousand Oaks, CA: Sage.
Lash, Scott and John Urry (1988). *The End of Organized Capitalism.* Madison, University of Wisconsin Press.
Sassen, Saskia (1988). *The Mobility of Labor and Capital.* Cambridge, UK: Cambridge University Press.
—— (1991). *Global Cities: New York, London, Tokyo.* Princeton, NJ: Princeton University Press.
—— (1998). "Service Employment Regimes," in her *Globalization and its Discontents.* New York: New Press.
Terrence Hopkins and Immanuel Wallerstein, "Commodity Chains in the World-Economy," in *The Essential Wallerstein* (New York: The New Press, 2000), pp. 221–233.
Wallerstein, Immanuel (1974). *The Modern World System, Vol. I.* New York: Academic Press.
—— (2000). *The Essential Wallerstein.* New York: New Press.
Weber, Max (1946). "Class, status and party," which appears pp. 180–195 in *From Max Weber: Essays in Sociology,* translated by Gerth and Mills (New York).

18
A "New" Global Age, but Are There New Perspectives on It?

GEORGE RITZER

A reader might have at least two kinds of expectations of a volume such as this one. One is to anticipate finding well-known ideas explored, lines of thinking broadened, and research directions extended. Such a book becomes a valuable summary of not only recent work in the field, but an overview of much of it. It also often offers a sense of where the field has been and/or where it is headed. The other is to expect some brand-new ideas, directions of thought, and research initiatives. Admittedly, the latter is a rarity in anthologies such as this one because such work is more likely to appear in journal articles or research monographs, but the hope is always there. This anthology, like most of this genre, is more in line with the first set of expectations than the second. The essays that are included are heavily weighted in the direction of the conceptual and the theoretical reflections on extant work rather than offering any major breakthroughs. There is comparatively little that is empirical (among the exceptions is the essay by Chase Dunn and Jorgenson),[1] and that which

---

[1] *Editor's Note*: The "careful" reader will notice that there are many more "exceptions." Knorr Cetina's essay is based primarily on her own first-hand research of global financial markets; the last section of Sklair's essay offers a research framework inspired by his empirical study of transnational business practices in urban architecture; Friedman's theorizing and methodological prescriptions are based on his field work of many years; similar observations apply to the essay of Sassen; Arrighi's thesis is backed by World Bank data; Albrow takes off from his field work in London; Grew heavily draws upon extensive historical research; analogous observations apply to Kneller, Schaeffer, and Rossi's essays. This makes 11 out of 17 chapters that are based on empirical and/or historical data in toto or in crucial sections. Ritzer uses the term "empirical" in an unusually restrictive sense.

is represented is more on the order of normal science than paradigmatic break-throughs. Nevertheless, this anthology is of utility, at least in part because a number of major players in the field of globalization studies offer overviews and insights into their ideas as well as those of others.

In reflecting on the essays in this book I was put in mind of the work of two important contributors to the literature on globalization, Ulrich Beck and Martin Albrow (the latter also represented in this collection). They, and many others, have been critical of the continued existence and use of modern theories and concepts in an era beyond classical modernity (to Beck, reflexive modernity and to Albrow the "global age").

Beck (2001) has argued in many places that we continue to be in the thrall of, and to use, what he calls "zombie concepts." These are ideas that, like the zombies in the movies, are the living dead. That is, they are dead, or at least they ought to be, but in fact they continue to live (or at least to be in a state of something approaching life) and to be used in scholarly work. This, of course, is a highly critical view of social science in general, and the sociology of globalization in particular. Sociologists[2] are seen as looking at, thinking about, and theorizing a phenomenon (such as globalization) that in the eyes of many is a very new development, through the lenses of a number of old, if not moribund, ideas. The issue is: how can we gain a lively new sense of these nascent phenomena and developments through the use of concepts that are dead (or nearly so) and ought, in the eyes of some, to remain so.

This is a powerful critique of much work in the social sciences, but it is weakened by the fact that Beck, himself, continues to use such zombie concepts as, for example, "modernity," albeit "reflexive modernity."[3] However, even though Beck falls into the trap of using such concepts, that does not mean that we ought not to take his arguments and criticisms about the continued use of zombie concepts seriously.

A similar theme, albeit in different terms, informs Albrow's (1996) *The Global Age*. Albrow sees an epochal change underway by the 1990s (perhaps it has occurred by now?); we are moving from the Modern Age to the Global Age. However, he argues that we have great difficulty seeing, understanding and analyzing this transformation because we continue to operate from a modern perspective (which, among other things, actively seeks to conceal the change) and we persist in using modern concepts, ideas, and theories. Thus, in Albrow's view, we need a whole new conceptual and theoretical arsenal in order to deal with the Global Age in anything approaching an adequate manner.

In spite of the admonitions of thinkers such as Beck and Albrow, it is clear in this volume, and in the literature on globalization more generally, that in the main we continue to operate with, even to be imprisoned by, modern zombie like concepts and theories. Interestingly, one of the authors (James Rosenau) represented in this

---

[2] I focus on sociologists here, because most of the authors in this volume represent that discipline, but they are far from being the only social scientists to employ zombie concepts.
[3] The concept of reflexivity may also already be passing into the status of a zombie concept since it became popular in the early 1990s as a result of the work of Anthony Giddens (2000). This leads to the view that we may be living in an era in which concepts become zombie like at a much more rapid pace and much more quickly than ever before.

book, and guilty of this tendency himself, has elsewhere made much the same point: "Social scientists, like the people they study, are prone to habitual modes of behavior, and thus are more likely to cast their inquiries into habitual frameworks that are taken for granted than to treat their organizing principles as problematic" (Rosenau, cited in McGrew, forthcoming). I hasten to add that I am at least as guilty of this as anyone. For example, my thinking on the contemporary world in general, and globalization in particular, in terms of McDonaldization (Ritzer, 1993/2004) was heavily influenced by Weber's theory of rationalization. No theory is more modern (except perhaps for Marx's), and no idea goes more to the heart of the modern world, than rationalization. More recently, I dusted off and redefined the hoary old concept of "nothing" (Ritzer, 2004) in order to further theorize globalization. This is not to argue that there is not utility in using zombie concepts such as rationalization and nothing, as well as many of the ideas that appear in this volume, or even better redefining them for a new social world, but such ideas exist in abundance. Where are the new ideas, concepts, and theories? Whatever the answer to that question, I want to make it clear that the following critique of the work of some of my peers represented in this volume applies at least as well to my own work in this area.

That being said, I want to look at the essays in this volume, or at least most of them, in terms of the degree to which they find themselves in the "prison house" of modern concepts and theories (Jameson, 1975). Overlapping this, in part, is the degree to which the authors are locked into their own previous, undoubtedly modern, work.

The most notable example of the latter is Archer's "Social Integration, System Integration and Global Governance" in which she trots out, once again, a theory and concepts that have informed her work for decades. Not only that, but the theory (systems theory) and associated ideas are deeply entrenched, as Albrow (1996) argues, in a modernist perspective. In fact, she makes no bones about her goal of basing her chapter on the "harnessing one of the most fruitful generic frameworks to the analysis of globalization, its impacts upon prior social configurations and its consequences for posterior ones." Archer is simply more explicit about, and uncritical of, a reliance on extant modern perspectives than most others who do much the same thing. In addition, Archer is one of those who not only falls into the modernist trap, but also does little more than repeat previous modernist arguments. This is the case, even more clearly, with Rosenau's "Three Steps Toward a Viable Theory of Globalization" which repeats, perhaps verbatim, ideas explicated in his 2003 book, *Distant Proximities* (and relies heavily on such highly modern approaches as the micro–macro distinction and a levels-of-analysis approach).[4]

---

[4] *Editor's Note*: In this essay Rosenau adds the novelty of a third—"relational"—methodological step; this is an important novelty as it is evident in Friedman's and Albrow's emphasis on relational analysis. Sklair's systematic formulation of an empirically oriented research framework represents a significant addition beyond his previous works; besides, in this essay he adds "cosmopolitanism" as an additional component to his notion of "generic globalization."

Much the same is true of Sklair's "The Transnational Framework for Theory and Research in the Study of Globalization," which also largely repeats ideas to be found in his books (e.g., Sklair, 2002) (for clarifications on this claim see Footnote 4) and is operating from, embedded in, the most modern of theories, Marxian theory. This theory also informs, at least in part, Rossi's remarks, especially his dialectical orientation (also, not surprisingly given his well-known orientation, it is central to Kellner's analysis of 9/11 and Al Qaeda). More generally, Rossi's modern orientation is also reflected in his tendency, one that I often resort to in my own work (and, as we have seen, is employed by Rosenau), to look at the social world from the perspective of "levels" of social analysis. This creation of a hierarchical system of distinctions is a familiar modern ploy, almost as common as creating all sorts of binaries. ["Modern" and "postmodern" à la Ritzer is, of course, another binary ploy. *Editor's remark*]

Urry's "Global Complexities" also repeats arguments made in a recent book, albeit with a slightly different title, *Global Complexity* (2003). However, Urry's work has the merit of not simply trotting out a range of well-known modern sociological ideas, but rather seeking to bring into the discussion ideas and theories, for example, quantum theory and its unpredictabilities, developed in other fields. This may not be new theory, but it at least constitutes an effort to bring in ideas new to the field and to do something new in terms of thinking about globalization. Although both his work and his basic concept are far less well known (at least in sociology) than Urry's, Stichweh utilizes a concept—*eigenstructures*—that has heretofore been largely restricted to mathematics and statistics, in order to think about globalization. In lieu of new ideas, such an attempt is generally to be welcomed. However, in this case it is not clear what this terms adds analytically beyond extant terminology. In fact, Stichweh's essay is devoted to a series of well-known ideas and phenomena that he groups under that heading including the function system, formal organizations, networks, and so on. After surveying a range of these, he concludes that these *eigenstructures* are not (or are not simply) producers of uniformity, but also "nonlocal diversity." An interesting, if not unique idea, but one wonders what the concept of *eigenstructures* adds to our understanding of it.

Knorr Cetina revisits her now well-known research and thinking on global currency markets, but supplements it with an original (at least for me) analysis of the new terrorist societies from much the same orientation. The perspective used and developed, and it is an important one, is microglobalization, as well as the need to extend it to deal with "distantiated spatial configurations." This is especially important because the literature on globalization is dominated by far by a concern with macroglobalization. Although microglobalization is an important idea, it is largely derived from, and analyzed through, the lens of various modern theories,[5] most notably here Schutz's phenomenology. Even more telling is the fact that it is lodged in the general tendency in modern thinking to deal in binaries, in this case the macro–micro distinction. In her conclusion, Knorr Cetina seeks to make clear the need to deal with them in a more dialectical fashion (also, as we've seen,

---

[5] As is the idea of "distanciation," derived from Giddens's work.

an orientation embedded in ultra-modern theory), however, the fact remains that she continues to be clearly informed by, and to utilize, the macro–micro distinction. Again, I hasten to add that this distinction, as well as the dialectical relationship between micro and macro, has long informed my own theoretical orientation (Ritzer, 1991). However, the issue remains: are we well-advised to continue to use old ideas, even in new ways, in thinking about globalization, or do we need to develop new concepts and theories more appropriate to it and to what is presumed to be a new age?

Sklair is one who is to be applauded for attempting, over a number of years, to develop a new theoretical approach to globalization and for developing new theoretical ideas to be deployed in thinking about, and studying, that process. Most notable are his ideas (see also Robinson, 2004) of transnational practices, corporations, a capitalist class, and, most innovatively, a culture-ideology of consumption. Although these are useful ideas, as is the overall transnational perspective in which they are embedded, there is little that is new in the essay in this volume.[6] More troubling is the fact that these ideas are deployed within the framework of a very modern and fairly conventional Marxian analysis. Can Marx's ideas, no matter how much they are modified and expanded, be adequate for analyzing the new realities of the Global Age?

Not surprisingly, the anthropologist, Jonathan Friedman, makes the case for an anthropology of globalization. (And, equally unsurprisingly the historian Raymond Grew makes the case for the role of historical studies in gaining a better understanding of globalization.) Specifically he argues for what he calls a "global systemic anthropology" which, in spite of its apparent focus on the global system, continues to concentrate on the local. The idea that the global is somehow an entity separable from the local, one that can be studied apart from it, is rejected. Given this, it is again of little surprise that the anthropologist makes the case for ethnography (as does Albrow, see below), perhaps at multiple sites, as the method to study global systemic matters. In fact, Friedman is highly critical

---

[6] *Editor's Note*: As mentioned in Editor's Note 4, Sklair's essay adds new elements to his previous work. The same is true of other contributions to this volume in which Ritzer, however, finds no novel ideas of a "postmodern" type. The preoccupation with deciding what is modern or postmodern in theorizing seems to prevent Ritzer from realizing that various essays in this volume contain "emergent conceptualizations" in the study of globalization. The issue is that Ritzer's perspective is under the glare of the . . . flashy theorizing of Ulrich Beck, which, in this case, is based on a questionable (and empirically yet to be proven) theory of second modernity. One would have liked to see Ritzer engaged in a serious discussion of the foundational premises of Beck's (so-called) second modernity and related postnational (cosmopolitan) perspective. These questionable views (and their blinding effects on our critic) are carefully debated in the last chapter of this volume where more defensible (and more grounded) conceptualizations by various contributors to this volume are singled out and defended. (The ideological nature of certain types of cosmopolitanism is discussed in Friedman's essay in this volume.) The reader will have to judge for himself or herself what theorizing is genuinely novel (and empirically grounded) and what is glamorous (but empirically unsubstantiated). In the final essay I argue that Beck's structuration theory of individualization and his atomized conception of social structure exemplify the latter type of theorizing.

of those, who he often pejoratively labels ideologists, who see something very new here and attempt to conceptualize it in new ways using terms such as hybridity and translocality. He also calls those who are guilty of this (e.g., Robertson, Appadurai, Hannerz) "new globalizers." If, in fact, there is something new here (which Friedman tends to deny), aren't new globalizers exactly what we need? Friedman sees them as mistaking their own elite, translocal, jet-set life as "traveling intellectuals" for the life of the vast majority of people in the world that is still embedded in the local. Indeed, for Friedman (and most students of globalization) the central reality is that the global is embedded in the local.

Thus, Friedman seems hostile to the new ideas of the "new globalizers," but he goes beyond that to imply criticism of other new perspectives, especially postmodern (e.g., Deleuze and Guattari) and posttructural (i.e., Butler) theory. Such a stance is in stark contrast, as the reader will see, to the position adopted at the close of this commentary. Although Grew, as we have seen, also makes the case for his discipline (history) in the study of globalization, he is far less dismissive of other perspectives (including those who theorize transitions to the global world) than is Friedman and in fact sees a role for social scientific generalizations (produced by Friedman's "new globalizers"?) as long as they are informed by (and influence) historical research.

Chase-Dunn and Jorgenson are not hostile to new ideas, but they are involved in "normal" science and, as Thomas Kuhn showed long ago, such work is not designed to create anything dramatically new, but rather to add small increments to an established body of knowledge. Chase-Dunn and Jorgenson make it clear that they are focusing on an issue—structural globalization within the domain of investment—and that this builds on work on trade globalization and anticipates further research on political globalization.

Arrighi's essay is a nice complement to that of Chase-Dunn and Jorgenson in that he embeds his analysis in their work on structural globalization. However, he critiques this idea on the grounds that this process has been going on for centuries. In his view, it is ideological rather than structural globalization that accounts better for global inequality. Key to the problems faced by less-developed nations is the idea, attributed to Margaret Thatcher, that "There is No Alternative." Yet, if the key lies in ideology, it is clear that there are alternatives; there are other ideas. Specifically, less-developed countries have the option of choosing a different ideology than the cut-throat capitalism espoused by developed countries such as the United States. There is much of merit in Arrighi's essay, however, it, too, has the quality of normal science operating within the structural/ideological globalization paradigm. As such it cannot offer much that is new, but it can and does attempt to clarify what it is that we know.

Schaeffer purports to use both old and new theoretical frameworks to analyze practices in core nations and their impact on primary producers in the periphery. His approach adopts some of the basic principles of world-system theory and integrates them with concerns (especially with technology) of the sociology of agriculture. This, in turn, has implications for other well-known theories of dependency, environment, and globalization (e.g., that globalization does not lead necessarily to greater integration but also to disintegration between, for example, the core and the periphery of the world system). Although Schaeffer examines the interrelationship among a series of extant theories, and even integrates two of them, it is difficult to see what is "new" in his theoretical orientation unless it is an integration that has not been undertaken before. But even if it is, it underscores the fact that there is woefully little that is genuinely new in the study of globalization, but much that draws upon, pits against, and integrates extant theoretical ideas.

As mentioned earlier, Kellner's analysis of 9/11 and its relationship to globalization is embedded, as his work almost always is, in a neo-Marxian, dialectical approach. It is also, like much of his work, oriented to the concrete world of today rather than to the elaboration of abstractions. Of course, such an orientation is endemic to his Marxian orientation (although, many, perhaps too many, Marxists have been lured away from material realities and in the direction of great abstractions). To his credit, Kellner has generally refused to be pulled in this direction and has persisted in usefully analyzing the contemporary world through the analytical perspective of his neo-Marxian orientation. One may not agree with his politics, but almost everyone can admire his ability to apply abstract ideas to the quotidian, if we can think of 9/11 in that way.

I should note again, before proceeding, that much of this critique of the essays in this volume is based on the premise that we need new ideas, theories, and empirical approaches to the study of globalization, but I should at least suggest that it is also possible that the era of globalization is not so different after all and that such a need does not exist. Maybe Albrow and many others are wrong and we do not live in, or are not even seeing the emergence of, a new global age.

Sassen continues to embed her analysis of globalization, as she has since her work on global cities, in a sociology of spaces and places; a social geography. I think this is a promising direction; one that I have followed in some of my recent work. However, what is interesting, at least in this essay, is that Sassen writes about social geography without citing, or embedding herself, in the work that lies at the base of that tradition (say, Lefebvre, Foucault, Soja, Auge, and so on). In saying this I seem to be critiquing her for avoiding the problem—over-commitment to extant paradigms—for which I have been critiquing most of the other contributors to this volume. However, although it may be that Sassen's creativity in this area is traceable to the fact that she studies place without being restricted by the extant paradigms of the study of it, it is also possible that her insights into place and globalization would have been enhanced by more explicit engagement with it. In other words, there needs to be a balance of embedding oneself in one's predecessors and going beyond them.

Albrow's case for the use of ethnography in this volume is consistent with the emphasis on the lives of people in *The Global Age*, or as he puts it in this volume, the focus should be on "the immediacies of local social experience under globalized conditions," or their "lived social relations." What he and others of his circle are interested in studying is the way the global is "inscribed in everyday life." As attractive as this might be, it is certainly not a new focus, nor does it compensate for the fact that Albrow is on the one hand announcing the emergence of a new global age, but making the case for its study using one of the oldest social scientific methods.

Thus, this has largely been a critique of the essays in this volume for being locked into, or returning to, extant perspectives, theories, methods, and paradigms. There is nothing new or unusual about this in scholarly work in the social sciences, but what makes it notable is that this intellectual set of retrogressions is combined with the study of what most observers agree is a new social phenomenon, globalization. There is certainly much to be gained by using, perhaps in new ways, old tools, yet there also must be room, no a crying need for, new tools for the new global age. One will need to look long and hard to find those new tools in the essays in this volume (plenty of them by Albrow, Knorr Cetina, Rossi, Sklair, Sassen, Stichweh, Urry are pointed out in the Editor's final remarks) or for that matter in most of the rest of the approaches in the social sciences to globalization. The reason is that we not only remain locked into older ideas, but find it far easier to employ them in new contexts than to create new ideas.

I have already confessed to the fact that I am guilty of much of this myself, including in my studies of globalization. However, as I've been writing this, it has dawned me that in doing this analysis I have reverted to an earlier part of my academic career (Ritzer, 1975, 1991) and am here doing a metasociological and metatheoretical analysis of the chapters in this volume. Although I obviously think that is useful, it also clearly illustrates the problem that underlies this volume-as well as my critique of it.

The question is: Is it possible to overcome the burdens of our intellectual past and produce genuinely new concepts and tools to analyze a new or dramatically changed social world? Clearly, we have been able to do this in the past. Marx's theory of capitalism with its profusion of original ideas and concepts is the premier example. However, do we need to return to the ancient past of the discipline to find examples of this? Ironically, I think a more recent example is one that is either ignored or excoriated in this volume, and that is postmodern theory. Interestingly, even with its explosive creation of a plethora of new concepts and perspectives, postmodern social theory seems to be all but dead in the social sciences. Even in globalization studies, in spite of exceptions such as the work of Hardt and Negri (2000), there is little use of postmodern ideas and theories. How do we explain the dominance of old ideas and theories, and the seeming rejection of a set of new (postmodern) ideas and theories, in globalization studies in particular, and the social sciences more generally? The answer to that question is far beyond the scope of this undertaking, but the fact that the question is even raised tells us much about globalization studies in particular and the state of the social sciences in general.

References

Albrow, Martin. *The Global Age*. Stanford, CA: Stanford University Press, 1996.
Anthony Giddens (2000). *Runaway world*. London: Routledge.

Beck, Ulrich. "Interview with Ulrich Beck." *Journal of Consumer Culture* 1, 2, 2001: 261–277.

Hardt, Michael and Antonio Negri. *Empire*. Cambridge, MA: Harvard University Press, 2000.

Jameson, Fredric. *The Prison House of Language*. Princeton, NJ: Princeton University Press, 1975.

McGrew, Anthony. "Globalization in hard times: Contention in the academy and beyond." In George Ritzer, ed. *Blackwell Companion to Globalization*. Oxford: England, forthcoming.

Ritzer, George. *Sociology: A Multiple Paradigm Science*. Boston: Allyn and Bacon, 1975.

—— *Metatheorizing in Sociology*. Lexington, MA: Lexington Books, 1991.

—— *The McDonaldization of Society*. Thousand Oaks, CA: Pine Forge Press, 1993/2004.

—— *The Globalization of Nothing*. Thousand Oaks, CA: Pine Forge Press, 2004.

Robinson, William, I. *A Theory of Global Capitalism: Production, Class and State in a Transnational World*. Baltimore, MD: Johns Hopkins University Press, 2004.

Rosenau, James N. *Distant Proximities: Dynamics Beyond Globalization*. Princeton, NJ: Princeton University Press, 2003.

Sklair, Leslie. *Globalization: Capitalism and Its Alternatives*. Oxford, UK: Oxford University Press, 2002.

Urry, John. *Global Complexity*. Cambridge, UK: Polity, 2003.

19
"Globalization" as Collective Representation: The New Dream of a Cosmopolitan Civil Sphere

JEFFREY C. ALEXANDER

By friends and foes alike, globalization is hailed as a revolutionary, path-breaking, *weltgeschichte* phenomenon. It solves the world's economic problems or condemns more of the world's people to poverty. It creates equality and cooperation or frightfully deepens inequality and hegemonic domination. It opens the way for world peace or it ushers in a new and nightmarish period of terrorism and war.

Is it possible to pry "globalization" out of the clutches of the rhetorical binaries that define the passionate simplifications of symbolic life?

Globalization is, indeed, one of the central facts of our time. It is a reference that must become central to the social sciences, but has not yet. In this respect, Beck's claim that modern social science is hobbled by methodological nationalism bears serious consideration (Beck, 2000).

But globalization is too important to be left to the "globalizers," to the entrepreneurs of globalization, whether economic, political, or intellectual, who have created what might be called "the discourse of globalization." The members of this carrier group make use of the facts of globality to suggest that the traditional rules of the game no longer hold, whether these are the traditional social "laws"

Editor's Note: Instead of a commentary on the whole book, Alexander and Collins have provided two essays that offer antithetical views to Beck's thesis (and Ritzer's "wondering") on the need of a new paradigm for globalization research. Having completed the major lines of my conclusive argument before I received Alexander's and Collin's chapters, in the conclusion I refer to excerpts from their essays to indicate concurring or parallel critiques they offer of Beck's and Ritzer's positions.

that link capitalist markets with economic inequality and undemocratic political power with domination, or traditional ideas of the modern disciplines of social science.[1]

About such apocalyptic or utopian claims we must be very cautious. Globalization is not an alternative reality that makes previous knowledge and social reality irrelevant. It is a long emerging if only recently risible and represented reality, a social phenomenon that in itself is neither sacred nor profane. It must be put back inside history and social science.

To begin this process, we might start with a compelling phrase of Anthony Giddens, one of globalization's leading intellectual ideologists. Globalization marks, according to Giddens (1990), a compression of space and time. To this I would wish to add a relatively friendly amendment. Compression affects not only the pragmatics but the semantics of communication, the basic meaning units, the symbolic languages upon which interactions depend. There exist not only new technologies of movement and communication but more condensed and transcendent cultural logics, such as democracy and human rights, that spread common understandings and structures of feeling more widely than before. It is by the compression of space, time, and meaning that globalization creates a significantly more expansive field of action and organization.

The question, however, is whether such an expansion marks a new order of magnitude, as Giddens and the other entrepreneurs of globalization suggest, such that radically new knowledge is necessary? If the answer to this question is no, and I believe it is, then why has in incremental change in scale so frequently been represented as a change of exponential magnitude? Could it be that this shift in the representational order itself represents the fundamental and radical change? If so, it is an aspect of globalization to which globalizing intellectuals have not paid sufficient attention.

We return later to this shift in the field of representation. Let us speak first of the mundane process of globalization. My hypothesis is that globalization should not be understood as something radically new. It marks rather another step in the millennia-long compression of time/space/meaning, and the corresponding expansion in reach of the institutions that represent them, that is, the extension of political, economic, and cultural organization and power (Mann, 1986).

In fact, far from being radically new knowledge, this process of compression/expansion already formed the central subject of modernization theory in the middle of the last century. More than any other historical transformation, it was the movement from "particular" and "local" to the "universal" and "national" that fascinated modernization theorists, who framed it as the movement from traditional to modern society. In retrospect, from the perspective created by postmodern critique, we can see this binary as both tragic and absurd. The first side of the

---

[1] I have in mind such globalizing intellectuals as Giddens, Held, Beck, Keane, and Kaldor (see Footnote 9). See later in this essay for a discussion of this intellectual carrier group and their theoretical and empirical claims.

binary represents a vast simplification, ignoring the extraordinary variation between different forms of earlier societies, for example, the giant power reach of early empires. The other side of the binary is also highly exaggerated. Nation and universal are as contradictory as synonymous. As for the much-heralded modernity of the 20th century, it turned out to be as barbaric as any recorded in the annals of traditional history. Nonetheless, the modernization theorists were right in thinking broadly about an historical enlargement of scope. Insofar as we are moving toward a more global playing field, we are in the midst of this familiar process. Social organizations and cultural structures alike are expanding their scope and reach.[2]

By emphasizing the familiarity of this process, and how it was a central topic for modernization theory, I want to suggest that, whether italicized, capitalized, or followed with an exclamation point, globalization does not represent an abrupt change. To understand it, we need not invent new or alternative knowledge. Rather, we must better apply the theoretical and empirical ideas already available, which means to orient them in a more global way.

Every process evoked in the globalization literature has already been conceptualized in studies of social and cultural transformations from local to national scale, which have traced sometimes incremental, sometimes abrupt enlargements in economic, political, military, religious, legal, penal, and cultural life. How these processes work has been conceptualized in a manner that has little to do with the scale of the nation as such.

Let us consider, for example, the classical theoretical writings of Marx, Weber, and Durkheim, and their systemic understandings of such social phenomena as class formation, mode of production, division of labor, functional differentiation, bureaucracy, stratification, authority, and power. Were the concepts and propositions created by these writings, in contrast with their more restricted empirical referents, dependent on national scale? The empirical equation of their own societies—identified in terms of nation, civilization, or class—with progress, universalism, and rationality was often myopic. But the classical theorizing about the organizational and cultural processes involved in sustaining universalism and particularism can largely still stand. The same is true for much of the modern theorizing we have inherited from such sociological thinkers as Parsons, Elias, Goffman, and Geertz. They, too, dealt centrally with universalizing processes and compressions of temporal, spatial, and cultural scale, and their insights also provide foundations for thinking about the globalizing phase we are experiencing today.

But in the impassioned and simplified rhetorics of globalization more is involved than merely empirical claims. There are moral assertions about justice being possible for the first time or no longer being possible again. There is a sense of imminence, of an historical shifting that, for better or for worse, has

---

[2] For a sympathetic reading of the progressive elements of modernization theory, and the contextualization of its critics, see Alexander (1995).

already transformed, or is about to, the basic meaning of social life. I wonder, however, whether globalization has, in fact, had any particular normative purchase? Does the compression of space, time, and meaning translate into justice and the good life?

Let's do a thought experiment. You are a citizen of Florence in the year 1500 and you are visited by the angel of history and vouchsafed a vision of the different, nationally organized world that is to come. Deeply inspired by this new vision of universalism, you turn to your companion in the palazzo and exclaim:

> Hey, you're not going to believe this, but there's going to be, starting in a hundred years or so, the birth of an amazing thing called the nation-state, and everything henceforth will be organized on a gigantically different scale. There will be an extraordinary compression of time and space, and everything, I mean everything, will be subject to the new law of nationalization. Someday, everything we take for granted—about economic life, war, science, customs, politics, religion, education— will be based, not on this little puny city or even this region, but on the great entity that will be called the nation.

Would you have been right, in that long ago Florentine time, to be so excited? Did nationalization turn out to be anything so great? It did represent a new compression of space, time, and meaning, and it had immense historical significance. But was it liberating in the normative sense? Did it have any particular moral purchase? Should we have heralded it in the kind of utopian manner that the economic, political, and intellectual entrepreneurs speak about globalization today?

The enthusiasm of our Florentine ancestor may be excused. The movement toward the city-state had once promised enlightenment, freedom, and justice, and he was already beginning to feel its restrictive corruptions full face. The promise of expanding to the national field seemed to provide a way out of that urban cul-de-sac. The promise of the nation made universalism still seem possible, just as the promise of the city had before. But this new promise to make the universal concrete turned out no differently. The social and moral possibilities of nationalization were rather more limited than its ideologists had thought.

Similar caution applies to the phase of time-space-meaning expansion in which we are participating today. Globalization is a mundane process that, in the course of the 20th century, has created at least as much trouble as possibility. The reach of markets has dramatically expanded, producing and distributing on a wider scale than ever before. These economic processes, however, have contributed as much to exploitation and poverty as to wealth creation and economic participation. Information from distant parts of the world has become increasingly available in real-time, but it has not become free floating and universal. Even the most rapidly circulated and easily available information remains attached to particular worldviews, interests, and powers. Rather than having displaced enslaving religious dogmas for liberating reason, such globalizing ideologies as nationalism, communism, fascism, and economic liberalism have merely provided secular versions of equally heinous and dogmatic constraint. Like the earlier world-historical belief systems that emerged from the Axial age, these modern ideologies have created supplicants and priests. In the name of purification and world transformation, they have justified massive violence and created havoc and mayhem on a global scale.[3] It is hardly surprising, in light of this modernist legacy, that so-called traditional religion has recently found on the global stage a new life.

As the world's territory has been scaled down from empires and up from cities, globalizing rhetorics charged nation-states with the mission of democracy and equality. It has been much more likely, however, for the new nations to become iron cages of suppression, with the universalism of the "people" becoming a camouflage for primordiality of some primitive kind. If nations represented a new phase of time/space/meaning compression, their expansionary powers have not necessarily been linked to individual freedom or civil rights. The origins of international law in the Treaty of Westphalia brought the destructive wars of religion to an end, but it did so by underscoring national sovereignty (Clark, 1999; Lipschutz, 1992). The treaty gave freedom and respect not to individuals but to states. We live still according to the tradition of international law that has nothing intrinsically to do with human rights (Cushman, 2005). With the significant exception of the European Union, which itself remains a regionally restricted power, no larger, more impartial, more universalistic, and more democratic entity has yet taken over from the nation-state.[4]

These sober reflections about 20th century globalization are underscored when we consider war, the national form of organized violence so conspicuously neglected by classical and modern social theory. Has it not been the very compression of time, space, and meaning that has allowed destructive violence and mass murder to become so worldwide? The utopian vision of a cosmopolitan and boundaryless civil society eloquently espoused by Kant (1970 [1784]) emerged just as the ideal of a democratic civil sphere was becoming firmly instantiated in the revolutionary nation state. Napoleon advanced even as Kant wrote. Since that time, the imperial idea of reshaping the world in the name of universal ideals has been related to war, whether waged for a French warrior's vision of Europe, a Russian revolutionary's ideal of communism, a German dictator's scheme for a *Volk Gemeinschaft*, or a new and democratic world order envisioned by the United States.

Yet, if we must resist the impulse to fold normative aspirations for a "global imaginary" into some immanent empirical laws about globalization, we must try all the harder, as David Held (2004) quite rightly insists, to steer time/space/meaning compression in normatively more compelling ways. The present phase of globalization does open up new democratic possibilities. If the social and cultural processes involved in contemporary time space meaning compression are not radically new but mundane, it may well be that the sense of newness is in the name, in the signifier, and not the signified. What I am suggesting is that we understand "globalization" as a process of social representation.

---

[3] Eisenstadt's (1982) Weberian perspective on the manner in which free-floating intellectuals and transcendental, world-transforming ideologies emerged on a global level in the first millennium B.C. forms an important relativizing perspective for the current claims that are made for the newly emergent representation of globalization

[4] On how some of Europe's leading democratic intellectuals have recently employed the particularistic and simplistic tropes of "orientalism" to suggest European cultural and political superiority to America, see Heins (2005).

Why has "globalization" emerged as a dominant new imaginary? What discourse does it crystallize, what fears does it carry, and what hopes does it represent? "Globalization" appeared as a response to the trauma of the 20th century, in a moment of hope when it seemed, not for the first time, that the possibility for a worldwide civil society was finally at hand. Since before the Enlightenment, the idea of world peace has accompanied the expansion of organizational and cultural power. From the 17th century on, the political theory of high and organic intellectuals alike has articulated the idea of peaceful conflict resolution through the concept of civil power. The possibility for civil control, as opposed to military violence or political domination, can be traced back to the idea of the social contract, to the Lockean vision of consensual agreement and persuasion in contrast with the Hobbesian resort to force and fraud. Sociologically, the idea of civil society points to the idea of a liberal discourse that is at once critical and tolerant, and to institutions, from factual and fictional mass media to voting and law, that allow collectivities to be guided by symbolic communication among independent and rational citizens who feel bound by ties of solidarity and mutual obligation (Alexander, 2006).

In what has been called the long 19th century, during the "Age of Equipoise" that followed upon the end of the Napoleonic wars, there was the sense, not only among Euro-American elites, that such cosmopolitan peace was finally at hand.[5] It seemed possible to believe that, alongside the expansion of organizational and cultural power, "civilization" was becoming worldwide. That this civil utopian vision of a peaceful world was shadowed by the expansion of colonial conquest outside Europe is a fearful symmetry only visible from our own time.[6]

This dream of reason was shattered by the First World War. For intellectuals and artists, and thoughtful men and women on every side, the war exposed the barbarism that contradicted modernity's promise to create a more civil society.[7] If that first globalizing war exposed the ugly face of military nationalism that threatened cosmopolitan peace, so much more so did the totalitarianisms that emerged during its wake. The Second World War marked a globalizing battle over the very possibility for modern civil life.

In the wake of these war traumas, the victors promised to renew the dream of cosmopolitan peace.[8] The utopia discourse of world civil society was even embedded in formally democratic institutional regimes, the quasi-world governments of first the League of Nations and then the United Nations. The ideas for these repair efforts were provided by such high intellectuals as Bertrand Russell

---

[5] For the long 19th and short 20th centuries, see Eric Hobsbawm (1990, 1994); for the Age of Equipoise see Burn (1964). An earlier version of the second half of this chapter appeared in Alexander (2006b).

[6] For the self-deceptive conflation of the model of democratic citizen with patrimonial subject during the colonial era, see Mamdani (1996).

[7] For how 20th century social theory responded to the ennui and traumas of the century's first half, see Alexander (1990).

[8] In the following, I draw upon Alexander et al. (2004), which suggests that the construction of cultural trauma—defining the pain, the perpetrators, the victims, and the antidote—is a central path by which collectivities sustain and develop collective identity.

and implemented by such organic intellectuals as Ralph Bunche. Yet, the carrier groups for these efforts at renewing the cosmopolitan dream were the victorious national hegemons themselves. Such an infrastructure of national power belied the aspirations for a global civil order. When strains at the level of nation-states became too intense, the League of Nations was destroyed. It had been hobbled from its beginnings, of course, by America's refusal to join. The United Nations was undermined even more quickly by the division of the postwar universalizing spirit into the fighting camps of the Cold War. The rhetoric on both sides of this great divide rang the bells of international peace, but in the background one could always hear the sounds of war.

When the Third World War of the short 20th century was finished, there were once again utopian hopes for the repair of civil society and the creation of world peace. The utopian representation "globalization" first emerged in the late 1980s, as the Cold War wound down. As this new collective representation gained power, in the decade following, it looked as if a world civil society were finally at hand. This time around, the high and organic intellectuals were former activists and peaceniks, post-Marxist and liberal leftists who had campaigned for peace against the Vietnam war in the United States, for "Europe," and against national boundaries on the continent, and for nuclear disarmament on both sides. International law would be based, not on the rights of sovereign nations, but on individual and human rights. National force was pledged to multinational, not national interest, to a new world order in which peace and civil respect would reign. The Security Council of the United Nations was approached as if it were a global democratic forum in which rational discussion could affect the distribution of wealth and the application of power.[9]

---

[9] It was Giddens' *Consequences of Modernity*, in 1990, that most forcefully introduced the idea that "globalization" characterized contemporary late modernity. Giddens brought Ulrich Beck, another intellectual central to this discourse, to LSE, and it has primarily been a group of post-Marxist British intellectuals, including, with Giddens and Beck, Mary Kaldor, John Keane, and David Held, who brought the idea of civil globality into centrality in the 15 years since. Mary Kaldor emphasizes the importance of the 1980s European disarmament and peace movements in "The Ideas of 1989: The Origins of the Concept of Global Civil Society" (Kaldor 2003a), and she points to such early collaborations as Kaldor, Holden, and Falk, *The New Détente* (1989). The work of hers that discusses globalization in a manner that can most clearly be seen as casting it as an idealistic "collective representation" is *Global Civil Society: An Answer to War* (2003b). The representation process emerging from the end of the Cold War can be seen in Keane's work (1988, 1991, 2003) Moving into this arena of representation slightly later, Held's influential writings have clarified and highlighted the democratic dimensions of Giddens' globalization concept, (e.g., 1995, 2004; and Held and McGrew 2002). All these writings mix normative elaborations about the scope and desirability of a global civil society with empirical data about its structural processes and analytic dimensions. Held's work is especially striking in this regard, for, although it makes broad incursions into the empirical domain, it is explicitly imbedded in normative political theory. At the other end of the empirical/ normative continuum is the *Global Civil Society* project, the edited volumes that, since 2001, have been produced annually at the London School of Economics by Mary Kaldor, Helmut Anheier, and Marlies Glasius. This tightly organized and highly collaborative project, funded in large part by the Ford Foundation, has projected the "representation" of democratic globalization from London to activists, students, and intellectuals throughout the world.

Once again, however, this moment of equipoise was underpinned by a national infrastructure. It was the victors in the Cold War who were most excited about globalization; the losers were more interested in national reconstruction and restoring regional strength. It was the President of the United States, Bill Clinton, who gave commencement addresses on civil society as the key to world peace. It was NATO that intervened in Kosovo. It should not be surprising that this most recent dream for cosmopolitan peace reigned for scarcely more than a decade. The postwar collective effervescence in which globalization became such a powerful new representation came to an end with the election in America of George W. Bush, which was soon accompanied by a neoconservative discourse of empire. National interest was unabashedly reasserted, global agreements cancelled, and global conferences and institutions boycotted. As the President and neoconservative politicians and intellectuals handled and channeled the national trauma of September 11, 2001, it highlighted anticivil violence and global fragmentation and pointed to a Hobbesian struggle between civilizations. Collective violence once again came to be waged by nations and blocs, with divisive rather than unifying effects for the world scene.[10]

These events were experienced by the intellectuals promoting globality, and by its organized carrier groups, not merely as disappointment but betrayal. For explanation, many turned to anti-Americanism, the long-standing culture structure that divides good and evil by polluting the United States and purifying any collectivity, ideology, or region that comes to represent the other side.[11] No matter how culturally satisfying, however, this interpretation elides the systemic processes at play. The structures and the ideologies of the world are still primarily organized nationally, and hardly at all in a globally civil way. As long as this organizational structure is maintained, if and when other states amass extraordinarily asymmetrical power, they will undoubtedly act in a similar way.

To accept anti-Americanism as explanation rather than as interpretation, moreover, misses the ambiguous and often productive role that this cultural trope often has played. To pollute America as a hegemon is to make deviant anticivil actions as such, not merely the United States. By creating a stark if simplifying contrast between "American" action, on the one side, and a more civil sort of

---

[10] For the neoconservative discourse of empire, see, e.g., Boot (2001), D'Souza (2002), and Kagan (2003). For an overview of this revival and an ironic yet forceful liberal-realist case for American imperial power as, in principle, the only viable force for progressive transformation in a Hobbesian world, see Ferguson (2004). The most sophisticated and influential conservative argument against the very possibility for a global civil society is undoubtedly Huntington's (1996). which made its first appearance as a widely influential article in *Foreign Affairs* (1993). Huntington employs a primordial understanding of culture to develop a seemingly scientific case that the world's distinctive civilizations are based on religions that can never be reconciled, which means that, rather than moving toward global civil order, the future of international politics will revolve around prolonged conflict for hegemony.

[11] For a systematic empirical interpretation of French anti-Americanism during the postwar period, see Kuisel (1993) and, more generally, Buruma and Margalit (2004).

global power, this binary has the effect of allowing the purifying power of the globalization representation to be sustained. In February, 2003, in the days just before the American invasion of Iraq, the meaning of this cultural confrontation, and the stakes involved, were clearly displayed on the front page of the *New York Times*. Reporting the massive demonstrations that had unfolded throughout the world on the previous day, a *Times* correspondent wrote: "The fracturing of the Western alliance over Iraq and the huge antiwar demonstrations around the world this weekend are reminders that there may still be two superpowers on the planet: the United States and world public opinion." Apparently factual, this statement must be seen rather as interpretive reconstruction. It framed these empirical events in a globally civil way. They are presented as transpiring on the public stage of the world, and America is portrayed, not as an elect but as a particularistic nation, confronting not the evil of an Iraqi dictator but the world as a civil, rationally organized society: "President Bush appears to be eyeball to eyeball with a tenacious new adversary: millions of people who flooded the streets of New York and dozens of world cities to say they are against war based on the evidence at hand."

There is not a world government to curb a hegemonic state bent on defending its interests as nationally conceived. The nascent global civil sphere has none of the institutions that, in a fully functioning democracy, allow public opinion to produce civil power and thus regulate the state, such as independent courts, party competition, and elections. Yet this nascent global civil sphere does have access to institutions of a more communicative kind. Despite different languages and separated ownership and organization, national news stories construct extranational events in a manner that often reveals a high level of intertextuality, creating the common understandings and interpretations that allow there to be putatively global events. These "factual" understandings are sustained by the intense circulation around the globe of "fictional" mass media, which are far from being merely entertaining in their cultural effects. These fictional media are movies, television dramas, novels, music, and the international brands whose consumption is creating a more common material culture worldwide.

It is within this symbolic and institutionally constructed sea of global public opinion that there emerges the world stage, on which transpire polls, demonstrations, social movements, scandals, corruptions, terrorism, electoral triumphs, and tragedies, performances which palpably create the very sense that there is a supranational life. It is within this febrile and often highly unstable membrane of global consciousness that international institutions and nongovernmental organizations create forms, not of governance in the state-political sense, but of governmentality, from agreements over labor conditions and world health to regulations about the environment and land mines. The rules and resources that sustain governmentality, as opposed to government, rest on consensus and agreement rather than on the violence-backed power of a state.[12]

---

[12] For this distinction, see, particularly, Held and McGrew (2002).

The dream of cosmopolitan peace has not died. The forceful hope for creating a global civil sphere remains. It is embodied in the collective representation of globalization, which has organizational integuments and political and economic effects. There is a global stage in which local events are evaluated, not only nationally or ethnically, but according to the standards of the civil sphere. Before this stage sits an idealized audience of world citizens. Sometimes the performances projected to this audience are initiated by avowedly global actors. More often, they reflect local scripts of national actors, which are projected on the world stage and evaluated according to the principles of cosmopolitan peace and by the discourse and interactions of civil life.

Since the first national institutionalizations of civil societies, there has been imagined the possibility for a civil sphere on a supranational scale. In the 17th century, the trope of "oriental despotism" emerged, reconfiguring colonialism into a fight for civil power on a global scale. In the middle of the 18th century, the Lisbon earthquake became a trauma for Europe and offered a sentimental education for "all mankind." In the early 19th century, the moral movement against slavery achieved political success by generating moral empathy, extending solidarity and psychological identification to nonwhite others for the first time. In the mid-20th century, the narration and memorialization of the Holocaust formed a powerful basis for expanding moral universalism, establishing genocide as a principle for evaluating national, ethnic, and religious power. At the end of the 20th century, globalization emerged as a new representation on the fragile public stage of world life.

Globalization refers to a process of space/time/meaning compression that is ongoing. These expansions have not yet, by any means, created the basis for globality in the sense of a supranational civil society, as the recent revival of nation-centered rhetorics and practices of national hegemony have demonstrated. Nonetheless, globalization is a new and powerful social representation. It has performative force, and it has emerged for good sociological reasons. Even if it is sharply contested, the dream of cosmopolitan peace can never be entirely suppressed.

References

Alexander, Jeffrey 1990. "Between progress and apocalypse: Social theory and the dream of reason in the twentieth century," pp. 15–39 in *Rethinking Progress: Movements, Forces, and Ideas at the End of the Twentieth Century*, edited by Jeffrey Alexander and Piotr Sztompka. London: Unwin Hyman Limited.

—— 1995. "Modern, ante, post and neo: How intellectuals have tried to understand the crisis of our time," pp. 6–64 in *Fin-de-Siecle Social Theory: Relativism, Reduction, and the Problem of Reason*. London: Verso.

—— 2006a. *The Civil Sphere*. New York: Oxford University Press.

—— 2006b. *Global Civil Society, Theory, Culture and Society 23* (2–3): 521–524.

Alexander, Jeffrey, Ron Eyerman, Bernhard Giesen, Neil Smelser, and Piotr Sztompka. 2004. *Cultural Trauma and Collective Identity*. Berkeley: University of California Press.

Beck, Ulrich 2000. "The cosmopolitan perspective: Sociology in the second age of modernity," *British Journal of Sociology 51* (1): 79–105.

Boot, Max 2001. "The case for an American empire," *Weekly Standard* October 15, pp. 27–30.

Burn, William Lawrence 1964. *The Age of Equipoise: A Study of The Mid-Victorian Generation*. New York: Norton.

Buruma, Ian and Avishai Margalit 2004. *Occidentalism: A Short History of Anti-Westernism*. London: Atlantic Books.

Clark, Ian 1999. *Globalization and International Relations Theory*. Oxford, UK: Oxford University Press.

Cushman, Thomas 2005. "The conflict of the rationalities: International law, human rights and the war in Iraq," *Deakin Law Review 10* (2): 546–570.

D'Souza, Dinesh 2002. "In praise of American empire," *Christian Science Monitor* April 26, p. 11.

Eisenstadt, S. N. 1982. "The axial age: The emergence of transcendental visions and the rise of clerics," *European Journal of Sociology 23* (2): 299–314.

Ferguson, Niall 2004. *The Rise and Fall of the American Empire*. London: Penguin.

Giddens, Anthony 1990. *Consequences of Modernity*. Cambridge, UK: Polity.

Heins, Volker. 2005. "Orientalizing America," *Millenium*. Journal of International Studies *34* (2): 433–448.

Held, David 1995. *Democracy and the Global Order: From the Modern State to Cosmopolitan Governance*. Cambridge, UK: Polity.

—— 2004. *Global Covenant: The Social-Democratic Alternative to the Washington Consensus*. Cambridge: Polity.

Held, David and Anthony McGrew 2002. *Governing Globalization: Power, Authority, and Global Governance*. London: Polity.

Hobsbawm, Eric 1990. *Nations and Nationalism since 1780*. Cambridge, UK: Cambridge University Press.

—— 1994. *The Age of Extremes: The Short Twentieth Century, 1914–1991*. London: Michael Joseph.

Huntington, Samuel 1996. *The Clash of Civilizations and the Remaking of World Order*. New York: Touchstone.

—— (1993). "The clash of civilizations?" *Foreign Affairs* 72 (Summer): 22–49.

Kagan, Robert 2003. *Of Paradise and Power: America and Europe in the New World Order*. Knopf.

Kaldor, Mary 2003a. "The ideas of 1989: The origins of the concept of global civil society," pp. 50–78 in *Global Civil Society: An Answer to War*. Cambridge, UK: Polity.

Kaldor, Mary 2003b. *Global Civil Society: An Answer to War*. Cambridge, UK: Polity.

Kaldor, Mary, Gerard Holden and Richard Falk. 1989. *The New Détente: Rethinking East West Relations*. London: Verso.

Kant, Immanuel 1970 (1784). "Idea for a universal history with a cosmopolitan purpose," pp. 41–53 in *Political Writings*. Cambridge: Cambridge University Press.

Keane, John 1988. *Democracy and Civil Society: On the Predicaments of European Socialism, the Prospects for Democracy, and the Problem of Controlling Social and Political Power*. London, New York: Verso.

—— 1991. *The Media and Democracy*. Cambridge, UK: Polity.

—— 2003. *Global Civil Society?* Cambridge, UK: Cambridge University Press.

Kuisel, Richard 1993. *Seducing the French: The Dilemma of Americanization*. Berkeley: University of California Press.

Lipschutz, Ronnie 1992. "Reconstructing world politics: The emergence of global civil society," *Millenium 21* (3): 389–420.

Mamdani, Mahmood 1996. *Citizen and Subject: Contemporary Africa and the Legacy of Late Colonialism*. Princeton, NJ: Princeton University Press.

Mann, Michael 1986. *The Sources of Social Power, A History of Power from the Beginning to A. D 1760*. Cambridge, New York: Cambridge University Press. Volume I.

Tyler, Patrick E. 2003. "A new power in the streets: A message to Bush not to rush to war," *New York Times*, February 17, A1.

20
Rationalization and Globalization in Neo-Weberian Perspective

RANDALL COLLINS

There is no deep structural difference between modernity and so-called postmodernity. The latter is an extension of the same trends. That means it is an extension of the same long-term processes, the same causal dynamics, although carried further and producing new concrete manifestations.

This will become clear as we look at the most important structural transformations of societies since about 1600 in European societies. In many ways these structural transformations also developed about the same time in Japan, which casts another light on the ways in which these processes have been global.

I list four features briefly, then consider their underlying causal dynamics:

1. State penetration and bureaucratization of society
2. Mass mobilization of the people by new networks, and social and political movements
3. Self-transforming capitalist growth
4. Religious secularization: or more generally, proliferation and de-monopolization of the means of cultural production

---

Editor's Note: Randall Collins has written a chapter that, among other important points, challenges the notion that globalization has introduced a discontinuity in social processes and, therefore, demands a new sociological paradigm (Beck's thesis and Ritzer's "wonder").

I received Collins' paper when my conclusive argument was already formulated. However, I refer in my conclusion to crucial passages that suggest new or parallel critiques of Beck and Ritzer's positions.

I summarize the results of the last 25 years of historical sociology largely in the Neo-Weberian school. In contrast, the idea of postmodernism comes from a different intellectual movement, late Marxians or disillusioned Marxists; in France, where the movement began, postmodernists essentially were post-Marxians. When they said the grand narratives are dead, what they chiefly were concerned about was that Marxism is dead as a master theory of historical trends. But they continued to think in a Marxian vein because they never learned much other historical sociology. Weberian historical sociology has never been well known in France. As disillusioned Marxists they no longer believed that a revolution brought about by contradictions in the capitalist economy will ever happen; instead they turned back to the Hegelian roots of Marxism, reviving the dialectic but no longer expecting metaphysical emancipation; by amalgamating this Hegelian dialectic with structuralist semiotics, many postmodernists joined in the cultural turn that no longer looks at social organization or at social action, but sees the social world as a reflection of a disembodied cultural codebook in the sky. In this cultural-postmodernist vision, there are different codebooks for different historical periods: one codebook for the premodern period; another codebook for modernity; yet another codebook for postmodernity. How history actually moves from one historical period to another was a rather idealistic conception for most postmodernists. There is just a series of epistemological ruptures, as if philosophers were the dictators of the movement of history; a Zeitgeist of views and practices that morphs from one cultural epoch to another; as if history were just changes in a series of metaphysical ideas. For some postmodernists, though, the Marxian dynamic remains primarily; postmodernism is regarded as the form taken by late capitalism.

In contrast to this postmodernist or late structuralist movement, neo-Weberian historical scholarship has been developed mainly by sociologists in the Anglophone world. This movement is neo-Weberian in emphasizing there are three interrelated forms of social organization and social action: economic, cultural, and political. In the last 30 years, neo-Weberian sociology has made its most important breakthroughs on the political dimension: it is often called the state-centered approach. Among its major scholars are Theda Skocpol (1979) and Jack Goldstone (1991), who developed the state-breakdown theory of revolution; Charles Tilly (1991, 1995), Michael Mann (1986–1993), and others who developed the military/fiscal theory of the state; an offshoot of this is the state penetration theory of modernity, which gives rise to a theory of the mobilization of social movements (for a summary of this research see Collins, 1999: Ch. 1) Moreover, social movement research is part of the theory of social networks; and social network theory is central to what in America is called the "new economic sociology" developed by Harrison White (1981, 1992, 2002), Mark Granovetter (1985), Viviana Zelizer (1994), and others (Guillén et al., 2002). This might also be called the "network-embeddedness" school of research. What are conventionally regarded as economic markets are actually networks, divided into market niches that control competition and shape innovation.

I would like to underline here the distinctiveness of this larger movement, both in the theory of the state, social movements, and economic sociology: its emphasis is upon forms of social organization, and on their dynamics. It is about how forms of organization grow, come into conflict, and change the social landscape of organizations; it is about the growth and widespread penetration of bureaucracy; about the decline of rival traditional forms of organization, especially kinship networks and households; about the further growth of new forms of organizing, that is, social movement networks, which rise and fall, expand and contract, but nevertheless pass along the network form of organization to still newer movement networks. And it is about the network structure of the capitalist economy, which has always taken the form not of individual businesses, but an interorganizational network of economic producers shaping their identities from each other in a field of competitive niches that defines a market; here too organizational forms are dynamic, rising and falling but always transmitting a structure of competitive niches to be filled by new organizations and new products.

In sum: the Neo-Weberian movement in sociology is concerned with the dynamics of *organizational forms:* the state, the military, tax-collection, households, social and political movements, and social and economic networks. Instead of being culture-centered, like postmodernists and *French* structuralists; instead of being economy-centered, like traditional Marxists; it is organization-centered. It is dynamic, because organizations are the way in which social action takes place; struggles of organizations determine what happens historically. Above all, Neo-Weberian sociology is state-centered, because the state has been the prime mover in the sequence of transformations beginning 400 years ago; but it also shows how processes set off by state penetration into society produce reactions and set the stage for new kinds of organizations, above all social movements and economic networks, which react back against the state, and set off further developments in their own right.

Above I listed four main trends (state penetration and bureaucratization; mass mobilization of networks; self-transforming capitalist growth; and cultural secularization). Here I concentrate on two main causal processes behind the trends, one based in the state, the other in capitalist growth; the other two trends can be largely derived from them.

State Penetration, Bureaucratization, and Mass Mobilization

The state-centered dynamic started in Europe in the 16th and 17th centuries, continuing for several centuries, in what is called the military revolution. Armies became bigger and more heavily equipped with cannons and other guns; armies had increasing supply problems, and developed organization for large-scale logistics. All these changes made armies more expensive; the largest item in state budgets during these centuries was military costs, plus financial debts from past wars. In response, states began to bureaucratize: first by bureaucratizing the military itself, especially its armaments branches, supplies, and logistics. Another branch of bureaucratization occurred in the civilian government, as tax-collection organization became larger and more formalized.

State bureaucracy, starting in the military sphere, penetrated more and more of society. In part the bureaucracy aimed at revenue extraction; in part, it began to break down the independence of local households by inscribing their members as potential soldiers. State bureaucracy also expanded to provide infrastructure for transportation and communication, pulling local enclaves of society into a larger network centered on the state and its capital cities. States began to promote and regulate the economy with conscious concern for military resources, initially in the form of mercantilist policies, and later protectionism and other policies for economic growth.

(An earlier version of the state-penetration theory was developed by Norbert Elias (1939/1983). However, Elias lacked the fiscal and bureaucratic mechanism of state penetration, concentrating on the influence of centralizing court societies upon the spread of civilizing manners.)

A second wave of bureaucratization and state penetration took off as the state apparatus began to be put to other uses. State penetration awakened new forms of political and social action. Elites often resisted the growth of state power and its revenue demands; such resistance was a component of most of the European revolutions. But even a victorious revolutionary group found itself in command of the state apparatus, which they then proceeded to put to use for their own policies. State organization has grown after every revolution. State penetration also created the mobilizing conditions for the emergence of social movements. New networks and movements were facilitated by providing transportation and communication that could link persons together, as well as breaking down the patrimonial household structure that kept most people localized and out of contact with their counterparts elsewhere. Some of these new movements were relatively private, concerned only with cultural interests such as art, literature, or science. Other movements organized new religious sects or attempted to revive older religions. Still other movements mobilized to contest state power itself, or to use state power against their enemies: both economic classes and ethnic or national groups were organized by the same process of expanding resource mobilization. The main effect was to expand formal political participation, to make every individual a citizen of the state, and hence subject to state regulation.

Movement mobilization further reinforced the trends towards state penetration and bureaucratization. Political and social movements now had a target for their actions: they could attempt to create attention in the national arena, and if successful to make the state bureaucracy carry out their own interests. A bourgeois political faction could demand economic protection and support; a liberal faction could demand the state bureaucracy be turned to providing welfare services. These state agencies now further penetrated into private society, taking over new activities, and pulling individuals out of families as citizens subject to new regulations and recipients of new services. Public education, health, and welfare, as well as many other forms of regulation were the result of an alliance of state agencies expanding from above, and demands from below to use state organization to promote group interests. Groups interested in prohibiting alcohol, for example, could not have been effective as long as the state was small and outside the sphere of ordinary life in households and communities; such movements became strong in the early 20th century as state bureaucracy became widespread.

State bureaucratization and penetration outgrew its original military dynamics. Once the state had penetrated local households, the resulting mobilization of individuals to form social and political movements led to further expanding bureaucracy and state penetration. Today social movements, whether to protect the environment, promote rights for minorities, stamp out corruption, or any other cause, all embody their successes in new bureaucratic regulations penetrating society. In addition, social movements themselves become new forms of bureaucracy; to become large and permanent, any movement needs to acquire a organization with a permanent office staff, engaged in raising money, communications, and recordkeeping. Big successful movements become heavily bureaucratized, as we see in the history of labor unions; but all other movements also create bureaucratic organization to advertise their cause and recruit new members. Most people's contact with a social movement today is with its fund-raising bureaucracy. In sum, there is a circular relationship because state penetration, bureaucratization, and social movement mobilization all feed back on each other.

Entrepreneurial Market Capitalism or "Rationalized" Capitalism

The second big historical dynamic of modern times has been a distinctive form of capitalism: capitalism that contains a built-in mechanism of self-sustained growth. As Weber pointed out, capitalism existed in several forms, and long before the modern West. What *Weber* called "rationalized capitalism" exists where all the factors of production—land, labor, material, and financial capital—are free to move on a competitive market, protected from political confiscation, and united in the hands of entrepreneurs (Weber, 1923/1961; Collins, 1986: Ch. 2). This model is similar to Schumpeter's (1911/1961; Collins, 1986: Ch. 5) theory of modern capitalism as organized around entrepreneurs who make new combinations of productive resources. It is also similar to recent economic sociology's emphasis on networks of market actors who seek out innovations that give them a distinctive, noncompetitive market niche during the early period of their innovation; because their innovation is later imitated by other businesses, there is an endless push towards further innovations to produce new temporarily monopolistic niches.

Weber called this form of capitalism "rationalized" because all the factors of production move on a market of purely economic considerations, and thus are subject to a higher degree of calculation and planned innovation. In contrast, Weber noted two main forms of capitalism that were not rationalized: one that he called "political," or "adventure," or "robber booty" capitalism, which typically involved using military power to conquer colonies, win monopolies, or carry out long-distance trade at a high level of risk. The second form he called "traditional" capitalism, where producers, merchants, and customers maintained their same networks over a long period of time, without expanding or innovating. Neither of these two forms of capitalism had a built-in dynamic for capitalist growth, nor did they innovate in the means of production and distribution. Only a "rationalized" capitalist market, characterized by entrepreneurs combining markets for all the factors of production, has this dynamic of self-sustaining growth.

Both of the two big causal dynamics I have outlined—state penetration, and entrepreneurial capitalist markets—were pathways to "rationalization." Weber used the term in a number of different senses; in a more limited sense, rationalization characterizes bureaucratic administration, because it regularizes activities by making them subject to formal rules and recordkeeping. Capitalist entrepreneurs were not necessarily rationalized, in the organizational sense; early entrepreneurs were often family enterprises, but incorporating some elements of bureaucratic planning and accounting. Capitalist enterprises became organized as bureaucracies relatively late, largely at the beginning of the 20th century; before that time the main agent of bureaucratic rationalization was state agencies. In the 20th century, all organizations have become bureaucratized, in the capitalist sector, the state sector, and the "nongovernmental organization" (NGO) sector alike.

I omit here a detailed explanation of how the capitalist dynamic of self-sustained growth originally took off. Weber in his mature works (much later than his famous early work on the Protestant ethic) presented a complex, multicausal model; it involves both a political component, and a religious component. The political component of this causal model concerns the struggles by which the factors of production were freed from obstacles that kept them from moving on the market; very briefly, this part of the capitalist take-off was an offshoot of the state penetration discussed above, but with a distinctive conjuncture of forces in which private business interests got control of the state apparatus in order to protect their property interests. The religious component, as I have explained in earlier publications (Collins, 1986: Ch. 3; Collins, 1997), is concerned less with individual motivations (such as the Protestant ethic) and more concerned with the growth of entrepreneurial organizations in the religious sector itself; a restricted enclave of religious organizations (including both Catholic monasteries in Europe, and Buddhist monasteries in Japan) became wealthy entrepreneurs and pioneered the organizational forms of markets which spilled over into the secular, nonreligious economy.

The long-run results of bureaucratization are the same, both via state penetration, and via the expansion of omni-penetrating market capitalism. Both government bureaucracy and private capitalist bureaucracy have increasingly penetrated society, taking away the privacies of family and household organization; even when there are movements of resistance, against either state penetration or capitalist penetration, these movements organize themselves in a form that promotes further bureaucratic organization and regulation. Bureaucratization is the master trend of modern history.

Secularization of the Means of Cultural Production

We have already seen the main mechanisms by which religious secularization has come about. Secularization does not mean disappearance of religion; it is the displacement of religion from a central place in community life. In premodern societies, religion was the only well-organized means of cultural production. This religious monopoly on cultural production has been eroded by all the processes I have reviewed above. (a) State bureaucracy and penetration of society replaced many religious institutions with new governmental ones: the arena of political culture per se; the culture of journalism, and the circulation of discourse about political action came to take up the public attention that previously had been directed to religious ceremonies. State penetration also set up secular schools and displaced religion from control of education. (b) Secular social movements grew up alongside religious movements. New religious movements have been abundant in modern societies, but they have had to share the public attention space with many other movements. (c) Entrepreneurial omnicapitalism creates its own cultural markets; capitalist entrepreneurs treat culture just like any other commodity, to be sold in whatever market niches can be constructed. Of course, religious culture can use the same markets; religious books were the first big book markets; more recently there are markets for religious music, religious TV shows, and Internet sites. What is lacking is the former monopoly position that a dominant religion once had; now it is only one cultural product among others. If religion was once, as Durkheim (1912/1964) explained, the rituals holding communities together, its rituals have been displaced by a huge array of secular institutions that are temporary, often ephemeral, and hold together only small portions of the population (Collins, 2004). In this respect, religions are in the same position as any other form of contemporary culture, including science. Some persons believe it; others do not; there is no social structure to force everyone to pay attention to the same thing. Secularization and cultural pluralization are results of the same long-term structural transformation as state penetration, mass mobilization, and omnicapitalism.

The Dynamics of Early Modernization in Sengoku and Tokugawa Japan

The historical narrative I have given so far has been a Europe-centered one. European forms of state penetration, bureaucratization, and entrepreneurial capitalism have spread throughout the world. However, there are also some indigenous forms of structural change that resemble this pattern in several respects. I briefly summarize an analysis of Japanese structural change concentrating on the Tokugawa period from 1600 onwards and the Sengoku period of warring states that preceded it (1460–1580) (Collins, 1998; Ch. 7; see also Ikegami, 1995; Morris-Suzuki, 1994; Nakane and Oshii, 1990; Colcutt, 1981; McMullin, 1984). The beginnings of a capitalist market economy are found in the Sengoku, especially in the powerful Buddhist monasteries of the Pure Land sects; these acted not only as military powers, but as economic entrepreneurs. Important commercial towns such as Osaka and Sakai grew up around monasteries, under their military protection; they developed through the spilling-over of the religious economic networks into a secular market economy. The confiscation of Buddhist property at the end of the Sengoku is structurally similar to the Protestant Reformation in Europe: not so much because of a cultural change, but because the accumulated resources and the organizational forms of the religious economies were put into a secular economy, which now began its own pathway to economic growth. The Tokugawa period was a time of expansion of the market economy and its penetration throughout most of the country; although it did not give rise to industrial capitalism, there were many areas of innovation of market processes including the expansion of large-scale business enterprises. The so-called miracle of Japan's rapid catching up with the European economy after the Meiji revolution would not have been possible without being prepared by this extensive rationalization of the Japanese economy in the previous period.

The state penetration and bureaucratization dynamic was not as extensive in Japan as in Europe. But the Tokugawa regime, although it was organized to uphold a feudal coalition of the daimyo lords under the ceremonial control of the central court, also introduced many features of bureaucratization. The huge armies of the late Sengoku period, which required considerable logistical organization, remained largely delegated by the Tokugawas in the form of obligations by the daimyo; at the same time, these warriors, although not forming a centralized army, were subjected to a great deal of formalized regulation. Daimyo schools as well as administrative structure took up much of the time of warriors in ceremony and paperwork. The Tokugawa was less a feudal regime than an absolutist regime pretending to be a feudal regime, while instituting widespread regulation of society. The decree requiring all Japanese to register themselves with a Buddhist temple was part of this state penetration; it was used to keep records not only on the Buddhist monasteries and prevent them from becoming wealthy and powerful again, but also to regulate the religious lives of the populace.

Although there is not so much of a military/fiscal dynamic in Tokugawa Japan, compared to the rise of a large tax-collecting bureaucracy in Europe, state fiscal problems were an important part of Tokugawa administrative politics. The growth of a merchant economy, largely out of the control of the fiscal policies of the Tokugawa regime and the daimyo lords, kept the government organization in a condition of fiscal strain throughout most of the 1700s; these problems gave rise to various proposals for reform (such as those made by Ogyu Sorai), which were in effect proposals to expand the scope of government regulation. This extensive state penetration did not fully take place until after the fall of the Tokugawas.

The combination of Tokugawa state pacification and partial bureaucratization, and the growth of the market economy, also gave rise to the expansion of new social networks and movements. These were largely cultural movements (documented in Ikegami, 2005) the spread of private circles for aesthetic activities such as linked poetry (*haikai*); an expanding marketplace for books and for art; a huge market of private schools for various kinds of skills (Rubinger, 1982; Dore, 1965); and what Ikegami calls "fashion politics." Social movements also developed, chiefly in the form of religious and intellectual movements: the Ancient Learning movement, the National Learning movement, and various new religious sects. Although many of these ostensibly had the character of looking backwards to the past, they were neoconservative movements, not archaic revivals. Often they were cultural innovators in the guise of restoring tradition. Social movements are a modern phenomenon, not a traditional one; it takes modern mobilizing conditions for movements to become organized and to spread widely. Modernity is not necessarily a cultural ethos proclaiming itself as modern; just as often it takes the form of movements that put themselves in resistance to contemporary culture. The existence of neoconservative movements is an indicator of structural modernization. On the whole, the ethos of Tokugawa Japan was already that of a secular society, experiencing proliferation of the means of cultural production. In most important respects, Japan had its own pathway to modernity, with processes parallel to those in the West.

Postmodernism as Intensification of Neo-Weberian Trends

Postmodernism does not add any structurally new features of society, but only intensifies the main trends.

(1) State penetration and bureaucratization continue to new levels. The chief feature of bureaucracy is formal rules and recordkeeping. This continues to expand for both technical and political reasons. Technologically, the growth of computerization as well as video and other forms of recording have made government agencies able to collect and store much more information than before; state agencies penetrate private lives with records of education, employment, health, and welfare, not to mention criminal and military records and various forms of political surveillance. This happens also in the nongovernment sphere; political fund-raising organizations keep records of the political sympathies of persons who might give money or attend their meetings. The political dynamic, as we have seen, involves not only state expansion from above, but mobilization of social movements from below; and these foster their own bureaucracies and their own regulatory regimes.

What makes this development seem postmodern is the proliferation of competing and overlapping forms of recordkeeping and regulation. Governments split into numerous branches, often working at cross-purposes. Social movements create their own private bureaucracies, private would-be governments, that add to the cacophony of competing forms of regulation. Postmodern bureaucracy is disorderly, chaotic, and self-contradicting bureaucracy; but that is nothing new. Bureaucracies never worked perfectly; they always give rise to new forms of conflict. The postmodern era only expands these feature so far that they become widely visible.

It is sometimes argued that organizations have outgrown the national state, and that this is a form of postmodern globalization. But this too continues a trend. Weak federated state structures have existed at least since the early modern period in the West; the German empire grew out of intermediate steps such as the customs union of the early 19th century; the Federal government of the United States was also a weak structure for a long time, until the world wars and the domestic political mobilizations of the 20th century. The huge array of transnational governmental organizations existing today, ranging from the European Union to the United Nations, various trade and security pacts, the International Labor Organization (ILO), the World Trade Organization (WTO), the Group of 7, and so on – these are all efforts, with varying degrees of effectiveness, attempting to expand the sphere of regulations on the world scale, or in particular parts of the world. There was a similar pattern in the earlier historical growth of states. International NGOs do the same thing. All these organizations produce a version of global state penetration; and each of these organizations attempts to regulate, thereby spreading bureaucracy.

(2) Mass mobilization of networks, social movements, and political factions. If postmodernism is characterized by a proliferation of language games, a multiplicity of perspectives without a single authoritative vision, this is the result of the mobilization of a large number of networks and movements. It is not simply an intellectual development invented by philosophers. The trend of modern history is not to the Left, nor indeed to the Right; Marxians, Liberals, and Fascists alike were wrong about the direction of history. The direction of modern history is not on the level of particular ideological contents at all; the trend is a structural one, the continually increasing mobilization of networks and movements themselves. For each five- or ten-year period, often there is one social movement that is new or rapidly mobilizing, which claims for itself the dominant ideology, as if it were the wave of the future. But in reality there always exist competing movements; and the conditions that allow the mobilization of some movements—increasing communications, ease of travel, mass education, and the like—ensure that every new social movement will be succeeded by something different. Moreover, movements borrow tactics and themes from each other, even borrowing across ideological lines. Thus traditional religious movements, family values movements, and other neoconservative movements all use the same methods of recruitment networks, fund-raising, mass media publicity, demonstrations, and political campaigns as do liberal, left-wing and ultramodernist movements. The antiabortion movement in the United States uses many of the same tactics that the civil rights movement used in the 1950s and 1960s; new Christian religious movements in the United States use the same kinds of group psychology techniques, music, and dramatic presentation as did the hippie rock concerts.

There are two results of this proliferation of multiple movement mobilizations. No social movement can make itself dominant; none can realistically claim to be the direction of future history, as the labor movement or the nationalist movements of the 19th and early 20th centuries used to claim. Instead there is a gridlock of competing movements; this not only blocks political change, but it also gives rise to the cultural consciousness that the world has no single underlying reality. The multiplicity of social movements promotes a multiplicity of worldviews; it leads to relativism and reflexivity, which is expressed most self-consciously in the skeptical, self-undermining epistemologies of postmodernist intellectuals. In social reality, however, this multiplicity is only on the level of culture. On the structural level, there is a clear social reality: the proliferation of bureaucratic organizations, omni-market capitalism, and mobilized networks and movements. There is nothing mysterious or unknowable about the underlying structure that produces the postmodern cultural situation.

(3) The basic structures of entrepreneurial capitalism have extended, penetrating new markets and further encroaching on private life. This is not a new trend. The basic structure of modern "rationalized" capitalism is the bringing together of all the factors of production onto markets subject to entrepreneurs making new combinations. Brand names and rival identities in a market are not new; they are the mark of the Schumpeterian entrepreneur throughout the history of modern capitalism. The penetration of capitalist marketing into homes via telemarketing, Internet spam, and the proliferation of advertisements at sporting events and in schools and everywhere else, is the intensification of an old trend. This is sometimes regarded as the result of a high-tech revolution, the information age, the era of information technology (IT). But these technologies are developed by the same process that have always brought technological innovation in modern capitalism: the processes of rationalization, calculation, and planning of production and distribution. Information technology is another phase of capitalism just as were the steam engine and railroad revolution, the chemical and electrical revolution, the automobile revolution, the airplane revolution, and so on. Each has involved market competition, niche-seeking, and the struggle for monopolization into big bureaucratic organizations. We can predict that after the IT revolution will come another technological revolution as another set of products is created and marketed by capitalist entrepreneurs.

It is sometimes argued that the contemporary postmodern era is more global than before. But capitalist economies have always had a global long-range organization; what is new is only an intensification of global networks (Chase-Dunn, 1998; Chase-Dunn and Hall, 1991; Frank, 1998; Abu-Lughod, 1989; Gereffi, 1994). Another argument for the uniqueness of the postmodern era is that it represents a shift from Fordist mass production to flexible production of a wide array of consumer products. But this is to overstate the degree of change. The basic structure of entrepreneurs making new combinations for all factors of production continues as before. Over the centuries, capitalism has shifted its weight from the extractive sector (agriculture, mining) to the sector of bulk goods production, and more recently to the service sector. This tertiary sector includes not only the production of ephemeral consumer goods that previously would have been luxuries; it also includes the massive sector of bureaucratic work, including electronic recordkeeping; the IT revolution is chiefly a matter of expanding the bureaucratic service sector of the economy. Another major sector of the service economy is the entertainment business in all its ramifications, ranging from film, video, music, Internet games, as well as the gambling industry (the last is currently the fastest-growing industry in the United States). All of these are the same old capitalist entrepreneurs, continuing pushing into new market niches. There is nothing about the early 21st century that would have surprised Schumpeter in the 1920s. The chaos of ephemeral products may seem postmodern, but the underlying mechanism is the same.

Conclusion

Weber distinguished between formal and substantive rationality. *Formal rationality* is the process of regulation by formal rules and recordkeeping that is propelled by state penetration and bureaucratization, and also by omnimarket penetrating capitalism. *Substantive rationality* is subjective rationality, the ability to understand the world in logical calculable order from means to ends. Substantive rationality is often undermined by formal rationality. The proliferation of multiple organizations, movements, and capitalist enterprises, all formally rational in their procedures, leads in the aggregate to a feeling of substantive irrationality in the entire society. This is what postmodernists have spoken about as the loss of a common unifying code of cultural understanding. In Weber's terms, postmodernism is just the combination of long-term trends of formal rationalization and its resulting substantive irrationality.

References Cited and Bibliography

Abu-Lughod, Janet L. 1989. *Before European Hegemony. The World System A.D. 1250–1350*. New York: Oxford University Press.
Chase-Dunn, Christopher 1998. *Global Formation. Structures of the World Economy*. Boston: Rowan and Littlefield.
Chase-Dunn, Christopher, and Thomas D. Hall 1991. *Core/Periphery Relations in Precapitalist Worlds*. Boulder, CO: Westview Press.
Collcutt, Martin 1981. *Five Mountains: The Rinzai Zen Monastic Institution in Medieval Japan*. Cambridge, MA: Harvard University Press.
Collins, Randall 1986. *Weberian Sociological Theory*. New York: Cambridge University Press.
—— 1997. "An Asian Route to Capitalism: Religious Economy and the Origins of Self-Transforming Growth in Japan." *American Sociological Review* 62: 843–65.
—— 1998. *The Sociology of Philosophies: A Global Theory of Intellectual Change*. Cambridge, MA: Harvard University Press.
—— 1999. *Macro-History: Essays in Sociology of the Long Run*. Stanford, CA: Stanford University Press.

—— 2004. *Interaction Ritual Chains*. Princeton, NJ: Princeton University Press.

Dore, Ronald P. 1965. *Education in Tokugawa Japan*. Berkeley: University of California Press.

Durkheim, Emile 1912/1964. *The Elementary Forms of Religious Life*. New York: Free Press.

Elias, Norbert 1939/1983. *The Court Society*. New York: Pantheon.

Frank, Andre G. 1998. *ReOrient: global economy in the Asian age*. Berkeley: University of California Press.

Gereffi, Gary 1994. "The international economy and economic development." In Neil Smelser and Richard Swedberg (Eds.), *Handbook of Economic Sociology*. Princeton, NJ: Princeton University Press.

Goldstone, Jack A. 1991. *Revolution and Rebellion in the Early Modern World*. Berkeley: University of California Press.

Granovetter, Mark 1985. "Economic action and social structure: The problem of embeddedness." *American Journal of Sociology* 91: 481–510.

Guillén, Mauro F, Randall Collins, Paula England, and Marshall Meyer (Eds.) 2002. *The New Economic Sociology*. New York: Russell Sage Foundation.

Günter, Frank Andre 1998. *ReOrient: Global Economy in the Asian Age*. Berkeley: University of California Press.

Ikegami, Eiko 1995. *The Taming of the Samurai: Honorific Individualism and the Making of Modern Japan*. Cambridge, MA: Harvard University Press.

—— 2005. *Bonds of Civility: Aesthetic Networks and the Political Origins of Japanese Culture*. Cambridge, UK: Cambridge University Press.

Mann, Michael 1986–1993. *The Sources of Social Power*. Vols. 1 and 2. Cambridge, UK: Cambridge University Press.

McMullin, Neil 1984. *Buddhism and State in Sixteenth Century Japan*. Princeton, NJ: Princeton University Press.

Morris-Suzuki, Tessa 1994. *The Technological Transformation of Japan: From the Seventeenth to the Twenty-first Century*. Cambridge, UK: Cambridge University Press.

Nakane, Chie, and Shinzaburo Oishi (eds.) 1990. *Tokugawa Japan. The Social and Economic Antecedents of Modern Japan*. Tokyo: University of Tokyo Press.

Rubinger, Richard 1982. *Private Academies in Tokugawa Japan*. Princeton, NJ: Princeton University Press.

Schumpeter, Joseph A. 1911/1961. *The Theory of Economic Development*. New York: Oxford University Press.

Skocpol, Theda 1979. *States and Social Revolutions*. New York: Cambridge University Press.

Tilly, Charles 1991. *Coercion, Capital, and European States. A.D. 990–1990*. Oxford, UK: Blackwell.

—— 1995. *Popular Contention in Great Britain 1758–1834*. Cambridge, MA: Harvard University Press.

Weber, Max 1923/1961. *General Economic History*. New York: Collier.

White, Harrison C. 1981. "Where do markets come from?" *American Journal of Sociology* 87: 517–47.

—— 1992. *Identity and Control: A Structural Theory of Social Action*. Princeton, NJ: Princeton University Press.

—— 2002. *Markets from Networks*. Princeton, NJ: Princeton University Press.

Zelizer, Viviana 1994. *The Social Meaning of Money*. New York: Basic Books.

21
From Cosmopolitanism to a Global Perspective: Paradigmatic Discontinuity (Beck, Ritzer, Postmodernism, and Albrow) Versus Continuity (Alexander and Collins) and Emergent Conceptualizations (Contributors to this Volume)

Ino Rossi

Introduction and Précis of this Conclusion

The question has been raised as to whether the conceptualization of globalization offers a test case for the continuing usefulness of our existing paradigms and concepts. Janet Abu-Lughod suggests that a refinement of traditional concepts and paradigms is in order and it would suffice. Ritzer, however, offers a detailed critique of most of the essays based on the possibility that we may "need new ideas, theories, and empirical approaches to the study of globalization," simply because Martin Albrow has written about the new "global age" and Beck has theorized a discontinuity between the first and second modernity (post 1960s), globalization being one of the key processes of the second modernity. After showing how he (Ritzer) and most of the researchers on globalization, including the contributors to this volume, do not measure up to the standard of new ideas and theories, he concludes his critique by suggesting "that it is also possible that the era of globalization is not so different after all and that such a need does not exist."

No such doubt is entertained by Jeffrey Alexander or Randall Collins who put forward the notion of cultural (Alexander) and structural (Collins) continuity of modernity in direct contradiction to Beck's thesis on the sharp discontinuity between two modernities and between the national and the transnational perspectives. Alexander sees a continuity between the cultural themes of modernization (Beck's first modernity) and globalization theory (a component of Beck's second modernity) and he is quite firm on the notion that to analyze globalization we must continue using ideas already available by orienting them in a more global way.

Collins' essay makes analogous points on the basis of the continuity in the structural processes of self-transforming capitalism. Alexander finds nonsensical the notion that traditional sociological concepts were "scaled to nation-state" and, therefore, they are inapplicable to the analysis of transnational processes (a thesis central to Beck's thinking). Alexander and Collins' essays were offered in lieu of commentaries. They are welcome additions to this volume, because they concur with and add new arguments for the position that I had already reached on the basis of a detailed critique of Beck's writings. I must add that Albrow agrees with Beck's notion that we need new concepts, but neither Albrow or Alexander or Collins agrees with Beck's notion that globalization entails the demise of the nation-state and, therefore, the demise of traditional sociological concepts; the latter, according to Beck, are presumed to become "zombielike" when applied to postnational processes.

A systematic critique of Beck's cosmopolitanism is in order, because it is supposed to represent a challenge to much of the sociological enterprise. What does cosmopolitanism consist of and what is the basis for asserting that it should replace the allegedly defunct national perspective?

This final essay is organized around the following questions. (1) First, is there a new paradigm, or are there at least new concepts, to study globalization, and, if any, what is their theoretical and/or empirical basis? The answer is that current scholarship is largely scanty on new conceptualizations, however, various essays in this volume contain interesting new concepts and many of these concepts are based on empirical research (contrary to Ritzer's claim that the essays offer no new concepts or much empirical data); (2) secondly, what are the more promising new concepts proposed so far in the literature at large and in the essays contained in this book? The answer is that, as Ritzer suggests, Ulrich Beck and Martin Albrow are the most vocal thinkers on the need for new conceptualizations. It is shown also that Beck and Albrow agree on the novelty of the globalization process, the need of new concepts, and even on the use of some new concepts. Albrow, however, does not advocate a wholesale dismissal of the traditional sociological apparatus. I find more promising Albrow's line of thinking, although both Beck and Albrow are at the beginning of their innovative efforts; (3) thirdly, does postmodernism offer a useful perspective and/or concepts, as Ritzer seems to suggest? Ulrich Beck says no and Albrow cautions us against a relational and fictitious theory of social relations; (4) Fourthly, is the present state of global theorizing confronted by the dilemma of having to choose between the old "methodological nationalism" or the "methodological cosmopolitanism" of Ulrich Beck? Alternatively, is the linking of the national and transnational perspective a better strategy to follow? The latter strategy would facilitate an upgrading of traditional concepts with, perhaps, a formulation of new ones. The answer to this question will be that Beck's thesis on the demise of the nation-state and of "methodological nationalism" is refuted by the empirical research of Albrow, Friedman, Knorr Cetina, and Sassen who find that the "global" is partially embedded in the "national." The just-mentioned essays and those of Rosenau, Stichweh, Rossi, and Albrow offer alternative approaches to conceptualize the relationship between national and transnational processes; this relationship is alternatively explained in this volume in terms of interaction, or interpenetration, or embeddedness, or multilevel and dialectical relationships. Finally, an analysis of foundational sociological concepts and references to contemporary research in sociology will challenge the notion that much of the traditional analytic apparatus was contained within the contours of the nation-state and, therefore, it is inadequate to explain transnational processes.

On the Complexity of Globalization and the Need of a New Paradigm

Abu-Lughod makes important points in favor of the continued usage of traditional paradigms:

> On the debate concerning whether today's globalization represents a quantum leap or merely an increase in scale and intensity facilitated by the enhanced annihilation of space by time, [Grew] comes out on the side of history, suggesting that the study of prior moments of integration (and disintegration) can yield important insights into present trends. Case studies of earlier times and different places can, at the minimum, deepen our perspectives on globalization.

From this methodological stance, traditional paradigms and concepts must remain valid for the analysis of the antecedents of contemporary globalization, and, at least of a starting point for the study of contemporary globalization. Abu-Lughod is of the opinion that we are at the preparadigmatic state of the art: "globalization" is too frail of a concept to sustain the heavy theoretical/methodological burden usually attributed to it (and here she refers to Sklair's essay); moreover, globalization is too complex and amorphous a process to be amenable to precise framing and hypotheses testing (and here she refers to Rosenau's essay). Abu-Lughod's comments are well taken and they also offer a reasonable classification of the approaches utilized in this volume on the basis of a typology of traditional paradigms. Alexander is very explicit and direct with his thesis that globalization does not represent an abrupt change from modernity. To understand globalization, we do not need to invent new or alternative "knowledge"; rather, we must apply the theoretical and empirical ideas already available by orienting them in a more global way.

On the other end of the theoretical spectrum, we find Ritzer apparently afflicted by a self-imposed castigation for having himself used old, "zombielike" concepts in his published works on globalization. He suggests that similar guilty feelings ought to be shared by everyone else who has touched on the topic of globalization, with the exception of Ulrich Beck and Martin Albrow. We must applaud Ritzer's strong invitation to think innovatively, but we become disappointed by his failure to make a clear argument that we are in dire need of dismissing traditional paradigms and by his failure to suggest any new concept of his own.

But how would we know whether traditional paradigms and concepts are no longer sufficient or in, Beck's terminology, when they become zombielike (Beck et al., 2004)? Ritzer has written eloquently on this matter. In a 1975 essay (Ritzer, 1975: 7) he stated that

A paradigm is a fundamental image of the subject matter within a science. It serves to define what should be studied, what questions should be asked, how they should be asked, and what rules should be followed in interpreting the answers obtained. The paradigm is the broadest unit of consensus within a science and serves to differentiate one scientific community (or sub-community) from another. It subsumes, defines, and interrelates the examples, theories, methods, and instruments that exist within it. . . .

How does a paradigm emerge in the scientific community? Ritzer quotes Merton's (1967) famous essay "The Bearing of Empirical Research on Sociological Theory," where

He [Merton] suggests that social research provides many important functions which help to shape the development of sociological theory. According to Merton (1967: 157), research initiates, reformulates, deflects, and clarifies sociological theory. Empirical research not only tests theoretically derived hypotheses, it originates new hypotheses whenever unexpected observations are made. It is this serendipitous (accidental discovery) pattern to which we referred to when we discussed the role of induction in theory construction. Research reformulates sociological theory whenever new data exert pressure on the researcher to reconceptualize the variables under consideration. Merton (1967: 162) points out that sometimes conceptual schemes do not adequately take all facts into account—they consider some data irrelevant. When new research emphasizes the importance of these data, the conceptual schemes must be extended and reformulated in order for the theories to become more inclusive. . . .

In his short commentary to this book Ritzer does not allude to a single piece of research or data in the field of globalization that appears to "pressure" him (or us) to revisit old concepts and/or to develop new ones. Bypassing the standard he had clearly laid out in 1975, Ritzer leaves us only with references to Beck and Albrow's positions. Yet, one should ask, why doesn't he discuss the plausibility of Beck's arguments, considering that on the basis of those arguments Ritzer and the rest of us ought to post the sign "closed for embalming" on our sociological offices and printing presses? To pick up the challenge bypassed by Ritzer, I have reread carefully the suggestions made so far by Ulrich Beck and Martin Albrow. I have found Beck's approach stimulating, but highly debatable on key assumptions and theoretical analyses and, most importantly, with lacking any empirical substantiation. At the same time, I find Albrow's formulations quite interesting and promising along the lines of a paradigmatic shift.

The Transnational Paradigm of Ulrich Beck and Martin Albrow. Whither Postmodernism?

Beck's Second Modernity and the Twin Processes of Globalization and Individualization

Beck has been very vocal in various articles and books on the need to establish a cosmopolitan or postnational framework because, according to him, the national perspective that prevailed in what he calls "first modernity" reduces the sociological concepts of the first modernization to a zombielike status when applied to transnational processes. According to Beck, traditional sociology was based on the assumption that society equals (or is contained within) the nation-state. According to this "container model," society is composed of a number of interlocking social institutions:

> A reliable welfare state; mass parties anchored on class culture; and a stable nuclear family. These institutions are supported by, and in turn support, a web of economic security woven out of industrial regulation, full employment and life-long careers. And the entire arrangement is rendered intelligible to his members by a clarity of thought based on several clear distinctions [called "boundaries" elsewhere]: between society and nature; between established knowledge and mere belief; and between the members of society and outsiders (Beck et al., 2003: 1–2).

We encounter here the first oversimplification in Beck's thesis. Is it altogether true that for traditional sociology all social relations are "contained" within the boundaries of the nation-state? What about the many international organizations and the various intercontinental links of communication and transportation of the 19th century that greatly contributed to the internal dynamics of nation-states? What about the transnational spreading of the Enlightenment-based cosmopolitanism, liberalism, socialism, romanticism, religious universalisms, fascism, nationalism, and of the independence movements that deeply transformed the sociopolitical dynamics as well as the fortune or decline of nation-states? And what about the various political and military alliances and the vast international network for trading and banking, and the numerous technological innovations that criss-crossed national borders?

Beck asserts that in traditional or nation-centered sociology individuals are theoretically free and equal, "but their freedom and equality are molded by social institutions." Does Beck imply that socialization has been understood by traditional sociologists as a passive indoctrination? Or does he arbitrarily consider structural theories of socialization as the only legitimate ones, ignoring interactional and phenomenological theories of the sociological tradition? Moreover, for Beck "first modern societies unfold themselves on the basis of a scientifically defined concept of rationality that emphasizes instrumental control" (p. 4). Has this emphasis subsided in contemporary societies? If Beck refers to the poverty of sociological imagination, then, we must remember that the counter-critique of "substantial rationality" of Mannheim has been part of sociological thought for a long time. The list of one-sided characterizations of traditional sociology becomes longer and longer throughout this chapter.

Beck argues that various processes are responsible for the emergence of the second modernity and the advent of the postnational perspective:

(a) Globalization undermines the economic foundations of modern society, and with it the idea of society as a nation-state; this is because many political and cultural aspects of globalization change the relationship between local and global, between domestic and foreign, and "affect the very meaning of national borders—and, with that, all the certainties upon which nation-state society is based" (p. 6).

I prove later on that the sociological notion of society was never delimited by national borders as such, and that national borders never limited the applicability and validity of most sociological concepts. Moreover, one can counteract that the fascist dictatorships of the first part of the 20th century were based on certainties, but those certainties led to national disasters, whereas the League of Nations worked for collective security and the preservation of peace. As a matter of fact, the League of Nations was credited for aiding World War I refugees, and for improving world health and labor conditions, and for curbing international narcotics and prostitution. So, at the time of what Beck calls "first modernity" the transnational order was already of crucial importance in the internal dynamics of nations; perhaps, we could have averted two World Wars and the demise of important nation-states, if nation-states had taken the transnational order more seriously.

(b) According to Beck, other processes are responsible also for the advent of the second modernity since the 1960s: "several ascriptive patterns of collective life . . . have gradually lost their legitimacy," such as class, family, and ethnicity (Beck & Beck-Gernsheim, 2002: 206), and such processes as universalization of freedom and equality, transformation of gender role, the breakdown of full employment, and ecological crises. Beck makes the point that such a structural break with the past is explained by some authors in terms of developments in subsectors of society, for instance, in information technology. Beck places in this category of explanations the theories of postindustrial society, information society, and network society. Postmodernists explain the change in terms of the loss of key certainties in the cultural sphere (Beck et al., 2003: 13). On the contrary, for Beck these trends mark the advent of the second modernity that calls for a sociology of reflexive modernization or remodernization that entails a restructuration and reconceptualization of social processes (p. 3). Postmodernism is rejected by Beck for limiting its explanation to the loss of uncertainties in the cultural sphere. (I wonder whether Ritzer ever read this rather systematic essay that Beck co-authored with Bonss and Lau, and that undermines Ritzer's penchant for postmodernism as, perhaps, the last remaining savior of sociology). Ulrich Beck continues that we are now experiencing a "metachange," whereby "the experiential and theoretical co-ordinates change at the same time as basic institutions." We have to discover "the new rules of the game for our political and social systems" (p. 13). In collaboration with Bruno Latour, Beck has spelled out the new rules of the game as follows:

(a) Multiplicity of boundaries: during the first modernity there were "unambiguous and institutionally guaranteed boundaries between social spheres, between nature and society (p. 22), between science and superstition, between life and death, between Us and the Others (p. 19). With the advent of the second modernity, these boundaries become optional and multiple; therefore, conflicts arise over the drawing of the boundaries so that we now experience an uncertainty over both institutional boundaries and subject's boundaries,

(b) We also have multiple rationalities (or multiple claims to knowledge) in so far as extra-scientific criteria of boundary drawing are recognized (p. 19), contradictory scientific camps emerge, and the unexpected becomes expected. Currently, ad hoc decision making becomes institutionalized,

(c) A quasi-subject emerges: the subject is no longer pregiven and delimited by boundaries that are clear and need only to be interpreted. With the advent of multiple and shifting boundaries the subject must make quick choices and create his or her own network (p. 25); the subject is no longer a master of the environment within prescribed boundaries, but becomes a quasi-subject that is both the result as well as the producer of its own network and situation; the net is produced by individuals, but at the same time,

Subjectivity is a product of self-selected networks, which are developed, through self-organization, into spheres that enable self-expression, and reinforce it through public recognition. Both the self and the public develop in tandem. Instead of being the planner and ruler of its own life and being guided by pre-given principles, the subject is transformed into a constitutive part of a context that determines its subjectivity, and within which it exercises joint decision-making power. Quasi-subjectivity, thus, describes a situation of socially constructed autonomy that is understood and experienced as such (p. 25).

Beck recognizes that his categories must be empirically grounded if they are to be used to analyze the characteristics of the second modernity. Hence, in his 2003 co-authored article Beck has announced research projects on the epistemology of uncertainty, the sociology of ambiguity, and the political economy of uncertainty that have been launched in Munich (p. 29). I have written to Beck whether any preliminary findings from this research are available, a research that appears difficult to operationalize. Neither Beck or the other two co-authors of that article have replied to my inquiries.

Beck's Notion of Individualization

Beck's notion of individualization is central to understanding what drastic changes he theorizes in the social structure of the second modernity. These notions have been explained at length in his co-authored book *Individualization* (Beck & Beck-Gersheim, 2002) and in successive articles that have appeared in *Theory, Culture and Society*.

According to Beck, the old sociology (Durkheim and Parsons) explained social integration through values or joint material interests or through national consciousness (p. 17–18) so that "the self always had to be subordinated to patterns of collectivity" (p. 28). During the first modernity social roles were clearly defined and provided clear guidelines to individual life; in other words, individualism was institutionalized or routinized or embedded in social institutions; for instance, the market was a structure of individuation. Obviously, Beck chooses to ignore the large literature produced by the sociological traditions on role confusion, role conflict, and deviance.

More recently, Beck has emphatically stated that during the sociology of the first modernity, individuation was largely determined by the situation and that self-understanding was suspicious (Beck & Willms, 2004: 23). Again, Beck seems to reduce traditional sociology to the structural paradigm by ignoring, among others, phenomenological, existential, and critical paradigms.

According to Beck, with the advent of the era of unemployment, destruction of nature, and world-risks, social integration has disappeared and it must be redis-covered/reinvented through self-interpretation, self-observation, self-discovery, and self-invention. People's integration depends on their ability to shape the future so that individualization and integration are mutually exclusive (Beck & Beck-Gernsheim, 2002: 19). Now we live in the midst of conflicts among different cultures, in hybrid traditions, "in contradictory transnational and personal identities and risks" (p. 26).

> The social structure of the global life of one's own thus appears together with continual differentiation and individualization, or to be more precise, with the individualization of classes, ethnic groups, nuclear families and normal female biographies. In this way, the nationally fixed social categories of industrial society are culturally dissolved or transformed. They become—zombie categories—which have died yet live on (p. 27).

A "self-culture" emerges with indeterminacy, unpredictability, and insecurity. Social structure becomes ambivalent or rather we have a society without social structure that is accompanied by a lot of insecurity (p. 42). Individualization becomes atomization (p. 207) as the individual is cut off from traditional security; for instance, the traditional family has been broken down as a result of free choice, more models to follow, divorce, therapy, and conjugal succession (p. 206 ff.).

One can counter-argue that Beck's notions of pervasive insecurity and atomization appear to be variations of the phenomena of mass society and alienation that have been abundantly documented by what Beck calls traditional sociology. Moreover, traditional sociology documented new social forms that are continuously being created. In my opinion, we must resist the temptation of reducing societal complexity to the simplicity of theoretical constructs. We know, for instance, that in the American cultural tradition we have a duality of individualism/collectivism, materialism/humanism, freedom/conformity (Spindler et al., 1990), and, perhaps, we should add, a tension between individuation and individualization.

I for one theorize that a differentiated understanding of legitimate sources of knowledge is not an indicator of the breakdown of social structure and social boundaries. On the contrary, it is an indicator of the emergence of more articulated and sophisticated individuals that become capable of drawing on different sources of knowledge for different purposes and in different spheres of life. In Chapter 16, I advocate a more sophisticated role for a reflexive agency and I argue that a capacity for multiple identities is demanded by the intercultural tasks that are typical in our globalizing society. Certainly, these notions provide more constructive tools than the notion of a fragmented "quasi-subject" that is at the mercy of, or co-mingled with, an atomized social structure.

What is the role of the individual in the new social structure? Beck states that in the second modernity "more in each individual situation has to be consciously chosen. Choice has become not only a more important but also a more constitutive element of the individual situation. We can no longer treat volition as an epiphenomenon" (Beck and Willms, 2004: 24). At this point, Beck's conceptualization seems close to the perspective of the old humanistic sociology and is at odds with the structural definition of individualization or "quasi-subjectivity." However, in his book on individualization, Beck explains that it does not speak of an individualism or an individuation that entails the autonomy of the individual. In the second modernity roles dissolve and gender, racial, and class distinctions become fluid and flexible. Each individual must construct his or her own life from fluid elements; nothing is pregiven, all is negotiated (64–65).

Jeffrey Alexander strongly disagrees with the whole idea of a sharp discontinuity between modernization theory and the theorizing of globalization:

> Globalization is too important to be left to the 'globalizers', to the entrepreneurs of globalization, whether economic, political, or intellectual, who have created what might be called 'the discourse of globalization'. The members of this carrier group make use of the facts of globality to suggest that the traditional rules of the game no longer hold, whether these are the traditional social 'laws' that link capitalist markets with economic inequality and undemocratic political power with domination, or traditional disciplinary ideas of the modern disciplines of social science. About such apocalyptic or utopian claims we must be very cautious. Globalization is not an alternative reality that makes previous knowledge and social reality irrelevant. . . .

Later on Alexander continues as follows: ". . . My hypothesis is that globalization should not be understood as something radically new. It marks rather another step in the millennia-long compression of time/space/meaning, and the corresponding expansion in reach of the institutions that represent them, i.e., the extension of political, economic, and cultural organization and power."

Jeffrey Alexander argues for a continuity of sociological perspective between modernization theory and globalization theory on the basis of the historical enlargement of scope from the "particular" and "local" to the "universal" and "national":

> . . . Far from being a radically new development, this process of compression/expansion [of time/space/meaning] already formed the central subject of modernization theory in the middle of the last century. More than any other historical transformation, it was the movement from the "particular" and "local" to the "universal" and "national" that fascinated modernization theorists, who framed it as the movement from traditional to modern society. . . . The modernization theorists were right in thinking broadly about an historical enlargement of scope. Insofar as we are moving toward a more global playing field, we are in the midst of this familiar process. Social organizations and cultural structures alike are expanding their scope and reach. . . . Every process evoked in the globalization literature has already been conceptualized in studies of social and cultural transformations from local to national scale, which

have traced sometimes incremental, sometimes abrupt enlargements in economic, political, military, religious, legal, penal, and cultural life. These processes have been conceptualized in a manner that has little to do with the scale of the nation as such.

Randall Collins makes a clear and strong case for a structural continuity between what Beck calls first modernity and second modernity:

> ... There is no deep structural difference between modernity and so-called post modernity. The latter is an extension of the same trends. That means it is an extension of the same long-term processes, the same causal dynamics, although carried further and producing new concrete manifestations. ... The long-run results of bureaucratization are the same, both via state penetration, and via the expansion of omni-penetrating market capitalism. ...

Collins develops this argument in reference to the position of postmodernists:

> ... Postmodernism does not add any structurally new features of society, but only intensifies the main trends. ... Postmodernism is characterized by a proliferation of language games, a multiplicity of perspectives without a single authoritative vision, this is the result of the mobilization of a large number of networks and movements. It is not simply an intellectual development invented by philosophers.

Collins makes the general point that

> ... the direction of modern history is not on the level of particular ideological contents at all; the trend is a structural one, the continually increasing mobilization of networks and movements themselves ... in reality there always exist competing movements.... Thus traditional religious movements, family values movements and other neo-conservative movements all use the same methods of recruitment networks, fund-raising, mass media publicity, demonstrations, and political campaigns as do liberal, left-wing and ultra-modernist movements.... The multiplicity of social movements promotes a multiplicity of world views; it leads to relativism and reflexivity, which is expressed most self-consciously in the skeptical, self-undermining epistemologies of postmodernist intellectuals. In social reality, however, this multiplicity is only on the level of culture. On the structural level, there is a clear social reality: the proliferation of bureaucratic organizations, omni-market capitalism, and mobilized networks and movements. There is nothing mysterious or unknowable about the underlying structure which produces the postmodern cultural situation.

Collins' position has the merits of relating the cultural to the structural level of social reality, even though someone might detect an hint of priority of the structural over the cultural.

Collins' Neo-Weberian position encompasses also the technological engine of globalization:

> This is sometimes regarded as the result of a high-tech revolution, the information age, the era of information technology (IT). But these technologies are developed by the same processes that have always brought technological innovation in modern capitalism: the processes of rationalization, calculation and planning of production and distribution. Information technology is another phase of capitalism just like the steam engine and railroad revolution, the chemical and electrical revolution, the automobile revolution, the airplane revolution, and so on. In Weber's terms, postmodernism is just

the combination of long term trends of formal rationalization and its resulting substantive irrationality.

For Beck, on the contrary, irrationality is the hallmark of the social fragmentation of the second modernity. In fact, Ulrich Beck backs the thesis of a sharp discontinuity between modernization and globalization with a very peculiar and unsubstantiated theory of social structure and individuality as distinguishing characteristics of the second modernity. According to Beck, the structure based on clear role-sets is replaced by disembedded and institutionalized individuation which is the same as the fluid structure of the second modernity. "We now have the institutionalization of individual options, the necessity of choosing among them, and the indeterminateness of the final outcome" (p. 66). Individualization is a social phenomenon because it takes place with and against others, "It is defined by the normative claims of co-individualization" (p. 67). Hence, disembedded and institutionalized individualism does not imply that the individual becomes a more authentic self. According to Beck, self-chosen life does not occur on the basis of subjective criteria, but occurs "because individuals have been institutionally forced to construct their lives to a qualitatively new degree, resulting in a more indeterminate existence. . . . Life construction is now a key part of social constructions, of social structuration" (p. 68). Here, Beck reveals once more his structural bias by proposing a variation of structuration theory, but a variation that individualizes social structure and, so it dissolves the notion of society. This kind of theorizing calls to our mind Albrow's warning about the relational notion of society (see later on).

Globalization increases social contradictions, but for Beck contradictions foster individualization (p. 84). It is no longer true that integration is the basis for freedom; rather freedom (a socially forced self-chosen life) is the basis of integration (p. 88). Integration is no longer produced by control norms, but by constitutive norms (p. 89).

> Individualization can no longer be understood as a merely subjective phenomenon whose deeper reality is revealed by objective class analysis. Individualization no longer only affects the superstructure of ideology and false consciousness, but also the economic substructure of "real classes." For the first time in history, the individual rather than the class is becoming the basic unit of social reproduction (p. 101).

Is the individual sneaking in through a back window? But to which notion of individual is Beck referring? There is no need to worry; Beck makes clear his difference from Talcott Parsons and the old individuation theory. "We have to realize that this sort of institutionalized individualism represents a radical departure from Talcott Parson's idea of a linear, self-reproducing system. What makes an "individualizing structure" (my italics) so paradoxical at first sight is precisely that it is a non-linear, open-ended, ambivalent, and continuous process" (p. 101). We have come full circle: institutionalized embedded individualism is a synonym of individualizing structure, and the (traditional) subject is being replaced with a structural quasi-subject.

Beck's analysis is an hard pill to swallow in a time when we experience a great expansion of education, mass media, grass-root movements, global civil society, and wide-spreading awareness of nuclear risks and of cross-national terrorist networks. How can all these phenomena be reckoned with the notion that the individual is perishing under the forced choice imposed by a pluralized social structure? On the contrary, one should argue that increased education and diffusion of knowledge via digital media equip individuals with more sophisticated views of the so-called traditional boundaries; and a more sophisticated understanding of traditional boundaries is facilitated by the enhanced accessibility to sophisticated sources of knowledge. Hence, instead of relativization of knowledge one can argue that we have a more sophisticated understanding (and development) of knowledge and a greater availability of bodies of knowledge that equip us to cope with increasing societal complexity and modern dilemmas. It is precisely the increased sophistication of the individual that produces a more nuanced conception of social structure. Hence, the level of complexity of social structure and the sophistication of the individual go hand in hand.

Once more, Beck appears to contradict himself when he admits that "existential uncertainty" (Beck and Beck-Gernsheim, 2002: 210) does not lead to egoistic individualized subcultures, but to a new ethics of solidarity and "altruistic individualism" (212). One is left wondering how this statement is consistant with the individualization of social structures and the atomization of the quasi-subject.

In conclusion, the hypothesized breakthrough of a new paradigm and the "zombie status" of old concepts, such as individual, social role, family, class, and social structure are based on a questionable theorizing of social structure. Alexander and Collins provide more convincing interpretations of contemporary trends.

Ulrich Beck on the Presumed Demise of the Nation-State and the Need of Methodological Cosmopolitanism

As previously mentioned, Beck's theoretical perspective on globalization is based on the basic premise that the era of nation-state is ending. The second modernization, "the shape of which is still being negotiated," calls into question the very foundation of the state by stripping away its boundaries: the economic, political, and cultural boundaries of the state are shattered respectively by expansionary market forces, legal universalism, and the technical revolution. The second modernity "ends up stripping away the nation – and welfare state . . . In so doing, modernization is calling into question its own basic premises (Beck et al., 2003: 2). This process will eventually undermine every aspect of the nation-state: the welfare state; the power of the legal system; the national economy . . . and the parliamentary democracy that governed the whole . . . (p. 3). Hence, the second modernity does not represent an example of continuous change, but a discontinuity, an historical break, a radical change and a crisis in the very foundations and coordinates of society (pp. 8–9).

Beck opposes his own methodological constructionism, where nature and the object are not "other" (Latour), to "methodological nationalism" that assumes that "the nation-state is the power container of social processes and the national being the key-order for studying major social, economic and political processes" (2002a: 21). In his 2004 *Conversations* with J. Willms, Beck states the following:

My central contention is that sociology developed in the container of the nation-state. Its categories of perception, its self-understanding, and its central concepts were all molded to its contours, and because the concepts thus engendered refuse to die, the sociological imagination is now inhabited by zombie categories. They haunt our thinking. They focus our attention to realities that are steadily disappearing. And they haunt our empirical work, because even the subtlest empirical work, when framed in zombie categories, becomes blind empiricism (Beck & Willms, 2004:19).

The notion of the nation-state as a container molding sociological concepts deserves careful scrutiny because of its implications for the validity of sociological concepts. We already quoted J. Alexander denying the notion that the theorizing of modernization thinkers had "little to do with the scale of the nation." An analysis of the historical origin and meaning of the "nation-state" as well as of the foundational concepts of sociology provides a strong support for rejecting the "container" notion of the nation-state for sociological theorizing. First of all, what does the notion of "state" entail? Historians tell us that city-states existed in the civilizations of Mesopotamia, Assyria, Persia, Rome, the Ottoman empire, and China. These city-states were communities with political independence, but with loosely defined borders and exclusionary political participation. Since the peace of Westphalia of 1648 the European "state" became a territorial state with clearly defined borders and "intensive power" over all its territory (Mann, 1986: 7–10). The 1933 Montevideo Convention declares that the "state" as a person of international law should possess the following characteristics: (a) a permanent population; (b) a defined territory; (c) government; and (d) a capacity to enter into relations with the other states. This statement makes clear that the "state" is first and foremost a legal entity within the realm of customary international law. The term "government" derives from the Greek "steering" and means a power to make and enforce laws; hence, the term "government" indicates that the state has the ability to impose sovereign will across its own territory and has the monopoly of the legitimate use of force. Besides having autonomy in domestic affairs, the state is also free from the interference of other states. The state was said to have acquired "extensive power" when it began building empires overseas.

What does the term "nation" add to the notion of "state"? The online *Oxford English Dictionary* defines "nation" as "a large aggregate of communities and individuals united by such factors as common descent, language, culture, history, or occupation of the same territory, so as to form a distinct people. It entails also a common cultural identity." "Nation" refers to the people that form a political state. How did "nation-state" come into being? Some scholars argue that it was "print capitalism" that disseminated common symbols and a shared sense of the past; people who never met could identify with their own "imagined communities" (Anderson, 1991). For Ernest Gellner (1983) the emergence of national cultures and languages was mainly the byproduct of industrialization and commerce. The state also played an important role in the emergence of "nation-state" by fostering national education. Finally, historians focus on the French Revolution for introducing the notion of "nation in arms," national conscription, and the ideology of nationalism.

"Nation-state" indicates a "political community in which the state claims legitimacy on the grounds that it represents the nation" (Baylis & Smith, 2001: 621). More generally, we can state that the "nation-state" properly speaking is a container of (1) a culturally homogeneous population, (2) under one sovereign authority, (3) within a given territory. Strictly speaking, "nation-state" is an historical, juridical, and political science concept, where the notion of "container" refers to the boundaries of territorial jurisdiction and cultural homogeneity of the people living within its territory; the latter characteristic, however, has been always subject to a great variation.

The foundational concepts proposed by the fathers of sociology had a much wider analytic scope than the territorial and cultural boundaries that distinguish one nation-state from another. Foundational sociological concepts were "constructed" to differentiate between the traditional and modern stages of societal evolution on the basis of fundamental characteristics that cut across a large number of societies. In other words, what interested the founders of the discipline was not what separates one society from another, but cross-societal characteristics that cluster a large number of societies according to evolutionary stages. For instance, Comte dealt with modes and sources of knowledge when he proposed the theological, metaphysical, and positive stages of social evolution; each stage was common, of course, to a large number of societies and states. Emile Durkheim dealt with the evolution from traditional to modern societies in terms of the prevailing type of social solidarity. The social homogeneity of traditional societies supported a mechanical solidarity and a strong collective consciousness. The division of labor and related social differentiation gave room to the organic solidarity of modern societies, where people need each other because of specialization of tasks. Solidarity, division of labor, collective consciousness, social norms, anomie, egoistic suicide, deviant behavior, and repressive and restitutive laws are fundamental concepts that cut across the jurisdictional and cultural boundaries of individual nation-states for the simple reason that they are meant to differentiate among socially homogeneous and socially heterogeneous types of societies; again, each type of society encompasses a large number of societies and/or nation-states.

Similar arguments hold for Weber who discussed the difference between traditional and modern types of societies in terms of three ideal types of domination: charismatic (familistic and religious in nature), traditional (patrimonialism and feudalism), and legal (modern state based on law and the form of rational administration called bureaucracy). Again, anybody can see that these types of domination transcend political borders because they are applied transnationally to a large cluster of societies that share the same type of domination. "Rationalization" is for Weber the defining characteristic of capitalism that, again, is understood to be the dominant mode of organization of a large number of societies that shared certain economic practices. Weber's comparative analyses of Confucianism and Puritanism as two contrasting types of rationalization clearly show the transnational character of the concept. The territorial and cultural borders of individual societies are irrelevant for most foundational concepts in sociology, because they were designed to identify clusters of societies by societal types or stages of societal evolution.

In conclusion, it does not make sense to pretend that sociological paradigms are constrained within the boundaries of the nation-state or to suggest that we have experienced a transition from a national to a transnational perspective because of a presumed demise of the state (a claim that is amply refuted later on). Sociology has always dealt and still does with both transnational and national processes, and the latter have been effectively analyzed in terms of the concepts of authority, domination, and state.

Let us consider one more example of what Beck calls "zombie concept." Max Weber uses the concept of class as does Marx, and here we touch on one example of Beck's favorite example of zombie concepts. For Beck, the concept of class has become a zombie concept because the sociological analysis of class structure was contained within the boundaries of the nation-state. Beck argues that global elites, the poor, and exploited migrants live today in a transnational framework, that is, in their country of origin and in the "guest" country:

> They are positioned simultaneously in two different frameworks that are both enlarged and brought into a new relation with each other through their mediation. This ambivalent and transnational placement completely stamps their lives and their identities. . . . Class concepts, no matter how subtle, simple can't capture the existing complexity of radically unequal living situations, either within nation-states societies or between them (Beck & Willms, 2004: 105).

We can see that Beck mixes up two analythically distinct concepts, class and ethnicity. To begin with, even within the nation-states of the first modernity, poor ethnic groups were living in economically and ethnically heterogeneous societies: consider the different socioeconomic gradients of diverse ethnic groups within national boundaries, the differential rate of assimilation of different ethnic groups, and the intergenerational differences in cultural assimilation of each ethnic group. Secondly, class analysis is still very helpful to understand contemporary transnational situations. Max Weber was concerned with explaining social order, regardless of jurisdictional and cultural boundaries. Social order is based on social ranking (social stratification) on the basis of class, status, party. Culture comes in under the notion of "status" (i.e., in terms of cultural ranking), and not in terms of homogeneity or heterogeneity that, properly speaking, pertain to considerations of ethnic or cultural identity. For Weber and Marx social class is determined by the economic relationship to the market, such as owner, renter, employee, and so on, wherever market relations occur.

As I discussed in the first chapter of this volume, the "market" as a mechanism for trading or exchanging goods and services on the basis of supply and demand was known in a large variety of societies: it has been documented by anthropologists in aboriginal societies, by historians in the so-called high civilizations of Greece, Rome, the Hellenistic world, Islamic and Byzantine empires, Italian city-states, and way down in the expansionary states of the colonial and postcolonial world. There is no more transnational concept than this one, although the form and the importance of the market mechanism greatly differed in these societies; trading practices gradually evolved over the millennia from being a secondary form of economic activity with the "administered trade" of world-empires to become the predominant form with the "market trade" of the world-economy in the 16th century (Wallerstein, 1979/97: 6).

Similarly, "social class" was not invented by Karl Marx, but it was already known to the Greeks, re-emerged in the European social thought and, again, after the French Revolution (ibid. p. 282). It is surprising to see Ulrich Beck denying the transnational validity to a concept that has been useful from the time of the Greeks up to the 20th century. It goes without saying that different modalities of social classes prevail in different periods in history and/or in different societies that differ in economic characteristics and not just in national borders. The reason is that class is defined by groups' economic relationships to the market regardless of the national boundaries within which the economic relationships take place. Besides failing to disentangle "class" from "ethnic identity," Beck also fails to make a distinction between "class" and "class consciousness:" "class refers to the economy which is worldwide, but class consciousness is a political, hence primarily national, phenomenon" (ibid. 61). I may concur with Beck that Wallerstein's characterization of class consciousness as "primarily national" should be submitted to some recalibration. Would, however, Beck's critique of the notion of class (as inapplicable in the postnational era) apply also to the notion of class consciousness?

There is plenty of evidence for arguing that national resentments against structural discrimination are quickly spreading beyond national borders inasmuch as social inequities and injustices are transnationally compared and experienced; as a result of transsocietal comparisons and solidarities, class consciousness within nation-states is heightened. Let us stick to the example that Beck gives. Poor immigrants realize quickly that, no matter what different national settings they live in, they are always powerless in terms of market relations. Doesn't this strengthen the class consciousness of the still "home-based" pool of potential migrants as well as the class-consciousness of those who have migrated? This is one example of how the transnational perspective is based on and how is it fueled by the national perspective, and vice versa. Otherwise, how would we explain, for instance, the spilling over of recent urban rioting from France to other European countries?

Is there a need to discuss the transnational validity of Marxist concepts? His notions of capitalism, mode of production, private ownership, relations of production, profit, capital accumulation, proletariat, wage labor, class consciousness, and alienation are as transnational as the concepts we have examined so far and as much as "capitalism" is an ancient and a transborder process.

Let us now revert to Beck's theses. He argues that the old methodological nationalism is no longer adequate to explain a society that takes place in a debounded space, where the distinctions between national/international, inside/outside perspectives do not make any sense (2002b: 53). But the national perspective was never the sociological perspective par excellence, except in case study analysis. So one is puzzled by Beck's criticism of traditional sociological concepts as zombie-categories : (p. 54).

The fundamental concepts of "modern societies" must be re-examined. Household, family, class [see Albrow also below], social inequality, democracy, power, state, commerce, community, justice, law, history, politics must be released from the fetters of methodological nationalism and must be reconceptualized and empirically established within the framework of a cosmopolitan social and political science which remains to be established.

(On the notion of "zombie" categories see also Beck & Beck-Gernsheim, 2002).

Class for Marx and Weber was not "contained within nation-state;" as a matter of fact, Karl Marx discussed capitalist class and working class by using historical material from France, Germany, England, and so on. Marx's distinction between feudal and capitalist modes of production was based on a comparative and cross-societal analysis as much as Weber's analysis. Emmanuel Wallerstein's world-system is essentially comparative with its notions of central and peripheral countries. A large part of sociological analysis has remained explicitly comparative with many journals and series of volumes carrying the name "comparative" in their titles, and there is a standing "Research Committee in Comparative Sociology" in the International Sociological Association, and an ongoing "World Value Survey" project. One wonders how it is even conceivable to understand sociological concepts as bounded by the nation-state.

Clearly, the notion of class (or rather class consciousness) can be spared the honor of zombie status if we consider that international concerns enter in the formulation of national interests and goals. De facto, the presumed country-specific class situation has already built-in transnational elements. Consider, for instance, the national impacts of the large number of international associations or federations of brotherhoods or unions for migration (IOM), fair labor, machinists, chemical workers, metal workers, transport workers, industrial workers, and so on. Without suggesting that trading associations are about fostering a Marxian notion of class consciousness as such, we can certainly argue that they foster a transnational perspective in the definition of human rights and worker rights within nation-states. I am arguing that a postnational conception of the transnational, akin to one proposed by Beck, logically would impose a zombie label to traditional sociological concepts. On the contrary, an interactive conceptualization of the national and transnational perspectives produces a refinement and an upgrading of the concept of class consciousness. A similar argument can be put forward for the notion of "household" that Beck has also volunteered to the zombie status. Witness the U.S. Census redefinition and extension of this concept to include multicultural and multiethnic diversity.

Finally, a quick glance at current research shows that it is premature to declare the death of the concept of "social class": see, for instance, Sklair and Robinson's empirical analyses of transnational class (Sklair, 2001), and, at least in the case of Robinson, of transnational class and transnational state (2003). It is true that class has different socioeconomic configurations in various societies and that capital is denationalized, whereas labor is still place-dependent (Beck & Willms, 2004: 104). This analysis reflects an empiricist misplacement, if we want to use Friedman's perspective; socioeconomic contingencies are different in different societies, but the power differential between dominant and dominated social strata are structurally analogous in different societies.

A more serious discourse would have to be entertained about Beck's notion of individualization. I do not see any convincing evidence that the boundaries among nations, genders, and classes have all vanished and are in such a constant redefinition and state of flux that they cannot provide any certain frame of reference or can find any legitimating grounds. The interaction among the local (ethnic and religious), national, and international levels of societal dynamics entails an overlapping, complementarity, and interactive redefinition of boundaries that are, therefore, not dissolved, but made flexible and enriched with new elements. This type of conceptualization is consistent with the redefinition or extension of the traditional notion of individuation as implied, for instance, by Martin Albrow's human responsiveness, preparedness, and sustainability and by Rossi's multiple identity that is fostered by intercultural performances (see Ch. 1). As to Beck's notion about the demise of the nation-state, there are plenty of scholars arguing for the continued importance and the transformed role of the nation-state (see, for instance, Martin Wolf, 2001). Seán Ó Riain (2000) summarizes his recent review essay of the sociological literature on "States and Markets in an Era of Globalization" with the following statements.

> States and markets shape one another at the national and world-system levels and . . . globalization is transforming that relationship. . . . Globalization has undermined many of [the state controls of trade and capital flows] so that states must increasingly integrate themselves into local and global networks. States are experimenting with organizational and strategic changes nationally and internationally in order to respond to a networked economy and polity.

Far from concluding to a state demise, this analysis documents the key role of the state in the introduction of national and international organizational changes and in seeking integration with local and global networks.

Collins' paper makes this point very clearly and cogently. In reviewing the neo-Weberian scholarship of the last 30 years, which he defines as "state-centered," Collins states that this research has focused on the transformation of economic, cultural and political forms of social organization: witness Skocpol and Goldstone's state-breakdown theory of revolution, Tilly and Mann's military/fiscal theory of the state, and the works in the areas of social network theory and new economic sociology. Whereas traditional Marxists focus on economics and French structuralists and postmodernists on cultural forms, neo-Weberians focus on the dynamics of the organizational forms that we call the state, the military, tax-collection, household, social movements, and socioeconomic networks, (I should clarify that French structuralists focus on social structure also, avoiding the disconnect of culture from social structure that Collins detects in postmodernists; see Rossi, 1974, 1982.) For Collins, social action is generated by organizational dynamics or, in more general terms, "struggles of organization determine what happens historically." More specifically, Collins argues that during the last 400 years the state has been the prime mover of social transformations.

The state's penetration into society has set into motion new organizations, social movements, and economic networks that react against the state; such an interactive sequence has kept going on for centuries.

Personally, I wouldn't conceptualize the state as the sole or prime mover of history. Otherwise, how could we explain the ascendance of craftsmen, artisans, and towns against the central political authority in the Italian city-states, and the ascendance of the bourgeoisie against the King of England and the consequent origin of the Magna Charta in the 13th century? What about the ideologies of liberalism, romanticism, fascism, and socialism (and of universalizing religions in pre-modern times) as mobilizers of sociopolitical action? In actuality, history has been set in motion by the interaction among political organizations, social strata, and ideational systems (civilizations, religions, ideologies) (see Ch. 1 in this volume). However, the point is well taken that history is not just a flow of ideas playing out in a metaphysical world.

Collins's essay discusses four main trends documented by neo-Weberian sociology: state penetration and bureaucratization; mass mobilization of networks; self-transforming capitalist growth; and cultural secularization. Collins takes postmodernism to task for not producing any structurally new features of society, but for pointing out only an intensification of some major trends. In direct contradiction to Beck's position, Collins finds that the multiplications and overlappings of social organizations, chaotic and self-contradictory bureaucratic elements, and conflicting regulations are not new social forms as postmodernists (and Beck) claim, but just a continuation and expansion of previous forms. The multiplication of transnational organizations is also an outcome of the historical growth of the state. The proliferation of languages and perspectives that postmodernists talk about is a result of numerous networks and social movements.

In any event, the multiplicity of views, relativism, and reflexivity that postmodernists theorize about refer to the cultural level, whereas, Collins argues, at the level of structure there is a proliferation of bureaucracies, market capitalism, and networks. Entrepreneurial capitalism, rationalization, and information technology are continuing manifestations of the self-transforming power of capitalism, and in this sense there exists a deep structural continuity among these forms of social transformations. I would be remiss if I did not notice that entrepreneurship, rationalization, individualism, laissez-faire capitalism, and citizenship indicate some of the cultural components of capitalism. Stated differently, there is no structure apart from culture and vice versa; hence, in my view there should be no need to opt for a structural or a cultural priority as an analytic perspective, because structure and culture are two interactive and co-constitutive principles of social action.

Collins refers also to the post-world war institutions that would seem to support Beck's qualification of globalization as transnational: "It is sometimes argued that organizations have outgrown the national state, and that this is a form of postmodern globalization. But capitalist economies have always had a global, long-range organization; what is new is only an intensification of global networks."

Another argument for the alleged uniqueness of the postmodern era is that it represents a shift from Fordist mass production to a flexible production of a wide array of consumer products. Collins argues that this is an overstatement of the degree of social changes. The basic structure of entrepreneurs making new combinations of the factors of production continues as before: the shift from agricultural to manufacturing to tertiary activities are continuing manifestations of the same old capitalistic push to search for new market niches. "The chaos of ephemeral products may seem postmodern, but the underlying mechanism is the same." Conceivably, the real issue to be determined is whether the same old self-transforming capitalism has finally produced qualitatively new social structures. Personally, I have not read anything in Beck's analysis that cannot be accounted for in terms of new-Weberian scholarships as conceptualized by Randall Collins.

We show shortly that the empirical research cited by Sassen and Knorr Cetina in their essays leads them to deny the demise of the nation-state and to reject the dichotomy between the national and the global, because the latter is found partially embedded within national processes. There is a lot of truth in the importance of the transnational perspective, which is clearly central in one form or another in Albrow, Rossi, Sassen, Sklair, Stichweh, and Urry's chapters in this book. But the transnational perspective does not have to be conceptualized as incompatible with and/or superseding the usefulness of the national perspective. We show also that the relationship between the national and the transnational perspective is open to different conceptualizations. Let us first briefly discuss the position of Martin Albrow, the other scholar invoked by Ritzer as the other champion of a transnational perspective that supersedes the national one.

Albrow's Global Shift

In the paper delivered in 2002 at the International Sociological Association meeting Martin Albrow (2002) outlines elements of his paradigm in four clear principles:

(a) Society must be analyzed in terms of transnational and transborder relations. Both Beck and Albrow agree on the existence of relations delinked from state boundaries and on the making of new boundaries. Albrow adds that we are moving toward (or is he hoping for?) a new form of world society, global citizenship, and, perhaps, the emergence of global statehood.

(b) Nowadays, we give a lessened importance to "opinion and market research, age and sex, birthplace" as identifiers of individuals; the latter become "empty sites of arbitrary attributes" and class ceases to be an issue of "national political party affiliation:" similarities with Beck's position are clear here. However, for Albrow we have a shift "from class to identity politics" that implies a breaking away from any group boundary. Identity depends on the choice of life style, group membership, or nation, and it aspires to globality, to "identify with mankind as a whole." The notion of breaking away from boundaries and of a choice among new boundaries is common with Beck, but the key mechanisms for Albrow are identity and identity politics. I much prefer Albrow's notions because they are more compatible with the notion of individuation rather than with Beck's individualization.

(c) The new cross-boundary links are weak and fluid, and they can be analyzed in terms of networks and flows. Beck, however, discards both of these notions.

(d) We must have a nuanced view of social relations that are not "self-sustaining social units. Wholes are, then, seen as conditioned by their relations with other units in a global field, which in turn raises a series of questions on dissolutions and transformations." Yes, the flux of globalization induces "uncertainties of belief and self-identity, time and space compression permits more frequent communications," but this "does not alter the fact that relationships in the normal case endure in both absence and presence" (physical presence of people in interaction). Like Simmel, Albrow returns to

The idea of social relations as the site for social processes. . . . But we are now moving beyond the early assimilation of his ideas into the interactionist account of the self towards a concern for the construction of collectivities in a global social field. Here we may expect important contributions from cultures that have emphasized social relations as the medium through which individuals conceive their goals and in which collectivities coalesce. Asian and African traditions of social thought will be able to exert a far more effective influence on global society than it was possible in the old Western individual/ society frame of thought.

This is a provocative hypothesis. I did not come across an emphasis on the role of culture in Beck's recent writings, whereas Albrow speaks of the free floating of culture that parallels the delinking of society from the state. "Again this only reasserts the age-old autonomy of the human spirit, the capacity for expressions and ideas to cross boundaries, physical or social." I find this humanistic reference a bit refreshing after the encounter with Beck's structuration theory of individualization. For Albrow the globe is set as a value alternative to national symbols and this dispenses with inclusion and exclusionary processes (which are present in Beck); generalized trust can invigorate global civil society, citizenship, and community. "In understanding society beyond boundaries we are bound to look, then, to social relations as the carriers of values rather than to values as boundary maintenance. The integrity of a person or group is sustained in transactions with others rather than in declarations of good intention."

Notice that Albrow's argument is not based on the demise of the nation-state as such, but on the importance of transborder or global relations.

Albrow's essay in this book makes important additional clarifications. He proposes to replace Park and Burgess's definitions of primary and secondary relations that are based on social contact and spatial terms, because certain social relations can be face to face and be impersonal at the same time.

Moreover, closest friends can live far away and yet they can be close via new communication media. These media also permit one to establish a known identity with an unknown person who lives far away (for instance, with another president, a veteran, a homeless person). So in a globalized world where territorial referents are not important, identity becomes a central category of social relations; class becomes a special case of identity. Local definitions of gender, class, and ethnicity can be bypassed by the negotiation of "identities anywhere in the world that offer potential for common understandings, personal development and the basis of collective action." Hence, global or tertiary relations play a major role.

In my view it is in this expanded, rather than in a substitutional sense, that the global perspective must replace methodological nationalism. Gender, class, ethnicity, and other sociological concepts can be redefined and extended with the transnational perspective. I do not see Albrow denying this anywhere, and much less do I see Albrow dismissing in a wholesale fashion traditional concepts as "zombie concepts."

Albrow states that "The global frame is instantiated repeatedly in everyday interactions. . . . The primary, secondary and tertiary are inscribed in daily relations in any place, and equally each has a potential global stretch." There is no hint here of historical break or dichotomous thinking, but an extension of relations and a mediation of all social relations by global relations.

He proposes a new scheme of social relations on the basis of intimacy, instrumentality, and identity that dispenses with the boundaries of proximity and the notion of community. *Socioscape* is a concept introduced to encompass the lived experience of all social relations in a locality, that is, relations that entail proximity and any other order of relations. In other words, socioscape includes any attachment to a place that occurs on the basis of elective belonging regardless of physical distances or territorial boundaries.

Albrow clarifies that socioscape is the local intersection of sociospheres, the latter consisting of the wider relations of the occupants of the socioscape. Sociosphere does not connote specific locations, although it requires space and material conditions of activation. Socioscape and sociosphere are freed of community, national, and territorial boundaries. In my interpretation we can still use community and nation for delimitated analyses, but they need to be complemented with concepts of a wider perspective as soon as we realize that a full account of communities and nations requires attention to global considerations.

From my perspective I like to stress Albrow's definition of socioscape as "comprising mainly the lived experience of the social relations of [all] people in locality." Whereas I insisted in Chapter 16 on "place" as constituted by the interaction of people, I referred to people that are both in a physical and virtual interaction. Here we find that Albrow's definition of "locality" includes all people who influence a specific social interaction, that is, people in physical proximity and anybody else that affects "the quality of social interaction ... in which the actors are implicated." In other words, Albrow's socioscape does not seem to eliminate the notion of locality or of an interactively constituted "place," but it makes explicit that such interaction can be based on physical (territorial) or transterritorial (typically virtual) links. This is an example of extension and upgrading of sociological concepts as opposed to relegating them prematurely to a zombielike status.

(e) Albrow speaks also of a new pragmatics that has analogies with Beck's shift from class to risk society (1992). We move from the optimism of science and technology to pessimism, from risk avoidance to the risk taking of the Club of Rome. "... A loss of confidence in the power of human beings to direct the course of history now goes hand in hand with a growing sense of the importance of contingency, of events that fall outside the normal course of expectations, unpredicted by theory, yet with unraveling consequences." Contingency is, of course, at the center of Beck's individualization and atomized social structure, but this is not the view taken by Albrow who continues as follows. "At the same time the shifting future reference in human action puts a premium on trust and faith rather than prevision. The immanent character of making the future in the present stresses values rather than means in the routine productions of daily life."

(f) Sociology in public policy. The broader consequences of the global shift for sociology have been to intensify an interest in its potential for policy purposes.

> The reason there is urgency now for a new sociological paradigm, is not because society has come to dominate every other consideration. Rather, defective understanding of society interferes with the full realization of human end. . . . The cutting edge work now will be done on transnational structures of trust, social capital and the invention of new institutions, discourse and strategic vision, mediation of conflict, narrative and identity formation, the robustness and durability of structures of social relations, the embeddedness of the domains of economy, culture, environment, state in society, the direction of self-development and orientation to the future. . . .

We have here a strong list of components of a new paradigm without any shadow of obsession with zombielike concepts, and there is plenty of room for a humanistic endeavor.

The abstract offered in the "Sociological Abstracts" of the paper delivered by Albrow at the International Sociological Association, Brisbane, Australia (ISA) in 2002 reads as follows.

> The (re)discovery of the globe in the second half of the twentieth century, culminating in the dominant discourse of globalization in the 1990s, has required us to review and upgrade the conceptual apparatus and thematic foci bequeathed to us by the founders of our discipline. Deterritorialization, transnationalism, time/space compression have challenged the old modern agenda where society and the nation-state were treated as co-terminus. A global orientation has led us to reassess human agency in terms of response, preparedness and sustainability rather than purposes, projects and progress. The crisis of Western sociology has mirrored the crisis in the

West's relations with the rest of the world. We are now constructing a sociology for all the peoples of the globe that acknowledges the limitations of Western centered visions.

Albrow's focus is not on the fragmentation and individualization of modern society, but on the importance of deterritorialization and transnationalism (notice here an affinity with Sklair's position) and on the importance of human agency in terms of preparedness and sustainability.

We have here an example of a paradigm in the making that utilizes upgraded traditional concepts together with new ones. Before discussing the relationship between old and new concepts and between the national and transnational perspective, let us briefly analyze another source of inspiration that George Ritzer mentions as a neglected perspective that may harbor significant potential for the analysis of globalization.

Can Postmodernism Be the Savior, as Ritzer Seems to Suggest?

A long time analyst of postmodernism, Douglas Kellner (2003), concludes one of his recent essays as follows.

> I have suggested that we are living in a period between the modern and something new for which the term "post-modern" stands as a marker. One could, of course, describe the tensions between global and the local, the modern and the post-modern, and the old and the new, as a process of post modernization, of increasing complexity, fragmentation, indeterminacy, and uncertainty. Yet it is my position that although a post-modern turn is visible, continuities with the modern are so striking that it is a mistake to posit a post-modern rupture and exaggerate discontinuities. . . . . Capitalist relations of production still structure most social orders and the hegemony of capital is still the structuring force of most dimensions of social life. Dramatic change and innovation have been part of modernity for centuries, as has technological development and expansion. . . . Globalization can be articulated with both theories of the modern and the post-modern because we are currently involved in an interregnum period between an aging modern and an emerging postmodern era (Best & Kellner, 1997). In this period of transition, in a borderlands between two epochs, globalization signifies both continuities with the past, with modernity and modernization, as well as novelties of the present and the already here future.

One can, of course, extend this consideration to the necessity of dealing with the national and trans-national to explain the global. Kellner continues as follows.

> One could, of course, describe the tensions between global and the local, the modern and the postmodern, and the old and the new, as a process of post modernization, of increasing complexity, fragmentation, indeterminacy, and uncertainty. Yet, it is my position that although a post-modern turn is visible, continuities with the modern are so striking that it is a mistake to posit a post-modern rupture and exaggerate discontinuities.

Similar moderation is suggested by James H. Mittelman (2002), ". . . In the near term, there is no looming Kuhnian crisis in the sense of an impending overthrow that would quickly sweep away reigning paradigms . . . we have entered an interregnum between the old and the new."

Beck sees the need to theorize a new paradigm of the second modernity, but he does not find it in postmodernism. Postmodernism tells you why the old ways of drawing boundaries were based on hidden and unjustifiable assumptions or that their nature has changed, but it does not tell you how social life continues. Beck continues by saying that postmodernism is useful to explain aspects of global culture, but not as a theory of social structure. (Beck & Willms, 2004: 25).

We saw that Beck's conceptualization of contemporary social structure is open to serious questions and lacks empirical support. The postmodernist position is not in a much stronger shape as demonstrated by Collins's criticism on the separation of culture from its structural base that is typical in postmodernist works:

> . . . Many postmodernists joined in the cultural turn which no longer looks at social organization or at social action, but sees the social world as a reflection of a disembodied cultural codebook in the sky. In this cultural-postmodernist vision, there are different codebooks for different historical periods: one codebook for the pre-modern period; another codebook for modernity; yet another codebook for post modernity. How history actually moves from one historical period to another was a rather Idealist conception for most postmodernists. There is just a series of epistemological ruptures, as if philosophers were the dictators of the movement of history; a Zeitgeist of views and practices which morphs from one cultural epoch to another; as if history were just changes in a series of metaphysical ideas. For some postmodernists, though, the Marxian dynamic remains primarily; postmodernism is regarded as the form taken by late capitalism.

What is missing from postmodernist analyses is for Collins the central role of self-transforming capitalism that keeps on producing new structures and a proliferation of overlapping structures.

> The proliferation of multiple organizations, movements, and capitalist enterprises, all formally rational in their procedures, lead to a feeling of substantive irrationality in the entire society. This is what postmodernists have spoken about as the loss of a common, unifying code of cultural understanding. In Weber's terms, postmodernism is just the combination of long term trends of formal rationalization and its resulting substantive irrationality. . . . The chaos of ephemeral products may seem postmodern, but the underlying mechanism is the same.

Much of Collin's critique of postmodernism applies also to Beck's skewed analysis of the constitutive processes of the second modernity.

Albrow's essay in this book seems to agree on the central importance of not forgetting the social structure in issuing the following warning, "It has become an almost standard post-modern challenge to conventional sociology to discard the concept of society because of its association with the statistic project of modernity, even to regard society as a modern construct." Albrow warns us that

> The fluidity and negotiability of social relations should not be confused with fictitiousness, and the idea of society should not be equaled with the self-definition of the nation-state. The relative decline of the nation-state should only encourage us to

recognize the reality that is suppressed, namely that human society is worldwide and the only boundaries in social relations are the ones we make ourselves.

Notice that the nation-state is not in demise; it is, perhaps, in relative decline or, as we show later on, it assumes new functions as older ones are superseded. After all, we know that if the G-8 pull out their financing of the IGOs, we may not have much left besides the old nation-state. More crucial is Albrow's rejection of the relativization and individualization of society or of the self-definition of nation-state that we have previously discussed. For Albrow a global shift does not entail a rejection or a neglect of the national, but a focus on transterritorial social relations that make human society worldwide.

Against the False Dichotomy of the National Versus the Cosmopolitan Perspective: Empirical Evidence and Theoretical Arguments Offered in This Volume

We have seen that Beck advocates an abandonment of the national perspective on the basis of the demise of the nation-state and a radical transformation of the social structure. Having already criticized Beck's theory about the social structure of the second modernity, I argue now that the thesis on the demise of the nation-state is not sustainable either on the basis of historical and sociological analysis.

Historical Role of the State in the Establishment of the IGOs

It was the international community that founded the modern state in Westphalia, and it is the modern state that founded and continues to support the global infrastructure, such as the United Nations, IMF, WB, and other IGOs. Neither the state or the IGOs can be historically understood apart from the other: contemporary intergovernmental organizations cannot be understood independently of the states that established them, or can the contemporary transformation of the state be understood independently of transnational processes. Hence, it would not make sense to privilege the national over the transnational perspective, or the other way around, as an analytic perspective, inasmuch as both national and transnational forces are at work in today's world and influence each other. For this reason I am uncomfortable with the notion that methodological cosmopolitanism should replace methodological nationalism; I rather contend that nationalism as a methodological perspective should be open to and interact with transnationalism. Similarly, I am uncomfortable with the notion that the old state boundaries have been dissolved and are being continuously reconstructed so that people cannot ever know with certainty the delimitations or even the legitimacy of the new boundaries. The reality is that the functions of the state are continuously transformed and redefined, but the regulations and organizational structures of the IGOs are also; the two types of processes feed on each other. (It goes without saying that transnational processes include more than the working of the IGOs.)

Against the Duality of the "National" Versus the "Transnational":
The Essays of Knorr Cetina, J. Friedman, Sklair, Stichweh, Urry,
Rosenau, Sassen, Albrow, and Alexander

At this point I reread various essays of this book, especially after I saw Beck
(2002a: 23) quoting Sassen's writings in support of his postnational cosmopolitan perspective. Beck forcefully argues against the notion of considering
globalization

> As an additive and not substitutive aspect of nation-state society. . . . Globalization
> includes globalization from within, globalization internalized, or, as I prefer to say,
> "cosmopolitanization of nation-state societies." So, this misunderstanding can be
> solved: under conditions of globalization the national is no longer the national. The
> national has to be rediscovered as the internalized global.

Right after this statement, Beck quotes Sassen's article (Sassen, 2000) in
the *British Journal of Sociology* as supporting his own formulation of the cosmopolitan perspective that replaces the state-centered perspective. However, in
that article Sassen argues that in current globalization we have two types of
processes: processes that occur within state boundaries, but that are not national
processes, and, at the same time, national firms, capital and culture which are
more and more located outside natural territories (foreign territories or digital
space): "This localization of the global, or of the non-national, in national territories, and of the national outside national territories, undermined a key duality
running through many of the methods and conceptual frameworks prevalent in
social sciences, that the national and the non-national are mutually exclusive."
Beck does not see that this passage challenges his central contention that
methodological cosmopolitanism should replace rather than be added to methodological nationalism. Beck goes on inferring from Sassen's text that "there is no
need to investigate the global totally globally. We can organize a new purpose-
ful historically sensitive empiricism on the ambivalent consequences of globalization in cross-national and multi-local research networks" (p. 24). Instead of
speaking about empiricism and ambivalences of globalization Beck should have
more accurately stated that globalization consists not just of the "cosmopolitiza-
tion of nation-state societies" (or the rediscovery of the national as "internalized
global"), but also of what can be called the territorialization of transnational
practices. Having conceptually broken away from the national and local, Beck
cannot quite explain how the study of national and local processes reveal the
working of transnational processes.

Sassen's chapter in this volume adds important clarifications based on her
extensive empirical research. For economy of space it suffices to quote from the
introduction and the conclusion of her essay where she argues that the national is
inseparable from the global. In the introduction she states the following. " . . .
I develop the question of place as central to many of the circuits constitutive of
economic globalization. This opens up the conceptualization of the global economic
system to the possibility that is partly embedded in specific types of places and

partly constituted through highly specialized cross-border circuits." Later on in the same introduction she speaks of the "combination of the global and place . . . and of the partial embeddedness of the global in the national. . . ." In the conclusion of her essay she refers again to ". . . The practices and dynamics that, I argue, pertain to the constituting of the global, yet are taking place at what has been historically constructed as the scale of the national and subnational. . . ."

At this point she seems to explicitly refer to Beck without mentioning his name: "this type of analysis suggests a different—though by no means incompatible— research strategy from that which calls for transnational analysis as a response to methodological nationalism." Sassen states that transboundary formations make "the nation as container category inadequate;" we cannot ignore "the fact of multiple and specific structurations of the global inside what has historically been constructed as national." She calls for a "detailed study of national and subnational formations and processes and their recoding as instantiations of the global." Current data and research technologies are useful, but we need different conceptual structures, such as "transnational communities, global cities, post-colonial dynamics." Sassen's conceptualizations are predicated on the rejection of the dichotomy of the national versus transnational "because the national is highly institutionalized and is marked by sociocultural thickness . . . structurations of the global inside the national entail a partial, typically highly specialized, and specific denationalization of particular components of the national." For these reasons we need to study the national to discover and understand the global and for these reasons Beck's research strategy runs the risk of missing an important component of the global.

Yet, all this seems to escape Ritzer who acts surprised by the fact that Sassen uses paradigms from social geography without being sufficiently anchored in extant paradigms. Hold and behold, Ritzer seems to flatly contradict his patron saint, Ulrich, when he adds the following principle: "There needs to be a balance of embedding oneself in one's predecessors and going beyond them." Ritzer should realize that his principle not only chastises his patron saint (for having promoted to zombie status all his predecessors), but also that it represents quite well the strategy followed by the contributors to this volume: far from advocating a wholesale rejection of the "national" (and traditional concepts a la Beck), they use the "national" (and some traditional concepts) together with new concepts to document and explain the "transnational" that they document within the "national."

To return to Sassen, Ritzer does not seem to notice that beside using traditional concepts, Sassen also attempts to follow the second part of his principle, attempting to "go beyond one's predecessors." At the end of her essay Sassen expresses the possibility that not even "the analytic vocabulary of transnationalism, postcoloniality, hybridity" may be adequate for globalization analysis; elsewhere she also mentions the territorialization of transnational processes and the denationalization of some state functions. Sassen builds on traditional concepts and adds new concepts, but of a less controversial nature than, for instance, Beck's individualization.

Knorr Cetina's essay is consistent with Sassen's opposition to the dichotomy of the national (and local) versus the global. In fact, she suggests "The view that the texture of a global world becomes articulated through microstructural patterns that develop in the shadow of (and perhaps liberated from) national and local institutional patterns."

Yet, Ritzer scolds Knorr Cetina for continuing to be informed by the macro – micro distinction, even if of a dialectical version. Has he read the following passage from the conclusion of her essay?

> Microglobalization implies that the micro (in the sense of microprinciples of patterning) and the macro (in the sense of global scope and extension) should not be seen as two levels of empirical reality that stand in contrast to one another. Rather, the micro in the form indicated instantiates the macro; microprinciples enable and implement macroextension and macroeffects. . . . What appears necessary today is that we rechart the territory of microsociology once again in ways that include distantiated spatial configurations.

Knorr Cetina argues for an extension of the micro viewpoints that are anchored at the level of the local, and for the situation as the prime social reality to larger settings. "If the hallmark of microsociology in the past was its emphasis on local social forms, one should now open the door to corresponding research on genuinely global forms." The interpenetration of the local, national, and global could not be formulated in a clearer way and the same is true for Knorr's rejection of an empirical dichotomy between micro- and macroprocesses. A similar position is taken by Knorr Cetina in other writings (Knorr & Bruegger, 2002; Knorr Cetina, 2005). One wonders why Ritzer does not perceive that a microsociology that includes distantiated spatial configurations goes beyond the traditional micro – macro distinction.

J. Rosenau's essay offers a methodology (if not the conceptualization) on how to bridge the local/national/global levels of interaction via the micro, macro, micro/ macro, macroanalysis of social interactions. This conceptualization is obviously based on traditional concepts.

Sklair's essay adds to his previous writings the notion of cosmopolitanism as a defining characteristic of globalization together with transnational social space. He distinguishes his own transnational approach from the international (state-centrist) approach and from the globalist approach.

> Although the inter-nationalist approach exaggerates the power of the state, the globalist approach fails to theorize correctly the role of the state and the inter-state system under conditions of capitalist globalization. Globalists (like state-centrists) are unable to analyze adequately the changing role of state actors and agencies in sustaining the hegemony of capitalist globalization. In particular, as I argue below, globalists and state-centrists both fail to conceptualize the state as a site of struggle and to probe adequately the relations between the state, its agents and institutions, and the transnational capitalist class. The transnational approach to globalization is the synthesis of the collision of the flawed state-centrist thesis and the flawed globalist antithesis.

In his empirical research Sklair bypasses the dichotomy of the national versus cosmopolitan aspects of globalization by positing transnational practices (TNPs) as the fundamental unit of analysis of his globalization framework, a framework that he clearly formalizes in the chapter he wrote for this book.

As mentioned, Stichweh's approach represents another strategy that avoids the dichotomy of the old (national) versus new (transnational) perspective. His multilevel structures (eigenstructures) do not replace old structures, such as local and national structures, but incorporate them through higher forms of integration. Stichweh's argument is based on a cumulative model of social structure. Eigenstructures reproduce preexistent cultural diversity, while creating new social and cultural patterns of their own. The new structures reduce the informational relevance and the frequency of activation of old structures; the latter are not eliminated, but pushed back over long stretches of historical time.

John Urry's essay in this book also clearly avoids a dichotomous thinking. For him global complexity consists of two types of global hybrids: global networks and global fluids. The first hybrids consist of enduring and predictable connections among people, technologies across distant spaces and times that overcome regional boundaries. The global fluids consist of money, digitized information, and social movements that "result from people acting upon the basis of local information" and are deterritorialized and create their own context for action. For Urry global complexity consists of global networks, global fluids, national societies, supranational states, civilizations, and international organizations. "The intensely fluid and turbulent nature of the global complexity" results not in the demise of the state, as Beck claims, but in a bigger role for the state in support and regulation of new spatial configurations; state structures have multiplied to deal with the multiplicity of overlapping fluids that move across borders. The role of the state remains central to the global dynamics with added structures and functions. At the same time, "states have shifted away from governing a relatively fixed and clear-cut national population resident within its territory and constituting a clear-cut and relatively unchanging community of fate. . . . Shifts toward global networks and fluids transform the space beyond each state that they have to striate." Hence, for Urry no understanding of globalization is possible without understanding the stronger and more diversified role of the state, and the state must not be understood as a fixed and impenetrable "container" à la Beck.

Alexander reminds us what happened to the cosmopolitanism that was resurrected right after the end of World War II:

The election in America of George W. Bush, . . . was soon accompanied by a neoconservative discourse of empire. National interest was unabashedly reasserted, global agreements cancelled, and global conferences and institutions boycotted. As the President and neoconservative politicians and intellectuals handled and channeled the national trauma of September 11, 2001, it highlighted anticivil violence and global fragmentation and pointed to a Hobbesian struggle between civilizations. Collective violence once again came to be waged by nations and blocs, with divisive rather than unifying effects for the world scene. . . . The structures and the ideologies of the world are still primarily organized nationally, and hardly at all in a globally civil way. As long as this organizational structure is maintained, if and when other states amass extraordinarily asymmetrical power, they will undoubtedly act in a similar way. . . . There is not a world government to curb a hegemonic state bent on defending its interests as nationally conceived. The nascent global civil sphere has none of the institutions that, in a fully functioning democracy, allow public opinion to produce civil power and thus regulate the state, such as independent courts, party competition, and elections.

... Globalization refers to a process of space/time/meaning compression that is ongoing. These expansions have not yet, by any means, created the basis for globality in the sense of a supranational civil society, as the recent revival of nation-centered rhetorics and practices of national hegemony have demonstrated. . . .

Alexander concurs with the contributors I have just mentioned in rejecting the notion of the demise of the state: we are witnessing the reemergence of national interests in international relations and of a primarily national organization of world structures and ideologies. We notice that both Sklair and Urry prefer to speak of the "state" and Alexander of the "hegemonic state" and "empire" rather that of "nation-state." The position of Jonathan Friedman's essay on the postnational perspective and on the very notion of nation-state introduces a new element in the discussion. To begin with, his

global systemic approach is consistent with the positions we have been discussing: "the local is always part of the global in this framework, and this does not mean that the local is produced by the global. On the contrary, the global is not something other than the local, on an higher plane. The global simply refers to the properties of the systemic processes that connect the world's localities, and this includes their formation as more or less bounded places. There is no global space floating above the local. The global is a purely structural concept. . . . Any global approach that assumes that the global is an empirical field in its own right is a victim of misplaced concreteness. And yet this is precisely the nature of much of the globalization literature. The notion that the global is somehow postnational or transnational is precisely this kind of error.

At this point, Friedman connects the notion of transnational as postnational to evolutionary and ideological biases. "It [this kind of error] is one harboring its own evolutionary bias; once we were local but now we are global. We have gone beyond all that, now. . . ." Friedman speaks also of the ideology and the cult for "the translocal expressed as transnational, border-crossing, postnational." This is "a classificatory or interpretative device of intellectual observers rather than a product of research into the emic intentional and nonintentional realities of the global/local arena." It is quite obvious that there cannot be transnational communities without national ones: "This is trivial but equally easily forgotten or ignored by those who have invoked the prophecy of a new postnational world." Friedman explains the evolutionary and ideological biases of the transnational as follows.

There is an evolutionary assumption which seems to function as the doxa for much of this discourse . . . this is the notion that we move from the local to the global as if to a higher stage of world history. Just as with the older notion of civilization, those who belong to the global are truly évolué. They have left the 'rednecked' masses behind and have entered the new world of the cosmopolitan, a world, not a position, in which all the values of humanism, democracy and human rights, cultural pluralism, and hybridity, catchwords of global organizations from CNN to UNESCO have been adopted by what we would characterize as a new organic intellectual class, the *Neue Mitten* as it is called in Germany, for whom the most serious problems in the world are in their own downwardly mobile national populations who are becoming so terribly local, and even xenophobic, the new notion *classes dangereuses*.

For Friedman the ideological nature of the transnational is built on an ideological conception of "nation":

> The discourse of cultural globalization has a strong ideological component, what I have referred to elsewhere as a global vulgate. . . . It consists in an assault on the family of terms that convey closure, boundedness, essence; all expressions of the same basic problem related to the assumed Western nature of such categories. The root metaphor is the category of the nation-state itself.

At this point, Friedman seems to attack what I have previously identified as the cultural boundaries of nation-state:

> The latter [the nation] is represented as a closed unit, whose population is homogeneous and whose mode of functioning is dominated by boundedness itself, by territoriality, and thus, by exclusion. The notions of national purity, ethnic absolutism, and all forms of essentialism are deducible from the root metaphor. But in order for this metaphor to work, the nation-state has first to be reduced to a culturally uniform totality. Now Gellner's notion of the homogeneity of the nation-state was not about cloning, but about the formation of shared values and orientations, primarily related to the public sphere. When this notion is culturalized it suddenly implies total cultural homogenization, that is, the formation of identical subjects. It is via the essentialization as well as individualization of the culture concept that the latter is transformed into a substance that is born or at least possessed by people . . . the subject is, in this sense, filled with culture. . . . As in a certain biological individualism, culture is shared to the degree that individuals are filled with the same or different cultural substance; that is, the collective is a product of the similarity of its individuals. This is clearly a replication of 19th century racialism. . . . The new critique, which seeks to unbound the old categories consists largely of inserting the prefix "trans-" into all such formerly closed terms. Thus: translocal, transcultural, transnational all stress the focus on that which is beyond borders, all borders.

Friedman finds fault with those anthropologists who contrast modernity and colonialism (characterized by a homogeneity imposed from above) to postcolonialism and globalization (that are presumed to destroy the categories of place, locality, and society). "The contemporary world is one of hybridity, translocality, movement and rhizomes . . . the terms trans-X + hybridity + globalization form a conceptual totality." For Friedman this ideological and political discourse is put forward by an intellectual elite that consists of academicians, media people, politicians, diplomats, and high officials of NGOs.

> It is the discourse of global elites whose relation to the earth is one of consumerist distance and objectification. It is a birds-eye view of the world that looks down upon the multiethnic bazaar or ethnic neighbourhood and marvels at the fabulous jumble of cultural differences present in that space. Hybridity is thus the sensual, primarily visual, appropriation of a space of cultural difference. It is the space below that thus becomes hybridized, even if, for the people who occupy that space, reality is quite different. And it is the space-for-the-observer, or rather for the consumer/appropriator of that space.

From this perspective national identity becomes dangerous and indigeneity must be considered dead. For Friedman this kind of ideological discourse occurs

> In periods in which declining hegemony, increasing class polarization, mass migration and the globalization of capital coincide, and the class polarization produces a confrontation between indigenizing downwardly mobile classes and new cosmopolitanizing elites. The latter identify with the world rather than with their nation states which are declassified as dangerously racist. This is a discourse that supports global control and global governance, which has even strived to transcend the demos in democracy (—) in favor of a new centrism of respectability, one that accounts for the emergence of new dangerous classes.

Friedman locates this ideology in the context of the advocated Third Way as an alternative to the radical left and the radical right.

Alexander also refers, although in somewhat different terms, to the ideological component of the globalization discourse.

> ... In the impassioned and simplified rhetorics of globalization more is involved than merely empirical claims. There are moral assertions about justice being possible for the first time or no longer being possible again. There is a sense of imminence, of an historical shifting that, for better or for worse, has already transformed, or is about to, the basic meaning of social life. I wonder, however, whether globalization has, in fact, had any particular normative purchase? Does the compression of space, time, and meaning translate into justice and the good life? ...
>
> ... Globalization is a mundane process that, in the course of the 20th century, has created at least as much trouble as possibility. The reach of markets has dramatically expanded, producing and distributing on a wider scale than ever before. These economic processes, however, have contributed as much to exploitation and poverty as to wealth creation and economic participation. Information from distant parts of the world has become increasingly available in real-time, but it has not become free floating and universal. Even the most rapidly circulated and easily available information remains attached to particular worldviews, interests, and powers. ...

Briefly stated, the globalization process has mostly benefited strong nations, and contemporary national interests are no less hegemonic and brutal than the old colonialism; here a reference to the global uneven development documented by Arrighi's essay is much à propos. Is cosmopolitanism, then, a more insidious form of nationalism? There is a phalanx of writers, scholars, and commentators who propagate or would defend this thesis; Douglas Kellner is a good representative of this cohort, as his essay in this volume amply documents.

Globalization Theory and Sociology of Knowledge: Ritzer's Posture

In conclusion, various essays in this volume undermine the following central premises of Beck's methodological cosmopolitanism either on the basis of straight empirical research or of theoretical analysis: the demise of the role of the state with the advent of globalization; the need to replace the national

perspective with a postnational (cosmopolitan) perspective; the notion that sociological concepts are contained within the boundaries of the nation-state and,
consequently, they become useless for the analysis of transnational processes.
One is puzzled as to how the major thrust of so many chapters in this book has
gone unnoticed by Ritzer: much of the empirical research and theoretical analyses presented in this volume point at the unsustainability of the position of his
mentor (for this occasion), Ulrich Beck. On the other hand, Ritzer could find
some solace in the theoretical and empirical support provided by the essays of
this volume for the continuing validity of such traditional categories as "noth-
ingness" and "rationality" that he has abundantly used in his works. We may
have, after all, succeeded in sparing from Ritzer's publications the dubious promotion to a zombielike status and reserve instead such a privileged status for
Beck's notions of individualization and postnational cosmopolitanism.

One more thing about Ritzer's posture cannot go unnoticed. The fascination
with sensationally novel concepts prevents Ritzer from seeing not only the anti-
Beck thrusts and novel theoretical elements contained in this book, but also
important additions and clarifications that the chapters by Sklair, Rosenau, and
other contributors bring to their previous writings. As I have already underlined,
Sklair's essay adds "qualitatively new forms of cosmopolitanism" to the components of "generic globalization" that he had discussed in his 2002 book; importantly, in the essay prepared for this book he provides a systematic formulation of
a research framework. Rosenau adds a third step to the methodology of globalization research that he had discussed in his 2003 volume.

I am not suggesting a Ritzer conspiracy, but we know from the sociology of
knowledge, that embedded paradigms can make one less sensitive to new
or emerging concepts. Actually, this was my experience with the first reading of
Levi-Strauss' works. I myself started my early career with a perspective that led
me to criticize in my doctoral dissertation those works, among other reasons, for
their metaempirical and unverifiable character. Then came various sessions I
organized on Levi-Strauss' structuralism at the American Anthropological
Association meetings, where I was exposed to the "structuralist" interpretation of
Levi-Strauss by his disciples and sympathizers based at the University of Lavalle.
I reread Levi-Strauss's works as the study of the concrete logic underlining cultural systems and my conclusions changed quite drastically (see Rossi, 1974,
1982). What I am suggesting is that Ritzer's embeddedness within traditional categories—at the same time that he detests their zombie character—may have prevented him from seeing the "emerging" characters of various theoretical elements
contained in this book. An additional explanation can be found in the fact that
these essays offer radical and empirically based critiques of Beck's theses largely
in traditional sociological language. Ritzer's performance demonstrates how difficult it is for himself to achieve that balance that he recommends to others, "the
balance of embedding oneself in one's predecessors and going beyond them" at
the same time.

As previously mentioned, Ritzer also seems to overlook the fact that the positions put forward in this book are based on solid empirical knowledge either in

the sense of personal empirical research (Albrow, Friedman, Knorr Cetina, Rosenau, and Sassen) or of civilizational (Stichweh) or historical and survey research (Rossi). What is more striking is that we are strongly advised by Ritzer to consider abandoning the national perspective and all the concepts it has, presumably, produced just on the basis of an highly subjective theorizing of contemporary social structure. Not only are Beck's interpretations highly debatable, but they also lack any empirical support. My repeated efforts to seek out the results of his announced empirical research have produced no results.

From a "Cosmopolitan" to a Global Perspective

Let's summarize the major points and research findings discussed so far. (1) Friedman and Alexander have placed in evidence the ideological nature of certain conceptions of the national and transnational or cosmopolitanism. I should make explicit that I use here the term "cosmopolitanism" in the sense of Beck's postnational transnationalism that is supposed to replace a defunct nationalism; (2) there is no empirical support for the thesis on the demise of the state. Extensive empirical research described and summarized in some of the chapters in this volume show the increased importance of certain state functions and the emergence of new state functions. Sassen and Knorr Cetina empirically document that certain transnational processes are embedded within state boundaries. In actuality, some state functions are denationalized (embeddedness of the national in the transnational), and new state functions have been emerging. Alexander refers to recurring cycles of cosmopolitanism at the service of nationalistic interests. Collins discusses the ongoing state penetration of society as a central component of self-transforming capitalism. All this evidence indicates that a sound understanding of national processes remains an indispensable avenue to document certain transnational processes; (3) there is no theoretical rationale for the notion of the nation-state as a "container" that limits the analytical power of sociological concepts to intrastate processes. We have seen that the sociological perspective transcends the political (jurisdictional) and cultural delimitations of the notion of nation-state. We have also seen that sociologists prefer to use the categories of domination, authority, and power and that these concepts are used as "ideal types" for comparative (and cross-societal) analyses.

What kind of analytic apparatus does emerge from the theoretical points and research findings of these essays? Following is a list of concepts that can be used to formulate an articulate global approach. (1) Albrow's deterritorialized notion of three types of social relations based on the notion of "identity" and "elective belonging" that represents a shift from class to identity politics. The fact that Ritzer fails to call attention to these important ideas that Albrow discusses in this volume is quite surprising inasmuch as Ritzer considers Albrow as one of the two innovators in globalization research; (2) the new concepts of emergent, institutionally light, flowlike, self-organizing, and temporal nature of the structures of global connectivity, scopic systems (Knorr Cetina), supersystemic organizing systems and eigenstructures (Stichweh), self-organizing systems (Urry), and the various new categories proposed by Sassen; (3) the incorporation of certain phenomenological and postmodernist ideas on the materiality of practices as an added "constructionist" perspective to the Durkheimian categories of space and time (see Chapter 16); (4) Friedman, Albrow, and Rosenau's locally and existentially situated strategies of ethnographic analysis as well as their emphasis on the importance of the ethnographic study of the particular to understand the global; (5) various concepts from historiographic research (Grew) and social geography (Schaeffer, Sassen); (6) the definitional clarifications contained in the chapters of Archer, Arrighi, Chase-Dunn and Jorgenson, and Kellner as well as important operational definitions on political and economic aspects of globalization contained in the chapters of Arrighi, and Chase-Dunn and Jorgenson; (7) the usage of system theory (Stichweh) and the dialectic extension of Weberian and Parsonian ideas (Rossi) to build a framework for the analysis of globalization.

I am not attempting to build an integrated perspective out of these elements, but to point out that a global perspective based on the interaction of national and transnational processes can provide an overall umbrella for these various theoretical elements. I use the term "global perspective" to differentiate my position from Beck's cosmopolitan or postnational perspective.

Albrow and Sklair concur with Beck that we need to adopt a transnational perspective, and Sassen is sympathetic towards such a perspective. However, Sklair and Sassen do not radically abandon old concepts, but utilize them together with new concepts when empirical research demands them. Among the contributors to this book, Martin Albrow is the one who is outright in favor of the thesis that we need new concepts. We have seen that his focus on identity, values, and human agency is much more palatable and empirically sustainable than Beck's individualization of social structure. All in all, "when it comes to good research there is no single correct vocabulary" (Albrow, 2002: 6), and in fact there is a sharp disagreement on which new conceptual elements ought to enter in the global paradigm: for Beck individualization is a key, for Albrow "identities in a global frame," for Sklair transnational practices; for Sassen transnationalism, embedded nationalism, denationalization, postcolonialism, and hybridity; for Urry global networks and global fluids; and for Knorr Cetina scopic systems.

The essays by Alexander, Friedman, Knorr Cetina, Rossi, Sassen, and Stichweh clearly reject the radical break between the national and the transnational that is posited by Ulrich Beck. As a matter of fact, these contributors to the book find the national and the transnational inextricably connected to each other; in my view, either one of them is indispensable to fully explain the other: the transnational is uncovered in the national and the national in the transnational, and, more important, they interactively (via conflicts, negotiations, and accommodations) calibrate and strengthen each other.

It appears to me that the multidimensional and dialectical framework I proposed in Chapter 1 to analyze societal dynamics (see Table 1.3 in particular) encompasses the national and transnational foci of analysis without positing an artificial dichotomy among them. Table 1.3 starts the analysis from the national perspective to argue that we cannot understand the dynamics of any society without interrelating a double type of analysis: first, an analysis of how cultural, political, and economic processes interact with each other at each level of societal concerns (the local, national, and international); second, an analysis of the interface among local, national, and international concerns. From this point of view no artificial separation among the local, national, and international makes sense, because only the study of their reciprocal influence permits an adequate understanding of each one of them. Simply put, the international is part of the national because international issues are major items in nations' agendas. Conversely, the national is part of the international because international processes and structures are the outcomes of negotiations and compromises among competing national interests.

Whereas Sassen and Knorr Cetina speak about the embeddedness of the global in the national and Stichweh about the superimposition of structures, I prefer to posit a co-constitutive dialectical interaction among local, national, and international processes (see Rossi 1993). Refinement of traditional concepts and novel theorizing may logically follow from this dialectical integration of the national and the transnational; however, I am skeptical of taking as a starting point of analysis a fabricated demise of the nation-state that is replaced by a fragmented and individualized view of social structure. The latter perspective would, of course, reduce many traditional concepts to a zombie status, but there is not an ounce of empirical evidence in support of such a perspective.

We remember Beck speaking of "internalized globalization" that consists of the rediscovery of the national as internalized global. In reality, the national has never disappeared, but it has contributed more and more to create, support, and modify international agendas as they are necessary for the functioning of the modern nation-state. We can, perhaps more properly, speak about a "nationalized international" that is part of the internal dynamics of the nation-state; we should also speak of an internationalized national that is part, for instance, of IGO and NGO agendas. The undeniable fact is that the ongoing world dynamics is an outcome of the interaction (and all too often a struggle) between national and international forces. In this sense, I prefer to speak of a global perspective that is different from and in opposition to the postnational perspective of Beck. For me the global perspective consists of explaining national and transnational processes not separately or in succession, but simultaneously in terms of their reciprocal interaction. As much as the national perspective is not adequate by itself, so we cannot adopt a transnational perspective that totally rejects the national perspective. Stichweh prefers to explain the relationship between the national and the global in terms of eigenstructures, that is, structures that are superimposed on older structures without replacing them (see Stichweh's paper). I prefer to explain globalization in terms of a reciprocally constitutive interaction (conflict, negotiation, adaptation) among local, national, and international concerns of world's societies (see Rossi's Chapter 1).

Obviously, we are at the beginning of global theorizing, and global processes may turn out to be so transformative as to demand that paradigmatic turn that George Ritzer seems to crave. The opposite views of contemporary social structure offered by Beck and Collins indicate that globalization might become a ground for theory testing and theory development. We must be grateful to Ritzer for trying hard to resensitize our embedded perspectives, even as he admits that "It is also possible that the era of globalization is not so different after all and that such a need [for new ideas, theories, and empirical approaches] does not exist."

Ritzer seems to intend to drill us for . . . hypothetical (hoped for?) paradigmatic changes! It may be good and well that we should be in a state of readiness for new conceptualizations. But shouldn't new perspectives be submitted to close scrutiny, especially when they pretend to be so provocatively iconoclastic? Secondly, a certain zest for novelty provides dynamism and relevance to our disciplines. But shouldn't our zest be sensitive enough to be able to detect the novel under old clothes as well? One would surmise that such readiness is line with the (all of a sudden "balanced") posture of Ritzer, that we have to calibrate our embeddedness within our predecessors with an attempt to go beyond them. There seems to be a basic temperamental divide between the facile enthusiasts for radically novel theorizing (even when it is based on an imaginary and implausible atomization of social structure and a structuration of individuality) and those among us who prefer to take a hard look at the empirical evidence first. Let the proof of the pudding remain with a close study of empirical reality; but let it be a study of real and not fictive social relations, as per Albrow's advice, and a study that does not ignore the structural transformations of self-propelling capitalism, as per Collins' advice.

Postscript One: On Recent Critiques of Beck's Theories of Second Modernity and Individualization

As of November 2007 some empirical tests of Beck's notion of second modernity have appeared. Paul De Beer (2007) operationalized Beck's notion of 'individualization' in three components, - detraditionalization, emancipation, and heterogenization. He defined "emancipation" as a declining influence of social groups and institutions on individual attitudes and behaviour that is expected to result in a greater freedom of choice for people than were possible in more traditional times (heterogenization). De Beer analyzed 1980 and 2002 survey data on cultural change in The Netherlands and concluded the following: "only the hypothesis of detraditionalization is confirmed by the data. The emancipation hypothesis is, however, unambiguously refuted by the available data, while the data are not conclusive with respect to heterogenization. Hence, the empirical support for the individualization trend is much weaker than is often supposed" (From the abstract of the article).

In a forthcoming essay (Rossi 2008) I discuss in detail other recent empirical refutations of Beck's theses,- namely the uncertainty of the individual in a fragmented social structure that is replaced by fictive relations. Ceplak (2006), Chtouris et al. (2006), and Banks (2006) show that, according to various European surveys, young people and other segments of society are firmly anchored on the traditional institutions of family, friendship, and free political institutions. After a careful analysis of American survey data Baker (2004) concludes the following: "The evidence shows overwhelmingly that America has not lost its traditional values, that the nation compares favorably with most other societies, and that the culture war is largely a myth" (Baker 2004). Data from the extensive "world values surveys" conducted during the last two decades are no less reassuring. In a recent work Inglehart and Welzel (2005), who have published various works based on these surveys, conclude as follows: "A massive body of cross-national data demonstrates that (1) socio-economic modernization, (2) a cultural shift toward rising emphasis of self-expression values, and (democratization) are all components of a single underlying process: human development. The underlying theme of this process is the broadening of human choice" (p. 2). In their works and in the various reports published on the web site of the "World values survey" (http:// www.worldvaluessurvey.org/) I did not find any evidence that the institutions of what Beck calls the first modernity are breaking down and falling in a state of chaos. Inglehart and Welzel conclude that "economic growth, rising levels of education and information, and diversifying human interactions increase people's material, cognitive, and social resources, making them materially, intellectually, and socially more independent". Far from living in a state of uncertainty, people in post-modern society experience "rising levels of existential security and autonomy" that lead them to emphasize individual liberty, freedom of self-expression and self-realization, civil and political liberties; these values lead to the growth and transformation of democracy. "Never before in history have the masses experienced levels of existential security comparable with those that have emerged in postindustrial societies.... . This unprecedented high degree of existential security enables people to focus increasingly on goals beyond immediate survival" (p 28, 45, 56). There is no doubt that the post-industrial and postmodern world documented by the "world values surveys" is antithetical to the one imagined by Ulrich Beck, who has not produced yet, to my knowledge, the empirical analyses he had promised us in 2003 (Beck et al. 2003).

I should briefly allude to another concept that Beck seems to prefer in explaining "globalization". He has been arguing for a notion of cosmopolitanism that replaces the old ontological distinction between "us" and "them" with an inclusive distinction of "us" and "them", and with a "dual locatedness for all". "Both culturally and politically, people experience and live out apparently contradictory identities and loyalties, without this being experienced as contradictory either in a person's own mind or in others' expectations" (Beck 2005: 36). "Differences, contrasts and boundaries must be fixed and defined in an awareness of the sameness in principle of the others.... Cosmopolitanization, thus understood, comprises the development of multiple loyalties as well as the increase in diverse transformational forms of life". (Beck 2006: 9). One wonders how fictive is the nature of the 'dual locatedness' and 'the sameness in principle of the others' since, according to Beck, the old institutional boundaries and, presumably, cultural and civilizational boundaries have been blurred or dismantled with the advent of the second modernity. Against these notions of a blurred world of the first modernity and a fictively reimagined world of differences, I simply suggest that contemporary confrontations of civilizational and geopolitical nature lead to a re-interpretation and heightening of differences. In the forthcoming paper (Rossi 2008) I argue that *sameness* (global awareness of a common humanity and a common survival need) derives from the sharp realization of *differences*:

complementary differences in nations' cultural and economic resources that produce reciprocal exchanges; competitive differences in the race for world hegemony and for scarce resources of strategic importance that generate the need for negotiation and compromise to avoid mutual destruction. Instead of an "awareness of the sameness in principle of the others" (Beck), we have an awareness of a basic sameness produced by our differences from the others. We come to the vivid realization that national and civilizational differences generate strong bonds of complementarity and interdependence among us all. In this sense "difference" is bound to remain the strong propeller of our "sameness", - a "sameness" that is inclusive of multiple identities, yes, but identities that are molded by and subordinated to the common imperative for global survival.

Postscript Two: On Roland Robertson's Position

Roland Robertson was also on the list of possible contributors. In an October 20, 2005 email to me Robertson stated the following.

> I am a little inclined to agree with [the position] that we may not need any new concepts/ paradigms for the study of globalization. On the other hand, there are deep divisions within the field as to such crucial matters as: the beginnings of globalization—e.g., the Roman Empire; the dimensions of globalization—e.g., roughly the Parsonian scheme; the relationship between the so-called global and the so-called local; how best to approach the similarity vs. difference debate. In a phrase, I don't think we need neither a new paradigm—nor even major adjustments in our conceptual language. We do, nonetheless, need to take more decisive attempts to tackle the central thematic issues and try to transcend the heavy weight of the disciplines.

The reader must be aware by now that the crucial issues identified by Robertson are at the core of the essays of this book: the historical view of globalization; the embedded and reciprocally co-constitutive interaction of the national and transnational; the refinement and integration of theoretical elements derived from Marx, Weber, Durkheim, Parsons, phenomenology, structuralism, world-system theory, postmodernism; the bearing of the anthropological (Friedman), historical (Grew), international relations (Rosenau), and sociological perspectives on the globalization process.

At the closing of this adventure, we must all realize that unless we develop an integrated and cross-disciplinary discourse we shall continue writing about globalization without grasping what are the truly global dimensions of our age and what their consequences are. At first, the intradisciplinary diatribe about new versus old paradigms seems much less urgent than a cross-disciplinary discourse among disciplinary genres and, most important, than a genuine dialogue among the North and the South of our lopsided globe. Yet the realization of the continuing usage by the global North of cosmopolitan ideologies at the service of its nationalistic interests is a precondition for establishing a genuine dialogue between the North and the South.

References Cited and Bibliography

Albrow, Martin 2002. "The global shift and its consequences for sociology." Invited paper delivered at the *Special Session of the 13th World Congress of the International Sociological Association in Brisbane*, 7–13 July, 2002 on "Advancements in Sociological Knowledge Over Half a Century."

Anderson, Benedict. 1991. *Imagined Communities: Reflections on the Origin and Spread of Nationalism*. London: Verso.

Baker, Wayne E. 2004. *America's Crisis of Values: Reality and Perception*. Princeton University Press.

Banks, Mark 2006. "Moral Economy and Cultural Work", *Sociology*, 40 (3): 455–472.

Baylis, John and Steve Smith, eds. 2001. *The Globalization of World Politics: An Introduction to International Relations*. New York: Oxford University Press.

Beck, Ulrich 2000. "The cosmopolitan perspective: Sociology and the second age of modernity," *British Journal of Sociology*, 51 (1) (January): 79–105.

—— 2002a. "The cosmopolitan society and its enemies," *Theory, Culture and Society*, 19 (1–2): 17–44.

—— 2002b. "The terrorist threat: World risk society revisited," *Theory, Culture and Society*, 19 (4): 39–55.

—— 2005. *Power in the Global Age*. Translated by Kathleen Cross. Polity Press. Malden, Mass.

—— 2006. *The Cosmopolitan Vision*. Translated by Ciaran Cronin. Polity Press. Malden, Mass.

Beck, Ulrich and Elisabeth Beck-Gernsheim. 2002. *Individualization: Institutionalized Individualism and Its Social and Political Consequences*. London: Sage.

Beck, Ulrich, Wolfgang Bonss, Christopher Lau 2003. "The theory of reflexive modernization: Problematic, hypotheses and research programme," *Theory, Culture and Society*, 20 (2): 1–33.

Beck, Ulrich and Johannes Willms 2004. *Conversations with Ulrich Beck*. London: Polity.

Best, Steven and Douglas Kellner 1997. *The Postmodern Turn*. Guilford.

Ceplak, Metka Mencin. 2006. "Values of young people in Slovenia: The search for personal security". *Young*, 14 (4): 291–308.

Chtouris, Sotiris; Anastasia Zissi, Efstratios Papanis, Konstantinos Rontos. 2006. "The state of youth in contemporary Greece". *Young*, 14 (4): 309–322.

Collins, Randall 2005. "Rationalization in neo-Weberian perspective," paper delivered at Waseda University.

De Beer, Paul. 2007. "How Individualized are the Dutch?". *Current Sociology*, 55 (3): 389–413.

Gellner, Ernest. 1983. *Nations and Nationalism*. Oxford, UK: Blackwell.

Inglehart, Ronald aand Christian Welzel. 2005. *Modernization, cultural change and democracy: the human development sequence*. New York: Cambridge University Press.

Kellner, Douglas 2003. "Globalization and the postmodern turn." http://www.gseis.ucla.edu/courses/ed253a/dk/GLOBPM.htm

Knorr Cetina, Karin 2005. "Complex global microstructures: The new terrorist societies," *Theory, Culture and Society*, 22 (5): 213–234.

Knorr Cetina, Karin and Urs Bruegger 2002. "Global microstructures: The virtual societies of financial markets," *American Journal of Sociology*, 107: 905–950.

Mann Michael, 1986. *The Sources of Social Power, Vol. 1. A History of Power from the Beginnings to A. D. 1760*. Cambridge, UK: Cambridge University Press.

Merton, Robert K. 1967(1949). *Social Theory and Social Structure*, Enlarged Edition. New York: Free Press.

Mittelman, H. James 2002. "Globalization: An ascendant paradigm?" *International Studies Perspectives*, 3 (1) (February).

Mythen, Gabe 2005. "Employment, individualization and insecurity: Rethinking the risk society perspective," *The Sociological Review*, 53 (1): 129–149.

Ó Riain, Sean 2000. "States and markets in an era of globalization," *Annual Review of Sociology*, 26 (August): 187–213.

Ritzer, George 1975. "Sociology: A multiple paradigm science," *The American Sociologist*, 10(3) (August): 156–167.

Robinson, William I. 2003. *Transnational Conflicts: Central America, Social Change, and Globalization*. New York: Verso.

Rossi, Ino (Ed.) 1974. *The Unconscious in Culture: The Structuralism of Claude Levi-Strauss in Perspective*. New York: Dutton.

—— (Ed.) 1982. *The Logic of Culture: Advances in Structural Theory and Method*. South Hadley, MA: J. F. Bergin.

——. 1993. *Community Reconstruction after an Earthquake: Dialectical Sociology in Action*. 1993. Westport, CT: Praeger.

——. 2008. *"Globalization and negotiated global awareness: Whither individualization?"* Forthcoming in "Uncertainly and Insecurity in the New Age", edited by Mario Toscano and Vincent Perillo. Milan (Italy): Franco Angeli.

Sassen, Saskia 2000. "New frontiers facing urban sociology at the millennium," *British Journal of Sociology*, 51 (1): 143–160.

Sklair, Leslie. 2001. *The Transnational Capitalist Class*. London: Blackwell.

Spindler, George Dearborn, Henry T. Trueba, Louise S. Spindler, Melvin D. Williams, Eds. 1990. *American Cultural Dialogue and Its Transmission*. New York: Taylor & Francis.

Wallerstein, Immanuel. 1979/97. *The Capitalist World-Economy: Essays by Immanuel Wallerstein*. Cambridge, UK: Cambridge University Press.

Wolf, Martin 2001. "Will the nation-state survive globalization?," *Foreign Affairs*, (Jan/Feb), 80 (1).

"World Values Surveys", network of social scientists coordinated by the World Values Survey Association http://www.worldvaluessurvey.com/

Index

Printed in the United States
100497LV00001B/4/A

9 780387 757193